DISCARD

© AVALON TRAVEL

D0965344

Contents

MOON HANDBOOKS

NEW JERSEY

LAURA KINIRY

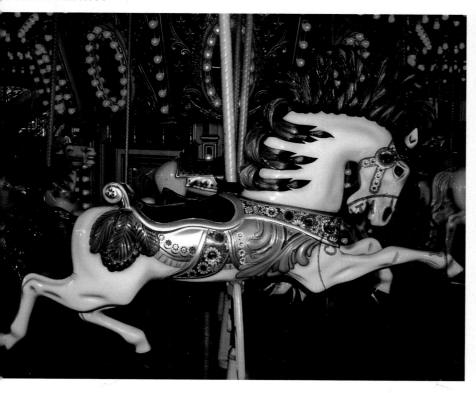

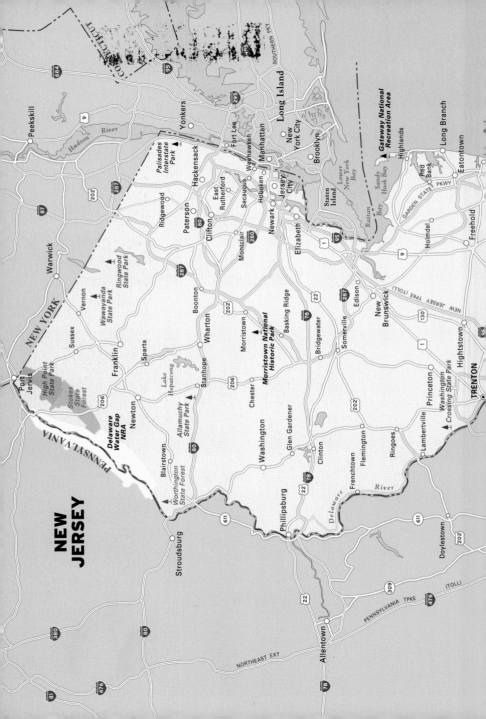

Discover New Jersey

Iconic and misunderstood, individual and resilient, New Jersey is one of the country's best-known and misrepresented states. Away from the grays and browns of its smokestacks, the notorious toll roads, and the tarnished freight cars, visitors may be surprised to find a place of stunning beauty and diversity.

New Jersey has been described as "a barrel tapped at both ends," and it's true that the state is often considered little more than a throughway. But depart from the highways and you'll see cranberry bogs and blueberry thickets, apple orchards, and colonial homes with herringbone designs.

After years of jokes, New Jersey is finally finding comfort in its skin. Historic towns have gained new life through Main Street improvement programs, and cities like Hoboken and Atlantic City have morphed into cosmopolitan centers. Downtown stretches like Collingswood and Red Bank are finally coming of age.

The urban landscape offers a mere glimpse into New Jersey's variety. Beyond it there are old mining villages and hillsides home to black bears, deer, squirrels, and beavers, wetlands where blue heron, Canada geese, and osprey fly, and miles and miles (and miles) of coastline.

It's difficult to get unintentionally lost in New Jersey. Drive a few hours and you'll eventually hit water, or New York. If you want to disappear, that's another story: The Kittatinny Mountains offer backcountry

trails; unmarked roads wind through the Delaware Bayshore; and over one million acres of Atlantic cedar, scrub, oak, and pine forest spread virtually untouched across Central and South Jersey.

In a place where the Devil is legendary, Muffler Men (and women) tower over roadways, and an elephant resides at the Shore, New Jersey continues to surprise. The state's overwhelming place in the hearts of its musicians and its leading role in TV and films, such as *The Sopranos* and Kevin Smith feature films, confirms its longevity.

New Jersey's people can be brash and opinionated, but they are also big-hearted and proud. Years of defending themselves have given residents a hard-bitten sense of unity, and Jersey girls have earned themselves a place in the American psyche.

New Jersey offers opportunities for historians, outdoor enthusiasts, art collectors, pop culture fans, beach bums, shoppers, antique buyers, families, artists, and musicians, to name a few. It's a state too often disregarded and begging to be discovered. Shouldn't you be the one to do it?

Planning Your Trip

New Jersey is perfectly poised as a day-trip destination or weekend excursion from New York City, Philadelphia, and much of the country's Mid-Atlantic. Due to each region's varying cultural and geographic offerings, it pays to think about activities you're interested in pursuing before visiting.

► WHERE TO GO

The Gateway Region

Across the Hudson River from New York City, the Gateway is New Jersey's most cosmopolitan region. To truly experience it, a Hoboken visit is a must. Peruse the Washington Street shops, then hop a train to Jersey City for a movie at the restored Loews Theater. The Spanish and Portuguese restaurants in Newark's Ironbound neighborhood are the way to go for drinks or a more substantial meal. Newark Museum, along with Montclair, South Orange, and Summit, offer convenient urban escapes.

The Skylands

New Jersey's northwest corner is perfect for outdoors lovers. Skiers and snowboarders should check out Mountain Creek and High Point State Park, while hikers should visit the Delaware Water Gap National Recreation Area. Central Piedmont and the Lambertville area are ideal for cyclists, and fly-fishing is best at Big Flat Brook. Several hot air ballooning companies offer trips above Hunterdon County. Shopping for antiques is a popular regional pastime, with shops in Lambertville, Frenchtown, and Chester.

The Jersey Shore

Where to begin? From the north at Sandy Hook, work your way south to Asbury Park (the birthplace of Jersey Shore music),

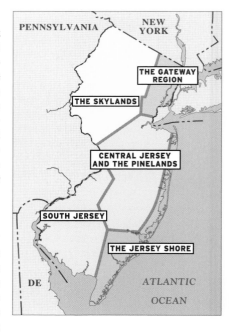

Ocean Grove, and Spring Lake, then detouring to Point Pleasant for an evening on the boards. From the south, start at Cape May. Set aside ample time to explore this Victorian hot spot before a northern Ocean Drive to see Wildwood's doo-wop architecture, nosh on caramel popcorn along Ocean City's Boardwalk, and take in Atlantic City's nightlife. For an all-inclusive beach vacation, Long Beach Island is your place.

winter in South Jersey

Central Jersey and the Pinelands

A Central Jersey trip is incomplete without visiting historic Trenton, New Jersey's state capital. While here, swing by Princeton University to see the famed campus along with historic Revolutionary War sites and Albert Einstein's home. On the region's eastern side, Red Bank is a must. Adrenaline junkies will want to beeline for Six Flags and the world's tallest, fastest roller coaster, while nature lovers can canoe through the Pinelands, New Jersey's most pristine natural treasure.

South Jersey

Shopping and dining opportunities abound in Collingswood and Haddonfield, along with Mullica Hill, offering one of New Jersey's best antique-store selections. Burlington County, Woodbury, and Salem are brimming with historic sites, but for the region's extensive glass history a trip to Millville's Wheaton Arts Center is recommended. For sea life, check out Camden's Adventure Aquarium or Cumberland County's Delaware Bayshore region, also great for birding and cycling.

▶ WHEN TO GO

New Jersey is a year-round destination, but the ideal time for visiting is May–June or September–October when temperatures cool and the majority of attractions remain open.

Summer is essential for a true Shore experience, if you don't mind humidity, crowds, and hard-to-find parking spaces. Boardwalks are in full swing, beaches are packed, and bars and restaurants are bursting with daily specials. New Jersey's remaining regions offer varying ways to keep cool, including canoeing and kayaking, river tubing, and water parks.

The state comes alive during December holidays with village festivals, extended shopping, and the start of the winter sports season. In fall, local farms run pumpkin-patch hayrides and corn mazes. Autumn is also a good time for cranberry bog excursions and photographing the state's magnificent burned-orange and red foliage.

► BEFORE YOU GO

What to Take

New Jersey is a casual place, although many of its restaurants have dress codes excluding sneakers, tank tops, T-shirts, baggy pants, and hats. Some restaurants require a tie and jacket, but these are few.

For winter visits, a warm coat, hat, gloves, and a scarf are musts, and it's always a good idea to bring along an umbrella. During summer, shorts, tank tops, and T-shirts are the norm. "Down the Shore" tends to be a bit cooler and windy—carry a windbreaker and pack long pants. Beach attire typically consists of a swimsuit, flip-flops, a beach towel, and a shirt and shorts for cover-up. Beachgoers commonly lug makeshift living rooms onto the sand: folding chairs, a beach umbrella, and a tote packed with sunscreen, an iPod, bottled water, and a novel. Bug spray helps keep summer's nasty greenflies at bay. A notable temperature shift occurs in autumn—don't forget a light jacket.

Paterson's Great Falls, Gateway Region

Transportation

New Jersey is 150 miles long and 69 miles wide at its widest point, about 1.5–2 hours' drive across and 2.5–3 hours' drive from top to bottom. While public transport is viable for exploring small stretches like the Gateway's Gold Coast, a car is essential for travel between regions or through the state's more remote areas, like Warren County and the Pinelands. Toll roads are the bane of New Jersey driving, with fees along the New Jersey Turnpike, Garden State Parkway, Atlantic City Expressway, and between many shore towns.

New Jersey springs to life Memorial Day Weekend, when the state's entire population seemingly climbs into cars and heads down the Shore. This mass exodus becomes a weekly ritual through Labor Day, making west-east and Parkway traffic unbearable Friday evenings and Saturday mornings; plan ahead.

Point Pleasant Beach

Explore New Jersey

► THE BEST OF NEW JERSEY

New Jersey is packed with so many historic sights, urban enclaves, recreational regions, and quirky attractions that a few weeks are required to really delve into things. Unfortunately, most visitors have 10 days to devote at best. Don't worry—that's plenty of time for a good state overview, allowing brief stopovers at places you may want to concentrate on during future visits. The best times of year for touring are late spring, early summer, or fall, when prices are lower, crowds are minimized, most establishments host at least limited business hours, and temperatures are generally pleasant. This tour begins in the Gateway Region but can easily be started from Philadelphia, Trenton, or even from Cape May, by way of the Cape May–Lewes Ferry. In addition to usual suitcase necessities, you may want to bring camping gear to enjoy the recommended outdoor sleeps.

Day 1

Begin at Ellis Island, catching the ferry from Liberty State Park. Spend the afternoon touring the immigration museum and maybe searching for your ancestors' names. Afterward, hop over to Hoboken's Washington Street for dinner. Spend your evening at the city's new W Hotel.

Day 2

Drive I-80 west across the state to the Delaware Water Gap. Spend the day exploring this naturally scenic region, heading north to visit High Point State Park and the state's highest peak. Stay at Hope's Inn at Millrace Pond, or in summer, camp at one of the numerous area resorts.

Day 3

South along Route 519 takes you past meandering hills and open farmland into Milford. Take time to explore the town before continuing into Frenchtown, where bike rentals are available at Cycle Corner Bicycle Shop for easy cycling south along the D&R Canal, en route to Lambertville. Spend the evening in Frenchtown's Widow McCrea B&B.

Day 4

Head south again—this time in your car—to Trenton, for a day of museum hopping.

WEEKEND GETAWAYS

Tony's Freehold Grill

There's perhaps no U.S. state better suited for a weekend getaway than New Jersey, conveniently sandwiched between New York City and Philadelphia. The following trips are accessible from the area's major points, and at most require an extra tank of gas and a few additional hours' driving time.

FROM NEW YORK CITY

Friday, drive west to the Skylands and a stay at Milford's romantic **Chestnut Hill on the Delaware.** Enjoy dinner at nearby **Milford Oyster House.**

Following breakfast, head south to explore **Frenchtown** and **Stockton,** continuing on to **Lambertville** for antique shopping, gallery browsing, and a late lunch at **Lambertville Station.**

Your evening is reserved for a scenic **balloon ride** with Alexandria Balloon Flights, complete with a champagne toast. Follow it with a quiet night on the B&B's veranda or a couple of beers at Milford's **Ship Inn.**

Sunday, travel east for a relaxing afternoon at **Round Valley Recreation Area.** Return to New York.

FROM PHILADELPHIA

Take the Atlantic City Expressway to Route 9 North and **Historic Smithville** for two nights at the **Colonial Inn Bed & Breakfast.** Enjoy dinner and drinks at the **Smithville Inn.**

Saturday, drive north along Route 9, connecting with Route 542 east into the **Pinelands.** Spend an afternoon exploring **Wharton State Forest** before dining at Leeds Point's **Oyster Creek Inn.**

Sunday, stroll Smithville, if you haven't already, then head west for brunch at the **Renault Winery.** Enjoy wine tasting before returning to the Pinelands along Route 563. Stop by **Batsto,** a restored mining and glassmaking village, then continue north to Route 70 West en route to Philly. Stop for a bite at Cherry Hill's **Caffe Aldo Lamberti.**

FROM TRENTON

Travel across New Jersey's center to **Red Bank** for two nights at the **Oyster Point Hotel.** After check-in, head downtown for dinner and cocktails at **Teak.**

Start Saturday dining at **No Ordinary Café** and browsing downtown's shops. Afterward, drive east toward **Sandy Hook** for an afternoon at the beach and a snack at the **Sea Gull's Nest.** Later visit the Highlands, taking in lovely views from the **Twin Lights of Navesink.** Return to Red Bank for more dining and nightlife.

Depart for Freehold and an early lunch at **Tony's Freehold Grill,** then continue west along Route 537, stopping at Jackson's **Outlet Village** before returning home.

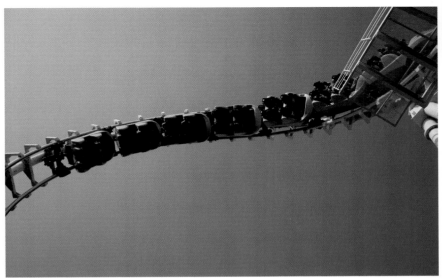

flipping for Wildwood

Day 5

From Trenton drive east to Princeton. Walk around Princeton University campus, browse the shops, and enjoy pub-style dining at the Yankee Doodle Tap Room.

Day 6

Visit Grounds for Sculpture in nearby Hamilton Township, where you'll want to spend a few hours wandering before heading south along I-295 to Camden County. Check into the Haddonfield Inn, and enjoy an Italian dinner in nearby Collingswood.

Day 7

Beeline southeast to Cape May, where you can meander around the historic district, take a trolley tour, or simply sunbathe. For a peaceful evening, choose from one of the many Victorian bed-and-breakfasts and spend your time on the front porch people-watching. If it's entertainment you're after, head north to Wildwood, where you can cruise the boardwalk, ride the roller coasters, and stay the night in one of the city's famed and endangered doo-wop motels.

Day 8

Enjoy a leisurely drive north along Ocean Drive, passing through Stone Harbor, Avalon, and Sea Isle City, before arriving in Ocean City, where you may want to stop for a slice of pizza along the boards. Continue on to Atlantic City and enjoy late-afternoon shopping at the Pier, riding in one of the Boardwalk's rolling chairs, or playing your cards at the blackjack table. Stay the night in the Chelsea Hotel.

Day 9

Hop on the Garden State Parkway heading north, and exit at Route 72 west for an afternoon of Pinelands canoeing. Camp at one of the nearby resorts.

Day 10

Back on the Garden State Parkway heading north, stop for lunch in Downtown Red Bank before returning to the Gateway Region.

► ON THE SHORE

One hundred twenty-seven Atlantic coastline miles are a lot of beach to choose from. How do you know you're heading to the town or city best suited to your style, preferences, and needs? This guide will help you plan the ultimate shore vacation, whether you're a beach bum, music lover, surf junkie, or all of the above plus a family of four.

To start, Manasquan and Long Beach Island offer the shore's best surf. For privacy, there's LBI's Island Beach and Cape May Point's Higbee Beach. Atlantic City, Wildwood, and Strathmere beaches all have free access. Sandy Hook's North Beach has a Manhattan backdrop, while its Gunnison Beach is clothing-optional. Belmar and Asbury Park both have beautiful stretches of pristine sand. At a half mile wide, Wildwood hosts New Jersey's largest beaches. Cape May's Sunset Beach is the only New Jersey beach to watch the sun rise and set over the water. LBI's Harvey Cedars is known for its bay beach. Fishers will want to head to Belmar, Keyport, Point Pleasant Inlet, and the Delaware Bayshore's Fortescue for good fishing. Read on...

History

Lighthouses exist along the coast, including the Highlands, Long Beach Island, and Cape May. For architecture, don't miss Cape May's Victorians, Ocean City's Spanish-style downtown and boardwalk, Beach Haven's Cedar-shingled historic district, and Asbury Park's art deco diamonds in the rough. Brigantine, Ocean City, and Long Beach Island are the places to learn about coastal shipwrecks, and you can also visit Cape May Point's Sunset Beach to see Atlantus, a sunken concrete ship. Asbury Park and Wildwood have two of the most prolific music histories along the East Coast. Cape May and Long Branch, where James Garfield died, are associated with presidential history. Atlantic City has one of the most fascinating life stories of any city existing. Stop by the Boardwalk's Atlantic City historical museum to learn more.

Lodging

Cape May is New Jersey's bed-and-breakfast capital, with dozens of lodgings to choose from. Upscale Spring Lake's B&Bs,

horseshoe crabs laying eggs along Fortescue's coast

NEW JERSEY POP

For quirky roadside attractions and pop-culture history, New Jersey is king. Hit the state's back roads and byways for a tour unlike any other:

MUSIC HISTORY
Head to **Hoboken** for a self-guided **Sinatra tour;** stroll Springsteen's adopted hometown of **Asbury Park;** and visit the 1950s-inspired **Wildwoods,** where Chubby Checker first twisted and Dick Clark's *American Bandstand* spent summer vacations.

THE BIG AND SMALL SCREENS
Tour the Gateway's **"Soprano Land"** with the New York City-based bus tour; dine at *Garden State's* **Medieval Times** in the Meadowlands; stop by the Skylands' **Blairstown,** filming locale of the original *Friday the 13th;* and drive through Vineland and the Shore's Cape May County seeking out spots from *Eddie and the Cruisers.* **Kevin Smith** lovers, don't miss Red Bank and surrounding Monmouth County.

JERSEY ELITE
See **Albert Einstein's** former home and workplace in **Princeton;** visit poet **Walt Whitman's** deathbed and tomb in **Camden;** and explore **Thomas Edison's** former factories in **Edison**

and **West Orange. Grace Kelly's** childhood summer home still stands at **Ocean City's** 26th and Wesley Avenue, and the **Lindbergh** "Trial of the Century" courthouse remains on **Flemington's** Main Street.

KITSCHY AND QUIRKY
Take a **Meadowlands' ecotour** while searching out Jimmy Hoffa's remains; see a live snake den at the Skylands' **Space Farms Zoo and Museum;** go west at Netcong's **Wild West City** theme park and South Jersey's **Cowtown Rodeo;** and go inside **Margate's Lucy the Elephant,** the country's only multistory beachfront pachyderm. Want more? Hunt the **Pinelands' Jersey Devil** and visit the *Hindenburg* crash site, then head over to Grover's Mill, home to Orson Welles' infamous *War of the Worlds'* **Martian landing.**

JERSEY RUINS
Tour among mansion remnants in **Palisades Interstate Park;** see the Skylands' remains of Hamburg's **Gingerbread Castle** and Oak Ridge's **Fairytale Forest** (off Route 23); and seek out **forgotten towns** scattered throughout the Pinelands.

---

although smaller in number, are just as grand. For more affordable inns with ocean breezes, check out Ocean Grove. Into mid-'50s modern architecture? Don't miss Wildwood. Try Atlantic City for penthouse suites.

For Families
Ocean City Beach and Point Pleasant Beach are ideal for kids. The former hosts activities like sand-sculpting contests and hermit-crab races throughout summer, while the latter features beachfront family movies and an aquarium. Both host terrific family-friendly boardwalks with amusements, arcades, and some of the best shore food around (fried Oreos, anyone?).

Shopping
Newly reinvented Atlantic City offers the shore's best shopping opportunities, including the Walk, the Quarter, and the Pier. For antiques, check out Asbury Park's Cookman Avenue or shops along Route 9, west of Long Beach Island and again around Sea Isle-Cape May. Spring Lake's Third Avenue has numerous worthwhile shops, as does tiny Bay Head.

Nightlife
What you consider nightlife will determine where you'll go. For bars spelling Jersey, stick to Seaside Heights and Wildwood. Belmar's bars are a bit more refined, as are

JERSEY CRAVINGS

Not only is it the de facto diner capital, New Jersey's assortment of ethnic enclaves offers culinary options galore. You just have to know where to look.

DINERS

Diners exist statewide, although they vary in quality and offerings. Here are some of New Jersey's best.

Best Late-Night Haunts

Stop in for coffee, sandwiches, or sliced pie after midnight at the Gateway's **Meadowlands Diner,** Hoboken's **Malibu Diner,** Jersey City's **White Mana,** and South Jersey's **Colonial Diner** in Woodbury.

Most Authentic

For a true diner experience (long counter, booths, chrome fixtures) you can't beat the following: Jersey City's **Miss America Diner,** Summit's **Summit Diner,** Tony's Freehold Grill in Central Jersey, Barnegat's **Moustache Bill's,** and **Angelo's** in Glassboro, South Jersey.

Best Eats

Don't miss the burgers at Clifton's **Tick Tock** and South Jersey's **Phily Diner** and **Marlton Diner;** cheese bread at Bordentown's **Mastoris;** desserts at Cherry Hill's **Ponzio's;** and sliders at Hackensack's **White Manna.**

INTERNATIONAL FLAIR

Whatever your taste, you'll find it in New Jersey.

Italian

Italian eats are prevalent throughout the Garden State. Hotspots include Trenton's **Chambersburg District,** downtown **Hoboken,** South Jersey's **Haddon Avenue,** and the Shore's **Bradley Beach.**

South American and Caribbean

Newark's **Ironbound District** is the place for

the Gateway's Summit Diner

South American, Spanish, and Portuguese fare. Head to the Gateway's **Union City** for the state's finest cubano sandwiches.

Indian and Middle Eastern

Jersey City's **Journal Square** and Edison's **Oak Tree Road** are home to some of the best Indian eateries in the tristate region. You'll find the best selection of Middle Eastern eateries in **Paterson.**

Asian

Fort Lee and **Palisades Park** are best known for their Korean cuisine, and **Edgewater** hosts one of the area's best Japanese marketplaces. For Thai eats, try the Skylands' **Somerville** and South Jersey's **Voorhees;** for Chinese, visit **Edison** and **Route 1** between Princeton and New Brunswick.

Atlantic City

Sea Isle's, Avalon's, and Stone Harbor's. Live Jersey Shore bands? There's no better place than Asbury Park; it is rock-and-roll history. For New York City–style clubbing, Atlantic City can't be beat. It's also the place to catch big-name acts like Dylan and Elton John. If you're looking for luxe, it's Atlantic City again, along with Long Beach Island, which has recently earned the nickname "the Jersey Shore Hamptons." While there, swing by Daddy O—it's a must.

Seafood

New Jersey's oceanfront locale makes it a great location for sampling seafood. Some of the freshest seafood is served dockside in Point Pleasant Beach, Belmar, Long Beach Island's Viking Village and Harvey Cedars, and Sea Isle City.

▶ TRAIL MIX

New Jersey offers a variety of outdoor opportunities, and whatever you're into—birding, cycling, hiking, canoeing, kayaking, scuba diving, or winter sports—you'll find something to suit your tastes. Rivers, lakes, and streams are plentiful statewide, making New Jersey a popular place for water activities, and as far as mountainous terrain, scenic roads, wetlands, marshlands, open land, and open sky, the state has you covered.

Cycling

The Skylands' Ringwood State Park and its Ridge and Valley Region's Jenny Jump State Forest offer excellent mountain biking trails, and during summer months Vernon's Mountain Creek transforms into a downhill two-wheel haven. The roads around Morris County's Great Swamp and the Central Piedmont's Round Valley Recreation Area are ideal for cycling. Casual riders

Mountain Creek's snow-tubing hill on a clear day

have plenty of opportunities, including the Delaware River towns' D&R Canal towpath, Central Jersey's 5.5-mile Edgar Felix Bike Path, and the Henry Hudson Bike Trail from Keyport to the Atlantic Highlands. For more of a challenge, try the Gateway's Henry Hudson Drive, lined by Palisades Interstate Park's sheer cliffs.

Hiking

Short day hikes are in supply statewide, and there are several longer, more strenuous routes that challenge even experienced hikers. For trails both scenic and easy, try South Jersey's Belleplain State Forest and Parvin State Park, Central Jersey's Washington Crossing State Park, or Morris County's Jockey Hollow. The Pinelands' 50-mile Batona Trail traverses a few area forests, but its flat terrain and numerous entry points make it accessible for even casual hikers. Experienced-hiker trails include the Skylands' incongruent Highland Trail, the 20-mile Sussex Branch Trail, and the 27-mile Paulinskill Valley Trail, as well as many smaller trails at Gateway's Palisades Interstate Park that can be conjoined. All offer rewarding views coupled with vast expanses of changing scenery.

a great egret at Brigantine's E.B. Forsythe National Wildlife Refuge

Bird-Watching

As part of the Atlantic Flyway migratory route, New Jersey is an excellent spot for birding. Some of the state's best opportunities are within Morris County's Great Swamp, also home to the Raptor Trust; and the Brigantine division of the E.B. Forsythe National Wildlife Refuge. Both are best visited during spring and fall. Cape May Point and Cumberland County are exceptional birding locales. The region hosts both a Winter Eagle Festival and May's World Series of Birding annually. Long Beach Island's Island Beach State Park and Sandy Hook are two other birding favorites. They're both great places for spotting waterfowl, raptors, and ospreys. The Meadowlands' marshes are a good place to bird-watch from the comfort of a canoe or kayak.

Winter Sports

Skiing and snowboarding prevail in New Jersey's Skylands, where the Vernon Valley hosts both Hidden Valley, a family-oriented albeit semiprivate ski club, and Mountain Creek, ideal for downhill skiers of all levels and a favorite spot among hard-core snowboarders. Mountain Creek also features a snow-tubing park. For anyone who enjoys cross-country skiing there are trails statewide, most notably in the Ridge and Valley Region's High Point State Park, South Jersey's

an osprey nesting in Cumberland County

Belleplain State Forest, Central Jersey's Washington Crossing and Monmouth Battlefield State Parks, and the Pinelands' Brendan T. Byrne State Forest.

Adventure Activities

New Jersey is no New Zealand, mind you, but the state does host a couple of adrenaline-rush activities. Skydiving takes place in Skylands' Sussex County, near Central Jersey's Allaire State Park, and just outside South Jersey's Washington Township in Williamstown. For a heart-stopping experience over water, Wildwood hosts the Silver Bullet speedboat, as well as parasailing, also available in Beach Haven and Avalon.

Washington Crossing State Park

▶ KIDDING AROUND

A wide range of historical parks, living-history farms, museums, boardwalks, aquariums and zoos, natural sights, roadside attractions, and pleasant shore towns make New Jersey a wonderful state for a family to explore together. Some destinations, such as the Cape May Zoo, are free, while others offer kid-friendly discounts.

Day 1

Begin your trip in South Jersey with a visit to Camden's Adventure Aquarium and adjacent Children's Garden, then drive north for overnight lodging in Mount Laurel. PAWS Farm Nature Center, a play station and petting farm where kids learn without ever knowing it, is located nearby.

Day 2

Hop on I-295 north en route toward Trenton to explore the city's Old Barracks Museum and visit New Jersey's State House for a lesson in civics and history. During summer you might also try nearby Howell Living History Farm, offering agricultural demonstrations interesting to young and old.

Trenton's Old Barracks Museum

a late spring afternoon on the Ocean City boardwalk

Day 3

Drive east to Six Flags Theme Park for a safari drive-through and a day at the amusements. Stay at a nearby hotel, or continue east to the Shore.

Day 4

South along the Garden State Parkway will bring you to Storybook Land, just west of Atlantic City. It really is fun for all ages (especially during winter holidays), although teens may prefer checking out nearby Smithville's interesting specialty shops. Afterward, make the trip into Ocean City for an evening of boardwalk strolling, miniature golf, and skee ball.

Day 5

Spend the morning collecting shells along the beach, then take a leisurely drive along Route 9 south to Stone Harbor's Wetlands Institute. Explore the marshlands, visit the aquarium, maybe even head out in a canoe. You may also want to visit the nearby Cape May Zoo, a free park that's home to tigers, bears, and lemurs. Scour Cape May Point's Sunset Beach for "diamonds" before driving onto the Cape May–Lewes Ferry, heading back toward Philadelphia via Delaware.

THE GATEWAY REGION

Mention New Jersey to most people and they picture the urban Northeast—a congested conglomeration of highways, high density, smokestacks, and smog that seems little more than a New York City suburb. It's true New Jersey's Gateway Region is only a bridge and tunnel away from the Big Apple, and that the two regions share much of the same history. Together they represented a gateway of freedom for millions of immigrants arriving to Ellis Island, and Germans, Italians, and Irish settled on both sides of the Hudson River in unprecedented numbers, building neighborhoods filled with sidewalk storefronts and brick and brownstone homes. Like New York City, Newark quickly established itself as a major urban center, becoming one of the world's leading manufacturing cities. And Paterson was established as the first

planned industrial center in the United States. Gateway towns like the suburban Oranges and mountainside Montclair eventually became refuges for the civilian urban overflow.

While today's Gateway region has morphed into a Manhattanite escape from the city's astronomical rents, its personality remains strictly Jersey. As the state's smallest region, the Gateway's offerings are more diverse than all of New Jersey's other regions combined. There's Jersey City's Little India, Union City's Little Havana, Newark's Portuguese, Spanish, and South American Ironbound district, Hoboken's Irish pubs, and Paterson's Middle Eastern cafés. The Gateway's also the state's most cosmopolitan region, offering some of New Jersey's best shopping, including boutiques along Hoboken's Washington Street, Ridgewood's

THE GATEWAY REGION

HIGHLIGHTS

(**Ellis Island:** Located in Upper New York Harbor, this New World welcoming place belongs not only to New York and New Jersey, but to the millions of immigrants who first arrived on its shores (page 28).

(**Hoboken:** Once down-and-out, the mile-square city has sprung back to life tenfold, most notably along Washington Street's 14 blocks where boutiques and specialty shops, cafés, bars, restaurants, and superb people-watching opportunities are the norm (page 33).

(**Palisades Interstate Park:** Jersey's side of a joint state recreational palace is 12 miles of sheer cliffs and wooded canopies, making it easy to forget you're right across the river from the country's largest city and smack in the center of the country's most densely populated region (page 40).

(**Ecotours in the Meadowlands:** It seems like a stretch, but these former dumping grounds have cleaned up their act and image and are now an ecotourism hot spot. Bring along the binoculars, and keep your eyes peeled for shore birds — along with Jimmy Hoffa's remains (page 42).

(**Newark Museum:** New Jersey's largest museum is jam-packed with art and science exhibits that include world-renowned sculpture, hungry piranhas, Red Planet star shows, and one of the greatest Tibetan collections in the western hemisphere (page 49).

(**Tick Tock Diner:** There's no better place to begin a tour of New Jersey's famous diners than the Tick Tock — a shiny chrome space with booths and counter seating as well as the juiciest burgers in town (page 60).

LOOK FOR (TO FIND RECOMMENDED SIGHTS, ACTIVITIES, DINING, AND LODGING.

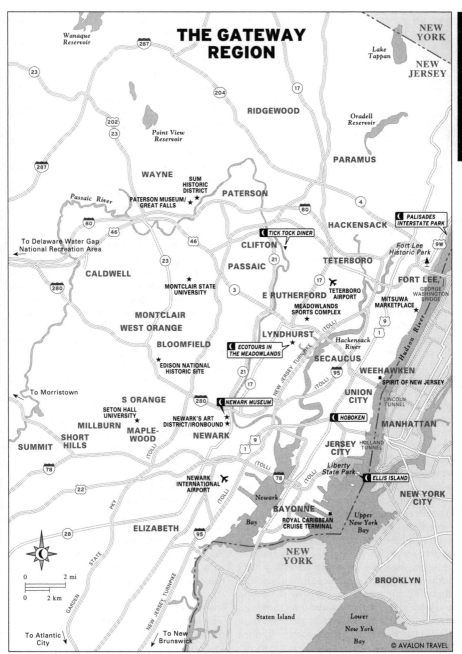

specialty shops, the Mall at Short Hills, and the Secaucus outlets. And what about sports? The Gateway's Meadowlands are home to both the New York Giants and New York Jets football teams and the New York/New Jersey Red Bulls soccer team, and Newark houses both ice hockey's New Jersey Devils and minor league baseball's Newark Bears. With so much going on, locals need opportunities to escape. Thankfully, there's Palisades Interstate Park, a thin stretch of Hudson riverside land offering some of the New Jersey–New York metropolitan region's best road cycling and hiking.

When describing local geography it's pretty much impossible to overlook the Gateway's dense highway system, but there are also mountainous outskirts and sheer Palisade cliffs. The Meadowlands are actually one of the region's greatest natural resources, with canoeists and kayakers, naturalists, and birders recently reacquainting themselves with the area's vast wetlands, marshes, and rivers.

Next time you catch a *Sopranos* rerun on A&E, think about all the things Tony could be doing instead of driving along that turnpike. There's an entire Gateway to explore.

PLANNING YOUR TIME

Most Gateway visitors arriving by way of Newark International Airport are simply passing through with little time to spend. Others cross the Hudson River for an afternoon, day, or weekend excursion. The Gateway's overall area is pretty small, and (sans traffic) it can be covered easily in a relatively short time. It makes sense to visit the region for a day or a weekend, adding an extra day or two for a more comprehensive area view. Easily accessible from most East Coast cities, the Gateway Region makes an easy round-trip. Public transport is better here than anywhere else in the state.

Begin your day trip from New York City with a ferry ride to Hoboken. Enjoy breakfast along Washington Street, pursue the shops, and admire the city's exquisite brownstone architecture. Afterwards, stop by the waterfront Hoboken Historical Museum for a look at the displays, or pick up a map at the museum's front desk and head out on a self-guided Sinatra walking tour.

From the Hoboken Terminal catch a PATH train into downtown Jersey City, stopping off at the Grove Street Station to check out the Jersey City Museum. You may prefer continuing on to Journal Square instead for a tour of the old Stanley Theatre and Indian eats along Newark Avenue. Another option is the PATH into downtown Newark for a stroll along Ferry Street, also known as Portugal Avenue, before spending the afternoon at the Newark Museum. Return to Ferry Street for dinner and sit back and enjoy. Don't worry if you've missed the ferry; you can catch a PATH train back into Manhattan from Newark, Jersey City, or Hoboken until approximately midnight.

If planning a weekend trip and traveling by car, spend the evening at one of Jersey City's waterfront hotels, and drive up the Gold Coast into Palisades Interstate Park the following day. While there, keep an eye out for remnants of millionaires' mansions. Park for a picnic, or go hiking along the scenic cliffs.

If you have an extra day, spend it in the Urban Northeast. Shop in Ridgewood, stop for a photo op at Paterson's Great Falls, then head south into Clifton for lunch at the Tick Tock Diner. Afterwards, pay a visit to the Montclair Art Museum, or continue on into West Orange for an afternoon at Turtle Zoo. If you're ready for more shopping, drive over to Short Hills and spend, spend, spend at New Jersey's most fantastic mall.

INFORMATION AND SERVICES

The Gateway hosts several convenient welcome centers, including **Liberty State Park Tourism Welcome Center** (New Jersey Turnpike Exit 14B, 201/915-3440). Despite its name, the center provides information on accommodations and attractions throughout the region and is located close to Newark Liberty International Airport and New York City. The **Montvale Welcome Center** (201/391-5737), situated at the state's northern border by Garden State Parkway mile marker 172, works best for those entering New Jersey from New York State. The **Satellite Information Center** (Newark Liberty International Airport, Terminal B, International Arrivals, Door 11, 973/623-5052) is the ideal stopping point for international airport arrivals. A fourth center is the New Jersey Turnpike's **Vince Lombardi Travel Plaza and Information Center** (201/943-8757), located between Exits 17 and 18, north of Route 3 and south of Route 46.

GETTING THERE AND AROUND

The **Lincoln Tunnel** connects Weehawken with Manhattan's Midtown, and the **Holland Tunnel** connects Jersey City's Newport neighborhood with New York City's Canal Street. The bicycle- and pedestrian-friendly **George Washington Bridge,** a double-decker suspension bridge, connects Fort Lee to the Bronx. Tolls for both the bridge and tunnels run $8 for autos, with discounts for E-Z Passholders.

NY Waterway (www.nywaterway.com) operates ferry service between New York City and numerous New Jersey Gold Coast cities, including Weehawken, Edgewater, Hoboken, and Jersey City. **Newark Liberty International Airport** (888/397-4636, www.panynj.gov) is the region's major transport hub for out-of-state arrivals and is connected by train to Newark's Penn Station and midtown Manhattan.

Newark Pennsylvania Station is a hub for NJ Transit and Amtrak trains as well as Greyhound and interstate transit buses. **PATH** (800/234-7284, www.panynj.gov/path) trains and the **Hudson-Bergen Light Rail** (800/772-2222, www.mylightrail.com) connect Gold Coast cities, as well as Newark, to each other and to New York City.

NJ Transit (800/772-2222, www.njtransit .com) runs commuter trains throughout the Gateway Region with stops in most larger towns; main transfer points are Hoboken Terminal and Secaucus Junction.

Prominent auto routes running through the region include I-280 (the Urban Outskirts), I-80 (the Urban Northeast), the New Jersey Turnpike, and the Garden State Parkway. Routes 17 and 3 connect most Meadowlands towns. A good way to enter the Gateway Region is from the north, taking Palisades Interstate Parkway south from New York State into New Jersey. This will ease you into the urban waterfront towns of Fort Lee, Edgewater, Weehawken, and Hoboken before introducing expansive Jersey City.

Jersey City and the Gold Coast

Though some people turn up their noses at Jersey City, this Hudson River locale offers spectacular Manhattan views along with fine dining and nightlife options, a spacious park, several wonderful museums, and cultural events year-round. The city is North Jersey's own financial center and home to much of New York City's overflow—a dense population of people, commerce, business, and backgrounds offering some of the area's best Big Apple alternatives.

Situated on a peninsula between the Hackensack and Hudson Rivers and the Newark and New York Bays, sprawling 14.8-square-mile Jersey City is located so close to Manhattan's downtown district that it's often referred to as "the sixth borough." By all accounts, Jersey City has vastly improved from what it was just over a decade ago. The city has completely revamped its waterfront, adding mixed-use properties and glass-walled towers, including the 42-story Goldman Sachs building, New Jersey's tallest structure. In downtown areas like Van Vorst Park, Hamilton Park, and Harsimus Cove, brownstones that were once occupied by squatters have been renovated into million-dollar pads.

Once a great transportation and manufacturing hub, Jersey City remains a convergence point for many of the region's major routes and

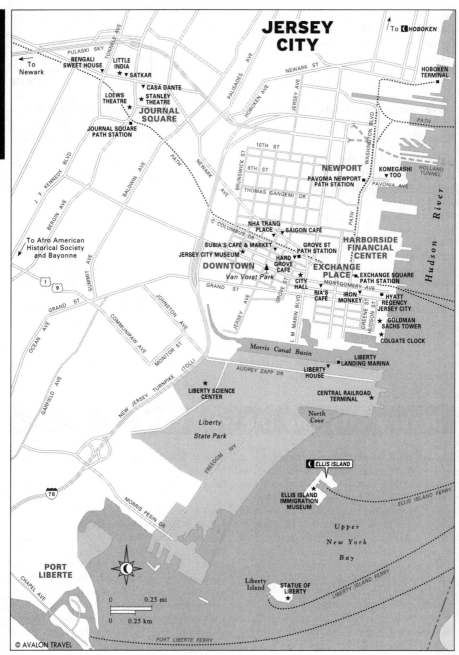

JERSEY CITY

To HOBOKEN

PULASKI SKY

To Newark

BENGALI SWEET HOUSE
LITTLE INDIA
★ ▼ SATKAR
▼ CASA DANTE
★ STANLEY THEATRE
LOEWS THEATRE ★
JOURNAL SQUARE
JOURNAL SQUARE PATH STATION ■

HOBOKEN TERMINAL

NEWARK ST

PATH

NEWPORT
PAVONIA NEWPORT PATH STATION ■
10TH ST
8TH ST
THOMAS GANGEMI DR

KOMEGASHI ▼ TOO
PAVONIA AVE
HOLLAND TUNNEL

To Afro American Historical Society and Bayonne

NHA TRANG PLACE ▼ ★ SAIGON CAFÉ
SUBIA'S CAFÉ & MARKET ▼
JERSEY CITY MUSEUM ★
DOWNTOWN
Van Vorst Park
HARD ▼ GROVE CAFÉ
GROVE ST PATH STATION

HARBORSIDE FINANCIAL CENTER
EXCHANGE PLACE ■ EXCHANGE SQUARE PATH STATION
★ CITY HALL
MONTGOMERY AVE
RIA'S ▼ CAFÉ
IRON ▼ MONKEY
● HYATT REGENCY JERSEY CITY
★ GOLDMAN SACHS TOWER
COLGATE CLOCK ★

Morris Canal Basin
LIBERTY LANDING MARINA ■
AUDREY ZAPP DR
LIBERTY ▼ HOUSE
★ LIBERTY SCIENCE CENTER
CENTRAL RAILROAD TERMINAL ★

Liberty State Park

North Cove

ELLIS ISLAND

ELLIS ISLAND IMMIGRATION MUSEUM ★

Upper New York Bay

Liberty Island
STATUE OF LIBERTY ★

PORT LIBERTE

Hudson River
Hudson River

ELLIS ISLAND FERRY
LIBERTY ISLAND FERRY
PORT LIBERTE FERRY

0   0.25 mi
0   0.25 km

© AVALON TRAVEL

train lines. A good thing, because Jersey City is not a walkable place—neighborhoods are scattered, streets are potholed, and traffic rules lax. Rather than a definitive center, the city has many small enclaves hosting numerous nationalities, including Irish, Italian, Puerto Rican, Russian, Indian, and Asian.

SIGHTS
The Financial Waterfront
Easily visible from New York City, Jersey City's waterfront stretches over several miles from the **Newport** neighborhood south of the Holland Tunnel down through Liberty State Park and into **Port Liberte,** a mixed-use residential space that's one of the city's newest communities. The city's financial hub, **Exchange Place,** stands tall along the waterfront center, directly across the Hudson from New York City's Wall Street. Jersey City's revitalization is most notable here, with a new hotel and New Jersey's tallest structure—the **Goldman Sachs Tower**—soaring high at the end of Hudson Street. Across the street in an otherwise empty

© LAURA KINIRY

Colgate Clock, a Jersey City landmark

lot stands the octagonal **Colgate Clock.** Fifty-five feet in diameter, it's said to be the world's largest clock, and once stood atop the now-demolished Colgate-Palmolive building. This local icon continues on as a reminder of prosperous days past—something the city has been attempting to re-create, with notable success.

Like many financial centers, Exchange Place turns into a ghost town after 5 P.M. weekdays, but occasional festivals and fairs keep things lively on weekends year-round. There is not a ton to see here, but the recent development explosion makes this a pleasant place to walk around.

Van Vorst Park
Van Vorst Park is a Jersey City historic district and one of the city's nicest neighborhoods. Central to downtown, it's only a short PATH ride west of the Financial Waterfront, and it can be easily explored from the Grove Street Station. The neighborhood is small, but its streets are lined with cafés, restaurants, and restored brownstones, including several gorgeous structures along York Street. In the neighborhood's center stands its namesake community park (Montgomery St. and Jersey Ave.), home to a seasonal flea market. The park also serves as main rehearsal venue for summer shows by the **Hudson Shakespeare Company** (hudsonshakespeare.org). The **Jersey City Free Public Library** (472 Jersey Ave., 201/547-4500, Mon.–Thurs. 9 A.M.–8 P.M., weekends 9 A.M.–5 P.M.) and City Hall (280 Grove St.), both nearby, are good reference points for navigating the area.

Van Vorst Park hosts one of the city's best museums, the **Jersey City Museum** (350 Montgomery St., 201/413-0303, www.jerseycitymuseum.org, Wed.–Fri. 11 A.M.–5 P.M., Sat.–Sun. noon–5 P.M., Thurs. 5–8 P.M., $4 adult, $2 senior and student), a modern structure housing a permanent collection of 19th- and 20th-century fine art and historic objects as well as an ever-changing contemporary exhibit. A museum highlight is the local history collection, which includes a collection of glass and ceramic works by the American Pottery

Company and the Jersey Glass Company, and detailed studies of Jersey City's environmental and cultural geography by landscape painter August Will and pictorial photographer William Armbruster.

Liberty State Park

Created in 1976 for the U.S. Bicentennial, 1,200-acre Liberty State Park (www.liberty statepark.com, daily from 6 A.M.) is one of the region's most popular recreation spots. It feels massive, although large portions of the park remain closed to the public. Fortunately its prime waterfront stretch is accessible and is often packed on weekend afternoons with Frisbee players, picnickers, and travelers en route to Ellis Island. The park hosts numerous walking trails and dining options, several historic sites, an IMAX theater, and a high-tech museum worth the admission price.

The two-mile waterfront **Liberty Walk** connects Liberty State Park's north and south portions, offering sweeping view of the Hudson, including Ellis Island and Manhattan, and a unique profile view of the Statue of Liberty. Boats are launched from **Liberty Landing Marina,** where **water taxis** (201/985-1164) are available for bay cruises and cross-river trips to New York City. History buffs will appreciate the **Central Railroad of New Jersey Terminal** or CRNJT (201/915-3440). Located along Liberty Walk in the park's northeast corner, it was once the main transport center for thousands of arriving immigrants. Today, CRNJT serves as a welcome center, hosting changing displays relating to the immigrant journey.

In the park's northwest corner stands the recently reinvented **Liberty Science Center** (222 Jersey City Blvd., 201/200-1000, www .lsc.org, Mon.–Fri. 9 A.M.–5 P.M., weekends and holidays 9 A.M.–6 P.M.), one of the area's finest attractions. The center reopened in July 2007 after a nearly two-year renovation, completely revamping itself as a think-globally, act-locally resource for living, learning, and working. Exhibits are multifaceted. Want to learn more about a display? Dial your cell phone to hear recorded staffers share additional details. The center also hosts Exhibit Live, an online exhibit accessible from your home computer, meaning the center's open—in a way—24/7. In-house exhibits include a 10-foot-long Graffiti Expressions Wall, where visitors can tag or draw with digital paint, and Wonder Why, a collection of favorites from the former museum, like a rock wall and an animation stand. The center also features a digital 3-D theater, as well as an IMAX Dome theater screening Discovery Channel–type films. Entry to Liberty Science Center is $15.75 adult, $11.50 senior and child under age 12, and $5 for teachers, with a separate IMAX entry price of $9, $8, and $7. It's possible to attend an IMAX theater show without exploring the center, though if you'd like to do both, a combination ticket costs $22.75 adult, $17.50 senior, and $12 for teachers.

Statue Cruises (877/523-9849, www .statuecruises.com, $12 adult, $10 senior, $5 child 4–12) runs ferry service between Liberty State Park, Ellis Island, and Liberty Island (home to the Statue of Liberty), from roughly 9 A.M.–5 P.M. daily year-round, with extended service during the summer months.

The Hudson-Bergen Light Rail Line stops at the park's northwest corner, close to the Liberty Science Center. From here catch NJ Transit Bus 305 for various points within the park.

◖ Ellis Island

In 1998 the U.S. Supreme Court ruled the bulk of 27.5-acre Ellis Island, including former hospital wards and the superintendent's home, are New Jersey property. But for a thorough visit it only makes sense to cross state borders.

Over 40 percent of Americans can trace their ancestry through Ellis Island, the nation's premier immigration station from its opening in 1892 well into the 20th century. The **Ellis Island Immigration Museum** (212/363-3200, www.ellisisland.org, daily 9:30 A.M.–5:15 P.M., extended hours during summer, free), part of the greater Statue of Liberty National Monument, honors the millions of American immigrants who arrived through these gates: People like Bob Hope, the Von Trapp family, and many of our grandparents and great-grandparents. Located within the Main Building of the former immigration station complex, the museum houses a series of self-guided exhibits that include immigrant photos, letters, and personal artifacts such as luggage and clothing. There's also a Wall of Honor inscribed with the names of over 700,000 immigrants, gifts of prosperity from family and friends. Visitors can tour the immigration station's original baggage room, railroad ticket office, and registry room, as well as a third-floor dormitory, all restored to their turn-of-the-20th-century appearance.

In 2001 the museum introduced the American Family Immigration History Center, where descendants can trace their Ellis Island ancestry with the combined aid of computers and personal assistants. Once found, it's possible to obtain a photo of the ship they sailed on along with a copy of its original passenger list.

Ferry rides (877/782-9849, www.statue cruises.com) to Ellis Island cost $12 adult and $5 child, with parking available at Liberty State Park. There is no admission fee to visit the island. A museum "food court" is open for snacks.

Journal Square

To reach Journal Square (www.thenewjournal square.com) from downtown, drive west through what looks like bail bond central, or hop a PATH train to Journal Square Station. Once a vibrant city center, the neighborhood is attempting to reinvent itself. Some retail shops are spread among the neighborhood's old garages, but there is nothing notable. Instead, Journal Square's main draws are its two historic theaters and its dense stretch of Indian shops and eateries—known as Little Bombay or India Square—along Newark Avenue. Signs help to orient you, although the area is hard to mistake.

Successfully avoiding a 1987 scheduled demolition, the once-multiplexed **Loews Theater** (54 Journal Sq., 201/798-6055, www.loews jersey.org) has been glamorously restored to its original 1929 appearance and now hosts independent and classic films, live drama,

children's theater, jazz, and swing shows. It's said Frank Sinatra credits his 1930s attendance of a Bing Crosby show at Loews as his catalyst for entering show business. Jehovah's Witnesses acquired the grand 1928 **Stanley Theater** (2932 Kennedy Blvd., 201/377-3100), one of the country's largest movie theaters, as an assembly hall in 1983. Easily recognizable from the street by its copper marquee and large arched windows, its interior has been lovingly restored and is really quite spectacular; it is well worth a visit for anyone who appreciates architecture and design. Drop-in tours are given daily 8 A.M.–5 P.M., and admission is free.

South of Journal Square in the city's Greenville neighborhood is the **Afro-American Historical Society Museum** (1841 Kennedy Blvd., 201/547-5262, Mon.–Sat. 10 A.M.–5 P.M., closed Sun.). Located on the second floor of the **Greenville Public Library,** it's New Jersey's only museum dedicated solely to African American history. Civil rights posters, a large quilt collection, and a display of Pullman Porter (an African American labor union) memorabilia are among the more than 800 artifacts.

Just north of the square is Little Bombay or India Square, a colorful enclave of Indian eateries, markets, and retail shops tucked along Newark Avenue.

FESTIVALS AND EVENTS

Jersey City hosts dozens of festivals throughout the year, many of them at waterfront **Exchange Place** near the Colgate Clock or at Liberty State Park. These include July's **Jersey City Caribbean Carnival,** August's **Pride Parade** (www.jclgo.org/index1.htm), and September's **Greek Festival** and **Italian Festival.** For specifics, call the Division of Cultural Affairs (201/547-6921). The long-running **Black Maria Film and Video Festival,** hosted by **New Jersey City University** (www.njcu.edu), is also a local favorite.

Perhaps the city's best-known event, the annual **St. Patrick's Day Parade,** held on or around St. Patrick's Day, begins with a morning breakfast and mass followed by an early afternoon parade along Kennedy Boulevard. Festivities culminate at Journal Square, where slurring renditions of "When Irish Eyes are Smiling" repeat well into the evening.

Farmers Markets

Jersey City hosts several weekly farmers markets during warmer months. **Journal Square Farmers Market** (Journal Sq., 201/798-6055, Wed. 11 A.M.–7 P.M.) takes place mid-July–late November. Jersey Fresh fruits and vegetables and a variety of baked goods are available. Stop by if you're in the neighborhood. Additional markets include the waterfront **Newport Pavonia Farmers Market** (Pavonia E. St., 973/879-2696, Tues., Thurs., Sat. 11:30 A.M.–6:30 P.M., late June–late Nov.), downtown's **Friends of Van Vorst Park Farmers Market** (Jersey Ave. and Montgomery St., 201/433-5127, Sat. 8 A.M.–2 P.M., mid-June–late Nov.), and **Harvest Square Farmers Market** (201/432-2128, Tues. 3–6 P.M., mid-July–late Oct.), held at St. Patrick's Roman Church.

ACCOMMODATIONS

Jersey City hosts a few waterfront hotels conveniently located near transit lines and ferry ports. They're ideal jumping-off points for exploring the city's neighborhoods as well as the greater Gold Coast region. These hotels cater primarily to business travelers, and rates drop substantially on weekends.

$150-300

Right across the river from New York City and within walking distance of the Pavonia-Newport PATH Station, the newly renovated **Courtyard by Marriott Jersey City** (540 Washington Blvd., 800/346-8357, www.marriott.com, $189–369) offers clean rooms on 10 floors along with an indoor pool and free wireless Internet and an on-site breakfast café.

At the nearby all-suite **Doubletree Club Suites Jersey City** (455 Washington Blvd., 201/449-2400, $209–379), rooms include a living area, microwave, fridge, and wet bar. A bar and grill are located off the lobby, although room service is available for those preferring to stay put. The hotel is directly across the street from the upscale Newport Centre Mall.

$300-450

In addition to superb Manhattan skyline views, the 14-story **Ⓒ Hyatt Regency Jersey City on the Hudson** (2 Exchange Pl., 201/469-1234 or 800/233-1234, www.hyatt.com, $239–469) offers spacious modern rooms with fridge and *New York Times* daily delivery. Additional amenities include an on-site gift shop/convenience store, ATM, and a heated indoor pool. Unfortunately, connecting to the Internet will cost you.

FOOD AND NIGHTLIFE
The Financial Waterfront

Each one of Jersey City's waterfront enclaves has its own bars and eateries. With so much construction going on, new establishments open seemingly overnight.

The Newport Complex hosts the sleek **Komegashi Too** (99 Town Square Pl., 201/533-8888, www.komegashi.com, $9–24), a traditional Japanese and neofusion restaurant with expansive harbor views. Weekend brunch comes highly recommended, as does the signature nigiri sushi. Komegashi Too is open for lunch noon–2:30 P.M. Monday–Friday, and for dinner 5–10:30 P.M. Monday–Thursday, 5–11 P.M. Friday and Saturday, and 4–10 P.M. Sunday. Brunch hours are 12:30–3 P.M. Saturday and 1–4 P.M. Sunday.

Downtown

Cuban American **Hard Grove Cafe** (319 Grove St., 201/451-1853, www.hardgrovecafe.com, Mon.–Fri. 11 A.M.–1 A.M., Sat. 8 A.M.–1 A.M., Sun. 8 A.M.–10 P.M., $13–22) is kitschy, colorful, and downright fun. Located on the corner of Columbus and Grove Streets right across from the PATH station, it's a great starting point for exploring Van Vorst Park. Besides, their mojitos are billed as the best in town.

Two of the city's best Vietnamese restaurants are located along Newark Avenue. Sprawling **Nha Trang Place** (249 Newark Ave., 201/239-

1988, Sun.–Thurs. 10 A.M.–10:30 P.M., Fri.–Sat. 10 A.M.–11 P.M., $8–14) offers beloved traditional dishes for reasonable prices, along with on-site parking. It's rumored the Village People hang out at smaller **Saigon Café** (188 Newark Ave., 201/332-8711, Mon.–Thurs. 11 A.M.–10 P.M., Fri.–Sat. 11 A.M.–11 P.M., Sun. 2–10 P.M., $6–18), where *pho* is the specialty but tamarind soup is just as popular. Owner Ms. Lee is a café staple.

For fresh juices, vegan dishes, or a healthy snack to go, visit **Subia's Organic Cafe and Market** (506 Jersey Ave., 201/432-7639, Mon.–Fri. 8 A.M.–8:30 P.M., Sat. 8 A.M.–7:30 P.M., Sun. 8 A.M.–6:30 P.M., $7–11). Favorite in-house dishes include vegetarian meatloaf and spicy "buffalo" sticks made from soy. Organic coffee is also served.

Tiny **Ria's Cafe** (24 Mercer St., 201/915-0045, Tues. 11 A.M.–2:30 P.M., Wed.–Sat. 11 A.M.–10 P.M., Sun. 10 A.M.–4:30 P.M., $9–18) serves freshly prepared Dominican dishes and hosts a popular weekend brunch. The frittatas are excellent, but prepare to wait at this BYO—service can be spotty.

Coffee comes strong at **Beechwood Cafe** (290 Grove St., 201/985-2811, Mon.–Fri. 7 A.M.–10 P.M., Sat. 8 A.M.–10 P.M., Sun. 8 A.M.–9 P.M. summer, Mon.–Fri. 7 A.M.–9 P.M., Sat. 8 A.M.–9 P.M., Sun. 8 A.M.–8 P.M. other seasons, $5–12), a local hangout serving a varied selection of sandwiches and sweets. Settle in with a book or swing by with friends for weekend brunch. On your way out, stop by their adjoining market to browse the selection of kitchenware.

Housed within a converted Brownstone, **◖ The Iron Monkey** (97 Greene St., 201/435-5756, www.ironmonkey.com, Mon.–Wed. 11:30 A.M.–midnight, Thurs.–Sat. 11:30 A.M.–1 A.M., Sun. 11:30 A.M.–10 P.M., $11–15) serves a rockin' menu of American-European fare on multiple floors, including a rooftop sundeck offering Hudson River views. Go for the mac and cheese ($11) with mascarpone and wild mushrooms, or simply stop in for a brew at the downstairs pub, where live bands entertain. Brunch is served until 4 P.M. on weekends.

Though specializing in American fare, the **Liberty House** (Liberty State Park, 76 Audrey Zapp Dr., 201/935-0300, www.liberty houserestaurant.com, Tues.–Sat. lunch noon–3 P.M., dinner from 5 P.M., Sun. 11 A.M.–5 P.M., Sunday brunch 11 A.M.–2 P.M., $19–36) also features both a sushi bar and a raw bar. There's a glass-enclosed wine cellar in the lobby, and lengthy glass windows afford diners excellent waterfront views. Situated within Liberty State Park, the restaurant inevitably attracts a tourist crowd, but that hasn't stopped locals from visiting.

Journal Square

Unless you're in the mood for Indian cuisine, Journal Square offers little in the way of dining options. There is, however, one standout exception: **Casa Dante** (737 Newark Ave., 201/795-2750, www.casadante.com, Mon.–Thurs. 11:30 A.M.–10 P.M., Fri. 11:30 A.M.–closing, Sat. 4 P.M.–closing, Sun. 2–9 P.M., $16–40). Just a couple of blocks northeast of the square, it is classic southern Italian that can do no wrong. Though the restaurant recently underwent extensive renovation, those remembering its earlier days will recognize the stained glass windows and mahogany walls.

For Indian food, there's no better place in the city than Newark Avenue's Little India, stretching from Kennedy Boulevard west to Tonnele Avenue. Dozens of Indian markets and eateries line the street on either side, and really, it's hard to go wrong. Vegetarian and vegan snacks, known as *chaats,* are neighborhood specialties. Originating in north India and Gujarat, these fried dough pockets usually come filled with potato, chopped onions, and spices (though texture, sweetness, and ingredients can vary) and topped with a dollop of yogurt or other sauces. They cost $1.50–5. The **Bengali Sweet House** (836 Newark Ave., 201/798-9241, www.bengalisweet.com) is a good place to sample *chaats* along with a selection of Bengali, Punjabi, and Gujarati sweets.

One of the city's most popular Indian restaurants is the vegetarian **Satkar** (806 Newark Ave., 201/963-6309, Tues.–Sun.

10:30 A.M.–9:30 P.M., $3.50–8.50), serving up southern Indian dishes like potato-and-onion-filled *masala dosa* ($5.50) and vegetable *uttapam* ($5.50), a thick pancake topped with grilled veggies. For southern Indian cuisine that includes an expansive *dosa* (the Indian version of a crepe) menu, try the **Dosa Hut** (777 Newark Ave., 201/420-6660, Mon.–Fri. 11 A.M.–10 P.M., Sat.–Sun. 10 A.M.–10 P.M., $5–11). **Rasoi** (810 Newark Ave., 201/222-8850, www.rasoiindianrestaurant.com, lunch Tues.–Fri. 11:30 A.M.–3 P.M., Sat.–Sun. 11:30 A.M.–4:30 P.M., dinner Mon.–Thurs. 5–10 P.M., Fri.–Sun. 5–10:45 P.M., $9–15) offers spacious dining and a full bar, and their northern Indian menu features a large vegetarian selection.

Diners

Not to be mistaken for Hackensack's White Manna (notice the extra *n*), Jersey City's **White Mana** (470 Tonnele Ave., 201/963-1441, daily 24 hours, $3–11) is a compact rounded-front diner with an add-on, built as "the diner of the future" for the 1939 World's Fair. It has been cooking up burgers since 1946. The 1940s O'Mahony-manufactured **Miss America Diner** (322 West Side Ave., 201/333-5468, Mon. 5:30 A.M.–9:30 P.M., Tues.–Fri. 5:30 A.M.–9 P.M., Sat. 5:30 A.M.–8 P.M., Sun. 5:30 A.M.–4 P.M., $5–14), built in the streamline style, serves quintessential American fare along with Italian dishes like chicken Parmesan.

GETTING THERE AND AROUND

Jersey City is seven miles east of Newark, easily reachable by car from Newark Liberty International Airport via I-78. If traveling from Manhattan, take the Holland Tunnel from Canal Street, which will bring you out at Jersey City's northeastern waterfront. The city is a 10-minute train ride from Manhattan's Wall Street, and **PATH** (800/234-7284, www.panynj.gov, $1.75 one way, $3.50 round-trip) trains connect Jersey City with New York City, Hoboken, and Newark. Both **NJ**

Transit (800/772-3606, www.njtransit.com) and **Amtrak** (www.amtrak.com) run trains from Newark Liberty International Airport to Newark's downtown Penn Station. Here, transfer to a PATH train for stops within Jersey City. If arriving from other points along the Gold Coast, catch the **Hudson-Bergen Light Rail** (800/772-2222, www.mylightrail.com), which travels south from Weehawken into Jersey City, continuing on to Bayonne.

NY Waterway (800/533-3779, www.nywaterway.com) operates commuter ferries between Midtown Manhattan ($6.50 one way) or New York City's World Financial Center ($5 one way) and Jersey City's Paulus Hook (Hudson St. near Exchange Place). Additional routes run between Midtown Manhattan and Jersey City's Newport neighborhood ($6.50 one way), and between Manhattan's Wall Street and Port Liberte ($8.50 one way). Ferries operate roughly 7 A.M.–7 P.M. weekdays.

Unless you're focusing on a specific neighborhood, having a car or making use of Jersey City's public transport is essential. **PATH** stations are located at Pavonia-Newport, Grove Street (downtown district), Exchange Place, and Journal Square. **Hudson-Bergen Light Rail** has stops at Pavonia-Newport, Harborside Financial Center, Exchange Place, Essex Street, and Liberty State Park, and trains run approximately every 10 minutes.

In Liberty State Park, ferries run from **Liberty Landing Marina** (201/985-8000, www.libertylandingmarina.com) to nearby Ellis Island and the Statue of Liberty.

BAYONNE

Just south of Jersey City is Bayonne, a 5.39-square-mile city serving as New York City's cruise ship terminal for Royal Caribbean and Celebrity cruise lines. Bayonne has also succeeded in attracting the motion picture industry: Numerous TV shows and movies have been filmed here, including *War of the Worlds*, HBO's *Oz*, and the *Strangers with Candy* movie. Still, there's little reason to visit unless you're stalking a celebrity or taking to the seas. In either case, be sure to have a look at the architecturally powerful steel-arch **Bayonne Bridge** while here. Completed in 1931, it connects the city to Staten Island's Port Richmond.

Cruise Ship Terminal

Cape Liberty Cruise Port (14 Port Terminal Blvd., 201/823-3737, www.cruiseliberty.com) is the "New York City" terminal for **Royal Caribbean Cruise Lines** (www.royalcaribbean .com) and **Celebrity Cruises** (www.celebrity cruises.com). Both run ships to Bermuda, the Caribbean, Canada, and New England.

Getting There and Around

Numerous **Hudson-Bergen Light Rail** (800/772-2222, www.mylightrail.com) stops connect Bayonne with Jersey City, Hoboken, and Weehawken. Once aboard, the light rail connects with PATH trains and transit lines in numerous Gold Coast locations.

◖ HOBOKEN

Once known as New Jersey's down-and-out Mile Square City, Hoboken has been completely revitalized with restored brownstones, luxury flats, and some of the best drink and dining this side of the Hudson. The city is predominantly Irish and Italian, like much of the state, and is isolated by the Hudson River to the east and the Palisades to the west and separated from Jersey City by railway yards. Thankfully, Hoboken makes full use of its tiny space while commemorating its history. Squint and you may glimpse the ghosts of longshoremen once working at the city's shipyards, or catch a hint of the corruption that plagued the town throughout the mid-20th century. Still, urban hipsters priced out of Manhattan have migrated west, reinventing Hoboken as the Big Apple's little brother, a Jersey-fied version of the city that never sleeps. It's a persona that suits the city well.

Hoboken is a pretty place: one-way streets, brick sidewalks, and brownstones—some painted in shades of gray, white, or blue—stacked three or four stories high. Many of the homes have handrailed front stoops, jutting windows, and small side yards, and it is

© LAURA KINIRY

Hoboken's brownstones

common to see bicycles locked outside. Until recently, most of these homes also had superb harbor views. That has changed with the construction of waterfront condos, townhouses, and shopping plazas, a typical Gold Coast occurrence. But as you move west from the water, gentrification seems to fizzle out, and the city becomes more industrial.

Washington Street is the city's undisputable hub—a wide bustling thoroughfare packed with shops, Irish bars, and in the summer, sidewalk seating—and one of the city's main draws. Brownstones line the street's 14 blocks, which pick up momentum as they continue south, culminating in a conglomeration of cafés, boutiques, and coveted parking spaces.

History

Colonel John Stevens purchased Hoboken's land for $90,000 in 1784 as a home away from home for New Yorkers. The city was incorporated in 1855 and became a thriving shipping and commercial port, welcoming companies such as Hostess, Lipton Tea, and Maxwell

House. Hoboken was once home to a large German population, who were forced to flee when World War I began, abandoning shops and businesses and sending the city into a financial downward spiral. By the time of the prohibition era, River Street was lined with saloons, and organized crime ran rampant. Along the waterfront Hoboken's docks were teeming with corruption, a situation accurately depicted in Elia Kazan's 1954 film *On the Waterfront,* starring Marlon Brando, and it took until the 1980s for the city to regain its footing. New Yorkers began relocating here for affordable rents with proximity to the city. A long-defunct commuter ferry started operating again. Soon retail boutiques and gourmet restaurants opened, and Hoboken was reborn.

Hoboken is home to a number of firsts, including the first organized baseball game at the waterfront's Elysian Fields, the country's first brewery, opened in 1642, and the world's first zipper, invented at Hoboken's Automatic Hook and Eye Co.

Sights

Housed within the Bethlehem Steel Shipyard's former machine shop, the **Hoboken Historical Museum** (1301 Hudson St., 201/656-2240, www.hobokenmuseum.org, Tues.–Thurs. 2–9 P.M., Fri. 1–5 P.M., Sat.–Sun. noon–5 P.M., $2 adult, child free) pays tribute to the city's fascinating history. Displays include a 12-foot-tall coffee drop, part of a Maxwell House "Good to the Last Drop" sign that once stood atop the company's downtown coffee plant, and images from the filming of *On the Waterfront.* While here, be sure to pick up a copy of the Hoboken self-guided walking map, or for Ol' Blue Eyes fans, a Sinatra-centric map highlighting 23 of the city's crooner-related spots, including **St. Francis Church** (308 Jefferson St., 201/659-1772, www.stfrancis hoboken.com), where he was baptized.

Frank Sinatra is Hoboken's golden boy. Born in the city in 1915, the country's most famous crooner resided at **415 Monroe Street** in the city's Little Italy until he was 12. Though his childhood home no longer stands, a bronze star placed by the Hoboken Historical Society

commemorates the spot. Frank may have left Hoboken permanently in 1939, but the city never forgot him. His name is associated with local restaurants, area attractions, and downtown streets. Just off Hudson Street is the waterfront **Sinatra Drive,** offering some of the city's best cross-river views. Head south around the bend and you'll come to Sinatra Park, where 1954's *On the Waterfront* was filmed. Today, it's a popular festival locale.

Festivals and Events

Hoboken's painters, jewelers, musicians, and other artists and crafters open their studios to the public the second Sunday of each month for **Artists' Open Studio Days** (201/795-5000, www.monroecenter.com, noon–5 P.M.).

The **Hoboken Italian Festival** (www.hobokenitalianfestival.com) takes place annually for four days on the weekend after Labor Day. Held in Sinatra Park, the festival derives from Italy's Feast of the Madonna Dei Martiri and is over 75 years old. Highlights include a cannoli-eating contest and an evening procession of the Madonna statue. Another popular Italian festival, **Saint Ann's Feast,** is held for seven days each July, kicking off with a mass at St. Ann's Church.

Since 1996 the **Hoboken Farmers Market** (Washington and Newark Sts., Tues. 3–7:30 P.M., late June–late Oct.) has been the place to visit for organic produce and fresh baked goods.

Shopping

Fourteen blocks is a long stretch, but **Washington Street** makes good use of it with a bevy of boutiques and specialty stores.

For True Religion jeans and Allison Burns handbags try **Peper Inc** (1028 Washington St., 201/217-1911, www.peperapparel.com). This well-established boutique has been selling fun and fashionable (albeit pricey) duds for men and women since 1995. Stop by **The Wishing Tree** (706 Washington St., 201/420-1136, www.thewishingtreehoboken.com) for a full stock of soaps, candles, and artsy jewelry. Sea Monkeys thrive at **Big Fun Toys**

(602 Washington St., 201/714-9575, www
.bigfuntoys.com), along with an assortment of
whoopee cushions, potato guns, and pocket
air hockey. There's also a selection of goods
for tots and teens.

Locals rave about the customer service at
Down to Earth (527 Washington St., 201/656-
7766, www.dtehoboken.com), a clothing
boutique for both sexes. At **Via Mode** (404
Washington St., 201/217-6727, www.viamode
.com) it's all about shoes. Complement your new
Yes London pants from **Define** (610 Washington
St., 201/427-9844, www.defineclothing.com)
with a pair of Carlos Santana heels, or pick out
a set of Uggs sandals to go with that recently
purchased American Apparel (80 Hudson St.,
201/656-4441, americanapparel.net) T-shirt.

Sure, it's not on Washington Street, but
Aaraa (106 5th St., 201/386-0101, www
.aaraa-usa.com) is still worth a stop. This
Indian-inspired shop stocks handmade linens
and silks, many which have been individually
hand-embroidered. Home accessories include
pillows as well as bedspreads that can be custom tailored for all you kings and queens.

Recreation and Entertainment

Movies Under the Stars (201/420-2207)
screen Wednesday evenings June–August in
Pier A Park, at the foot of Sinatra Drive.
Those in town for an afternoon visit might
opt for kayak rentals at **Sinatra Park,** which
also hosts a café.

Accommodations

Scheduled to open in February 2009, Hoboken's
25-story **W Hotel** (225 River St., 201/253-2400,
www.starwoodhotels.com) will feature 225
modern rooms, each with a state-of-the-art entertainment system, wireless Internet, and a signature Munchie Box minibar. Some rooms have
Manhattan skyline views. This luxury property
will be the city's first—and only—hotel. For
additional options visit Jersey City.

Food

Hoboken has one of the state's finest restaurant selections. Everything from Asian fusion

to traditional Italian can be found along
Washington Street and the blocks nearby.
May–October many of the eateries set up outdoor sidewalk seating, and people-watching
ops are at an optimum.

EUROPEAN

Occupying the first floor of a five-story corner
brownstone is Hoboken's oldest continuously
operating bar and restaurant, **Elysian Cafe**
(1001 Washington St., 201/798-5898, www
.elysiancafe.com, Mon.–Thurs. noon–11 P.M.,
Fri. noon–2 P.M., Sat. 10 A.M.–2 P.M., Sun.
10 A.M.–11 P.M., $16–23). Much of this French
bistro's decor has been restored to its original
1895 appearance. Request a seat next to one of
the wall-length windows to take advantage of
afternoon light, and don't leave without trying the French onion soup. The café features
a just-as-popular upscale bar that hosts live
music and has a bar menu available a full hour
after the dining room closes.

Pizza is king at the cozy **Margherita's Pizza
& Cafe** (740 Washington St., 201/222-2400,
Tues.–Thurs. 11:30 A.M.–10:30 P.M., Sat.
11:30 A.M.–11:30 P.M., Sun. 12:30–9:30 P.M.,
$10–17), but large portions of homemade pasta
are also well received. This BYO features an
outdoor patio for sweltering summer nights.

Leo DiTerlizzi and his wife Tessie had always been fond of Sinatra (Leo and Frank
were old friends), as evidenced by **Leo's
Grandevous** (200 Grand St., 201/659-9467,
www.leosgrandevous.com, lunch weekdays
11:30 A.M.–2 P.M., dinner Sat. 5–11 P.M. and
Sun. 4–10 P.M., $7–16, cash only), a corner
Italian eatery with a Frank-filled jukebox and
dozens of Blue Eyes images plastered on the
walls. One of Hoboken's oldest family-owned
and operated restaurants, Leo's opened in 1939,
and though neither the original owners nor
Frank are still around, the place lives on as a
neighborhood institution.

NEW AND TRADITIONAL AMERICAN

Stop by the casual **Frozen Monkey Cafe** (526
Washington St., 201/222-1311, www.frozen
monkeycafe.com, Mon.–Thurs. 8 A.M.–11 P.M.,

Fri.–Sat. 9 A.M.–midnight, Sun. 9 A.M.–11 P.M.) for a crab cake panini ($9) or double mocha in the company of an ever-changing art display. Frozen Monkey's got the goods on breakfast too with white-chocolate pancakes ($5) and eggs scrambled with pepperoni and smoked Gouda cheese ($4.50).

Originally known as the 14th Street Diner, the since-remodeled **Malibu** (247 14th St., 201/656-1595, www.malibudiner.com, daily 24 hours, $6–24) is Hoboken's only 24-hour diner, featuring all-day breakfast, a recently added specialty drink bar, and on-site parking. Campy **Robongi** (520 Washington St., 201/222-8388, Mon.–Sat. 11 A.M.–11 P.M., Sun. 11:30 A.M.–11 P.M., $11–30) is Hoboken's spot for good sushi and friendly service. BYO.

For the best porterhouse in town head to **Frankie & Johnnie's** (163 14th St., 201/659-6202, www.frankieandjohnnies.com, Mon. 5–10 P.M., Tues.–Thurs. 5–11 P.M., Fri.–Sat. 5–11:30 P.M., Sun. 4–9 P.M., closed Sundays during summer, $21–37), a 140-seat steakhouse established in 1926. Built as a longshoremen's saloon, the restaurant's interior has retained many of its original features, including its tile floor and tin ceiling. Don't miss the piano player on weekends. Valet parking is available.

Housed in an old brownstone diagonal to its sister property Elysian Cafe, **Amanda's** (908 Washington St., 201/798-0101, www.amandas restaurant.com, dinner Mon.–Thurs. 5–10 P.M., Fri.–Sat. 5–11 P.M., Sun. 5–9 P.M., brunch Sat.–Sun. 11 A.M.–3 P.M.) is my pick for romance. This New American restaurant offers a wonderful wine selection to pair with dishes like tofu stir-fry ($19) and pistachio-crusted swordfish ($28). And don't worry about a dress code: You'll feel just as comfortable in Lucky jeans as in a dress suit.

ASIAN

For Asian eats try the popular **Satay** (99 Washington St., 201/386-8688, daily 11:30 A.M.–11 P.M., $7–16). Though its exterior is nondescript, its food is spectacular. Go for the *itik palam*—duck with plum sauce ($11.95)—and follow up with a bowl of deep-fried ice cream ($3.75). Open daily.

LATIN-AMERICAN

Colorful **Zafra** (301 Willow Ave., 201/610-9801, www.zafrakitchens.com, Mon.–Thurs. 9 A.M.–10 P.M., Fri. 9 A.M.–11 P.M., Sat.–Sun. 10 A.M.–10 P.M., brunch Sat.–Sun. 10 A.M.–3 P.M., $16–24) is a fun BYO serving Cuban-Latino fare. For a small fee they'll turn your bottle of wine into a delicious pitcher of sangria. Outdoor seating is available April–November.

Crowds never abate at **Lua** (1300 Sinatra Dr. N., 201/876-1900, www.luarestaurant .com, dinner Mon.–Wed. 5–11 P.M., Thurs. 5 P.M.–midnight, Fri.–Sat. 6 P.M.–midnight, Sun. 5–10 P.M., $20–25), a 150-seat restaurant and 360-degree bar with exceptional views of Manhattan's skyline. Cuisine is Latin-inspired and includes tapas and tamales as well as innovatively prepared seafood and steak. Come here to be seen or to sample one of more than two dozen tequilas, but not for conversation.

You can't beat ◖ **Cucharamama's** (233 Clinton St., 201/420-1700, www.cucharamama .com, Tues.–Sat. 5–11 P.M., Sun. noon–4 P.M. and 5–10 P.M., closed Mon., $12–25) lively atmosphere and exquisite South American fare. Start with the calamari, and then move on to the day's fish special paired with a glass of Spanish wine. Meals are cooked in a wood-fired oven, but the restaurant's clay-tiled floor keeps things cool. During warmer months wall-length windows open out onto sidewalk seating.

Nightlife

Manhattan's evening alternative, Hoboken is packed with neighborhood watering holes, Irish pubs, and hipster bar-restaurants. There's plenty live music scattered throughout town, and food is a standard complement to bottles, drafts, and martinis.

Trendy **Madisons Bar and Grill** (1316 Washington St., 201/386-0300, www.madison barandgrill.com, Mon. 11:30 A.M.–10 P.M., Tues.–Fri. 11:30 A.M.–11 P.M., Sat. 11 A.M.–11 P.M., Sun. 10 A.M.–10 P.M.) is known for its Tuesday-night martini madness—when crowds pack the long bar for half-price specials—and

Sunday jazz brunch. The decor is classy, spiced with black-and-white photos and fringed lampshade chandeliers. For live music there's no better place than **Maxwell's** (1039 Washington St., 201/653-1703, www.maxwellsnj.com, Sun.–Thurs. 5 P.M.–midnight, Fri.–Sat. 5 P.M.–1 A.M., Sun. 11:30 A.M.–4 P.M.). This Hoboken institution features local and big-name bands like Girl in a Coma, and tickets come cheap. There's plenty of seating, along with a full food menu and a Sunday soul kitchen fixed-price special ($13.95) 5–8 P.M.

Hoboken is filled with Irish pubs, but one to try is **O'Donoghues on First** (205 First St., 201/798-7711, www.odonoghues.com, Mon.–Fri. 4 P.M.–2 A.M., Sat.–Sun. noon–2 A.M.). This fun place hosts cover bands and DJs and doubles as a sports bar, with large-screen TVs, darts, and Ping-Pong. Weekly specials include free buffalo wings and $3 pints all night.

Alternative types will dig the **Gold Hawk** (936 Park Ave., 201/420-7989, www.thegold hawk.com, Sun.–Thurs. 5:30 P.M.–2 A.M., Fri. and Sat. 5:30 P.M.–3 A.M.), a large space hosting weekly events like the Writer's Hang, a singer-songwriter performance series, and the new People's Open Mic. This pub-lounge combo offers a nice beer selection and nightly drink specials. Don't leave before checking out the old radio collection behind the bar.

Catch the Yankees, Mets, football, *and* soccer at **Black Bear Bar & Grill** (205 Washington St., 201/656-5511, www.black bearbar.com, Sun.–Thurs. 11 A.M.–2 A.M., Fri.–Sat. 11 A.M.–3 A.M.), two stories with two bars and 50 TVs.

Services
Steven's Park at 4th and Hudson Streets is Hoboken's first free public wireless Internet park. Details on connecting to the network are available on the city's official website, www .hobokennj.org.

Getting There and Around
Hoboken is situated along the Hudson River waterfront between Jersey City and the Holland Tunnel to the south and the Lincoln Tunnel to the north. **PATH** trains traveling from New York City or Jersey City stop in Hoboken at the **Hoboken Terminal** (1 Hudson Pl.) and run Monday–Friday 6 A.M.–11 P.M., weekends 9 A.M.–7:30 P.M. The **Hudson-Bergen Light Rail** connects at Hoboken Terminal and continues north with stops at 2nd Street and 9th Street along the city's west side before reaching Weehawken.

Hoboken's **Crosstown Bus** runs through the city weekdays 7 A.M.–7 P.M. approximately every half hour, stopping at Hoboken Terminal. Fare is $0.50.

NY Waterway operates a commuter ferry ($4 one way) between Hoboken South (near the transit terminal) and Manhattan's Wall Street daily 6 A.M.–9 P.M., and another between New York's Midtown and Hoboken's 14th Street on weekdays 6 A.M.–11 P.M. and weekends 10 A.M.–9 P.M. Ferries from New York City's World Financial Center serve both locations.

WEEHAWKEN
Weehawken, west of the Lincoln Tunnel and just north of Hoboken, consists of two sections: a modern low-level waterfront and the original downtown district atop the Palisades. The borough is famous for a July 11, 1804, standoff between Aaron Burr and Alexander Hamilton, costing Hamilton his life.

With mixed-use residences and ongoing construction, Weehawken's waterfront resembles other Gold Coast communities, although the borough's upper residential neighborhood—filled with narrow side streets and spacious yards—is lovely. A paved cliff-side walkway offers aerial views of the neighborhood below along with a panorama of the Manhattan skyline, but head west a block or two to **Park Avenue**—Weehawken's once main thoroughfare—and the borough adopts an abandoned-city sort of feel.

Water Excursions
The **Spirit of New Jersey** (Lincoln Harbor, 866/483-3866, www.spiritcitycruises.com) runs year-round lunch ($32 and up) and dinner

view of Manhattan's skyline from Upper Weehawken

($79 and up) cruises along the Hudson and East Rivers, passing the Statue of Liberty and the Brooklyn Bridge.

One of New Jersey's tall ships, the **Richard Robbins** (973/966-1684, www.classicsail .com), over a century old, sets sail from Lincoln Harbor Yacht Club a couple of times monthly. Trips range from a $59 Father's Day brunch excursion to a $199 overnight cruise.

New York Waterway (Lincoln Harbor, 800/533-3779, www.nywaterway.com) hosts $22 round-trip shuttle service to Yankees' games throughout baseball season. Food and drink are available on board.

Accommodations

The ten-story ◖ **Sheraton Suites on the Hudson** (500 Harbor Blvd., 201/617-5600, $189–429) stands along the Hudson River just a few steps from New York Waterway and a five-minute trip to Midtown Manhattan. On-site amenities include a full bar, lounge, and grill, a gift shop, and a heated indoor pool. Rooms come with a complimentary morning buffet, and often have a superb view. Because of its accessibility, the hotel makes a great alternative to a New York City stay.

Food

For authentic Northern Italian, try **Paula at Rigoletto** (3706 Park Ave., 201/422-9500, Tues.–Sun. 5–10 P.M., Sun. 10 A.M.–3 P.M., $13–26), a 40-seat BYO located in the borough's downtown district. Paula was Bruce Springsteen's personal chef for two years.

Arthur's Landing (1 Pershing Cir., 201/867-0777, www.arthurslanding.com, Sun.–Mon. 5–9 P.M., Tues. 4:30–10 P.M., Wed.–Thurs. 5–10 P.M., Fri.–Sat. 5–10:30 P.M., brunch Sat.–Sun. 11:30 A.M.–2:30 P.M., $22–36) dishes up New American cuisine amid breathtaking views of the Manhattan skyline. The waterfront restaurant offers a pretheater package ($50 per person) that includes early dinner (5–6:30 P.M.), valet parking, and a round-trip ferry into New York City (six minutes one way).

Getting There and Around

Weehawken is 10 minutes north of Hoboken by car. The **Hudson-Bergen Light Rail** stops at Weehawken's Lincoln Harbor and continues south through Hoboken, Jersey City, and into Bayonne. One-way fares are $1.90 adult and $0.95 child.

UNION CITY

Situated atop the Palisades cliffs west of Hoboken, Union City has the distinction of being the most densely populated city in the United States. Its nickname, "Havana on the Hudson," derives from its large Latino population, making up more than 80 percent of the city's residents. Cubans, Colombians, Ecuadorians, and Dominicans are among the many ethnicities that reside here. Downtown is considered an Urban Enterprise Zone, with sales tax lowered to 3 percent in efforts to revitalize the local economy.

Latino culture centers around **Bergenline Avenue,** a narrow one-way street lined with Cuban eateries, religious trinket shops, and family-owned bodegas. All the tightly constructed brick and clapboard buildings, people, and activity can make the avenue feel a bit claustrophobic, but for an authentic Latin experience it's worth a visit.

Food

Casual **El Unico Restaurant** (4211 Park Ave., 201/864-3931, 5 A.M.–9:30 P.M. daily) serves Latin-American fare at unbeatable prices: You can stuff yourself for under $5. But don't come for the atmosphere; it's the eats that make this place a local landmark, with fried plantain, *pollo asado* (roast chicken), and cubano sandwiches—they're all here.

The excellent **Beyti Kebab** (4105 Park Ave., 201/865-6281, www.beytikebab.com, daily 11:30 A.M.–10 P.M., $13–23) is credited as the New York City metro area's first Turkish restaurant, opening in 1983 as a butcher shop. Today, there's also an adjoining market and a sweet shop supplying all of the restaurant's baked goods. Kebabs, lamb chops, and gyros are the norm, along with a belly dancer on Saturday after 9 P.M. (excluding summer).

Getting There

Catch a Hudson-Bergen Light Rail train to 49th Street and Bergenline Avenue, or from Weehawken drive Route 495W to the Park Avenue exit. Union City is about a half mile west.

EDGEWATER

Edgewater's been completely transformed over the last several years, its once unremarkable waterfront becoming a showcase of modernity replete with high-rises and townhouses. The borough is home to a large Asian population, most notably Japanese.

Mitsuwa Marketplace

If you're into reading manga comics and dining on *bento* boxes, you'll love Mitsuwa Marketplace (595 River Road, 201/941-9113, www.mitsuwa.com). This Japanese shopping center stocks everything from cosmetics (Shiseido, 201/313-1400) to ceramics (Utsuwa no Yakata, 201/941-1902) to bamboo blinds

(Mars New York, 201/945-1134), along with sake, sweets, and sushi. A marketplace highlight is the Borders-style **Sanseido Bookstore** (201/941-1564), packed with colorfully packaged teen reads, novels, celebrity mags, and anime in both Japanese and English. You can literally spend hours here.

Food

Line up for **Mitsuwa Supermarket's** freshly made spring rolls and cream crab cakes, then snag a table at the popular food court—Sunday mornings fill up quickly. Across the parking lot is the waterfront **Matsushima Restaurant** (595 River Rd., 201/945-9450, lunch daily from 11 A.M., dinner daily from 5 P.M., $20–30), a Japanese steakhouse and local sushi favorite (though be sure to pack your wallet).

Nestled along an artsy little stretch of Old River Road is **Rebecca's** (236 Old River Rd., 201/943-8808, Tues.–Sat. 5:30–10 P.M., Sun. 4–9 P.M., closed Mon., $20–30), a cozy BYO serving Cuban-Caribbean fare in a converted house. If you visit during summer months, be sure to request a seat on the backyard patio.

FORT LEE

Fort Lee straddles the Palisades cliffs, ascending steeply from the Hudson and working its way through a hodgepodge of architectural styles, including Victorian clapboards and modern high-rises. Main Street, the borough's main thoroughfare, is home to many of the Asian eateries—specifically Korean—that Fort Lee is currently known for.

Fort Lee played a part in the American Revolution and hosted a portion of the locally beloved Palisades Amusement Park (www.palisadespark.com) for over 80 years. The borough's best-known role, however, was as the country's silent movie capital (Fort Lee Film Commission, www.fortleefilm.org) from 1905–1920, before producers and directors made their way out West for the better climate and greater personal control. To honor the nearly three dozen movie studios once operating in the area, many Fort Lee streets have been renamed for silent screen stars, including

Theda Bara Way, which shares its name with Linwood Avenue. Features filmed in the area include *Robin Hood* (1912), *The Vampire* (1913), and *Poor Little Rich Girl* (1917).

The George Washington Bridge connects Fort Lee to the Bronx and is a strong downtown presence.

Fort Lee Historic Park

At the southern tip of Palisades Interstate Park is 33-acre Fort Lee Historic Park (Hudson Terr., 201/461-1776, park daily 8 A.M.–sunset, visitors center Wed.–Sun. 10 A.M.–5 P.M., closed Jan.–Feb.), an American defense site against British troops during the Revolutionary War. A visitors center features several displays relating to the fort's role in the Revolution. A couple of evidently handmade exhibits are a bit lackluster, though others—like a small-scale model of predevelopment Palisades—are impressive. Outside are nature trails, overlooks, and artillery reproductions. A $5 parking fee is charged during special events.

Food

North Jersey's *Bergen Record* claims that Fort Lee is "fast becoming the leading destination for Asian food in North Jersey," with more than a dozen Asian restaurants and eateries. The bulk of them stand near the top of Main Street and along Broad Street in nearby Palisades Park. Many are open 24 hours.

Catering to a largely Asian clientele is **Hiura** (400B Main St., 201/346-0110, closed Wed.), a Japanese BYO known for its sushi. Coffee, pastries, and Asian-style cakes are served at the popular **Parisienne Bakery & Cafe** (250 Main St., 201/592-8878, Mon.–Sat. 8 A.M.–8:30 P.M., Sun. 8 A.M.–8:30 P.M.), located on the corner of Main and Center. Try one of the Beard Papa cream puffs—they're fresh, tasty, and oh-so-good.

Customers flock to **Restaurant So Kong Dong** (130 Main St., 201/242-0026, 10 A.M.–10 P.M. daily, $6–12) for *soondubu* ($7) or "soft-tofu stew," a gurgling egg-topped soup that comes in nearly a dozen varieties, some that

will even please meat lovers, accompanied by rice and an assortment of side dishes.

Vietnamese BYO **Mo' Pho** (212 Main St., 201/363-8886, www.saigonmopho .com, Tues.–Sat. 11:30 A.M.–9:30 P.M., Sun. 1–9:30 P.M., closed Mon., $11–17) is known for its *pho,* a hearty noodle soup with a variety of vegetarian and meat toppings to choose from. In nearby Palisades Park **So Moon Nan Jib** (238 Broad Ave., 201/944-3998, daily 6 A.M.–3 A.M., $9–22) allows guests to grill their own Korean barbecue at tables over hot coals.

Getting There

Fort Lee is just north of Edgewater on the western side of the Bronx-connecting George Washington Bridge. The bridge has a bike and walking path leading into Fort Lee.

◖ PALISADES INTERSTATE PARK

Sheer cliffs and the Hudson River Line either side of this long sliver of parkland, stretching 12 miles to the New York state border and no more than half a mile wide on its Jersey side. Palisades Interstate Park (201/768-1360, www .njpalisades.org) is part of a greater collection of parks and historic sites encompassing over 100,000 acres that New Jersey shares with New York. The park offers some wonderful cycling, hiking, and cross-country skiing opportunities, and has long been an oasis for New Yorkers and Gold Coast residents needing retreat from urban life. Interesting and informative guided tours are offered here year-round.

Hiking

Palisades Interstate Park's Jersey side features more than 30 miles of hiking trails, including the **Shore Trail,** which follows the Hudson River bank for nearly 3.5 miles before meeting **Huyler's Landing Trail,** a historic trail (used in 1776 by British General Cornwallis to surprise the Revolutionaries) ascending the Palisades cliffs; and the **Long Path,** a higher-elevation trail running the length of the entire New Jersey side of the park and continuing

NORTH JERSEY'S MILLIONAIRES' ROW

Although most of the 15 mansions that lined Palisade Interstate Park's diabase cliffs are long gone, it's still possible to spot their remains between Route 9W and Palisades Interstate Highway. Known as Millionaires' Row, these Gilded Age estates were the homes of prestigious folk such as John Ringling of circus fame and George A. Zabriskie, New York's Pillsbury Flour director. Philanthropist John D. Rockefeller purchased the majority of Palisades homes in the 1930s, razing them for a better cross-river view, but explorers can still uncover stone steps, pillars, and a foundation wall or two tucked among foliage. They're fun to uncover, especially with a knowledgeable guide. The Palisades Park Commission's historian Eric Nelsen often leads free two-hour tours through the area. For more info, call 201/768-1360 or visit www.njpalisades.org.

Tudor-style Penlyn, the last of the estates, remains as park headquarters.

into New York. The trails range from easy to strenuous, depending on direction, though a handful of intersecting paths allow for alternate hiking opportunities. Each trail is marked by an individual color blaze. In winter, skiing is allowed.

Henry Hudson Drive

One of the Gateway Region's best cycling spots is seven-mile Henry Hudson Drive, a north-south scenic route open to bicyclists and motor vehicles mid-April–mid-November. Weekend afternoons throughout summer, dozens of cyclists take advantage of the uphill challenge, along with shade provided by dense tree canopies lining the eastern roadside. The Palisade Park Commission requires bikes have at least 24-inch tires and that all cyclists wear a helmet and be over age 14.

An old stretch of Route 9W runs through the northern half of the park's New Jersey portion near the State Line Lookout, where the **Lookout Inn** (201/750-0465), a year-round snack stand and book shop, operates. The road is open to cyclists but closed to autos.

The Meadowlands

The so-called "Armpit of America" has made great strides in cleaning up its image. Thirty square miles of wetlands, estuaries, marshes, and for the past half century, loads of development, the Meadowlands were a notorious dumping ground for trash, toxins, and the occasional body. Buried beneath its land are the remains of New York City's original Penn Station, and according to legend, organized crime leader Jimmy Hoffa. Incinerated trash heaps, mosquito infestations, and mercury-polluted rivers have long been synonymous with the Meadowlands, but these days a new word comes up: ecotourism. Over 250 bird species and 60 fish and shellfish species reside or pass through here, and 8,400 acres have been established as a wildlife preserve. Meadowlands boat tours and canoe trips are now being offered, and

people are booking months in advance, perhaps hoping to glimpse a lost legend or two.

In addition to the wetlands, the Meadowlands consist of 14 towns, including East Rutherford and Rutherford (home to the Meadowlands Sports Complex), and Secaucus, known for its outlets and as a transit transfer point.

Conservation efforts aside, Meadowlands development continues as a new upscale retail entertainment plaza is in progress.

MEADOWLANDS SPORTS AND ENTERTAINMENT COMPLEX

During the late 1970s and early 1980s, New Jersey's Meadowlands (www.meadowlands .com) morphed into a central hub for the area's professional sports teams. Basketball's New

Jersey Nets were first to arrive, followed by ice hockey's Jersey Devils and football's New Jersey Giants and the New York Jets. Today, the complex is also home to a racetrack and pro soccer's New York/New Jersey Red Bulls, though it's smack in the middle of another rebirth. The Devils left town for Newark in 2007, the Nets may leave for Brooklyn, N.Y., as early as 2009, and the two football teams are set to receive a brand new stadium in 2010. Even the long-standing Continental Area has changed, recreating itself as the Izod Center. But perhaps the Meadowlands' biggest change is the addition of a sprawling shopping and entertainment complex called **Xanadu** (www.meadowlands xanadu.com), still under construction at this writing. At 4.8 million square feet, Xanadu will include an Egyptian-themed 18-screen multiplex theater, 30-lane bowling center, 287-foot-high Ferris wheel, runway fashion shows, a children's play area called Wanadoo, a luxury hotel, and the country's first Snow Dome, an insulated 28-degree venue for skiers and snowboarders featuring 165,000 square feet of snow, a half pipe, an equipment rental lodge, and a children's snow play area. It's no wonder why, despite so many turning wheels, the Meadowlands remain one of the region's biggest draws.

The Meadowlands Event Information Hotline (201/935-3900) offers information on current and upcoming games and events at both Giants Stadium and the Izod Center. Ticket purchases can be made through Ticketmaster (201/507-8900 or 212/307-7171, www.ticketmaster.com). For the Meadowlands Racetrack, call 201/843-2446.

Giants Stadium

Currently home to the NFL's **New York Giants** (201/935-8111, www.giants.com) and **New York Jets** (516/560-8200, www.new yorkjets.com) as well as Major League Soccer's **New York/New Jersey Red Bulls** (877/727-6223, www.nyredbulls.com), Giants Stadium (201/935-3900) is the Meadowlands' largest showcase, seating more than 80,000. The stadium hosts large-scale musical acts and

attractions year-round, such as Van Halen and New Jersey's State Fair.

The Izod Center

Formerly known as the Continental Airlines Arena (201/935-3900, www.meadowlands .com), the 20,000-seat Izod Center opened in 1981 with six sold-out Springsteen shows and has since hosted hundreds of concerts, figure skating performances (including Disney on Ice), circuses, and more. It's home to basketball's **New Jersey Nets** (800/765-6387, www .njnets.com).

One of the Meadowlands newest performing venues, **The Izod Center Theater** follows a statewide trend of introducing more intimate performing venues to larger spaces. Theater seating ranges from 4,000 to 9,000.

Meadowlands Racetrack

The 40,000-seat Meadowlands Racetrack (Meadowlands Sports Complex, East Rutherford, 201/843-2446, www.thebigm .com) hosts live harness and thoroughbred racing year-round. General parking is free, and grandstand admission is only $1 ($1.50 for reserved seating, $3 for clubhouse admission).

OTHER SIGHTS AND RECREATION
The Meadowlands Environmental Center

Get information on area birding and local tours, meander the marsh discovery trail, or relax at the Meadowlands Environmental Center's (2 DeKorte Park Plaza, 201/460-8300, www.njmeadowlands.gov/ec/, free) Memorial Butterfly Garden. The Environmental Center is primarily an administration center, although it does house a classroom and interactive learning center and hosts various events, such as a Black Maria film festival, throughout the year. A science observatory is currently in the works.

◖ Ecotours

What's so strange about ecotouring the Meadowlands? Well, a lot. But that doesn't mean it's a bad idea. In fact, it's one of the best additions to local tourism in recent years. The New Jersey Meadowlands Commission (201/460-6440, www.meadowlands.state .nj.us) offer both **pontoon boat tours and canoe trips** along the Hackensack River and Mill Creek Marsh. Keep an eye out for waterfowl (and Jimmy Hoffa's remains) as you glide through this delicate region. Two-hour guided pontoon-boat trips (suggested donation $15 per person) leave from the River Barge Park and Marina in Carlstadt. Each boat accommodates up to 12. Three-hour guided canoe trips (suggested donation $15 per person) begin at Secaucus's Mill Creek Point Park or Hudson County Park at Laurel Hill. Check the website for current schedules. Both tours are extremely popular—reservations are a must.

Captain Bill Sheehan is in large part responsible for the Meadowlands' ecotourism transformation, so it's little wonder that his **Hackensack Riverkeeper** (231 Main St., 201/968-0808, www.hackensackriverkeeper .org, $25 adult, $10 child) ecotours are extremely popular. Fifteen-seat pontoon vessels launch from Secaucus's Laurel Hill County Park, floating down the Hackensack River and its tributaries toward Jersey City. Every tour includes a trip to **Saw Mill Wildlife Management Area,** a haven for herons, egrets, and ospreys. Hackensack waters remain polluted, so stay put—keep your eyes to the sky instead for a possible bald eagle sighting. Tour routes vary depending on the time of day, but they each last about 2–3 hours. Advance reservations are highly recommended.

The Riverkeeper also offers guided birding walks ($10 adult, $5 child), canoe and kayak rentals ($25 paddler, $10 passenger), guided paddles ($30 paddler, $15 passenger), and hosts volunteer cleanups during warmer months.

Teterboro Airport and Aviation Hall of Fame

Located 12 miles from Manhattan, the Port Authority's Teterboro Airport is the region's oldest operating airport. It's also home to the recently expanded **New Jersey Aviation Hall of Fame Museum** (400 Fred Wehran Dr., 201/288-6344, www.njahof.org, Tues.–Sun. 10 A.M.–4 P.M., $7 adult, $5 child), a showcase of vintage airplanes and various aviation-themed exhibits, including military and spaceflight displays. The airport sits within a large residential area, and increasing runway traffic has lead to community run-ins.

Medieval Times

An easy drive from the Meadowlands Sports Complex, Medieval Times (149 Polito Ave., 888/935-6678, www.medievaltimes.com, $54.95 adult, $39.95 child) is much loved by renaissance faire enthusiasts and college students. Two-hour 11th-century dinner shows feature horse-riding knights, trumpeters, and jousting matches, along with a utensil-free dinner of spareribs and garlic bread served by wenches and serfs. It all takes place in a cavernous 1,350-seat castle-like structure. It is entirely kitschy, but loads of fun.

© LAURA KINIRY

Medieval Times, a dinner theater from the Middle Ages

SHOPPING

Secaucus is synonymous with bargain shopping, and the best place for it is at the **Secaucus Outlets** (877/688-5382 or 201/348-4780, www.harmonmeadow.com/pages/secaucus page.html), situated between Route 1-9 and Highway 3. Stand-alone stores include Calvin Klein (201/223-9760), Gucci (201/392-2670), and Kenneth Cole (201/319-0140). Others, such as Liz Claiborne (201/770-1435), Samsonite (201/863-1366), and Geoffrey Beene (201/617-8082) operate within the enclosed **Harmon Cove Outlet Center** (20 Enterprise Ave.).

The borough's **Harmon Meadow Plaza** (off Rte. 3 and NJ Turnpike, 201/392-8700, www.harmonmeadow.com) mixes retail and office space with hotels, restaurants, and a couple of multiplex movie theaters. It's also home to the Meadowlands Exposition Center, hosting trade shows and festivities year-round. Plaza shops include Pier 1 Imports (201/319-1110), Linens 'n Things (201/866-6065), and Harmon Meadow Jewelry Exchange (201/864-9666), and dining options range from burger-slingin' Houlihan's (201/330-8856, 11 A.M.–midnight Mon.–Fri., 11 A.M.–1 A.M. Fri. and Sat., and 11 A.M.–11 P.M. Sun.) to Chipotle Mexican Grill (201/223-0562, 11A.M.–10 P.M. daily).

ACCOMMODATIONS

Though the Meadowlands host a bevy of hotel and budget accommodations, most preferred establishments are centered around the Sports Complex and within Secaucus's shopping district.

$150-300

Conveniently located next to the outlets, just off the Turnpike, and right across the river from the Meadowlands sports and entertainment complex, the 14-story **Crowne Plaza Meadowlands Hotel** (2 Harmon Plaza, Secaucus, 877/898-1721, $136–200) is a good all-around option for exploring the area. There's an on-site restaurant and lounge as well as a seasonal outdoor pool. Some rooms include views of New York City. Choose between three levels of lodging: guest room, executive club level, and suite.

The nine-story **Embassy Suites Hotel** (455 Plaza Dr., Secaucus, 201/864-7300, $134–299) is ideally situated within Harmon Cove and has both a restaurant and lounge. All rooms include refrigerator, microwave, and separate living area.

For a bit of pampering try the nine-story ◖ **Renaissance Meadowlands Hotel** (801 Rutherford Ave., Rutherford, 201/231-3100, $169–309). This smoke-free lodging features newly renovated guest rooms, each with flat-screen TV, free high-speed Internet, and complimentary Starbucks coffee. A heated pool and an on-site steakhouse with an extensive wine menu are additional perks.

Courtyard by Marriott (455 Harmon Meadow Blvd., Secaucus, 201/617-8888, www.marriott.com, $259) offers spacious rooms, each with a separate seating area. The hotel is located within Harmon Meadow Plaza next door to the Meadowlands Exposition Center. An Outback Steakhouse, which also provides room service, is just off the hotel lobby.

FOOD

The Meadowlands offer options for those who prefer savoring meals and others who treat them like just another Turnpike toll.

One of New Jersey's most revered restaurants, East Rutherford's classy **Park & Orchard** (240 Hackensack St., 201/939-9292, www.parkandorchard.com, lunch Mon.–Fri. noon–4 P.M., dinner Mon.–Fri. 4–10 P.M., Sat. 4:45–10 P.M., Sun. 2–9 P.M., $16–29) serves healthy-sized Italian dishes, stir-fries, and a selection of vegetarian casseroles using only whole foods, fruits, and vegetables. Their wine list is exceptional.

The place to come on a special date, romantic BYO ◖ **Café Matisse** (167 Park Ave., Rutherford, 201/935-2995, www.cafematisse.com, Mon.–Thurs. from 5 P.M., Fri.–Sun. from 5:30 P.M.) serves an extensive menu of American Eclectic and European dishes, along with a fixed-price grazing menu featuring smaller appetizers and entrées (the mid-road four-course grazer is $75 per person). The atmosphere is color-soaked and eclectic and includes a seasonal outdoor garden.

A visit to the Meadowlands isn't complete without a trip to the classic **Meadowlands Diner** (320 Rte. 17, 201/935-5444, daily 24 hours, $5–15), a local institution serving awesome pizza, pancakes, and burgers.

GETTING THERE AND AROUND

Multilevel Frank R. Lautenberg Rail Station (100 Laurel Hill Dr.), or **Secaucus Junction,** links eight of NJ Transit's 11 transit lines. From here catch trains to Rutherford (Orient Way and Park Ave.) and Teterboro (Williams Ave. and Rte. 17).

Route 17 runs north-south among numerous Meadowlands towns, but prepare yourself for traffic any time of the day. Taking neighborhood back roads or hopping on the NJ Turnpike are alternatives, though Route 17 remains the most direct route to northern towns. Secaucus, the Rutherfords, and Lyndhurst are accessible to one another by Route 3.

Newark and Vicinity

If you've only experienced Newark on the way to and from the airport, chances are you'll never want to return. But New Jersey's largest city isn't all traffic, shipping crates, smog, and smokestacks. It's also home to a vibrant downtown arts district, a bustling ethnic neighborhood filled with superb restaurants, and New Jersey's largest museum. Construction remains underway throughout downtown Newark, which over the last decade has seen a complete revamping, including the addition of a minor-league ballpark and a state-of-the-art entertainment center.

Of course, New Jersey's Brick City—nicknamed so because of the high percentage of brick homes once located here—still has problems. Crime remains a concern (though percentages have dropped considerably since the start of the new millennium), streets can be difficult to navigate, and litter is often strewn about the streets. But in the end, it's no so bad being Newark. Though wisecracks continue, so does the city's reinvention, and those who explore it may be surprised. Neighborhoods and attractions are well marked. Public transport is plentiful. In fact, Newark serves as a major connecting hub for New York City, Trenton, and Philly, along with many of New Jersey's outlying areas. And there's plenty to do once you arrive.

Newark is home to five colleges and universities, including Rutgers's Newark branch and New Jersey's Science and Technology University. The city's roster of famous alumni includes Frankie "Castelluccio" Valli, Queen Latifah, and Philip Roth, the Pulitzer Prize–winning author who sets many of his short stories and novels in New Jersey's Gateway region.

South of Newark is Elizabeth—an older industrial city that survived British attacks during the Revolutionary War and continues to retain many of its original structures. These days Elizabeth is known for its shopping options and makes an easy afternoon excursion from downtown Newark. In fact, nearly half of Newark Liberty International Airport lies within Elizabeth's boundaries.

History

New Haven colony leader Robert Treat and a group of Connecticut dissidents settled Newark in 1666, trading Hackensack Indians $750 worth of guns, swords, blankets, beer, and additional bartered goods for the land. The city opened its first hotel in 1670 at the present site of Grace Episcopal Church, and the College of New Jersey—which later became Princeton University—operated in Newark 1747–1756.

Newark grew into one of the world's great manufacturing capitals and was known as a

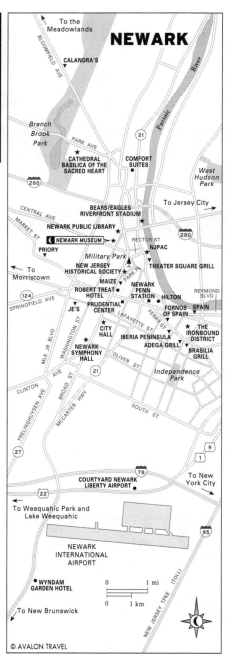

hotbed of invention. Samuel Whitehead, the city's first shoemaker, arrived in the 1680s. Azariah Crane opened Newark's first leather tannery in 1698. Local resident Thomas Cort invented the world's first tennis shoe, and inventor Seth Boyden perfected the process for crafting patent leather, beginning a trend that would include over 150 citywide manufacturers. While shoe production would later move north, Newark's tannery business exploded due to a local excess of tamarack trees, used for producing Russian and Moroccan leather. Thomas Edison invented the ticker-tape machine in Newark. The city is also founding home of Prudential Insurance (1875).

One of Newark's main revenue industries was brewing, and during the late 19th century local Ballantine Brewery became the sixth largest brewery in the United States. Pabst Blue Ribbon also maintained a city presence. The massive amber bottle once identifying their company still exists today.

From the late 19th century through World War II, thousands of African Americans arrived from the South looking for work in Newark's factories. As the city's population soared, its infrastructure folded. Unemployment became an issue. By the 1960s police brutality was common, further heating Newark's already-tense atmosphere. When the city tore down its African American Central Ward neighborhood to make room for Newark's University of Medicine and Dentistry, it was the last straw.

Riots occurred in 125 U.S. cities in 1967, but the worst were in Detroit and Newark. On Newark's third day of rioting the National Guard arrived, and state troopers opened fire on rioters. The rioting set in motion an era of urban flight continuing through the 1970s.

In 1986 Newark elected its second African American mayor, Sharpe James, who was responsible for much of the city's ensuing reconstruction, including the building of the New Jersey Performing Arts Center. James served five consecutive terms before leaving in July 2006. In July 2007 he was indicted on 25 counts (and later convicted on five counts) that included mail fraud, wire fraud, and conspiracy.

Neighborhoods

Newark consists of five wards (districts used for orientation and political purposes), each made up of several smaller neighborhoods. Visitors tend to stick mostly within Newark's Downtown Arts District, Ironbound, and Branch Brook Park, located within the East and North Wards, but it's good to know a bit about each of them, especially when trying to find your bearings within the city.

The aptly named West Ward lies west of the Garden State Parkway. It's home to **Vailsburg,** a traditionally Irish, Italian, and German neighborhood once considered the city's political capital. Two of Newark's most revered movie palaces—the Stanley, now a church, and the Mayfair—were also found here.

Newark's South Ward contains Weequahic, the once-Jewish neighborhood that resident Philip Roth immortalized in many of his short stories and novels. The area changed demographics following the 1967 riots. It's now home to a large African American community.

The city's East Ward is Newark's most commonly visited district, home to the ethnically diverse Ironbound neighborhood, Newark Penn Station, and the Downtown Arts District. Most of the city's attractions, downtown hotels, and dining options are found here, along with the 21-block **James St. Commons,** a historic district including portions of James, Bleeker, and Warren Streets.

North Ward is home to Branch Brook Park as well as **Ahavas Shalom Synagogue,** Newark's last remaining synagogue. Newark's fifth ward is the Central Ward, located west of the city's downtown center.

SIGHTS AND RECREATION

Most activity in Newark takes place in the city's East Ward, requiring a decent but comfortable walk from Newark Penn Station. To reach sights located within the North Ward, hop on the Newark City Subway at the station.

Military Park

Downtown's six-acre Military Park (Broad St. between Rector St. and Raymond Blvd.,

---

MAKING LIKE A MOLTISANTI

OK, so we're on the fence about what happened to Tony. Was he offed? Did he relocate to Florida? Or is it simply old dog, some new tricks with him? Maybe a *Sopranos* tour will help shed light on where North Jersey's favorite mob boss ended up, even if that place is at the bottom of the Passaic River. The **On Location** (www.screentours. com) four-hour bus tour visits 40 *Soprano*-related places, including the diner where Christopher was shot, Father Phil's parish, and Satin Dolls, a.k.a. the Bada Bing strip club, where you actually get a chance to go inside. Tours leave from Manhattan (Sat.-Sun. 2 P.M., $42 per person), so you'll have to make your way across the Hudson River only to come back to the Jersey side (Nothing's ever easy with this family, *capisc?*). And just like you'd expect from a Sopranos tour, the departure location isn't revealed until you pay. And you'd better pay, know what I'm sayin'?

800/843-6420) serves as a tiny oasis at Newark's city center. While in the area, purchase a pretzel from one of the street vendors and stop in to see the **Wars of America Monument,** created by Mount Rushmore artist Gutzon Borglum. The statue has been a part of the park since 1926.

Newark Penn Station

Newark Penn Station (Market St. and Raymond Plaza, 800/772-2222) is both a major transportation hub and an architectural masterpiece. Combining art deco and neo-classical styles, it was dedicated in 1935 and is the second Penn Station to stand here. While waiting for your connection, have a look at the sculptured ceilings and transportation medallions along the walls.

Cathedral Basilica of the Sacred Heart

The Roman Catholic Cathedral Basilica of the Sacred Heart (89 Ridge St., 973/484-4600, www.cathedralbasilica.org) is the fifth-largest cathedral in the United States. A French Gothic structure known for its exquisite stained glass windows, the Cathedral hosts the **Cathedral Concert Series,** a variety of vocal and instrumental performances held throughout the year (check the website for a current schedule). Cathedral Basilica appears in *The Sopranos* opening credits. It's located just east of Branch Brook Park and south of Park Avenue.

New Jersey Historical Society

Founded in 1845, the statewide New Jersey Historical Society (52 Park Pl., 973/596-8500, www.jerseyhistory.org, Tues.–Sat. 10 A.M.–5 P.M., free) houses multiple-floor displays focused on New Jersey residents past and present, and on what makes New Jersey "New Jersey." Changing exhibits highlight what it means to be from the Garden State. For an overall view of state history, this place can't be beat. The Society also hosts an on-site library, open Wednesday, Thursday, and Saturday, noon–5 P.M., as well as various neighborhood walking tours throughout the year.

Newark Symphony Hall

Originally built as a Shriner temple in 1925, Newark Symphony Hall (1020 Broad St., 973/643-4550, www.newarksymphonyhall .org)—with its sculpted limestone facade and massive Ionic columns—remains a grand site. It's home to the 2,800-seat **Sarah Vaughan Concert Hall,** a main auditorium named to honor the late locally born jazz singer, as well as a 1,000-seat Terrace Ballroom and a 200-seat black box theater. Concerts, plays, and church services are hosted here year-round.

Newark Public Library

The recently renovated Newark Public Library (5 Washington St., 973/733-7800, www.npl.org, Mon., Fri.–Sat. 9 A.M.–5:30 P.M., Tues.–Thurs. 9 A.M.–8:30 P.M. autumn–spring, Mon.–Fri. 9 A.M.–5 P.M., Wed. 9 A.M.–8:30 P.M., Sat. 9:30 A.M.–1:30 P.M. summer) is New Jersey's largest public library and features a wonderful resource selection, including the New Jersey

Hispanic Research and Information Center, the James Brown African American Room, and the Charles F. Cummings New Jersey Information Center. The library hosts interesting exhibits year-round, with some of the more recent being a Super Cool Exhibition of Shopping Bags, and Gone but Not Forgotten: Selected Views of Newark and New Jersey Cemeteries. Newark Public Library also plays a secondary role in Philip Roth's short story "Goodbye, Columbus."

Bears and Eagles Riverfront Stadium

Newark's 6,200-seat minor-league ballpark, Bears and Eagles Riverfront Stadium (450 Broad St., 866/554-2327, www.newarkbears.com, $8–10), is named for the city's original two minor-league teams: The Newark Bears, who played throughout the 1930s and 1940s, and the Negro League Newark Eagles, a team until 1950. The Bears is also the name of the present Atlantic League ball club, not associated with any major-league team. The stadium, dubbed "the Den," was built in 1999 and also includes a concert stage. Kids run bases on Sundays.

To reach the stadium without a car, catch the Newark Subway directly from Penn Station.

Prudential Center

Nicknamed "The Rock" (165 Mulberry St., 201/507-8900, www.prucenter.com) for Prudential's familiar slogan (Get a piece of the . . .), the new home of ice hockey's **New Jersey Devils** opened October 27, 2007, with a game against the Ottawa Senators. The Devils lost, but the arena has since been going strong. Seating approximately 17,625 people, Prudential Center's red and gray exterior pays tribute to the city's bricklaying and railroad heritage as well as the home ice hockey team. There are 750 flat-screen televisions spread throughout the arena. Acts like Tom Petty and the Heartbreakers and Cirque du Soleil perform throughout the year.

New Jersey Performing Arts Center (NJPAC)

Credited as the spark that started Newark's

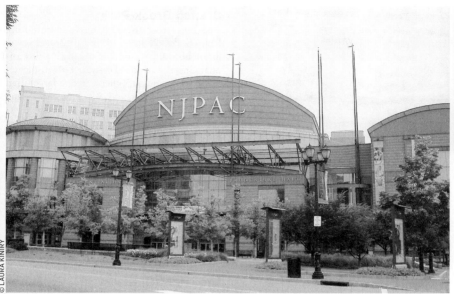

New Jersey Performing Arts Center, the spark of downtown Newark's revitalization

upward spiral, the New Jersey Performing Arts Center (1 Center St., 888/466-5722, www.njpac.org) opened in 1997 and remains the Downtown Arts District's crowning jewel. The center consists of two theaters—the 2,750-seat **Prudential Hall** and the more intimate 500-seat **Victoria Theater,** home to the **New Jersey Symphony Orchestra.** Performances range from jazz to dance to concerts by Yo-Yo Ma and Pink Martini. Guided tours of the theaters, the center's grand lobby, and backstage areas are available by calling 973/297-5857 or emailing tours@njpac.org.

Summer months you can catch free music at the center's outdoor **Theatre Square.**

◖ Newark Museum

With 80 galleries dedicated to arts and science, the Newark Museum (49 Washington St., 973/596-6550, www.newarkmuseum .org, Wed.–Fri. noon–5 P.M., Sat.–Sun. 10 A.M.–5 P.M. Oct.–June, Sat.–Sun. noon–5 P.M. July–Sept., $9 adult, $6 child, AAA discount) is New Jersey's largest, housing everything from a fire museum to a former brewery. Its permanent collection includes African art galleries and Hudson River School landscapes, along with neoclassical sculptor Hiram Power's 1847 statue *The Greek Slave* and Joseph Stella's exquisite five-paneled painting *Voice of New York Interpreted* (1920–1922). The museum's most prolific exhibit is its eight-gallery Tibetan art collection, the largest such collection in the western hemisphere. Displays include a Tibetan Buddhist altar consecrated by the 14th Dalai Lama, a hands-on Tibetan culture display, and a mural depicting Tibet.

Newark Museum is also home to a minizoo featuring more than 100 domestic and exotic animals, such as red-bellied piranhas, cotton-top tamarins, dwarf mongooses, and boa constrictors. **The Alice and Leonard Dreyfuss Planetarium** ($3 adult, $2 child) hosts astronomy shows year-round. Adjacent to the main museum is the restored 1885 brick and limestone **Ballantine House,** former home to members of a prominent local brewing family. Now a National Historic Landmark, visitors are invited to explore its two floors depicting 19th-century period life.

the enormous Newark Museum

In 2009 the museum will honor its centennial with a yearlong celebration of special programs and exhibits.

The Ironbound

Named for the railway tracks encompassing the neighborhood, Newark's Ironbound District (www.goironbound.com) is a vibrant ethnic community home to the country's largest Portuguese population as well as numerous Spaniards and Brazilians. The Ironbound is always buzzing, even on weekday afternoons, with foot traffic, delivery trucks, and a dialectical symphony. Seemingly independent from the rest of Newark, the district hosts its own retail stores, service shops, bar, restaurants, and supermarket. **Ferry Street,** dubbed "Portugal Avenue," is the district's commercial hub.

Though Ferry Street may appear less than grand during the day, don't let it stop you from browsing the shops and markets and stopping at one of the dozens of restaurants, bars, and cafés for an afternoon meal. The experience is worth it.

The Ironbound is situated a few blocks southeast of Newark Penn Station.

Branch Brook Park

The best time for visiting four-mile-long Branch Brook Park (973/268-2300, www.branchbrookpark.org) is during April's annual Cherry Blossom Festival. This display of 3,500 white and pink cherry trees is larger than Washington, D.C.'s, and coincides with Japan's own cherry blossom festival. For two weeks each year the park hosts traditional Japanese music and dance celebrations, as well as art demonstrations in origami and bonsai.

Branch Brook Park was designed by Central Park architect Frederick Law Olmsted and is located within Newark's North Ward. To get here from the Downtown Arts District, take Broad Street north to Bloomfield Avenue, turning left onto Park Avenue. The Newark City Subway, accessible from Newark Penn Station, also stops here.

SHOPPING

Regardless of its big-city status, Newark doesn't have a lot of notable shopping ops. Instead, nearby Elizabeth hosts the bulk of the region's retailers.

Elizabeth

The nearly 12-square-mile industrial city of Elizabeth, just south of Newark, is often paired with its northern neighbor. In fact, a good portion of Newark Liberty International Airport and a number of Newark-centric hotels are within Elizabeth's borders. Elizabeth is best known as being home to **Jersey Gardens** (651 Kapkowski Rd., 908/354-5900, www.jerseygardens.com, Mon.–Sat. 10 A.M.–9 P.M., Sun. 11 A.M.–7 P.M.), the state's largest outlet mall. The Gardens opened in 1999 and features more than 200 shops, eateries, and attractions spread across two indoor levels. There's a small theme park with kiddie rides, arcade games, and a makeshift fossil dig, and a multiplex movie theater along with designer outlets like Lucky Brand Jeans (908/352-4970), Filene's Basement (908/629-0652), Guess (908/659-0826), and H&M (908/436-9300).

A 10-minute shuttle to Jersey Gardens

leaves from Newark International's AirTrain station every 30 minutes, Monday–Saturday 10 A.M.–8 P.M. and Sunday 11 A.M.–6 P.M., and returns every quarter-past and quarter-to the hour. Passengers must each purchase a $5 token for the airport return trip, available inside Filene's Basement and at the Concierge Desk on the lower level by Entrance D.

One of North Jersey's two **IKEA** (1000 IKEA Dr., 908/289-4488, www.ikea.com, Mon.–Fri. 10 A.M.–9 P.M., Sat. 9 A.M.–9 P.M., Sun. 10 A.M.–8 P.M.) furniture stores is conveniently located off the New Jersey Turnpike's Exit 13A (along with Jersey Gardens). Relish the fact that you're not in traffic while dining on Swedish meatballs in the cafeteria above.

ACCOMMODATIONS

The city's accommodations range from no-nonsense airport hotels to convenient downtown locales, though nothing particularly stands out. For something away from the urban bustle without traveling too far, nearby Plainfield offers a wonderful bed-and-breakfast option.

$100-150

Center to Newark's Downtown Arts District is the 170-room **Best Western Robert Treat Hotel** (50 Park Pl., 973/622-1000, www.best western.com, $100–120). The building itself is more than a century old but has held up surprisingly well. Rooms are small but cozy and come with complimentary breakfast, high-speed Internet, and satellite TV. For those who like to check in and stay in, there's a restaurant on-site.

$150-300

Downtown's 86-room **Comfort Suites** (1348 McCarter Hwy., 973/481-5200, www.comfort suites.com, $150–215) features clean smoke-free rooms that come with complimentary continental breakfast. A shuttle is available 24/7 for rides to and from Newark International Airport. The hotel is within walking distance of the city's minor league ballpark, although it's a short hike to the Arts District and area restaurants—nothing that public transport can't fix.

Completely renovated in 2008, the five-story **Wyndham Garden Hotel** (550 Hwy. 9, 877/999-3223 or 973/824-4000, $116–249) includes a Michael Graves–designed coffee-maker, wireless Internet, and contemporary Be Well bedding in every room. A complimentary 24-hour shuttle is available to and from nearby Newark Airport, and there's a car rental service on-site.

Courtyard Newark Liberty Airport (600 Rtes. 1 and 9 S., 973/643-8500, $124–244) offers complimentary 24-hour airport shuttle service and features both an on-site deli and breakfast café. Room service and local restaurant delivery are available.

Approximately 20 miles west of Newark Airport, the ◖ **Pillars of Plainfield Bed and Breakfast** (922 Central Ave., Plainfield, 908/753-0922, www.pillars2.com, $185–250) offers a delightful urban alternative. Housed in a restored 1870 Victorian-Georgian mansion in the town's Van Wyck Brooks Historic District, the inn features six individually styled guest rooms and a long-term studio rental, along with a book library and a music room ideal for sipping sherry and snacking on cookies. When the weather's warm, head outdoors for a walk among the property's dogwood and cherry trees and a rest on the covered veranda. Quiet hours begin at 10 P.M.

Downtown Newark's **Hilton Newark Gateway at Penn Station** (1 Gateway Center, Raymond Blvd., 973/622-5000, $165–350) connects with the train station via a walkway, making it an extremely convenient overnight stay for visits to Jersey City, Hoboken, and New York City, as well as Newark. The Ironbound District's bars and restaurants are right outside its doors. Although the hotel is over 20 years old, rooms have been newly renovated and each includes a flat-screen TV as well as Crabtree and Evelyn's toiletries and deep-soak tubs.

FOOD
Arts District

Situated on the ground floor of the Robert Treat Hotel, **Maize's** (50 Park Pl., 973/733-2202, www.maizerestaurant.com, Mon.–Fri. 7 A.M.–midnight, Sat. 8 A.M.–midnight, Sun.

11 A.M.–10 P.M., $19–27) selection of continental cuisine includes seared sea scallops and lamb porterhouse, along with several vegetarian dishes. Stylishly decorated with blown-glass pieces and a row of bench seating, the restaurant has been used as a *Sopranos* filming location. Both Maize and its cigar bar are popular with the after-work crowd.

Just off from NJPAC's main lobby is the **Theater Square Grill** (NJPAC, 1 Center St., 973/642-1226, www.theater-square-grill .com, Mon.–Fri. 11:30 P.M.–2:30 P.M., dinner Tues.–Fri. 5–9 P.M. and in conjunction with weekend performances, $23–29), an upscale eatery serving New American entrées like Niman Ranch pork chops with sweet corn flan and sugar snap peas. The restaurant also features a more casual French-inspired bistro and **Calcada,** a seasonal outdoor eatery with wrought iron tables and strewn white lights. Alfresco offerings include a selection of salads, sandwiches, and wood-oven pizzas. There's also an express menu.

Surrounding Downtown

Consistently voted one of Newark's best eateries, **Je's** (34 Williams St., 973/623-8848, Tues.–Sat. 8 A.M.–7:30 P.M., Sun. 9 A.M.–7:30 P.M., closed Mon., $7–15), a small storefront space south of the central Arts District, is the place to load up on soul food and family-style comfort cooking like fried chicken and mac-and-cheese. Devout customers include Queen Latifah and Shaquille O'Neal.

Located a couple of blocks west of the Ironbound, **The Priory** (233 W. Market St., 973/242-8012, lunch Mon.–Fri. 11:30 A.M.–3 P.M., dinner Wed.–Sat. 5–10 P.M., brunch Sun. 10 A.M.–5 P.M.) is known for its Southern-style daily lunch buffet, along with an exquisite Sunday creole brunch. Jazz, piano, and gospel are performed weekly at this converted Gothic church.

Just west of Branch Brook Park, local stalwart **Calandra's Italian & French Bakery** (204 First Ave., 973/484-5598, www.calandrasbakery.com, daily 6 A.M.–9 P.M.) offers freshly baked biscotti, deep-dish pies, chocolate cakes, and some of New Jersey's best bread loaves (don't miss the panelle), made fresh opening to close.

The Ironbound

The most difficult thing about dining in the Ironbound is deciding which restaurant to choose.

Romantic **Fornos of Spain** (47 Ferry St., 973/589-4767, www.fornosrestaurant.com, Mon.–Fri. 11:30 A.M.–10:30 P.M., Sat.–Sun. noon–11 P.M., $13–34) serves large portions of classic Spanish dishes like *mariscada,* a shellfish stew. Seasonal garden seating and private parking are available.

The name means "wine cellar" in Portuguese, and with over 180 wines to select from, (**Adega Grill** (130 Ferry St., 973/589-8830, www.adega grill.com, Mon.–Thurs. 11:30 A.M.–10 P.M., Fri.–Sat. 11:30 A.M.–11 P.M., Sun. noon–10 P.M., $20–43) doesn't disappoint. The Spanish and Portuguese cuisine is outstanding, and the decor, which includes stone pillars, wrought iron gates, and roaring fires, calls to mind a medieval castle. Still, a trip to modernity's not far off: Just stop by the restaurant's sleek **One Thirty-Two** lounge. Its low-slung ceiling and plush deco furnishings will transport you to the 20th century at least.

Behind the velvet curtains of **Brasilia Grill** (132 Ferry St., 973/589-8682, www.brasiliagrill .com, daily 11:30 A.M.–11 P.M.) guests consume endless *rodizio* ($22), an all-you-can *carnes* fest originated in southern Brazil. The dining room is spacious, but soccer fans may want to take their meals in the bar.

The grand **Iberia Peninsula** (63–69 Ferry St., 973/344-5611 or 973/344-1657, www.iberi arestaurants.com, Mon.–Wed. 11 A.M.–2 A.M., Thurs.–Sat. 11 A.M.–3 A.M., Sun. noon–2 A.M., closed Tues., $16–38) is also known for its *rodizio,* brought continuously to your table until you say stop. The restaurant's sibling establishment, the original **Iberia Tavern & Restaurant** (80–84 Ferry St., 973/344-7603, Mon.–Wed. 11 A.M.–2 A.M., Thurs.–Sat. 11 A.M.–3 A.M., Sun. noon–2 A.M., closed Mon., $16–38), specializes in *paella á valenciana,* or rice garnished with seafood. The two restaurants share a massive brick exterior and a parking lot, along with some of the neighborhood's best sangria, offered in red or white for $18 a pitcher. And they both have breathtaking interiors: the Peninsula with its cathedral ceilings, and the Tavern with a beamed ceiling, brick walls, and mounted sconces throughout.

On the edge of the Ironbound is popular **Spain** (419 Market St., 973/344-0994, www .spainrestaurant.com, Mon.–Thurs. 11:30 A.M.– 10 P.M., Fri.–Sat. 11:30 A.M.–11 P.M., Sun. noon–10 P.M., $12–18), a fun and boisterous corner space featuring Spanish eats like *vieiras rellenas* (crabmeat-stuffed scallops) and *cola de langosta* (broiled lobster tail).

Elizabeth
In business since 1969, family-run **Tommy's Italian Sausages and Hot Dogs** (900 2nd Ave., 908/351-9831, $3–7) is a take-out store-front renowned for its stewed-onion chili dog and the Italian Dog, a deep-fried hot dog topped with peppers, onions, and potatoes stuffed into pita-like pizza bread.

INFORMATION
Newark is home to the *Star-Ledger* (www .nj.com/starledger), one of the state's most prominent newspapers.

GETTING THERE AND AROUND
Newark Liberty International Airport (parking 888/397-4636, information 973/ 961-6000, www.panynj.com) is located south of Newark's business district, three miles outside the city straddling the Newark-Elizabeth border. From here, hop aboard a NJ Transit train for an easy ride into downtown Newark, or to connect with **Newark City Subway** at Newark Penn Station. The subway runs nearly four miles north along a former portion of the historic Morris Canal, with a stop at Branch Brook Park. The PATH train from downtown Manhattan, by way of downtown Jersey City, also connects at Newark Penn Station.

For drivers, Newark is easily reached via the New Jersey Turnpike, and from the east by the **Pulaski Skyway** connecting to Jersey City. Newark's downtown district is considered walkable, though it may be a stretch for some. Street parking in the Ironbound can be difficult—once you find a space, stay there. There are several parking garages in the area; they run $1–2 per half hour, $10–20 per day.

The Upper Northeast

Above the Meadowlands and west of the Gold Coast, New Jersey's urbanized Northeast begins petering out in a series of suburban stretches, Main Street villages, and a dense urban center or two. The area's best dining options are in Ridgewood, with a few standouts in Paramus and Hackensack. Accommodations mostly center along Route 17.

Information
The *Bergen County Record* (www.bergen .com) is the local newspaper.

Getting There and Around
I-80 travels east to west through the Gateway's Upper Northeast and is easily accessible from both the New Jersey Turnpike and the Garden State Parkway. Traffic congestion persists throughout the region, but the worst stretch by far is Route 17 from the Meadowlands north through Hackensack and Paramus. Pay attention.

HACKENSACK AND PARAMUS
Though both traffic and sprawl are inevitably part of Hackensack and nearby Paramus, the area's attractions and shopping ops may be worth it. Unfortunately, Route 17—an out-dated, congested highway—is the main road for reaching them. Bergen County's blue laws banning the Sunday sale of most nonfood and

nondrug items, including clothes, furniture, and home appliances, affect both Hackensack and Paramus—take note before heading to IKEA.

Sights

The **New Jersey Naval Museum** (Court and River Sts., Hackensack, 201/342-3268, www.njnm.com) is home to the **USS Ling**, a 312-foot-long, 2,500-ton BALAO class submarine open for tours ($7 adult, $3 child). The museum itself houses a fine collection of historic photographs and personal items from Navy sailors, along with a shrine to the more than 3,500 Navy sailors who lost their lives during World War II. German Seahund torpedoes and a Patrol Boat Riverine once used in Vietnam are displayed on the outer grounds. Unfortunately, property owners have recently asked the museum to vacate in order to sell or develop the land. Though the museum is still in operation as of this writing, it's best to call ahead before visiting. Hours of admission are weekends only 10 A.M.–4 P.M., with the last submarine tour beginning at 3:15 P.M. Poor weather may cause the grounds to close, so call ahead.

South of Paramus in the town of River Edge is **Historic New Bridge Landing** (1201 Main St., River Edge, 201/343-9492), where General George Washington led his troops across the Hackensack River to escape British forces during the Revolutionary War. The site was granted state park status in 2004, making it one of New Jersey's newest state parks. In addition to the commemorative site, the park is home to three Dutch Colonial sandstone structures: the 1774 **Campbell-Christie House**, the 1794 **Demarest House**, and the 1752 **Steuben House** (1209 Main St., 201/487-1739), one of the region's numerous "Washington slept here" locations and the only one of the three buildings to remain in its original location. All three homes are property of the **Bergen County Historical Society** (201/343-9492, www.bergencountyhistory.org), which, until recently, operated the latter as a museum. An April 2007 nor'easter caused significant damage to both the home and its collection, closing it until further

notice. The Campbell-Christie House is open the second Sunday of the month.

Originally built as an 18th-century farmhouse, **The Hermitage** (335 N. Franklin Turnpike, Ho-Ho-Kus, 201/445-8311, www.thehermitage.org, $5 adult, $4 child, 6 and under free) hosted Aaron Burr's wedding and served as one of George Washington's headquarters during the American Revolution. Today, a National Historic Landmark, the home was reconstructed in the mid-19th-century as a Greek revival mansion, incorporating parts of the original stone structure into its walls. The Hermitage museum is open year-round Monday–Friday 9 A.M.–5 P.M. with tours offered Wednesday–Sunday 1–4 P.M.; the last tour begins at 3:15 P.M. A museum store is open during tour hours.

In the boundaries of Paramus's Van Saun County Park is the small **Bergen County Zoological Park** (216 Forest Ave., Paramus, 201/262-3771, daily 10 A.M.–4:30 P.M.), home to mountain lions, elks, alligators, boa constrictors, the endangered Andean condor, and other birds, reptiles, and mammals found only in the Americas. Admission ($2.50 adult, $1.50 ages 3–14) is only charged Wednesday–Sunday and on holidays May–October. The rest of the year admission is free.

Located on the Bergen Mall's lower level, **The Bergen Museum of Art and Science** (Rte. 4 E., Paramus, 201/291-8848, www.thebergenmuseum.com, Tues.–Thurs. and Sat. 10 A.M.–5 P.M., $5 adult, $3 child under 12) displays many of Bergen County's art, culture, and scientific contributions, including a mastodon skeleton (the museum owns two) discovered in the 1960s during the construction of a nearby highway. Additional displays include a handcrafted miniatures exhibit and temporary exhibits like Century Icons and Soviet Dissident Art.

The **New Jersey Children's Museum** (599 Valley Health Plaza, Paramus, 201/262-5151, www.njcm.com, daily 10 A.M.–6 P.M., $10) is divided into more than 30 cubicle-like rooms, each hosting an interactive theme. Kids can play house in a life-size dollhouse, run a pizzeria, or create pictures on a light mosaic described as "a giant Lite-Brite for kids."

Shopping

Sticking to the New Jersey norm, Bergen County is filled with chain stores and shopping stores, though a few retailers warrant their own mention.

Why pay the bridge toll when you've got **The Shops at Riverside** (One Riverside Sq., Hackensack, 201/489-2212, www.shopriver side.com) for your New York finds. Tiffany & Co., Boss Hugo Boss, and Burberry, along with upscale chain restaurants McCormick & Schmick's and Morton's Steakhouse, are all represented at this two-story shopping mall. Unfortunately, the county blue laws keep most stores shuttered on Sundays. Barnes & Noble is the exception.

Paramus's **Westfield Garden State Plaza** (1 Garden State Plaza, Paramus, 201/843-2121, http://westfield.com/gardenstateplaza/) features *five* department stores, including Lord & Taylor, Nordstrom, and Neiman Marcus, along with hundreds of retail shops. J. Crew, Jessica McClintock, and Kenneth Cole New York are each represented. American Apparel, Urban Outfitters, and Fossil are on their way. Dine at California Pizza Kitchen or Napa Valley Grille.

New Jersey's home to two **IKEA** stores, both within the Gateway Region. This location (100 IKEA Dr., Paramus, 201/843-1881, closed Sun.) is situated just off Route 17 in Paramus.

Famous for their newsprint-like mail-order catalogs filled with sleeping bags, tents, and camp cooking utensils, **Campmor** (810 Rte. 17 N., Paramus, 201/445-5000, www.campmor .com) maintains a retail space in Paramus. The showroom is packed with outdoor gear and accessories like backpacks, canoes and kayaks, and skiing, snowboarding, and cycling equipment. Suppliers include Kelty, Timbuk 2, and Camelbak.

Recreation

Situated in the Shops at Riverside, the full-service **Fountain European Spa** (Rte. 4, West Hackensack, 201/327-5155, www.fountain europeanspa.com) has more than 20 treatment rooms, along with whirlpool tubs for couples and an on-site spa boutique. Hair removal, deep-tissue massage, and seaweed body wraps are all available, as well as special massages and facials for athletic and acne-prone teens.

Accommodations

Many area visitors prefer staying overnight in the nearby Meadowlands or even around Newark Airport for easy highway accessibility and convenience, but for something a bit closer try Paramus's **Comfort Inn & Suites** (211 Rte. 17 S., 201/261-8686, www.comfort innparamus.com, $180–220). It's centrally located, the rooms are clean, and the entry lounge is particularly comfortable. Stays include daily hot breakfast daily and use of high-speed Internet.

Food

Paramus and Hackensack offer plenty of fast food, chain, and diner options, but there are also a few unique standouts.

Adorable **White Manna** (358 River St., Hackensack, 201/342-0914, Mon.–Sat. 8:30 A.M.–9 P.M., Sun. 10 A.M.–6 P.M.), cousin to Jersey City's White Mana (minus an *n*), has only 21 seats. Pull up a stool at the U-shaped counter and order a slider ($1), a small but juicy (oh-so-juicy) onion-topped burger served on Martin's famous potato rolls. You'll be happy you did.

Wondee's Fine Thai Food Noodle (296 Main St., Hackensack, 201/883-1700, www .wondeenj.com, Tues.–Fri. 11 A.M.–10 P.M., Sat. 11:30 A.M.–10 P.M., Sun. and holidays noon– 8:30 P.M., $8.50–15) is a BYO foodie favorite. Entrées include meat, chicken, and tofu dishes, along with frog legs and quail. Items can be spicy—be sure to specify.

Solari's (61 River St., Hackensack, 201/487-1969, www.solarisrestaurant.com, Mon.–Fri. 10 A.M.–2:30 P.M., Sat. 10 A.M.–10 P.M., $17–25) serves classic northern Italian dishes like cheese tortellini ($19) and shrimp scampi ($20) in a bright spacious setting. Live music and dinner shows are the norm.

For something unusual, check out **Chakra** (W-144 Rte. 4, Paramus, 201/556-1530, www.chakrarestaurant.com, lunch Mon.–Fri. 11:30 A.M.–2:30 P.M., dinner Mon.–Wed. 5–10 P.M., Thurs.–Sat. 5–11 P.M., Sun. 5–9 P.M., $19–34), a massive dimly lit restaurant where New American dishes like diver scallops and a half rack of lamb are served to guests in pillowed booths draped with sheer silk curtains, pulled taut for privacy. Hanging sconces, white candles, and towering palms contribute to the conspicuous setting. A late-night menu is also available throughout the week.

Services

Hackensack University Medical Center (30 Prospect Ave., Hackensack, 201/996-2000, www.humc.com) is one of New Jersey's largest and highest-rated hospitals.

The 24-hour **Oradell Animal Hospital** (580 Winters Ave., Paramus, 201/262-0010, www.oradell.com) is one of the United States' largest animal hospitals and the Gateway region's premier pet-care facility. In addition to general medicine and surgery, the hospital offers dental and dermatological treatment, nutritional counseling, and bereavement support.

Getting There and Around

NJ Transit's Pascack Valley Line has stops in Hackensack at Essex and Anderson Streets. Catch the **Hackensack Shuttle** (Mon.–Fri. 5:53 A.M.–7 P.M., Sat. 10 A.M.–4 P.M.) from either station to access various points throughout town. Paramus is best explored by car.

PATERSON

Secretary of Treasury Alexander Hamilton created Paterson as the first planned industrial city in the United States in 1791, utilizing the waters of its Great Falls for textile manufacturing. Its current population of 149,000 is New Jersey's third largest, smaller only than Newark and Jersey City. From its beginnings Paterson was an ethnically diverse place, a mecca for

© LAURA KINIRY

Paterson pays homage to its founder, Alexander Hamilton.

immigrants arriving to work in its factories. In addition to textiles the city became a proficient producer of handguns, railcars, and silk, earning it the nickname "Silk City" in the late 1800s. Paterson once housed over 800 silk operations.

The city has retained its industrial feel, though not much else. Early-20th-century fires destroyed a large portion of Paterson's commercial district, to be resurrected in the form of massive beaux arts buildings. These structures are now in danger, as a battle continues over preserving them or tearing them down and replacing them with modern units. Some property owners have covered the remaining buildings with cheap facades, damaging what might be the only key to Paterson's successful revitalization.

Paterson has the distinction of being the country's most strike-ridden city, scene of over 137 strikes from 1880 to 1900. When businesses moved south to escape the unions, Paterson suffered a blow from which it has never recovered. Still, the city seems to hold a special place in the hearts of current and former residents, including deceased poets William Carlos Williams and Allen Ginsberg. Williams, a Pulitzer Prize winner, wrote the epic poem "Paterson" as a monument to the city, while Ginsberg—a Williams admirer—scribed the much shorter "Paterson" in his honor. Ginsberg's friend Jack Kerouac depicted the main character of *On the Road* as a Paterson resident.

Architecture and history buffs will appreciate Paterson, though others may want to avoid it. The city is crowded with cars and people, even on weekday afternoons, and Market Street, though packed with multistory structures housing storefront after storefront, offers little draw for visitors. Awnings are faded, sidewalks have heaved, and litter and parking meters are plentiful. That being said, Paterson supposedly has some of the best Middle Eastern eateries around. But for those visiting the museum and the Great Falls, skip the Market Street exit and take Main Street instead.

© LAURA KINIRY

Paterson's Great Falls

Great Falls State Park

Paterson's Great Falls are the area's main natural attribute and the reason for the city's establishment. Once used as an energy supplier for Paterson's manufacturing, the Great Falls are the second largest waterfall by volume east of the Mississippi. In 2004 the falls and over 100 surrounding acres, including the nearby **SUM Historic District,** became known as Great Falls State Park (973/225-0826, www.nj.gov/dep/parksandforests/parks/great-falls.htm). Visitors can walk a small footbridge overlooking the 77-foot falls, take a photo with Paterson native Lou Costello's statue, or walk among historic brick buildings still bearing the names of various textile machines. New York–based landscape architecture and urban design firm Field Operations recently won a competition to redesign the park, and the Department of Environmental Protection approved their master plan in July 2008. For now, Great Falls doesn't feel like the safest area, but then again no portion of Paterson does.

Paterson Museum

One of Paterson's historic district highlights is its Paterson Museum (2 Market St., 973/321-1260, www.thepatersonmuseum.com, Tues.–Fri. 10 A.M.–4 P.M., Sat.–Sun. 12:30–4:30 P.M., $2 adult, child free), easily recognizable by the locomotive parked out front. The museum hosts several interesting local history displays, including photographs of Paterson during its Silk City reign, a collection of Colt pistols and firearms, patent medicines acquired from an early-20th-century South Paterson drugstore, and an exhibit on Gasoline Alley, a row of garages between the city's 17th and 18th Streets that survived until the 1990s. The museum also hosts Irish inventor John Philip Holland's 1881 Fenian Ram, considered the world's first true submarine.

Lambert Castle

Located within **Garret Mountain Reservation County Park** west of Paterson, Lambert Castle (3 Valley Rd., 973/247-0085, www.lambertcastle.org) is a unique example of medieval revival architecture as well as the home of the

Passaic County Historical Society. During the early 20th century the castle belong to Paterson silk mill owner Catholina Lambert, an avid antique and art collector. Many of her belongings, along with changing exhibits pertaining to Passaic County, are displayed inside. The castle museum is open 1–4 P.M. Wednesday–Sunday. Hours for the Historical Society library are 1–4 P.M. Wednesday–Friday and the second and fourth Saturdays of the month, closed mid-October through mid-December. Admission for either is $5 adult, $3 child; with purchase of one, admission to the other is free.

Wayne

Sprawling Wayne Township served as muse for pop group Fountains of Wayne, who supposedly named themselves after an iconic lawn furnishings and garden center along Route 46. The area is without a cohesive center, though it's home to both **William Paterson University** (300 Pompton Rd., 877/978-3923, www.wpunj.edu) and **Dey Mansion** (Preakness Valley Park, 199 Totowa Rd., 973/696-1176, www.passaiccountynj.org/historicalhousemuseums.htm, $1 adult, child free), a colonial estate that served as George Washington's Revolutionary War headquarters during July, October, and November 1780. Mansion tours take place Wednesday–Friday 1–4 P.M., weekends 10 A.M.–noon and 1–4 P.M. The park is open Wednesday–Sunday 8:30 A.M.–4:30 P.M.

Getting There and Around

NJ Transit's **Bergen County Line** runs from both Hoboken Terminal and Secaucus Junction to Paterson's transit station, located at Market and Ward Streets. The station is within walking distance of both Paterson Museum and Great Falls State Park, though I recommend driving if it's an option. From the Gold Coast region take I-80 west and exit at Main Street. To reach Wayne from Paterson, continue on I-80 west for about 4.5 miles to Route 23, Exit 53 (for Wayne, Butler, and Verona).

RIDGEWOOD

Known for many fine restaurants and shops and its walkable downtown, upscale Ridgewood is worth a trip. The village main street, Ridgewood Avenue, is lined with low-slung brick and clapboard structures housing a mix of boutiques, chain retailers, and service stores. Ridgewood's train station is conveniently located downtown, but a slight incline from the shops may make the return walk a bit challenging. Large old homes—including several in craftsman style—surrounding the village center are worth a look.

Shopping

Ridgewood's shopping options consist of retail stores and independent boutiques.

For vinyl toys, Count Chocula bobble heads, and DIY designs, check out the fun **Brain Candy** (26 Chestnut St., 201/447-3200, www.braincandyshop.com). Those in the market for ecofriendly footwear or a new pair of New Balance sneakers will want to stop by **Ecco/Village Tannery** (125 E. Ridgewood Ave., 201/444-2885, www.villagetanneryshoes.com). **Yansi Fugel** (66 E. Ridgewood Ave., 201/493-7060, www.yansifugel.com) is home to chic sculpted pants, cashmere pullovers, ruffle tuxedo blouses, and drop-waist sheath dresses for women.

A wonderful local bookstore, **Bookends** (232 E. Ridgewood Ave., 201/445-0726, www.book-ends.com) hosts year-round author events and features New Jersey's largest stock of autographed books.

Mango Jam (41 N. Broad St., 201/493-9911, www.mangojamonline.com) specializes in unique home decor like swanky magnets and decorated dinnerware, as well as perky garden scents and treats for your pooch. It's not just the name **Happy Tuesday** (210 E. Ridgewood Ave., 201/447-0074, www.happytuesday.com) that attracts patrons: This bright specialty store stocks handmade greeting cards, crafted candles, and distinct handcrafted jewelry guaranteed to make you smile.

Day Spas

Ridgewood is an ideal place to get pampered, especially after a day perusing the shops. Day spa **Araya Rebirth** (10 Garber Sq.,

201/445-7005, www.araya-rebirth.com, Tues. and Thurs. 10 A.M.–8 P.M., Wed. and Fri. 10 A.M.–6 P.M., Sat. 9 A.M.–5 P.M., closed Sun.–Mon.) provides custom facials and reflexology massage, along with specialized treatments such as "ear candling," an old home remedy that help rid clients of extraneous ear wax.

Ridgewood European Day Spa (30 Franklin Ave., 201/447-1600, www.ridge woodspa.com, Mon. 10 A.M.–4 P.M., Tues. and Thurs. noon–9 P.M., Wed. 9 A.M.–9 P.M., Fri.–Sat. 9 A.M.–5 P.M., closed Sun.) offers spoiling treatments like ultracalming facials and hot-stone massage.

Food

Ridgewood's eateries range from casual coffeehouses to elegant restaurants, with several chain establishments strewn throughout.

Reputable BYO **Village Green** (36 Prospect St., 201/445-2914, www.villagegreen restaurant.com, lunch Mon.–Fri. 11:45 A.M.–2 P.M., dinner Tues.–Thurs. 5:30–9:30 P.M., Fri.–Sat. 5:30–10 P.M., Sun. 5–8 P.M. except summer, $23–39) specializes in tasting menus and small flavorful dishes that make good use of fresh ingredients. The interior has the feel of a refined Bavarian hall.

Before reaching the namesake portion of the menu at **Country Pancake House** (140 E. Ridgewood Ave., 201/444-8395, Mon.–Thurs. 7 A.M.–9:30 P.M., Fri.–Sun. 7 A.M.–10 P.M., $7–15), you'll already have been tempted with cheese blintzes, omelets, frittatas, *waffle* frittatas, and Benedicts. And while they're all delicious, the pancakes are what you're here for. Bring dough (it's cash only) and an appetite; it's so difficult deciding between buckwheat pancakes and the chocolate-lover's mix, you may choose both.

Stop by cozy **Natalie's Cafe** (24 S. Broad St., 201/444-9020, nataliescafe.com, Mon.–Sat. 10 A.M.–10 P.M., closed Sun., $6.95–11.95) for lunchtime burgers and wraps, or hold off till dinner for comforting dishes like chicken pot pie ($19) and baby back ribs ($19). The restaurant recently relocated from its former address across the street, converting the old space into a bakery and pasta house.

Situated beside the train station, BYO **Latour** (6 E. Ridgewood Ave., 201/445-5056, $21–29) is both elegant and adorable, graced with high ceilings, crisp white linens, and dark wood floors. Classic French cuisine is perfect but pricey; to get the most for your money, opt for the five-course fixed-price tasting menu ($44.50 per person) evenings Tuesday–Thursday and Sunday. The restaurant is open for lunch Tuesday–Friday 11:30 A.M.–2:30 P.M., dinner Tuesday–Thursday 5–10 P.M., Friday 5–11 P.M., and Sunday 4–9 P.M. Saturday night seatings take place at 6 P.M. and 8:30 P.M., and the restaurant is closed Monday.

Getting There

NJ Transit's **Bergen County Line** runs from both Hoboken Terminal and Secaucus Junction to Ridgewood Transit Station, located in the downtown village at Garber Square and West Ridgewood Avenue.

The Urban Outskirts

West of the Gateway's Gold Coast are the Watchung Mountains, home to a series of affluent New York City commuter suburbs. The area is a nice reprieve from the dense waterfront cities—a good place to come for a drive or meal. Both Summit and Montclair offer superb dining options, the latter seeing an influx of new eateries almost monthly. While not hosting a ton of lodging options, both West Orange and Summit do have a few recommendable choices—though depending on your plans it may be more convenient to drive the short distance to one of Newark's airport hotels. Montclair and Short Hills, home to perhaps New Jersey's finest mall (and New Jerseyans *love* their malls), offer excellent shopping opportunities. The area hosts several attractions worth visiting, including Montclair's art museum, Edison's West Orange Lab, Millburn's New York–caliber theater, and two popular universities.

UPPER MONTCLAIR AND CLIFTON

Perched above downtown Montclair is Upper Montclair and the Spanish-style **Montclair State University,** which crosses over Watchung Road, spreading into nearby Clifton and Little Falls. The school is mainly a commuter campus for thousands of students and features both its own Jersey diner and a minor-league ballpark.

◖ Tick Tock Diner

One of New Jersey's most beloved—and photographed—diners, slick and shiny Tick Tock Diner (281 Allwood Rd. and Rte. 3, Clifton, 973/777-0511, open 24/7, $5–15) is spacious and sunny inside, with ample counter space and an extensive menu. The diner's "Eat Heavy" motto is taken in all seriousness, and burgers come huge. Suits, thirtysomethings, and senior couples cozy into booths, reminiscing about past meals at their favorite hangout.

Yogi Berra Stadium and Museum

Tucked into the hillside Montclair State University, Yogi Berra Stadium (Valley Rd. and Norman Ave., Upper Montclair, 973/746-7434, $8–10) is New Jersey's smallest minor-league ballpark, home to the independent **New Jersey Jackals** (www.jackals.com) minor-league team. The stadium, built in 1998, is named after former Yankees catcher, baseball manager, and Montclair resident Lawrence "Yogi" Berra, three-time winner of the American League MVP. Official seating is approximately 3,800, with a general admission lawn behind outfield accommodating an additional 4,000.

Adjacent to the stadium is the **Yogi Berra Learning Center and Museum** (8 Quarry Rd., Little Falls, 973/655-2378, www.yogiberra museum.org, $6 adult, $4 student), an educational facility and exhibit space stressing sports as an essential learning tool. Sports-based education programs are offered through the museum year-round, along with events like book signings and sports drawing workshops. Berra's signature and handprints are preserved in the cement out front, though it's plausible you'll catch Yogi in person. The museum is open Wednesday–Sunday noon–5 P.M., noon–7 P.M.

© LAURA KINIRY

Clifton's Tick Tock Diner, the ideal place for a rainy afternoon

during Wednesday–Sunday home games, and two hours prior to every Jackals home game. It's closed on major holidays.

Other Sights

Trek on up to one-acre **Montclair Hawk Lookout** to watch the region's annual fall hawk migration. A viewing platform dedicated by the New Jersey Audubon Society sits atop Upper Montclair's First Watchung Mountain, along Edgecliff Road a couple blocks west of Upper Mountain Avenue, and is open September–November.

For approximately three weeks each year, usually from mid-May through early June, volunteer-run **Presby Memorial Iris Gardens** (Mountainside Park, Upper Montclair Ave., Upper Montclair, 973/783-5974, http://presby irisgardens.org) celebrates the blooming of more than 4,000 iris varieties with a series of garden parties, art exhibits, and walking tours. Visitors are welcome to visit the gardens daily, dawn to dusk, year-round.

Mount Hebron Cemetery (Valley Rd., Upper Montclair, 973/744-1380) plays permanent host to a few minor celebrities, including John Charles Barclay (1856–1934), inventor of the electric telegraph, and the actress Shirley Booth (1898–1992).

Getting There

Montclair State University has its own NJ Transit commuter station, but trains only stop here during the week. To get here board the Montclair-Boonton Line at New York City's Penn Station, about a 40-minute ride, and exit at Montclair State University. Watchung Avenue separates Upper Montclair from Montclair (south).

MONTCLAIR

Often cited as New Jersey's most liberal small town, Montclair has a lot going for it. Less than 14 miles west of New York City, the township is a hotbed of diversity, filled with interesting shops, restaurants, clubs, and coffeehouses. Downtown centers along Bloomfield Avenue, a long, heavily trafficked stretch beginning in nearby Bloomfield and continuing west into Caldwell and Verona. North of downtown the streets slope upward, providing Montclair the appeal of a Rocky Mountain town and some of New Jersey's highest property values. Although a commuter bus does stop here and NJ Transit has numerous stations in the outlying township, it's not an easy place to explore without a car. The Montclair Center Business Improvement District (www.montclair center.com) is a great resource for learning more about the township's offerings, as is the continually updated and interesting Montclair blog *Baristanet* (www.baristanet.com).

Montclair Art Museum

Housed in a neoclassical Greek revival structure, the diverse collection of the Montclair Art Museum (3 S. Mountain Ave., 973/746-5555, www.montclairartmuseum.org, Tues.–Sun. 11 A.M.–5 P.M., $8 adult, $6 senior and student) includes Andy Warhol paintings, works by local artist George Inness and the Hudson River School, and an extensive Native American artifact collection with jewelry, baskets, and weavings. Expanded in 2001, the museum hosts all-ages drawing, painting, and sculpture workshops, as well as an art reference library with over 50,000 books, periodicals, and resource materials. The library is currently open by appointment only Wednesday–Friday 10 A.M.– noon and 2:30–4:30 P.M., closed in August.

Themed museum tours take place every third Saturday of the month, and free admission is offered each Friday 11 A.M.–1 P.M.

Van Vleck House and Gardens

Begun as a private estate more than 125 years ago, Van Vleck Gardens (21 Van Vleck St., 973/744-4752, www.vanvleck.org, daily 9 A.M.–5 P.M., free) is known for its lovely rhododendron and azalea displays. The gardens surround an early-20th-century Mediterranean-style villa built for a member of the Van Vleck family, three generations of which lived on the nearly six-acre land before it was handed over to the Montclair Foundation. In addition to self-guided garden tours, visitors are treated to garden art shows and activities year-round, including outdoor summer concerts.

Grover Cleveland Birthplace

Grover Cleveland's Birthplace (207 Bloomfield Ave., Caldwell, 973/226-0001, Wed.–Sun., hours vary so call ahead, free), located in the nearby borough of Caldwell, was the first home of the only U.S. president elected to two nonconsecutive terms. The country's most complete collection of Cleveland artifacts is displayed here, including his baby cradle and fishing gear.

Entertainment

Cafés and old-style theaters are both part of Montclair's quasi-urban streetscape.

Originally opened as a stage venue in 1922, the historic **Wellmont Theatre** (5 Seymour St., 973/783-9500) operated as a single-screen movie house for many years before converting into a triplex and finally closing in 2006. After a multimillion-dollar makeover the theater reopened in fall 2008 as a 2,000-seat concert venue run by the owners of New York City's Bowery Ballroom and Andy Feltz, who brought shows to Manhattan's Beacon Theater for two decades. Stay tuned.

At the heart of Bloomfield Avenue is **Montclair-Claridge Cinemas** (486 Bloomfield Ave., 973/470-2589), a converted six-plex specializing in first-run features and art-house films. The theater is operated by Clearview Cinemas, who run many of the Gateway's former single screens.

Comfortable **Cafe Eclectic** (444 Bloomfield Ave., 973/509-9179, Mon.–Thurs. 11 A.M.–midnight, Fri. 11 A.M.–1 A.M., Sat. noon–1 A.M., Sun. 1 P.M.–midnight) is the kind of place you'll want to curl up with a book and stay a while; that's if you don't mind congregating with hordes of high school teens. They serve a mean cubano sandwich and the coffee is good, especially when iced or flavored. Free wireless Internet and a weekly karaoke night really liven things up.

About a 10-minute drive from downtown Montclair, **The Remedy** (401 Broad St., Bloomfield, 973/566-0404, Tues.–Sun.

10 A.M.–11 P.M., closed Mon.) features a fine selection of espresso drinks and herbal-based "cures," along with breakfast sandwiches and baked goods. Latte art complements dark wood furnishings and a checker-print floor, though the private outdoor courtyard is just as nice. The café also provides free wireless Internet.

Shopping

The bulk of Montclair's shops are located along lengthy Bloomfield Avenue, Church Street (a short diagonal stretch hidden behind Bloomfield's storefronts), and Glenridge Avenue.

You'll find every kind of bead at **Montclair Beadworks** (43 Church St., 973/744-3202, www.montclairbeadworks.com), including ceramic raku beads, semiprecious stones, and Swarovski crystal. The shop hosts beading classes for both kids and adults throughout the year. **Modern Yarn** (32A Church St., 973/509-9276, www.modernyarn.com) carries yarns from Vietnam and South America, along with hemp yarns and bamboo knitting needles. Don't miss the handbags crafted from recycled inner tubes.

For mineral makeup, organic facial treatments, and lavender bath gel, stop by **Ecco Bella** (50 Church St., 877/696-2220, www.eccobella.com), Montclair's natural beauty center for more than a decade. New York City transplant **Just Kidding Around** (507 Bloomfield Ave., 973/233-9444, www.kiddingaroundnyc.com) is the place for picking up bathtub finger paints, pedal taxicabs, and NASA flight suits—all for kids, of course. Children's clothing consignment shop **Milk Money** (76 Church St., 973/744-0504, www.milkmoneylove.com) features fashions by Lands' End, Baby Gap, and Ralph Lauren, along with strollers, portable cribs, and high chairs.

Craving scones and clotted cream? Visit **London Food Company** (416 Bloomfield Ave., 973/783-6688, www.londonfoodco.com), where you'll also find Cadbury bars, Branston pickles, and large jars of Marmite.

A community stalwart for over 20 years, **Montclair Book Center** (219-221 Glenridge Ave., 973/783-3630, www.montclairbook

center.com) is three stories overflowing with new, rare, collectible, and out-of-print books. While browsing, don't forget to catch a peek at the stamped-tin ceiling. The smaller **Watchung Booksellers** (54 Fairfield St., 973/744-7177, www.watchungbooksellers.com) specializes in new releases and features a wonderful book room for kids. The shop hosts poetry evenings, readings, and variety book clubs for lovers of history and science fiction.

Euro Glass & Art Gallery (27 S. Park St., 973/744-4004, www.euroglassart.com) is the outlet store for Euro Glass Art, a distributor and promoter of European glassworks. Even if you're not in the market for purchase, it's worth stopping in to browse the fine selection of fused-glass plates, etched vases, and hand-blown Murano glass.

Food

Seems there's always a restaurant coming or going in Montclair. The township has a wonderful selection of eateries, most centered along and around Bloomfield Avenue.

For Mediterranean eats and gyros in particular, head to **Greek Delights** (14 Park St., 973/783-9100, www.greekdelightsnj.com, Mon.–Thurs. 11 A.M.–9:40 P.M., Fri.–Sat. 11 A.M.–10:40 P.M., Sun. noon–8:40 P.M., $6–16), claimed by knowledgeable foodies as the best around.

Montclair hosts a number of Thai restaurants, including **Tuptim Thai Cuisine** (600 Bloomfield Ave., 973/783-3800, www.tuptimthaicuisine.com, lunch Tues.–Fri. 11:30 A.M.–2:30 P.M., dinner Mon.–Thurs. 5–10 P.M., Fri.–Sat. 11:30 A.M.–11 P.M., Sun. 4:30–10 P.M., $10–18), a BYO with a good vegetarian selection and authentic Thai decor.

◖ **Nouveau Sushi** (635 Bloomfield Ave., 973/746-0399, www.nouveausushi.com, dinner hours only, $13–24) serves high-end sashimi that is simply outstanding even beyond the New Jersey market. The menu also includes a selection of hot and cold fusion dishes, grilled meat and vegetable skewers, and delish *mochi* ice cream.

Culinary art is the specialty at **Aozora** (407 Bloomfield Ave., 973/233-9400, www.aozora

fusion.com, Sun.–Thurs. noon–10:30 P.M., Fri.–Sat. noon–11 P.M., $14–35), a stunning BYO serving a seasonal menu of Japanese-French fare, including sushi and sashimi.

Superb even by Montclair standards, **Fascino** (331 Bloomfield Ave., 973/233-0350, www.fascinorestaurant.com) offers a modern twist on Italian cuisine. Seasonal tasting and à la carte menus include dishes like buttermilk baked chicken breast with black truffle pesto ($25), and squid ink tagliatelle with eggplant and black tiger shrimp ($24). Dinner is served 5–9:30 P.M. Monday–Thursday and 5–10:30 P.M. Friday and Saturday. Closed Sunday.

Located in nearby West Caldwell, **Wazwan Indian Restaurant** (691 Bloomfield Ave., 973/226-3132, www.wazwan.net, Tues.–Thurs. noon–9 P.M., Fri.–Sat. noon–10 P.M., closed Sun.–Mon., $10–21) prepares expertly spiced Kashmiri cuisine, including a selection of vegetarian entrées, along with mouth-warming chai.

Recently reopened under new ownership, **Mexicali Rose** (10 Park St., 973/746-9005, Mon.–Thurs. 11:30 A.M.–11 P.M., Fri. 11:30 A.M.–midnight, Sat. 11 A.M.–midnight, Sun. 11 A.M.–11 P.M., $12–20) has reclaimed its title as the local king of Tex-Mex. Kid-friendly, festive, and filled with color, BYO tequila and they'll mix you a margarita on the spot.

Held at the Walnut Street Train Station, the **Montclair Farmers Market** (Sat. 8 A.M.–2 P.M., late June–Nov.) features more than a dozen vendors selling Jersey fruits and vegetables like organic beets and carrots, grass-fed beef, free-range chickens, beeswax candles, and more. For a healthy on-the-go snack the remainder of the week, stop by **Whole Foods** (701 Bloomfield Ave., 973/746-5110).

Nightlife

Montclair is not a bad place for a little night music. Options range from university hangouts to Soho-style digs, and cuisine always comes with the territory.

Montclair's New York City–style **Diva Lounge** (373 Bloomfield Ave, 973/509-3000, www.divalounge.com, Wed.–Sun. 6 P.M.–2 A.M.) features multiple rooms heavy with velvet and dim with lights. The lounge features a full bar and dinner menu. Music varies from Latin to hip-hop to soul, depending on the evening. Dress codes and cover charges vary, so call ahead.

While it's reputed for its Sunday jazz brunch, **Trumpets Jazz Club-Restaurant** (6 Depot Sq., 973/744-2600, www.trumpetsjazz.com, Tues.–Thurs. 6 P.M.–12:30 A.M., Fri.–Sat. 6 P.M.–1:30 A.M., Sun. 11:30 A.M.–3 P.M. and 7 P.M.–midnight, closed Mon. year-round, closed Sun.–Tues. July–Aug., $12–25) is also the swankiest supper club in town, and has been for more than 20 years. Dinner is served during shows ($8–35), which take place throughout the week except Monday, beginning at 7:30 P.M. Tuesday–Thursday and Sunday, and at 8:30 P.M. Friday and Saturday.

Popular with the Montclair State crowd, **Just Jake's Bar & Restaurant** (30 Park St., 973/655-8987, www.justjakes.com, lunch and dinner Tues.–Sat. 11:30 A.M.–10 P.M., Sun. 11:30 A.M.–9 P.M., brunch Sun. 11 A.M.–2:30 P.M., $7.50–22, brunch $4.50–12) specializes in live music, affordable drinks, and casual American cuisine, with a late-night menu for after-hours stragglers. The outdoor patio is a great place to while away a summer afternoon.

Getting There

Montclair is 14 miles west of New York City and easily reachable by NJ Transit's **Montclair-Boonton Line** running from New York City, Secaucus Junction, and Hoboken Terminal, with several area stops including Watchung Avenue. Unfortunately, none of the stops are convenient for accessing the downtown center on foot. **DeCamp** (101 Greenwood Ave., 973/783-7500, www.decamp.com) operates a commuter bus (Rte. 33) from New York City with a stop in downtown Montclair (Gates and Bloomfield Aves.), about a 35-minute ride. Call or check the website for updated fares and schedules—bus runs are limited on weekends.

WEST ORANGE

Suburban West Orange Township climbs over First Watchung Mountain, eventually joining with South Mountain Reservation. In addition to attractive Tudor-style homes, large estates, and terraced streets, the township hosts a couple of fine eateries and attractions, not least of which is a National Historic Site.

Edison National Historic Site

Inventor Thomas Edison opened a manufacturing plant in West Orange while he was in his 40s, operating it until his death in 1931. The preserved structures along with Edison's estate and burial ground have been declared a National Historic Site (Main St. and Lakeside Ave.) open to the public. Following several years of renovation, visitors can tour the plant's newly restored laboratory complex (still under construction as of this writing), which is made up of nearly a dozen sites, including an exact replica of Black Maria, the world's first motion picture studio. Other buildings include a chemistry lab, a physics lab-turned-visitors center, and the main laboratory housing Edison's personal library. Thousands of artifacts such as motion picture projectors and phonographs are on display. Edison National Historic Site is the larger of New Jersey's two Edison sites; the second is located in Edison Township's Menlo Park section.

The public is also invited to tour Edison's estate, **Glenmont** (12 Honeysuckle Rd., 973/324-9973, www.nps.gov/edis). Call the Glenmont Information Desk (973/324-9973) noon–4 P.M. Friday–Sunday throughout the year.

South Mountain Reservation

Situated on the Watchung Mountains, 2,048-acre South Mountain Reservation (973/268-3500) is a multiuse recreation area once traversed by George Washington, doubling as a watershed and nature preserve. Spread among West Orange, Millburn, and Maplewood, the park features numerous hiking trails along with the indoor hockey rink **Richard J. Codey Arena at South Mountain** (560 Northfield Ave., 973/731-3828) and the **Turtle Back Zoo** (560 Northfield Ave., 973/731-5800, www.turtlebackzoo.com, $8 adult, $4 child and senior), home to wolves, wallabies, bobcats, and bears, as well as a wide array of birds, including eagles, owls, and a condor. The zoo features a petting station, veterinary hospital, and train ride at no extra cost, and hosts events year-round, including a summer guided night tour. In addition, more room has been added recently for the occupants, including an environmentally integrated black bear habitat. Winter zoo hours are daily 10 A.M.–3:30 P.M. with extended seasonal hours Monday–Saturday 11 A.M.–5:30 P.M., Sunday 10 A.M.–4:30 P.M.

Accommodations

Opened in 2002, the three-story **Residence Inn West Orange** (107 Prospect Ave., 973/669-4700, www.marriott.com, $150–200) stakes its claim as New Jersey's first solar-powered hotel. Referred to as "the mansion," it features spacious rooms and high-speed Internet access, and hosts courtyard barbecues during summer months. The hotel is entirely nonsmoking.

Food and Nightlife

Pal's Cabin Restaurant (265 Prospect Ave., 973/731-4000, www.palscabin.com, Mon.–Fri. 7:30 A.M.–10:30 P.M., Sat. 11 A.M.–11 P.M., Sun. 11 A.M.–10 P.M., $10–25) began during the Great Depression as a hot dog stand. Today, the family-owned eatery serves half-pound hamburgers ($8) alongside cuts of New York strip steak (14 ounces for $26) in an attractively rustic and historic setting.

A favorite for weekend dim sum, **China Gourmet** (468 Eagle Rock Ave., 973/731-6411 or 800/652-6688, Mon.–Thurs. 11:30 A.M.–9 P.M., Fri. 11:30 A.M.–10 P.M., Sat. 11 A.M.–10 P.M., Sun. 11:30 A.M.–9 P.M.) features live jazz monthly.

Owned and operated by drummer Cecil Brooks III and his wife Adreena, **Cecil's Jazz Club** (364 Valley Rd., 973/736-4800, www.cecilsjazzclub.com, daily noon–2 A.M.) hosts live jazz, blues, Latin, and swing performances throughout the week, with a gospel show Sunday evenings. No-cover Tuesday night jam sessions, beginning at 9 P.M., are a favorite among local musicians. Food is served daily noon–2 A.M., and most shows run about $7–10.

SOUTH ORANGE

With a revitalized downtown resembling an alpine village, South Orange is worth a peek (excuse the pun). Its transit station looks like a miniature castle, and the Swiss-style Village Hall calls to mind beer steins and mountain goats. Craftsman-style and pitched-roof homes ascend up the mountainside along the township's outer streets. It's like something out of a fairy tale.

South Orange is home to **Seton Hall University** (400 S. Orange Ave., 973/761-9000, www.shu.edu) and is located 15 miles from New York City.

Festivals and Events

Held summer weekends for one month annually in South Mountain Reservation's (accessible by South Orange Ave.) Tulip Springs Section, the **New Jersey Renaissance Fair** (732/271-1119, www.njkingdom.com) provides admittance into a costumed world of knights and maidens. The makeshift village offers plenty of purchase opportunities, including wonderful handmade crafts and clothes, but browsing is just as fun. Admission is $15 adult (or $22 for a two-day pass), $9 senior, and free for children 10 and under.

Somewhat surprisingly for outsiders, the Urban Outskirts are a haven for jazz musicians. South Orange's center for the Department of Recreation and Cultural Affairs, also known as **The Baird** (5 Mead St., 973/762-0748, http://southorange.org/TheBairdArts), celebrates this art and its local talents by hosting jazz concerts the last Saturday of each month January–May, along with an annual **Giants of Jazz Festival** in October.

Food and Entertainment

South Orange's university-town status makes finding casual food and drink easy, especially around the transit station.

One of New Jersey's dozen or so microbreweries, **Gaslight Brewery & Restaurant** (15 S. Orange Ave., 973/762-7077, Mon.–Tues. 3 P.M.–midnight, Wed.–Sun. 11:30 A.M.–midnight, $7.50–28.95) temps local residents and

© LAURA KINIRY

alpine architecture in South Orange Village

college crowds with Philly burgers, Bavarian-style dishes, and some excellent beer. This is your place for live music and shuffleboard.

A little bit restaurant, coffeehouse, art gallery, and live entertainment space, easygoing **Goat Cafe** (21 S. Orange Ave., 973/275-9000, http://thegoatcafe.typepad.com, Tues. 10:30 A.M.–9 P.M., Wed.–Thurs. 10:30 A.M.–11 P.M., Fri. 10:30 A.M.–11:30 P.M., Sat. 10 A.M.–11:30 P.M., Sun. 10 A.M.–10:30 P.M., $5.50–8) offers something for everyone—there's even an all-organic menu for kids. Take in performances ranging from hip-hop dancing to stand-up comedy, or share tapas with friends. Admission is charged on show nights and ranges $5–10 depending on the performance.

Getting There

South Orange's transit station is conveniently located at 19 Sloan Street within the downtown village, and is accessible from New York City, Secaucus Junction, or Hoboken Terminal on NJ Transit's Morris and Essex Morristown Line.

MAPLEWOOD, MILLBURN, AND SHORT HILLS

The affluent communities of Maplewood, Millburn, and Short Hills are filled with charming hillside homes and attractive main streets lined with specialty shops and service centers. Maplewood's train station even features its own concierge (973/763-7155). Although the neighborhoods feel somewhat exclusive, they're worth exploring, especially if you can fit in a show at Millburn's outstanding live performance theater. Bona fide shoppers will love the Mall at Short Hills, one of New Jersey's most luxurious shopping centers.

Shopping and Entertainment

With five anchor stores including Bloomingdale's, Nordstrom, and Saks Fifth Avenue, the two-story **Mall at Short Hills** (Rte. 24 and JFK Parkway, 973/376-7350, www.shopshorthills.com) is easily the grand dame of New Jersey indoor shopping complexes. This is not your typical mall selection—Betsey Johnson, Ralph Lauren, Diesel, and Anthropologie are all represented—and with no sales tax on clothes and shoes in New Jersey, you've got New York shopping Garden State–style.

Founded in 1934, Millburn's **Paper Mill Playhouse** (Brookside Dr., 973/379-3636, www.papermill.org) is New Jersey's official state theater, running top-caliber productions of musicals and children's plays year-round. Its reputable status and proximity to New York City make the playhouse a sought-after venue for TV and movie actors expanding to Broadway. Gourmet sandwiches are served before shows and throughout intermission. An interesting fact: The playhouse was named for a paper mill that once operated on the site.

Food

We're all a little Irish, aren't we? For true pub and grub, stop by downtown Maplewood's **St. James's Gate Publick House** (167 Maplewood Ave., 973/378-2222, www.stjames gatepub.com, daily 11:30 A.M.–2 A.M.), offering an extensive selection of draft beers and Irish whiskeys, along with a menu that includes shepherd's pie ($13) *and* bangers and mash ($13). There's a jukebox filled with Irish tunes and live Irish music on Sunday afternoons; even the pub's tables come from Ireland. I promise, if you're not already Irish when you walk in here, by the time you walk out you'll be green.

Getting There

NJ Transit has stops in Maplewood (between Dunnell Rd. and Maplewood Ave.), Millburn (35 Essex St.), and Short Hills (25 Chatham Rd.). All three stations are accessible from New York City, Secaucus Junction, and Hoboken Terminal by way of the Transit's Morris and Essex Morristown Line.

SUMMIT

When the "Summit of Short Hills" train first arrived during the 19th century's early half, the city of Summit got its name. Located along the Passaic River, Summit later became a resort getaway for New York City escapees. Bulbous trees and grid-laid streets occupy the city's downtown, along with two- and three-story red, brown, and white brick buildings filled with shops and restaurants. Summit's train station is conveniently located in the city center, making for an easy stroll around its wonderfully vibrant downtown.

New Jersey Center for the Visual Arts

Part of the Summit community since 1933, the nonprofit New Jersey Center for the Visual Arts (68 Elm St., 908/273-9121, www .njcva.org, Mon.–Fri. 10:30 A.M.–4:30 P.M., Sat. noon–4 P.M., closed Sun., $1 donation) is an art school, exhibition space, and art park combined. Classes are offered year-round in ceramics, jewelry-making, printmaking, and photography, and emerging and established artists display rotating works in the interior galleries. Outdoors is a 5,040-square-foot sculpture park where works of two contemporary artists appear annually.

Accommodations

Since the late 19th century Summit's **Grand Summit Hotel** (570 Springfield Ave., 908/273-3000, www.grandsummit.com, $175–340) has been choice accommodation for area visitors. The hotel is currently undergoing a multimillion dollar renovation: Guest rooms on the lower level are receiving new hardwood floors, and all 149 rooms are getting flat-screen TVs and Bose Wave radios. Mattresses and pillows are also being replaced and recovered with 300-thread-count linens. The hotel includes an on-site steak and seafood restaurant, with additional perks such as wireless Internet, weekday afternoon high tea, and complimentary chocolate-chip cookies.

Food

Summit has plenty of dining options to choose from, ranging from diner fare to fancy Italian restaurants. Most eateries are within walking distance of one another and downtown's transit station.

In a state where the diner is royalty, the **Summit Diner** (Summit Ave. and Union

commuter bicycle parking in downtown Summit

Pl., 908/277-3256, daily 5:30 A.M.–8 P.M., $5–10) stands as king. It's compact and cozy, a bit greasy in places, with only a wall of booths and a line of counter seats. New Jersey diner expert Peter Genovese describes it as the best diner to "bring a newcomer to." A clientele of local characters and the Taylor ham, egg, and cheese sandwiches are standouts.

Dine on exquisite northern Italian dishes like asparagus risotto ($16) and pan-roasted salmon ($19) at local favorite **Fiorino Ristorante** (38 Maple St., 908/277-1900, www.fiorinoristorante.com, Mon.–Thurs. 11:30 A.M.–10 P.M., Fri. 11:30 A.M.–11 P.M., Sat. 5–11 P.M., closed Sun., $16–34). A superb wine list and fresh daily specials are more reasons to visit. Just look for the entrance's bright-yellow awning.

New Italian is the specialty at **Adagio Ristorante** (401 Springfield Ave., 908/277-1677, www.adagioristorante.net, lunch Mon.–Fri. 11:45 A.M.–2:45 P.M., dinner Mon.–Thurs. 5–10 P.M., Fri.–Sat. 5–10:30 P.M., closed Sun., $16.95–34.95), located within downtown Summit's historic Roots Building. Choose from an elegant dining room, a casual tavern with high-back booths and its original terrazzo floor, or the Vault, a private space for groups of eight (10 on weekends) or more ($57 per person).

New York City's **Monster Sushi** (395 Springfield Ave., 908/598-1100, www.monster sushi.com, Mon.–Fri. 11:30 A.M.–10 P.M., Sat. noon–10 P.M., Sun. 3–9 P.M., $14–28) has overtaken Summit with teriyaki combos, tempura dishes, and vegetarian-friendly "monster rolls." There's even a menu for the little ones.

Specializing in steak and seafood, the Grand Summit Hotel's **Hunt Club Grill** (570 Springfield Ave., 908/273-7656, lunch Mon.–Sat. 11:30 A.M.–2 P.M., dinner daily 5–10 P.M., brunch Sun. 11:30 A.M.–2:30 P.M., $17–35) serves a popular Sunday champagne brunch and features seasonal outdoor seating, a casual tavern menu, and live music on the weekends.

Getting There

Summit is located west of Millburn. The town's transit station stands at Union Place, near the intersection of Broad and Elm Streets. If riding public transit, take the Morris and Essex Morristown Line from New York City, Secaucus Junction, or Hoboken Terminal.

THE SKYLANDS

For anyone looking to experience a New England–style vacation without leaving the Mid-Atlantic, New Jersey's Skylands region is your place. Just a short drive from the urban Gateway, it's a world away geographically, brimming with mountains and hills, state parks, and plenty of recreational opportunities. Here in New Jersey's northwest corner is the state's largest lake, its highest point, and some of the East Coast's most scenic stretches. Like parts of South Jersey, the region is filled with farmland, though rather than flatlands they meander over hillsides, soon giving way to a mountain stretch that's home to hundreds of black bears. Toward the New York State border stands a series of old mining towns, one holding the distinction of being "the World's Fluorescent Rock Capital," and west along the Delaware lies a stretch of charming river towns. With its rolling terrain and lightly trafficked scenic roads, the Skylands host some of the states best cycling opportunities, along with ideal spots for swimming, hiking, fishing, tubing, skiing, and even hot-air ballooning.

But the Skylands aren't *all* beauty. The region is home to its fair share of history, including the country's first national historic park, Morristown, honoring the place where General George Washington spent two long winters during the Revolutionary War. And Flemington, in the Skylands' Central Piedmont, was the site of "the trial of the century," leading to the conviction of carpenter Bruno Hauptmann for the kidnapping and murder of aviation hero Charles Lindbergh's infant son. The Skylands are also where you'll

THE SKYLANDS

HIGHLIGHTS

◖ **Mountain Creek:** With half-pipes, snow tubing, waterslides, and downhill mountain biking, this remade ski mountain is all action winter, spring, summer, and fall (page 76).

◖ **High Point State Park:** Home to New Jersey's highest point, High Point offers panoramic tristate views along with a stretch of the Appalachian Trail and some of the area's best cross-country skiing (page 86).

◖ **Delaware Water Gap National Recreation Area:** One of the country's most visited national parks, there's no better place for hiking, cycling, exploring, and simply getting away (page 88).

◖ **Great Swamp:** Birders have it made at this 7,500-acre refuge, also a great place for spotting wildlife. The surrounding roads are good for bicycling too (page 98).

◖ **Ballooning:** Soar over the countryside in New Jersey's most picturesque region and you'll easily forget you're in the country's most densely populated state (page 106).

◖ **Shopping in Lambertville:** This artsy riverfront city is a walkable spree of antiques stores, art galleries, and specialty shops, and it's one of the most attractive places around (page 113).

LOOK FOR ◖ TO FIND RECOMMENDED SIGHTS, ACTIVITIES, DINING, AND LODGING.

find some of New Jersey's best oddities, including quirky Space Farms Zoo and Museum and the remnants of an old childhood favorite, Hamburg Gingerbread Castle. As for shopping, Lambertville, Frenchtown, and Chester feature some of New Jersey's best selections of art and antiques.

Outdoor recreation definitely tops the list of reasons for a Skylands visit. The Vernon Valley has recently remade a fledgling downhill ski area into a world-class ski resort, and cross-country skiing is popular throughout the area. Campgrounds and camping resorts are plentiful here, and you'll also find some of New Jersey's only backcountry campsites and mountain bike trails.

One visit to the Skylands will have you rethinking that theory about New Jersey being all highways and exits. You may also have found a new vacation destination.

PLANNING YOUR TIME

New Jersey's Skylands are a great weekend destination, especially from New York City and throughout New Jersey or Eastern Pennsylvania. If you're into outdoor activities, this is your place. The region offers plentiful recreation opportunities and camping facilities, although if you prefer your outdoors from a comfortable B&B veranda, the Skylands has them too. If you plan on sticking to a specific area, like the Vernon Valley or the Delaware

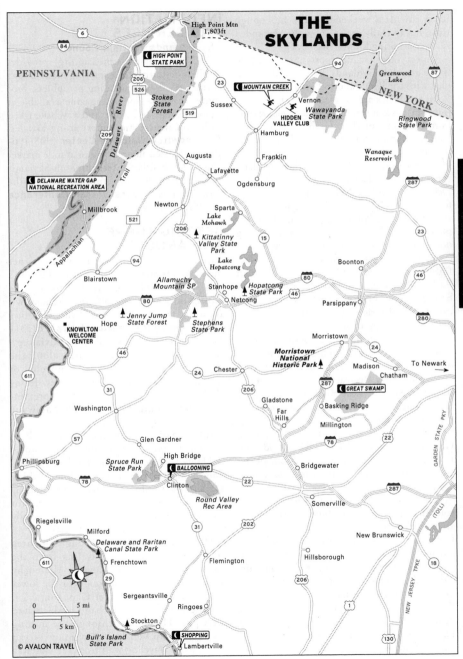

THE SKYLANDS

High Point Mtn
1,803ft

**THE
SKYLANDS**

PENNSYLVANIA

HIGH POINT
STATE PARK

Stokes
State
Forest

MOUNTAIN CREEK

Greenwood
Lake

NEW YORK

Sussex

Vernon

HIDDEN
VALLEY CLUB

Wawayanda
State Park

Ringwood
State Park

Hamburg

Wanaque
Reservoir

DELAWARE WATER GAP
NATIONAL RECREATION AREA

Augusta

Franklin

Lafayette

Ogdensburg

Millbrook

Newton

Sparta
Lake
Mohawk

Kittatinny
Valley State
Park

Boonton

Lake
Hopatcong

Blairstown

Allamuchy
Mountain SP

Stanhope

Hopatcong
State Park

Parsippany

Hope

Jenny Jump
State Forest

Netcong

KNOWLTON
WELCOME
CENTER

Stephens
State Park

Morristown

Morristown
National
Historic Park

GREAT SWAMP

Madison

Chatham

To Newark

Chester

Washington

Gladstone

Far
Hills

Basking Ridge

Millington

Glen Gardner

Phillipsburg

Spruce Run
State Park

High Bridge

BALLOONING

Clinton

Bridgewater

GARDEN STATE PKY

Round Valley
Rec Area

Somerville

Riegelsville

Milford

Delaware and Raritan
Canal State Park

Frenchtown

Flemington

Hillsborough

New Brunswick

NEW JERSEY TPKE (TOLL)

Sergeantsville

0   5 mi

0   5 km

Ringoes

Stockton

Bull's Island
State Park

SHOPPING

Lambertville

© AVALON TRAVEL

River towns, a weekend should be enough time, but to really get to know the Skylands I suggest devoting four or five days.

Unless you're a winter-sports enthusiast (and if you are, the Highlands' Vernon Valley coupled with the Ridge and Valley Region's High Point State Park are the places to be), try starting your weekend in or around Lambertville, home to some of the region's best lodging choices. Get an early start Saturday morning for perusing the wares at Route 29's Golden Nugget Antique and Flea Market. Athletic types have several alternatives: Drive up to the Delaware Water Gap National Recreation Area for a day of hiking (or spend the night at Hope's Inn at Millrace Pond and go from there), or plan a day of kayaking, canoeing, or tubing down the Delaware River from Frenchtown (or canoeing and kayaking from nearby Clinton's Raritan River). On Sunday, head east through Basking Ridge for a visit to the Raptor Trust before continuing north into Morristown to explore the historic sites and museums or simply stroll through town.

Campers have plenty of campground resorts and state park sites to choose from throughout the Skylands, including backcountry sites at Round Valley Recreation Area. You might start your weekend near High Point State Park in the state's northwest corner and work your way south through the Delaware Water Gap the following day. On Sunday, return to the Gateway or New York City via Ringwood State Park, possibly stopping en route at one of the area's mining museums for a unique underground tour.

Add a few extra days to your itinerary and you can fit in Allamuchy Mountain State Park, along with a visit to Sparta, Clinton, or Lake Hopatcong. Mountain bikers should check out Ringwood, Wawayanda, and Allamuchy Mountain State Parks, along with Mountain Creek's Diablo Freeride Park. The region's best dining options are in Lambertville, Milford, Frenchtown, Morristown, and Central Piedmont's Somerville. For shopping, head to Lambertville, Frenchtown, and Flemington, queen of the outlet stores.

INFORMATION AND SERVICES

The **Skylands Tourism Council** (800/475-9526, www.skylandstourism.org) provides excellent resources for exploring New Jersey's northwest corner, including pamphlets, brochures, a free seasonal magazine available at regional shops and stops, and a website filled with informative and entertaining articles. The **Knowlton Welcome Center** (908/496-4994) is located along I-80 east at mile marker 7 in Columbia. For information on Skylands parks and hiking opportunities, contact the **New York-New Jersey Trail Conference** (201/512-9348, www.nynjtc.org).

GETTING THERE AND AROUND

Tucked into New Jersey's northwest corner the Skylands may seem like one of the state's most inaccessible regions, but towns like Phillipsburg, Flemington, and Frenchtown are all easy to reach from Pennsylvania's **Lehigh Valley International Airport** (3311 Airport Rd., Allentown, PA, www.lvia.org), an hour at most by car. Towns along the Skylands' eastern border are connected to Newark and New York City by New Jersey public transit and are within close proximity to **Newark Liberty International** (www.newarkairport.com).

NJ Transit (www.njtransit.com) rail lines travel as far west as Morristown, Gladstone, and High Bridge (three miles north of Clinton) from New York City before ending, making much of the southeast Skylands accessible by public transport. Still, a car is essential for thorough exploration of the region, especially for visiting the state parks and forests.

Major roads running through the area include east-west I-80, traveling from the Gateway's Meadowlands toward Allamuchy Mountain State Park through to the lower tip of the Delaware Water Gap; Route 23, heading west from the Urban Outskirts into the Upper Highlands, through the mining towns and onto Vernon Valley; Route 46, an old thruway traveling west from the Gateway

Region toward the Delaware Water Gap's lower portion; and to the south I-78, a direct route from Newark Airport south to the Central Piedmont—an easy alternative for reaching Bridgewater, Somerville, Morristown, and all of the Delaware River towns—and continuing past Clinton en route toward Phillipsburg and Easton, Pennsylvania.

Major north-south routes include scenic Route 206, traveling north from South Jersey's Hammonton past Chester, Allamuchy State Park, Netcong, and Augusta as well as Stokes State Forest and High Point State Park before crossing the Delaware into Milford, Pennsylvania; and I-287, easily accessible by way of I-78 west from Newark Airport, heading south into Bridgewater and Somerville, and north into Morristown before intersecting with I-80 and Route 23.

Traffic can get heavy throughout the region, but other times it's like you're the only one on the road. The highways are much more bearable than in New Jersey's Gateway region, but it's important to keep an eye out for deer crossing, especially at dusk. Unfortunately, deer carcasses along the roadsides serve as hefty reminders. Route 206 is one of New Jersey's most scenic drives and makes for a great afternoon excursion. Routes 23 and 46 are a bit older and are built-up. For roads that get you where you need to be quickly, stick to the interstates: I-287, I-80, and I-78.

The Highlands

Said to attract more annual visitors than Yellowstone National Park, New Jersey's Highlands are a northern geologic extension of the Blue Ridge Mountains—a heavily forested area marked by sheer cliffs, lakes, and streams, and a natural water source for much of the Northeast Corridor. The region was once heavily mined, and many industry-formed towns remain scattered throughout.

The Highlands eastern border lies at Ringwood State Park, typically considered part of the Gateway Region due to its Passaic County locale, traveling west through Vernon Valley, and south towards glacial lakes and the remains of the historic Morris Canal. Area highlights include Ringwood's botanical gardens—New Jersey's only such gardens—as well as Vernon Township skiing and snowboarding venues, the mining towns of Franklin and Ogdensburg, and the central Highlands' Allamuchy Mountain State Park. Dining options are relatively limited; chain eateries are plenty, but for quality meals your best bets are Sparta and the central region. For lodging, try Vernon's resort area and the central lake region; options range from campgrounds to B&Bs to condo-style rentals.

Getting There and Around

To reach the Highlands from New Jersey's Gateway Region, hop on Route 23, which intersects with Route 24 en route to Vernon Valley's resort area. Route 517 heads south through Ogdensburg to Sparta, continuing on to Route 206 and the bulk of the central Highlands' state parks as well as Wild West City. I-80 runs west from New York City directly to the central Highlands' parks, including Allamuchy Mountain and Stephens State Parks.

RINGWOOD STATE PARK

Spreading east across the Bergen County line at the foot of the Ramapo Mountains, just below the New York State border, 4,044-acre Ringwood State Park (1304 Sloatsburg Rd., 973/962-7031, www.state.nj.us/dep/parksand forests/parks/ringwood.html, free, $5 parking fee weekends Memorial Day–Labor Day) is one of the state's most varied, hosting two historical mansions and New Jersey's official botanical garden. Known for its excellent mountain biking trails, the park also offers opportunities for kayaking, boating, swimming, hiking, cycling, horseback riding, fishing, and hunting.

New Jersey Botanical Garden and Skylands Manor

Built in the English Jacobean style found throughout the English countryside nearly 400 years ago, the native stone Skylands Manor serves as centerpiece to the 94-acre Botanical Garden (Morris Ave., 973/962-7527, www .njbg.org, daily 8 A.M.–8 P.M.), the state's official garden situated at the foot of the Ramapo Mountains. Built in the 1920s, the mansion has 44 rooms, a carved staircase, and several large windows showcasing 16th-century stained glass medallions. The gardens were dedicated in 1984 and contain woodland paths, terraced gardens, a crabapple vista, and 400 lilac varieties from around the world, including Asia and the Middle East. Self-guided tour maps are available at the **Carriage House Visitors Center,** open weekdays and some Sundays May–September, or you can catch one of the free guided tours leaving from the visitors center Sundays at 2 P.M. May–October. Guided tours of Skylands Manor ($5) are offered one Sunday each month March–December; visit www.njbg.org/tours.shtml for exact dates.

Ringwood Manor

North of the botanical garden and across Sloatsburg Road stands Ringwood Manor (973/962-7031, www.ringwoodmanor.com), a gothic revival mansion originally built for one of North Jersey's most prominent iron masters. The mansion is filled with 19th-century period furniture and paintings, and is open for self-guided touring Wednesday–Sunday 10 A.M.–3 P.M. year-round. The surrounding grounds include sitting gardens, stone fences, and a small footbridge. An old blacksmith shop still stands on the premises.

Sports and Recreation

South of Skylands Manor is a turnoff for 74-acre spring-fed **Shepherd Lake,** open to swimmers and boaters seasonally. A lifeguard is on duty Memorial Day–Labor Day, and kayak and rowboat rentals are available at the on-site boathouse (973/962-6999). Bathhouses, a concession stand, and picnic tables are also located nearby. The park's fishing opportunities include trout-stocked **Ringwood Brook** and Shepherd Lake, where anglers can also cast for sunfish, pickerel, largemouth bass, and catfish.

Ringwood State Park features over a dozen hiking and multiuse trails, ranging in length 0.5–5 miles and with varying degrees of difficulty. Trails are well marked with colored blazes. For something of a challenge, begin near Skylands Manor with the five-mile **Crossover Trail,** designated by a white blaze, and combine it with the **Ringwood Ramapo Trail** for a half-day loop. An in-depth description of this and other Ringwood hiking trails can be found on the New York–New Jersey Trail Conference website, www.nynjtc.org.

Ringwood offers some of New Jersey's best mountain biking opportunities, partially due to trail maintenance by local **Ramapo Valley Cycling Club** (www.rvccmtb.com). Options include all-level double tracks and several single tracks for experienced riders only. A 7.5-mile mostly single-track trail begins at Shepherd Lake.

Getting There

Ringwood is about one hour and 40 minutes from New York City. To reach the park, take I-287 to Exit 57 and follow the signs.

WAWAYANDA STATE PARK

Perhaps New Jersey's wildest state park, Wawayanda (885 Warwick Turnpike, Hewitt, 973/853-4462, $5 weekdays, $10 weekends Memorial Day–Labor Day) encompasses nearly 35,000 acres brimming with swampland, forests, and steep mountain terrain, and is home to a black bear or two. Removed from the bustle of the lower state, the park offers suitable retreat for hikers, campers, and water enthusiasts who flock to 225-acre Lake Wawayanda, an enclosed lake popular with boaters, fishers, canoeists, kayakers, and swimmers. There are more than 40 miles of marked hiking trails, including a 20-mile stretch of the Appalachian Trail, and killer views from atop **Wawayanda Mountain.** Mountain bikers take to the park's fire roads, although single- and double-track trails do exist. Wawayanda is also a good place for winter recreation; cross-country skiing and snowshoeing are both popular park activities. Group camping sites are available April–late October.

Lake Wawayanda

The lake's 225 acres make for ideal recreation year-round. Swimmers take to its waters in summer, when a concession stand and restrooms are open and lifeguards are on duty most afternoons Memorial Day–Labor Day. Rowboats, paddleboats, and canoes are available for rent as well. Between the lake and Wawayanda Creek, fishers will find brown and rainbow trout, yellow perch, largemouth bass, pickerel, catfish, sunfish, crappie, bowfin, and since 2006, landlocked salmon. In winter, frozen waters are handed over to ice fishers and skaters.

Getting There

Wawayanda's proximity to Vernon Township is deceiving. The park's main entrance is on its east side, accessible by the Warwick Turnpike. To reach the entrance travel Route 23 north from New York City to Route 513/Union Valley Road and head north through West Milford. The road soon turns into Route 513/White Road and bears left, eventually intersecting the Warwick Turnpike. Make a left onto Warwick Turnpike; the park is about four miles down on your left.

VERNON

Winter sports are big business in the Skylands, especially in Sussex County's **Vernon Township,** also known as Vernon Valley. Although the Valley's ski tourism originated in 1964, it only began taking off recently. The region's longest vertical drop is a mere 1,040 feet, but its proximity to Manhattan, along with a revived world-class ski resort and ample new real estate, have turned Vernon into a desirable vacation destination. Skiing and snowboarding share equal winter spotlight, while golfing and water rides take over during summer.

Without an official Main Street, Vernon's downtown centers along Routes 94 and 515 and is made up of mostly service stores and fast-food chains. Vernon's best dining options are at Crystal Springs Resort.

Sports and Recreation

Vernon's smaller, more family-oriented ski locale, the **Hidden Valley Club** (44 Breakneck Rd., 973/764-4200, www.hiddenvalleynj .com, Mon.–Thurs. and Sat. 9 A.M.–9 P.M., Fri. 9 A.M.–10 P.M., Sun. 9 A.M.–5 P.M.) recently went semiprivate, meaning that once winter memberships (available for purchase during off-seasons) reach 250, weekends become members-only. Nonmembers can still hit the slopes on weekdays (full-day pass $25 adult, $20 child) or weeknights ($25 adult, $20 child).

Topping out at nearly 1,500 feet, Hidden Valley's main mountain features a 620-foot vertical drop and a dozen trails—ranging from the easy Chicken Delight to the double-diamond Newman's Chute—to choose from. The Browse Along Trail, which is the park's longest, runs 0.75 mile. Hidden Valley also hosts a snowboarder and free-skier terrain park with both a C-rail and rainbow rail, and offers ski lessons ($25 per hour group lesson) and rental equipment.

During summer Hidden Valley runs a private swimming club and a tennis academy, and hosts mountain bike races sanctioned by USA Cycling. There's both a grill and a cafeteria on-site.

Saddle up at **Legends Riding Stable** (Rte. 94, 973/827-8332, www.saddleupatlegends .com, Sat.–Mon. 9 A.M.–3:45 P.M.), offering extensive horse-riding trails for all skill levels. The ranch is located directly across Route 94 from Crystal Springs Mineral Hotel and accepts cash only.

Accommodations

A few wonderful bed-and-breakfasts are scattered throughout the area, but book early; space is limited (especially during cold winter months—Vernon's high season).

Close to the resorts, the Federal-style 1887

Alpine Haus Bed & Breakfast Inn (217 Rte. 94, 973/209-7080 or 877/527-6854, www.alpinehausbb.com, $110–225) gives guests the option of settling into the snug living room or sitting back on the second-story covered porch, where they can linger over a complimentary country breakfast in summer. Each of the eight guest rooms come decorated with antique furnishings, along with a private bath, TV, telephone, and wireless Internet. Two suites, including one that's wheelchair accessible, are located in a separate guesthouse behind the main inn.

Housed in a lovely 1831 Colonial mansion, **Apple Valley Inn Bed & Breakfast** (967 Rte. 517, Vernon, 973/764-3735, www.app1evalleyinn.com, $130–150) features six guest rooms, each with a TV and DVD player, air-conditioning, and wireless Internet, and a few with a private bath and fireplace. Breakfast is served at a long family-style dining table and can later be walked off in the mansion's private gardens, complete with a creek and small footbridge. The inn also features a wraparound second-story veranda.

With only two guest rooms and two suites, its important to book ahead for the **◖ Glenwood Mill Bed & Breakfast** (1860 Rte. 565, Glenwood, 973/764-8660, www.glenwoodmill.com, $150–225), a fully renovated inn occupying a 200-year-old former gristmill just south of the New York State border. Room amenities include a private bath, sitting area, and gas fireplace, and guests have complete access to the inn's Great Room, an open dining-living space with beamed ceilings and hardwood floors. The mill's former power source, an 18-foot waterfall, remains on the property, along with a charming garden and a babbling brook.

◖ MOUNTAIN CREEK

The thought of New Jersey downhill winter sports was something of a joke before Mountain Creek (200 Rte. 94, 973/827-2000, www.mountaincreek.com) burst onto the scene. Canada-based company IntraWest purchased the property in 1998, renaming it and

Mountain Creek's snow-tubing hill

completely remaking it into the four-season resort it is today. Part of Mountain Creek's allure is its devotion to snowboarding: Approximately half the park is dedicated to the sport, including five terrain parks and an Olympic-size halfpipe. Skiers are adequately cared for as well, with 46 trails on four mountains. Most of the intermediate and black-diamond slopes are on South Peak, while beginners will want to head up Vernon Peak. The park features 11 lifts, including an eight-person open-air gondola, along with a snow sports school with top-notch instructors. Snow-tubers have their own hill across the highway from the main resort, just beyond the parking lot.

Downhill runs give way to mountain bikers tackling Diablo Freeride Park during the summer months, and the resort's mountainside water park draws ample crowds.

Skiing

Mountain Creek's Main Park—a fee-designated area for advanced skiers—centers around South Peak. For anyone still working on their turns and jumps, the easier Vernon Peak and Half Peak are open to all. Call 973/827-2000 for up-to-date weekday and weekend rates and twilight skiing.

Mountain Creek Waterpark

With more than 26 rides and attractions, Mountain Creek Waterpark (200 Rte. 94, 973/827-2000, www.mountaincreekwater park.com, daily Memorial Day–Labor Day, $32.99 adult, $22.99 under 48 inches tall) attracts its fair share of revelers, including young kids who can't get enough of the Tide Slide and Junior Rapids. For adrenaline junkies there's plenty, including an 18-foot Bombs Away free-fall carved straight out of the mountainside and the four-story High Anxiety tubing ride. While the side-by-side Sidewinder is best saved for your favorite competitor, thrill-seeking couples will want to ride double on the Vortex, a pitch-black rapids tunnel with a 360-degree loop. Twilight tickets ($22) are offered up to three hours before the park closes. Check the website for exact park hours.

Diablo Freeride Park

Downhill mountain bikers have it made at Diablo Freeride Park (200 Rte. 94, 973/864-8420, www.diablofreeridepark.com, Fri.–Sat. 9 A.M.–4 P.M. May–June and Sept.–Nov., Mon.–Fri. 11 A.M.–7 P.M., Fri.–Sat. 9 A.M.–4 P.M. July–Aug., $36 full day), New Jersey's only downhill mountain biking park. A high-speed open-air gondola serves 50 downhill and free-ride trails on a mountain with a 1,040-foot vertical drop. And when you're done for the day, there's a bike wash for rinsing off the caked-on mud, unless you'd rather save it for posterity. Full-day bike rentals are available for $69–109.

Accommodations

In addition to Mountain Creek lodging, Vernon's bed-and-breakfasts and Crystal Springs Mineral Hotel offer convenient overnight alternatives.

A world-class resort needs upscale accommodations, which Mountain Creek has sufficiently covered with **Black Creek Sanctuary** (200 Rte. 94, 973/209-7080, www.mountaincreek .com, $169–279 s, $319–629 d), a series of Adirondack-style townhouses clustered within a gated community. Each one- to three-bedroom guesthouse comes equipped with a full kitchen, gas fireplace, and outdoor deck, as well as several TVs and wireless Internet.

Mountain Creek's recently constructed **Appalachian Grand Lodge** (200 Rte. 94 (973/864-8000, www.mountaincreek.com, $159–269 s, $289–609 d) stands at the foot of the ski mountain, acting as the resort's first truly ski-in/ski-out hotel. Rooms range in size from studio to two-bedroom, and all include a fireplace, kitchen facilities, wireless Internet, and complimentary breakfast. Some rooms feature private balconies overlooking the mountain, but they'll cost you. Bicycle and ski rentals as well as a swimming pool are located on-site.

Food

Mountain Creek offers a couple of easy dining options. Visitors can pick up simple sandwiches or morning bagels at the **Discovery Deck Bar,** situated below the slopes, or sit down for something a bit more substantial at **The Mountain Express.** For those 21 and over (or accompanied by a parent) there's **Hex2 Bar & Restaurant,** known as "the Hex," serving burgers, fries, and plenty of beer. For further information on any of the eateries call 888/767-0762 or visit www.mountaincreek.com.

Getting There

Mountain Creek is approximately 1.5 hours' drive from New York City. From the George Washington Bridge take Route 23 to Route 94 and turn north. The resort is just south of Vernon's Routes 94 and 515 downtown intersection.

CRYSTAL SPRINGS RESORT

Another fairly new resort transforming the local community is the exclusive Crystal Springs (100G Port Royal Dr., Vernon, 973/827-5996, www.crystalgolfresort.com), an upscale golf and spa resort spread between Vernon and Hamburg. Crystal Springs hosts six golf courses ranging from easy to challenging, several restaurants, a hotel, a spa facility, and townhouses. There's even a golf school on the property. The resort's main golfing hub, site of the newly constructed **Watermark Country Club,** is located along Route 94 in northern Hamburg. **Minerals Hotel and Elements Spa** is three miles north in Vernon Township. If you're looking for pampering, this is your place.

Golf Courses

Crystal Springs hosts seven championship golf courses within five miles of each other; around here carts are more common than cars. Courses include the top-rated public course **Ballyowen** (105-137 Wheatsworth Rd., Hamburg, 973/827-5996), described by *Golfweek* as one of the top 50 golf resorts in the world; **Black Bear** (128 Rte. 23, North Franklin, 973/827-5996), site of the **David Glenz Golf Academy;** and **Crystal Springs,** listed on *Golf Digest's* 2006 "Top 50 Most Challenging Golf Courses in America" list. Additional courses include the kid-friendly **Minerals Family Golf Center, Wild Turkey, Great Gorge Country Club,** and **Cascades Golf Course.** Call 973/827-5996 or visit www.crystalgolfresort.com to schedule a tee time at any of the seven courses.

Elements Spa

Located within Vernon's Great Gorge Resort, Elements Spa (2 Chamonix Dr., 973/827-5996, www.crystalgolfresort.com) offers golfer-designed pedicures and salt body scrubs followed by a bath inspired by the tropics. Even the spa's clapboard-and-stone exterior is soothing.

Accommodations

Guest rooms at Crystal Spring's 175-room **Minerals Hotel** (2 Chamonix Dr., Vernon, 973/827-5996, $169–444) range from rooms with queen beds to presidential suites complete with a fireplace and a separate bedroom. Things tend to get a bit loud in the evening, but if you miss your beauty sleep, you can still have that rested glow with complimentary use of the Sports Club's whirlpool tubs.

Food

Crystal Springs offers a range of dining options, with the following two being its best.

Sporting sleek new stonework and granite decor, **Kites Restaurant** (973/864-5840, $16–32) remains the most relatively casual Crystal Springs eatery. Located in the Great Gorge Resort, this American eatery and bar tends to get rowdy on weekends. The restaurant opens for à la carte breakfast weekdays 7 A.M.–11 A.M. and buffet style on weekends 7 A.M.–11 A.M. An all-day lunch and dinner menu is served Sunday–Thursday 11:30 A.M.–9 P.M., Friday–Saturday 11:30 A.M.–10 P.M.

For a true experience, book a table at **Restaurant Latour** (Crystal Springs Country Club Clubhouse, 1 Wild Turkey Way, Hardyston, 973/827-0548, Thurs. 5–9 P.M., Fri.–Sat. 5–10 P.M., Sun.–Wed. 4–8 P.M., $63–84), a French-inspired eatery showcasing a seasonally changing menu prepared with fresh local ingredients, including locally grown produce and meat and fish from the Delaware Valley. Latour's expansive wine list comes presented in two cork-covered binders, with selections retrieved from the Restaurant's private cellar that houses more than 54,000 bottles. The price of an entrée includes an appetizer and dessert.

Getting There and Around

Crystal Springs is about a 1.5-hour drive from New York City and just five minutes south from Vernon's downtown intersection of Routes 94 and 515.

HAMBURG, FRANKLIN, AND OGDENSBURG

South of Vernon, Route 94 passes through Hamburg, a small borough dubbed "Children's Town" to honor the now-abandoned cake-like castle on an east-end side street, once one of the country's oldest children's theme parks. Further on you'll come to Franklin and Ogdensburg, known collectively as northern New Jersey's mining country. The area is home to fluorescent rocks found nowhere else in the world. None of the downtowns offer much to look at; instead their beauty resides in the history and geology still explored today.

Mining Museums

Once home to iron and zinc mines and quarries, Franklin is best known for its fluorescent rocks, many of which exist nowhere else on earth. In fact, the borough has been dubbed the world's "fluorescent minerals capital," and this legacy is well represented at the unassuming **Franklin Mineral Museum** (32 Evans St., 973/827-3481, www.franklinmineralmuseum .com), tucked along a backstreet beside an 1879 engine house. Created as a mineralogy, geology, and paleontology educational aid, the (literally) cool space is staffed by ardent rock geeks thrilled to be sharing their passion with others. For this alone it's worth a visit. The museum is open 10 A.M.–4 P.M. Monday–Friday, 10 A.M.–5 P.M. Saturday, and 11 A.M.–5 P.M. Sunday March–November. Admission is $7/ adult, $4/child 3–12, and $5/senior. A combined museum entry and rock collecting runs $12/adults, $7/child, and $8/senior, which includes a collecting bag and two pounds per paid admission. Additional collecting fee is $1.50 per pound.

The museum features a main floor display dedicated to local rocks, a hall with more than 5,000 worldwide mineral specimens, and a gift shop stocked with informative books, colorful polished rocks, and a $5 bag filled with as many rocks as you can fit in it. A two-story mine replica is the museum highlight. Tours ($6 adult, $3 child) are given hourly.

At the nearby **Buckwheat Dump,** visitors can chisel magnetite, zincite, and franklinite of their own from various rock specimens left here by mid-1800s zinc miners. Collecting runs $1.50 per pound after an initial entrance fee ($6 adult, $4 child), but there are also combination museum-tour and rock-collecting tickets available ($11 adult, $6 child).

Ogdensburg is known for its sterling zinc mining, something you'll get close and personal with at the **Sterling Hill Mining Museum** (30 Plant St., 973/209-7212, www.sterlinghill .org, 10 A.M.–3 P.M. daily Apr.–Nov., tours at 1 P.M. daily, $10 adult, $7.50 child). The museum, featured on the Travel Channel's *Cash and Treasures* series in 2007, includes exhibits of actual mining equipment and dynamite casings, as well as a tour taking you into a genuine mine that was closed down in 1986. In operation since 1990, the museum also houses the Workman's Lunch Box, filled with picnic tables and a small snack shop, and a gift shop (daily 10 A.M.–3 P.M. Apr. 1–Nov. 30) selling fool's gold, petrified wood, and locally mined rocks. Once inside, you can't go too far without a guide. Tours of the mine are offered daily at 1 P.M. April–November 30, and at other times by chance or by appointment. Regardless of the outside temperature, the mine gets cold (it *is* underground), so dress accordingly.

Camping

Spacious **Beaver Hill Campground** (Big Spring Rd., 973/827-0670 or 800/229-2267, www.beaver hill.com, May–mid-Nov., from $34) has plenty of RV and tent sites, but only one facility with restrooms and showers. It's not a problem if you're an early riser, and the showers make up for the lack of additional amenities by having some of the warmest water around. This scenic campground attracts both mountain bikers and lots of families with small kids.

SPARTA

Sparta is adorable, although it's far from small. The nearly 39-square-mile township encompasses 11 private communities, but it's the largest of these—the one surrounding artificial **Lake Mohawk,** created as a 1920s summer resort—that's worth a visit. The community began with a mandate that every building must be different, including those in **White Deer Plaza,** the lakeside downtown. White Deer's architecture blends English Cottage, Tudor, and German influences together into a unique style dubbed "Lake Mohawk Tudor." The style is so unique that the plaza has earned a place on both the National and New Jersey State

CAN SWEETNESS BE SAVED?

Hamburg's vacant Gingerbread Castle, a former children's theme park

Gingerbread Homes are hard to resist – just ask Hansel and Gretel. A wicked old woman lured them inside her own candy house, deliberately built to bait such sweet-toothed kids. While the intentions of F. H. Bennett – the man behind Hamburg's Gingerbread Castle – weren't malicious, he did know that children (soon to be adults) would find such a place irresistible: so irresistible that the castle still stands after 80 years.

In a state known for roadside attractions, Hamburg's Gingerbread Castle is remarkable. Situated just off Route 94 – down Gingerbread Castle Road – in New Jersey's northwest corner, the castle was the brainchild of F. H. Ben-

nett, a local miller and baker credited with inventing both the Wheatsworth Cracker and Milk-Bone Dog Biscuits. Bennett commissioned Austrian designer Joseph Urban – whose prior achievements included an addition to Cairo's Abdin Palace, St. Petersburg's Alexander Bridge, and numerous Ziegfeld Follies sets – to build a fairy-tale palace for kids. According to Dr. Marion Wood, president of the Hamburg Historical Society and author of *All about Hamburg,* the castle was originally called the Gingerbread House, constructed primarily of concrete with a roof resembling candied frosting, and a hand railing that "turned to stone" if touched. An old postcard featuring the castle's image describes its "candystick towers, cake icing turrets, and sugar-panned windows." The castle took two years to build – from 1928 to 1930 – and cost $250,000.

While the Castle's exterior attracted visitors, it was the fairy-tale figurines placed throughout its interior and grounds that cemented its theme-park status: Humpty Dumpty sat contently on a garden wall; Snow White congregated with the seven dwarfs in one of the castle towers; and an old woman lived privately in an outdoor shoe. The castle even housed a witch's cauldron, said to contain the bones of little boys and girls who never left – a story relayed by local children who acted as tour guides, showing visitors around the castle and its grounds.

Hamburg Borough and the Gingerbread Castle became synonymous. Local streets – like Cinderella Street and Wishing Well Road – were named to reflect fairy tales, and street signs were reissued with castle depictions attached (a few still remain). Police officers and ambulance drivers began wearing castle patches on their uniforms, and the castle became the borough's official logo. Hamburg was dubbed "The Children's Town."

By the mid-1970s the aging castle had seen multiple owners and was losing favor to more modern attractions, like the newly opened Six Flags Great Adventure, a couple of hours south. After operating as a children's fairy-tale theme park for nearly 50 years, Gingerbread Castle finally closed in the late 1970s. It reopened for a few years as a haunted Halloween venue before a fire closed it permanently in 1993.

Attempts to restore the castle as a children's theme park haven't gotten far. New Jersey resident Frank Hinger and his wife, Lou, purchased the property in 2003 with plans to revitalize it, even securing a grant from Hampton Hotel's Save-a-Landmark program in 2004, which was used to repaint the castle exterior. But raising additional funds proved difficult. After unsuccessfully offering the castle on eBay, it was auctioned off in a sheriff's sale in January 2007 for approximately $680,000.

Vandalism has been an increasing problem in recent years. When the *Weird N.J.* boys visited a few years ago, the old woman was gone, but the shoe where she lived remained. A smiling Humpty Dumpty still sat on the wall, and the witch's cauldron stood ready to brew. Since then, says Dr. Wood, Humpty Dumpty has fallen, the shoe is uninhabitable (if it even exists), and the castle is an empty shell. "Even the stained glass windows were stolen," she said.

Local real estate developers Gene Mulvihill and Pat Barton are the Gingerbread Castle's current owners. Mulvihill, who owns the neighboring former Plastoid building and a share in nearby Ballyowen, the state's highest-rated public golf course, seems interested in preserving the castle. In a January 2007 article in the *New Jersey Herald,* Mulvihill states, "It's in [Hamburg's] blood. We're not going to rip the place down; that's not going to happen."

Last fall, a newly formed Hamburg Historical Commission interested in the castle's preservation led members of the New Jersey Historic Preservation Office through the structure, with Mulvihill's permission, attempting to draw attention to the borough's historic resources. But whether Hamburg's Gingerbread Castle will have a fairy-tale ending remains to be seen.

"The one thing I can tell you for sure is that we are going to restore the Gingerbread Castle," Mulvihill told the *New Jersey Herald.*

Life should be so sweet.

an example of Sparta's Lake Mohawk Tudor architecture

Historic Registers because of it. The entire community has a shore-away-from-shore feel, with a bit of New Hampshire and Vermont thrown in. There's even a short curvy boardwalk courtesy of the medieval-like **Mohawk Country Club,** a large reception hall at water's edge. Although the walkway is private, you're welcome to stroll it or take a seat along one of the numerous lakeside benches, as long as you're not acting up. Motorboats and waterskiers are common on the lake during summer months. While access to Lake Mohawk is limited for outside visitors, it's still something to see.

Tomahawk Lake

A few miles from White Deer Plaza along Stanhope Road is the turnoff for Tomahawk Lake (Tomahawk Trail, Sparta, 973/398-7777, www.tomahawklake.com), a long-running family-owned and operated 20-acre beach and water park. This place has everything! In addition to waterslides measuring over 500 feet tall, there are racing slides, a water coaster, and a 70-foot high-speed slide. Not into heights? Cool off under the tipping bucket, picnic at one of the shaded groves, or get toasty at the beer garden before heading to the tent arcades, 18-hole miniature golf course, and bumper boats. You could spend all day here, really. Seasonal hours begin weekends in May and go daily starting mid-June, usually weekdays 10 A.M.–5:30 P.M. and weekends 9 A.M.–7 P.M. Admission weekdays is $10 adult, $10 child, weekends $11 adult, $9 child and is cash only.

Food and Nightlife

There are several eateries in White Deer Plaza, including the ever-so-cute **Krogh's Restaurant and Brew Pub** (23 White Deer Plaza, 973/729-8428, www.kroghs.com, Mon.–Sat. 11:30 A.M.–10 P.M., Sun. noon–9 P.M.). Housed in the plaza's original tearoom and gift shop, Krogh's has been around since 1937, though it has gone through several owners since then. The fairy tale–esque structure is today a National Historic Landmark, and inside there's a little something for everyone: burgers, gourmet pizzas, pastas, seafood, and even Mexican fare, along with a brewed-on-site beer selection ranging from Golden Wheat to Nutty Brown. Live music is performed throughout the week. Across the street, locals flock to **Casa Mia** (20 White Deer Plaza, 973/729-6606, $3–16.50) for pepperoni pizza pies and delectable baked ziti slices. Casa Mia is open 10:30 A.M.–10 P.M. Monday and Tuesday, 10 A.M.–10 P.M. Wednesday and Thursday, 10 A.M.–11 P.M. Friday, 11 A.M.–11 P.M. Saturday, and noon–9 P.M. Sunday.

Just up from Tomahawk Lake is **Zoe's by the Lake** (112 Tomahawk Tr., 973/726-7226, www.zoesbythelake.com, dinner Tues.–Thurs. 5–9 P.M., Fri.–Sat. 5–10 P.M., Sun. 4–8 P.M., closed Mon., $23–31), a bright and airy upscale restaurant serving country dishes complemented by to-die-for desserts (warm upside-down chocolate soufflé, anyone?). Situated on the bank of Seneca Lake, Zoe's is known as much for exceptional cuisine as for its seasonal outdoor dining. An ever-changing three-course bistro dinner ($29 per person) is offered Tuesdays, Fridays, and Sundays.

ALLAMUCHY MOUNTAIN STATE PARK

A haven for anglers and fishers, the scenic 8,683-acre Allamuchy Mountain State Park (800 Willow Grove St., Hackettstown, 908/852-3790, free) features lakes and ponds swimming with sunfish, perch, pickerel, and largemouth bass as well as a trout-stocked stretch of the Musconetcong River, named one of the country's newest Wild and Scenic Rivers in 2006. Allamuchy is filled with marked and unmarked trails perfect for hiking, mountain biking, and horseback riding as well. While most of the unmarked trails are located in the park's northern section, the bulk of those that are easier to navigate begin within the Allamuchy Natural Area, a nearly 2,500-acre reserve intended to show the progression of hardwood forests. The park's **Cranberry Lake,** connected to the Musconetcong River, is popular with boaters, canoeists, and kayakers, who take to the three-mile water trail ending at the Saxton Falls Dam. If you've arrived without a boat, don't worry: a lakeside concession stand rents rowboats during summer months. Allamuchy is also home to the endangered Waterloo Historic Village, one of the last remnants of New Jersey's 19th-century Morris Canal (www.canalsocietynj.org).

Hiking

Trails include three miles of the Sussex Branch Trail, a 20-mile trail from Waterloo Road to Branchville, the main stretch of which lies within nearby Kittatinny Valley State Park. Ten miles of the in-progress **Highland Trail** also run through here, beginning from the park's northern tip and heading through to Stephens State Park. The trail combines new and established smaller trails and roads, eventually connecting New York's Storm King Mountain to Phillipsburg, along the Delaware River. The Allamuchy stretch is one of the park's more difficult trails.

Fishing

The park's stretch of the Musconetcong River offers some of New Jersey's best trout fishing opportunities. The river's stocked with brown, rainbow, and brook trout throughout the year. Other spots for in-park fishing include Cranberry Lake, Jefferson Lake, Allamuchy Pond, and Deer Park Pond, home to warmwater species like largemouth bass, sunfish, and pickerel.

Camping

Camping facilities are located at nearby 805-acre **Stephens State Park** (800 Willow Grove St., Hackettstown, 908/852-3790, Apr.–Oct., $20), east of Allamuchy State Park and 7.5 miles south of Route 206 along Waterloo Road (Rte. 604). The park hosts 40 tent and pop-up trailer sites, each with its own fire ring and picnic table. Restrooms are within walking distance.

KITTATINNY VALLEY STATE PARK

Ideal for mountain bikers, hikers, and anglers is 3,641-acre Kittatinny Valley State Park (4 Lake Aeroflex Rd., Newton, 973/786-6445, www.state.nj.us/dep/parksandforests/parks/kittval.html, daily dawn–dusk, free), a relatively small park filled with glacial lakes and limestone outcroppings and home to whitetail deer, wild turkeys, and muskrat. The park includes portions of two popular rails-to-trails conversions: the 26-mile multiuse **Paulinskill Valley Trail** and the 20-mile **Sussex Branch Trail,** both used by hikers, cyclists, and horseback riders, the latter used by cross-country skiers and dogsledders in the off-season. Kittatinny also includes more than eight miles of designated mountain bike trails.

The park's 119-acre **Lake Aeroflex** forms a headwater portion of the Pequest River, a favorite among fly-fishers. The lake is stocked with landlocked salmon and trout and is open to ice-fishers during the winter season. Because **Aeroflex-Andover Airport** (973/786-5100), an airport used by the New Jersey Fire Service, is located within park boundaries, aircraft watching has become a popular park activity.

STANHOPE, NEWTON, AND NETCONG
Wild West City

I don't know how PC it is, but Wild West City (Rte. 206 N., Netcong, 973/347-8900, www.wildwestcity.com, daily 10:30 A.M.–6 P.M. mid-June–early Sept., Fri.–Sat. 10:30 A.M.–6 P.M. May–mid-June and early Sept.–Columbus Day, $13.50 adult, $12.50 child) sure is interesting. Family-owned and operated for more than 50 years, this seasonal operation hosts live-action gunfights and big-bang holdups along a make-shift Western Main Street inspired by 1880s Dodge City, Kansas (to be fair, firearm-free programs are available for schoolkids with advance notice). Stagecoach, pony, and train rides are all available for an extra fee ($3 each), along with miniature golf, and there's a barnyard filled with Western critters like Sno-ball the pony and Gertrude the pig for kids to get friendly with. When all is said and done, who knows? You just may walk out of here with a brand new Stetson (ish) hat and a swagger in your step. Yahoo!

Lake Hopatcong

At 2,500 acres with 45 miles of shoreline, Lake Hopatcong is a sight to behold. New Jersey's largest freshwater lake, its waters inspired and operated as part of the Morris Canal waterway, a supply route connecting the Delaware River's Phillipsburg to Newark. Today, the lake is a favorite spot for recreation and is used by swimmers, boaters, and fishers as well as sailboats, canoes, and kayaks. Along the southwest edge of the lake is **Lake Hopatcong State Park** (973/398-7010, www.state.nj.us/dep/parksandforests/parks/hopatcong.html, Memorial Day–Labor Day, cars $6 weekdays, $10 weekends, $3 walk-ins and bikes), where you'll find a historical museum dedicated to the Morris Canal—which occupies the canal's old lock tender's house—as well as Lake Musconetcong, which operated as an additional Morris Canal water source.

With so much surrounding land, Lake Hopatcong is a natural for marinas, bait and tackle shops, delis, bars, and lodging, but the best place for swimming, picnicking, and easy accessibility remains the state park, in close proximity to Stanhope, Newton, and Netcong. To reach the park, take Exit 28 from I-80 or follow Route 183 in Netcong.

Accommodations

Newton's pleasant **Wooden Duck Inn** (140 Goodale Rd., Newton, 973/300-0395, www.woodenduckinn.com, $125–299) offers nine guest rooms, six within its main estate house and three in the accompanying carriage house. Rooms are bright, clean, and spacious, and each comes equipped with high-speed Internet, TV, air-conditioning, and a private bath. In addition to a seasonal in-ground pool, guests have access to puzzles and games and coffee, tea, or snacks any time. The inn is situated on 10 acres just north of Kittatinny State Park.

Tucked along a quiet residential street between Allamuchy State Park and Wild West City is the **Whistling Swan Bed & Breakfast** (110 Main St., Stanhope, 973/347-6369, www.whistlingswaninn.com, $120–249), a three-story Victorian with uniquely appointed era-themed guest rooms, a chair-lined wraparound porch, and a couple of comfy hammocks that may inspire you never to leave the property. For romance, book a room in the third-floor high-point suite. Complimentary sherry and soft drinks come with your stay.

Camping

Situated on 160 acres with its own 45-acre lake, **Panther Lake Camping Resort** (6 Panther Lake Rd., Andover, 973/347-4440 or 800/543-2056, Apr.–Oct.) is one of the Highlands' larger campgrounds. The lake is open for fishing and boating (with paddleboats available for rent) and hosts a small beach for swimming. Resort highlights include shuffleboard and a heated pool, though hot showers run extra. Panther Lake features 435 tent and RV sites ($39 for two people), each with water and electric, along with several cabins and stationary trailers available for overnight stays.

Tucked along the Sussex County foothills, **Green Valley Beach Campground** (68 Phillips Rd., Newton, 973/383-4026, www.greenvalleybeach.com, May–mid-Oct., $36 for two people) is a nice overnight option for exploring both the Highlands and the nearby lower Ridge and Valley Region. Grounds include an Olympic-sized heated pool and a private lake for fishing and boating, with paddleboats available to rent. The campground includes 250 wooded and open sites for tents and RVs.

Food

Along Route 206 is the region's only authentic German restaurant, the **Black Forest Inn** (249 Rte. 206, Stanhope, 973/347-3344, http://blackforestinn.com, Mon. and Wed. 4:30–10 P.M., Fri. 11:30 A.M.–2 P.M., 4:30–10 P.M., Sat. 11:30 A.M.–2 P.M., 5–10 P.M., Sun. 1–8 P.M., $18–28). Start with the smoked trout and then move on to more filling dishes, like traditional beef Stroganoff served alongside cabbage and potato dumplings. The main hall feels like the interior of a Bavarian castle.

Ridge and Valley Region

The Kittatinny Mountains line New Jersey's northwest corner, isolating the sprawling valleys lying beneath and giving way to one of the state's most prominent features—the Delaware Water Gap. The entire region is a haven for outdoor enthusiasts, with opportunities for hiking (including a portion of the Appalachian Trail), cross-country skiing, fly-fishing, canoeing and kayaking, and camping. Though somewhat limited, dining and hotel options do exist, but for greater selection head to the nearby Highlands.

AUGUSTA

Part of larger Franklin Township, Augusta is home to Culver's Gap—the only route through the Kittatinny Mountains for 30 miles. The area hosts a few notable attractions.

Olde Lafayette Village

Just east of Augusta is Olde Lafayette Village (75 State Rte. 15, 973/383-8323, www.lafayette villageshops.com), a colorfully themed shopping village filled with factory outlets, antique stores, and cafés. There's even a yoga studio. The village is a bit nicer aesthetically than the outlet centers in Flemington, but with a couple of worthwhile exceptions, the selection is nothing to go out of your way for. If you do visit, be sure to browse the shelves of the **Olde Village Book Cellar** (973/383-0040, www.oldevillagebookcellar.com), an independent bookstore that occasionally hosts author

readings, poetry open mics, and book clubs. Additional shops include **The Village Barkery** (973/300-0035) stocking earth-friendly toys for your pooch, home decor center **La Reverie** (973/383-0095), and the **Lafayette Cheese Shoppe** (973/579-4900).

Events

The **Sussex County Fairgrounds** (37 Plains Rd., Augusta) plays host to a couple of popular annual events. Late spring's **Michael Arnone's Crawfish Festival** (www.crawfish fest.com, $25 advance, $30 gate, under age 14 free with parent) is a three-day celebration of good ol' Louisiana fun, with live bands like the Zydeco Roadrunners and the Rocket 88's on four stages, and regional eats that include po'boy sandwiches, alligator sausage, and broiled crawfish (of course!). On-site camping is available throughout the weekend.

Although it's no longer called the Sussex County Horse and Farm Show, August's 10-day **New Jersey State Fair** (www.newjersey statefair.org, $5–10) still features such events as a rooster crowing contest, a beef obstacle course, and a horse show, along with carnival rides, chainsaw art, and live music.

SPACE FARMS ZOO AND MUSEUM

What began as a small store and wildlife center in the late 1920s has morphed into the quirky Space Farms Zoo and Museum (Rte. 519,

Beemerville, 973/875-5800, www.spacefarms .com, daily 9 A.M.–5 P.M. May 1–Oct. 31, $13 adult, $8.50 child), a 100-acre museum and private zoo. There's an antique car and motorcycle display, a collection of Civil War rifles, a miniature circus, an Eskimo exhibit, and a fluorescent mineral theater—and that's just in the museum. There are over 500 zoo animals, including lions, buffalo, lemurs, a hyena, and some retired circus bears. Space Farms has held several zoo records, including the longest-living bobcat (33 years) and puma (22 years) in captivity, but perhaps its most celebrated resident is a 2,000-pound, 12-foot-tall Alaskan Kodiak bear named Goliath. Goliath lived at the complex from 1967 until his death in 1991, but his upright stuffed figure remains on display. The annual August Teddy Bear Day is held in his honor.

◄ HIGH POINT STATE PARK

Seven miles north of Sussex, along the Kittatinny Mountain crest just south of the New York state line, is High Point State Park (1480 Rte. 23, Sussex, 973/875-4800, www.state.nj.us/dep/ parksandforests/parks/highpoint.html, $5 weekdays, $10 weekends, Memorial Day–Labor Day), home to the state's highest elevation. At more than 15,000 acres, this all-season park hosts ample opportunities for hiking, mountain biking, horseback riding, swimming, fishing, dogsledding, snowshoeing, and cross-country skiing. High Point is actually considered one of the state's prime skiing locales, covering its trails with artificial snow during colder months and housing the **High Point Cross Country Ski Center,** which rents out snowshoes, skis, and other winter sports equipment.

In addition to spectacular tristate views, the park hosts three natural areas, including the 1,500-acre **Dryden Kuser Natural Area.** This natural area, named for the park's land donors, contains what is thought to be the highest-elevation Atlantic white cedar swamp in the world.

High Point Monument

Let's face it: New Jersey is no Montana when it comes to mountain peaks, but it's not exactly Florida or Delaware either. The state's highest elevation is a respectable 1,803 feet above sea level. That's not too shabby, especially with 220-foot **High Point Monument** topping it off. Erected in the 1930s, the monument bears a striking though much smaller resemblance to D.C.'s Washington Monument. Visitors can climb to the top (daily 9 A.M.– 4:30 P.M. Memorial Day–Labor Day, Fri.– Sat. noon–4 P.M. Labor Day–Memorial Day) for an outstanding 360-degree view of New Jersey's Wallkill Valley, Pennsylvania's Pocono Mountains, and New York's Catskill Mountains. A nearby snack stand sells ice cream, hot dogs, and water.

Sports and Recreation
SUMMER RECREATION

High Point's spring-fed 20-acre **Lake Marcia** is open to swimmers during summer months. Lifeguards are on duty, and there's a snack bar and bathhouse nearby. The lake is also open to fishers, along with High Point's Sawmill and Steenykill Lakes. Look for trout, bass, and catfish among the three.

High Point hosts more than 50 miles of multiuse trails for hikers, mountain bikers, and horseback riders to enjoy. The trails vary in length 0.5–18 miles and even include a scenic stretch of the Appalachian Trail. Most are well marked by color blazes. For casual hikers, the 1.5-mile **Cedar Swamp Trail** is an easy loop within Dryden Kuser National Area, in the park's northern section.

The park offers a "scenic drive" for autos beginning near Lake Marcia. It's a short one-way route with plenty of rocks on view, but it's nothing too exciting.

SKYDIVE SUSSEX

High Point not high enough for you? Try Skydive Sussex (53 Rte. 639, Sussex, 973/702-7000, www.skydivesussex.com) for over-the-top aerial views. Trips begin at Sussex Airport and cost $175 for the first tandem jump.

WINTER SPORTS

High Point State Park (www.xcskihighpoint

.com) offers 9.3 miles of groomed cross-country ski trails as well as a 5-mile trail for snowshoeing. You can rent skis ($20 adult, $18 child weekend full day, $17 adult, $15 child weekend half day) and snowshoes ($17 adult, $15 child weekend full day, $15 adult, $13 child weekend half day) at the park's **High Point Cross Country Ski Center** (973/702-1222, Mon.–Fri. 9 A.M.–4 P.M., Sat.–Sun. 8 A.M.–4 P.M. Dec.–Apr.). Trail passes are also required; they cost $16 adult, $14 child for a full weekend day and $12 adult, $10 child for a weekend half day. The ski center hosts group lessons for cross-country skiers daily 10 A.M.–2 P.M. during the season.

High Point's **Center at Lake Marcia** sells hot soup and comfort meals, and has a fireplace perfect for cozying up to after a long day on the trails.

Accommodations

About a half hour's drive from High Point is Pennsylvania's **Cliff Park Inn** (155 Cliff Park Rd., Milford, PA, 570/296-6491 or 800/225-6535, www.cliffparkinn.com, $157–263), a lovely inn set on 500 acres. There are fourteen guest rooms of various sizes, each with wireless Internet, TV, a DVD player, down bedding, and complimentary breakfast. Some also feature sun porches and claw-foot tubs. The inn has its own nine-hole golf course as well as seven miles of nature trails, and on-site dining options ranging from bar fare to gourmet cuisine.

Additional overnight options close to High Point State Park exist in Vernon Township, about 30–40 minutes' drive east.

Camping

High Point features 50 tent sites along Sawmill Lake (Apr.–Oct., $20), each with a fire ring, picnic table, and nearby flush toilets. Two group campsites ($25–35) accommodate 25 and 35 people, each with pit toilets and drinking water. High Point also offers two rental cabins (mid-May–mid-Oct., $65 for up to six people) located on Steenykill Lake, each with a furnished living room, a woodstove, hot and cold water, a full bath, a kitchen, and

electricity. A group cabin (mid-May–mid-Oct., $155, two-night minimum) accommodates up to 28.

Food

Load up on hiking carbs at Sussex's **Holland American Bakery** (246 Rte. 23, Sussex, 888/401-9515, www.hollandamericanbakery.com/store, Tues.–Sat. 6 A.M.–6 P.M., Fri. 6 A.M.–9 P.M.), specializing in *speculaas* (traditional Dutch biscuits) and almond tarts. To find it, just look for the windmill out front. For breakfast, try the **Sussex Queen Diner** (289 Rte. 23, Sussex, 973/702-7321, 6 A.M.–10 P.M. daily, $5–16), a brick-and-stucco landmark that gets packed on weekends (could be the small booths). Get here early.

Information and Services

Just before the park entrance there is parking for the Appalachian Trail. A visitors center (on Route 23) is open daily 9 A.M.–4 P.M.

STOKES STATE FOREST

South of High Point is 16,067-acre Stokes State Forest (1 Coursen Rd., Branchville, 973/948-3820, www.state.nj.us/dep/parksandforests/parks/stokes.html). Known for its scenic mountain views—most notably from atop 1,653-foot Sunrise Mountain—the forest is also home to an attractive stretch of the multistate Appalachian Trail. Rugged terrain makes for good mountain biking, but Stokes is just as popular with hikers, fishers, and winter sports enthusiasts. The forest includes 525-acre **Tillman Ravine Natural Area** (Memorial Day–Labor Day, $5 weekdays, $10 weekends), home to several endangered species, including the cream- and brownish-gray-colored barred owl.

Visitors should take Route 206 four miles north from Branchville.

Camping

Stokes has 51 sites suitable for tents or trailers, each with picnic tables and fire rings ($20). Several of these sites are open year-round. The park also hosts nine group campsites (Apr.–Oct.) with capacities ranging 10–65 people.

© LAURA KINIRY

Delaware Water Gap

The nightly cost of each site is based on the number of people it accommodates. Additional facilities include nine year-round lean-tos ($30); 10 furnished cabins adjacent to Lake Ocquittunk with a half-bath, a wood stove, and running water, each accommodating up to four ($45); two eight-person cabins with showers ($85), and one 12-person cabin with two full baths ($125). All the cabins are available April–mid-December. To reserve a campsite or cabin, call the park office at 973/948-3820.

◖ DELAWARE WATER GAP NATIONAL RECREATION AREA

Approximately five million people explore the Delaware Water Gap National Recreation Area (570/588-2452, www.nps.gov/dewa) each year, making it one of the country's most-visited national parks. Spread between New Jersey and Pennsylvania, Water Gap encompasses 70,000 acres and 37 riverfront miles, including the Gap itself, a 1,400-foot-deep, 900-foot-wide natural divide between New Jersey's 1,527-foot Mount Tammany and Pennsylvania's 1,463-foot

Mount Minsky. The surrounding area—filled with green-covered mountains, meandering brooks and streams, and awesome panoramic views—is easily one of the most stunning spots in the Mid-Atlantic, let alone the entire East Coast. It's an ideal place for backpackers, hikers, cyclists, fishers, nature lovers, and wildlife enthusiasts who might catch glimpses of beavers, otters, groundhogs, and black bears. The river itself is popular with canoeists and kayakers, as well as divers and snorkelers.

Although Pennsylvania hosts the bulk of DWG hiking trails, along with a designated cycling trail, New Jersey offers a few trails of its own, including a portion of the Appalachian Trail. The New Jersey side also offers some wonderful scenic drives.

Sights

Nature inspires art, so it seems fitting to find **Peters Valley Craft Education Center** (Kuhn Rd., Layton, 973/948-5200, www.pvcrafts .org) tucked within the Delaware Water Gap Recreation Area along Route 615. This small village is really an arts and crafts campus where workshops in fiber arts, metalworking, photography, woodworking, and ceramics are held. A small retail store (19 Kuhn Rd., 973/948-5202, Thurs.–Tues. 10 A.M.–6 P.M.) stocks the works of resident artists alongside those of artists nationwide, and you can shop for glass beads, handmade paper, turned wooden bowls, and more. Upstairs is a free gallery displaying rotating exhibits year-round.

Peters Valley hosts an annual craft fair the last weekend in September at Augusta's Sussex County Fairgrounds.

Situated on the southern stretch of Old Mine Road is **Millbrook Village** (908/841-9531, www.millbrooknj.com, Sat.–Sun. 9 A.M.–5 P.M. Memorial Day–Labor Day), a re-created 19th-century farming village filled with old wood structures that could use a little TLC. Spangenberg Cabin serves as the main information center but is only open on summer weekends, when costumed interpreters are also on hand demonstrating era-specific skills. Despite having more than two dozen structures of historic significance, this is not one of the state's better living-history museums. That being said, Millbrook *is* strictly volunteer-run, and donations do help. The village is a good staring point for several area hikes.

Sports and Recreation

One of New Jersey's premier fly-fishing spots, **Big Flat Brook** runs through the Water Gap north to south from the area east of Layton alongside the park's eastern boundary, re-entering through the Walpack Valley into Flatbrookville, where it joins the Delaware River. Beginning at the Route 206 Bridge east of Layton and south for about four miles, the brook is fly-fishing only. There are additional access points, however, along Route 615 within park boundaries.

Oh, lucky hikers! New Jersey includes a portion of the famed Appalachian Trail. Running through the Pennsylvania part of the Water Gap's southern portion and crossing the Delaware River at the Kittatinny Point Visitor Center, the Appalachian Trail heads north into Worthington State Forest, lining

the western side of the Kittatinny Mountain Range. Water Gap campgrounds located along the trail are open to through-hikers on trips of two or more days only, so get walking. Around Millbrook Village are numerous smaller trails that access the Appalachian Trail, including the steep **Coppermine Trail,** beginning from the Coppermine Parking Area on Old Mine Road, which connects with the Appalachian Trail at Camp Road after about two miles. One of the area's easier hikes, the White-Blaze trail begins at the Route 602 parking lot a mile south of Millbrook Village and climbs for about 300 feet to a fire tower and excellent east-facing views.

There's more good hiking in the area surrounding **Blue Mountain Lakes** (Flatbrook-Stillwater Rd.), 2.5 miles north of Millbrook Village. Parking is available along Route 627.

Along with fishing, the Water Gap is a great place for snorkeling and diving, both permitted in the Delaware River, as long as you don't come within 50 feet of a boat or canoe launch. The Point of Gap at the park's southern end is a preferred diving area. Canoes and kayaks are also welcome on the river, and there's a boat launch near Kittatinny Point in the recreation area's southern section. **Kittatinny Canoes** (102 Kittatinny Ct., Dingmans Ferry, PA, 800/356-2852, www.kittatinny.com) runs canoe and kayak trips down the Delaware from seven locations within the upper tristate region, including **River Beach Campsites** (378 Rtes. 6 and 209) in Milford, Pennsylvania, 3.5 miles over the bridge from Montague on the recreation area's northern tip.

Camping

Worthington State Forest (along Old Mine Rd. in the recreation area's southern portion, 908/841-9575, Apr.–Dec., $20) offers 69 campsites, each with restroom and shower access. Twenty-three of the sites are for tent camping only. There are also three group sites (Apr.–Dec., $35), each accommodating up to 35 people. These include toilets, fire rings, and picnic tables.

The Water Gap is home to a couple of Appalachian throughway campsites, as well

THE SKYLANDS

as river sites for anyone exploring the area by kayak or canoe. For a list of sites currently open, visit the DWGNRA website (www .nps.gov/dewa) or call park headquarters at 570/588-2452.

Located toward the Gap's northern tip, year-round **Cedar Ridge Family Campground** (205 River Rd., Montague, 973/293-3512 or 800/813-8639, www.cedarridgecampground .net, from $20) provides a swimming pool along with a private lake for fishing and boating, with paddleboat rentals available. Just five minutes from I-84, the campground is popular with both drive-through visitors and Appalachian Trail through-hikers.

Food

For an out-of-the-way dining experience, you can't beat the **Walpack Inn** (Rte. 615, Walpack Center, 973/948-3890, www.walpackinn.com, lunch Sat.–Sun. 11:30 A.M.–2:30 P.M., dinner Fri.–Sat. 5–10 P.M., Sun. 3–8 P.M., $21–44), a large lone restaurant that suddenly appears along Route 615. Dishes are American and the decor is decidedly rustic, with mounted taxidermy and a mural depicting Native Americans. Eighteenth-century tools hang in the inn's entryway, and a greenhouse dining room provides an expansive view of the Walpack Valley and sneak peeks at deer grazing in the field. One of the best things about the inn is the freshly baked bread served with meals, so popular they sell loaves and bread mix to go.

Information and Services

New Jersey's **Kittatinny Point Visitors Center** (908/496-4458, daily 9 A.M.–5 P.M. Memorial Day–Labor Day, Sat.–Sun. 9 A.M.–5 P.M. Sept.–mid-Oct., closed winter) is located just off I-80 at the Water Gap's southern end, and includes a canoe launch, parking, and picnic area. Toilets *may* be available. **Dingmans Falls and Visitors Center** (daily 9 A.M.–5 P.M. Memorial Day–Labor Day, Sat.–Sun. 9 A.M.–5 P.M. Sept.–mid-Oct., closed winter) has restrooms and is a bit further north on the Pennsylvania side, across privately owned Dingmans Ferry Bridge ($1).

Getting There

To reach the Delaware Water Gap National Recreation Area, follow River Road/Old Mine Road north from I-80, or take Millbrook Road from Blairstown. You can also follow the signs along I-80. In the north, Route 206 connects with Delaware Mine Road, becoming Old Mine Road further south.

BLAIRSTOWN

Just outside the Delaware Water Gap's lower portion is Blairstown, a rural mountainside town with a attractive Main Street and unbeatable surroundings. For movie buffs, Blairstown served as backdrop for the original *Friday the 13th*. Look for downtown's old stone mill sidewalk tunnel in the film's opening scene. Blairstown has a decidedly Western feel, its two-story low-slung structures hosting some worthwhile restaurants and shops, including an independent bookstore. A neighborhood park on the east end of Main Street, complete with a waterfall and steel footbridge, is a nice place to regroup before heading out of town.

Sports and Recreation

Blairstown's **Double D Guest Ranch** (81 Mt. Herman Rd., 908/459-9044, www.doubled guestranch.com, Tues.–Sun. 9 A.M.–6 P.M. spring–summer, Tues.–Sun. 9 A.M.–4 P.M. fall–winter) offers one- and two-hour half-day and full-day horseback riding excursions daily except Monday. The two-hour ride ($65) tackles a portion of the 26-mile Paulinskill Trail, which runs partially through Kittatinny Valley State Park. Half-day rides ($90) explore Allamuchy Mountain and Swartswood State Parks.

Food

For a meal that's inexpensive and satisfying, visit the **Forge Restaurant** (Hwy. 94, 908/362-5858, Tues.–Thurs. noon–9:30 P.M., Fri.–Sat. noon–10 P.M., Sun. noon–9 P.M., $7–16), just outside of downtown. A local recommendation brought me to the juiciest barbecue chicken sandwich I've ever eaten, accompanied by thick steak fries for less than $7. The food is nothing fancy, but man, is it good.

HOPE

Along with South Jersey's Burlington City, Hope Village was one of the first planned communities in the United States. A Bohemian Protestant religious sect known as the Moravians founded the small village—now part of larger Hope Township—in the late 18th century. These settlers remained in the area for 39 years, 1769–1808, fleeing when smallpox struck the region. Today, many of Hope's original 16 buildings remain, either in their authentic state or since restored, including a 1769 gristmill operating as a restaurant and inn. Downtown's few square blocks are filled by limestone colonials with steep pitched roofs and brick dual fireplaces, some of which house antique stores. Still, the village is far from being a consumer hotspot.

Toward the lower end of the main street's hill is **Trout Alley,** known to the Moravians as "Locust Alley," a historic trail that's worth a stroll. On the opposite side of town is the **Moravian Cemetery,** which includes a small plot dedicated to the village's original Moravian settlers.

Hope Village was listed on Preservation New Jersey's (www.preservationnj.org) 10 Most Endangered List in 2005.

Historic Sights

For a better understanding of Moravian history, visit the **Hope Historical Society Museum** (Rte. 519, 908/637-4120, Sat. 11 A.M.–1 P.M., Sun. 1–3 P.M., June–Oct.). The Society provides a free self-guided map to Hope's Moravian architecture.

Help Our Preservation Effort, or HOPE (908/459-9177), occasionally hosts 90-minute walking tours ($8) of historic Hope village throughout the year; call for details.

Land of Make Believe

Just a mile from Hope Village is the Land of Make Believe (354 Great Meadows Rd., Rte. 611, 908/459-9000, www.lomb.com, Sat.–Sun. 10 A.M.–6 P.M. Memorial Day–mid-June, daily 10 A.M.–6 P.M. late June–Labor Day, $20 adult, $22 child 2–18), a family amusement park operating for more than 50 years. Though attractions in both the main park and adjoining Pirate's Cove water park are geared towards kids, most are sturdy enough to handle adults as well. In addition to old favorites like Old McDonald's Farm and the Candy Cane Forest, the park has added new hits like a towering freefall and an enclosed waterslide. Ride the carousel, visit the petting zoo, hide from the talking scarecrow, or don costumes at the **Middle Earth Theater** and participate in plays. It's all good fun, and what's even sweeter: The Land of Make Believe is one of those rare gems where adults get a cheaper deal.

Lakota Wolf Preserve

Recent winner of the New Jersey Environmental Tourism Award, the Lakota Wolf Preserve (89 Mt. Pleasant Rd., Camp Taylor Campground, Columbia, 877/733-9653 or 908/496-9244, www.lakotawolf.com, closed Mon., $15 adult, $7 child under 12, cash only) offers visitors an opportunity to view wolves in their natural habitat. It's a half-mile walk from the preserve's entrance to its observation deck (though bus transport is available), which sits at the center of four roaming wolf packs. In addition to arctic, tundra, and timber wolves, you may also catch glimpses of resident bobcats and foxes. The preserve is popular with wildlife photographers, who can book half-day or whole-day shoots.

Wolf Watch programs are presented twice daily at 10:30 A.M. and 4 P.M. in summer, and 10:30 A.M. and 3 P.M. fall and winter. Appointments aren't needed on weekends for individuals or families, but larger groups must have an appointment at all times; to make one call 877/733-9653.

Accommodations

Built in the late 1700s as an operating gristmill, the ◖ **Inn at Millrace Pond** (313 Johnsonburg Rd., 908/459-4884, www.innatmillracepond.com, $175–255) still contains its original waterwheel. The property features 17 colonial-themed guest rooms in three buildings: the gristmill, the 19th-century Millrace House, and a two-room wheelwright's cottage. Each room features wood floors and an area rug, and many have white walls and linens, contrasting beautifully with the dark wood furniture and ceiling beams. While all rooms have private bath and wireless Internet, only some have television. Additional perks include Room 17's cathedral ceiling, Room 4's fireplace, and an excellent on-site restaurant and tavern.

Camping

Tucked onto a 250-acre working farm in the Kittatinny Mountains, **Triple Brook Family Camping Resort** (58 Honey Run Rd., 908/459-4079, www.triplebrook.com, Apr.–Oct.) features 200 open and shaded tent and RV sites, along with an Olympic-size pool, an adults-only lounge, and shuffleboard and horseshoe courts. The resort is an ideal starting point for exploring Hope, Blairstown, and the Delaware Water Gap. Basic sites begin at $36 in-season.

Four-hundred-acre **Camp Taylor Campground** (85 Mount Pleasant Rd., Columbia, 908/496-4333 or 800/545-9662, www.camptaylor.com, mid-Apr.–late Oct., from $23) offers spacious tent and RV sites, along with a few rental cabins ($70 and up) and stationary RVs ($90 and up). Though adjacent to the southern Delaware Water Gap National Recreation Area, the ground features a few of its own hiking trails as well as a two-acre lake for swimming. It's also home to the Lakota Wolf Preserve. Hot showers are available for an additional fee.

Food

The **Village Cafe** (1 Millbrook Rd., 908/459-4860, Mon.–Fri. 11 A.M.–9 P.M., Sat.–Sun. 8 A.M.–9 P.M., $14–19) serves casual American fare in a converted clapboard home on the edge of town. Warmer weather brings alfresco garden seating.

Recently under new management, upscale **Millrace Pond** (313 Johnsonburg Rd., 908/459-4884, www.innatmillracepond.com, lunch daily 11:30 A.M.–5 P.M., dinner Sun.–Thurs. 5–9 P.M., Fri.–Sat. 5–10 P.M.) remains a regional favorite. Dine by candlelight on American dishes like New York strip steak ($28.25) and New England lobster pie ($31.50), with a glass of Australian Shiraz from the accompanying wine menu. Don't miss the basement tavern and its huge walk-in fireplace.

Getting There

Hope Village lies along Route 521 at the Route 519 junction, 15 miles west of the Delaware Water Gap. It's just a few minutes south of I-80. From Blairstown, take Route 521 south for 6.5 miles to reach the village center.

JENNY JUMP STATE FOREST

Just outside Hope village is Jenny Jump State Forest (330 State Park Rd., 908/459-4366, www.state.nj.us/dep/parksandforests/parks/jennyjump.html, free), 4,244 acres of mountainous wooded terrain marked by ancient moraines. Like nearby Stokes, the forest is known for its inspiring views, as well its large population of black bears. Jenny Jump is supposedly named for a girl, ambushed by a local Indian tribe, whose father called out for her to jump. The forest is a good spot for hiking, camping, and mountain biking, and fishers have both the trout-stocked Mountain Lake waters and Ghost Lake's supply of sunfish, catfish, and bass to choose from. Running along the forest is the eerily named Shades of Death Road, a favorite subject of *Weird N.J.* fans.

Greenwood Observatory

Jenny Jump is home to Greenwood Observatory (908/459-4366), where the United Astronomy Clubs of New Jersey (www.uacnj.org) host free Saturday evening astronomy programs for the public April–October. Each stargazing event is preceded by an 8 P.M. presentation that varies week to week. The observatory has a 16-inch Newtonian telescope and a retractable roof, along with a gift shop and a small astronomy museum. According to the Astronomy Clubs' website, Greenwood is one of New Jersey's few remaining dark sky locations.

Recreation

Jenny Jump hosts six miles of hiking-only trails and three additional miles of multiuse trails, ideal for mountain bikers. The 1.5-mile hikers-

NEW JERSEY'S BLACK BEAR FUTURE

It seems odd that the country's most densely populated state is also home to a thriving black bear population – but it's true. The number of black bears in New Jersey is estimated to be 1,600–3,400, with more than half residing in the state's northwest corner of Sussex, Warren, Passaic, and Morris Counties. Since 1980 their once-dwindling numbers have increased dramatically, fueled by the restoration of forest habitat, more comfort with humans, and, many argue, a lack of sufficient population control. This increase has created tension between local and state authorities, as well as among New Jersey residents.

In the last few years, black bears have been spotted in all of the state's 21 counties, and reports of human-related incidents are becoming more common. Most reports are generally minor, such as bears rifling through trash, stealing food, and occasionally harassing farm animals. But they've also gone so far as to kill house pets. In October 2004 a black bear attacked two Boy Scouts outside Blairstown, and in June 2008 a bear was shot and killed for approaching a group of picnicking school kids. The state's bear situation has become so notable, in fact, it was included as a story line in season 5 of *The Sopranos.*

Cited as a response to increasing black bear numbers, encounters, and expanding territory, New Jersey's Department of Environmental Protection allowed the state's first black bear hunt in 33 years to take place in 2003, amid vibrant opposition from environmental groups and animal rights activists who promote viable methods of population control, including increasing public education and awareness, possible relocation, and using contraception to stabilize bear numbers. The six-day hunt led to the issuing of 5,000 permits and the killing of 328 bears.

New Jersey Fish and Wildlife Division's proposed 2004 bear hunt was successfully blocked by Department of Environmental Protection Commissioner Bradley M. Campbell, who declared it an unnecessary means of population stabilization. The state's supreme court sided with Campbell, ruling that a bear hunt could only be reinstated if and when New Jersey's bear policy was brought up to date. As of 2005, a new five-year plan has been proposed and includes dividing the state into six bear-hunting zones with permits issued in correlation to the zone's bear population, establishing a seven-day hunting season set to expand to nine days in coming years, permitting farmers to shoot bears that have attacked their livestock, and capturing and killing bears who wander into "bear exclusion zones," especially regions close to New York City and Philadelphia, as well as the entire Jersey Shore.

Although the 2005 bear hunt was permitted, subsequent hunts have since been canceled. In September 2007, New Jersey's supreme court officially ruled against the 2005 plan, saying it did not follow several administrative procedures. The controversy continues, but for now New Jersey black bears are free to roam.

only **Summit Trail** offers a steady climb rewarded with awesome views. The trail joins with the 1.3-mile **Ghost Lake Trail,** carrying hikers on a descending path to Ghost Lake. The multiuse **Mountain Lake Trail** is the park's longest, a 3.7-mile trek along two heavily wooded loops.

Camping

Jenny Jump hosts 22 tent and trailer sites (Apr.–Oct., $20), all equipped with fire rings and picnic tables, and restroom and shower facilities a short walk away. Two group sites are also available: One accommodates up to 25 people ($25), the other 40 people ($40). Both are equipped with fire rings, picnic tables, and pit toilets. Eight year-round shelters ($10 per bunk, up to four people) are available near the top of Jenny Jump Mountain. They each feature a wood-burning stove, a furnished living area, two rooms with bunk beds, an outdoor grill and picnic table, and nearby restrooms and showers. For reservations, call the park office at 908/459-4366.

Morristown and Vicinity

The town of Morristown, along with nearby university town Madison and Basking Ridge, offer numerous cultural, historic, and natural sites to explore. All of their downtowns are walkable and within an easy drive of one another. Because of its size, Morristown offers the most eclectic restaurants, but for those preferring a quiet getaway, Basking Ridge is your place.

In addition to perhaps New Jersey's largest number of churches per square mile, Morristown is one of the state's most historic towns. It's a cosmopolitan place, filled with fun boutiques and trendy restaurants and centered around a town square, but during Revolutionary War times the town served as General George Washington's home-away-from-home for two

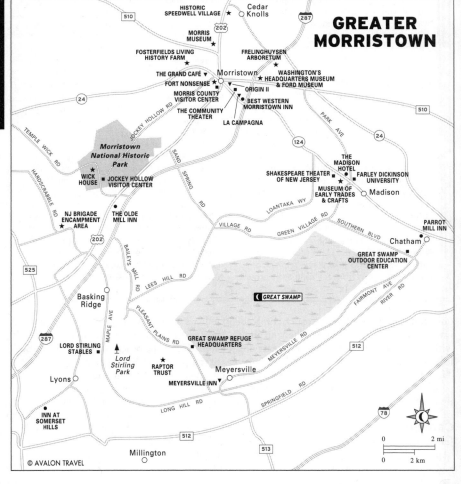

© AVALON TRAVEL

long cold winters. Although none of the war's battles were ever fought here, Washington and his army used Morristown's vantage point to survey the Brits in New York City.

Morristown is less than three square miles in size, but its downtown gives the impression of an endless stretch, with its tallest structures hovering around 10 stories. You'll fine a mixture of independent shops, restaurants, and chain retailers along South Street, most of them housed in colonial brick buildings with upper-floor apartments. Morris County's political seat, the town's early 19th-century Federal-style courthouse—a multistory brick building with a white bell tower—stands along Washington Street, and is the first stop on a self-guided walking tour provided by the visitors center (www.morristown-nj.org/history .html). Arguably downtown's best-known attribute is 2.5-acre Morristown Green, a town square with benches, walkways, and statues, not to mention a few homeless people. Outdoor movies often screen here evenings throughout summer.

MORRISTOWN NATIONAL HISTORIC PARK

Established in 1933, Morristown (www.nps .gov/morr/index.htm) is the country's first National Historic Park and the only one in New Jersey. The park is dedicated to preserving the history of General Washington and his troops' two long winters spent here during the Revolutionary War (1777–1778 and 1779–1780), and encompasses three distinct sections: Ford Mansion, Jockey Hollow, and Fort Nonsense.

Ford Mansion and Washington's Headquarters Museum

Just north of Morristown's downtown center is Ford Mansion, General George Washington's Revolutionary War headquarters during the brutal winter of 1779–1780. Landowner Jacob Ford Jr.'s widow allowed Washington use of Ford Mansion and its 200-acre estate, enabling him to keep close watch on British movements in nearby New York City. While the widow and her four children set up house

THE SKYLANDS

© LAURA KINIRY

Washington statue in front of Ford Mansion, Morristown

in one half of the mansion, Washington occupied the other. His guests to the estate included Martha Washington and the Marquis de Lafayette, the French soldier and statesman. While the Jacob Ford Mansion survived over time, other property buildings weren't so lucky: Today, only their foundations remain. Tours of Ford Mansion take place hourly 10 A.M.–4 P.M. except at noon. Admission to Washington's Headquarters Unit is $4/adult (good for seven days), free for children 15 and under.

Also on the property is the Washington's Headquarters Museum (230 Morris St., 973/539-2016, www.nps.gov/morr, 9 A.M.–5 P.M. daily), which recently underwent a multiyear renovation.

Jockey Hollow

While Washington stayed in Ford Mansion, 10,000 Revolutionary soldiers spent the freezing cold winter of 1779–1780 in nearby Jockey Hollow, five miles south. Though none of the original huts still remain, five reproductions have been placed on the property. Jockey Hollow is also home to the **Wick House** (daily 9:30 A.M.–4:30 P.M., free), a farmhouse used by American officers, including Pennsylvania General Arthur St. Clair.

In addition to its historic sites, Jockey Hollow is home to 27 miles of hiking trails and a two-mile auto tour. The **Jockey Hollow Visitor Center** (Tempe Wick Rd., 973/543-4030) is open daily 9 A.M.–5 P.M.; the park's entry and exit roads are open dawn–dusk.

SIGHTS
Historic Speedwell Village

Historic Speedwell Village (333 Speedwell Ave., 973/285-6550, www.speedwell.org) honors Speedwell Ironworks, one of North Jersey's major 19th-century industrial centers, and its proprietor, Stephen Vail. Little remains of the original 19th-century complex, but a collection of Vail's personal belongings, including photos, diaries, and maps, help illustrate his large contribution to New Jersey's industrial past. The present-day village encompasses 7.5 acres, including **Vail House,** which was the proprietor's

home, and the recently renovated factory, used by Samuel F. B. Morse and Vail's son Alfred to "perfect and demonstrate" the nation's first telegraph. Tours of the Vail House and factory are held Wednesday–Saturday 10 A.M.–5 P.M., Sunday noon–5 P.M. April–October, and admission is $4 adult, $3 senior, $2 child age 4–16.

Fosterfields Living History Farm

Living history is big business in New Jersey, and Morristown is no exception. At Fosterfields Living History Farm (73 Kahdena Rd., 973/326-7645, www.morrisparks.net, Wed.–Sat. 10 A.M.–5 P.M., Sun. noon–5 P.M. Apr.–Oct., $5 adult, $3 child), period-dressed interpreters re-create 19th-century farm life, such as traditional crop raising and livestock tending. Foster's Gothic revival home still stands on the property.

Morris Museum

One of New Jersey's most intriguing museums, the Morris Museum (6 Normandy Heights Rd., 973/971-3700, www.morrismuseum.org, Tues.–Wed. and Fri.–Sat. 10 A.M.–5 P.M., Thurs. 10 A.M.–8 P.M., Sun. 1–5 P.M., $8 adult, $6 child, free Thurs. 5–8 P.M.) combines art, science, theater, and history with a permanent collection of nearly 50,000 objects, including vintage costumes, a model railroad, re-created dinosaur skeletons—even a stuffed grizzly. Rotating exhibits, such as *Black Cinema: The Vintage Years* and *Line Drives and Lipstick: The Untold Story of Women's Basketball,* are displayed throughout the year. A Morris Museum highlight is its Mechanical Musical Instrument Collection, approximately 700 mechanical musical instruments and figures awarded to the museum by New Yorker Murtogh Guinness, a member of the Guinness brewing family, in 2003. On permanent display in the museum's new 4,300-square-foot gallery, opened in November 2007, the exhibit includes both miniature and life-size pieces from the early 16th to late 20th centuries, in forms that include Chinese tea servers, Moorish harpists, automatic banjos, and residential barrel organs, all of which provide their own distinct sound. Live demos of several Guinness Collection objects are held Tuesdays–Sundays at 2 P.M.

Frelinghuysen Arboretum

Anyone who enjoys beauty and the outdoors will like the 127-acre Frelinghuysen Arboretum (53 Hanover Ave., Whippany, 973/326-7600, www.arboretumfriends.org, daily 9 A.M.–dusk, free), a series of themed gardens listed on the National Register of Historic Places. The property once belonged to patent attorney George G. Frelinghuysen and his wife Sara, who was granddaughter of the founder of Newark's P. Ballantine Brewing Company. It was their daughter Matilda who turned the land into an arboretum. Hundreds of annuals and perennials bloom here throughout the year, and highlights include a rock garden, vegetable garden, and a Braille Trail for the visually impaired. Guided walking tours are available on weekends, and various cell phone tours are offered seasonally. The on-site **Haggerty Education Center** (daily 9 A.M.–4:30 P.M.) hosts year-round seminars and workshops.

The Stickley Museum at Craftsman Farms

In the early 20th century, arts and crafts pioneer Gustav Stickley acquired 650 acres for building and operating a self-sufficient boys' school. Although the school never materialized, Stickley and his family resided on the property until 1915 in a log home he designed. Both the home, which now operates as a museum, and 26 acres of the original property known as Craftsman Farms (Rte. 10 W., 973/540-1165, www.stickleymuseum.org, daily dawn–dusk, Apr.–Dec., $7 adult, $4 child), are open to the public. Museum tours take place at scheduled times daily during these months; call for an updated schedule.

NIGHTLIFE AND ENTERTAINMENT

Many of Morristown's restaurants features full bars and sometimes entertainment. The following establishments place nightlife first.

The sophisticated **Side Bar** (14 Washington St., 973/540-9601, daily from 4 P.M.) is for those who've outgrown cover bands and cigarette smoking and have since moved on to pianos and cigars. Entry requires proper dress and a minimum age of 25. A selection of appetizers and desserts from its neighboring sister establishment, Famished Frog, are available.

Catch performances by comedians, Shakespearean actors, traditional dancers, and musicians like Hot Tuna and Herbie Hancock at **Community Theatre at Mayo Center for the Performing Arts** (100 South St., 973/539-0345, www.communitytheatrenj.com), just a short walk from Morristown Green. Built in 1937 as a motion picture house, the theater began its present incarnation in 1994, and is also home to the **Colonial Symphony** (www.colonialsymphony.org), directed by Paul Hostetter.

ACCOMMODATIONS

Built in 1980, the **(C** **Best Western Morristown Inn** (270 South St., 973/540-1700 or 800/688-7474, fax 973/267-0241, www .bestwestern.com, $139–189) does an admirable job blending with its historic surroundings. This colonial-style inn boasts a lobby filled with antiques—including a framed print of Washington above the fireplace—although the guest rooms are more modern, each with high speed Internet and satellite TV. It's located one mile from downtown.

Nearby Chatham's **Parrot Mill Inn** (47 Main St., Chatham, 973/635-7722, fax 973/635-0620, www.parrotmillinn.com, $185) features 11 country-style guest rooms, each with a private bath, telephone, TV, and wireless Internet. The inn originally operated as a mill house along the Fishawack River before relocating to Chatham's Main Street, serving as home to the Parrot family for more than a century.

FOOD

Morristown's majority of eateries lie along downtown's South and Washington Streets, interspersed with interesting shops worth browsing while digesting your meal.

Named for a mountain range in Central Asia, Afghan **Pamir** (85 Washington St., 973/605-1095, www.pamirrestaurant.com, lunch buffet Mon.–Fri. 11:30 A.M.–2 P.M., dinner Mon.–Thurs. 4:30–10:30 P.M., Fri.–Sun. 5–11 P.M., $14–22) serves mildly flavored entrées complete with yogurt-dressed salads and a side of Afghan bread. The restaurant is rich in color and tapestries—a perfect setting for savoring that bottle of pinot you brought along.

Ideal for special occasions is █ **The Grand Café** (42 Washington St., 973/540-9444, www.thegrandcafe.com, Mon.–Thurs. 11:45 A.M.–9 P.M., Fri. 11:45 A.M.–10 P.M., Sat. 5:30–10 P.M., Sun. private parties only, $25–39), a fancy French bistro serving fabulous gourmet dishes and plenty of fine wine. In business for more than 25 years, everything about this Parisian-style townhouse is first rate, including the dress code. Cozy alfresco dining is available in warmer months.

With its tropical colors, striped booths, and flower display, **The Famished Frog** (18 Washington St., 973/450-9601, www.famishedfrog.com, Mon.–Thurs. 11:30 A.M.–10 P.M., Fri.–Sat. 11:30 A.M.–11 P.M., Sun. noon–9 P.M., $8–26) feels like a diner relocated to the rainforest. Meals at this casual space are simple and include signature eats like deep-fried onion straws ($7.49) and sizzling fajitas ($15.49–18.49). In addition to food, the Frog features monthly drink specials like the George Washington apple martini with Crown Royal and cranberry.

For sleek, stylish dining try **Origin II** (10 South St., 973/971-9933, www.originthai.com, lunch Tues.–Fri. 11:30 A.M.–3 P.M., Sat. noon–3 P.M., dinner Tues.–Thurs. 5:30–9 P.M., Sat. 5–10:30 P.M., Sun. 3–9 P.M., closed Mon., $11–27), A Thai-fusion restaurant with a fish tank up front and basement seating.

Highly revered **La Campagna** (5 Elm St., 973/644-4943, www.lacampagnaristorante.com, lunch Mon.–Fri. 11:30 A.M.–3 P.M., dinner Mon.–Sat. 5–10 P.M., Sun. 4–9 P.M., $18.95–28.95) complements exemplary service with superb Italian dishes, each prepared using only fresh ingredients that include parmesan cheese and buffalo milk mozzarella imported from Italy. This BYO occupies a double storefront and offers a scattering of seasonal sidewalk tables.

The Caribbean-like **Calaloo Café** (190 South St., 973/993-1100, www.calaloocafe.com, Mon.–Thurs. 11:30 A.M.–10 P.M., Fri. 11:30 A.M.–11 P.M., Sat.–Sun. noon–11 P.M., $8–19) is a fun, colorful indoor-outdoor space with real palm trees (shipped back to Florida during winter), and food that's a mix of American and island-inspired. Still, people watching, mai tais, and Jamaican tunes are this restaurant's best features, along with the **R Bar** (Wed.–Sat.) downstairs.

INFORMATION AND SERVICES
The **Morris County Visitor Center** (973/631-5151, www.morristourism.org, Mon.–Fri. 9 A.M.–4:30 P.M., Sat. 9 A.M.–1 P.M., June–Aug.) is located at 6 Court Street, two blocks north of the Green.

GETTING THERE
NJ Transit's **M&E Morristown Line** runs from New York City's Penn Station to downtown Morristown. The trip takes costs $10.50 adult one way. Morristown is located east of Route 202 and west of I-287 from Exit 35.

BASKING RIDGE
Just a few miles south of Morristown is Basking Ridge, a ritzy unincorporated community with a small downtown centered along South Finley Avenue, surrounded by large homes and woodland. It's a much quieter place than its northern neighbor, with a decidedly calmer feel. Basking Ridge is home to the Great Swamp, an enormous marshland that's a favorite among birders and naturalists. You'll also find a couple of good restaurants and lodging choices it the area.

█ Great Swamp
If not for a group of local conservationists, New Jersey's Great Swamp (241 Pleasant Plains Rd., 973/425-1222 or 973/425-7309,

www.greatswamp.org, http://greatswamp
.fws.gov/, daily dawn–dusk, free) might now
be an airport. Instead, the 7,500-acre marshland, considered little more than a royal "nuisance" during the Revolutionary War years, is
run by U.S. Fish and Wildlife as a "resting and
nesting" place for hundreds of bird species,
dozens of reptiles, amphibians, and fish, and
mammals such as white-tailed deer, coyotes,
and muskrat. A short walk along some of the
swamp's 8.5 miles of trails and boardwalks may
lead to beaver, stork, and bullfrog sightings, or
a chance peek at the evasive blue-spotted salamander and rarely seen eastern mud turtle.
The swamp is filled with mountain laurel,
ferns, and oak trees, and it encompasses some
smaller parks, including the wonderful Raptor
Trust. There's also a **bookstore and gift shop**
on-site (197 Pleasant Plains Rd., 973/425-
9510, daily 11 A.M.–5 P.M., closed July–Aug.).
Anyone who enjoys birding, wildlife, or simply
being outdoors should find the Great Swamp
worthwhile. The surrounding roads are
good for cycling as well, although you'll get
more out of a ride if you come prepared with
ample water and bug spray. For a free cycling
map to the Great Swamp area, visit the New
Jersey Department of Transportation at www
.state.nj.us/transportation/commuter/bike/
freeinfo.shtm.

The best times for visiting the Great Swamp
are during spring and fall, when mosquitoes
and ticks are at a minimum and wildlife
sighting is at a premium. Morning and late
afternoon are the best times of day to visit,
avoiding the noonday sun. Remember to bring
binoculars.

Privately funded 15-acre **Raptor Trust**
(1390 White Bridge Rd., Millington, 908/647-
2353, www.theraptortrust.org, daily dawn–
dusk, free, $2 donation accepted) is one of New
Jersey's special finds. Its large cages play temporary home to over 100 injured birds of prey,
including broad-winged hawks, peregrine falcons, turkey vultures, golden eagles, and my favorite, snowy owls. Visitors are invited to walk
the wooded grounds and view the birds in
their resting cages. Each cage is marked with a
plaque or plaques displaying information about
its resident, including its scientific name, size,
natural habitat, diet, migratory pattern, and
New Jersey species status. Even birds without a
typical state presence have found a home here,
shipped to the facility for treatment. Others
were injured while migrating. Birds that can't
be rereleased due to substantial injuries are
often used as foster parents for other birds, or
for breeding and education. There's also a cash-
only on-site gift shop.

Adjacent to the Great Swamp is Chatham's
40-acre **Great Swamp Outdoor Education
Center** (247 Southern Blvd., 973/635-6629,
Mon.–Fri. 9 A.M.–4:30 P.M.), where you'll
find a reference library, natural history displays, and additional nature trails. The center hosts educational workshops for both kids
and families.

Less than a mile (down a pebble road) from
Raptor Trust is Lord Stirling Park (190 Lord
Stirling Rd., Basking Ridge, 908/766-6471),
named for New Jersey's onetime surveyor
general and Revolutionary War major-gen-
eral William Alexander, the disputed Earl of
Stirling. The park is home to **Lord Stirling
Stables** (256 S. Maple Ave., Basking Ridge,
908/766-5955, daily 9 A.M.–5 P.M.), which offers introductory and advanced English and
Western saddle horseback rides, horse rentals,
and riding lessons year-round.

Food and Entertainment

The **Meyersville Inn** (632 Meyersville Rd.,
Gillette, 908/647-6302, Tues.–Thurs. 4–9 P.M.,
Fri.–Sat. 4–10 P.M., Sun. 11:30 A.M.–8:30 P.M.,
closed Mon.) serves traditional American fare
in a casual and tavern setting. Dine on evening dishes like blackened Cajun shrimp ($22)
and broiled salmon ($19), or come early for
the popular Sunday brunch ($17 per person),
where French toast baguettes and breakfast
wraps are the norm. Happy hour is Tuesday–
Friday 4–6 P.M. The Meyersville Inn is located
southwest of the Great Swamp.

Sharing 10 acres with the Olde Mill Inn is
the historic **Grain House Restaurant** (225
Rte. 202, Basking Ridge, 908/221-1150,

Mon.–Thurs. 11:30 A.M.–10 P.M., Fri.–Sat. 11:30 A.M.–11 P.M., Sun. 10 A.M.–9 P.M., $11–33), specializing in country American cuisine prepared with organic fruits and veggies, purified water, and grass-fed meats. The popular restaurant occupies a restored 18th-century structure that served as the property's inn 1930–1977 and features a creek-side outdoor garden with umbrella tables, as well as the indoor Coppertop Pub, a full bar with live music and superb martinis.

Accommodations

The conveniently located ◖ **Olde Mill Inn** (225 Rte. 202, Basking Ridge, 908/221-1100, www.oldemillinn.com, $179) features 102 guest rooms, including several Pure rooms equipped with carbon filter air cleaners, Energy Star lighting, and linens washed using unscented toxin-free laundry detergents. The Pure rooms are also the inn's most updated and attractive, except for maybe the two Grande Suites, and run only about $10–20 more per night. In its ode to receiving a good night's sleep, the Olde Mill also houses a relaxing piano lounge and a sunny conservatory where daily breakfast is served. The Grain House Restaurant is adjacent to the property.

The pet-friendly **Inn at Somerset Hills** (80 Allen Rd., Basking Ridge, 908/580-1300 or 800/688-0700, www.theinnatsomersethills.com, $199–239) hosts 111 spacious and elegant guest rooms, as well as an on-site bar and restaurant. Built in 2000, its sister property is Warren's Somerset Hills Hotel. The inn caters to corporate clients, so rates are significantly lower on weekends.

Getting There

To reach the Great Swamp from Morristown, take Route 202 south to North Maple Avenue, turn left, and follow the road until it becomes South Maple Avenue. Make another left onto Lord Stirling Road. After about two miles (on partially pebbled streets) the Raptor Trust Center will appear on your left. Pass the center and you'll come to Pleasant Plains Road. Turn left to reach the Great Swamp headquarters.

MADISON

Madison is an attractive university town with a bustling, walkable center. Brick buildings housing restaurants and boutiques line its Main Street, easily accessible from the nearby transit station. Madison earned the nickname "Rose City" for the rose-growing industry that once flourished here. Today, it's better-known as home to both **Fairleigh Dickinson's Florham Campus** (285 Madison Ave., 973/443-8500, www.fdu.edu) and **Drew University** (36 Madison Ave., 973/408-3000, www.drew.edu).

Museum of Early Trade and Crafts

Madison's nonprofit Museum of Early Trade and Crafts (9 Main St., 973/377-2982, www.rosenet.org/metc, Tues.–Sat. 10 A.M.–4 P.M., Sun. noon–5 P.M., $5 adult, $3 child) displays one-of-a-kind handcrafted artifacts, including toys, furniture, and musical instruments, along with rotating exhibits focusing on the works of New Jersey tradespeople. While the museum's collection is impressive, the building itself is spectacular: a 1900 Romanesque revival–style former library with vaulted ceilings, rounded archways, and detailed walls—it alone is worth a visit.

Shakespeare Theatre of New Jersey

For nearly half a century New Jersey's Shakespeare Theatre (www.ShakespeareNJ.org, June–Dec.) has honored England's prolific playwright by adapting his works for local audiences, and since 1990 they've been performing on the main stage at Drew University's **F.M. Kirby Shakespeare Theatre** (36 Madison Ave., 973/408-5600, www.drew.edu). Now the East Coast's longest-running Shakespearean theater, they also hold select summer performances outdoors at the **Greek Theatre** (2 Convent Rd., 973/236-2954), located on nearby Morristown's College of St. Elizabeth campus.

Food and Entertainment

With live jazz playing six nights a week,

Shanghai Jazz (24 Main St., 973/822-2899, www.shanghaijazz.com, $17–30) is Madison's music hotspot. Although there's usually no cover charge to enter, a per-person food and drink minimum ($15–35) does apply. Good thing there's a full bar, an Asian-inspired entrée menu, and dim sum delectables like steamed spring rolls ($8.95) and crispy crab dumplings ($8.95) to make the entire package worthwhile. The restaurant is open Tuesday–Sunday evenings (closed Sun. July–Aug.) with seatings Friday and Saturday evenings at 6:30 and 8:45 P.M.

The draw of the **Garlic Rose Bistro** (41 Main St., 973/822-1178, www.garlicrose.com, lunch Mon.–Fri. 11:30 A.M.–3 P.M., dinner Mon.–Thurs. 5–10 P.M., Fri.–Sat. 5–11 P.M., Sun. 4–9 P.M., $13.50–21.95) is its main ingredient, mixed into everything from soups to dessert. You don't have to be a fan of garlic to enjoy dishes like garlicious rigatoni in cream sauce ($15.95) and garlic rose crab cakes ($21.95), but it helps. The restaurant features several sidewalk tables preferable to the indoor dining area, since the oh-so-sweet scent is a little less severe.

A great place for sampling Southern fare is **Pop's Bar-B-Q** (42 Lincoln Pl., 973/301-0101, popscajun.net, Tues.–Thurs. 11:30 A.M.–9 P.M., Fri. 11:30 A.M.–9:30 P.M., Sat. noon–9:30 P.M., closed Sun.–Mon.), a New Orleans–style café and grill serving sizable oyster po'boys ($12) and starters like a stuffed poblano pepper ($11) and andouille mac and cheese ($7).

Getting There

NJ Transit's **Morris and Essex Line** from New York City's Penn Station stops at the Madison Train Station. To reach Madison from Morristown, take Route 124 southeast a little over 4.5 miles (about a 10-minute drive).

THE SKYLANDS

The Central Piedmont

Situated between New Jersey's urban east and its hard-to-reach western border is the Central Piedmont, a mix of office parks and attractive downtowns that are New York City–accessible (by way of NJ Transit), but distant enough to feel like they're twice removed. The region offers a fine selection of restaurants and shops, including Chester's antique stores and Flemington's outlets. While it's not heavy on B&Bs, there are several worthwhile overnight options to choose from. The Central Piedmont is a popular spot for hot-air ballooning, even hosting a hot-air balloon festival each July, and is easily accessible from Routes 22 and 202.

CHESTER

Antique aficionados will find a lot to do in Chester, a charming 18th-century borough just off Route 206. Chester's Main Street is brimming with antique and specialty stores, most of them housed in historic colonials and Victorians lining both sides of the road. Though not as compact as other towns, Chester is still walkable, and foot traffic is often heavy on weekends. You can easily spend an afternoon browsing the wares, many of which are set up outdoors on covered front porches and small front lawns.

Shopping

Most of Chester's shops exist along East Main Street, where you'll find everything from antique rocking chairs to vintage records.

Housing the handmade works of more than 70 regional artisans is **Hester Crafts & Collectibles** (26 Main St., 908/879-2900, www.chestercrafts.com). **Perfect Treasure** (30 Main St., 908/879-9622) offers custom embroidery and American Girl accessories. In business for more than 30 years, **Chester Timepiece** (58 Main St., 908/879-5421) sells grandfather, wall, and mantel clocks and offers in-shop repairs, although house calls are made for larger models. For blankets, rugs, and quilts (some even depicting Chester), try **Chester Country Furnishings** (60 Main St.,

THE SKYLANDS

© LAURA KINIRY

shopping for antiques in downtown Chester

908/879-4288). Chockfull of antique finds including Depression glass, dial telephones, and tin signs is **Pegasus Antiques** (98 Main St., 908/879-4792). **Hollyberries** (92 Main St., 908/879-8995) features authentic antique and reproduction furniture, including tables, cabinets, and armoires.

Housed within the Old Factory building, **Stained Glass Boutique** (76 Main St., 908/879-7351) is home to colorful glass sunflowers, sailboats, and hot-air balloons, along with stained glass window hangings awaiting refurbishing. The **Chester Carousel Antiques and Gifts** (125 Main St., 908/879-7141) features a varied antique selection of birdcages, dolls, and a vintage carousel horse. The shop also sells Byers' Choice Carolers.

Food

Tucked behind Main Street proper is **Benito's Trattoria** (44 Main St., 908/879-1887, Tues.–Fri. 11:30 A.M.–10 P.M., Sat. 5–10 P.M., Sun. 1–9 P.M., $15–24) a family-friendly BYO selling Northern Italian fare. Head over to **Taylor's Ice Cream Parlor** (18 E. Main St., 908/879-5363) for a locally made hand-scooped vanilla cone.

A nice stop for an afternoon shopping break is **Sally Lunn's Tearoom & Restaurant** (15 Perry St., 908/879-7731, www.sallylunns.com, Tues.–Fri. 10:30 A.M.–5:30 P.M., Sat.–Sun. 10:30 A.M.–6 P.M.). Select from an assortment of scones, soups, and sandwiches to accompany your pot of White Monkey Paw ($6) or Chocolate Mint ($3.95) tea, two of dozens to choose from.

Completely renovated and reopened over the last few years, Chester's historic **Publick House Inn** (111 Main St., 908/879-6878, daily 11:30 A.M.–10 P.M., $17–32) serves American brick-oven pizzas and Angus burgers along with seafood and steak specialties. The food has received mixed reviews, but the ambiance is unbeatable.

Getting There

Chester is located just off Route 206 along Route 513 (Main Street).

GLADSTONE-PEAPACK AND FAR HILLS

The Old Chester-Gladstone Road (Rte. 512) meanders past setback estates from Chester east into Gladstone-Peapack, a lovely borough filled with brick storefronts and a local market.

Both Gladstone and neighboring Far Hills are great for residential sightseeing—most homes are enormous, and amazing. The route is also great for cycling—light on traffic, with plenty of hills and greenery, although the shoulder is virtually nonexistent.

The USGA Museum and Archives

Home to the world's premier collection of American pro-golf memorabilia and artifacts, permanent exhibits at the **USGA Museum and Archives** (Liberty Corner Rd., Far Hills, 908/234-2300, www.usgamuseum. com, Tues.–Sun. 10 A.M.–5 P.M., $7 adult, $3.50 child) include the Hall of Champions, honoring every past USGA champ and championship, and a series of galleries highlighting iconic golf moments from the late 19th century until now. Golf clubs, balls, trophies, and medals are all on display, along with books and documents pertaining to the sport. The museum hosts an online photography store where copies of famed historic photos can be purchased, as well as a film and video archive available for commercial and noncommercial use. A nine-hole putting course was added in September 2008.

A museum highlight is the 30-minute docent-led tour of the USGA's Research and Test Center. Attendees visit the biomechanics labs, where a computerized golf-swing model is being created, and (weather permitting) have an opportunity to test modern and historically replicated golf clubs to hit balls on the center's driving range. Tours run less than 1 hour and take place weekdays at 2 P.M.; reservations are encouraged (908/234-2300, kgianetti@usga.org).

U.S. Equestrian Team Headquarters

Gladstone's Hamilton Farm is the official home of the U.S. Equestrian Team, or USET Foundation (1040 Pottersville Rd., 908/234-1251, www.uset.org). Visitors are welcome to explore the grounds, which are used for Olympic training, during weekday office hours (8:30 A.M.–4:30 P.M.) and on event-hosting weekends. June's **Dressage Festival of Champions,** a series of Olympic-style horse-and-rider events, is an annual highlight.

Accommodations

With 111 spacious guest rooms and suites and a fine restaurant and lounge, the grand **Somerset Hills Hotel** (200 Liberty Corner Rd., Warren, 908/647-6700, www.shh.com, $199–239) has become a popular place for wedding receptions. In addition to wireless Internet, all rooms include access to the hotel's health center. Room service is available and pets are welcome for an additional fee; rates are reduced on weekends.

BRIDGEWATER

Just north of Somerville, Bridgewater is often considered a county seat extension. It's a clean spacious place with numerous office parks, frequented by business travelers. Although Bridgewater is home to a few attractions and a spiffy shopping mall, your best bet for dining is to head into Somerville.

Commerce Bank Ballpark

Bridgewater's 6,100-seat Commerce Bank Ballpark (1 Patriots Park, 908/252-0700, www.somersetpatriots.com, $5–12.50) is home to the Somerset Patriots, a member of the Freedom Division of the Atlantic League of Professional Baseball since 1998. Built in 1999, the park has both a party deck and a picnic spot along with the Turf Club, a grassy area where fans can set up for game viewing near the Patriots bullpen. Food is plentiful but pricey.

United States Bicycling Hall of Fame

Across the street from the minor-league ballpark is Bridgewater's homage to the underappreciated sport of cycling, the United States Bicycling Hall of Fame (941 E. Main St., 732/356-7016, usbhof@optonline.net, www.usbhof.com, call or email for hours and admission cost). Take some time to admire the jerseys, bikes, trophies, medals, photos, and clippings highlighting the nation's cycling greats. The center hosts an annual induction ceremony honoring road, BMX, and mountain bikers along with outside contributors to the sport.

Bridgewater Commons

The place for one-stop modern shopping, Bridgewater Commons (400 Commons Way, 908/218-0001, www.bridgewatercommons .com) is New Jersey's first three-story shopping mall. Anchored by Macy's, Bloomingdale's, and Lord & Taylor, the over 170 shops include Sephora, Oakley, and J. Crew, along with restaurants, a multiplex AMC Theater (908/725-1161), and a modern outdoor village.

Accommodations

Focusing on business guests, **Hyatt Summerfield Suites** (530 Rte. 22, 908/725-0800, $239–339) features one- and two-bedroom suites equipped with kitchens, a 24-hour convenience store, and on-site video rentals, along with Wednesday night grilling socials throughout summer. A complimentary happy hour takes place Monday–Thursday. Rates (and added amenities) are reduced on weekends.

SOMERVILLE

One thing that'll catch your eye while traveling through historic Somerville is its courthouse, a massive beaux arts structure complete with Greek columns and a rounded dome topped with a gold statue of Justice. It stands on an expansive lawn past a long line of restaurants and service shops that make up the borough's Main Street. While shopping opportunities do exist, most notably in Somerville's Antique Shopping District on Division Street and along West Main Street, the borough's real attractions are its numerous reputable restaurants. While in town be sure to have a look at the many Gothic, Victorian, and Greek revival homes along Somerville's side roads, and don't miss the castle-like transit station on the way into town.

Wallace House

The Wallace House (38 Washington Pl., 908/725-1015) was less then four years old when it served as George Washington's 1779–1780 seasonal headquarters. Now more than 200 years old, this clapboard colonial has held up surprisingly well. Tours of the home are offered Wednesday–Saturday 10 A.M.–noon and 1–4 P.M., Sunday 1–4 P.M. year-round, or stop off in winter for an evening candlelight tour of both the Wallace House and the property's Old Dutch Parsonage (Wed.–Fri.).

Duke Farms and Gardens

Tobacco heiress Doris Duke (as in Duke University) created the exquisite 2,740-acre Duke Farms and Gardens (Rte. 206 S., 908/722-3700, www.dukefarms.org, daily noon–4 P.M. Oct.–June, $10 adult, $8 child), a series of internationally themed greenhouses, tree-lined walkways, and numerous sculptures and fountains, beginning with land she inherited from her father. She maintained, added to, and upgraded the property until her death in 1993. Today, the gardens are owned and operated by the Duke Farms Foundation. Known for its strict rules and regulations regarding public access, Duke Farms and Gardens is in the process of becoming more visitor-friendly while simultaneously making itself more environmentally friendly, including providing sustainably powered trams for tours and opening previously closed trails for public access. Various tours include free self-guided Walk on the Wild Side tours (Fri.–Sun. 10 A.M.–3 P.M.), and guided seven-mile bicycle tours (Sat. 8 A.M.–10 A.M. Apr.–Oct.) where participants provide their own mountain bikes and helmets. Twilight biking tours are also available.

Reservations are required for all Duke Gardens tours. Call or check the website for updated times and prices.

Festivals and Events

Somerville hosts the United States' oldest bike race, the four-day **Tour of Somerville** (www .tourofsomerville.org), each Memorial Day weekend. Events include a criterium—a bicycle lap race—and a cycling classic, culminating Monday with live music and the official bike tour. Weekend events are free.

July's annual **Quick Chek Festival of Ballooning** (800/468-2479, http://quickchk.balloonfestival.com, $17 adult, $7 child) takes place at Readington's Solberg Airport over three days. Up to 125 international hot-air balloons—including, in 2008, one resembling Darth Vader—ascend twice daily, weather permitting. If that's not enough, there's also live music, fireworks, and amusement rides.

Food

Somerville has a fine selection of restaurants, including several ethnic eateries. Tables may be a little snug at trendy BYO **Origin** (25 Division St., 908/635-1444, www.originthai.com, lunch Tues.–Sat. 11:30 A.M.–3 P.M., dinner Tues.–Thurs. 5–9:30 P.M., Fri.–Sat. 5–10 P.M., Sun. 3–9 P.M., closed Mon., $13–24), but the Thai-French fare is so intriguing you'll hardly notice. The restaurant has additional locations in Morristown and Basking Ridge. BYO **Chao Phaya** (9 Davenport St., 908/231-0655, http://chaophaya.com, Mon.–Thurs. 11:30 A.M.–9:30 P.M., Fri. 11:30 A.M.–10 P.M., Sat. noon–10 P.M., Sun. 4–9 P.M., $9–19) serves traditional Thai food in an intimate setting removed from Main Street.

One of Somerville's prized establishments, the multistory **Verve** (18 E. Main St., 908/707-8655, www.vervestyle.com, Mon.–Sat. 5 P.M.–closing, $22–40) serves New American–French entrées along with a varied selection of wines and martinis. In addition to its bright bistro, Verve also features a bar and a popular lounge that still has its black-and-white tile floor from Prohibition days. Live jazz plays on weekends; the bistro offers alfresco seating during the summer months.

Casual BYO **Martino's** (212 W. Main St., 908/722-8602, Tues.–Sun. 11:30 A.M.–10 P.M., closed Mon., $12–19) is known for its healthy portions of authentic Cuban fare, along with quick service and a lively owner. For Italian eats nothing beats **La Scala** (117 N. Gaston Ave., 908/218-9300, www.lascalafineitalian.com, lunch Tues.–Fri. 11:30 A.M.–3 P.M., dinner Tues.–Thurs. 5–10 P.M., Fri.–Sat. 5–11 P.M., Sun. 4–9 P.M., $17–24), a down-to-earth BYO

whose signature dishes include homemade lobster ravioli and grilled ostrich steak.

CLINTON

Straddling the banks of the Raritan River, scenic Clinton (once known as Hunts Mills) features one of New Jersey's finest historic Main Streets, a stretch of 19th-century Bavarian-inspired brick and clapboard buildings housing several worthwhile shops and eateries, including a waterfront restaurant. At street's end a flat iron bridge stretches across the river, carrying both foot and auto traffic alongside a 200-foot-wide waterfall. On either side stands a historic mill—Clinton's two most notable structures. The town received its current name in 1828 to honor Governor Dwight Clinton, sponsor of the Erie Canal.

Historic Mills

One of the state's most recognizable and photographed structures is Clinton's circa-1810 Red Mill, situated along the western bank of the Raritan River alongside the waterfall. Once a processor of wool, plaster, and graphite, and later used to generate electricity for limestone quarries, today it houses the **Hunterdon Historical Museum** (56 Main St., 908/735-4101, $6 adult, $4 child), four floors showcasing the county's commercial and agricultural heritage. The mill is part of the larger **Red Mill Museum Village** (www.theredmill.org), made up of a handful of restored and reproduced buildings including a circa-1860 schoolhouse and a log cabin. The property also includes the 19th-century Mulligan Limestone Quarry with a stone crusher, dynamite shed, and limekilns. The museum's changing exhibits have included vintage toy soldiers, dollhouses, and a collection of local rocks and fossils. Historic reenactments and other events are held seasonally. The museum and village are open Tuesday–Saturday 10 A.M.–4 P.M., Sunday noon–5 P.M. early April–mid-October.

Directly across the waterfall stands the **Hunterdon Museum of Art** (7 Lower Center St., 908/735-8415, fax 908/735-8416, www.hunterdonartmuseum.org, Tues.–Sun.

11 A.M.–5 P.M., $5 adult suggested donation), a contemporary art museum housed in an 1836 gray-stone gristmill that operated until 1952. Permanent and changing exhibits include modern prints, paintings, photographs, and sculpture from internationally recognized and regional artists; call ahead for docent-led tours. The museum offers on-site studio classes and workshops for all ages, and hosts a ground-level gift store selling silk totes, domino bracelets, and printed stationery.

(Ballooning

With so much wide-open countryside, Hunterdon County has become a popular place for hot-air ballooning. A couple of balloon companies are located just outside Clinton. **American Balloon** (908/534-5220, www .balloonride.net, $195 each 1–3 people, $175 each 4 or more people) offers daily flights year-round, depending on the weather. Balloons take off from the Clinton Elks ball field. Call to schedule a ride and to get directions. In business for more than 20 years, **In Flight Balloon Adventures** (888/301-2383, www.balloonnj .com) hosts popular morning or evening two-person flights followed by a champagne and hors d'oeuvres party ($590 per couple). The individual rate for three or more people is $215 per person. Flights leave from the Spain Inn II Restaurant in Asbury; call for directions. Taking off from nearby Pittstown, **Alexandria Balloon Flights** (Sky Manor Airport, 42 Sky Manor Rd., 888/468-2477, www.njballooning.com) offers standard flights for up to three people ($215 per person), as well as private flights for two ($595). Flights last about an hour, and conclude with champagne, soft drinks, and hors d'oeuvres.

Kayaking

Paddle down the Raritan in a canoe or kayak from **Pender's Boathouse** (9 Lower Center St., 908/735-6767, weekends 9:30 A.M.–4:30 P.M. summer). The shop is situated on the eastern riverbank just above the waterfall.

Spruce Run Recreation Area

New Jersey's third-largest reservoir is four miles north of Clinton in 2,012-acre **Spruce Run Recreation Area** (68 Van Syckel's Rd., 908/638-8572, www.state.nj.us/dep/parksand forests/parks/spruce.html). The 1,290-acre pool offers 15 miles of shoreline and is a great place for swimming, sunbathing, and kayaking during summer months. There's also an on-site book rental shack (908/638-8234). Fishers come here to catch trout, northern pike, sunfish, catfish, and carp. In winter it's ice fishers, ice boaters, and cross-county skiers.

Spruce Run is home to the nearly one mile of the **Highlands Millennium Trail** that will eventually connect the Delaware River with the Hudson River. Tent and trailer camping is allowed April 1–October 31 ($20).

Sixty-seven sites include fire rings and picnic tables, with restrooms nearby. The park is open year-round dawn–dusk, with an access fee Memorial Day–Labor Day of $5 weekdays, $10 weekends. Cyclists and walk-ins are $2 daily throughout the season.

Shopping

Clinton has some fun Main Street shops that are definitely worth a peek inside.

Local mainstay **Clinton 5&10** (36 Main St., 908/735-8515) sells everything from old-fashioned candies to Lionel trains to sunscreen. Score copies of *Weird N.J.* at the independent **Clinton Book Shop** (33 Main St., 908/735-8811, http://clinton.booksense.com) along with best sellers and summer reading classics. Book signings are held year-round. For fine-tip pens, specialty stationery, and greeting cards try **The Write Touch** (41 Main St., 908/713-9595). Small, crowded, and oh-so-cozy **Things We Like** (20 Main St., 908/730-9888) stocks apparel, cups, pins, and German spring toys. Teens peruse the latest Betsey Johnson designs and Lucky Brand jeans at multilevel **Mary's, Addicted Jeans, Rock the World Cafe** (43 Main St., 908/713-1134) before settling in for a crepe and cappuccino. And pets pull their guardians into **Fur Majesty** (18 Main St., 908/730-7977) for gourmet snacks and four-legged fashions. Kitties will especially love the catnip bar.

Owned and operated by Taiwanese native Chia Cheng "Charlie" Huang in nearby Pittstown, 40-acre **Chia-Sin Farms** (215 Quakertown Rd., 908/730-7123, http://the businesslinks.com/chiasinfarms/home.htm, daily 10 A.M.–6 P.M.) offers a pick-your-own selection of Chinese and East Asian vegetables such as Taiwan cabbage, yellow watermelon, and Chinese cucumbers, as well as medicinal herbs.

Accommodations

Within walking distance to downtown's shops and restaurants, the family-friendly **Holiday Inn Select** (111 W. Main St., 908/735-5111, www.hisclinton.com, $152–219) features free wireless Internet in public areas, along with check-in perks like complimentary lemonade and homemade cookies. There's both a café and dance club on-site.

Situated along I-78, the fairly new **Courtyard by Marriott Lebanon** (300 Corporate Dr., 908/236-8500, $139–204) offers clean smoke-free rooms with spacious work areas. A breakfast buffet is included in the room price. The hotel is just a couple of miles from both Clinton and Round Valley Recreation Area.

Camping

Situated along the Raritan Riverbank on 26 wooded acres, **Camp Carr Campground** (144 W. Woods-Church Rd., 908/782-1030, Apr.–Oct., from $30) hosts 30-odd RV and tent sites and runs a YMCA kids camp weekdays during summer months. Its convenient location near Clinton and Flemington along with gracious hosts makes scoring one of Camp Carr's hard-to-get sites worthwhile, as long as you're not planning to sleep in.

Food

Clinton's dining options are not exceedingly varied, but you will find some wonderful American eats and a couple of good ethnic restaurants.

With its waterfront view of Clinton's historic Red Mill, **The Old River House** (51 Main St., 908/735-4141, www.oldriver houserestaurant.com, Mon.–Fri. 8 A.M.–9 P.M., Sat. 7 A.M.–9 P.M., Sun. 7 A.M.–8 P.M., $15–21) is the perfect place to unwind after a day tackling New Jersey's highways. This scenic spot offers both indoor fireside dining and garden-style alfresco seating, with live entertainment and the occasional waddling duck during summer months. American cuisine includes seafood, steak, and vegetarian dishes. If you're in town for lunch, try the Little Falls salmon sandwich topped with caper aioli ($8.45). *Magnifique!*

Wasabi's (5 Main St., 908/238-9300, $15–25) sushi comes highly recommended. The place is tiny—only a handful of tables and an L-shaped sushi bar. The restaurant is open for lunch noon–3 P.M. Tuesday–Friday and dinner 5–9 P.M. Tuesday–Saturday. Closed Sunday and Monday.

For Thai food try **Pru Thai** (6 E. Main St., 908/735-0703, Tues.–Thurs. 11:30 A.M.–9:30 P.M., Fri.–Sat. 11:30 A.M.–10 P.M., Sun. 2–9 P.M., $9–18). Highlights include Drunken Man stir-fried noodles and *khoa pad:* fried rice with egg, tomato, and onions.

Family-owned **Towne Restaurant** (31 Main St., 908/735-7559, www.clintontownerestaurant .com, Mon.–Sat. 6 A.M.–4:30 P.M., Sun. 7 A.M.–2 P.M.) is a long-running local gathering spot with a loyal clientele. Stop here for a feta and spinach omelet ($6.75) before exploring town. Open for breakfast and lunch only.

Established in 1743, the recently renovated **The Clinton House** (2 W. Main St., 908/730-9300, www.theclintonhouse.com, Mon.–Fri. 11:30 A.M.–2:30 P.M. and 5–9:30 P.M., Sat. 11:30 A.M.–2:30 P.M. and 5–10 P.M., Sun. noon–8:30 P.M., $15.50–44.50) oozes history. A large whitewashed structure across the Raritan River from Clinton's Main Street stretch, it's home to numerous colonial-inspired dining rooms where traditional American dishes, including a small vegetarian selection, are served. The inn also houses its own bakery and bar.

Widely regarded as one of New Jersey's best restaurants, the award-winning **Ryland Inn** (Rte. 22, Whitehouse, 908/534-4011, www .therylandinn.com) has been closed since

February 2007 because of flood damage and the high cost of repair. Known for its French-American tasting menus ($100–140) prepared with organic ingredients grown in the property's outdoor garden, it's unclear if and when the restaurant will reopen; call ahead.

Getting There and Around

From the Bridgewater-Somerville area take Route 22 west toward Clinton. **Trans-Bridge Lines** (www.transbridgebus.com) runs buses from New York City's Port Authority Bus Terminal (212/564-8484) daily to Clinton, arriving at Clinton's Park and Ride (Route 31 and Center Street) in a little over an hour. Return buses run throughout the day. Round-trip tickets are $32.30 adult, $19.35 child if purchased from an agent, $20 one-way if purchased on board.

ROUND VALLEY RECREATION AREA

Four miles east of Clinton is scenic Round Valley Recreation Area (1220 Lebanon-Stanton Rd., 908/236-6355, www.state.nj.us/dep/parks andforests/parks/round.html), home to a more than 2,000-acre reservoir that, at 180 feet, is the state's deepest body of water. With its rolling green hills and tall trees, the park is genuinely peaceful, and it is one of only a few spots in New Jersey offering backcountry camping. Swimming is allowed in a separate day-use-only section of the reservoir during summer months, when lifeguards are on duty. The reservoir is also popular with fishers, hosting 19 fish species and an annual stock of trout, and its clarity and aquatic life make it one of the state's best freshwater lakes for scuba diving (Apr.–Oct., divers must be certified).

Round Valley hosts several multiuse trails open to mountain bikers, horseback riders, and hikers, along with a couple of short nature trails easy enough for casual strollers. The park also hosts 85 backcountry campsites accessible only to those traveling in on foot or by boat. Round Valley's surrounding region is ideal for **cyclists,** who can obtain a free map of the Round Valley Roundabout ride from the New

Round Valley Recreation Area

Jersey Department of Transportation (www .state.nj.us/transportation/commuter/).

Round Valley Recreation Area is open daily dawn–dusk year-round and is free to enter most of the year. Memorial Day–Labor Day admission is $5 per vehicle weekdays, $10 per vehicle weekends, and $2 for walk-ins and cyclists.

Recreation

In addition to the reservoir, a Round Valley highlight is its nine-mile **Cushetunk Trail,** traversing wooded stretches and exposed areas and rising to 500 feet above the shoreline. A moderate-difficult trail, its lower portion leads toward the park's backcountry campsites. Other hikes include the easy one-mile **Pine Tree Trail** and the 0.5-mile **Family Hiking and Biking Trail,** both popular with birders who might catch glimpses of ospreys, blue jays, and woodpeckers. Cross-country skiers make use of the trails in winter.

Backcountry Campsites

Round Valley hosts 85 backcountry tent sites (Apr.–Oct., $17), and eight group sites (Apr.– Oct., $25) each accommodating up to 25 guests. All sites are accessible by hiking a 3–6-mile portion of the moderately difficult nine-mile **Cushetunk Trail,** or by boat or kayak. They're located on the eastern end of the reservoir. Sites are pretty rustic, but there is drinking water available.

FLEMINGTON

Hunterdon's county seat is New Jersey's premier outlet center, a one-mile stretch replete with steep roofs, front porches, and traffic circles. Downtown is known for its Greek revival architecture, interspersed between brick buildings that provide the borough with a slightly industrial feel. Main Street bustles with judges, lawyers, and jurors most weekdays but is especially quiet on weekends, when visitors head to the outlying shopping centers for bargain buys. Flemington was the hometown of Danny "Phantom Dan" Federici, the E Street Band's organist and keyboard player who passed away in April 2008.

Greek Revival Courthouse

Although no longer used for its original function, Flemington's towering Greek revival courthouse is central to downtown's Main Street. With tall Doric columns and a whitewashed facade the 19th-century structure is quite impressive, although it wasn't architecture that earned it National Historic Landmark status. This famous courthouse was site of the 1930s Lindbergh baby kidnapping trial, and it was here that carpenter Bruno Hauptmann was convicted and sentenced to death for the kidnapping and murder of aviator Charles Lindbergh's son, whom he'd stolen from a second story nursery in the Lindberghs' Central Jersey Hopewell home.

The courthouse has since been restored to its 1935 trial-era appearance, and on weekends throughout October hosts reenactments of the "trial of the century" for public audiences. Visitors can even watch the performance from the jury box. For further details visit www .famoustrials.com or call 908/782-2610.

PRESERVED

© LAURA KINIRY

Flemington's historic courthouse

THE SKYLANDS

Schaefer Farms

Kid-friendly Schaefer Farms (1051 Rte. 523, 908/782-2705, www.schaeferfarms.com, daily 9 A.M.–6 P.M.) hosts family-oriented events year-round, including a holiday light show and October's Fright Fest hayride. The farm offers July blackberry picking and August raspberry picking, and also hosts its own produce stand in spring, summer, and fall. Free-cut flowers are popular sellers in spring.

Northlandz

Just north of Flemington Circle is the cavernous and remarkable Northlandz (Rte. 202, 908/782-4022, www.northlandz.com, Mon. and Wed.–Fri. 10:30 A.M.–4 P.M., Sat.–Sun. 10:30 A.M.–5:30 P.M., closed Tues., $13.75 adult, $9.75 child) a miniature train museum credited by Guinness as having "the largest model railroad ever." With its model mountains, mining towns, amusement parks, train wrecks (my four-year-old nephew Patrick would love this!), graveyards, and obligatory outhouses, this "Great American Railway" as it's dubbed is the creation of computer-game software developer and publisher Bruce Williams Zaccagnino, who, along with his wife Jean, continues to operate Northlandz daily. In addition to the railroad, which has eight miles of track and 300–400 bridges, the 16-acre space is home to a doll museum, art galleries, and a 5,000-pipe theater pipe organ that Zaccagnino often plays. If so much stimulation makes you hungry, stop by Northlandz Club Car Cafe for a hot dog.

Black River & Western Railroad

If you'd rather board a train than watch one, the Black River & Western Railroad (908/996-3300, www.brwrr.com, $14 adult, $7 ages 3–12) runs one-hour, 11-mile round trips between Flemington's Liberty Village Outlets and the town of Ringoes aboard steam and diesel locomotives. Special excursions include Haunted October's corn maze and pumpkin patch excursions, December's North Pole Express, and the occasional Great Train Robbery. Trains leave from Flemington Station at Liberty Village weekend afternoons May–December, and for special excursions year-round.

Recreation

Often described as one of the nation's most professional miniature golf courses, **Pine Creek Miniature Golf** (394 Rte. 31, West Amwell, 609/466-3803, www.pinecreekgolf .com) features two 18-hole courses without any fiberglass fanfare. The upper course is the easier of the two. The course is open weather permitting.

Hunterdon Ballooning (111 Locktown-Flemington Rd., 908/788-5415, www.hunterdon ballooning.com, $215 per person) runs hot air balloon excursions twice a day. Flights last about 45 minutes and include a champagne toast.

Shopping

Flemington has long been New Jersey's outlet capital, although it has lost much of its hype over the last decade or so, especially with the closing of downtown's Flemington Cut Glass, a local institution since 1908. Numerous outlet centers host a mix of stores, a few of which are worth visiting if you're in the area. Traveling between them requires some savvy traffic-circle navigation.

The first outlet mall in the United States is Flemington's **Liberty Village Premium Outlets** (1 Church St., 908/782-8550, www .premiumoutlets.com), an open-air shopping plaza with more than 60 outlet and factory stores, including Harry & David, J. Crew, Cole Haan, and L. L. Bean. Liberty Village is also home to dish and pottery retailers Royal Doulton and Le Creuset. Next door is **Feed Mill Plaza** (Rte. 12, 908/788-3816), home to Roman Jewelers and Bill Healy Crystal.

At the junction of Highways 202 and 31 on the Flemington Circle is **Kitchen Expo Plaza** (Rtes. 202/31, 908/782-7077, www .dansk.com). Formerly called Dansk Plaza, it houses both a Lenox Outlet and the popular California Grill restaurant.

Accommodations

Just off Route 202 one mile west of Flemington's downtown center is the **Hampton**

Inn (14 Royal Rd., 908/284-9427, $129–175), a standard hotel offering continental breakfast and a complimentary 24-hour snack bar with overnight stays. Access to both a heated indoor pool and high-speed Internet (wireless in public areas) is also included.

The centrally located **Main Street Manor** (194 Main St., 908/782-4928, www.main streetmanor.com, $180–215) is an easy walk to Flemington's historic courthouse and downtown restaurants. This Queen Anne Victorian was originally built for the Schenk Family, who've long held a place in local history. The inn features five bright floral-inspired guest rooms, each with air-conditioning, a private bath, and TV, along with first-floor common areas that include Victorian furnished parlors and an arts and crafts–style dining room, where guests are treated to homemade breakfast daily.

Food

While Flemington is not especially known for its restaurants, there are a few worthwhile options. For fine dining, venture outside the borough.

Tucked inside the newly named Kitchen Expo Plaza (formerly Dansk Plaza), **California Grill** (Kitchen Expo Plaza, Rtes. 202/31 Cir., 908/806-7141, www.californiagrillnj.com, Mon.–Fri. 11:30 A.M.–9 P.M., Sat.–Sun. 8 A.M.–9 P.M.) specializes in hearty salads and gourmet pizzas like the White Light, White Heat ($13.95), a three-cheese combo topped with pesto, spinach, mushrooms, and artichoke hearts. A doting staff and a long list of daily specials more than make up for the lacking decor. Locals love the cute and kitschy **Shaker Café** (31 Main St., 908/782-6610, www .shakercafe.com, Mon.–Fri. 7 A.M.–3 P.M., Sun. 9 A.M.–noon, $3.95–12) a BYO serving up simple soups, salads, sandwiches, and breakfasts in the heart of downtown. The café is also open for dinner Friday and Saturday evenings.

In late 2007 well-known area chef and Flemington native Jonas Gold spent three months transforming a downtown ice cream parlor into **55 Main** (55 Main St., 908/284-1551, www.55main.com), a New American

BYO serving internationally inspired dishes such as wasabi seared yellowfin tuna on gingered sticky rice ($25) and herb-crusted cod with anchovy tempura ($23). Seats on the sidewalk patio are best. Lunch is served 11 A.M.–4 P.M. Monday–Friday and dinner 5–9 P.M. Wednesday and Thursday, until 10 P.M. Friday and Saturday.

Nearby Ringoes is home to the **Harvest Moon Inn** (1039 Old York Rd., Ringoes, 908/806-6020, www.harvestmooninn.com, lunch Tues.–Fri. 11:30 A.M.–2:30 P.M., dinner Tues.–Thurs. 5–9:30 P.M., Fri.–Sat. 5–10 P.M., Sun. 1–8 P.M., closed Mon., $19–32), where guests are treated to elegantly prepared New American dishes in a traditional dining setting. The restaurant is housed in a former educational academy and features both a main dining room with seasonally changing entrées, and a tavern where lighter fare (not offered Sat.) and a three-course fixed-price menu (Tues.–Fri. before 6 P.M., $27) are served.

SERGEANTSVILLE

A speck in the larger Delaware Township, Sergeantsville is an inviting village with an old-fashioned **General Store** (609/397-3214) and the state's last pre-20th-century still-standing covered bridge. Downtown (if you can call it that) centers around the intersection of Routes 604 and 523, and the surrounding country roads are ideal for cycling, with light traffic, meandering hills, scenic views, and ample shoulder room.

Green Sergeant's Covered Bridge

While Green Sergeant's Covered Bridge (570 Rosemont-Ringoes Rd., 609/397-3240) is considered New Jersey's only remaining pre-20th-century covered bridge, it's not quite the original structure. The bridge was constructed in 1872 but was taken down after being damaged in 1960. Due to local preservation efforts the bridge was rebuilt a year later from the original materials. Listed on the National Register of Historic Places, it's situated along Route 604 west of Sergeantsville and handles westbound traffic only.

Accommodations

Set back along a country road between Flemington and Sergeantsville is the pet-friendly **Silver Maple Organic Farm and B&B** (483 Sergeantsville Rd., www.silver maplefarm.net, $135–175), a more than 200-year-old farmhouse on 20 acres that are home to chickens, pigs, ducks, and goats. The inn features four themed guest rooms and one suite—all with TV and DVD players, wireless Internet, and a private bath—plus an outdoor swimming pool that's popular with kids. A full country breakfast incorporating the farm's organic veggies and freshly laid eggs is prepared daily and served in the inn's colonial dining room.

Food

Across the street from the General Store is the circa-1734 **Sergeantsville Inn** (1 Rosemont-Ringoes Rd., 609/397-3700, www.sergeantsville inn.com, lunch Tues.–Sat. 11:30 A.M.–3 P.M., dinner Tues. 5–9 P.M., Wed.–Thurs. 5–10 P.M., Fri.–Sat. 4:30–11 P.M., Sun. noon–9 P.M., closed Mon.). This low-ceilinged stone structure was originally built as a private residence, and it was used as a grain shop and ice cream parlor before becoming a restaurant. Entrées such as organic salmon ($26), Kobe steak ($32), and the vegetarian tofu stir-fry ($17) are accompanied by an international wine selection and a martini menu that'll have you handing over the car keys. Lighter fare ($5–13) is offered in the adjoining tavern.

Lambertville and Vicinity

Hunterdon County's only city, Lambertville (www.lambertville.org) is well known for its art galleries, antique shops, and specialty stores, as well as some fine restaurants and a distinctly laid-back attitude. Situated along the Delaware River directly across from New Hope, Pennsylvania, a free auto and footbridge linking the two cities has made this joint destination one of the region's most alluring spots. Fortunately, since New Hope receives the bulk of tourism, Lambertville has retained most of its charm. Brick, stucco, and clapboard-sided Federal row homes—many of them painted in colonial shades of blue, brown, or turquoise—line downtown's streets. Most were originally built for factory workers in the 1800s and now teeter on the edge of sidewalks in varying states of disrepair. During the 1960s a lack of industry and a polluted Delaware caused many Lambertville residents to leave town, ultimately sparing the city's architectural and historic integrity. Its five-block downtown stretch invites afternoon strollers and window-shoppers, although the closer you get to the bridge, the more touristy things become.

Lambertville's "Washington slept here" site stands at 260 North Main Street. Now a private residence, it once belonged to the city's first resident, John Holcombe, who allowed General Washington to set up temporary headquarters here in 1778.

The D&R multiuse towpath runs through Lambertville, connecting the city to smaller towns north. It's an ideal way for outdoor lovers, including walkers, runners, and cyclists, to explore the area. Being a riverfront community, Lambertville is a good place to engage in water sports. Opportunities exist for rafting, tubing, kayaking, canoeing, and river-trolley touring.

SIGHTS

The **Lambertville Historical Society** (609/397-0770, www.lambertvillehistorical society.org) maintains **Marshall House** (62 Bridge St.), the boyhood home of James Wilson Marshall, who along with partner Augustus Sutter discovered gold in California. It's open for tours weekend afternoons April–October or by appointment. The society hosts several additional tours throughout the year, including an October house tour, a June garden tour, and guided city tours the first Sunday of each month beginning at 2 P.M. April–October.

Slightly removed from the city center is the

waterfront **River Horse Brewing Company** (80 Lambert Ln., 609/397-7776, www.river horse.com), a two-story brick brewing facility offering public tastings (daily noon–5 P.M., $1) and self-guided tours. There's also a small gift shop touting Team River Horse bike jerseys and seasonal beer six-packs. The "Hippo," another word for River Horse, sells in eight Northeastern states.

ENTERTAINMENT AND FESTIVALS

Bearing Lambertville's original name, **Coryell's Ferry Boat Rides** (22 S. Main St., New Hope, PA, 215/862-2050) treats guests to half-hour excursions on the Delaware in an open pontoon craft. Rides board across the river in New Hope—a quick walk across the bridge—and leave every 45 minutes, daily 10 A.M.–5:30 P.M. May–September.

April's annual **Shad Festival** celebrates the return of shad, or river herring, to the Delaware River with two days that are "all about the fish." Peruse the arts and crafts booths, settle in for live music and beer, sample local wines, and learn a thing or two about shad preservation.

◖ SHOPPING
Art Galleries and Specialty Shops

Lambertville is home to some of the state's best art. You'll find functional furniture, artisanal glass beads, and sculptures, paintings, and pottery all made by local artists, along with several boutiques selling handcrafted wares. Even if you're just browsing, expect to spend hours perusing the wares.

Down a side street filled with row homes and a former movie house turned apartment complex is **The Coryell Gallery at the Pork Yard** (8 Coryell St., 609/387-0804), an art gallery occupying a renovated sausage factory. For works by local artists, this is the place to come. Independently owned **Phoenix Books** (49 N. Union St., 609/397-4960) stocks a quality selection of rare, used, and out-of-print books specializing in subjects such as mythology, the military, and music. Their maze of stacks also includes cooking aids, mystery novels, and leather-bound books.

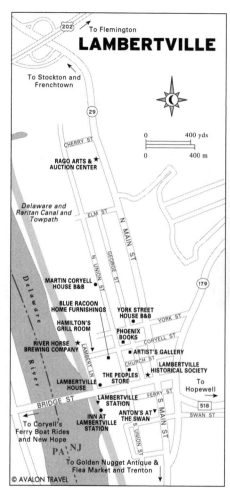

For truly functional folk art stop by **A Mano Inc. Contemporary Craft** (42 N. Union St., 609/397-0063, www.amanogalleries.com), located in Lambertville's former five-and-dime. Coffee tables come with colorful painted-on chess and backgammon boards, and Avner Zabari masterpieces double as chairs. Wearable art and kaleidoscopes are also sold.

Artist-owned and operated **Artist's Gallery** (32 Coryell St., 609/397-4588, www.lambert villearts.com) hosts rotating monthly exhibits by a wide variety of local artists. The gallery also offers classes during spring and fall. Hours are limited to Friday–Sunday 11 A.M.–6 P.M. or by appointment.

At **Antick** (54 N. Union St., 609/773-0287, antickfurnishings.com), master craftsman David Wilson uses traditional techniques to create gorgeous custom-designed replicas of 18th century furniture. The shop also sells handcrafted toys and felt dog portraits.

Greene & Greene Gallery (32 Bridge St., 609/397-7774, www.greeneandgreenegallery .com) displays functional blown glass and fiber arts, along with an intriguing array of jewelry, furniture, and ceramics. For tribal textiles, Czech glass beads, and Chinese dressing tables try **Sojourner** (26 Bridge St., 609/397-8849, www.sojourner.biz). Contemporary narrative painter Valeriy Belenikin displays his evocative still life, portrait, and landscape paintings at **Belenikin Fine Art Gallery** (5 Lambert Ln., 609/397-5855, www.belenikin.com).

After a five-year stint across the Delaware, **Blue Raccoon Home Furnishings** (6 Coryell St., 609/397-5500, www.blueraccoon.com/ about.html) has returned its wide selection of made-to-order upholstery and fabrics along with a distinct furniture and home-furnishing collection to the store's original Lambertville location. While here, keep an eye out for Blue Raccoon's English bulldog mascots, Dottie and Dash.

Antique Stores

South of downtown is the **Golden Nugget Antique and Flea Market** (Rte. 29, 609/397-0811, www.gnmarket.com, Wed., Sat., Sun. 8 A.M.–4 P.M.), an indoor-outdoor venue with 40 permanent shops and up to 200 outdoor vendors touting vinyl records, rare coins, baseball cards, and Pepsi glasses. Inside, browsable shops come crowded with old pinball games, Beanie Babies, and autographed celebrity posters. A few food stalls exist along one of the outdoor paths, including a kettle-corn shop and a small café.

Situated in downtown Lambertville, **The Peoples Store** (28 N. Union St., 609/397-9808) is a three-story co-op plump with secretaries, vintage swimsuits, oil paintings, jewelry, and additionally awesome finds. Travel Main Street north from downtown to reach **Rago Arts and Auction Center** (333 N. Main St., 609/397-9374, www.ragoarts.com), lodging both a private gallery displaying 20th-century crafted wares (call 609/397-1802 for showings) and an auction house hosting approximately 15 events annually, usually during spring and fall. Depending on the sale, items up for grabs may include arts-and-crafts furnishings, Tiffany blown glass, perfume bottles, and estate jewelry. Rago is situated in an old warehouse that once belonged to Jockey Underwear, and its proprietor has been an *Antiques Roadshow* appraiser.

ACCOMMODATIONS $150-300

Set back from Bridge Street along New Jersey's Delaware River bank is the **Inn at Lambertville Station** (11 Bridge St., 609/397-8300, www.lambertvillestation.com, $125–220), a boutique hotel with 45 rooms each individually designed to reflect a different world city. Accommodations range in size from standard to suite, and all include river views and continental breakfast delivered daily to your door. Although it is family friendly, the decor is a bit more formal than your average place.

At the colonial-style **York Street House B&B** (42 York St., 609/397-3007 or 888/398-3199, www.yorkstreethouse.com, $125–275), choose from six uniquely styled guest rooms, each adorned with period fixtures (Room 3 has a speaking tube that connects to the kitchen) and modern amenities like TV and air-conditioning. The inn's spacious lot features both a formal garden and a front porch lined with rocking chairs. Don't miss the full vegetarian breakfast served by candlelight.

The brick Federal-style **Martin Coryell House B&B** (111 N. Union St., 609/397-8981 or 866/397-8981, www.martincoryellhouse .com, $195–279) was once owned by descendents of Lambertville's original founder. Guest rooms are lovely, and each comes equipped with TV and a DVD player, air-conditioning, a writing desk, a private bath, and a fireplace or stove. It's the inn's personal touches, including locally roasted coffee, comfy bathrobes, and a three-course complimentary breakfast, that makes for returning guests.

$300-450

Built in 1812, the historic ◖ **Lambertville House** (32 Bridge St., 32 Bridge St., 888/867-8859, www.lambertvillehouse.com, $290–405) originally served as a stagecoach stop. Today, it's a boutique hotel listed on the National Register of Historic Places, located just a few yards away from the Lambertville–New Hope Bridge. Each of the inn's 26 guest rooms, inspired by the 19th century, features jet tubs and lighted makeup mirrors, and most come with a fireplace. Complimentary continental breakfast is served daily in the hotel's Country Breakfast room, although you can request it room-delivered. Once you see your room, you may not want to leave.

Lambertville's most romantic lodging is the **Chimney Hill Estate and Old Barn** (207 Goat Hill Rd., 609/397-1516 or 800/211-4667, www.chimneyhillinn.com. $215–419), situated on eight acres of property outside downtown proper. This 1820 country inn—popular with wedding parties—features 12 guest rooms and suites, many with fireplaces and all with private baths. The smaller rooms don't have TV or telephone, though you many consider this a plus. Homemade pancakes, French toast, and waffles are served by candlelight daily in the inn's colonial dining room. Saturday stays require a two-night minimum.

FOOD AND NIGHTLIFE

Lambertville offers a wonderful variety of dining options, most located within the city's downtown center.

Located at the foot of New Hope Bridge, **Lambertville Station** (11 Bridge St., 609/397-8300, www.lambertvillestation.com, lunch Mon.–Sat. 11:30 A.M.–3 P.M., dinner Sun.–Thurs. 4–9:30 P.M., Fri.–Sat. 4–11 P.M., brunch Sun. 10 A.M.–3 P.M. with buffet

10:30 A.M.–2:30 P.M., $21–29) is a spacious converted railway house serving substantial American eats in a split-level colonial-themed dining area, with a basement bar and seasonal alfresco seating both along the railway tracks and beside the canal. It's a popular spot for daytrippers; to score an outdoor table, arrive early.

Across the street is the casual **Full Moon Cafe** (23 Bridge St., 609/397-1096, Mon., Wed.–Fri. 8 A.M.–3 P.M., Sat.–Sun. 9 A.M.–4 P.M., closed Tues., $8–12), serving breakfast, lunch, and a weekend brunch known for its omelet selection. Dinner ($18.75–24.75) is offered only on the eve of a full moon.

Downtown's cozy and colorful (literally!) French bistro **Manon** (19 N. Union St., 609/397-2596, Wed.–Sat. 5:30–9 P.M., Sun. 5–8 P.M., closed Mon.–Tues., $20–27) features daily dishes like *poisson du jour* and bouillabaisse, along with a small specials menu. Settle under the *Starry Night*–inspired ceiling with your own bottle of wine and a pocket full of bills—it's cash only, but worth it.

Hidden behind the Coryell Gallery at the Pork Yard, ◖ **Hamilton's Grill Room** (8 Coryell St., 609/397-4343, www.hamiltons grillroom.com, Mon.–Sat. 6–10 P.M., Sun. 5–9 P.M., $18.50–35) specializes in grilled Mediterranean dishes and does so quite well. Meals are served in a lovely white-linen space with warm tile floors and excellent views of the D&R Canal below. Drinks are BYO, or you can enjoy a round across the courtyard while waiting for your reserved table; Saturdays often fill a month in advance.

Along downtown's southern outskirts is the romantic **Anton's at the Swan** (43 S. Main St., 609/397-1960, www.antons-at-the-swan .com, Tues.–Thurs. 6–9 P.M., Fri.–Sat. 6–10 P.M., Sun. 4:30–8 P.M., closed Mon., $15–32), treating guests to a changing menu of innovative American dishes like filet of beef with potatoes and gorgonzola ($32) amid rich colonial decor. The bar stays open an hour later than the restaurant.

Tucked into the basement of Lambertville Station is the **Station Pub** (609/397-8300), a cozy space decked in dark wood and pine-green leather booths. Grab a cocktail at the oval bar and settle in for one of Thursday night's local performances, or take advantage of the free Wi-Fi hookup. More live entertainment plays throughout the weekend, and a casual dining menu ($7–15) is available daily.

Nestled along the brownstone courtyard across from Hamilton's Grill Room is the **Boat House** (8½ Coryell St., 609/397-2244, Mon.–Sat. from 4 P.M., Sun. from 2 P.M.), a small bar adorned with old photos and paintings. Outdoor seating is available when weather permits.

GETTING THERE AND AROUND

To reach Lambertville from Flemington or Sergeantsville, take Route 523 southwest to Stockton, turning left on Route 29 and continuing south for nearly four miles. Lambertville is 15 miles north of Trenton, 70 miles southwest of New York City, and 40 miles northeast of Philadelphia. Buses are available from Trenton and several other points. Once here, visitors should have little trouble finding their way around downtown—plenty of signs point the way to shops and eateries. Lambertville's downtown streets have four-hour metered parking.

Trenton connects to Lambertville, as well as Stockton and Frenchtown to the north, by way of Route 29, a mostly pleasant two-lane drive. The stretch between Trenton and Lambertville can be dicey, with plenty of twists and traffic and hardly a shoulder. For this portion I recommend traveling Route 31 north from Trenton and connecting with Route 518 toward Lambertville instead. It is a bit out of the way, but worth it to avoid anxiety.

STOCKTON

About a 10-minute drive north of Lambertville is the much smaller Stockton, once known as Howell's Ferry, a charming river community with a few worthwhile shops and eateries. The town's center is at Main (Rte. 29) and Bridge Streets, where a free auto and pedestrian bridge crosses the Delaware, connecting the town with Pennsylvania's Center Bridge. Stockton is a popular stop for cyclists riding the D&R towpath through town, en route from Lambertville north to Frenchtown.

A nice reprieve from more touristy Lambertville, Stockton is a perfect place to put your feet up and sip a beer while the sun descends. Parking is free, and public restrooms are hard to come by.

Prallsville Mills

North of Stockton's town center, **Prallsville Mills** (Rte. 29 N., 908/397-3586) is a 19th-century mill complex once operated as part of the Delaware and Raritan Canal. Maintained by the Delaware River Mill Society, the property includes an 1877 stone mill (built to replace an early-18th-century wooden grist mill), an old grain silo, a sawmill, and the original machinery used to operate them. Today, the site hosts various artists and antique vendors, as well as events such as individual art shows and rummage sales, throughout the year.

Accommodations

Downtown's **Stockton Inn** (1 Main St., 609/397-1250, www.stocktoninn.com, $135–195) offers 11 newly renovated guest rooms, some above its historic eatery and others spread throughout the Carriage House, Wagon House, and Federal House. Most rooms include a fireplace. The Carriage House bedroom, with an outside porch, and the Stockton Suite, with Ralph Lauren bedding, are two of the nicest.

Situated on 300 acres of preserved farmland and forest east of downtown Stockton is the romantic ◖ **Woolverton Inn** (6 Woolverton Rd., 609/397-0802, www.woolvertoninn.com, $170–425), a 1792 stone manor estate with seven guest rooms, five cottages, and a guest loft. Each overnight stay comes with a three-course country breakfast, delivered to your room on request, as well as fluffy robes, a private bath, wireless Internet, and a complimentary copy of the *New York Times* Monday–Saturday. The lodging is some of the area's finest.

Food

Originally operated as an 18th-century stagecoach stop, the imposing **Colligan's Stockton**

Inn (1 Main St., 609/397-1250, www.stockton inn.com, $12–28) stands at the end of Bridge Street keeping watch over Stockton's small center. This three-story stone structure features hardwood floors, fireplaces, murals, a low-slung tavern, a front dining porch, and in back, a small waterfall and wishing well that served as inspiration for Rodgers and Hart's Broadway tune "There's a Small Hotel with a Wishing Well." While hearty American dishes are well prepared, the inn's real reputation comes from its historic significance. Reporters congregated here when covering the famous Lindbergh baby kidnapping trial in nearby Flemington, and writers Dorothy Parker, F. Scott Fitzgerald, and their Algonquin Round Table associates used the inn as a country meeting place. The inn was closed for a brief time in 2006 due to flooding but reopened under new ownership soon after. Guest rooms are available above the restaurant.

For comfort food there's no better place than **Meil's** (Bridge and Main Sts., 609/397-8033, www.meilsrestaurant.com, Sun.–Thurs. 8 A.M.–9 P.M., Fri.–Sat. 8 A.M.–10 P.M.). Grab a table by the baked goods and admire the Shad Fest poster collection while your chicken pot-pie ($14.75) cooks. Really hungry? Go for the Thanksgiving dinner ($24): turkey breast, mashed potatoes, stuffing, and cranberry sauce served year-round.

For a newspaper, mints, or a picnic lunch swing by **Stockton Food Store** (12 Bridge St., 609/397-0049), located alongside the B&R Towpath in Stockton's original train depot. Customers tend to bring their bikes along and set up at one of the outdoor tables for a mid-day reprieve.

Northeast of Stockton is the superb **Cafe at Rosemont** (88 Kingwood-Stockton Rd., Rosemont, 609/397-4097, www.cafeatrosemont .com, Tues.–Wed., Fri. 11 A.M.–9 P.M., Thurs. 11 A.M.–3 P.M., Sat.–Sun. 9 A.M.–9 P.M., closed Mon., $9–24), a comfy eatery with an ever-changing menu and daily blackboard specials. The café is known for its weekend brunch and as a stop-off for cyclists taking area rides. Wednesday's "Eat Global, Drive Local"

menu highlights three-course selections from a different country's cuisine each week. Past weeks have highlighted China, Australia, and Portugal.

Shopping

Family-owned and operated **Phillips' Fine Wines** (Bridge St., 609/397-0587, www.phillips finewines.com) features an extraordinary— and seemingly endless—selection of spirits, brews (including the Lambertville-based River Horse), and wines.

DELAWARE AND RARITAN CANAL STATE PARK

D&R Canal State Park (732/873-3050, www .dandrcanal.com, daily sunrise–sunset) includes nearly 70 miles of the original Delaware and Raritan Canal—built for freight-carrier transport between Pennsylvania and New York beginning in the early 1800s—including 22 miles of feeder canal connecting Frenchtown to Trenton. Thousands of Irish immigrants constructed the canal, and when dozens of them died from a cholera outbreak, they were buried on the nearby hillsides. The canal reached its peak in the 1860s and 1870s before losing business to railroads and closing permanently in 1932. What was left of the canal was placed on the National Register of Historic Places in 1973, and the entire V-shaped footprint was declared a state park in 1974. The D&R Canal stretches from Trenton (where it has been filled in) east to New Brunswick, and its feeder canal runs from Trenton north to Frenchtown. One of the park's most popular attractions is a towpath running alongside the feeder portion, west of Route 29 and parallel to the Delaware River. This multiuse path is used by all levels of cyclists, walkers, joggers, and in-line skaters, and offers an excellent auto travel alternative between Hunterdon County's riverfront towns.

Along both the canal's main and feeder portions, look for bridge tender houses, locks, and the occasional fossil find. Canoe and kayak rentals for paddling the canal's intact portions are available in Princeton (609/452-2403, $13 one-hour canoe, $16 one-hour 2-person kayak) and Central Jersey's Griggstown (908/359-5970, $13 one-hour canoe, $16 one-hour 2-person kayak).

Camping

D&R's only camping facilities are located just west of Stockton on **Bull's Island** (2185 Daniel Bray Hwy./Rte. 29, 609/397-2949, Apr. 1–Oct. 31, $20), a sizable island between the canal and the Delaware River. There are 69 tent and trailer sites with access to drinking water, restrooms, and showers. Picnic tables are plentiful, and a modern information center stocked with brochures is located nearby. Area flooding has caused the closure of Bull's Island several times recently. Check the park's website at www.dandrcanal.com for a current update.

Information and Services

The D&R's **Feeder Canal Office** (Rte. 29, 609/397-2949) is located by the lock near Bull's Island. The **Main Canal Office** (625 Canal Rd., 732/873-3050) is in Somerset. Dogs must be leashed in D&R State Park, and alcohol is not permitted.

Bull's Island has footbridge access to both New Jersey and Pennsylvania. The park has 30 access points, each with parking. These include spots in Trenton, New Brunswick, Lambertville, and Princeton. Delaware River access points (for electric motorboats) exist at Bull's Island and in Lambertville. Boats, including canoes and kayaks, are required to portage at all locks and at some bridges.

FRENCHTOWN

Frenchtown was named for Henri Mallet-Prevost, a French-speaking man from Switzerland. In 1805 Prevost built the town's first hotel where the Frenchtown Inn stands today, at the foot of the Pennsylvania Bridge. The little town boomed with the railroads but declined during the Depression, a development that ended up preserving its architecture appeal. Frenchtown remains an enclave for area artists, and New Yorkers searching out second homes have found their way here in recent years. Downtown is easily walkable and extremely

pleasant, lined by a series of colorful clapboards, stand-alone Victorians, and brick structures hosting a nice array of shops, galleries, and eateries. The town seems to have suffered a bit over the last few years, with high retail turnover and the closing of the National Hotel, a top-pick in this guidebook's last edition. Recent area floods are a likely cause for the change.

Shopping

Tucked along Race Street's brick-paved "Cartoon Corner" is **Stone & Company Antiques** (8 Race St., 908/996-4840), a shop overflowing with antique birdcages, textiles, and country decor. **The Studio** (19 Bridge St., 908/996-7424, http://greathomestyle.com/store/) stocks a varied selection of European-inspired furnishings alongside coffee-table books, music, and baby gifts. **Brooks Antiques** (24 Bridge St., 908/996-7161) features hooked rugs, ceramic dishware, hand-stitched dolls, dressers, and folk art paintings.

Frenchtown's art galleries include **Kissimmee River Pottery** (1 8th St., 908/996-3555, www.kissimmeeriverpottery.com), a pottery studio and gallery displaying functional ceramic pieces. Classes, workshops, and private studio time are offered throughout the year. Packed to the gills with fish and bird carvings, paintings, and bronze sculptures, **Decoys and Wildlife Gallery** (55 Bridge St., 908/996-6501, http://decoyswildlife.com) also offers custom framing as well as hosting annual events, including an open house each February.

Clothing boutiques include **Blue Fish at Barclay Studio** (62 Trenton Ave., 908/996-3720, www.barclaystudio.com). Located just south of the downtown center, Blue Fish sells hand-blocked natural-fiber collections that are easy to mix-match and layer. **Alchemy Creative Clothing and Gallery** (17 Bridge St., 908/996-9000, www.alchemyclothing.com) features the works of more than 50 designers of men's and women's clothing, as well as scarves, bags, shoes, and jewelry. The selection ranges from casual to glamorous, and clothing can be custom-suited. Rotating art exhibits are hosted year-round.

Stop by **Minette's Candies** (43 Bridge St., 908/996-5033) for all your truffle and fudge needs.

The well-kept **Beasley's Bookbindery** (106 Harrison St., 908/996-9993, www.beasleys bookbindery.com) can rebind your tattered copy of *For Whom the Bell Tolls.* They also sell handmade stationery and desk sets inspired by Beasley, or "the Baron of Kingwood," a wrinkly-faced pug born in 2003. Book signings and demonstrations take place year-round. Housed in a lovely 19th-century blue Victorian is the cozy **Book Garden** (28 Bridge St., 908/996-2022, www.bookgarden.biz), a multiroom store stocking both new and used books. The shop features an impressive local-interest selection, as well as a kids section and some window-side chairs for reading. Owner and proprietor Esther Tews opened the shop in 1999 after retiring from more than 20 years in health care. Her book sales contribute to the *New York Times* best-seller list.

For country decor, including ceramics, Americana, and faux fruits and vegetables try **Thistle** (38 Bridge St., 908/996-7080, www .shopthistle.com). **Nelson Bridge** (29 Race St., 908/996-6646, www.nelsonbridge.com) is a dream for modern-design lovers. The shop sells chaise longues, vortex benches, and lasso stools in geometric shapes and vibrant colors, along with coats, watches, and kitchenware. Some items have to be custom ordered, so check their website or call ahead.

Sports and Recreation

On hot and humid summer days, nothing beats drifting along the Delaware River in an inner tube. **Delaware River Tubing** (2998 Daniel Bray Hwy., 908/996-5386, www.delaware rivertubing.com), just south of Frenchtown, supplies the tubes, as well as pickup and drop-off transport on the river. Excursions run up to four hours in length, and include a meal from the "River Hot Dog Man" (www.river hotdogman.com)—a vendor providing snacks, sweets, sodas, and simple lunches from a floating stand en route. Groups leave weekdays between 10 A.M.–3 P.M., and weekends 9 A.M.–4 P.M. throughout summer. The cost is $17.95 adult weekday, $21.95 weekends. The company also offers six-person rafting trips along the Delaware ($22.95 adult weekdays, $27.95 weekends).

Across the river about seven miles south is **Bucks County River Country** (2 Waters Ln., Point Pleasant, PA, 215/297-5000, www .rivercountry.net), featuring kayaking and canoeing trips in addition to rafting and tubing. "Snuggle tubes" are available for lovebirds or parents traveling with kids, and full-moon night boating is occasionally offered for those 18 and over. Visit the website for exact dates and times. Seasonal two-, three-, and four-hour tubing excursions cost $18 weekdays ($21 snuggle tube), $21 weekends ($23 snuggle tube), and a four-hour rafting trip runs $22–25. A two-person canoe is $30 for six miles, a single kayak $35, and a tandem kayak $40. Sit-on-top kayaks range $41–45. Food is available.

The D&R Feeder Canal Towpath, stretching from Frenchtown south to Trenton, offers scenic cycling for bicyclists of all skill levels. If you haven't brought your own bike, stop by **Cycle Corner Bicycle Shop** (52 Bridge St., 908/996-7712, www.thecyclecorner.com) to rent one. The shop supplies mostly Giant sport and comfort mountain bikes, as well as youth bikes, tandems, kiddie trailers, and both a Revive and a recumbent. Rentals range $20–30 for two hours to $45–60 for a full day, and include a lock and a helmet. The shop also offers repairs, and is a popular meeting spot for local cyclists.

Yogis seek refuge at downtown's **Yoga Loka** (34 Bridge St. Suite 2, 908/268-7430, www .yoga-loka.com), a multiple skill-level Vinyasa studio hosting drop-in classes for $16. Pilates classes ($14) and meditation workshops (donation) are also available. Following your workout, stop by **Euphoria Studio** (15 Trenton Ave., 908/996-3399, www.euphoriastudio.com) for a custom massage ($90 for 70 min.) or deep-cleansing facial ($75 for 60 min.).

Accommodations

Housed in an 1878 Italianate Victorian, the wonderfully relaxing **Widow McCrea Bed**

& Breakfast (53 Kingwood Ave., 908/996-4999, www.widowmccrea.com, $100–220) features five antique-filled rooms and suites, along with a small private cottage, gardens, and a guest patio. Each overnight stay comes with a gourmet breakfast by candlelight and a complimentary bottle of wine. Light sleepers may want to request a room in back to avoid possible street noise.

Removed from downtown's center is the two-story **Guesthouse at Frenchtown** (85 Ridge Rd., 908/996-7474, www.french townguesthouse.com, $165–185), an 18th-century colonial available for single-family or two-couple overnight stays or long-term rentals. The 70-acre property includes its own hiking trail and a small outdoor dining area, and inside the home is a living room, fully equipped kitchen prestocked with breakfast goodies, and two bedrooms each with a queen bed, air-conditioning, cable TV, and a bath. There's a two-night minimum stay on weekends ($185); weekly rates run $1,100–1,300 during summer and holiday high seasons.

Food
Frenchtown is a good place to stop for a bite to eat, with several dining choices ranging from casual to upscale.

Built in 1838 on the site of the borough's first inn, **Frenchtown Inn** (7 Bridge St., 908/996-3300, www.frenchtowninn .com, $24–36) features the superb French-inspired culinary works of chef and owner Andrew Tomko. The historic space is home to three former dining rooms (lunch Tues.– Sat. noon–2 P.M., Sun. noon–3 P.M., dinner Tues.–Fri. 6–9 P.M., Sat. 5:30–9:15 P.M., Sun. 5–8 P.M., closed Mon.), along with a more casual bar-grill room (Tues.–Fri. 5–9 P.M., Sun. 3–8 P.M., closed Mon.) and seasonal outdoor seating. Reservations and proper attire are musts for the main dining areas.

Across from the inn is the **Bridge Café** (8 Bridge St., 908/996-6040, www.bridgecafe .net, Mon.–Thurs. 7 A.M.–3 P.M., Fri.–Sat. 7 A.M.–9 P.M., Sun. 7 A.M.–5 P.M., $7–12), a casual eatery and coffeehouse occupying Frenchtown's original train depot. Dine on healthy eats or fresh baked goods indoors or alfresco. They also serve ice cream.

Local residents can't say enough about **Cocina Del Sol** (10 Bridge St., 908/996-0900, Tues.–Thurs. 5–9:30 P.M., Fri.–Sat. 11:30 A.M.–3 P.M. and 5–10 P.M., Sun. 11:30 A.M.–3 P.M. and 5–8 P.M., $13–17.50), a Mexican BYO occupying a cozy basement space in the historic Gem Building. It's both the oldest and one of the few Mexican restaurants in the region.

If romance if what you're after, try **Race Street Cafe** (2 Race St., 908/996-3179, Thurs.– Sat. 10:30 A.M.–9 P.M., Sun. 10:30 A.M.–8 P.M., $18–26), a tiny BYO whose signature dishes include maple-glazed Long Island duckling and Maryland crab cakes, although the homemade menu changes weekly. Thursday is locals' night, with $12 home-style specials.

Getting There and Around
Frenchtown is midway between New York City and Philly, approximately 90 minutes each way. Buses from New York City's Port Authority Bus Terminal take one hour 45 minutes.

Deer are common along Route 29 between Stockton and Frenchtown. Remain alert while driving, especially at dusk and dawn. Sheer cliffs line the road to the east, and a few homes are tucked so closely to the ridge that they look as though they've been carved from rock.

MILFORD
About five miles north of Frenchtown is Milford, a small river community situated at the foot of a tree-covered bluff. Like the towns to its south, Milford has a bridge at the end of its main thoroughfare crossing into Pennsylvania. Larger than Stockton but smaller than Frenchtown, Milford's downtown's has notably improved over the last few years. More shops and eateries have moved onto Bridge Street, including natural-food store Healthy Habits and the Lovin' Oven bakery. With its mansard-roofed Victorians and forested backdrop, the town looks like it should exist somewhere along Oregon's coast.

Milford is home to a couple of wonderful restaurants and a darling B&B.

Accommodations

A short walk from the bustle of Bridge Street is the ◖ **Chestnut Hill on the Delaware** (63 Church St., 908/995-9761, www.chest nuthillnj.com, $115–275), a wonderful B&B with a riverfront deck where you can literally spend hours watching the waters pass by. Innkeepers Rob and Linda begrudgingly moved to New Jersey on a corporate assignment in 1982, turning a three-year stint into more than 20. They're only the third family to own the inn and have poured themselves into it, modernizing the kitchen but keeping the living area strictly Victorian. A large veranda overlooks the water, and the guest rooms—all with private baths, wireless Internet, and TV—are sizable enough for two.

Food and Entertainment

Milford is home to New Jersey's first brewpub, **The Ship Inn Restaurant and Brew Pub** (61 Bridge St., 908/995-0188, www.shipinn.com). Established in 1995, the building has been around since the late 1800s, previously operating as both a bakery and an ice cream parlor. The inn serves authentic British pub food (the owners are British) like three-piece fish and chips ($15.95) and shepherd's pie ($12.95), along with craft-brewed ales. They also offer a small organic menu. Three dining areas include one with brick walls and tin ceilings and "the deck," featuring window-side tables made from World War II–era ships' hatch covers, overlooking **Milford Creek.** Food is served Monday–Saturday noon–10 P.M., Sunday noon–9 P.M.

A great place for dinner, **Milford Oyster House** (92 Rte. 519, 908/995-9411, www .milfordoysterhouse.com, Wed.–Thurs., Sun.–Mon. 5–9 P.M., Fri.–Sat. 5–10 P.M., closed Tues., $20–30) specializes in seafood, with a small selection of meat dishes. The dining room features exposed stone walls and a fireplace. Casual diners will prefer the on-site tavern for burgers ($5.95), onion rings ($4.95), and an ice-cold brew.

Getting There

Route 29 ends at Frenchtown. To reach Milford, hop on Route 619, which turns into CR-519/Frenchtown Rd./CR-14 after about 3.5 miles. Stay straight to Bridge Street, a six-minute drive.

PHILLIPSBURG

Warren County's largest town is 3.2-square-mile Phillipsburg or "P-burg," as it's referred to locally, a longstanding transportation hub. In 1998, Phillipsburg was chosen as future site of the New Jersey Transportation Heritage Center, a "theme park" honoring New Jersey's transportation history. Like many worthwhile projects, the center is currently on hold. P-burg is already home to a couple of railway centers along with two bridges (one free, one toll) into Pennsylvania, and the town runs a scenic steam train for residents and visitors. Brimming with old brick buildings and weathered Victorian homes, P-burg looks like little more than an industrial river town, but insiders claim it is undergoing rebirth.

Currently, downtown is a designated Urban Enterprise Zone, meaning sales tax is lowered to 3 percent to aid with revitalization. Phillipsburg's historic business district, Union Square, lies just beyond the free bridge, with the Easton-Phillipsburg Toll Bridge a few blocks north.

P-burg's cast-iron Bullman Street Stairway

For history, transportation, and train buffs, a visit to Phillipsburg is a must. While in town, keep your eyes peeled for the **Bullman Street Stairway,** 100 steps leading clear up the hillside from Main Street, just south of Union Square. This cast-iron stairway has been a part of downtown P-burg since the early 1900s.

Transportation Museums

Phillipsburg is currently home to three railway organizations. The **Phillipsburg Railway Historians** (www.prrh.org, Sun. 10 A.M.–3 P.M., free) run a small renovated museum preserving local railway history, located atop the hill on South Main Street and open to the public Sundays throughout the summer. They also operate a miniature railway on summer weekends. Admission is free to ride the train and enter the museum, although donations are accepted. The **New York, Susquehanna and Western Technical and Historical Society** (877/872-4674, www.nyswths.org) operates Delaware River Railroad Excursions aboard open-window steam trains between P-burg and Carpentersville on weekends 11 A.M.–3 P.M. May–October ($14 adult, $7 child). Santa and Easter Bunny trains pull out of the station at appropriate times of the year.

The **Friends of New Jersey Transportation Heritage Center** (178 S. Main St., admin@njthc.org, www.njthc.org, Sat.–Sun. 11 A.M.–4 P.M., free) runs a small exhibit space and welcome center at a former passenger station stop for the Central Railroad of New Jersey and the Delaware. There's a model train display and photos of P-burg during its transportation heyday.

Festivals and Events

Each July Phillipsburg hosts the annual **Ole Town Festival** (www.phillipsburgdowntown .org), a local celebration with food, crafts, music and dance, and carnival rides, concluding with a fireworks display. The town also hosts the **Criterium Bike Race** (www .pburgcrit.com) each September.

Steam Train Excursions (100 Elizabeth St., www.877trainride.com, $14 adult, $7

child) along the Delaware River take place weekends May–October, leaving from downtown Phillipsburg. Additional rides are offered during the Christmas and Easter holiday seasons, and a corn maze train runs in fall.

Sports and Recreation

Warren County is another popular spot for hot-air ballooning. Two to try are **Balloonatics and Aeronuts** (7 Harmony-Brass Castle Rd., 908/454-3431 or 877/438-6359, www.aero nuts.com, $275 individual, $525 couple), with daily flights that often head over the Delaware River into Pennsylvania, and **Have Balloon Will Travel** (57 Old Belvidere Rd., 908/454-1991, www.haveballoonwilltravel.com, $525 couple, $210 each for 4 or more), sailing above Warren and Hunterdon Counties.

Downtown Phillipsburg's **Cycle Funattic** (403 S. Main St., 908/454-0432, www.cyclefunattic .com) hosts weekly group bike rides on Sunday mornings, leaving from the shop at 9 A.M.

Food

Opened in February 2006, **The Union Station Grill** (9 Union Sq., 908/387-1380, www.theunionstationgrill.com, Tues.–Thurs. 3–9 P.M., Fri.–Sat. 11:30 A.M.–10 P.M., Sun. 11:30 A.M.–8 P.M., closed Mon., $16–28) serves upscale meat, fish, and poultry dishes in a spacious dining room and bar; but for a true experience request a table in the renovated train car, former Penn Central coach number 1420.

For an easy meal, try **Jimmy's on the Delaware** (7 Union Sq., 908/454-2999, jimmysonthedelaware.com, Tues.–Sun. 11 A.M.–9 P.M., $1–8), situated at the foot of the Easton–Philipsburg free bridge. Jimmy's, named for a beloved hot dog stand that stood in its place more than a decade before, serves up hot dogs, burgers, soft drinks, and milkshakes at unbeatable prices.

Getting There

To reach Phillipsburg from Milford, take Route 519 for four miles and turn left onto South Main Street (NJ 122). It's about a 25-minute drive, most of it along scenic rolling hills.

THE JERSEY SHORE

For nearly two centuries, New Jersey's 127-mile Atlantic coastline has been a favorite vacation destination for Northeast travelers, and more recently, Canadians and Europeans. There's no denying that the Shore has got it going on. Every summer, New Yorkers and Pennsylvanians clog New Jersey's roadways, along with our own "bennies" and "shoobies," heading towards surf, sun, and fun that only exists along boardwalks and in the shore's casinos, restaurants, bars, and bays. Ladies slick back their locks trying to prevent the inevitable frizz, while guys ditch the suits for flip-flops and shorts. A week's worth of clothes fit into a weekend tote bag—coverage is minimal in the sticky shore heat. Blankets appear along beaches, parked with giant umbrellas and low-slung chairs, as kids break out the buckets and shovels, moms lather on the lotion, and paddleball players pair up along the rising tide. Banner planes advertising dollar drafts and surf-and-turf specials fly slowly overhead.

The Jersey Shore consists mostly of low-lying barrier islands surrounded by back bays and wetlands, although a few towns are located on the mainland. Beaches are sandy, and many have scrub-covered western dunes acting as barriers to high tides and storms. Erosion is a problem all along the shore. Cities and towns are constantly replenishing their beaches with money partially raised through beach tag sales, only to see their efforts washed away with the next big storm. Collecting shells is a popular beach activity. Most beaches are loaded with clam, conch, and oyster shells, and depending on month, the armor of horseshoe crabs and jellyfish.

© LAURA KINIRY

THE JERSEY SHORE

HIGHLIGHTS

◖ Sandy Hook and the Highlands: Where else in New Jersey can you swim in the ocean (naked, if you like) and bask in the backdrop of Manhattan (page 129)?

◖ Spring Lake: Calling to mind the grandeur of the Jersey Shore past, this elegant and classy beachfront town is the perfect spot to take a step back in time (page 146).

◖ Barnegat Lighthouse State Park: Tucked up in Long Beach Island's northern tip, this tiny state park is home to one of New Jersey's most endearing lighthouses, Old Barney, a 217-step watchtower offering unbeatable views (page 157).

◖ Atlantic City's Casinos: Move over, Vegas, the AC is back with a new slew of shopping, restaurants, spas, and hotels. And with its long-established rep as a sparkling senior center, there's nowhere to go but up (page 171).

◖ Lucy the Elephant: New Jersey's iconic pachyderm has weathered well over 100 years along Margate's coast, having done stints as a tavern and private residence before opening up as a museum. With a new coat of paint and freshly touched-up toenails, she has no plans to retire her trunk (page 183).

◖ Ocean City: The best little Shore town on this side of the country. My nephew thinks his granddad owns the boardwalk because of all the time my father spends there. Oh, how I wish he did (page 186).

◖ Wildwoods Boardwalk: As experiences go, this two-mile waterfront stretch – packed with amusements, stuffed prizes, fried-food stands, tacky T-shirt shops, and one of the surliest tram cars around – is unbeatable. Pair it with the neon lights and plastic palms of the surrounding doo-wop motels, and you've got yourself one kitschy weekend (page 198).

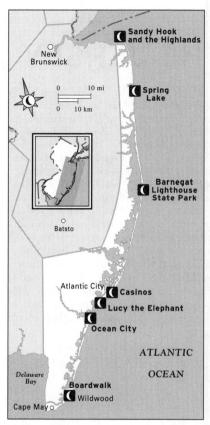

LOOK FOR ◖ TO FIND RECOMMENDED SIGHTS, ACTIVITIES, DINING, AND LODGING.

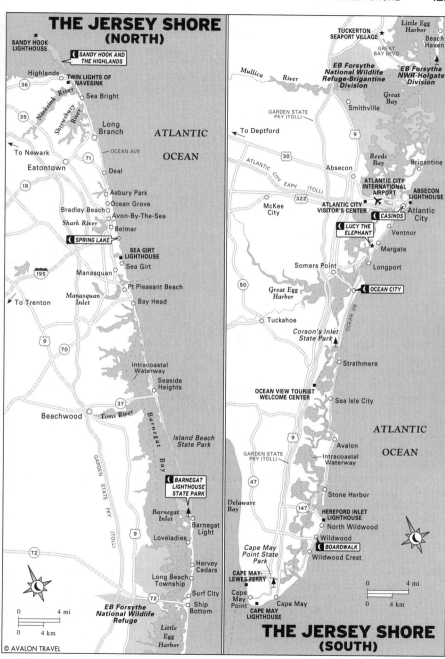

THE JERSEY SHORE (NORTH)

SANDY HOOK LIGHTHOUSE

SANDY HOOK AND THE HIGHLANDS

Highlands
TWIN LIGHTS OF NAVESINK
36
Sea Bright
35
Navesink River
Shrewsbury River

Long Branch

ATLANTIC OCEAN

To Newark
71
OCEAN AVE
Eatontown
Deal
18
Asbury Park
Ocean Grove
Bradley Beach
Avon-By-The-Sea
Shark River
Belmar
SPRING LAKE
195
SEA GIRT LIGHTHOUSE
Manasquan
Sea Girt
Manasquan Inlet
Pt Pleasant Beach
To Trenton
Bay Head
9
70

Intracoastal Waterway
Seaside Heights
37
Beachwood
Toms River
Island Beach State Park
Barnegat Bay
GARDEN STATE PKY (TOLL)
BARNEGAT LIGHTHOUSE STATE PARK
Barnegat Inlet
Barnegat Light
Loveladies
9
Harvey Cedars
72
Long Beach Township
Surf City
72
Ship Bottom
EB Forsythe National Wildlife Refuge
Little Egg Harbor

0   4 mi
0   4 km
© AVALON TRAVEL

TUCKERTON SEAPORT VILLAGE
Little Egg Harbor
Beach Haven
GREAT BAY BLVD
EB Forsythe National Wildlife Refuge-Brigantine Division
EB Forsythe NWR-Holgate Division
Mullica   River
Great Bay
Smithville
GARDEN STATE PKY (TOLL)
To Deptford
9
Reeds Bay
Brigantine
30
ATLANTIC CITY EXPY (TOLL)
Absecon
ATLANTIC CITY INTERNATIONAL AIRPORT
ABSECON LIGHTHOUSE
322
McKee City
ATLANTIC CITY VISITOR'S CENTER
CASINOS
Atlantic City
LUCY THE ELEPHANT
Ventnor
Margate
Somers Point
Longport
50
Great Egg Harbor
OCEAN CITY
Tuckahoe
OCEAN DR
Corson's Inlet State Park
Strathmere
OCEAN VIEW TOURIST WELCOME CENTER
Sea Isle City
ATLANTIC OCEAN
9
Avalon
Intracoastal Waterway
47
GARDEN STATE PKY (TOLL)
Stone Harbor
147
HEREFORD INLET LIGHTHOUSE
Delaware Bay
North Wildwood
Wildwood
BOARDWALK
Cape May Point State Park
Wildwood Crest
CAPE MAY-LEWES FERRY
Cape May Point
Cape May
CAPE MAY LIGHTHOUSE

0   4 mi
0   4 km

THE JERSEY SHORE (SOUTH)

THE JERSEY SHORE

Though New Jersey's native Lenape Indians spent time at the shore, the region didn't start becoming today's seaside resort until the 1850s, when railways bridged the gap between cities and beaches. At the same time, religious groups were establishing summer camps along the coast. The spiritual roots of places like Ocean City and Ocean Grove are evident along today's downtown streets, which don't allow liquor sales.

The Jersey Shore isn't *all* sun and games. Over the years, hundreds of shipwrecks have occurred off its coast; and in 1916, one of history's worst shark attacks took place in its waters. The Shore made news in the 1980s, when hospital-discarded hypodermic needles began washing up along its beaches. And more recently a local poll concluded that many people find the shore unfriendly (most people citing the "Jersey" attitude as the problem).

The Shore is a big place, and every New Jerseyan knows that a shore town or city can say a lot about you. While partiers head to Seaside Heights, Wildwood, and Belmar, families frequent Point Pleasant Beach and Ocean City. Couples tend to visit Spring Lake and Cape May, offering the best selection of bed-and-breakfasts statewide. Live music lovers make the drive to Asbury Park, and anyone preferring ritzy clubs and a little luxe (not to mention gambling) head to Atlantic City. New Yorker's stick to the Northern Shore while Philadelphians head to the Cape; the two meet up somewhere along Long Beach Island.

The best boardwalks—those with rides, souvenir shops, and deep-fried funnel cake—are in Point Pleasant, Seaside Heights, Atlantic City, Ocean City, and Wildwood; most towns without destination walkways, however, offer plenty of recreational activities to keep you occupied.

Remember, you don't have to be born in New Jersey to enjoy the Shore. Some locals may roll their eyes at weekenders "clogging" the beaches and stealing parking spots, but the shore belongs to everyone. So come Memorial Day, why not join the masses, heed the call, and head down the Shore? It's a bona fide Jersey experience.

PLANNING YOUR TIME

The Shore includes dozens of towns and cities with varying personalities. It's not a place you can, or should try to, cover in one visit. Most travelers stick to a particular town or region, though you may want to drive along the coast visiting highlights over the course of a week. One thing about the shore: It's versatile. It makes a perfect day trip, weekend escape, or seasonal excursion. But if your time is limited—say a day or weekend—choose a section near where you begin.

If arriving from New York City, stick to the Northern Shore or Barnegat Peninsula. Sandy Hook makes a good car-free day trip: It's accessible by ferry from Manhattan (summer only), and from there a bus will bring you to various peninsula points. For those traveling by car, continue the day with a coastal drive from Sea Bright to Spring Lake, a good place to stop if you're planning an overnight trip. Since prices at Spring Lake's bed-and-breakfasts can be steep during high season, consider backtracking to Ocean Grove for more affordable rates. On day 2, continue down the coast to Point Pleasant Beach for a stroll on family-friendly Jenkinson's Boardwalk. Or, for something a bit wilder, head into Seaside Heights for an afternoon at Breakwater Beach water park followed by a round of miniature golf and some wonderful people watching. The Garden State Parkway offers a quick return route to New York City.

From Philadelphia you'll get the most out of a day or weekend trip to the Cape or Long Beach Island. Cape May is a great spot for daytrippers. Enjoy breakfast in the city's historic district or at one of the beachfront eateries, then visit the Washington Mall Information Booth for details on the day's events and seats on one of the afternoon tours. Peruse the nearby shops, stroll along the Promenade, or admire the Victorian architecture before returning for your afternoon excursion. Following the tour you have a couple options: drive to Sunset Beach and search for Cape May diamonds before visiting nearby Cape May Lighthouse, or travel Ocean Drive north to Wildwood's boardwalk for pizza slices and people watching. Extend your day trip into a weekend and you can do it all. It's worth it just to spend a night in one of Cape May's several dozen Victorian B&Bs.

Many Jersey Shore establishments are shuttered in the off-season (Oct.–Apr.). For year-round Shore attractions, your best bets are Atlantic City and Cape May. With casinos, nightlife, shopping, and fine restaurants, it's easy to spend a weekend in Atlantic City without ever leaving, but if you're going a bit stir-crazy, head onto the mainland for tastings at one of the nearby wineries. As in summer, Cape May offers trolley tours and events throughout the Christmas holiday season. January and February are both quiet months, but things tend to pick up again come March.

During the height of summer many Shore accommodations require a 2–3 night minimum stay, usually on weekends. If possible, it's best to plan an overnight trip mid-week—accommodations are at their cheapest Tuesday–Thursday evenings. Take note that many dining establishments, especially along boardwalks, are cash-only.

Most Shore towns, including Belmar, Bradley Beach, Point Pleasant Beach, Beach Haven, Ocean City, Sea Isle, and the Wildwoods, offer weekly and seasonal rentals of homes, flats, and apartments, and local real estate agents tend to specialize in summer tourism (although many places are available for rent year-round, and the off-season is a *steal*). You can also go to New Jersey's http://craigslist.org and click on Jersey Shore housing for rental listings. The best time to search for your summer rental is January–March, when the selection is at it's best. Shore rentals go quickly.

Take note: Shore sand gets extremely hot during summer and can be unbearable to walk on without shoes. Invest in flip-flops.

INFORMATION AND SERVICES
Beach Tags
Most New Jersey beaches (Atlantic City and Wildwood are exceptions) require the use of beach tags Memorial Day–Labor Day. Daily costs range from $5–7 depending on the town. If you're planning a longer stay, it makes sense to purchase a weekly or seasonal pass, which will save you significant cash. Tags can usually be purchased at beachfront kiosks or by employees stationed at beach entryways. If there's no one around to collect your fee, it doesn't mean you're off the hook. Many beaches employ taggers to trudge up and down the sand checking tags as they go. You can try and feign sleep or run for a quick ocean dip when you see them approaching, but FYI—they're on to you, and will return at some point to see you cough up that cash. Yeah, it's a nuisance, but the money goes towards restoring the beaches for our future use. You can't argue with that. Still don't want to pay? Wait until after 5 P.M. when the lifeguards go off duty. You'll avoid the sun's stinging rays *and* the collection agency.

Since they're different from town to town and their designs are updated annually, New Jersey beach tags have become popular collectibles. You may think twice before tossing yours in the trash.

Visitors Centers
The Shore's only two welcome centers are located within the region's southern stretch. The **Atlantic City Welcome Center** (Atlantic City Expressway Mile Marker 3.5, Pleasantville, 609/383-2727) is situated along the Atlantic City Expressway right at the city's entry, and the Cape's **Ocean View Tourist Welcome Center** (Garden State Parkway Mile Marker 18.3 N/S, 609/624-0918) sits along the Garden State Parkway west of Sea Isle City. Both centers provide brochures, maps, and various pamphlets highlighting the local and surrounding regions.

Most New Jersey, Pennsylvania, and New York welcome centers provide information on the Jersey Shore. If you're already in the area and needing additional information, contact the local chamber of commerce.

Parking
Weekend parking during July and August is often a nightmare, especially in towns with

boardwalks. Private lots exist most places, but prices are steep ($10–20). It's best to reach your destination early, secure a parking spot away from the action (this limits the hunt), and stay put for a while. Weekdays aren't as bad, but if you plan on parking within easy walking distance to the shops or the beach, bring plenty of quarters—meters are the norm.

GETTING THERE AND AROUND

There are numerous ways to reach the Shore, depending on the town or city you're visiting. **NJ Transit's** (www.njtransit.com, 800/772-3606) North Jersey Coast Line runs trains daily from New York City as far south as Bay Head, with stops in Long Branch, Asbury Park, Bradley Beach, Belmar, Spring Lake, Manasquan, and Point Pleasant Beach. **SeaStreak** (732/872-2600 or 800/262-8743, www.seastreak.com) runs a daily commuter ferry from New York City to the Northern Shore's Highlands, and a daily summer ferry from Manhattan to Sandy Hook Gateway National Recreation Area.

Charter and bus tours from both New York City and Philadelphia are popular ways to reach Atlantic City, though Philly visitors can also catch NJ Transit's (www.njtransit.com) direct Atlantic City Line (ACL) from 30th Street Station. New Jersey residents can board the ACL at South Jersey's Lindenwold Station (901 Berlin Rd.). New York City's proposed Atlantic City Express Service (ACES) will operate between Penn Station and Atlantic City with one stop in Newark. As of this writing the plan is still undergoing review. Another way to reach the region is to fly. **Atlantic City International Airport** (609/645-7895, www.acairport.com) is a hub for **Spirit Airlines** (www.spiritair.com), which flies out of places such as Las Vegas and Florida. To reach the Cape without cross-state traffic, catch the **Cape May-Lewes Ferry** (800/643-3779, www.capemaylewesferry.com) in Lewes, Delaware. You'll be dropped off—car and all—just outside Cape May city.

If driving from North Jersey, the Garden State Parkway (a toll road) connects New York City and New York State, along with New Jersey's Gateway Region, to all of New Jersey's shore towns, traveling parallel to the state's eastern coastline straight through to Cape May. Traffic can get heavy during rush hour and summer weekends (especially Friday evenings), but otherwise it's a fairly no-nonsense route.

Another option from New York and North Jersey is Route 9 South (beginning as Rte. 1-9 in the Gateway Region). The road extends west of the Parkway until the Barnegat Bay region, where the two roads intersect. From here, Route 9 hugs the shoreline and remains there, for the most part, until the Cape region, when it once again crosses with the parkway.

The Atlantic City Expressway (accessible via Rte. 42) is the most straightforward route to Atlantic City and the Garden State Parkway for anyone arriving from Philadelphia, although the various tolls can add up. To reach towns along the Cape, a good option is Route 42 to Route 55, which leads into Route 47—a direct road into Wildwood. It's more scenic than the Parkway, though with only one lane heading each direction, traffic can easily back up. For Ocean City, take Route 49 west from Route 55.

Because of the large number of barrier islands and inlets, it's impossible to drive a straight north-south route along the Jersey Shore, although it is possible to explore the region in clusters. Route 36 travels east from the Highlands toward Sandy Hook and Sea Bright, turning south into Long Branch where it connects with local roads straight through to Manasquan. From here you can hop on Route 35 South and continue through Point Pleasant Beach and Seaside Heights straight into Island Beach State Park, where things get tricky. Although you can see Long Beach Island's Barnegat Lighthouse from Island Beach's southern tip, reaching it is not so easy. You have to backtrack to Seaside Heights and take Route 37 West to either Route 9 or the Garden State Parkway, traveling south to connect with Route 72 East, which will bring you to the Causeway Bridge connecting LBI to the mainland. The whole trip can take about an hour, but unless you have a boat it's the only way to do it. Scenic Ocean Drive connects greater Atlantic City with the southern Shore's Cape. It's a straight route with several toll bridges and stifling speed limits, but it's worth the ride. The drive is actually a series of local roads with various names, but it's instinctively easy to navigate. If you find yourself lost (all the better), don't hesitate to ask directions. Really, it's a straight shot.

The Northern Shore

Stretching from Sandy Hook's northern tip south to Manasquan, New Jersey's Northern Shore is a conglomeration of stately mansions, recovering (and recovered) cities, live-music venues, party bars, religious retreats, and romantic B&Bs. A decidedly New York and North Jersey hangout, this is where you'll find some of the Shore's best clubs and surfing locales, along with some excellent shopping opportunities. Beach erosion has reduced the size of the northernmost beaches, leading to the establishment of private beach clubs from Sea Bright (south of Sandy Hook) straight through to Long Beach. Further south, lakes and inlets separate the beach towns and lend postcard views. The Northern Shore is wider than much of the Jersey coast, creating a blend of beach town and residential suburb that continues straight through to the Point Pleasant Canal.

Information and Services

The free *Upstage* magazine (www.upstage magazine.com) provides local show listings and entertainment news for Jersey's Northern Shore. Look for it in stores.

For Northern Shore beach house weekly and seasonal rentals try **Diane Turton, Realtors** (www.dianeturton.com), with locations in Sea Bright, Ocean Grove, Avon-by-the-Sea, and Spring Lake, or **The Mary Holder Agency** (www.maryholder.com), in Bradley Beach, Sea Girt, and Manasquan.

Getting There and Around

NJ Transit's **North Jersey Coast Line** leaves from New York's Penn Station, Hoboken Terminal, and Newark's Penn Station, stopping in Long Branch, Asbury Park, Bradley Beach, Belmar, Spring Lake, and Manasquan before continuing on to the Barnegat Peninsula.

◖ SANDY HOOK AND THE HIGHLANDS

On the upper portion of a barrier split protruding 11.2 miles north from the city of Long Branch sits seven-mile Sandy Hook Peninsula. Often mistaken as a town, Sandy Hook is actually part of the greater 26,000-acre New Jersey–New York **Gateway National Recreation Area;** a 1,665-acre natural formation of salt marshes, coves, forest, and beaches dividing Raritan Bay from the Atlantic Ocean. In 1974 Sandy Hook's southern portion—already a state park—joined with its northern half, home to a decommissioned U.S. defensive fort, and the two became part of the vast recreation facility.

There's plenty to do in Sandy Hook. Beaches on both the ocean and bay sides offer opportunities for swimming, sunning, birding, and water sports, and a multiuse trail perfect for walkers, runners, cyclists, and skaters runs the peninsula's entire length. Sandy Hook's North Beach offers a backdrop of the Manhattan skyline, and just south of it stands the remains of the former fort and military battery. A mile inland is the country's oldest continuously operating lighthouse, and farther south, the Atlantic Coast's highest density of holly forest, along with the state's only clothing-optional beach.

Most visitors combine a trip to Sandy Hook with one to the nearby Highlands, a seafaring town located on New Jersey's mainland, just over the Highlands Bridge. It's a natural pairing—west of the Sandy Hook Peninsula, the Highlands look like a European city rising

BENNIES VERSUS SHOOBIES

So you haven't spent every summer day since birth at the Shore, your folks didn't inherit a beach home from their parents, you don't recognize your seasonal neighbors or the people who own the upstairs flat, and you've never worked on the boards. You're obviously not a local — so which are you, a benny or a shoobie?

"Benny" is the name adopted for day-trippers along New Jersey's northern coast — an acronym for those arriving from the Great Northeast. The exact origin is unclear, but the word is a possible stand-in for "Bayonne, Eliza-

beth, and Newark," or even "Bergen, Essex, and New York." Along New Jersey's Cape and southern coast, "shoobie" is the designation of choice, a name based on the day travelers who used to arrive down the Shore with their lunches secured firmly in shoeboxes. Although both terms may be taken as derogatory, they're often viewed lightheartedly — in Sea Isle City there's even a restaurant named Shoobies. Still, if you'd rather not be mistaken for either, wear the sunscreen, lose the socks, and don't spend an hour on your 'do before hitting the sticky, salty air.

from the hillside, beckoning visitors. Besides, this is where you'll find the area's B&Bs, along with a few wonderful dining choices.

Sights

Sandy Hook hosts the majority of local attractions, though the Highlands host a magnificent twin lighthouse that's worth seeing.

In service since 1764, **Sandy Hook Lighthouse** (Gateway National Recreation Area) is the oldest operating lighthouse in the United States. It is also one of New Jersey's smaller lighthouses, a 103-foot octagonal tower positioned more than a mile inland from Sandy Hook's northern tip. Free tours are conducted every half hour by the New Jersey Lighthouse Society, weekends noon–4:30 P.M. April–November. The lighthouse is also open during New Jersey's annual October Lighthouse Challenge, but if you plan to climb it, get here early (or late). Lines at this lighthouse are particularly long.

On Sandy Hook's northern half stand the remains of **Fort Hancock,** a U.S. coastal fort built to protect New York Harbor. Army personnel testing Sandy Hook Proving Ground's military artillery resided here. There was also a hospital, a school, a bakery, and a bowling alley. When Nike missiles, and later intercontinental missiles, replaced batteries fortified with disappearing guns, Fort Hancock was

declared surplus, and by 1975 it was all but abandoned. Today, there's an ongoing battle between preservationists and environmentalists to determine the future of these structures. Should they be restored, or should the land be returned to its natural state? Several of the buildings are currently occupied for research and educational purposes. Nearby still stand the decayed and weather-torn remnants of the old battery defenses.

Visitors can learn more about Fort Hancock's past by stopping by **Fort Hancock History House,** a restored 1898 lieutenant's residence situated along the bayside **Officer's Row.** The house is open weekends 1–5 P.M. and hosts a "Christmas during World War II" celebration each December. To find out more, or for information on the seasonal museum and bookstore located nearby, contact the Sandy Hook Visitor Center (732/872-5970).

At the north end of Officer's Row sits the 20-inch **Rodman Gun,** a Sandy Hook landmark and the largest smooth-bore muzzleloader ever made.

Sandy Hook is considered one of New Jersey's best birding spots, with over 340 bird species living or migrating through annually, including flycatchers, buntings, loons, and grebes, and rarities like the swallow-tailed kite and Townsend's warbler. New Jersey's Audubon Society established the **Sandy Hook Bird Observatory**

(20 Hartshorne Dr., 732/872-2500, Tues.–Sat. 10 A.M.–5 P.M., Sun. 10 A.M.–3 P.M. Sept.–June, Tues.–Fri. 10 A.M.–5 P.M., Sat. 10 A.M.–3 P.M., closed Sun. July–Aug.) in 2001 to provide information on area birding spots and recent bird sightings. The center also hosts a small bookstore and gift shop.

Topping the Highlands' hillside 200 feet above sea level and the Raritan Bay are the **Twin Lights of Navesink** (Lighthouse Rd., Highlands, 732/872-1814, http://twin-lights .org), two turreted brownstone lighthouses connected by a long low-lying base. Not your typical tall and narrow structures, the Twin Lights look pretty ordinary when approached from the parking lot. To get their full effect, walk around front. It's also where you'll have the best view (without entering the lighthouse) of Sandy Hook and the sea below, and on a clear day, Manhattan. Built in 1862, the twin lights—one blinking and one stationary—helped distinguish the area for sailors. Both lights were decommissioned in 1949, although the north tower received a commemorative light in 1962. Self-guided north tower tours are allowed daily 10 A.M.–5 P.M. Memorial Day–Labor Day, and Wednesday–Sunday 10 A.M.–5 P.M. the remainder of the year. Admission is free. The south tower is open during the state's annual Lighthouse Challenge in October.

Beaches

Sandy Hook has miles of ocean beaches open to swimmers and sunbathers. The best swimming spots include the south beaches near Areas C and D, and **North Beach,** where wave-jumping comes with a Manhattan backdrop and a view of airplanes descending into JFK Airport. One of New Jersey's best-known beaches is also located nearby: Just south of the Hook's ocean midway, **Gunnison Beach** is the state's only clothing-optional beach. And just so you don't stumble across it unexpectedly, a warning sign reading BEYOND THIS POINT YOU MAY ENCOUNTER NUDE SUNBATHERS offers a heads-up.

Sandy Hook's beaches are open to the public all year, although there's a $10-per-vehicle parking fee (10 A.M.–4 P.M.) to enjoy them during summer months.

Sports and Recreation

The one-mile **Old Dune Trail,** beginning at Area D near the visitor center, offers a nice area overview, meandering near the coast through a densely populated 200-year-old holly forest. Before beginning, stop by the visitor center for an information packet describing possible flora sightings. A six-mile paved multiuse path, opened in 2004, runs the length of the peninsula. It's flat and easy to use, although wind exposure can be a nuisance.

Surf fishing is a popular activity along the Hook's Atlantic side, and a beach dedicated to the sport lies just north of Area D. Proper licensing is required. Windsurfing, kayaking, and sailing can all be enjoyed bayside, where you'll find a couple of small coves.

Accommodations

Bring your pooch for a stay at the Highlands' **SeaScape Manor B&B** (3 Grand Tour, Highlands, 732/291-8467, www.seascape manorbb.com, $119–195), with four lovely guest rooms all with private baths. The inn serves a complimentary gourmet breakfast in the dining room or seasonally on the outdoor deck, but you can also request it in-room. Stays include free use of SeaScape's beach tags.

Housed in a 1910 brick Victorian, the **Grand Lady by the Sea** (254 Rte. 36, Highlands, 732/708-1900 or 877/306-2161, www.grand ladybythesea.com, $139–249) offers six rooms, most with private baths, a few with ocean views, and all with complimentary breakfast. The inn has been renovated with original wood moldings and pocket doors, and there are subtle antique touches throughout. Perks include rental bikes and organic coffee.

Food and Entertainment

Sandy Hook's only dining establishment is located above the refreshment stand next to the visitor center. The **Sea Gull's Nest** (Area D, Hartshorne Dr., 732/872-0025, dawn–dusk summer, $6.50–10) serves casual

American fare on an outdoor deck overlooking the ocean. In addition to a full bar, the Nest closes each day with a recorded rendition of "God Bless America."

Just south of Sandy Hook is Sea Bright's **Donovan's Reef** (1171 Ocean Ave., 732/842-6789, www.donovansreefseabright.com), an area institution since 1976. Rumor has it that condos are moving in, and 2008 may be Donovan's last year. Here's hoping they're still slinging drinks as you read this. Donovan's attracts both Gen Y and Gen Xers, who gather at the outdoor tiki bar for live music and dancing, spilling over onto the establishment's private beach. An on-site grill selling burgers ($5.50) and shrimp-in-the-basket ($8.75) helps keep inevitable drunken antics at bay.

Located within a restored 100-year-old Highlands' bayside inn, popular **Doris & Ed's** (348 Shore Dr., Highlands, 732/872-1565, www.dorisandeds.com, Wed.–Fri. 5–10 P.M., Sat. 5–11 P.M., Sun. 3–10 P.M. Sept.–June, Tues.–Fri. 5–10 P.M., Sat. 5–11 P.M., Sun. 3–10 P.M. July–Aug., closed Mon. year-round, $30–50) specializes in fresh seafood and a selection of quality meat dishes—including a $68 Kobe beef special—along with more than 300 wines to choose from.

Another beloved seafood establishment, family-owned **Bahrs Landing Restaurant** (2 Bay Ave., Highlands, 732/872-1245, www.bahrs.com, Mon.–Thurs. 11:30 A.M.–10 P.M., Fri.–Sat. 11:30 A.M.–10:30 P.M., Sun. 11:30 A.M.–9 P.M. summer, hours vary slightly the rest of the year, $17–30) has been in business since 1917. Head indoors for fine dining, outdoors for kid-friendly chuckwagon-style meals and waterfront views.

Information and Services

Housed in a former 1894 U.S. Lifesaving Station, **Sandy Hook Visitor Center** (732/872-5970, daily 10 A.M.–5 P.M.) is located in Area D, two miles north of the park entrance. There's a bookstore, exhibits, and public restrooms on the premises, and a refreshment stand open April–October. Alcohol is allowed within park boundaries—but no glass containers.

Getting There and Around

SeaStreak (732/872-2600 or 800/262-8743, www.seastreak.com) and **New York Waterway** (800/533-3779, www.nywaterway.com) operate 30-minute Beach Excursion ferries (approx. $43 adult, $20 child round-trip) from New York City to Sandy Hook and back, daily throughout summer. A free shuttle for ferry riders operates from Area D to designated stops throughout the park, though you can also bring your bike aboard the ferry ($3 one way) and use it for commuting once you arrive. The company also runs ferries between the Highlands (Conner's Ferry Landing) and New York City's Wall Street or 34th Street daily year-round (6 A.M.–10 P.M.), with a limited weekend schedule. Round-trip fares are $43 adult (no child fare is offered) during peak weekday hours (before 9:30 A.M.), and $35 adult, $19 child on weekends.

A daily shuttle bus ($1, free for ferry passengers) operates around Sandy Hook during summer months, stopping at beaches and park sites throughout the peninsula, including Fort Hancock Museum, North Beach, and Gunnison Beach.

LONG BRANCH

What began as an elitist gambling resort and became a vacationing spot for big money men like railroad financier Jay Gould and seven U.S. presidents, including Ulysses S. Grant, Rutherford B. Hayes, and James A. Garfield, has emerged from a period of economic blight, finally regaining its niche as an upscale resort community. Recently the "Friendly City" has wiped out much of its waterfront property, rebuilding from the ground up (a preservationist's nightmare) with money invested by state and federal agencies. High-rises and condos now occupy prime beachfront real estate. Signs of "progress" are everywhere along the water, but take Broadway west and the city's struggling past is evident. Wild West legends Annie Oakley and Buffalo Bill both spent time in the city, as did actor Edwin Booth (of Washington, D.C.'s Booth Theatre) and the Gould and Astor families, but with so much reinvention, finding a hint of their history is difficult. Long Branch is about an hour's drive from New York City.

Sights

Long Branch's noncommercial waterfront walkway offers unbeatable views, but only because it's east of the city's recent construction boom. Although it's at street level, the walkway rises about six feet above the sand, and there's a dedicated bike path running beside it. Along the walkway is a monument honoring 20th U.S. President James A. Garfield, who died in Long Branch after retiring here to recuperate from an assassination attempt in Washington, D.C.

Built in 1881 as a house of worship for visiting U.S. Presidents, St. James Historic Chapel—now known as the **Church of Presidents**—is home to the **Long Branch Historical Museum** (1260 Ocean Ave., 732/229-0600, www.churchofthepresidents .org), and is located directly across the street from where James A. Garfield died. Due to the church's deteriorating condition, the museum's collection—which includes Ulysses S. Grant's gun cabinet and game table, and the church's original pipe organ—was removed in 1999. Plans are currently underway to restore the church and reopen it to the public.

Pier Village (732/528-8509, www.pier village.com), a waterfront residential and retail complex housing over 30 boutique stores and restaurants, began accepting tenants in 2005. Stores include local surf shop **Aloha Grove** (732/263-0100, www.alohagrove.com), **Atlantic Books** (732/571-4300), and craft art gallery **Arrivée** (732/222-9366, www.arrivee gallery.com).

In nearby Oceanport, **Monmouth Park Racetrack** (Oceanport Ave., 732/222-5100, www.monmouthpark.com, 11:30 A.M.–5 P.M., $2 adult, child free) features live thoroughbred horse racing throughout summer and into the shoulder seasons. The racetrack is a favorite TV filming locale, with cameos in both *The Sopranos* and *Law & Order*. ATMs and a gift shop are located on the first floor, and the track hosts several restaurants and concession stands.

Beaches

Much of Long Branch's oceanfront is considered private, so for sunbathing and body boarding head to **Seven Presidents Oceanfront Park** (Ocean Ave. at Joline Ave., 732/229-7025 or 732/229-0924 in summer, $6), also featuring volleyball courts and a skateboard park. Long Branch hosts a handful of other public beaches, including North Bath Avenue, West End Avenue, and Morris Avenue, all of which have public restrooms. The city's surfing beach is at Matilda Terrace. For a full list of Long Branch public-access beaches, call the **Greater Long Branch Chamber of Commerce** at 732/571-1833.

Daily beach tags cost $5 adult, $3 age 13–17, and 12 and under free. A season pass is $35 adult, $30 child age 13–17.

Accommodations

Located in the city's West End district near Monmouth Park Racetrack is the 12-room **Cedars and Beeches Bed & Breakfast** (247 Cedar Ave., 800/323-5655, www.cedarsand beeches.com, $160–250), a spacious Victorian with a wraparound covered porch perfect for escaping summer humidity. A bit of a hike from the beach, it is best suited for business travelers (high-speed Internet is available) and those looking to rejuvenate.

The upscale **Ocean Place Resort & Spa** (1 Ocean Blvd., 800/411-6493, www.ocean placeresort.com, $299–399) occupies prime waterfront property—and has its own private beach—but that doesn't mean you're required to take an ocean dip. With both an indoor and outdoor pool and an on-site spa, you've got plenty of luxuries to choose from. Rooms have private balconies (some with superb ocean views) and for an extra $150 your pet can come along too. There's also a restaurant, lounge, and seasonal low-carb café on-site.

Food and Nightlife

Tucked behind Long Branch's newer development, **Rooney's Oceanfront Restaurant** (100 Ocean Ave., 732/870-1200, www .rooneysocean.com, Mon.–Thurs. and Sun.

11:30 A.M.–10 P.M., Fri.–Sat. 11:30 A.M.–11:30 P.M., $16–45) is a gem worth finding. Its prime beachfront location offers sweeping ocean views, especially from the restaurant's bi-level outdoor deck. Standouts include Rooney's changing seafood specials and an expansive wine selection. Though attire varies, you'll probably want to forgo the shorts and flip-flops.

It may look like a dive, but **Brighton Bar** (121 Brighton Ave., 732/229-9676, www.cojack productions.com) has been a favorite live music venue for over 20 years. The bar showcases New Jersey bands and national acts ranging from jazz to rock for the 18-and-older crowd. Weekday performances are $7, weekend shows $9.

Getting There and Around

Long Branch is located off Exit 105 of the Garden State Parkway.

NJ Transit's North Jersey Coast Line operates from New York Penn Station with a stop at **Long Branch Train Station** (3rd Ave. between North Bath Ave. and Morris Ave.), just north of the **Monmouth Medical Center.** The trip takes approximately 1.5 hours one-way, and off-peak round-trip fare is $20.50 adult, $10.25 child. The station is a hike from the beach, so bring along a bike for transport.

ASBURY PARK

The crumbling and abandoned buildings, graffitied facades, and an overall sense of desolation may have some people asking, "What's the allure?" But Asbury Park has one, and now it looks as though things may finally be turning this city's way. The queen of New Jersey's Shore during the first half of the 20th century, Asbury Park entered a downward spiral when the state's Garden State Parkway opened in the 1950s, paving a route to beaches further south. The city was soon taken over by motorcycles and music, but what business that brought in was damaged for good in the 1970s, when race riots split Asbury Park in two and the city was abandoned, almost completely.

Thankfully, years of neglect have left many of Asbury Park's architecturally grand structures untouched, but whether this will hold true with the onslaught of new development is another story. Palace Amusements succumbed to the wrecking ball in 2004, and the Baronet Theatre, Upstage Club (where Springsteen *really* got his start), and even the Stone Pony have all been threatened in the name of progress.

It still holds true that Asbury has seen better days, but rarely does a city fight such a heartfelt battle to bring those days back. True, the city has been "up and coming" for a while, but results are finally showing. A notable gay community has breathed new life into Asbury Park, introducing shops and restaurants, a hotel and nightclub, and an annual gay pride parade. And along Cookman Avenue, storefronts are being filled by retro boutiques, coffeehouses, and art galleries. The boardwalk has seen endless construction through 2008, including brand-new shops, a makeover for the casino arcade and its carousel house, and even a miniature golf course.

Ocean Avenue remains riddled with potholes, and crime does occur, but there are plenty of reasons to visit Asbury Park. Not to linger on the boards after dark, mind you, but for the excellent restaurants, unique shopping ops, stunning architecture, the beach, history, art…and surely, the music.

Sights

In 2004 Asbury Park's new mile-long million-dollar **boardwalk** debuted as part of the city's new look, and in 2008 a whole slew of recently constructed shops were set to open, giving strollers plenty to explore between Convention Hall and the casino, connecting the walkway to Ocean Grove's. You won't be mistaking these boards for Seaside Heights or Wildwood any time soon, but you wouldn't want to. It's rare to have such a pleasant stretch of beachfront property practically to yourself, and it won't last long. Go on: take a stroll, ride your bike, peruse the shops, play a round of miniature golf (when was the last time you

ASBURY'S CLOWN

Tillie the clown is one of New Jersey's most iconic faces. Two nearly identical images, each 200 feet high, 13 feet wide, both strewn with neon tubes and sporting Cheshire-cat grins, prominently adorned Asbury Park's Palace Amusements' exterior, their blue eyes watching over residents and visitors since 1956. Over the years Tillie and Asbury Park became synonymous. He was featured in movies and TV shows such as *The Sopranos* and appeared in Springsteen publicity shots and on concert merchandise.

Tillie's life began through the artful hand of Leslie "Worth" Thomas, a graphic design artist hired by Asbury Park's Central Amusement Corporation to provide the Palace with a fun house feel. Thomas added a unique touch by painting the names of rides like Olympic Bob's and Tunnel of Love in curvaceous letters on the Palace walls. But while Tillie's faces came from his brush, they didn't come directly from Thomas's imagination.

Tillie's origin can be traced back to 1897, when a smiling caricature known as the Steeplechase Fun Face decorated Coney Island's Steeplechase Park Pavilion of Fun. Both the park and the fun face were destroyed by fire in 1907, but Steeplechase was rebuilt, and for the next four decades a Fun Face version appeared on everything from entry tickets to advertisements, although each portrayal was slightly different from the last. Eventually standardized in the 1940s, Fun Face disappeared when the park was demolished in 1964. But the faces of Steeplechase live on in Tillie. Even his name derives from ancestral roots: Tillie is short for George C. Tiylou, Steeplechase's founding father.

Palace life began for Tillie just as Asbury Park was reaching its end as a well-known vacation venue. Families started heading south to beach towns such as Beach Haven and Wildwood, and a new crowd began moving in. By the 1970s the bikers, street gangs, and music scene Springsteen immortalized in his lyrics had found a home in Asbury Park. But nothing seemed able to save the Palace, which soon fell like much of the city into disrepair. On November 27, 1988, the Palace closed its doors without warning, and Tillie's neon lights shone for the last time.

For almost a decade the Palace and Tillie stood untouched and seemingly forgotten, until the *Asbury Park Press* reported the building was in danger of collapsing and demolition was imminent. Within a day, thepreservation group **Save Tillie** (www.savetillie.com) was formed. Their original goal was to save at least one Tillie painting, removing it from the Palace intact and relocating it to another area of the city. Save Tillie has since grown into a nonprofit with hundreds of members and support from many local musicians, including Bruce. The group has expanded their efforts to preserving Asbury Park's unique architecture and history, like the Stone Pony, most famously associated with Springsteen.

In June 2004, Palace Amusements was demolished, but not before the group's volunteers saved Tillie. Unfortunately, the Palace property's current owners, Asbury Partners, have housed him in a poorly constructed leaky shed. Whether Tillie will have a future remains uncertain, but Save Tillie members are not giving up. For ways you can help save Tillie and Asbury Park's past, visit the group's website. And for a glimpse of Tillie in the meantime, check out Asbury Park's Wonder Bar: That crazy clown is still smilin' down.

heard *that* in Asbury?). Do it now, before you have to wait in line.

It's unclear what will happen to fortune-teller Madame Marie's little blue boardwalk shack now that she has passed away. The seer became famous when she appeared in the lyrics of Springsteen's song, "Fourth of July, Asbury Park (Sandy)," and her **Temple of Knowledge** (732/775-5327) has long been a photo-op favorite. When Marie (her real name was Marie Castello) died in late June 2008 at age 93, the city's Convention Hall lowered its flag to half-staff. Most recently Castello's daughter and daughter-in-law have been operating the temple. Whether they'll continue sharing fortunes without the matriarch, we'll have to wait and see.

Asbury Park's new and improved carousel house

Asbury Park is the birthplace of Jersey Shore music, and it's well known that this movement's main purveyor is none other than Brother Bruce. The **Asbury Park Public Library** (500 1st Ave., 732/774-4221, www.asbury parklibrary.org, Mon.–Wed. 11 A.M.–8 P.M., Thurs.–Fri. 9 A.M.–5 P.M., Sat. noon–5 P.M., closed Sun.) houses what's considered to be the largest collection of Boss memorabilia, including songbooks, tour books, newspaper articles, and academic papers, in the world. Much of the early collection was a gift from long-running (and awesome) Springsteen fan magazine *Backstreets.* Because library staff is limited, it's recommended you call and make an appointment to access the material before showing up. A list of the collection's current holdings is available on the library website.

Newark native and *The Red Badge of Courage* author Stephan Crane moved to Asbury Park in the late 1880s following his father's death. Crane penned his first short story at 508 4th Avenue. Designated the **Stephen Crane House** (732/775-5682, http://asburyradio .com/Cranehouse.htm, call for hours), the home now operates as a museum and performing arts space, hosting readings, plays, and movies.

Beaches

Asbury Park's daily beach tags cost $5 weekdays and weekends, age 12 and under free. A season pass costs $50. The city's beaches remain fairly deserted—you should have little trouble finding a place to lay your blanket. The best place to do so is in front of the boardwalk, between Convention Hall and the casino. The beach itself is lovely—a wide stretch of gleaming white sand—though for something a little livelier, walk through the casino to nearby Ocean Grove. A caveat: Their beaches are twice the price of Asbury's on weekends.

Shopping

Asbury's **Cookman Avenue,** the city's main street, is looking better than ever. A slew of new shops has moved in over the last few years, and while some favorites like Antic Hay Books (*sigh*) have closed their doors, the future shows tremendous promise. There are several antique stores to explore, as well as art galleries, clothing boutiques, and a shop selling retro kitchenware.

Wish You Were Here! (612 Cookman Ave., 732/774-1601, www.wishyouwerehereap.com) features a candy counter filled with goodies—chocolate-covered cherries, dark chocolate oozing with absinthe, and frosted cookies made to look like local icon Tillie the Clown—although its memorabilia collection is just as sweet. Pick up a miniature mechanical Ferris wheel or Asbury Park paintings by local watercolorist P. J. Carlino.

For hemp handbags, organic cotton T-shirts, and formaldehyde-free nail polish, stop by **Organic Style** (621 Cookman Ave., 732/775-1051, www.organicstyleshop.com). Afterward, swing over to **Crybaby Art Gallery** (717 Cookman Ave., 732/869-0606, www.crybaby artgallery.com) to browse cutting-edge works of pop, surrealist, and graffiti art.

Mike's Beach House (619 Cookman Ave., 732/988-6088, www.mikesbeachhouse.net) is the place to find Shore souvenirs like postcards, saltwater taffy, and custom wooden Asbury Park signs. Proprietors of the retro-fashion boutique **Allan & Suzi** (711 Cookman Ave., 732/988-7372) have dressed celebs including Robin Williams and the *Sex and the City* cast in their vintage finds. Stock includes Gucci, Prada, and Jimmy Choo shoes.

Tucked into the **Shoppes at the Arcade** in the former Woolworth Building, **Flying Saucers Retro Kitchenware** (658 Cookman Ave. Unit 13, 732/202-8848, www.flyingsaucers online.com) carries a fabulous selection of kitchen folk art, Fiesta ware, Kit-Cat Klocks, mixing bowls, and more. Also among the shops is the original (and operational) **Palace Amusement B&W Photo Booth.** You just *know* Bruce has been in there at some point.

Antique Emporium of Asbury Park (646 Cookman Ave., 732/774-8230, www.antique emporiumofasburypark.com) houses over 60 antique vendors, including the arts and crafts–era furniture of **Tristan's Antiques** (www .tristansantiques.com). The Antique Emporium supplies to B&Bs, stage designers, and major motion picture companies. The 5,000-square-

foot **Studebakers—Antiques and Collectibles Mall** (1201 Main St., 732/776-5565) is home to 30 antique and collectible dealers, as well as the **Rumble Seat Tea Room,** an ideal spot to savor your kitchenware purchases and Civil War finds.

Up on the boardwalk, **Asbury Galleria** (3rd Ave. Boardwalk Pavilion, 732/869-9977, www.asburygalleria.com) features Jersey Shore books and photos by longtime local resident Milton Edelman. Asbury Park's urban surf shop **Lightly Salted** (3rd Ave. Boardwalk Pavilion, 732/776-8886, www.lightlysalted surf.blogspot.com) opened in August 2008. In addition to custom boards and alternative coastal art, expect a place to chill. I'm stoked about **Hot Sand** (5th Ave. Boardwalk Pavilion, 732/927-5475, www.hotsandap.com), the city's hands-on glass studio. In addition to workshops in glassblowing and glass fusing, Hot Sand offers studio rental, hosts events, and sells handmade glass works inspired by Asbury Park. For a boardwalk bike rental there's now **Brielle Cyclery** (5th Ave. Boardwalk Pavilion, 732/502-0077, www.briellecyclery.com), open daily throughout summer.

Entertainment and Nightlife

Opened in 1923, the beachfront's 3,600-seat **Convention Hall** is impressive—a red-brick art deco structure built by the architects responsible for New York City's Grand Central Terminal. Joined to it by the Grand Arcade extending over the boardwalk, the street-side 1930 **Paramount Theatre** is just as stunning. Both venues are listed on the National Register of Historic Places and host concerts, festivals, and conventions throughout the year. The Paramount Theatre is the acoustically superior of the two, and the Convention Hall is a bit more rugged, with no heat or air-conditioning. The latter has become a favorite rehearsal venue for Springsteen and the E Street Band. Fans who don't manage to score a ticket can simply set up on the sand below and listen to the show.

Made famous by the Boss, Asbury Park's **The Stone Pony** (913 Ocean Ave., 732/502-0600, www.thestonepony.com) didn't actually

THE JERSEY SHORE

Asbury Park's historic Paramount Theatre and Convention Hall

© LAURA KINIRY

open until 1974, a year after Bruce released *Born to Run.* The building was originally occupied by a restaurant called Mrs. Jays, later becoming the Magic Touch disco bar, which was abandoned by the time John P. "Jack" Roig and Robert "Butch" Pielka decided to open the Pony. In addition to its Springsteen association, the Stone Pony gets cred for its rockin' house band, the Asbury Jukes, often cited as one of the world's greatest bar bands. The band still performs here. See a show at the Pony—it's like bathing in rock and roll.

Live bands take stage at **The Saint** (601 Main St., 732/775-9144, www.thesaintnj .com, $7–15) 5–7 days a week. Since 1994, this 175-capacity 18-and-over club has been the place to see up-and-comers, including Jewel and Stereophonics. There are 20 brews on tap, and all-age weekend matinees. The Asbury Music Company, parent company of the Saint, presents annual awards recognizing the best local talent.

A long-running bowling alley that has been converted into one of the hippest, hottest, baddest clubs in town, **Asbury Lanes** (209 4th Ave., 732/776-6160, www.asburylanes.com, Wed.–Sat. 8 P.M.–2 A.M.) is worth a trip. Punk nights and some fabulous art shows, including a 2007–2008 exhibit of painted bowling pins, are held year-round, and the lanes are still in use. The club's past live shows have included a Burlesque Bikini Blowout, the Yard Dogs, and Big City Bombers. To enter the club is age 18, to drink age 21, unless noted otherwise.

One of New Jersey's largest gay clubs is situated on the bottom floor of the renovated Empress Hotel. **Paradise** (101 Asbury Ave., 732/988-6663, www.paradisenj.com, Wed.–Thurs. 4 P.M.–2 A.M., Sat.–Sun. noon–2 A.M.) features two dance floors, two stages, and an outdoor pool with a hanging disco ball. Poolside happy hour is held weekday afternoons throughout summer.

Accommodations

In keeping with the city's revitalization theme, Asbury Park's historic **Berkeley Oceanfront Hotel** (1401 Ocean Ave., 732/776-6700, www .berkeleyhotelnj.com, $83–137) has been completely renovated with a new lobby, stylish guest rooms, and poolside private cabanas and tiki bar. It's quite a change from the worn and weathered hotel that stood here before. Granted the building is still old, but the decor is fun and modern. There's even a pool table in the lobby.

Just south of Asbury Park, Ocean Grove offers dozens of B&B options.

Food

Sunset Landing (1215 Sunset Ave., 732/776-9732, daily 7 A.M.–2 P.M., $6–11) is an Asbury Park classic, a family-owned diner/surf shack that serves a killer breakfast and also rents out canoes for use on Deal Lake, where the eatery is located. Cookman Avenue's **Twisted Tree Cafe** (609 Cookman Ave., 732/775-2633) bakes and serves vegan cupcakes, breads, muffins, and more, alongside a vegetarian menu dotted with bean wraps ($8) and hummus sandwiches ($8). Replenish your tummy, then order yourself a chai latte and stay a while.

The Boardwalk's iconic Howard Johnson's structure has been renovated and now houses the **Salt Water Beach Café** (732/774-1400, www.saltwaterbeachcafenj.com, Sun.–Thurs. 11 A.M.–10 P.M., Fri.–Sat. 11 A.M.–11 P.M., $11–30), offering a selection of artisanal sandwiches and upscale entrées. Visitors can nosh on softshell crab or pulled-pork sandwiches while admiring the crashing waves.

Ocean Grove transplant **Moonstruck** (517 Lake Ave., 732/988-0123, www.moonstrucknj.com, Wed.–Thurs. and Sun. 5–10 P.M., Fri.–Sat. 5–11 P.M., closed Mon.–Tues., $15–33) has been luring Asbury Park crowds with its romantic terraces, exquisite Mediterranean fare, and awesome views since 2004. Housed in a refurbished three-story shore home, the restaurant features a main-floor cocktail lounge and two upper-level dining areas, both with wraparound porches overlooking Wesley Lake. Get here early—reservations aren't accepted.

Asbury's Main Street still has a ways to go, but a good start is **Bistro Olé** (230 Main St., 732/897-0048, www.bistroole.com, dinner Tues.–Thurs. and Sun. 5–10 P.M., Fri.–Sat. 5–11 P.M., closed Mon., $19–29), a colorful and boisterous BYO with a gregarious host and tasty Spanish-Portuguese dishes—like seared sea bass topped with pesto and breadcrumbs ($29)—galore. Seating is first come, first served.

Getting There and Around

Asbury Park is 40 miles south of Manhattan, just off Exit 102 southbound (100A northbound) of the Garden State Parkway. The **Asbury Park Train Station** is at the south end of Cookman Avenue, an easy stroll to downtown's shops and within reasonable walking distance to the boardwalk.

OCEAN GROVE

Founded in the late 19th century as a Methodist summer camp, "God's Square Mile" has remained successfully true to its roots. While strict blue laws—such as no driving on Sundays—have been lifted, others—like restricted Sunday-morning beach use—remain in effect. The Great Auditorium is the city's center, a popular religious revival venue surrounded by narrow streets, all packed by multistory Stick Victorians in various states of repair. Across from the beach stand faded gingerbread clapboards, their long porches piled atop one another to utilize the ocean breezes. Just north of the auditorium are the canvas tents of Ocean Grove's original settlers. Each with a pitched roof and porch awning, they're still in use by seaside vacationers.

The Grove has been considered part of Neptune Township since the 1980s, but it retains its own downtown filled with ice cream stands and specialty shops. A noncommercial boardwalk runs along the beach, connecting with Asbury Park's boardwalk to the north. Affordable bed-and-breakfasts are scattered throughout town, many of them more like hostels or boarding hotels than boutique lodging. Patients released from an area mental hospital in the 1980s and gays migrating in from neighboring Asbury Park have added a whirlpool mix to local demographics—one that, by most accounts, nobody seems to mind.

THE JERSEY SHORE

Bed-and-breakfasts are scattered throughout Ocean Grove.

Sights

Connecting with Asbury Park's boardwalk to the north, the noncommercial Ocean Grove **boardwalk** is strictly for strolling.

Ocean Grove's centerpiece, the 6,500-seat **Great Auditorium** (21 Pilgrim Pathway, 732/775-0035 or 800/773-0097), is impossible to miss. This massive (almost as large as a football field) wood structure, built as a house of worship, hosts family-friendly shows such as the poodle-skirt-swaying Doo Wop Revue and acts like the Smothers Brothers, as well as religious services. Across the street is the **Auditorium Pavilion,** an open-air gazebo hosting book sales and a weekly church service.

Alongside the Great Auditorium is **Tent City,** over 100 canvas tents originally leased to Methodist church members—the Grove's founders—during the late 19th century. The tents are still owned by the Ocean Grove Camp Meeting Association, although you don't have to belong to the church to rent one. You do, however, have to sign your name to an extremely long waiting list—more than 20 years.

Many of the tents feature colorfully striped awnings perched above their entryways, and bicycles and beach chairs hang from their sides. Almost all have been added to over the years. Sneak a peek inside and you'll see they're just like other homes—quilt-covered beds, comfy couches, and plenty of knickknacks. You haven't seen Ocean Grove unless you've seen Tent City.

Beaches

Ocean Grove's daily beach tags are $7 weekdays, a whopping $12 weekends, under age 12 free. There are both weeklong ($35) and season ($70) passes available as well. On Sundays, beach use is restricted until noon. Fishing is allowed from beach jetties; the best times for fishing are 5 A.M.–7 A.M. and after 8 P.M.

Events

Ocean Grove Historical Society (732/774-1869, www.oceangrovehistory.org, Mon. and Wed.–Thurs. 10 A.M.–4 P.M., Fri.–Sat. 10 A.M.–5 P.M.) hosts numerous events year-round, including annual summer and

Christmas **House Tours,** and 90-minute **Historic District Walking Tours** (Wed. and Fri. 1 P.M., Sat. 11 A.M., June–mid-Sept.), which include visits to Tent City and the Great Auditorium. Tours begin in front of 50 Pitman Avenue, the Society museum.

Shopping

Take some time to peruse Main Street's shops, stopping off for an ice cream cone along the way.

Main Street is home to several collectibles shops, including the country-style **Favorite Things** (52 Main Ave., 732/774-0230, www.1800foragift.com). Housed in an old Victorian, the selection includes hand-painted furniture, period lace, and quilted bags. There's also an old-fashioned chocolate and candy counter for sweet-toothed passers-by. Year-round **Comfort Zone** (44-46 Main Ave., 732/869-9990, www.comfortzone-og.com) stocks aromatherapy candles, body lotions, and home accessories such as stained glass window hangings. Funky **Kitsch and Kaboodle** (76 Main Ave., 732/869-0950) features Burt's Bees lip balms alongside retro Barbies and vintage tableware. For all things Victorian, stop by **Gingerbreads Teas & Treasures** (49 Main Ave., 732/775-7900), also the place for Steiff stuffed animals and baby toys.

Located on the first floor of the Majestic Hotel, **Ocean Grove Surf Shop** (19 Main Ave., 732/869-1001, ogsurfshop.com) is a retro surf shop stocking clothing, boards, and accessories. Surf lessons are held during shop hours (daily 9 A.M.–7 P.M. summer). Call ahead to schedule, and check online for a 24-hour surf report.

Accommodations

The prettiest part of Ocean Grove—near the Great Auditorium—is also where you'll find many of the bed-and-breakfasts. Rooms tend to be small and lack modern amenities, although this is reflected in more affordable prices. Ocean Avenue establishments offer some of the best views, not to mention a cool ocean breeze.

One of Ocean Grove's newer B&Bs, the four-story **Henry Richard Inn** (16 Main Ave., 732/776-7346, www.henryrichardinn.com, $85–95) features single and double units with in-room sinks and a shared bath, along with two fully contained apartments. A full complimentary breakfast is served daily.

In addition to ocean breezes, the seasonal corner-lot **House by the Sea** (14 Ocean Ave., 732/774-4771, $85–135) offers a fabulous beachfront view from its front porch. There are no room telephones or TVs, and only a limited number of private baths. The living is simple but good.

Half a block away from the Great Auditorium is the 36-room **Manchester Inn** (25 Ocean Pathway, 732/775-0616, www.themanchester inn.com, $105–290), New Jersey's first solar-powered inn. This multistory white Victorian, once two separate buildings, has received accolades for its Murder Mystery Weekends, held in later spring and early fall. Many of the rooms rely on ocean air and ceiling fans for cooling, and a lengthy covered front porch with rocking chairs offers afternoon and evening relief. Although some bathrooms are shared, all rooms have their own sink. The inn offers half-day rates and free wireless Internet. Complimentary hot breakfast is served daily.

One of the town's smaller B&Bs, the eight-room **Carriage House** (18 Heck Ave., 732/998-9441, www.carriagehousenj.com, $125–180) occupies a renovated century-old Victorian along a quiet street. All the rooms feature a private bath, TV, and air-conditioning, and the larger ones have working fireplaces. This smoke-free inn is unable to accommodate kids.

An easy walk from the beach is **Lillagaard Hotel** (5 Abbot Ave., 732/998-1216, www.lillagaard.com, $120–175), an imposing 22-room Victorian with an English Countryside feel. Each room is uniquely designed with hand-painted murals, and there's a TV room, a library, and a dining room where complimentary breakfast is served. Air-conditioning comes with every room; private baths accompany most rooms.

With wraparound porches and sweeping

ocean views, the year-round Victorian **Ocean Plaza** (18 Ocean Pathway, 732/774-6552, www.ogplaza.com, $185–325) is a coveted establishment. Sixteen guest rooms and three suites each come equipped with modern amenities like TV and a VCR, central air, and private bathrooms—features that are hard to come by at the bulk of Ocean Grove B&Bs. A daily continental breakfast can be enjoyed from the second-story veranda during warmer months, offering fine people-watching opportunities below.

Food

The bulk of Ocean Grove's eateries are along Main Street, although several are scattered among the town's B&Bs. Most eateries around here tend to keep things casual, catering to the Shore appeal.

For breakfast try downtown's **Starving Artist at Days** (47 Olin St., 732/988-1007, Mon.–Sat. 8 A.M.–3 P.M., Sun. 8 A.M.–2 P.M., closed Wed., $6–12), also serving lunch throughout the week (except Wed.). The Artist dishes out theatrical entertainment, such as the musical *Godspell*, in its outdoor Victorian Garden.

The intimate **Raspberry Café** (60 Main Ave., 732/988-0071, Tues.–Thurs. 11 A.M.–7 P.M., Fri.–Sat. 11 A.M.–3 P.M. and 5–9 P.M., $8–25) offers a small lunch and dinner selection alongside a creative assortment of starters and salads. Sandwiches include an open-faced portobello with sautéed spinach ($8), and a three-cheese grilled cheese with tomato ($8).

Century-old **Nagles Apothecary Café** (43 Main St., 732/776-9797, daily 8:30 A.M.–9 P.M., closed Tues., $5–10) is a former pharmacy that has evolved into a classic American eatery complete with soda fountain and some of the best ice cream around (go for the peanut butter swirl). The café includes indoor and outdoor seating, and a take-out window that's popular even on rainy days.

On the Majestic Hotel's ground floor is the European-style **Bia,** a recently renovated and revamped 60-seat bistro serving a variety of light fare and innovative entrées, like jumbo scallops over lobster ravioli ($28) and filet mignon wrapped in smoked bacon ($34). Hours are daily noon–10 P.M. with brunch Sunday 11:30 A.M.–4 P.M. seasonally, although the inn also offers year-round dining on its 24-seat enclosed heated porch.

Getting There and Around

Ocean Grove is located just off Exit 100 of the Garden State Parkway. NJ Transit's **North Jersey Coast Line** stops in Asbury Park just across the lake from Ocean Grove.

BRADLEY BEACH

Just south of Ocean Grove is Bradley Beach, a pleasant borough founded by middle-class Philadelphians and New Yorkers in the late 19th century. Today, it's filled with one- and two-story colonials that look as though they've been passed down through generations. Thankfully, local zoning laws prevent any additional buildup. A couple of beachfront brick structures seem misplaced, but Bradley Beach is otherwise attractive, comfortable, and friendly. There are several fine Italian restaurants downtown, and a short stretch of Mexican shops and eateries catering to the borough's significant Latino population. A beachfront promenade hosts benches, gazebos, a few food stands, a miniature golf course, and boccie ball courts (4th Ave.), and bicycles are allowed on the walkway midnight–10 A.M. Memorial Day–Labor Day. Several Bradley Beach restaurants are open year-round.

Beaches

Daily beach tags cost $7 adult, free for those 13 and under. A season pass costs $65. Food and beverages are permitted on the beach, but no alcohol. Fishing is allowed on beach jetties at Lake Terrace, Park Place, Brinley Avenue, and 2nd Avenue. A one-mile beach stretch between Third and Fifth Avenues is reserved for surfers only. There are public restrooms at Newark, LaReine, Third, and Evergreen Avenues, and showers along the beach. The borough hosts a gazebo concert series at Fifth Avenue and the ocean (www.bradleybeachonline.com) evenings throughout summer.

Accommodations

Just steps from the beach, the three-story Victorian **Bradley Beach Inn** (900 Ocean Ave., 732/774-0414, www.thebradleybeachinn.com, $105–165) offers eight simple guest rooms, most with flower duvets, several with ocean views, and two with an extra full-size bed (for families). Some bathrooms are shared.

The **Sandcastle Inn** (204 3rd Ave., 732/774-2875, www.sandcastleinn.us, $130–270) offers six simple guest rooms and two suites, each with a private bath and wireless Internet access. While some rooms, like the bright Wildflowers room, include air-conditioning, others depend strictly on the sea breeze. Use of two beach tags, chairs, and a beach umbrella is complimentary.

Food

Always-bustling **La Nonna Piancone's Cafe** (800 Main St., 732/775-0906, www.piancone .com, Sun.–Thurs. 8 A.M.–7 P.M., Fri.–Sat. 8 A.M.–9 P.M., $12–29) recently changed ownership, revamping its interior with a classy new upstairs fit for live entertainment. Having been family-owned and operated for more than 50 years, patrons are in for a few changes, although the Mediterranean restaurant's reputation as grandma's substitute kitchen is expected to stick. La Nonna also houses an on-site deli and a from-scratch bakery, so you can take your goodies to go.

Another Italian favorite is **Giamano's** (301 Main St., 732/775-4275, www.giamanos.com, Tues.–Sun. from 5 P.M., closed Mon., $15–25), a classy restaurant with a downstairs dining room and outdoor café, and a second-floor live music lounge known for its jazz and blues. Traditional dishes include pasta marinara ($13.95) and shrimp scampi ($23.95).

Bradley Beach staple **Vic's** (60 Main St., 732/774-8225, www.vicspizza.com, Tues.–Thurs. 11:30 A.M.–11 P.M., Fri.–Sat. 11:30 A.M.–midnight, Sun. noon–11 P.M.,

closed Mon., year-round, $13–19) has been dishing up superb thin-crusted pizzas and pastas doused in homemade sauce since 1947. With its paneled walls and a number board that lights when order are up, the interior doesn't seem to have changed much over the years, but this hasn't stopped crowds from coming. The joint gets packed even early in the evening, but ample indoor and outdoor seating makes for quick turnover.

Getting There and Around

NJ Transit's **North Jersey Coast Line** from New York City stops in Bradley Beach. The borough is located east of the Garden State Parkway, Exit 100. After exiting, take Route 33 to Ocean Grove. Bradley Beach is the next town south.

BELMAR

With a lively nightlife and a full social calendar, not to mention a spectacular beach, Belmar is bustling. Long known as a retreat for rowdy grads and college parties, the borough is in the midst of an image makeover. Regulations on the number of renters to each summer unit and club noise restrictions are evidence of Belmar's shifting population. Still, while afternoon activities, including several weekend festivals and the state's largest St. Patty's Day parade, are popular borough pastimes, nightlife reigns supreme in Belmar and neighboring **Lake Como.** Downtown is filled with bars and restaurants, many of which are open year-round. With so much going on, it's little surprise legendary Captain Kidd is rumored to have buried treasure here (no doubt after a night at the pub).

Belmar is located between the Shark River and the Atlantic Ocean, with Silver Lake to the north of town and Lake Como to the south. It's home to New Jersey's largest commercial marina and a mile-long semicommercial boardwalk.

Beaches

Belmar's daily beach tags cost $7, age 14 and under free. A season pass costs $50. Alcohol is not permitted. Parking along the beach is mostly metered, but free spots can be had if you're willing to walk.

The borough hosts designated beaches for each of its water sports. Surfing is allowed south of the 16th Avenue jetty and on both sides of the 19th Avenue jetty. Kayaks are permitted south of 20th Avenue. For boogie boarders, the best ocean beaches are between 13th and 19th Avenues. Surf fishers should hit the Shark River inlet.

In addition to the ocean beaches there's a sandy artificial beach at L Street along the Shark River.

Events

Belmar and Lake Como play joint host to the state's largest **St. Patrick's Day Parade** (www .belmarparade.com), complete with bagpipers and marching bands, paving way for a daylong celebration that includes traditional Irish fare and green beer galore.

Belmar's long-running two-day **New Jersey Seafood Festival** (Silver Lake Park on Ocean Ave. between 5th and 6th Aves., 732/774-8506, www.belmar.com), held annually in June, features more than 45 seafood vendors with samples of everything from crab cakes to fresh steamed lobster. An international wine tent serves to complement local fare. Free festival trolley service runs between Belmar Marina, the NJ Transit train station, the beach, and the festival grounds.

Score prizes for the most creative or elaborate sand sculpture at the **New Jersey Sand Castle Contest** (732/681-3700, www.belmar .com), held on the beach in early July. Anyone can participate, but be warned: There are some true sand masters at work.

After two years in Seaside Heights, the three-day **AVP Volleyball Tournament** (732/681-3700, www.belmar.com, http://web.avp.com) returned to Belmar in June 2008, and many residents are hoping it's back to stay. Part of a cross-country tour, the tournament attracts thousands to Belmar's beaches to see some of the world's best pro volleyball players serve, block, pass, and dig.

Free family movies screen Sunday evenings

throughout the summer at 8th Street beach, beginning at dusk. Visit www.belmar.com for a full schedule.

Sports and Recreation

The **Belmar Marina** (Rte. 35 and 10th Ave., 732/681-5005) is New Jersey's largest commercial marina. No wonder sportfishing is such a popular local activity—you've got dozens of charter boats and fishing party vessels to choose from. For deep-sea fishing try the 100-passenger *Suzie Girl* (732/988-7760), or for something smaller, the six-person sportfishing boat *Teri Jean II* (732/280-7364, www.terijean.com). For diving excursions call Dean Iglay at **Horizon** (732/280-3284). Bait and tackle shop **Fisherman's Den** (Rte. 35, 732/681-5005, www.fishermansdennj. com) rents motorboats for use on the Shark River ($59.95 per day). The river hosts flounder, fluke, and striped bass, as well as blue-claw crabs late in the summer season.

During summer months, bicycles are only permitted on the boardwalk before 8 A.M. and after 8 P.M.

Nightlife

Belmar is known for its nightlife, although it's not the all-night partying of Seaside or the nonstop gluttony Atlantic City can be. It's more of the drinking beer, snacking on wings, and chilling outdoors kind of nightlife, with some dancing (and shots) thrown in for good measure. The following spots are known for their nightlife, but all serve food during the day and early evening. Like most Belmar establishments they're open year-round.

Known as "Bar A" to insiders, Lake Como's **Bar Anticipation** (703-705 16th Ave., 732/681-7422, www.bar-a.com, daily 10 A.M.–2 A.M.) is open all year, but the party really picks up in summer, with beat-the-clock Tuesdays and original band night Wednesdays, Saturday night danceathons, and all-you-can-eat seafood Sundays. Revelers make the most of the outdoor deck, downing $2 drafts and munching on pizza, burgers, and spicy Cajun tidbits. Did I mention drink specials?

With more than 30 satellite HD TVs, a

pool-table room, 14 beers on tap, and a waterproof smoking area, the **Boathouse Bar & Grill** (1309 Main St., 732/681-5221, www.boathousebarandgrill.com, Mon.–Sat. 11 A.M.–2 A.M., Sun. noon–2 A.M.) has got to be the best sports bar in town. A seven-days-a-week Irish happy hour doesn't hurt matters, nor do specials like beach badge giveaways. Wireless Internet too? You could live here.

I'm guessing you're coming for the drinks, but **Patrick's Pub** (711 Main St., 732/280-2266) is also rumored to cook some of the best steaks at the Jersey Shore. This tavern features live bands weekly, along with a fine wraparound bar.

Accommodations

Belmar's overnight choices include hotels, B&Bs, and a couple of guesthouses, though the borough's inability to shake its party reputation keeps many places average at best. These are the borough's standouts, and both offer complimentary breakfast daily.

An easy walk from the beach is the **Morning Dove B&B** (204 5th Ave., 732/556-0777, www.morningdoveinn.com, $175–270), a converted 19th-century Victorian home with eight guest rooms—including two suites—and a solarium overlooking Silver Lake. All rooms have air-conditioning and private baths, and guests are allowed access to the inn's private garden.

Also bordering Silver Lake is **The Inn at the Shore** (301 4th Ave., 732/681-3762, www.theinnattheshore.com, $175–285), a family-friendly B&B with 11 uniquely styled guest rooms. This 19th-century Victorian features a wraparound porch dotted with gliders and rocking chairs, a freshwater aquarium (for the kids), and a quiet reading and writing area. Though decor goes the way of ruffled curtains and teddy bears, at least it's not gloomy. Some rooms have shared baths.

Food

It's easy to find something to snack on along Belmar's boardwalk, but for more of a restaurant feel head inland to downtown and along the Shark River.

For coffee and doughnuts stop by downtown's **Freedman's Bakery** (803 Main St., 732/681-2334)—you can't miss its retro sign. Take a seat at the counter or box the sweet stuff to go. Breakfast and lunch is served beginning at 6 A.M.

One of only several vegetarian restaurants in New Jersey, **Kaya's Kitchen** (817 Belmar Plaza, 732/280-1141, www.kayaskitchennj.com, $8–16) has quite a loyal following. Some dishes—like a "sloppy joe" sandwich smothered in barbecue sauce ($10), and country fried soy legs ($14.95)—are vegan-friendly and have even been known to convert meat eaters. Nachos ($9) and soy nuggets ($6) are especially good appetizers. Kaya's menu is both eclectic and extensive and includes a seasonal Sunday breakfast; BYO. Lunch hours are Tuesday–Saturday 11:30 A.M.–2:30 P.M., and dinner is Tuesday–Saturday 5 P.M.–10 P.M. Breakfast is served seasonally (Apr.–Oct.) Sunday 9 A.M.–1 P.M. Sunday night features an all-you-can-eat vegan buffet, 5 P.M.–9 P.M. Closed Monday.

Dining at **Brandl** (703 Belmar Plaza, 732/280-7501, www.brandlrestaurant.com, dinner Mon.–Thurs. 5–10 P.M., Fri.–Sat. 5–11 P.M., Sun. 5–9 P.M., year-round, $24–38) is more like being in the big city than at the Jersey Shore. Though its storefront exterior gives little indication, Brandl is completely cosmopolitan—in decor, taste, and price. A seasonally refined New American menu most always features chef Chris Brandl's signature crab cakes ($14), which guests can savor on the heated outdoor patio. Friday nights are reserved for live jazz; additional entertainment has included Sinatra nights and psychic readings.

One of Belmar's most beloved institutions is **Klein's Fish Market and Waterside Cafe** (708 River Rd., 732/681-1177, www.kleinsfishmarketonline.com, Sun.–Thurs. 11:30 A.M.–9 P.M., Fri.–Sat. 11:30 A.M.–10 P.M., brunch Sun. 11 A.M.–3 P.M., year-round, $11–22), in business since 1929. Grab an indoor table or a dockside seat outdoors overlooking the Shark River—either way the fresh no-nonsense seafood is fantastic. T-shirts and flip-flops are

THE JERSEY SHORE

standard attire, and a sushi bar adds a touch of the exotic. Sunday brunch ($18.95 adult, $5.95 child) also receives top ratings.

Matisse (13th and Ocean Aves., 732/681-7680, www.matissecatering.com, $24–36) offers seasonal fine dining with unbeatable oceanfront views. This Grecian-style BYO restaurant is a bit more refined than your typical boardwalk eatery. Dishes include sweet and spicy Szechwan shrimp and Canadian hard-shelled lobster. During fall and winter Matisse hosts a Sunday interactive brunch, inviting guests to enter the kitchen and choose from five hot entrées, which the chef then prepares. Summer hours are nightly 5:30–10 P.M. July–August, closed Tuesdays in June.

Getting There
Belmar is located off Exit 98 of the Garden State Parkway. Its train station is located at downtown's Belmar Plaza between Ninth and 10th Avenues, within easy walking distance of restaurants. To reach Belmar from New York City and the Gateway Region by train, take NJ Transit's North Jersey Coast Line.

◖ SPRING LAKE
A throwback to yesteryear, elegant Spring Lake remains one of the last authenticities of the grand ol' Jersey Shore. Both picturesque and peaceful, this affluent borough is brimming with Victorian homes, stately beachfront hotels, and bed-and-breakfasts that line the streets and surround the namesake lake. Downtown's Third Avenue hosts some of the Shore's best shopping, and a few of the North Shore's best restaurants are found here as well. Unlike most shore towns, Spring Lake is primarily a year-round residential community. Most visitors stay at one of the more than dozen recommendable accommodation options throughout town. The beachfront features a two-mile noncommercial boardwalk (the state's longest noncommercial boardwalk) made from recycled plastic and perfect for savoring ocean views.

Beaches
Spring Lake's daily beach tags cost $8, age 12 and under free. Tags are also available for a half season ($60) or full season ($100). During summer months no food or drink is permitted on the beach, but *New Jersey Monthly* suggests leaving a snack-filled cooler along the two-mile boardwalk until you're ready to chow down.

Events
The **Spring Lake Chamber of Commerce** (304 Washington Ave., 732/449-0577, www.springlake.org) sponsors an annual **Bed & Breakfast Christmas Candlelight Tour** in early December, along with various summer happenings. Visit their website for a complete schedule. The borough's **Community House Theatre** (3rd and Madison Ave., 732/449-4530, springlaketheatre.com, $26 adult, $20 child) hosts locally produced musicals and plays throughout the year. Recently performances include *The Producers* and *Gaslight,* a psychological thriller.

Shopping
The borough's shopping district is centered along downtown's Third Avenue. Although it's a bit of a walk from the beach, it's a pleasant one, and once here you'll find plenty of specialty shops, boutiques, galleries, and candy counters to keep you occupied. Downtown shops remain open until 8 P.M. the fourth Friday of every month throughout summer.

BOUTIQUES AND SPECIALTY SHOPS
Camel's Eye (1223 3rd Ave., 732/449-3636) stocks funky designer fashions and Crocs wide-toed shoes, bright bags by Hobo and Kipling, and an assortment of distinguishing hairclips. The tiny **Teddy Bears by the Seashore** (1306 3rd Ave., 732/449-7446) is packed with Jersey-centric hats, sweats, and T-shirts for adults and kids, in addition to Jersey Girl dolls and a teddy bear collection. Girls are queen bee at **Splash** (1305 3rd Ave., 732/449-8388), a favorite clothing boutique of hip moms and daughters.

Men who prefer plaid shorts, Venetian leather shoes, and alpaca sweaters should hit **Village Tweed** (1213 3rd Ave., 732/449-2723, www.villagetweedinc.com), a Spring Lake institution since 1977. For surf and skate fashionistas there's **Third Avenue Surf Shop** (1206 3rd Ave., 732/449-1866, www.3rdavesurf.com), carrying clothing and gear from designers like Oakley, O'Neill, and Smith.

Home and body boutique **Urban Details** (1111 3rd Ave., 732/282-0013, www.urban-details.com) sells handblown glass and jewelry, along with wind chimes, clean-burning candles, and milk shampoo.

GALLERIES AND ANTIQUES

Located just north of the main shopping strip, **Thistledown Gallery Framing** (1045 3rd Ave., 732/974-0376) showcases fine art, including acrylics, watercolors, and lithographs, of local and national artists. The gallery specializes in framing and offers limited-edition prints for purchase.

Evergreen Gallery (308 Morris Ave., 732/449-4488) displays and sells a wonderful array of photography, fine art, and mixed-media works created by New Jersey artists.

Allison's Attic (1317 3rd Ave., 732/449-3485) carries a fun selection of 20th-century antiques, including a Mickey Mantle–signed blueprint of Yankee Stadium and a framed dinner menu from Spring Lake's former Monmouth Hotel.

CANDY STORES

Chocolate comes in all shapes and sizes at **Jean Louise Homemade Candies** (1025 3rd Ave., 732/449-2627), a Spring Lake landmark for more than 85 years. While the chocolate-covered strawberries are to die for, you also have chocolate-shaped baseball gloves, seashells, and elves to choose from. For saltwater taffy and chocolate pops shaped like cartoon characters, try **Third Avenue Chocolate Shoppe** (1138 3rd Ave., 732/449-7535) across the street. Their "chicken legs" on a stick are a must!

Accommodations

Historic hotels, inns, and B&Bs are both plentiful and worth the splurge in this upscale resort. Approximately a dozen of them are registered with the **Historic Inns of Spring Lake** (732/859-1465, www.historicinnsof springlake.com), which hosts events that include the award-winning **Authors and Inns Tour** each June.

The **White Lilac Inn** (414 Central Ave., 732/449-0211, www.whitelilac.com, $179–359) features nine guest rooms ranging from the woodsy Vermont cabin room to the Studio, doused in the rich red hue of a box of Valentines chocolates. Rooms include cable TV and air-conditioning, and some come with old-fashion soaking tubs.

Close to Spring Lake's train station and downtown shopping district is the **Chateau Inn and Suites** (500 Warren Ave, 732/974-2000, www.chateauinn.com). Housed in a late-19th-century building, the 37-room boutique hotel has been updated with modern amenities, including high-speed Internet, plasma TVs, and marble bathtubs. Some rooms have patios, fireplaces, and French doors. In addition to overnight rates, the inn offers celebratory packages such as spa trips and romance-themed room service.

The elegant **Normandy Inn** (21 Tuttle Ave., 732/449-7172, www.normandyinn.com, $149–399) is a late-19th-century Italianate villa listed on the National Register of Historic Places. With 16 rooms and two suites, all decorated in a classic Victorian motif, this is one of the borough's larger B&Bs. Despite its throwback decor, all rooms feature private baths, TVs, high-speed Internet, and air-conditioning, and some have Jacuzzis and fireplaces. A gourmet breakfast prepared by chefs from the French Culinary Institute (no, you're not dreaming) is served to guests restaurant-style.

Spread on prime oceanfront property is the historic 73-room **Breakers Hotel** (1507 Ocean Ave., 732/449-7700, www.breakershotel.com, $220–435), an imposing white clapboard more than a century old. The hotel's beach is private, although there's also an in-ground pool with dining nearby. Size and location make the Breakers a popular place for wedding receptions and conferences, and noise can sometimes be a problem—requesting a room away from the banquet hall may help. All rooms come with high-speed Internet access and a fridge, and many offer incredible ocean views.

Only a block from the beach is **Ashling Cottage B&B** (106 Sussex Ave., 732/449-3553, www.ashlingcottage.com, closed Jan.–Feb., $215–295), a 19th-century Victorian with 11 uniquely designed guest rooms and a glass atrium where visitors can linger over morning meals. The rooms, fairly bright and simple in decor, are spread over three floors (those on the bottom floors are largest). Guests are allowed use of the inn's bicycles during their stay, and there's also a hammock for snoozing, and a covered front porch perfect for an afternoon reprieve.

Housed in an 1888 shingled Victorian originally built as the borough's Grand Central Stables, the **❰ Spring Lake Inn** (104 Salem Ave., 732/449-2010 or 800/803-9031, www.springlakeinn.com, $219–399) is a find. There are 16 guest rooms, each painted in rich hues that complement their themes. Personal touches include a telescope in the Moonbeam Room, a sleigh bed in the Tower View, and the Lighthouse Room's maritime decor. Guests can spend the afternoon rocking in chairs on the inn's 80-foot covered porch, taking advantage of complimentary beach tags and towels, or using the inn's gym passes. The borough's beach and boardwalk are only a block away. Most rooms come equipped with a private bath, and all feature full breakfast daily.

Food

Spring Lake hosts a couple of upscale restaurants, along with more casual eateries along its downtown Third Avenue strip.

The Gulf Coast–inspired BYO **Island Palm Grill** (1321 3rd Ave., 732/449-1909, www.islandpalmgrill.com, Tues.–Sat. 11 A.M.–3 P.M. and 5:30–9 P.M., Sun. 10 A.M.–2 P.M. and 5:30–9 P.M. summer) features an ever-changing menu of dishes like lobster ravioli in lump-crab brandy sauce ($25) and plantain-crusted grouper ($24). A gracious staff helps with your selections.

Tucked within the lakefront Hewitt-Wellington Hotel (www.hewittwellington.com), BYO **Whispers** (200 Monmouth Ave., 732/974-9755, www.whispersrestaurant.com, daily 5:30 P.M.–midnight, $29–34) provides a feast of culinary offerings in a lavish elegant setting. Globally inspired dishes range from a relatively simple grilled salmon filet with mango salsa ($29) to a double-cut pork chop topped with Applewood bacon barbecue sauce ($29).

Situated on the ground floor of the historic Sandpiper Inn is the trendy **Black Trumpet** (7 Atlantic Ave., 732/449-4700, www.theblacktrumpet.com, lunch daily 11:30 A.M.–2 P.M. summer beginning in May, dinner Mon.–Thurs. 5–9 P.M., Fri.–Sat. 5–10 P.M., Sun. 4–8 P.M., $20–31), a BYO serving up New American cuisine with a creative flair. Chefs Mark Mikolajczyk and Dave McCleery are both alums of nearby Whispers, and seafood is their specialty. Of course desserts are just as fabulous, and are prepared either at your table or fresh in the kitchen daily. If you need further incentive to take on extra calories, remember, you can always walk along the beach afterward: It's literally right out the door.

Families flock to **Who's on Third?** (1300 3rd Ave., 732/449-4233, $5–21), a downtown deli and grill serving breakfast and lunch, as well as dinner in-season. Score a stool at the lunch counter and sit back with a pork roll sandwich while admiring framed images of baseball's greats.

Getting There

Spring Lake is located off Exit 98 of the Garden State Parkway. The borough's train station, accessible from New York City by NJ Transit's North Shore Line, is within walking distance of downtown's Third Avenue. The ride is approximately two hours from start to finish.

SEA GIRT AND MANASQUAN

Just south of Spring Lake is Sea Girt, an affluent community filled with sizable homes, manicured lawns, and an unusually high number of parked Mercedes. Although it doesn't offer much of a Shore feel, that's easy to find in nearby Manasquan, a cozy borough replete with funky beach shacks and bungalows, and more of a jeep-driving crowd. Long boards, beach cruisers, and hippie teens are in great supply here, giving Manasquan a sort of Santa Cruz, California, feel. The borough has both ocean and inlet beaches, and hosts some of the best surfing in the state.

Sea Girt Lighthouse

Built in 1896 to bridge a 40-mile gap between the Twin Lights of Navesink and Long Beach Island's Old Barney, the nonoperational Sea Girt Lighthouse (Ocean and Baltimore Blvd.) was the last live-in lighthouse constructed along the country's Atlantic Coast. The structure itself—an inconspicuous though pretty brick Victorian across the street from the beach—is easily overlooked, but once you find it, historic maps, photos, and lighthouse memorabilia make the inside worth a peek. Tours are conducted Sundays through mid-November (2–4 p.m.) and include the lighthouse keeper's office, the Fresnel lens room, and the tower. For further details, call the lighthouse message line at 732/974-0514.

Beaches

Sea Girt's daily beach tags cost $7 adult, age 12 and under free, and a season pass costs $70. For Manasquan, daily beach tags cost $6 adult weekdays and $7 weekends, age 12 and under free; a season pass costs $60.

One of the best surfing spots along the entire Jersey Shore is Manasquan's **Inlet Beach,** also a favorite fishing locale and one of the state's most easily accessible beaches. There's ample handicap parking nearby and a wooden walk that crosses the sand to a viewing area, ideal for mobility-impaired people.

Accommodations

Opened in 2004, Manasquan's **Inn on Main** (152 Main St., 732/528-0809, www.innon mainmanasquan.com, $199–269) stands along the town's small bustling Main Street. This boutique hotel features 12 individually styled rooms, each with its own personality.

Room 301 gets the morning sun, while rooms 204 and 304 are perfect for those traveling with kids. The country decor of room 201 is a grandparent favorite.

Food

Between Sea Girt and Manasquan you'll have plenty of restaurants to choose from. Most casual spots are located along Manasquan's waterfront, while more upscale eateries are scattered throughout Sea Girt and Manasquan's downtown Main Street, some distance from the ocean beach.

Sea Girt's seasonal **◖ Parker House** (1st and Beacon Ave., Sea Girt, 732/449-0442, www.parkerhousenj.com, $10–27) is an area institution, a glorious old clapboard Victorian strung with white lights during summer months, offering live music, dancing, and tavern-style dishes served outdoors on its wraparound veranda. The converted home was built in 1878 and continues to house apartment units up top. In addition to pub food there's an upscale steak and seafood restaurant on the structure's main floor, right above a tavern and below a nightclub. During the day the Parker House attracts families and beachgoers, but nights are taken over by a 20- and 30-something crowd; a group, I might add, that likes to drink.

Just south of Sea Girt on the drive into Manasquan is **Surf Taco** (121 Parker Ave., 732/223-7757, www.surftaco.com, Sun.–Thurs. 11 a.m.–9 p.m., Fri.–Sat. 11 a.m.–9:30 p.m., $2.95–9.95), a Shore semi-chain serving Cal-Mex eats in a brightly painted surf shack. Order at the counter, then grab a table in back among the local teen crowd.

Across the street from the beach where Manasquan's inlet and ocean meet, the flip-flop casual **Riverside Café** (425 Riverside Dr., 732/223-2233, $7–12) offers indoor and outdoor seating, along with burgers, grilled sandwiches, and some of the best chocolate shakes around.

Gracing downtown's Main Street is stylish **Mahogany Grille** (142 Main St., 732/292-1300, www.themahoganygrille.com, Mon.–Thurs.

THE JERSEY SHORE

5–10 P.M., Fri.–Sat. 5–11 P.M., Sun. 4–9 P.M., $24–36), a white-linen restaurant serving some of the Shore's best cuisine. Entrées include filet medallions in red wine syrup ($32) and peppercorn-crusted tuna with sweet brown rice ($30). Proper dress is required. Call for off-season hours.

Local hangout **Green Planet Coffee** (78 Main St., Manasquan 732/722-8197) serves organic and fair-trade coffee along with a small selection of pastries. Local artwork hangs on the walls, but you may be too busy connecting to the free Wi-Fi to notice.

Getting There
NJ Transit's **North Jersey Coast Line** stops at Manasquan's train station, just east of Main Street. To reach Manasquan by car, take Route 35 to the Manasquan Circle, following Atlantic Avenue East until it ends. Make a right onto Broad Street and follow it to the end. Turn left onto Main Street.

The Barnegat Peninsula

Referred to as Barnegat Peninsula from its days before the Point Pleasant Canal was added, this stretch of land starts north at Point Pleasant and continues to the southern tip of Island Beach State Park. North and Central Jersey's best boardwalks are found here, along with one of the most pristine and extensive white-sand beaches along the entire Jersey coast.

POINT PLEASANT BEACH
Not to be mistaken for the nearby borough sharing its name, family-friendly Point Pleasant Beach began as a fishing village that gained popularity once the railroad came to town, and only increased in appeal when the Garden State Parkway opened. Grassy-lawn Cape Cods and bungalows are the typical town residences. Downtown hovers around Arnold, Bay, and Richmond Streets, where there are several restaurants and bars and at least one coffeehouse. Still, the boardwalk is the town's main attraction, especially for kids and teens.

Sights
It may not be the Shore's longest walkway, but **Jenkinson's Boardwalk** (300 Ocean Ave., 732/892-0600, www.jenkinsons.com) packs a lot in for its size. Its two ends are mostly noncommercial, perfect for joggers and casual strollers. For action, head toward the center—a conglomeration of custard stands, pizza places, carnival games, and casual bars built up on both sides in seaworthy shades of green, blue, and pink. Jenkinson's hosts an aquarium and an outdoor amusement park geared towards kids (www.jenkinsons.com, opens daily at noon during summer), but perhaps its best attraction is the **Fun House** ($5), two stories of trick mirrors, moving floors, air blasts, and a rotating tunnel—the kind John Travolta and Olivia Newton John dance on at the end of *Grease*.

Open year-round, privately owned **Jenkinson's Aquarium** (300 Ocean Ave., 732/899-1212, www.jenkinsons.com, Mon.–Fri. 9:30 A.M.–5 P.M., Sat.–Sun. 10 A.M.–5 P.M., $10 adult, $6 senior and child) is a class-trip favorite. First-floor exhibits include tropical fish, sharks, gators, and underwater penguins, while the second floor features a rainforest exhibit with macaws, hissing cockroaches, poison dart frogs, and pygmy marmosets—the world's smallest monkeys. Scheduled shark feedings are open to the public throughout the year.

Beaches
Daily beach tags cost $6.50 on weekdays, $7.50 adult, $2 ages 5–11 on weekends. An adult season pass costs $80, and $45 ages 5–11. Point Pleasant's beaches are both public and private access. There's a small fee to access public beaches along the south end of town. To use the beaches in front of the boardwalk, tags must be purchased directly from Jenkinson's. Stations exist at most entryways.

Fun House, Jenkinson's Boardwalk

in February's annual **Polar Bear Plunge** (732/213-5387), an ocean dip raising money for the Special Olympics.

Movies on the Beach (732/892-0600) are screened on scheduled summer evenings at Jenkinson's beach in front of the boardwalk. Past flicks have included *National Treasure: Book of Secrets* and *Enchanted*.

Since 1975, September's **Festival of the Sea** (www.pointpleasantbeach.com/seafood festival.htm) has signaled summer's end with a showcase of arts and crafts and antiques, local foods, and loads of entertainment. Free shuttles run from the boardwalk to downtown festival grounds.

Sports and Recreation

The charter boat *Diversion II* (http://njscuba .net) takes pro divers to explore artificial reefs and real shipwrecks off New Jersey's coast. For more information contact Captain Steve Nagiewicz by email at steve@njscuba.com.

The **New Jersey Sailing School** (1800 Bay Ave., 732/295-3450, www.newjersey sailingschool.com) offers multiday lessons in basic sailing ($319), bareboat chartering ($579), and coastal navigation ($249). Most workshops are held during summer months, but a few are available in the off-season. Check the website for a complete schedule.

The inlet between Point Pleasant Beach and Manasquan, also known as "The Wall," is one of the area's best fishing spots, and a good place for charter boat rentals. Two to try are **Gambler Fishing** (59 Inlet Dr., 732/295-7569, www.gamblerfishing.net), with twice-daily fluke-fishing trips and night bluefish trips illuminated by underwater lights, and **Purple Jet Sportfishing Fleet** (Canyon River Club, 407 Channel Dr., 732/996-2579 or 800/780-8862, www.purplejet.com), running six-person Atlantic Ocean charter trips. Need fishing supplies? Stop by **Alex's Bait and Tackle** (9 Inlet Dr., 732/295-9268, www.baitandtackle .tv). Public restrooms are located on the inlet's eastern side.

Daredevils may want to try **Point Pleasant Parasail** (Ken's Landing, 30 Broadway,

Surfers gather off-hours at the Pocket along Point Pleasant's inlet to catch waves, but surfing-permitted beaches are difficult to find during on-hours. Your best bet is to drive down to Manasquan. Alcohol is not permitted on Jenkinson's Beach (except in front of the Tiki Bar), but coolers are allowed.

Entertainment and Events

The Southern-style *River Belle* (732/892-3377, www.riverboattour.com) riverboat leaves on two-hour sightseeing tours ($17 adult, $8.25 child) along Barnegat Bay and Point Pleasant Canal daily except Sunday during July and August. Advance tickets are recommended. Additional cruises, such as a Pizza and Fireworks Cruise ($33 adult, $22 child) and a Murder Mystery Dinner Cruise ($62), are scheduled throughout summer. The *River Belle* is docked along the Point Pleasant Canal, leaving from Broadway Basin (47 Broadway Pt.).

Ditch your winter parka, don your skimpiest suit, and join dozens of other maniacs

THE JERSEY SHORE

732/714-2359, www.pointpleasantparasail .org). Solo flights 500 feet above the sea cost $65; if you'd rather go side-by-side with a friend, it's $120. Ocean "dips" are offered for the more adventurous.

Accommodations

Although it's nothing fancy, Point Pleasant Beach's **Windswept Motel** (1008 Beach Ave., 732/899-1282, windsweptmotel.net, $168–258 s, $203–293 d) gets high marks for cleanliness and value. It's within walking distance of both the beach and the boardwalk, and there's a small pool on-site. Some rooms even have ocean views.

Close to Point Pleasant inlet is the family-owned **Surfside Motel** (101 Broadway, 732/899-1109, www.surfside-motel.com, $160–280). Clean standard rooms come equipped with a TV and a fridge, air-conditioning, and complimentary use of daily beach tags. There's also a heated in-ground pool roadside.

The upscale **White Sands Oceanfront Resort & Spa** (1205 Ocean Ave., 732/899-3370, www.thewhitesands.com, $260–765) features both a beachfront motel and a fancier hotel across the street. With two outdoor pools and a private beach, the 74-room motel is the more family-friendly of the two, while a highlight of the 56-room hotel is an adults-only spa. Shared amenities include an Italian steakhouse, fitness club, martini and frozen-drink bar, and an on-site liquor store.

Food and Nightlife

For a hot dog and cold beer, stop by **Jenkinson's Inlet Restaurant** (1 Point Pleasant Beach, 732/892-0234) on the north end of the boardwalk. Its decorative surfboards and open-air bar give off sort of an island feel—and with the ocean stretched before you, it'll be closing time before you known it. Central to the boards is **Jenkinson's Pavilion** (300 Boardwalk, 732/899-0569) a large space hosting several bars and eateries, including a full-service American restaurant, a sushi bar, and an always-packed fast-food counter serving exceptional pepperoni pizza slices ($4).

Tucked away in the rear is **Martell's Tiki Bar** (312 Boardwalk, 732/892-0131, www.tikibar. com, call for hours), *the* place for frozen margaritas and daiquiris. Enjoy them ocean-side along the pier or beach on sticky summer evenings while live bands perform. The pavilion opens daily at 11 A.M. during summer. Tiki bar hours vary so call ahead, or check out the website's webcam to see what's happening in real time.

For gourmet pizza try local favorite **Joey Tomatoes** (Central Ave. and Boardwalk, 732/295-2624, daily in summer, $3–15). Order a slice of chicken parm and linger at one of the boardwalk tables while enjoying supreme people-watching.

Since the 1950s, **Co-op Seafood & Market** (57 Channel Dr., 732/899-2211, daily 10 A.M.–9 P.M. summer, daily 10 A.M.–6 P.M. off-season, $8.50–15) has been serving fresh fish straight from the boats of the local fishers who own it. Just a handful of tables line the inside windows of this small no-frills

sign for the kitschy Circus Drive-In along Route 35

© LAURA KINIRY

establishment, but there's plenty of picnic seating out front. Portions are large, and the staff is both knowledgeable and friendly.

A bit north of Point Pleasant Beach along Route 35 is the glorious **Circus Drive-In** (1861 State Rte. 35, 732/449-2650, www.circus drivein.com, daily 11 A.M.–9 P.M.), a must-stop for fans of roadside architecture and fat pork-roll clubs ($5.99). The 1954 Circus is one of New Jersey's (and the country's) last remaining carhop eateries, and it's in tip-top shape. Pull in for a malted shake and a Wild Animal (ground beef) special ($6.39)—a smiling-clown sign and a circus tent awning leads the way.

Getting There

Point Pleasant Beach is located off Exit 98 (southbound) or Exit 90 (northbound) of the Garden State Parkway. NJ Transit's **North Jersey Coast Line** arrives from New York City at Point Pleasant's downtown train station at Arnold Avenue and Route 35. The station is only a few feet away from downtown's shops and eateries and a few blocks from the beach and boardwalk.

BAY HEAD

It's easy to understand where Bay Head got its nickname, "The New England of the Jersey Shore": With its weathered wood-shingled homes and a charming main street, this hamlet feels like an ideal fit for Martha's Vineyard. Barnegat Bay passes beneath downtown's tiny Bridge Avenue, home to a handful of specialty shops and a sweet bakery, and just north along Lake Avenue, bayside benches offer reprieve among ducks and various shorebirds. For anyone needing a vacation from their vacation, this is the place to come.

Beaches

Daily beach tags cost $6 adult, age 12 and under free. An adult season pass cost $65 or $45 for a half-season. Parking throughout town is free. Due to its small size and lack of tourist attractions, Bay Head offers no public restrooms or changing rooms. Food and beverages are prohibited on the beach.

Shopping

Most Bay Head shops are centered along Bridge Avenue, with a handful of stores scattered throughout town.

Old-fashioned **Mueller's Bakery** (80 Bridge Ave., 732/892-0442, www.muellers bakery.com) smells of baked butter cookies and cheese-filled pastries. Lines can be long, so get here early.

For beach-blanket and tote-bag combos, handmade Jersey Girl plaques, and a variety of antiques and collectibles, check out **Cobwebs** (64 Bridge Ave., 732/892-8005). Both a gift shop and art gallery, **The Jolly Tar** (56 Bridge Ave., 732/892-0223) carries specialty writing paper and hand-carved decoys, and keeps a full-time bridal consultant on staff.

Walking through the **Shopper's Wharf** (70 Bridge Ave., 732/295-4333), a former historic theater, is like entering a cartoon village: Store exteriors are painted to look like they're outdoors. Selections in this makeshift miniature town include the tiny tea and coffee shop **Bay Head Blends,** beach-themed jewelry store **Memory Shoppe,** and the **Chocolate Shoppe** (732/899-2870), selling homemade chocolates and fudge for more than 30 years.

Accommodations

The Queen Anne–style **Bentley Inn** (694 Main Ave., 732/892-9589 or 866/423-6853, www.bentleyinn.com, $164–249 s, $194–279 d) features 19 brightly colored guest rooms, most with a shared bath and all with a TV and VCR, air-conditioning, and individual sitting areas. The inn is known for its expansive covered porches and a dining solarium where guests dine on Belgium waffles and caramelized French toast. Use of the inn's bikes is complimentary.

Conover's Bay Head Inn (646 Main Ave., 732/892-8748, www.conovers.com, $175–320) hosts nine antique-filled guest rooms and three suites, all with a private bath, TV and VCR, and air-conditioning. Fresh baked goods are offered daily to enjoy outdoors in the inn's English garden or with afternoon tea.

Food

Nestled below Bay Head's **Historic Grenville Hotel** (345 Main Ave., 732/892-3100, www.thegrenville.com, Mon.–Fri. 11:30 A.M.–2:30 P.M. and 5–9 P.M., Sat. 11:30 A.M.–2:30 P.M. and 5–9:30 P.M., Sun. 9:30 A.M.–1:30 P.M. and 5–9 P.M., $18–40), the Grenville restaurant is this hamlet's fine-dining gem, a place to celebrate anniversaries and promotions. New American dishes come served in a Victorian setting or along an expansive front porch. The Sunday brunch buffet is a highlight.

Getting There

Bay Head is located off Exit 98 (southbound) or Exit 90 (northbound) of the Garden State Parkway. New Jersey Transit's **North Jersey Coast Line** runs from New York City to Bay Head, this small seaside hamlet being the last stop on the line.

SEASIDE HEIGHTS

It has been over a decade since Seaside Heights played host to MTV's summer beach house. If this gives any indication of what the town was like, things haven't changed. Dance clubs pumping pulsating music till the early morning, seedy motels advertising prom-night specials, and a tacky boardwalk topped with Muffler Men (those multistory fiberglass giants sometimes seen standing along secondary highways), Jäger bars, and casino arcades pretty much sum it up. For anyone wanting to partake in the Seaside spirit, stop by a boardwalk shop and buy yourself a "what happens in seaside stays in seaside" T-shirt, or one that reads "not only am i cute, but i'm italian, too." Then primp for the numerous security cameras and hit the piers for one long carnival ride. You'll have a story to tell.

Unless this is your designated shore town (which is kind of like a middle name for New Jerseyans), the boardwalk and amusement piers are the only real reasons to visit Seaside, along with a few interesting bars and clubs. Dining and accommodations are not Seaside's highlights, although a couple of bars offer a decent food selection and you can always grab a snack on the boardwalk. There are a few motels in town that are by no means luxurious, but are OK should you decide to stay. If you don't mind driving, it's worth it to book a room in Bay Head or Point Pleasant to the north and visit Seaside for the day.

Boardwalk

People are strange, you say? You haven't seen anything until you've visited Seaside Height's boardwalk. A wilder version of the Cape's Wildwood, this boardwalk attracts the ballsy, busty, and beefy, who are happy to display their wares. Built up on both sides with amusement piers, arcades, fried-food stands, bars, carnival games, and T-shirt shacks, it's definitely a sight to see. Why not take it all in from above? A mile-long skyway extends along the walkway's beach side, advertising cool breezes from its open-air seats.

Goth teens tend to congregate where the boardwalk narrows, connecting with the recycled plastic planks of Seaside Park's beachfront.

On the boardwalk's south side is the ocean-facing **Casino Pier** (800 Ocean Terr., 732/793-6495, www.casinopiernj.com), home to a log flume, pirate's cavern, glass house, and one of the boardwalk's best attractions, the Gothic-style **Stillwalk Manor** dark ride. The pier also hosts **Rooftop Wacky Golf,** an 18-hole miniature golf course presided over by the Happy Half-wit Muffler Man. Casino Pier is open every day in July and August and through most of June, and weekends during the shoulder seasons beginning mid-March and ending mid-September. Each ride costs a varying number of tickets (3–10), available for purchase on-site.

Was Pac-Man fever driving you crazy during the '80s? Then consider Casino Arcade's **Flashback Arcade,** tucked behind the carousel house, a must-stop. Centipede, Ms. Pac-Man, Track and Field, Pole Position—they're all here, and keeping with the yesteryear theme, most games play for $0.25. Ventilation is a problem, but most players are too overcome with joy to notice.

Casino Pier's carousel house is home to one

of only two American carved antique carousels remaining in New Jersey. The **Floyd Moreland Carousel** (732/793-6489, www.magical carousel.com, $2) features over 2,000 bulbs, nearly 20 paintings, and a Wurlitzer Band organ with 105 wooden pipes.

At Casino Pier's recently renovated **Jenkinson's Breakwater Beach** (800 Ocean Terr., 732/793-6488, www.casinopiernj.com, $22.95 adult, $18.95 child 3-hour admission) waterslides wiggle, plunge, shoot, and loop. Less-adventurous types take to the hot-springs pools and lazy river, or sit steady at one of the new private cabanas ($60 for 3 hours). There's also a good-sized kids' play area.

With over 40 rides, including bumper cars, a loop roller coaster, and the 225-foot freefalling Tower of Fear, **Funtown Pier** (1930 Boardwalk, 732/830-7437, www.funtownpier.com, $25 for 45 ride tickets) lives up to its name. A lot of the rides are for kids, but the giant Ferris wheel and go-karts belong to anyone. The pier is open throughout summer.

Beaches

Daily beach tags cost $5 adult, age 12 and under free. The beach is free for everyone Wednesdays and Thursdays. Seaside's adult season beach passes are a steal at only $35. There's metered parking on the streets; spaces in lots cost $5–10.

In nearby Seaside Park, just south, a day at the beach is $8 adult, age 11 and under free.

Events

Casino Pier hosts free summer fireworks every Wednesday beginning at 9 P.M.

In need of a laugh? Check out September's annual **Clownfest** convention (www.clown fest.com). Although the five-day event consists mostly of classes and competitions, the boardwalk parade, held on the final Sunday, is open to all. Painted participants are easily spotted throughout town, until packing 12-deep into their buggies for the drive home.

Accommodations

Motels are Seaside's primary overnight options,

and while there are plenty of them, a large percentage are uninhabitable. Following are a few of your best options for staying in Seaside, although Bay Head and Point Pleasant Beach both offer a greater selection and are only a short drive away—so you can skip the endless party for a good night's sleep.

Yes, the walls are wood-paneled, but rooms at the **Colony Motel** (65 Hiering Ave., 732/830-2113, www.seasidecolonymotel.com, $99–149) are clean and spacious. This lodging was recently selected by *The Washington Post* as the place to stay in Seaside. Amenities include air-conditioning, fridges, microwaves, and an in-ground pool.

In a commendable effort to keep noise to a minimum, the 23-room **Luna Mar Motel** (1201 N. Ocean Ave., 732/793-8991 or 877/586-2627, www.lunamarmotel.com, $148–198) strictly enforces the policy that anyone age 21 and under must be accompanied by an adult. Focusing on families and couples, the motel offers quiet rooms and efficiencies, most with newly renovated baths and furnishings. There's a swimming pool on-site.

Food and Nightlife

For a taste of New Jersey the way the rest of the world imagines it (gold chains, fringe T-shirts, big hair, accents), there's no place better than Seaside. This doesn't mean every Seaside establishment is Jersified—there are a few local bars where the state stereotype is a minority. These are usually the best places to grab a bite to eat as well. Like other New Jersey shore towns, many Seaside Heights establishments taper business hours beginning in the fall until January, when they're locked and bolted until spring.

For Seaside Heights in all its glory, swing by **Merge** (302 Boulevard, 732/793-3111), a downtown dance club featuring its own private champagne bar. When resident DJ Richie Rydell spins underground club tunes, rumor is the girls-to-guy ratio is 10 to one.

The **Saw Mill Restaurant & Tavern** (1807 Boardwalk, 732/793-1990, www.sawmillcafe .com) is a boardwalk institution, and the best place in town to grab a slice of pizza—they're enormous! The restaurant has gone through numerous changes over the years, including an expansion (complete with a sushi bar) that some say makes the place less cozy, but it's still adequately loved. Upstairs is the 21-and-over **Green Room,** the town's best live-music venue. Theme nights include $2 Tijuana Tuesdays and Krazy Kup Thursdays, with $3 32-ounce beer refills all night long.

If a little respectability is what you're after, try **Klee's Bar and Grill** (101 Boulevard, 732/830-1996, www.kleesbarandgrill.com), an Irish pub offering a variety of casual eats, including pizza, burgers, and a house-made Klee's Pot Pie ($10.95). Live music is featured in the bar on weekends. Klee's **Next Door Cafe,** literally next door, serves breakfast (daily 7 A.M.–noon).

Getting There
Seaside Heights is located off Exit 82 of the Garden State Parkway.

ISLAND BEACH STATE PARK

One of New Jersey's most pristine coastal stretches, 3,003-acre Island Beach State Park (Seaside Park, 732/793-0506, www.njparks andforests.org/parks/island.html) hosts 10 miles of white-sand beaches, a wildlife preserve, natural trails, freshwater bogs, and maritime vegetation. Situated between the Atlantic Ocean and Barnegat Bay, this narrow barrier strip is a major stop along the Atlantic Flyway, a bird migration route, making it a hot spot for birders. The park is home to New Jersey's largest nesting osprey colony, and peregrine falcons, waterfowl, and warblers all travel through. Red foxes and turtles reside here, and additional seasonal visitors include butterflies, and in nearby waters, bluefish and striped bass. Island Beach is also a good spot to glimpse bottlenose dolphins during summer months, as well as the occasional harbor or gray seal (Dec.–Mar.).

The park has three sections: a northern natural area, a central recreational zone, and a southern natural area, containing the majority of the wildlife habitat. The northern zone's access is somewhat limited—it has been set aside as protected coastal habitat.

Sports and Recreation
There are eight less-than-a-mile-long nature trails scattered throughout the park, including one beginning from the central zone's year-round comfort station, and another leaving from the bird blind in the southern zone's Area 20. Interpretive exhibits along each trail offer insight into the park's natural and cultural offerings. Bicycle lanes run parallel to the road for cyclists. Horseback riding is permitted October–April on the six southernmost miles of Ocean Beach.

The park's central recreation zone features a mile-long beach designated for swimming, with lifeguards, a concession stand, first-aid station, and bathhouses open Memorial Day–Labor Day.

Scuba diving is permitted along a 2.5 mile stretch off the park's southern zone, beginning from Barnegat Inlet and heading north. Divers are required to first register with the park service. The southern tip of Ocean Bathing Area 3 in the central area is designated for surfing and windsurfing. Surfing is also allowed from Parking Area 2 south to the inlet.

Island Beach offers some of the Shore's best saltwater sportfishing—especially for striped bass and bluefish—and the southern tip of the park overlooking Barnegat Bay Lighthouse (the lighthouse is about an hour's drive, as access is limited to mainland routes) is reserved for fishing. Beach parking is allowed for those carrying permits; four-wheel drive is preferable. Sportfishing is also allowed at the central zone's Bathing Area 2 during the off-season.

The southern natural area also offers the park's best bird-watching ops (waterfowl are best sighted May–Oct.), as well as a boat launch for canoes and kayaks at Area 21. In summer, guided canoe and kayak excursions take place along Barnegat Bay, exploring the nearby Sedge Islands—a marine conservation zone where sighting may include nesting ospreys, falcons, and wading birds.

Daily educational programs are offered

throughout summer at Ocean Swimming Area 1. These may include all-age beach tours, fishing the Barnegat Bay, and learning about the local food chain. For an updated schedule, phone the park's nature center (732/793-1698).

Information and Services

Vehicle admission fees are $6 on weekdays, $10 on weekends Memorial Day–Labor Day, $5 daily in the off-season.

Island Beach offers selected tours and programs daily July–August, beginning from the central zone's First Pavilion visitors center at Ocean Bathing Area 1. For ranger assistance, call the park office (732/793-0506) or 911 in an emergency.

Public restrooms are scattered throughout the park, including at the park entryway, in the middle and southern portions of the central recreation zone, and in numerous spots along the southern natural area. A year-round facility is located at Lot A-7 in the central recreation zone, which also hosts a wooden walkway to the sea suitable for visitors with disabilities. Big-wheel rolling chairs are available at the central zone's Ocean Bathing Areas 1 and 2 pavilions during summer, and from the park service (offices are located between the two beaches) in the off-season.

Beach picnicking with grills is allowed in the central zone south of the designated swimming area. Picnickers must supply their own grills.

Long Beach Island and Vicinity

Long Beach Island, also known as LBI, is a thin barrier island stretching for 18 miles along the Jersey coast, with only one access bridge. The island is made up of several distinct towns, each attracting a different type of visitor. While LBI was once notorious for its dangerous coastal waters and the dozens of shipwrecks because of them, the island has more recently become known as "New Jersey's Hamptons," with parts of the island now appealing to vacationers used to trendy restaurants and boutique hotels. You can still find casual cedar shacks, surfing enclaves, campy eateries, and family-oriented entertainment throughout the island, and it's all brought together by one long boulevard.

Due to LBI's length and its lack of roadways and access points, traffic backs up easily. It's best to book a room in or near the island's region you plan on exploring; otherwise you'll spend much of your vacation in the car. The towns mentioned below run north–south along LBI.

There are several camping resorts and worthwhile attractions along the mainland's Route 9, just over the island's causeway bridge. It's a beautiful region and much more low-key than LBI during summer months. You might consider staying at one of the campgrounds

and driving over to LBI in the morning or afternoon.

Getting There

To reach Long Beach Island take Exit 63 off the Garden State Parkway. There's only one bridge to LBI.

BARNEGAT LIGHT

Other than its southern tip, Barnegat Light is probably Long Beach Island's least inhabited stretch. Situated at the top of the island across the inlet from Island Beach State Park, Barnegat Light (separate from the mainland's Barnegat Township) has a population of less than 1,000 and is smaller than one square mile in size. It's home to one of New Jersey's most photographed structures.

◀ Barnegat Lighthouse State Park

Thirty-two-acre Barnegat Lighthouse State Park (Barnegat Light, 609/494-2016, www.state.nj.us/dep/parksandforests/parks/barnlig.html, daily dawn–dusk), sits along LBI's northern tip, where the Atlantic Ocean and Barnegat Bay meet. It's a picturesque place

THE JERSEY SHORE

© LAURA KINIRY

Old Barney, the Barnegat lighthouse

filled with long sandy stretches and a maritime forest, as well as an interpretive center, a maritime forest nature trail, and plenty of waterfront property. Along the inlet separating Barnegat from Island Beach State Park (a few hundred yards by sea, an hour by car) is a 1,033-foot concrete walkway ideal for strolling, and often used by fishers casting for bluefish, weakfish, and flounder. The park is a popular spot for wildlife viewing, and seasonal birds are regular visitors. Waterfowl appear during summer shoulder seasons, shorebirds arrive for the high season, and warblers make their way through in fall. December–March it's possible to sight gray and harbor seals along Barnegat beaches. Thousands of monarch butterflies find temporary shelter in the maritime forest in late summer and early autumn. The park does not offer a public beach.

Barnegat is home to one of the state's most beloved lighthouses, a 172-foot, 217-step, red-and-white structure affectionately known as **Old Barney** (daily 9 A.M.–4:30 P.M. Memorial Day–Labor Day, Wed.–Sun. 9 A.M.–3:30 P.M.

Labor Day–Memorial Day, $1). Said to be New Jersey's most photographed lighthouse, Barney was erected in the 1850s when sailors complained its predecessor could be mistaken for a passing ship. Today, visitors can climb to the top of Barney's deactivated light tower for spectacular 360-degree views. Not to worry—numerous exhibit rooms serve as rest areas for those ascending (and descending) the spiral stairs.

Viking Village

Founded in the 1920s by Norwegian fishermen and renamed in 1972, Viking Village (19th St. and Bayview Ave., 609/494-0113) is home to a small row of shanty-style shops, including antiques purveyor **The Sea Wife** (609/361-8039, www.theseawife.com), and **Viking Outfitters** (609/361-9111), a clothing store for sea captains. Thirty-eight boats dock at Viking Village, which is one of the East Coast's largest fresh-fish suppliers, producing $25 million worth of seafood products annually. In conjunction with the Southern Ocean County Chamber of Commerce the village offers free dock tours Fridays at 10 A.M. throughout summer.

A bit of local trivia: Viking Village is home to the *Lindsay L* fishing vessel, which portrayed the *Hanna Bodan* in the 2000 movie *The Perfect Storm.*

Beaches

The best beach access in Barnegat Light is below 20th Street. Beach tags run $5 daily, $20 weekly, and $35 for the season. Those age 12 and under don't require beach tags. Beach wheelchairs are available for rent at Borough Hall (10 W. 10th St., 609/494-9196), and there's handicap parking at Ninth and 29th Streets. There are public restrooms at Barnegat Lighthouse State Park and at 10th Street and Bayview Avenue. Food and alcohol are permitted on the beach.

Accommodations

Tucked along a side road near Barnegat Lighthouse State Park is **Sand Castle** (710 Bayview Ave., 609/494-6555 or 800/253-0353, www.sandcastlelbi.com, $295–425), a modern luxury B&B best suited for couples. Five guest rooms and two suites come equipped with private baths, fireplaces, and a TV and DVD player, and each has its own private entry. Guests get complimentary use of the inn's bicycles—perfect for working off the gourmet breakfast served each morning. Added perks include a heated pool and a rooftop deck.

Food and Nightlife

On the far side of the lighthouse parking lot is **Kelly's Old Barney Restaurant** (3rd St. and Broadway, 609/494-5115, $6–11), a cozy nautically themed restaurant serving a simple menu of American eats like burgers, fries, and grilled cheese on white bread. Prices are reasonable, and there's outdoor seating in back. Kelly's is cash-only and is open seasonally.

Moustache Bill's Diner (8th and Broadway, 609/494-0155, $7–15) is an island favorite, an old-school diner crowded with locals and shoobies who pack in for pancakes, omelets, and grilled Reuben sandwiches. Open for breakfast and lunch only, hours are Thursday–Monday 6 a.m.–3 p.m., Tuesday–Wednesday 6 a.m.–11:30 a.m. June–September, and Friday–Sunday 6 a.m.–3 p.m. during the off-season. The diner is closed January–mid-March.

Viking Village's **Viking Fresh Off the Hook** (1905 Bayview Ave., 609/361-8900, www.vikingoffthehook.com, call for hours, $6.95–24.95) lives up to its name, selling deliciously straight-from-the-boat seafood (you can actually watch it coming ashore) accompanied by fries, slaw, or smashed potatoes. Hours vary throughout the year.

HARVEY CEDARS AND LOVELADIES

Harvey Cedars began as a whaling station, though today it's a mostly residential ocean and bayside community hosting a couple of excellent dining options. Its neighbor Loveladies is part of the larger Long Beach Township, a conglomeration of island communities scattered along LBI. Loveladies is named for Thomas Lovelady, a local man who owned a nearby island in the late 19th century. The neighborhood suffered considerable damage during LBI's infamous 1962 three-day storm, with many of its homes destroyed completely. They've since been rebuilt bigger and better, raised high on pilings and blocking beach views. You'll still see the occasional single-story home in Loveladies, but it's rare. As one of the island's thinnest portions, Loveladies doesn't have much to offer visitors, and public beach access is limited. While Loveladies is completely without restaurants, there are a couple of excellent dining options in Harvey Cedars. Overnight accommodations are hard to come by in both towns—try Barnegat Light to the north, or if you're up for a drive, head south about 13 miles to LBI's Beach Haven, home to the island's best lodging selection. Several worthwhile stays are scattered in between.

Beaches

Harvey Cedars offers both ocean and bay beaches. Daily tags for use at both cost $6, free for those age 12 and under. Restrooms are located at the bayfront **Sunset Park** (W. Salem Ave.) along with volleyball and boccie courts, a baseball field, and a paved fitness track. There's a beach access ramp for disabled people at Mercer Avenue and 80th Street, along with handicap parking. Beach surf chairs for those with limited mobility are available through the local borough (609/361-9733). There's a children's beach at 77th Street and the bay.

Loveladies beach is $5 daily, free for those under age 12 and over 65. Much of Loveladies' shoreline is considered private. Public access points are located in only a handful of spots, including Coast Avenue, Loveladies Lane, and Seashell Lane. Loveladies's public restrooms are located at Harbor South.

Events

The **Long Beach Island Foundation of the Arts and Sciences** (609/494-1241, www.lbifoundation.org) hosts an annual August **Seashore Open House Tour** ($30) featuring some of Loveladies's finest homes. A summer concert series is held Wednesday summer

THE JERSEY SHORE

evenings at Harvey Cedars's **Sunset Park** (W. Salem Ave.) on the bay.

Food

LBI has earned the nickname "New Jersey's Hamptons" thanks in part to restaurants like **Plantation** (7908 Long Beach Blvd., Harvey Cedars, 609/494-8191, www.plantation restaurant.com, lunch daily 11:30 A.M.– 2:30 P.M., dinner Sun.–Thurs. 4:30–9:30 P.M., Fri.–Sat. 4:30–10:30 P.M., $10–25), a Key West–inspired year-round eatery specializing in rum-infused drinks and contemporary fusion dishes, like Brazilian fish and chips with paprika fries ($23) and wasabi-crusted Chilean sea bass ($36). The refined island decor is much more Bogie and Bacall than Monchichi.

Next door is the informal **Harvey Cedars Shellfish Company** (7904 Long Beach Blvd., 609/494-7112, harveycedarsshellfishco.com), a BYO seafood market with picnic tables for dining that has been in business since 1976. The Company opens at 4:30 P.M. nightly during summer, with limited hours during off-season.

SURF CITY

Tiny Surf City—it covers less than one square mile—has a wonderful laissez-faire quality. Filled with residential shacks and casual eateries, you'll feel perfectly at home in flip-flops and T-shirt attire toting a board on the back of your bike.

Beaches

Beach tags cost $8 daily (under age 12 and over 65 free). Surf City's designated surfing beach is between North First and North Third Streets; its designated fishing beach is North 23rd– North 25th Streets. A bayside bathing beach exists near 15th Street and Barnegat Avenue. Beaches can be accessed from any side street. Public restrooms are located at **Borough Hall** (813 Long Beach Blvd., 609/494-3064).

Sports and Recreation

For surrey and bicycle rentals try **Surf Buggy Center** (1414 Long Beach Blvd., 609/361-3611), and for miniature golf, **Surf City Island**

Golf (603 Long Beach Island Blvd., 609/494-1709, $4–5). Surf City has a **surf-only beach** between First and Second Streets—look for the flags. Local bait and tackle shop **Surf City Bait & Tackle** (317 Long Beach Blvd., 609/494-2333) is one of many island shops selling clamming licenses.

Accommodations, Food, and Nightlife

One of LBI's oldest hotels, the **Surf City Hotel** (8th St. and Long Beach Island Blvd., 609/494-7281, www.surfcityhotel.com, $160–230) is a massive white clapboard practically swelling with salty air. In addition to air-conditioned rooms, each with a TV and a fridge, and a disability-equipped cottage, the hotel houses a pub, adjacent liquor store, restaurant, and even a clam bar. While live entertainment plays most summer evenings and Sunday afternoons, it's the hotel's happy hour that draws the most varied clientele, including New York City commuters and sock-and-sandal-clad shoobies. Before leaving, pick up a logo-topped sun visor at the hotel's souvenir stand.

For a breakfast that satisfies, try the year-round **Scojo's** (307 N. Long Beach Blvd., 609/494-8661, $7–14), also open for lunch and dinner.

SHIP BOTTOM AND LONG BEACH TOWNSHIP

Long Beach Township comprises a number of smaller areas, including Brant Beach (south of Ship Bottom), Spray Beach, Brighton Beach, and Beach Haven North. Ship Bottom is the island's centermost borough, the place where Route 72 drops you onto LBI. For this reason, Ship Bottom is more commercial than the rest of the island, and it lacks the community feel you'll find in other boroughs. Businesses have popped up sporadically along the wide main street, catering to summer's inevitable weekend traffic.

Beaches

Long Beach Township's daily beach tags cost $5 daily, $20 weekly, and $35 for the season;

Ship Bottom's are $7 daily, $17 weekly, and $35 for the season. Public restrooms are located within Ship Bottom's Borough Hall (1621 Long Beach Blvd., 609/494-2171), 10–12th Streets at the bay, and Branch Beach's Bayview Park (68th St.). Many of Ship Bottom's beaches are wheelchair-accessible. Alcohol is permitted on both beaches.

Sports and Recreation

One of the Mid-Atlantic coast's largest windsurfing shops, **Island Surf & Sail** (3304 Long Beach Blvd., Brant Beach, 609/494-5553, www.islandsurf-sail.com) rents wakeboard, windsurfing, and surfing equipment, and offers lessons in all three, along with kiteboarding (check the website for prices). Kayaks are also available.

Opened in the 1950s as a tiny local surf shop, Ship's Bottom's **Ron Jon Surf Shop** (201 W. 9th St., 609/494-8844, www.ronjons.com) has morphed into a glossy national retail franchise. Island old-timers who haven't visited recently won't recognize the flagship store—looming large like Oz at the causeway entry. LBI's original still sells boards, gear, and hip summer fashions, but if history is what you're after, it's buried beneath the jams and T-shirts.

Accommodations, Food, and Nightlife

Located at the base of the island's entry bridge, BYO **La Spiaggia** (357 W. 8th St., 609/494-4343, www.laspiaggialbi.com, $25–38) offers upscale Italian eats and outstanding service, a few steps above your typical Jersey Shore dining experience. With this in mind it's best to forgo the tank tops and flip-flops for more appropriate attire. The restaurant is open for dinner only, Tuesday–Sunday from 5 P.M. during summer, Wednesday–Sunday spring and fall; call for winter hours.

A local institution for half a century, **Joe Pop's Shore Bar** (2002 Long Beach Blvd., 609/494-0558, www.joepops.com, daily) is the island spot for seeing area bands like Big Orange Cone, Steamroller Picnic, and the loveable Nerds. In addition to nightly drink specials, the bar serves an extensive menu of simple American eats. Call ahead for off-season and exact hours.

Literally the first thing you see when arriving on Long Beach Island is the octagonal **Quarter Deck** (351 W. 9th St., 609/494-9055), a massive nightclub, restaurant, and motel combo with an outdoor deck and karaoke on weekends. Live music includes the Springsteen tribute band B-Street, and Vanilla Ice (ice baby).

Long Beach Island's first boutique hotel and restaurant, **Daddy O** (4401 Long Beach Blvd., 609/494-1300, www.daddyohotel.com, $235–325 s, $275–425 d) opened in August 2006 to rave reviews. Occupying the site and structure of a former 80-year-old hotel, this deceivingly retro clapboard and cedar space features 22 modern guest rooms on its second and third floors, and a New American bar and eatery beneath. Doused in deep browns and whites, rooms are small but stylish, and each comes equipped with halogen reading lamps, a flat-screen TV, and access to the rooftop deck, which also hosts private parties. Daddy O's sleek dining establishment (daily 11:30 A.M.–2:30 P.M., dinner daily from 4 P.M.) offers alfresco seating during warmer months (both the hotel and restaurant are open year-round) and an island-inspired menu of dishes, including pan-seared mahimahi ($26), and lump crab cakes with shoestring fries ($25).

BEACH HAVEN

Toward LBI's southern tip is Beach Haven, a predominantly residential borough hosting the island's only amusement pier. The Haven includes a small historic district with a museum and dozens of century-old cedar Victorians, as well as a wonderful local theater and adjoining ice cream parlor. Keeping with its family image, the borough has a strict 11 P.M. curfew for minors.

Sights

For more than a quarter century **Fantasy Island Amusement Park** (320 W. 7th St., 609/492-4000, www.fantasyislandpark.com) has been entertaining LBI visitors. Enjoy a

THE JERSEY SHORE

bird's-eye view aboard the Ferris wheel, get queasy on the swinging Sea Dragon, or sit cozy on the carousel. Later, test your eye at an old-school shooting gallery before gorging on funnel cake and soft-serve cones. An indoor casino arcade features hundreds of slot machines, skee-ball courts, and giant crane games. Cash in your ticket wins for some of the best arcade prizes along the shore. Fifteen bucks will get you a roll of twenty tokens, and most rides require 3–5. The park opens Saturday–Thursday at 6 P.M., Fridays at 2 P.M. throughout summer. The arcade opens at noon.

Stop by the **Long Beach Island Museum** (Engleside and Beach Aves., 609/492-0700, www.lbi.net/nonprof/lbimusm.html, $3 donation) to get an understanding of island history, including information on its whaling community beginnings and details on the three-day storm of 1962, which destroyed a large percentage of the island's homes and forever altered its physical geography. The museum provides self-guided tour brochures for Beach Haven's historic district, and hosts guided

neighborhood tours ($8) throughout summer. Hours are weekends 2–4 P.M. May–June and early September, daily 10 A.M.–4 P.M. July and August. They're also open Tuesdays year-round; just knock on the back door.

The **Edwin B. Forsythe National Wildlife Refuge's Holgate Unit** (www.fws.gov/north east/forsythe/), an endangered piping plover nesting site, occupies LBI's southern tip. It's open for visits during nonnesting season (Sept.–Mar.), and is the perfect place for a quiet beach stroll.

Beaches

Beach Haven's beach access costs $5 daily, $15 weekly, and $25 for the season. Beaches can be accessed from anywhere, but Centre Street Beach has a wheelchair ramp. Restrooms are available at Centre Street and Dock Road, Schooner's Wharf, and in the Bay Village shopping area. Alcohol and picnics are prohibited on the beach, though it's alright to bring along a small sandwich.

A special toddler beach is located on the bay at Taylor Avenue, where there's also a playground and basketball courts.

Entertainment

Home to Ocean County's only professional theater, Beach Haven's beloved **Surflight Theatre** (Engleside and Beach Aves., 609/492-9477 or 609/492-4469, www.surflight.org, $29 adult, $9 child) has been running musical and stage productions such as *Kismet, Mister Roberts,* and *Oklahoma!* for more than 50 years. The theater has 450 seats, and performances—including children's theater ($9)—run throughout summer and fall, as well as the December holiday season.

True theater fans start the night at next door's **Show Place Ice Cream Parlor** (200 Centre St., Beach Haven, 609/492-0018, www .surflight.org/showplac.htm, daily from 6 P.M. summer), an old-fashioned ice cream parlor with checkered floors, candy-striped walls, and fabulous themed specialties like the Phantom of the Opera chocolate sundae, topped with a mask of marshmallow. But the best part about

Beach Haven's historic district

THE SHORE'S BACK ROUTE

Between the Shore's barrier islands and the mainland, beginning south from the Manasquan River, lie a series of salt water bays, natural inlets, rivers, and manmade canals connecting all the way to Texas. Called the **Intracoastal Waterway,** this Congress-authorized stretch acts as a toll-free route protecting boats from Atlantic seas and storms. New Jersey's portion, a back-bay wonderland bordering Route 9, often goes undiscovered. Here are some of its local roadside highlights:

HURRICANE HOUSE

An area institution, the Hurricane House (688 East Bay Ave., Barnegat, 609/698-5040, Mon.-Fri. 11 A.M.-10 P.M., Sat.-Sun. 7 A.M.-10 P.M.) has an interesting history. Originally built as a Victorian home, the property became a pool hall in 1918 after a fire destroyed the original structure. By 1920 it was a general store, morphing into the Hurricane House restaurant sometime in the 1970s. The business eventually closed, only to reopen as a restaurant and ice cream parlor in 2001. Recently, the Hurricane House underwent a complete interior renovation. Burgundy walls, high-backed booths, and a piano (and player) have been added, bringing back the establishment's original look and feel. Casual American eats (and ice cream) are served throughout the day.

TUCKERTON SEAPORT VILLAGE

Across Little Egg Harbor from Long Beach Island is 40-acre Tuckerton Seaport (120 W. Main St., 609/296-8868, www.tuckertonseaport.org, $8 adult, $3 child 6-12), a restored living-history village and New Jersey's only one dedicated to maritime culture. Opened in 2000, Tuckerton Seaport has all the makings of an authentic seaport village: docks, decoy carvers, and boat builders, along with 16 waterfront buildings. There's even a lighthouse, modeled after one that originally stood on Tucker's Island, off Long Beach Island's southern tip, but was washed away in a 1927 storm. The seaport is home to the **Jacques Cousteau National Estuarine Research Center,** hosting a visitors center and public maritime exhibits. And if traffic along Route 9 is too backed up, you can always arrive by boat.

Tuckerton Seaport Village is open daily 10 A.M.-5 P.M. during summer, Friday-Sunday 11 A.M.-4 P.M. in the off-season.

CAPTAIN MIKE'S MARINA

Located along Great Bay Boulevard just south of Tuckerton Seaport, Mike's (fourth bridge along Great Bay Blvd., 609/296-4406, www.captmikesmarina.com) was established in 1937 and serves as the region's premier place for boat and kayak rentals. Choose among 16- to 19-foot Carolina skiffs, wooden garveys, and 18-foot Pontoon boats. Prices range $75-190 for weekday boat rentals, and $25 for a two-hour single kayak rental. Guided kayaking tours ($45 per person, Wed. and Fri.) teach about the local habitat by taking participants through the marshes and wetlands. The area is popular with birds — you may even see nesting ospreys. Reservations for boat rentals and tours are strongly recommended.

Mike's is also home to a full-service bait and tackle shop, dry storage, and boat ramps.

OYSTER CREEK INN

Oyster Creek Inn (41 N. Oyster Creek Rd., 609/652-8565, Tues.-Sat. 4-9 P.M., Sun. 1-9 P.M. summer, $15-27) is an old-style fish house located along the back roads of Leeds Point and is an experience beyond the food (which is superb). The cedar-shake building that the restaurant and bar occupy is among two dozen such residential and fishing shacks situated along the area's back-bay marshlands, and the inn's outdoor deck is perfect for idling time while watching boats slip upstream. Oyster Creek's interior hosts familiar wood-paneled walls, with oyster crackers and horseradish atop every checkered-cloth table. The restaurant is known for its seafood: fried, grilled, broiled, and cooked to perfection. The casual Crab Room serves drinks and a raw bar menu. Get here early; reservations aren't accepted.

THE JERSEY SHORE

this place is its singing teenage staff, whose framed photos hang at the entrance. Donning the outfits of a barbershop quartet, they provide both double scoops and double octaves, and it's almost required that someone in your party join in the fun.

Shopping

Shoppers will want to check out Beach Haven's **Bay Village and Schooners Wharf** (9th St. between Ocean and Bay Aves., on the bay, 609/492-2800), an open-air multilevel shopping village with a wood-shingled seafaring theme. Shop for pajamas aboard an old sea schooner, or peruse for kites, candy, and ecofriendly gifts.

Sports and Recreation

LBI's double-decker paddlewheel *Crystal Queen* riverboat (Centre St. and Bayfront, 609/822-8849 or 609/492-0333 in-season, www.blackwhalecruises.com, May–Oct.) offers sightseeing cruises along Little Egg Harbor Bay and day trips to Atlantic City. One-hour evening bay cruises take place daily at 7 P.M. and 8:30 P.M. July–September.

Seasonal **Thundering Surf Waterpark** (Taylor and Bay Aves., 609/492-0869, www .thunderingsurfwaterpark.com, daily 9 A.M.– 7:30 P.M. July–Aug., $21.95 for two hours) is home to six giant waterslides, dancing fountains, a lazy "crazy" river, and the kiddie play land Cowabunga Beach. When you're ready to dry off, head over to the adjacent **Settler's Mill Adventure Golf** (daily 9 A.M.–11 P.M. July–Aug.), two 18-hole miniature golf courses ($7.50 and $9.95), both with a maritime theme. Call ahead for June and September hours.

Local water sports include **Beach Haven Parasailing** (2702 Long Beach Blvd., 609/492-0375, www.bhparasail.com), sportfishing with **June Bug Charters** (Beach Haven Yacht Club, Engleside Ave. at the bay, 856/778-0200 or 609/685-2839 cell, www .fish-junebug.com) or **L.B.I. Fishing Charters** (Morrison's Beach Haven Marina, 2nd St. and the bay, 609/492-2591, www.lbifishing charters.com), and **kayak rentals** from

Holgate Marina (83 Tebco Terr., 609/492-0191), just south of Beach Haven.

Founded in 1987, LBI's **Alliance for a Living Ocean** (2007 Long Beach Blvd., 609/492-0222, www.livingocean.org) promotes understanding and protection of the local aquatic ecosystem. In addition to various educational and craft programs offered for adults and kids throughout summer, the alliance hosts three-hour ecotours around the bay on select days July–August; call for details.

Accommodations

Beach Haven's historic district is home to the borough's B&Bs, along with a couple of worthwhile motels.

The **Victoria Guest House** (126 Amber St., 609/492-4154, www.lbivictoria.com, $220–265 s, $235–280 d) offers spacious period-themed rooms—many with four-poster beds—at one of two side-by-side locations, depending on the time of year. Both homes are less than a one-block walk to the beach and include wireless Internet, home-baked goods, and private baths. The summer home also allows use of an in-ground pool.

Don't let the updated Victorian exterior fool you; **Julia's of Savannah** (209 Centre St., 609/492-5004, www.juliasoflbi.com, $260–325) is plentiful with antiques. Air-conditioned rooms are small but cared for, with beds that make you want to stay put. Amenities include private baths and a full breakfast, and a lovely wraparound porch that catches the sea breeze. A first-floor room with a private porch is available for guests with disabilities.

Rooms at the beachfront **Engleside Inn** (Engleside Ave. at the oceanfront, 609/492-1251 or 800/762-2214, www.engleside.com, $244–365 s, $290–446 d) are spacious, if not a bit dated, ranging in size from single motel rooms to two-room efficiencies. Ocean views are prominent in many of the larger rooms. The inn hosts its own outdoor beach bar secluded by dunes, as well as a sushi bar and the highly rated Leeward Room, an American fine-dining restaurant.

Food

Stop into **Slice of Heaven** (610 N. Bay Ave., 609/492-7437, $3–20) for a slice of cheese steak–topped pizza, or order an entire pie—the baked ziti pie rocks. Friday and Saturday evening hours extend until 4 A.M. during summer.

Not sure what to have for breakfast? At the pig-themed **Uncle Will's Pancake House** (3 S. Bay Ave., 609/492-2514, daily 7 A.M.–1 P.M., dinner Thurs.–Sun. 5–9 P.M., summer) you'll have your pick. A local institution, Uncle Will's conjures up creative morning meals like peach pancake platters and stuffed French toast, and if you're lucky, serves them along with a ceramic pig that'll stay by your side as you eat. Caribbean-inspired dinners ($17–25) are also worth a try.

The seasonal **Chicken or the Egg** (207 N. Bay Ave., 609/492-3695, www.492fowl.com, daily 24/7 summer, $6–10) dishes out a full diner-style menu of breakfasts, sandwiches, soups, salads, and platters. Large wood booths act as hidden havens during early mornings, when locals scarf down peanut-butter-cup pancakes and egg sandwiches following late nights at the bar. Decor is—you guessed it—poultry themed.

Long a foodie favorite, **The Gables** (212 Centre St., 609/492-3553, www.gableslbi.com, daily 9 A.M.–3 P.M. and 5:30–10 P.M. summer, Fri.–Sat. 9 A.M.–3 P.M. and 5:30–10 P.M. off-season, closed Jan.) came under new ownership in 2005, opening a year later better than ever. The restaurant occupies the former dining room in a century-old home, just downstairs from a B&B. Romance is everywhere, from the dining room's wood-burning fireplace to its candlelit tables and original wood plank floors. Guests can also dine or sip tea in an outdoor Victorian garden, surrounded by flowers and a bubbling fountain. The eclectic menu features both prix fixe and à la carte selections that change daily, but may include dishes like handmade potato gnocchi and butter-poached Maine lobster.

MAINLAND
Camping

While no camping facilities exist on LBI, there are a few mainland resorts close enough to be considered overnight alternatives.

Family operated for more than 40 years, **Baker's Acres Campground** (230 Willets Ave., Parkertown, 609/296-2664 or 800/648-2227, www.bakersacres.com, May–Nov.) features 300 shaded sites set along the eastern edge of the Pinelands. The campground also hosts two in-ground pools, and offers hot showers and volleyball nets for play. Rentable cabins and cottages have recently been added. Sites cost $34–44 a night depending on amenities.

Approximately eight miles west of LBI, **Sea Pirate Family Campground** (Rte. 9, West Creek, 609/296-7400, www.sea-pirate.com, May–Oct., $35–52) features an indoor-outdoor sports complex with Ping-Pong, a baseball diamond, and a basketball court, as well as motorboat and kayak rentals and annual events, such as July's '50s Night and Sock Hop, held throughout summer.

THE JERSEY SHORE

Atlantic City

The city that was once "America's Playground" is now "Always Turned On," at least according to its latest marketing campaign. Whatever the case, Atlantic City is one for the books. From its humble beginnings as a fly-infested sand dune little more than a century ago, the city has made a name for itself across the country and throughout the world. Atlantic City may call to mind images that aren't always good, but this beachfront property is responsible for much of the Americana we know and love: Miss America, boardwalks, Monopoly, amusement piers, and supposedly even saltwater taffy. From the Rat Pack to the crack pack, Vanessa Williams to the Donald, Atlantic City has seen it all. Its history is dotted with diving

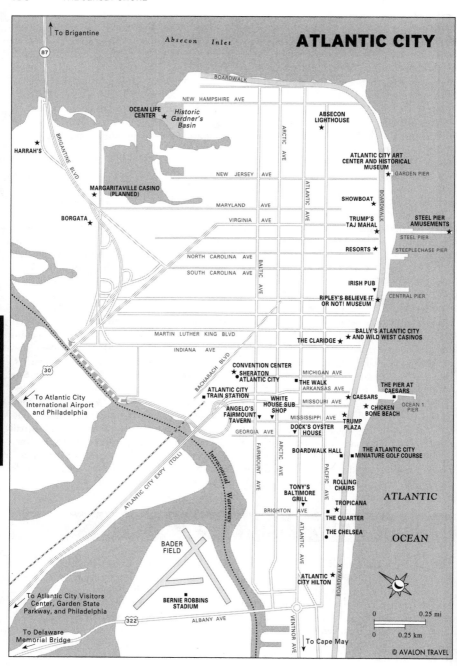

ATLANTIC CITY

To Brigantine

Absecon Inlet

BOARDWALK

NEW HAMPSHIRE AVE

OCEAN LIFE CENTER ★

Historic Gardner's Basin

ABSECON LIGHTHOUSE ★

ARCTIC AVE

HARRAH'S ★

BRIGANTINE BLVD

NEW JERSEY AVE

ATLANTIC CITY ART CENTER AND HISTORICAL MUSEUM

★ GARDEN PIER

MARGARITAVILLE CASINO (PLANNED) ★

ATLANTIC AVE

SHOWBOAT ★

BOARDWALK

MARYLAND AVE

BORGATA ★

VIRGINIA AVE

TRUMP'S TAJ MAHAL ★

STEEL PIER AMUSEMENTS ★

STEEL PIER

BALTIC AVE

NORTH CAROLINA AVE

RESORTS ★

STEEPLECHASE PIER

SOUTH CAROLINA AVE

IRISH PUB ★

RIPLEY'S BELIEVE IT OR NOT! MUSEUM ★

CENTRAL PIER

MARTIN LUTHER KING BLVD

BALLY'S ATLANTIC CITY AND WILD WEST CASINOS ★

INDIANA AVE

THE CLARIDGE ★

BACHARACH BLVD

CONVENTION CENTER ★

SHERATON ATLANTIC CITY ★

MICHIGAN AVE

To Atlantic City International Airport and Philadelphia

THE WALK ■

ARKANSAS AVE

THE PIER AT CAESARS ■

ATLANTIC CITY TRAIN STATION ■

MISSOURI AVE

CAESARS ★

OCEAN 1 PIER

WHITE HOUSE SUB SHOP ■

CHICKEN BONE BEACH ★

ANGELO'S FAIRMOUNT TAVERN ▼

MISSISSIPPI AVE

TRUMP PLAZA ★

DOCK'S OYSTER HOUSE ▼

GEORGIA AVE

BOARDWALK HALL ■

FAIRMOUNT AVE

ARCTIC AVE

THE ATLANTIC CITY MINIATURE GOLF COURSE ■

Intracoastal Waterway

TONY'S BALTIMORE GRILL ■

PACIFIC AVE

ROLLING CHAIRS ■

ATLANTIC OCEAN

BRIGHTON AVE

TROPICANA ★

THE QUARTER ■

ATLANTIC AVE

THE CHELSEA ●

ATLANTIC CITY EXPWY (TOLL)

BADER FIELD

OCEAN

To Atlantic City Visitors Center, Garden State Parkway, and Philadelphia

ATLANTIC CITY HILTON ■

BERNIE ROBBINS STADIUM

To Delaware Memorial Bridge

ALBANY AVE

VENTNOR AVE

BOARDWALK

0   0.25 mi

0   0.25 km

To Cape May

© AVALON TRAVEL

horses and Chicken Bone beaches, historic hotels and a Steel Pier that just won't quit.

After decades of decline, Atlantic City seems to be regaining some of its groove. Over the last ten years the city has added boutique shopping centers and killer spas, a casino that rivals Vegas, and some of the best new restaurants in the state, all the while holding onto many of the establishments that once made it one of the country's top seaside resorts. Some complain that AC is pulling a Vegas with its swanky stores, open-air bars, and attempts to become a foodie destination, but why shouldn't it? Vegas hasn't fared too poorly. Since the 2003 opening of the Borgata Resort, the city that for years drew almost exclusively senior citizens is again attracting the young—luring singles with top-shelf martini bars, tightly clad cocktail waitresses, and plenty of nightlife.

There's so much to do in Atlantic City and its surrounding region that it's worth sticking around a bit. When the buzz of computerized casino slots becomes unbearable there's always the Boardwalk, beach, and shops to explore, not to mention an awesome historical museum, a bayside village, minor-league baseball, a 65-foot-tall elephant, and nearby golf courses, wineries, and nature preserves. And that's if you're not hungry or in town for a festival or show. There's no shortage of hotel rooms and restaurants, but for the best dining, venture outside of the main casinos, where food tends to be overpriced and underwhelming. Cocktails are easy to come by any time of day or night.

History

When the first passenger train arrived in Atlantic City from Camden, New Jersey, on July 1, 1854, "America's Playground" was born. And the city spent no time messing around. AC grew quickly, both architecturally and population-wise. Taverns, boarding homes, and grand hotels sprang up throughout town. During the late 19th and early 20th centuries, Atlantic City was the place to be. The world's first boardwalk came into existence, and amusement piers appeared every few blocks. At Heinz Pier, H. J. Heinz (of ketchup fame) gave away free pickles and pickle lapel pins for 46 years, and the Million Dollar Pier entertained spectators with kangaroo boxing, magic performances by legendary magician Harry Houdini, and the famous High Diving Horse Act, featuring a woman and horse diving together from a 40-foot platform into a pool.

Unfortunately, by the mid-20th century, Atlantic City's heyday had ended. Its grand hotels had fallen into disrepair, and visitors were no longer coming. Looking for a way to improve their situation, city officials approved gambling in 1976. Atlantic City became the first U.S. location outside Las Vegas where a person could place a legal bet. As part of the agreement, all casinos had to include a hotel complex with at least 50 guest rooms. Revenue began pouring in. But what was happening behind the casino's windowless walls didn't reflect what was going on along Atlantic City's streets; life in Atlantic City hadn't improved. Under the Boardwalk a community of gamblers and addicts were establishing makeshift

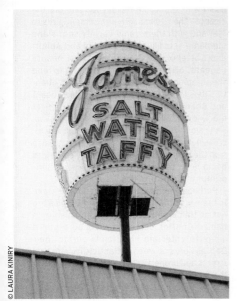

© LAURA KINIRY

a New Jersey original

THE JERSEY SHORE

THE HOTTEST COMMODITY IN TOWN

Only one walkway holds the indubitable distinction of being named Boardwalk with a capital *B*: That is Atlantic City's Boardwalk, the first known creation of its kind. Originally built in 1870, its purpose was not a commercial endeavor but simply a way of preventing beach strollers from tracking sand into hotel lobbies and railway cars. The Boardwalk was the brainchild of Alexander Boardman, a railway conductor and owner of Atlantic City's Ocean House hotel. Concerned about the damage his hotel's fine furnishings were undergoing by the same people he was bringing to enjoy the Shore's amenities, Boardman and fellow proprietor Jacob Keim gathered local hotel owners to discuss the problem. Boardman suggested a "raised platform" where visitors could stroll while still viewing the ocean, and the idea was met with overwhelming approval. City council financed the project with $5,000 in redeemable scrip. On June 26, 1870, the world's first boardwalk opened to the public.

the Steel Pier along Atantic City's Boardwalk

Made of wooden planks 1.5 inches thick, the original Boardwalk was 10 feet wide and pieced together in 12-foot sections, each board laid lengthwise 18 inches from the ground. Although not the most likely material for salty air and weather-beaten shores, the wooden planks had an obvious purpose: to be easily removed and stored away after each summer season. While this preserved them from the harsh winter elements, it didn't protect the boards from the masses of visitors they attracted, nearly twice the amount of vacationers Atlantic City had seen in the previous 16 years. Within 10 years the structure had worn thin, and a new boardwalk was built.

With this new boardwalk came relaxed commercial zoning. Previously restricted to thirty feet from the walkway, the Boardwalk's consumer potential could now be fully realized. Businesses jumped at the opportunity. As new establishments fought for space, two more walkways came and went, resulting in a fifth and final Boardwalk built in 1896. It was this Boardwalk – raised to five feet above ground, widened to 40 feet across, and attached to a steel bar base structure with hand railings (people were constantly falling off the boards onto the beach) – given the street name "Boardwalk." It's the same structure used today.

While Atlantic City's present-day fame comes from its role as Vegas on the beach, the Boardwalk enjoyed a heyday long before the casinos. The city brought amusement piers to life, and with them came variety shows and big-name acts like Harry Houdini and Abbott and Costello. The Boardwalk's first beauty pageant, originally held as a ploy to extend the summer season, paved the way for Atlantic City's long-running Miss America Pageant and Boardwalk Parade. The city built a five-block-long Convention Hall (now Boardwalk Hall) along the boards in 1929 to host the increasingly popular pageant festivities. It's also said the world's first saltwater taffy came into being here, "invented" by a candy store proprietor after a storm flooded his shop.

Perhaps the Boardwalk's most notable claim to fame is as the hottest property to land a top hat or thimble. In 1934 an unemployed man named Charles Darrow developed a board game to entertain his friends during their Depression-era woes. Atlantic City's actual streets and properties were chosen to decorate the board, with Boardwalk being the most lucrative square. The game's name? Monopoly.

homes, and crime still ran rampant across the Monopoly board. But inside, busloads of tourists were enjoying a world of free drinks, jingling shot machines, and all-you-can-eat buffets. To better understand how casinos have changed AC, consider this: The city's entire population is smaller than the number of people the casinos employ.

Atlantic City's rep became that of a day-tripper destination for senior citizens and a place for after-prom parties. And the city seemed content with this until the Borgata opened in 2003. Suddenly investors saw opportunity. Now there are worthwhile shops, exciting clubs, sleek restaurants, spas, and some wonderful new hotels spread throughout town. AC still has a long way to go toward adjusting its image and improving its streets, but it seems to be heading in the right direction.

For a better understanding of Atlantic City just before and after the casino boom, rent *The King of Marvin Gardens,* starring Jack Nicholson and Bruce Dean, and *Atlantic City,* with Susan Sarandon and Burt Lancaster. AC, exposed in all its urban-grit glory, plays a starring role in each.

THE BOARDWALK

Atlantic City's six-mile-long, 60-foot-wide Boardwalk with a capital *B* is both the world's first boardwalk and New Jersey's largest, brimming with casino arcades (and casinos), palm-reading stands, hourly massage houses, knickknack shops, a couple of amusement piers, and the obligatory T-shirt shops and greasy food pits. The Boardwalk's famed **Rolling Chairs,** large wicker seats on wheels pushed by chatty men and women willing to cart you wherever you like (for a fee), are everywhere. The cost of rides varies depending on the rolling chair company, but usually run about $5 (plus a tip) for the first five Boardwalk blocks, increasing in $5 increments for every five blocks after. Discounts are offered on half-hour and hour tours. Most chairs seat two and are cash-only. If you have the time and money, it's a worthwhile experience. Rolling chairs have been part of the local landscape for more than a century.

While no one is entirely sure where the name "saltwater taffy" came from, most people agree the confection was born in Atlantic City. Here on the boards there's no better place than **Fralinger's** (1325 Boardwalk, 609/344-0442), unless of course you're a longstanding fan of **James Salt Water Taffy** (1519 Boardwalk, 609/344-1519, www.jamescandy.com). Maybe you're more of a fudge person? Then **Steel's Fudge** (1633 Boardwalk, 609/345-4051, www.steelsfudge.com), in business on Atlantic City's Boardwalk since 1919, is your place.

Since Mr. Peanut is one of the city's unofficial mascots, it's only fitting that the walkway's numerous **Boardwalk Peanut Shoppes** (609/272-1511, www.boardwalkpeanuts.com) are favorites among visitors. Look for one in Resorts and Trump Plaza.

Though a popular Boardwalk attraction, the much-hyped **Ripley's Believe It or Not! Museum** (New York Ave. and Boardwalk, 609/347-2001, www.ripleys.com, daily 10 A.M.–10 P.M. May–Aug., Mon.–Fri. 10 A.M.–6 P.M., Sat.–Sun. 10 A.M.–8 P.M. Apr. and Sept., $15 adult, $10 child 5–12) is nothing if not touristy. If you miss it here you can catch the same sorts of oddities displayed in Orlando, Florida, or at San Francisco's Fisherman's Wharf.

Atlantic City Art Center and Historical Museum

Atlantic City has a varied and interesting history, and the best place to uncover it is the Atlantic City Historical Museum (New Jersey Ave. at Boardwalk, 609/347-5837, www.acmuseum.org, daily 10 A.M.–4 P.M., free), situated at the north end of the Boardwalk's commercial strip. Operating alongside the Atlantic City Art Center (both museums are free), the historical museum's permanent exhibit, "Atlantic City: Playground of the Nation," provides a great overview of the city's prosperous past, and there's a nice collection of Miss America memorabilia. The museum's newest exhibit, "Shore Deco: Atlantic City Design Between the Wars, 1919–1939," opened summer 2006. Museum visitors will receive a souvenir Heinz pickle pin, a replica of those handed out by H. J. Heinz himself at the Boardwalk's turn-of-the-20th-century Heinz Pier. The nearby AC Art Center features three exhibit galleries and a shop selling local work, including Wheaton Village glass.

Boardwalk Hall

Opened in 1929, Atlantic City's landmark Boardwalk Hall (2301 Boardwalk, 609/348-7000, www.boardwalkhall.com) played official host to the Miss America Pageant from 1933 until 2004, longer than any other venue. Although the pageant has since left town (and New Jersey), Boardwalk Hall remains a sought-after showcase, hosting high-profile concerts such as Van Halen's reunion tour, Jimmy Buffet, and Madonna, along with conferences year-round. Even if you're not in town for a concert or event, stop by the Hall to have a peek at the world's largest pipe organ, with over 33,000 pipes, built 1929–1932. Tours of the organ and a theater-type organ, located in Boardwalk Hall's ballroom, are given monthly by the Atlantic City Convention Hall Organ Society (www.acchos.org); visit their website for details.

Boardwalk Recreation

Directly across from Boardwalk Hall is **The Atlantic City Miniature Golf Course** (1 Kennedy Plaza, 609/347-1661, www.ac minigolf.com), home of the 2005 Harris Cup National Miniature Golf Championship. This 18-hole course was recently updated with new Astroturf and sand traps, providing it with a pro-golf feel and a steady flow of players on summer weekday afternoons.

A highlight of the year-round **Central Pier Arcade & Speedway** (St. James Pl. and Tennessee Ave., 609/345-5219) is its large selection of redemption arcade games, where players can rack up tickets to trade for prizes. The pier is also home to go-karts, and a "Shoot the Geek" paintball game that uses live targets.

Since 1898 the **Steel Pier** (Virginia Ave. and 1000 Boardwalk, 866/386-6659, www.steel pier.com, Mon.–Fri. 3 P.M.–midnight, Sat.–Sun. noon–1 A.M. mid-June–Aug., Sat.–Sun. noon–1 A.M. May–mid-June and Sept.–Oct.) has been bringing the hordes to Atlantic City, and somehow it (thankfully) continues going strong. Its last year was supposed to be 2006, but the amusements have been given ongoing reprieve by the pier's owner, Donald Trump, who plans to eventually redevelop it with a hotel, condos, and restaurants. Ride the Giant Slide, fly up in a helicopter, and stare amazed at the Skycycle Trapeze—a couple performing motorcycle stunts on a 60-foot-high tightrope—while you still have the chance.

OTHER SIGHTS
Absecon Lighthouse

Absecon Lighthouse (31 S. Rhode Island Ave., 609/449-1360, www.absenconlighthouse.org, daily 10 A.M.–5 P.M. July–Aug., Thurs.–Mon. 11 A.M.–4 P.M. Sept.–June, $7 adult, $5 senior, $4 child) is New Jersey's tallest lighthouse and the country's third-tallest. For a glimpse of Atlantic City before gambling took over, even preceding its days as America's Playground, come here. The attractive 228-step structure was built in 1857 and still has its first-order Fresnel lens. In the late 1990s the lighthouse underwent major restorations and now includes a replica of the light keeper's house, a museum, and a gift shop.

Atlantic City Convention Center

Opened in May 1997, the **Atlantic City Convention Center** (1 Miss America Way, 609/449-2000, www.accenter.com) hosts many of the city's largest fairs and festivals, including the biannual antique and collectible fair Atlantique City, Atlantic City's Classic Car Show, and an annual beer festival. The center features five second-floor showrooms and more than 500,000 square feet of contiguous exhibit space, as well as its own Sheraton Hotel. It's located just off the Atlantic City Expressway next to the train and bus stations.

BEACHES

Atlantic City's beaches are free, no tags required. Alcohol is permitted on the beach. Public restrooms are located along the

Boardwalk at Bartram Avenue, Albany Avenue, Chelsea Avenue, Mississippi Avenue, New Jersey Avenue, New Hampshire Avenue, and Caspian Avenue. Changing stations are available at Albany Avenue and South Carolina Avenue. The casino beach bars have showers available for public access. To reserve a surf chair for those with limited mobility (access ramps exist at various points along the Boardwalk), call 609/347-5312.

The beach directly in front of Missouri Avenue and Boardwalk is known as **Chicken Bone Beach,** named for the thousands of African American families who vacationed here in the early 1900s with their chicken-filled picnic hampers. Rat Pack performer Sammy Davis Jr. would join them while in town. The Chicken Bone Beach Historical Foundation hosts free jazz concerts at Kennedy Plaza, between Mississippi and Georgia Avenues, throughout summer.

◖ CASINOS

Most of Atlantic City's approximately dozen casinos are set along the Boardwalk, with a few located along the bay en route to Brigantine. The city doesn't have a lot of room left for construction, although the October 2007 Sands Casino implosion has left a gaping hole soon to be filled with a Pinnacle Entertainment megacasino.

Atlantic City's casinos are all-inclusive, 24-hour establishments where the sun don't shine and the customers don't quit till their pockets are empty. Each of the casino resorts offers hotel rooms, restaurants, lounges and bars, shops, live showcase theaters, nightclubs, and often arcades, along with slot machines, poker and blackjack tables, roulette wheels, keno, and private gambling rooms galore. Free drinks are usually available to anyone spending money on the casino floor. New Jersey's 21-and-over gambling laws are strictly enforced, and no one under 21 is even allowed on the casino floors. Underage visitors are, however, permitted in the hotels, restaurants, and shopping halls.

Each casino has its own parking garage. Spaces cost $4–7, but most garages will give you two receipts upon entry: one as proof of payment and the other to use for complimentary parking at a second casino. Don't hesitate to request a second receipt if you only receive one.

Most casinos offer some sort of VIP card with substantial room and food discounts depending on the amount of time and money you spend. If planning a trip to a particular casino, inquire about obtaining a card at the customer service desk.

Atlantic City's jitney bus service offers round-the-clock transport between the casinos, and it's a good option for getting from the Boardwalk to bayside casinos if you've arrived by train or simply prefer leaving your car parked. If you're sticking strictly to Boardwalk casinos, walking from beginning to end is a stretch but doable. Otherwise, the Boardwalk Rolling Chairs offer a memorable alternative. A little-used walkway connects the three bayside casinos.

Borgata

The cream of Atlantic City's casino crop and also the latest edition to its skyline, the bayside Borgata is most responsible for glamming up AC and attracting younger crowds. If this is the city's fountain of youth, than water's flowing from every Chihuly-blown chandelier hanging in the casino's entryways. Scantily clad Borgata Babes deliver drinks on the casino floor, and surrounding the slots and game tables are high-end boutiques, decadent restaurants, and some of the hottest bars in town.

The 1,100-seat **Music Box** (800/736-1420) is Borgata's intimate live showcase, a great place for catching a performance by Alanis Morissette or Herbie Hancock. For more of a stadium crowd, check out Bob Dylan or the Black Crowes at the 30,000-square-foot **Event Center.** As casinos go, the Borgata's got some of the best restaurants of any in town. Fine dining establishments include **Ombra** (Tues.–Thurs. and Sun. 5–10 P.M., Fri.–Sat. 5–11 P.M., $20–38) famous for its wines (over 14,000 bottles) and cheeses; **Bobby Flay Steak** (Mon.–Thurs. 5–11 P.M., Fri.–Sat. 5 P.M.–midnight, Sun. 4–11 P.M., $29–50), the Food Network personality's first-ever steakhouse; and **Old**

Homestead (Mon.–Thurs. 5–11 P.M., Fri.–Sat. 5 P.M.–midnight, Sun. 4–11 P.M.), purveyor of the 20-ounce Kobe burger ($41). For something more affordable try a wood-oven pizza ($13–16) from **Wolfgang Puck Tavern** (Wed.–Mon. 5–11 P.M., closed Tues.) or **Bread + Butter** (Sun.–Thurs. 7 A.M.–10 P.M., Fri.–Sat. 7 A.M.–4 A.M.), offering white-bread sandwiches like portobello and provolone ($7.50) and pepperoni and American cheese ($7.50) that don't break the bank. Reservations for each can be made by calling 866/692-6742.

Curtains are all that separate 24-hour **B Bar** from the casino floor action, so for something more exclusive check out **Mixx** (Fri.–Sat. 10 P.M.–till the party's over,) a dimly lit dance club with a DJ spinning world beats.

Harrah's

Standing just before the Brigantine Bridge in Atlantic City's Marina District, Harrah's (777 Harrah's Blvd., 609/441-5000, www.harrahs .com) is removed from much of downtown's casino bustle. I grew up visiting Harrah's, playing Pac-Man in the arcade while my grandmother hit the slots. Though Grandmom had since moved on to Showboat, Harrah's has continued appealing to me. Maybe it's nostalgia, but it's more likely the constant upkeep employed to keep up with more centralized establishments. One of the best additions to any AC casino in recent years is Harrah's new 172,000-square-foot glass-dome-enclosed Olympic-size swimming pool surrounded by poolside cabanas, six hot tubs, and $1 million worth of greenery. The pool is for hotel guests only (21 and over, daily 7 A.M.–7 P.M.) during the day, but at night it transforms into a pulsating DJ club open to anyone (21 and over) with $10 or $20 to spare. On the casino floor is the stylish 24-hour **Xhibition Bar,** a circular lounge that's another fairly new venue.

Hunger setting in? Harrah's hosts the popular seafood restaurant **McCormick & Schmick's** (609/441-5579, Mon.–Sat. 11:30 A.M.–midnight, Sun. 11:30 A.M.–11 P.M., $15–25) and **The Taste of the Shore Food Court** (Mon. 10 A.M.–midnight, Tues.–Thurs.

9:30 A.M.–2 A.M., Fri.–Sat. 9:30 A.M.–3 A.M., Sun. 9:30 A.M.–1 A.M., $5–15), a sampling of all that's oh-so-good but bad for you, including Philly soft pretzels, hoagies, and Ben & Jerry's ice cream.

Harrah's Atlantic City sister casinos are Bally's, Caesars, and Showboat. The **Total Rewards Shuttle** runs patrons between each of the four properties.

Showboat

Since opening in the late 1980s, the Mardi Gras–themed Showboat Casino (801 Boardwalk, 609/343-4000, www.harrahs .com) had been a steady favorite with the senior slot crowd, though things changed with the resort's 2005 **House of Blues** (609/236-2583) opening. With big-name billings like B. B. King, stage acts such as *Tony n' Tina's Wedding,* and a Cajun-style House of Blues restaurant serving up slow-smoked baby back ribs ($24), chicken potpie ($15), and an awesome Sunday gospel brunch, the Boardwalk's northernmost casino suddenly got hip. An entire casino wing has been devoted to the multistory venue, nightclub, and restaurant, which also includes a souvenir shop and a slew of themed slot machines.

Showboat's other notable eateries include the **French Quarter Buffet** (Sun.–Tues. noon–9 P.M., Fri. 4–10 P.M., Sat. noon–10 P.M.), serving a Saturday-night Louisiana seafood festival ($26), and the casual **Mansion Café** (Sun.–Thurs. 7 A.M.–11 P.M., Fri.–Sat. 7 A.M.–2 A.M., $15–25), a good place for breakfast or a burger. Accommodations include the **New Orleans Tower** and the **House of Blues Studio,** which, for the loft-style bedroom, fully-stocked bar, and state-of-the-art sound system it offers, is surprisingly affordable ($360 August midweek).

The casino's Atlantic City sister properties are Bally's, Caesars, and Harrah's.

Taj Mahal

A Trump contribution to AC's skyline, the illustrious Taj (1000 Boardwalk at Virginia Ave., 609/449-1000, www.trumptaj.com) opened in 1990 with much fanfare, its onion-shaped domes and Aladdin-style lettering making it easily recognizable among the city's box-shaped buildings. The Taj is probably AC's most ornate casino, decorated in deep reds and purples accentuated in gold, with enormous chandeliers hanging in the entry halls and gambling rooms bearing names like Dragon Place and Sinbad's. Restaurants and nightclubs are also theme-based, like the extraordinary **Casbah** (800/234-5678, casbahclub.com, Fri. 10:30 P.M.–5 A.M., Sat. 10:30 P.M.6 A.M.), consistently rated the city's best dance club, and the Asian-inspired **Dynasty** (nightly from 6 P.M., $14–30), home to sushi rolls and sake martinis. The Taj features 75 regular poker tables and 14 tournament tables, second in size only to AC's Borgata.

Trump Taj Mahal is also home to the **Mark G. Etess Arena** (609/449-5150), often used for big-draw boxing matches, and **Xanadu Showroom,** where Earth, Wind, and Fire and the Monkees have performed. Additional casino highlights include AC's **Hard Rock Cafe** (1000 Boardwalk, 609/441-0007, Sun.–Thurs. 11 A.M.–midnight, Fri.–Sat. 11 A.M.–1 A.M.), the affordable all-you-can-eat **Sultan's Feast** buffet and **Casbar** bar and lounge (Fri. 9 P.M.–2 A.M., Sat. 9 P.M.–4 A.M.), located downstairs from the Casbah nightclub.

Resorts

Atlantic City's first-ever casino, the art deco Resorts (1133 Boardwalk, 800/336-6378, www.resortsac.com) debuted in 1976 in the renovated and restructured Chalfonte-Haddon Hall Hotel (a Quaker-owned hotel that once banned alcohol sales) and has been plodding along since. The casino is a sister property to AC's Hilton Casino, both owned by Colony Capital, whose additional properties include Las Vegas's Hilton Casino and Bally's Casino in Tunica, Mississippi. Resorts hosts more than 2,500 slot machines and 80 table games and features over 100,000 square feet of casino space as well as a 388-room, 27-story recently constructed hotel tower called **Rendezvous.** It can be easy to forget Resorts' long history with Atlantic City; that is, until

Resorts, Atlantic City's oldest casino

© LAURA KINIRY

you step outside its Boardwalk entry. Here, at the **Entrance to the Stars,** are the cemented signatures and handprints of famed comedians and musicians, most—like Steven Martin, Lou Rawls, and Barry Manilow—dating back to the late 1970s and early 1980s, when Atlantic City was still priming to surpass Vegas as the number 1 casino resort.

Resorts hosts a nice range of restaurants, including the upscale Italian **Capriccio,** a more casual **Gallagher's Burger Bar** (Thurs.–Sun.) and an all-you-can-eat buffet. The **Boogie Nights** nightclub, open Fridays and Saturdays, plays '70s and '80s classics (from the casino's heyday) amid bellbottom outfits and dancing roller girls. Clubbers can sip on Donny Almonds before getting groovy under spinning disco balls. Entertainers such as Tom Jones, Jerry Seinfeld, and Chris Isaak perform at the casino's 1,350-seat **Super Star Theatre** year-round.

Bally's Atlantic City

Built on the site of the historic Marlborough Blenheim Hotel, Bally's (1900 Pacific Ave.,

609/340-2000, www.harrahs.com) is a three-part casino complex made up of the original casino building, the nearby **Claridge Casino,** and the campy **Wild West Casino,** opened in 1997. The resort is expected to change names to either the Horseshoe or the Rio, although no exact timeline has been established. Due in part to the diversity of its casino floors, Bally's tends to attract a mixed-age crowd.

Bally's highlight is its Wild West Casino, a kitschy, colorful, Western-themed space decorated with steam train murals, Wells Fargo wagons, and a gold digger's wishing well. Off the main casino floor is the **Mountain Bar,** a 24-hour watering hole with a 90-foot-long bar, faux cacti, and a tiny train that circles the seating area. Live acts perform nightly throughout summer. Located upstairs, the **Virginia City Buffet** (Sun.–Thurs. 11 A.M.–9 P.M., Fri. 11 A.M.–10 P.M., Sat. 11 A.M.–11 P.M., $15–25) is a popular dining venue with older crowds.

During summer months the Wild West Casino gets second billing to Bally's **Bikini Beach Bar** (609/340-2909), arguably the best of AC's remaining beachfront venues. Umbrellaed tables, palm trees, and private gazebos leave plenty of space for yellow-bikini-clad cocktail servers to deliver drinks and Philadelphia meatheads to ogle without obstruction. DJs spin most weekday nights, and bands perform on weekends.

The resort's older Claridge wing (once a favorite of Frank Sinatra) is home to the **Blue Martini Bar,** with a menu of more than 100 martinis and a built-in frosted ice rail to keep drinks cool.

Caesars

Caesars (2100 Pacific Ave., 800/443-0104, www.caesars.com) opened in 1979 as Atlantic City's second casino, and remains one of its best known. The resort has recently undergone massive renovations, including a new facelift and the construction and opening of its upscale Pier Shops at Caesars on the historic Million Dollar Pier, across the Boardwalk from the main casino. Caesars is known for its vast slot machine selection; with more than 3,400

it's one of the city's largest. Its Roman Empire motif extends throughout the resort: Slot machines bear names like Cleopatra's Garden, the Centurion Tower provides overnight stays, and cover bands jam regularly at **Toga** (daily 11 A.M.–6 A.M.)

Caesars' restaurants include the Italian **Primavera** (Sun.–Tues. 5:30–10 P.M., Fri.–Sat. 6–10 P.M., $26–48), and the **Bacchanal** (Fri.–Sat. 6–10:30 P.M., $64.95 per person) serving a fixed-price six-course Italian meal along with strolling musicians and a never-ending wine bottle served by a Royal Maid.

Caesars' sister properties include Harrah's Atlantic City and Showboat.

Trump Plaza

Renovated in 2006, Trump Plaza (Mississippi Ave. and Boardwalk, 609/441-0608, www .trumpplaza.com) is home to one of the city's few remaining beach bars, along with the kid-friendly **Rainforest Café** (609/345-5757, $10–18), accessible from the boards. The resort's central Boardwalk location makes it popular with casino hoppers who access their spots on foot. Several years ago the main floor smelled like a mix of fast food and cigarette smoke, but that's set to change with Atlantic City Casinos' smoking ban, effective October 2008. Trump Plaza's **Liquid Bar** (800/677-7787) is a worthwhile stop, as is the Italian **Evo** (609/441-0400, daily 10 A.M.–11 P.M., $17–22), a white-linen restaurant with Boardwalk seating.

Trump Plaza remains one of the city's more lackluster casinos, though this changes seasonally with the opening of the summertime **Beach Bar,** a spacious waterfront setup with umbrella tables and open-air bars. Live music includes DJs, cover bands, and a Thursday-night Battle of the Bands.

Tropicana

Located at the Boardwalk's southern end, Tropicana Casino & Resort (S. Brighton Ave. and the Boardwalk, 609/340-4000 or 800/843-8767, www.tropicana.net) is one of the walkway's better casinos, though it was almost no more: In December 2007 the New Jersey Casino Control Commission refused to renew the Trop's gambling license, but the casino remains open under trustee supervision. Built in the early 1980s, the Tropicana has done a great job of keeping up with the times. A nongambling upscale shopping and dining addition called the Quarter and consistent renovations have scored this casino a hipper, younger crowd. With more than 2,000 guest rooms, the Tropicana is also one of Atlantic City's largest hotels.

In the center of the Trop's casino floor is the **Rumba Lounge** (daily 11:30 A.M.–3 A.M.), a panoramic-view bar with plasma TVs and live entertainment on weekends. And in the **Tropicana Marketplace** there's **Firewaters** (609/344-6699, www.firewatersbar.com), a sports bar catering to beer drinkers with 50 draft selections and more than 100 bottles. The martinis aren't so bad either.

Karaoke lovers can venture over to the Quarter's zebra-print **Planet Rose** (609/344-6565) for 365-day sing-alongs of more than 10,000 songs. The nearby **Comedy Stop** (877/386-6922, www.comedystop.com, $23) hosts an all-age espresso bar along with selected family-friendly shows for those 12 and over, and adult-only comedy entertainment throughout the week. Also in the Quarter is the crimson-coated **Red Square** (609/344-9100, www.chinagrillmgt.com/redSquareNJ/main.cfm), a vodka bar and restaurant dressed with curtain-draped tables and a photo-worthy chandelier. A statue of Lenin greets patrons on their way in. Food is served Sunday–Thursday noon–11 P.M., Friday–Saturday noon–midnight.

ENTERTAINMENT

For a flashback to Atlantic City's playground days, why not take in a ballgame at **Bernie Robbins Stadium** (545 N. Albany Ave., 609/344-8873, www.acsurf.com, $8–12), formerly called the Sandcastle. Opened in 1998, the 5,900-seat ballpark is home to Minor League Baseball's Atlantic City Surf, an independent club. It's located just off Route 322/40 on the city's southwest side.

Tropicana's **IMAX Theater** (800/843-8767, www.imaxtheaterattropicana.com, $12–14) has a 3,500-square-foot screen stretching eight stories high and a 12,000-watt digital sound system. It's the only operating theater in a city once known for them, and is located in the Tropicana Quarter.

Atlantic City Cruises (800 N. New Hampshire Ave., 609/347-7600, www.atlanticcitycruises.com, $17–33 adult, $8.50–17 child) offers cruises of 1–2 hours throughout the summer months, including dolphin-watching trips, morning skyline cruises on the ocean, and weekday happy-hour tours.

Spas

It's been only recently that Atlantic City has developed a niche reputation for spas, but there are already several fine locations to choose from. The Borgata's **Spa Toccare** (609/317-7555, Sun.–Fri. 6 A.M.–8 P.M., Sat. 6 A.M.–9 P.M.) is AC's only spa to offer the new Soft Pack system, a flotation table that warms the body while simultaneously simulating weightlessness. It increases the body's absorption rate while receiving wraps like the Firm ($115), used for reducing cellulite appearance and improving skin elasticity. On Saturdays, Spa Toccare is open to registered hotel guests only. Opened in 2008, the Water Club's two-story **Immersion** (www.theborgata.com) features a 25-yard infinity-edge lap pool and 360-degree floor-to-ceiling views from its 32nd-floor location. Tropicana Quarter's apothecary spa **Bluemercury** (www.bluemercury.com) offers 15 private rooms and treatments like the Fast Blast, a 30-minute facial glycolic peel and vitamin oxygen blast ($85); and a hydrating honey–shea butter wrap followed by a essential citrus-oil massage ($130). Opened in 2008, the Elizabeth Arden **Red Door Spa** (609/441-5333) at Harrah's offers pedicure treatment zones and separate male and female "wet zones" with steam, sauna, and Jacuzzi pools, along with co-ed relaxation areas.

NIGHTLIFE

Atlantic City is one of the state's few, if not only, 24/7 destinations. A visit to the city wouldn't be complete without a little nightlife. While there's always something happening at the casinos (for a list of options see the *Casinos* section) and on beaches throughout summer, those who'd like to experience the real AC should venture inland, away from the glitzy nightclubs and the crashing waves.

Downtown

Up on the boards just north of the Tropicana is **Flames** (2641 Boardwalk, 609/344-7774, http://flamesac.com), a long and narrow space decorated in neon tube lighting and flat-screen TVs. Though Flames doubles as a surprisingly good Mediterranean restaurant, thumping techno tunes secure its clubby ambiance even early in the afternoon. Specialty drinks include the ever-popular Sex on the Beach and the Tutti Frutti, a concoction of tequila, Midori, rum, and cranberry juice.

If you're looking to disappear, the **Irish Pub** (164 St. James Pl. at Boardwalk, 609/344-9063, www.theirishpub.com, $3–7) is the place to do it. A good old-fashioned down-and-dirty sort of place just west of the Boardwalk, it offers cheap eats and drinks and very little sunlight. The pub even rents out überbasic rooms ($20 for a bed and running water) in a Victorian above the bar, and provides an all-weather smoking patio, so you *really* never have to leave.

The brainchild of hip-hop mogul (and Beyoncé hubby) Jay-Z, Atlantic City's **New York 40/40 Club** (2120 Atlantic Ave., 609/449-4040, www.the4040club.com, Mon.–Fri. 5 P.M.–4 A.M., Sat.–Sun. noon–5 A.M.) opened along downtown's outlet shopping Walk in October 2005. Part dance club, part sports bar, part lounge and restaurant, the multilevel space manages to mix athletic memorabilia with subdued sleekness and pull it off well. The club has four VIP rooms and more than 30 TVs.

EVENTS

Get your motor running for February's annual **Antique and Classic Car Auction & Flea Market** (Atlantic City Convention Center, 800/227-3868, www.acclassiccars.com/events

.html, $20), a four-day auto extravaganza. Hundreds of vintage vehicles are on display, along with hot rods, specialty cars, and an on-site auto parts swap meet. There's a side antique show of jewelry, furniture, and collectibles for anyone just along for the ride.

Some consider it to be the world's toughest swim race, which is probably why it keeps getting canceled. When weather and ocean conditions are right, several dozen men and women take to the waters for August's **Around the Island Marathon Swim** (www.acswim.org), a 22.5-mile race around Absecon Island in the Atlantic Ocean and the back bay. The event takes 7–9 hours on average to complete. Can't afford the time? Uh-huh. Why not cheer on your would-be competitors from outside Harrah's Casino, at the foot of the Brigantine Bridge?

Twice-annual **Atlantique City** (www.atlantiquecity.com) billed as "the largest indoor art, antique, and collectibles fair in the world," is one of the best in the country, a collection of books, bottle openers, clocks, cereal boxes—even coin-operated fortune-telling machines—and everything's for sale. The festival takes place in March and October at Atlantic City's Convention Hall.

SHOPPING

Worthwhile shops are a recent addition to Atlantic City's portfolio, but the city has since been wasting no time establishing its reputation as a retail destination. While most casinos have dedicated commercial space, their selection—most notably in the older casinos—is often overpriced, not to mention tacky. Things are beginning to change, but for now AC's best retail is away from the slots downtown, in the Tropicana Quarter, and along the Pier.

The Quarter

Tropicana's Cuban-inspired Quarter (Brighton and Boardwalk, 800/843-8767, www.tropicana.net/thequarter) is a multilevel shopping, dining, and entertainment plaza filled with planted palms and rounded street lamps, and sporting a painted sky ceiling that makes it feel as though you're strolling along a Havana Street. There's no need to step inside a casino to explore this Cuban paradise—while it's part of the Tropicana complex, it's completely self-contained. Restaurants and bars center around Fiesta Plaza, the integral fountain and square, and at night their occupants spill onto the circular balconies as if the party were truly spreading outdoors.

The Quarter is home to an Imax theater, Atlantic City's only movie theater, along with retail shops such as Chico's and Brooks Brothers. The specialty shopping is some of the city's best, with stores like **The Spy Store** (609/348-1500), stocking body recorders and surveillance cameras; **Klassic Kollectables** (609/344-1191), home to autographed photos and Betty Boop souvenirs; the aptly named **Hat Emporium** (609/348-1777); and **Bluemercury Apothecary** (609/347-7778), where you can pick up bottles of Kiehl's Ultimate Thickening Shampoo and Trish McEvoy moisturizer.

The Walk

Just a few steps away from Atlantic City's train and bus depot and convention center is a neon-lit open-air bargain shopper's paradise. Stretching along Michigan Avenue between Baltic and Artic Avenues, the Walk (609/343-0081, www.acoutlets.com, Mon.–Sat. 10 A.M.–9 P.M., Sun. 10 A.M.–8 P.M.) is home to factory and outlet stores such as Guess, Nike, Converse, Brooks Brothers, and Banana Republic, interspersed with eateries like Stewart's Root Beer to help keep energy levels up.

The Pier

Though you may have fond memories of the faux ocean liner once standing in its place, **The Pier Shops at Caesars** (1 Atlantic Ocean, 609/345-3100, www.thepiershopsat caesars.com, Mon.–Thurs. 11 A.M.–10 P.M., Fri. 11 A.M.–11 P.M., Sat. 10 A.M.–11 P.M., Sun. 10 A.M.–9 P.M.) is a different beast entirely: more upscale, more diverse, and much more refined. This multilevel shopping plaza is home to such high-class stores as Apple, Betsey

Johnson, Burberry, and Gucci, along with area favorites Steven Madden and James' Salt Water Taffy. Restaurants include **Sonsie** (609/345-6300, www.sonsieac.com, daily 10 A.M.–closing), a Boston favorite serving dishes like strawberry-stuffed French toast ($12) and prosciutto and pepperoni calzone ($14) for breakfast and lunch, and spice-crusted yellowfin tuna ($27) for dinner; and **The Continental** (Mon.–Thurs. 11:30 A.M.–10 P.M., Fri.–Sat. 11:30 A.M.–midnight, Sun. 11 A.M.–10 P.M., $15–30), a retro populuxe eatery complete with a fire-pit lounge and menu of global tapas.

A glass skyway extending over the Boardwalk connects the Pier with Caesars casino.

ACCOMMODATIONS

With more than 15,000 guest rooms within city limits, Atlantic City has no shortage of overnight accommodations. That being said, some are far better than others. While change is on the rise, the city is first and foremost a casino resort—they want you on the floor, not in the bed—and hotels in general are not a reason to book a trip here. Still, there are some fine choices, many of which offer discounts to casino regulars and AAA members. For the best deals, call well ahead.

Though motels line the roads in and out of the city, they can be seedy. Try nearby Somers Point for affordable alternatives.

Casino Hotels

Atlantic City's casinos are required by law to include hotels, but they've long been a secondary feature to gambling. That's now changing, with many casinos building newer luxury hotel towers to attract younger crowds. These same casinos have held onto their older towers, so it's important to specify your room type and tower preference when making reservations.

While fluctuating room rates are common in every shore town, with prices highest on weekends and July–August, Atlantic City's hotel rooms can run anywhere from $99 to $500 per night, depending on whether you're a frequent casino patron, when you call (rates change daily), and whether you book your room as part of a package deal. Rates below are based on midweek high season.

$150-300

Constructed in 2003, the Showboat's **New Orleans Tower** (801 Boardwalk, 800/621-0200, www.harrahs.com, $189–239) is the best lodging choice for those planning trips to the Boardwalk's northern attractions, including the Atlantic City Historical Museum and the Steel Pier. Many rooms offer excellent ocean views, along with plush headboards and plasma TVs. For central Boardwalk attractions, including Boardwalk Hall, book a **deluxe room at Bally's** (1900 Pacific Ave., 800/277-5990, www.harrahs.com, $149–179). Amenities include ample closet space and dark wood furnishings.

Another fairly recent addition to AC's skyline is Tropicana's **Havana Tower** (S. Brighton Ave. and Boardwalk, 800/345-8767, www.tropicana.net/thequarter, $149–169), perched above shopping and dining mecca the Quarter. Rooms are clean but basic; they're a good choice for a one-stop shopping stay.

Resorts may be Atlantic City's first casino, but its 27-story art deco–style **Rendezvous Tower** (Resorts, 1113 Boardwalk, 800/336-6378, www.resortsac.com, $145–175) is still in its early years. Rooms are some of the city's largest, and include oversized bathrooms and double-sized showers. The tower also features 58 suites complete with panoramic ocean views. It's a popular place, so book early.

Currently Atlantic City's tallest structure, Harrah's new 44-story **Waterfront Tower** (777 Harrah's Blvd., 609/441-5000, www.harrahs.com, $199–259) features 500-square-foot rooms, each with 42-inch flat-screen TVs, separate seating areas, dark wood furnishings, and a granite and tile spa shower. The tower also hosts 112 suites complete with fireplaces and in-room theaters. Harrah's more affordable Marina Tower isn't so bad either, offering chic luxury rooms ($169–229) with hardwood floors and urban decor. And here's the best part: Overnight stays come with use of the resort's brand-new dome-enclosed Olympic-size pool.

$300-450

As Atlantic City's newest casino, it's hard to go wrong with the bayside **Borgata** (1 Borgata Way, 866/692-6742, www.theborgata.com, $279–299). Modern rooms are bathed in neutral colors and host floor-to-ceiling windows, and many offer spectacular views of the Boardwalk's neon skyline. Guests have access to an indoor pool and wet bar, along with ample shopping, eats, and gambling down below. Although prices may skyrocket over summer weekends, keep in mind that prices are for the room and not the number of occupants.

Even better than the casino accommodations is Borgata's new **Water Club** (1 Renaissance Way, 800/800-8817, www.thewaterclubhotel.com, $329–379), a 43-story boutique hotel opened in summer 2008. Each of the 800 rooms offers water views, along with 400-thread-count sheets, wireless Internet, and LCD TVs. But that's just the beginning. Guests also have access to five heated pools, a sunroom lobby lounge, and an on-site spa.

Noncasino Hotels

You'll find plenty of noncasino hotels catering to Atlantic City visitors, but only a few real standouts (including a brand-new hotel that'll spoil you rotten). About a half-hour's drive south, Ocean City offers several bed-and-breakfast options. There's also a good B&B in Ventnor, the next town south from Atlantic City.

$100-300

If you don't mind driving, the **Hampton Inn Atlantic City Bayside** (7079 Black Horse Pk. and Rte. 40, West Atlantic City, 609/484-1900, $95–140), located a few miles west of AC, is a clean, affordable overnight option with its own bayside beach. The hotel offers complimentary breakfast daily and wireless Internet throughout.

Attached to AC's Convention Center, beside the train station and within easy walking distance of the city's outlet shopping, is the 15-story **Sheraton Atlantic City** (2 Miss America Way, 609/344-3535, www.sheraton.com/atlanticcity, $99–183 s, $189–329 d), a lush hotel with art deco–designed rooms and comfy beds, and some excellent skyline views. In addition to a gift shop, swimming pool, and the city's only brewery-restaurant, the Sheraton hosts the largest collection of Miss America memorabilia in existence, including past contestants' evening gowns and shoes, in its lobby.

$300-450

Seems like stand-alone luxe lodgings in AC went the way of its America's Playground image, until ◖ **The Chelsea** (111 S. Chelsea Ave., thechelsea-ac.com) opened in 2008. The 20-story hotel, an adaptive refurbishment of both the Holiday Inn Atlantic City and the adjacent Howard Johnson's Hotel, is the city's first noncasino Boardwalk hotel opened since the 1960s. With its two Stephen Starr restaurants, a saltwater-inspired spa, fireplace lounges, and an entirely full-service beach, the Chelsea oozes glamour. Just sip a mojito in one of its bars, or book a poolside cabana, and you'll see. A flat-screen TV, minibar, bathrobes and bath amenities, and Wi-Fi are customary in every room, and many offer water views. But luxury doesn't come cheap: Rooms run $299–499 August midweek, and if you really want to splurge there's the ultimate penthouse suite ($3,500), complete with sweeping ocean views, a master bedroom, and a sunroom with floor-to-ceiling windows. Did I mention the kitchen, balcony, and 42-inch flat-screen TV?

FOOD
Downtown

Atlantic City's most cherished dining establishments exist outside the casinos and off the boards, spread through downtown.

Located in the heart of the city's Ducktown Italian district is **Angelo's Fairmount Tavern** (2300 Fairmount Ave., 609/344-2439, www.angelosfairmounttavern.com, lunch Mon.–Fri. 11:30 A.M.–3 P.M., dinner Mon.–Fri. 5–11 P.M., Sat.–Sun. 4:30–11 P.M.), about as far from the bright lights and big buildings defining present-day AC as you can get. A classic Italian family-owned eatery opened in 1935, Angelo's serves heaping portions of old favorites like

stuffed rigatoni ($12.95) and linguine and crab ($19.75), accompanied by bread and large house salads. The loud, bustling restaurant is separated from a cozy upfront bar by a door. Decor includes framed baseball photos and an autographed Sinatra shot.

Another old-school haunt, known for its 24-hour bar and standard pizzas, **Tony's Baltimore Grill** (2800 Atlantic Ave., 609/345-5766, www.baltimoregrill.com, $4–12) also serves an unbelievably affordable selection of seafood, sandwich, and pasta dishes. Not much has changed in the 40-plus years this place has been in business; not even the jukeboxes, which still play 45s.

You won't find a better sandwich shop than **White House Sub Shop** (2301 Arctic Ave., 609/345-1564, Mon.–Thurs. 10 A.M.–9:30 P.M., Fri.–Sat. 10 A.M.–10:30 P.M., Sun. 11 A.M.–9 P.M., $6–11). In business since 1946, this Atlantic City gem hosts out-the-door lines of folks waiting to get their hands on a Philly cheese steak or Italian sausage sub almost daily. Sinatra had become such a fan it's rumored he had their sandwiches flown to him while performing in Vegas. The towel Frank used in his last AC performance hangs sealed on the wall.

For more than a century, family-owned ◖ **Dock's Oyster House** (2405 Atlantic Ave., 609/345-0092, www.docksoysterhouse.com, Sun.–Thurs. 5–10 P.M., Fri.–Sat. 5–11 P.M., $24–53) has been delivering consistently appetizing seafood dishes. The raw bar is especially popular. A gracious staff and the best margaritas in town are both reasons to visit **Los Amigos** (1926 Atlantic Ave., 609/344-2293, www.losamigosrest.com, Mon.–Sat. 11:30 A.M.–1 A.M., Sun. 11:30 A.M.–10 P.M., 7–12), although the fish tacos ($10.95) aren't so bad either.

Attached to the Sheraton Hotel within walking distance of the train station is **Tun Tavern Brewery & Restaurant** (2 Miss America Way, 609/347-7800, www.tuntavern.com, Sun.–Tues. 11:30 A.M.–midnight, Wed.–Sat. 11:30 A.M.–2 A.M.) Atlantic City's first and only restaurant–brew pub. Cuisine includes steak, seafood, and signature entrées like chicken and shrimp marsala ($21.99), but the real highlight here is the drinks. Try the bitter Bullies Brown Ale or the aptly named Leatherneck Stout, or for something unusual, request a made-to-order fruit beer. Located in the city's quieter Gardener's Basin, the lax **Back Bay Ale House** (800 N. New Hampshire Ave., 609/449-0006, www.backbayalehouse.com, daily 11 A.M.–9:30 P.M. summer, $8–26) serves favored American eats like the eight-ounce Cheese Burger in Paradise ($7.99) along with a selection of beers and wines. Request a table on the second-story enclosed deck for superb sunset views.

The Quarter

Atlantic City's newer shopping centers also feature some of the city's best upscale dining experiences. Tropicana's Quarter is home to several, including restaurant and rum bar **Cuba Libre** (The Quarter, 609/348-6700, www.cuba librerestaurant.com, daily 11:30 A.M.–11 P.M., $18.50–32). With its dimmed lights, palm trees, balcony terrace, and grand staircase, this place feels more like it belongs in the Caribbean than on the Jersey coast—just what its designers were hoping for. Classy Cuban eats include *ropa vieja,* a shredded beef brisket stew, and seviche on toasted flatbread. Come evening, the restaurant morphs into a salsa dance club (Fri.–Sat. until 4 A.M.), spilling out onto the Quarter's square.

Originating in New York City, **Carmines** (The Quarter, 609/572-9300, www.carmines nyc.com, Sun.–Thurs. 11:30 A.M.–midnight, Fri.–Sat. 11:30 A.M.–1 A.M., $19–40) serves southern Italian specialties like rigatoni ($26.50) and manicotti ($27), along with vegetable and sausage sides, in family-sized portions made to share. The restaurant's classic decor includes framed celebrity shots and photos of former Miss America beauty queens. Winter hours vary; call ahead.

Semichain **Ri Ra** (The Quarter, 609/348-8600, www.rira.com, daily 11 A.M.–closing, $10–20) is as Irish as they come. Guests dine on beef 'n' Guinness stew ($12) and shepherd's pie ($12) in a darkened interior decked with salvaged Irish goods. Even the staff is Irish. The place morphs into a nightclub Thursday–Saturday 11 P.M.–3 A.M., with live bands and dance.

INFORMATION AND SERVICES

Visit the **Atlantic City Convention & Visitors Authority** website (www.atlanticcity nj.com) or call their hotline (888/228-4748) for up-to-date details on what's happening in and around the city. Once in town, the **Boardwalk Information Center** (Boardwalk Hall, Boardwalk and Mississippi Ave., daily 9:30 A.M.–5:30 P.M. year-round) has reps on hand to answer questions, and there's a fully stocked display of free hotel, restaurant, and activity flyers. You can also stop by the **Atlantic City Expressway Visitor Welcome Center** (Atlantic City Expressway Mile Marker 3.5, daily 9 A.M.–5 P.M. year-round) for information on the drive into AC.

GETTING THERE AND AROUND

The **Atlantic City Expressway** is the most direct and quickest route (sans weekend traffic) to AC from both South Jersey and Philadelphia. From Philly's Walt Whitman or Ben Franklin Bridge, exit onto I-295 south to Route 42, which leads directly to the Expressway. It's about an hour's drive from beginning to end, but bring lots of cash for tolls. A Pennsylvania alternative is the Commodore Barry Bridge (south of Philadelphia International Airport) to Route 322, which eventually joins the Black Horse Pike (Route 42) and becomes Albany Boulevard just outside Atlantic City. The road leads directly into the city.

For those traveling the **Garden State Parkway** from New York City and North Jersey, take Exits 40 or 38; if you're coming north from Cape May, take Exits 36 or 38.

NJ Transit trains run from the Philadelphia Amtrak Station and take 90 minutes one-way. A round-trip ticket costs $16. Free shuttle service is available between AC's transit terminal and the city's casinos. There's no train service from New York City, but it is supposedly in the works.

It's easy to find all-inclusive bus packages to AC from both Philadelphia and New York, as well as from numerous towns and cities throughout New Jersey. Churches, Elks lodges, synagogues—everyone seems to be running them, and you often get cash back from casinos in the form of slot credits or a meal.

Spirit Airlines (www.spiritair.com) flies daily into **Atlantic City International Airport** (609/645-7895, www.acairport.com) from cities like Las Vegas, Los Angeles, and Fort Lauderdale.

Once in the city, **Jitneys** (609/344-8642, www.jitneys.net, $2.25) are a good way to get around. These 13-passenger blue buses operate along various number- and color-coded routes throughout AC: Number 1 Pink travels back and forth along Pacific Avenue, Number 2 Blue and Number 3 Green both operate to and from the Marina and its bayside casinos, and the Number 4 Orange picks up and drops off at the Convention Center, train station, and bus terminal. Most Jitney's run 24/7 (the Number 4 Orange runs daily 7 A.M.–7 P.M.) and can be accessed from various points along Pacific Avenue (look for the color-coded signs adorning street corners one block west of the Boardwalk casinos).

Greater Atlantic City Region

Atlantic City's surrounding shore towns and mainland suburbs offer lax alternatives to their big-city neighbor. The region is home to some excellent golf courses, affordable accommodation, lively beaches, and a handful of wineries, not to mention top-notch restaurants in Margate.

BRIGANTINE

Just north of Atlantic City is the quiet island city of Brigantine (www.brigantinebeachnj.com), accessible only by Route 87, which runs along AC's bay. Although mostly residential, the entire north end of the city's nearly 10 miles remains undeveloped, protected as a wildlife habitat. The name Brigantine means "two-masted vessel," a fitting memorial to the hundreds of shipwrecks that occurred off the city's coast over the centuries.

Brigantine was home of the infamous **Brigantine Castle,** a "haunted" walk-through dark ride that stood on the former Seahorse Pier during the late 1970s and 1980s. The castle burned down in 1987 after having been closed for several years, but I can assure you, it lives on in the memories—and nightmares—of South Jerseyans everywhere.

E. B. Forsythe National Wildlife Refuge

Brigantine's E. B. Forsythe National Wildlife Refuge (Great Creek Rd., 609/652-1665, http://forsythe.fws.gov, daily dawn–dusk, $4 vehicle, $2 walk-in or bicycle, under 16 free) is a birder's paradise. Filled with salt meadows, marshlands, tall grass, and scrub, it's one of New Jersey's best places for spotting egrets, herons, geese, mallards, and other waterfowl. An eight-mile one-way dirt trail open to cars and bicycles is dotted with points of interest and includes several pullouts (the 15-mile-per-hour speed limit can be a problem for tailgaters). It also offers an interesting juxtaposing view of Atlantic City's casinos in the distance. There are several walking trails, although ticks, mosquitoes, and greenflies are problematic during summer months. The best times to visit are in May and October, when the Atlantic Flyway (a migratory bird route) is in full swing and bugs are at a minimum. Printouts describing trail points are available at the information kiosk, and restrooms are situated nearby. If the kiosk is closed, stop by park headquarters (just south of the driving loop's entrance, weekdays 8 A.M.–4 P.M.) for info and pamphlets. And don't forget your binoculars!

Other Sights

Brigantine's **Marine Mammal Stranding Center** (3625 Brigantine Blvd., 609/266-0538, www.marinemammalstrandingcenter.org, $1) cares for sea life such as dolphins, turtles, and whales injured along the Jersey coast, in the hope of rereleasing them. In operation for more than 20 years, the center is in danger of closing when its city lease expires in 2010, if local officials decide there's a more valuable use for the waterfront property. For now, guests can visit the **Sea Life Education Center** (Tues.–Sat. 10 A.M.–3 P.M. Memorial Day–Labor Day, winter hours vary) and view regional sea life in an underwater tank, along with locally found shells and marine mammal bones, and life-size replicas of marine mammals and fish.

Just down the road from Brigantine's Wildlife Refuge is the **Noyes Museum of Art** (733 Lily Lake Rd., Oceanville, 609/652-8848, www.noyesmuseum.org, Tues.–Sat. 10 A.M.–4:30 P.M., Sun. noon–5 P.M., $4 adult, under 12 free), recently celebrating 25 years. The museum is one of the southern Shore's largest and most well-respected, displaying both folk art and fine art pieces, including a collection of vintage bird decoys once belonging to founder Frank Noyes.

Beaches

Daily beach tags cost $7, $17 for the season, age 12 and under free.

ABSECON

Two miles west of Absecon Bay, Absecon is a mainland community close enough to both Atlantic City and its shore towns directly south to be a good overnight alternative. The area features a range of lodging choices from chain hotels to campgrounds.

Storybook Land

Situated along Route 42 (Black Horse Pike) west of Atlantic City, Storybook Land (6415 Black Horse Pike, Cardiff, 609/641-7847 or 609/646-0103, ext. 5, www.storybookland .com, $19.95) has been a favorite fairy-tale theme park for more than 50 years. Every kid (and adult) who's driven past the roadside castle and its property walls longs to get a glimpse inside. The park has expanded over the years but remains as charming as its beginnings. You can still visit the home of the Three Bears, tumble down Jack and Jill's slide, and tour Alice in Wonderland's Day-Glo cave, which opens out to a life-size maze of playing cards; and mechanical rides include a carousel, the Happy Dragon airlift ride, and Bubbles the roller coaster. It's a fun place to visit in summer, but it's breathtaking (literally) in winter, when hundreds of thousands of colored lights are displayed. A visit during the holiday season makes a great date or family outing—adults will enjoy the scenery as much as kids, a new generation that'll hopefully keep the park up and running for another half century.

Storybook Land's hours vary depending on the season, but are normally weekends 11:30 A.M.–5:30 P.M. in late March and April, daily 11:30 A.M.–5:30 P.M. in summer, and daily 2–9 P.M. during winter.

WINERIES

The Jersey Shore's climate produces long growing seasons and nutrient-rich soil ideal for vineyards. For this reason several wineries have popped up along the state's southern coast over the last couple of centuries.

Renault Winery

My, how you've grown, Renault Winery (72 N. Bremen Ave., Egg Harbor City, 609/965-2111, www.renaultwinery.com). Once a fairly modest establishment, this 1864 winery—one of oldest continuously operating wineries in the country—is now a massive resort, home to a championship golf course and the imposing Tuscany House Hotel and Restaurant. The winery and its restaurant remain my favorites, connected to one another by a lakeside European-style courtyard. Winery tours (609/965-2111) begin in the Fountain Room and continue onto the property's antique-glass museum, hospitality room, and later, the grape pressing room before concluding with wine tastings. If you're planning to visit over a weekend, don't miss the

Renault Gourmet Restaurant's Sunday brunch (10 A.M.–2 P.M., $19.95), a feast of decadent foods and mimosas set in a dimly lit castle-like space. Winery tours run approximately ever 20 minutes, beginning daily at 10 A.M., with evening hours on Friday and Saturday. Renault Gourmet Restaurant is open Friday 5–8 P.M., Saturday 5–9 P.M., and Sunday 10 A.M.–2 P.M. and 4:30–7 P.M.

Tomasello Winery

Founded in 1933, Tomasello Winery (225 White Horse Pike, Hammonton, 888/666-9463, www.tomasellowinery.com, Mon.–Wed. 9 A.M.–6 P.M., Thurs.–Sat. 9 A.M.–8 P.M., Sun. 11 A.M.–6 P.M.) is the largest of the state's more than 30 wineries, a family-run establishment specializing in red raspberry and blackberry dessert wines, and premium wines such as cabernet sauvignon and pinot noir. The winery has a free tasting room and a vintner's room where annual galas are held (check the website for a schedule).

Balic Winery

Chateau Balic (6623 Rte. 40, May's Landing, 609/625-2166, www.balicwinery.com) opened in the 1960s and today features more than 27 award-winning wines, including an American Cream Red and a pomegranate wine. A tasting room is open to the public Monday–Saturday 9 A.M.–8 P.M. and Sunday 11 A.M.–7 P.M.

GOLF

Golfing is a popular regional activity, and the greater Atlantic City area hosts several good courses. These are the best.

Harbor Pines Golf Club's (500 St. Andrews Dr., Egg Harbor Township, 609/927-0006, www.harborpines.com, $65–115 daily) 18-hole course is known for its wide fairways and wooded seclusion. On-site classes are offered for anyone wanting to improve their game (609/927-0006, ext. 10).

Fifteen minutes from Atlantic City, **Blue Heron Pines Golf Club** (W. Country Club Dr., Cologne, 609/965-1800, www.blueheronpines .com, $69–99) is an 18-hole championship golf

course awarded a 4.5-star rating by *Golf Digest* magazine.

Part of the exquisite 670-acre Seaview Marriott Resort just off Route 9 is **Seaview Marriott Golf Club** (410 S. New York Rd., Galloway, 609/652-1800, www.seaviewgolf .com), 36 holes divided between two courses, each in play since the early 20th century. The annual Shop Rite LPGA Classic takes place on the renowned Bay Course, and a gorgeous 297-room luxury hotel adorns the property. Rates run $29–129 depending on the time of day, week, and year.

VENTNOR, MARGATE, AND LONGPORT

Just south of Atlantic City are the towns of Ventnor, Margate, and Longport, three shore communities making up the remainder of Absecon Island and referred to locally as "Downbeach." Driving through them, you get a feel for what Atlantic City must've been like when it was "America's Playground," before its fall from grace and the advent of the casinos. Homes are grand and stately, and many have been around since the early 20th century. The three towns are much (*much*) more residential than their northern neighbor, filled with pleasant shops, ice cream parlors, greenery, and front yards, along with some excellent restaurants. The best attraction, however, stands tall in Margate: With her long trunk and white tusks you can't miss her. Her name's Lucy, and believe me, she's something worth seeing.

C Lucy the Elephant

No, you're not seeing things. That *is* a 65-foot-tall wooden elephant (9200 Atlantic Ave., Margate, 609/823-6473, www.lucythe elephant.org, $6 adult, $3 child) standing along Margate's shore. She goes by the name of Lucy (though with those tusks she's really a he), and she was one of three elephant structures built in the late 1800s in New Jersey and New York. Lucy came about in 1881 as a way of luring prospective buyers to Absecon Island, and has since withstood disastrous ocean winds, encroaching development, and time. Now a historic landmark, Lucy has survived her two wooden siblings by more than a century. Cape May County's zoomorphic structure burned down in 1896, while New York's Coney Island tore down their elephant, which operated as a hotel, in 1900. Lucy has been used as a tavern and private residence, and today as a multistory museum. Things haven't always been easy for Lucy: She's faced extinction numerous times, and was once pulled along Margate's streets for seven hours to settle at her current home. In 2006 the howdah on her back was struck by lightening, causing damage that cost $145,000 to repair. But at nearly 130 years old, Lucy is looking better than ever, with bright painted toenails and a fresh coat of paint. She's the most frequented nongaming attraction in the Atlantic City area—be sure to pay her a visit.

Lucy's open for tours Monday–Saturday 10 A.M.–8 P.M. and Sunday 10 A.M.–5 P.M. during summer. Call ahead for off-season hours.

For Lucy bobbleheads, books, DVDs, and miniatures, stop by the **Lucy Souvenir Cart** (Artic and Michigan Aves., Mon.–Sat. noon–8 P.M., Sun. 11 A.M.–5 P.M. summer, Sat.–Sun. 11 A.M.–5 P.M. off-season) along the Walk in Atlantic City.

Beaches

Beach tags for Ventnor and Margate each cost $15 for the season, free for those age 12 and under. Longport sells season tags for $30 and weekly tags for $10 ($5 senior), with age 12 and under free. Tags cannot be interchanged among the three towns. Margate has a public restroom at Huntington Avenue and the beach.

Sports and Recreation

Go old-school putt-putt style at the seasonal **Margate Miniature Golf** (211 N. Jefferson Ave., 609/822-0660). Rent clunky cruisers ($10 for a half day) and four-wheel surreys ($20 per hour) at Ventnor's **AAAA Bike Shop** (5300 Ventnor Ave., 609/487-0808, www.aaaabike shop.com), in business for over 25 years. Bicycling is allowed on Ventnor's boardwalk Sunday–Thursday 6 A.M.–noon and 5–7 P.M.,

and on Atlantic City's connecting Boardwalk daily 6 A.M.–10 A.M.

Ventnor's noncommercial boardwalk attaches to the south end of Atlantic City's, extending the famous "B" by nearly two miles. There's also a long public fishing pier.

Accommodations

With only 10 rooms, Ventnor's **Carisbrooke Inn Bed and Breakfast** (105 S. Little Rock Ave., 609/822-6392, www.carisbrookeinn .com, $171–246) offers a nice alternative to Atlantic City's bustling hotels. Each individually styled room has its own private bath, along with a flat-panel TV, DVD player (and access to the inn's DVD library), central air, and wireless Internet. Guests are treated to complimentary wine and refreshments each evening, served on the ocean-view deck during summer months and fireside in winter. The inn stands on the original spot of Ventnor's first hotel.

Food

For breakfast don't miss Ventnor's colorful **Ma France Creperie** (5213 Ventnor Ave., 609/399-9955, Mon.–Sat. 8 A.M.–9 P.M., Sun. 8 A.M.–3 P.M., $5–15), a traditional French crepe restaurant serving sweet and savory crepes along with a selection of salads and quiche.

Tomatoes (9300 Amherst Ave., Margate, 609/822-7535, www.tomatoesmargate.com, Sun.–Thurs. 5–10 P.M., Fri.–Sat. 5–11 P.M., $31–49) is known for its upscale Asian-influenced eats and sharp decor. While the sushi bar is impressive, it doesn't top this BYO's glass-enclosed climate-controlled wine cellar stocked with thousands of vintages.

Considered one of Margate's great restaurants, ◖ **Steve & Cookie's by the Bay** (9700 Amherst Ave., 609/823-1163, www.steveand cookies.com, Sun.–Thurs. 5–10 P.M., Fri.–Sat. 5–11 P.M., $17–49) is both classy and consistent, serving seafood-heavy New American dishes in a waterside locale offering fantastic over-the-inlet sunset views. Highlights include an oyster bar and a to-die-for chocolate peanut-butter pie ($7.50).

Getting There

To reach Ventnor take Garden State Parkway Exits 38 or 36 (southbound) or Exits 29 or 36 (northbound). For Margate and Longport use the Parkway's Exit 36. There's a toll to reach Margate from the mainland. No tolls exist between Atlantic City and Longport.

SMITHVILLE

Things weren't looking too good for Smithville a couple of decades ago. The town had changed ownership numerous times since its late-18th-century beginnings, and many of its buildings had fallen into disrepair. You wouldn't know that by visiting Smithville now, especially when stopping by its Village Greene (1 N. New York Rd. at Rte. 9, 609/652-7777, www.smithvillenj .com), a restored shopping village made up of historic structures brought together from throughout South Jersey, interspersed with brick lanes and centered around a small lake and boardwalk. Antiques, Christmas ornaments, Irish flags, and framed celebrity photos are all for sale here, and attractions include an arcade shooting gallery, a miniature train, a

and paddleboat rentals (609/748-6160). In addition, the Greene is home to several dining options (including a historic inn), a bed-and-breakfast that suites the surrounding theme, and a number of festivals and events throughout the year. Smithville has become a great daytrip and family destination. Kids will especially love the geese and ducks frequently backing up traffic on area roadways.

Shopping

With more than 60 shops and restaurants, you'll find plenty to do in Smithville. Notable stores include **Ireland and Old Lace** (609/404-0477, www.irelandandoldlace .com), home to cable-knit sweaters and gold Claddagh rings; UK novelty shop **The British Connection** (609/404-4444); a smattering of craft and antique shops such as **Country Folk** (609/652-6161) and **Crafting Cellar** (609/404-3333); specialty soap purveyor **Little Egg Harbor Soap** (609/652-9300, www .LittleEggHarborSoap.com); and pooch-perfect **PawDazzle Pet Boutique** (609/748-7110). Shops are open daily year-round, with summer

© LAURA KINIRY

Smithville, along Route 9

hours Monday–Wednesday 10 A.M.–6 P.M., Thursday–Saturday 10 A.M.–8 P.M., and Sunday 11 A.M.–6 P.M.

Accommodations

It's easy to turn a trip to Smithville into a relaxing shopping weekend, especially if spending the night at the Village Greene's **Colonial Inn Bed & Breakfast** (615 E. Moss Rd., 609/748-8999, www.colonialinnsmithville.com, $149–199), situated next to the main parking lot. The inn offers eight traditionally styled guest rooms, all with private baths and bubble tubs, outdoor decks, and a TV and DVD player, and some offer panoramic views of the property's Lake Meone. Shops and restaurants are literally right outside your door, and a coffee shop is housed on-site. Overnight stays come with complimentary breakfast.

Food

A Smithville highlight is the **Smithville Inn** (Rte. 9 and Moss Mill Rd., 609/652-7777, www.smithvilleinn.com, Mon.–Thurs. 11:30 A.M.–9 P.M., Fri.–Sat. 11:30 A.M.–9:30 P.M., Sun. 10 A.M.–8 P.M., $18–29), a historic 1787 property with a patio room overlooking Lake Meone. It's one of the Greene's few original structures, and both decor and cuisine are traditional, with multiple fireplaces, exposed wood beams, and dishes like flaky-crust chicken potpie and Chesapeake crab cakes.

For those in the market for more casual fare, visit **Fred & Ethel's Lantern Light Tavern** (609/652-0544, Mon.–Thurs. 11:30 A.M.–2 A.M., Fri.–Sat. 11:30 A.M.–3 A.M., Sun. 11:30 A.M.–midnight, $9–18), also located in the village. This family-friendly place—named for Smithville's original founders, Fred and Ethel Noyes—hosts a popular weekday happy hour and serves a standard menu of American burgers, soups, and platters. Live music plays most weekends.

The Cape

THE JERSEY SHORE

The Jersey Shore's southernmost beach towns are some of its best. Sure, I'm biased, but with places like family-friendly Ocean City, wildlife-friendly Stone Harbor, and stunning Cape May, it's hard to go wrong. It seems like there's a place for everyone along New Jersey's southern shore, including naturalists, adrenaline junkies, romantics, and historians. Ocean City and Wildwood offer two of the state's best boardwalks, and Cape May features some of New Jersey's finest eats. One of New Jersey's best drives is along the unofficial Ocean Drive, a stretch of road connecting Ocean City straight through to Cape May, passing through every shore town along the way. Bridges connect the islands, and each has a $1 toll payable in one direction.

◖ OCEAN CITY

Founded by Methodist ministers as a 19th-century religious summer retreat, Ocean City remains an all-around family favorite. In addition to an abundance of summer rentals, the city hosts wonderful eateries, dozens of activities (including the crowing of Miss New Jersey *and* Miss Crustacean), and one of the Shore's best all-around boardwalks. As Ocean City's biggest draw, the 2.5-mile walkway attracts quite a crowd, who come for its amusements, arcade games, shops, and old-school miniature golf courses. The boardwalk hasn't changed much in the 30-some years I've been frequenting it. It's been widened and rebuilt in parts, but the Music Pier remains, as do the historic movie theaters, Mac & Mancos pizza stands, and Kohrs Bros. ice cream windows.

Ocean City has long had a problem with beach erosion—sand seems to wash south toward Wildwood with every storm. The city spends millions (your beach tag dollars at work) to replenish the beaches, only to watch them disappear again…and again.

Ocean City's Spanish-style downtown center

stretches along Asbury Avenue around Ninth Street, and it includes several interesting shops and restaurants. On the city's northern tip is the Garden District, a residential neighborhood that more resembles towns like Margate and Ventnor than Sea Isle and Avalon to the south. Corsen's Inlet lies along Ocean Drive toward Ocean City's southern end. En route to Strathmere and Sea Isle, the park offers a quiet reprieve from the typical Shore action.

Boardwalk

If I were to offer New Jersey an award for best boardwalk, I'd give it to Ocean City. This 2.5-mile walkway has just the right mix: not too crazy, not too calm, with long empty stretches ideal for walkers and runners, and a central hub that's built up on one side with shops, hotels, snack stands, and attractions, without blocking ocean views. The historic Music Pier is the only true structure on the boardwalk's western side, and it's lovely—a Spanish-style architectural masterpiece that juts out into the ocean, adding to the walkway's scenic allure. Games of chance don't exist (this is a religious town), but the amusement rides, shooting galleries, miniature golf courses, and multitude of fried-food options can keep you busy for hours. Some of my favorite boardwalk shops include **Air Circus** (1114 Boardwalk, 609/399-9343), which carries an awesome selection of colorful kites; the pricey but fun to browse **Only Yesterday** (1108 Boardwalk, 609/398-2869) collectibles store; **Islander** (922 Boardwalk, 609/398-3069), stocking one of the walkway's most varied clothing selections; and **7th Street Surf Shop** (654 Boardwalk, 609/391-1700, http://7thstreetsurfshop.com), offering daily summer surf lessons at 8 A.M. and 10:30 A.M. on the Seventh Street Beach ($35 per person). For one of the best boardwalk experiences, get up early and rent a beach cruiser to ride the boards before 11 A.M., breaking at one of the walkway's eateries for breakfast. Info on bicycle rentals is available under *Sports and Recreation.*

Other Sights

The **Discovery Seashell Museum** (2717 Asbury Ave., 609/398-2316, www.shellmuseum .com, Mon.–Sat. 10 A.M.–8 P.M., Sun. noon–6 P.M. Apr.–Oct., free) is a fun place to browse any time, but it's especially so on a

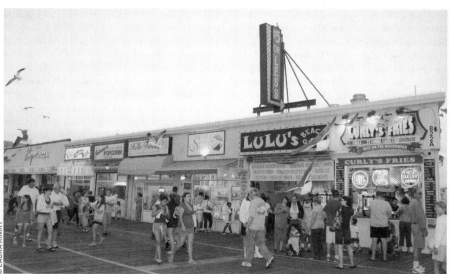

© LAURA KINIRY

Ocean City's boardwalk at dusk

© LAURA KINIRY

giant Ferris wheel, Gillian's Wonderland Pier, Ocean City

drizzly summer day. More of a store than a museum, there are hundreds of thousands of shells from around the globe here, along with giant coral and shark's teeth. Seashell-decorated change purses, shell necklaces, and carved-shell rings make great souvenirs.

Located in the city's large Cultural Arts Center alongside an aquatic and fitness center and a public library is the **Ocean City Historical Museum** (1735 Simpson Ave., 609/399-1801, www.ocnj museum.org, Mon.–Fri. 11 A.M.–4 P.M., Sat. 11 A.M.–2 P.M. May–Nov., Tues.–Fri. 10 A.M.–4 P.M., Sat. 11 A.M.–2 P.M. Dec.–Apr., donations accepted), the best place to visit for local history. Don't miss the museum's *Sindia* display, commemorating the British ship that crashed off the 16th Street beach in the early 1900s with more than $1 million in valuables rumored to be onboard. Less than 25 years ago parts of the ship could still be seen in the water, but today it's completely submerged in sand.

Beaches

Beach tags cost $5 daily, $10 weekly, and $20

for the season. There are public restrooms at the Boardwalk Music Pier, and on First, Sixth, 12th, 34th, and 58th Streets. Remember, this is a dry town; no alcohol is allowed.

The city's best surfing beaches are at Seventh Street and 16th Street. Twenty-four free shuffleboard courts are located at Fifth Street and Boardwalk.

Events

Ocean City hosts dozens of events and activities during summer months, with additional events scheduled year-round. For more details call 609/525-9300.

The Cape's fine sand serves as a wonderful artistic medium, and Ocean City offers two chances to give your sculpting abilities a go. Though the first event takes place in July, I recommend you wait for the second, Ocean City's official August **Sand Sculpting Contest.** Starting at 9 A.M. on the Sixth Street beach, it's part of a day-long celebration culminating with the **Miss Crustacean Pageant,** a crowning of the year's most fetching hermit crab. No worries if your crab ain't a looker—there's also a hermit crab race.

Need a laugh? Check out April's annual **Doo Dah Parade.** Elvis impersonators and bagpipe blowers join more than 300 basset hounds as they wiggle their way down the street en route to the boardwalk's Music Pier. Comedy acts take center stage afterward. In May the city celebrates a seaside version of Groundhog Day with **Martin Z. Mollusk Day.** If hermit crab Martin sees his shadow, summer will come one week early. The celeb crustacean is joined by the Ocean City High School marching band, along with performance artist Suzanne Muldowney, also known as Shelley the Mermaid, or Underdog.

Find out which lucky lady wins a chance to be Miss America at June's **Miss New Jersey Pageant,** held at the boardwalk Music Pier. July's annual **Weekend in Venice** (609/525-9300) kicks off with the **Merchants in Venice Seafood Festival,** an evening of culinary delight held along downtown's Asbury Avenue. The following night, one of the world's longest boat parades takes place along the bay from the Longport Bridge to Tennessee Avenue. It's part of the **Night in Venice** celebration, and it's a sight to behold.

Candlelit **Ghost Tours of Ocean City** (9th St. and Asbury Ave., 609/814-0199, www .ghosttour.com, $14 adult, $8 child) are held nightly (except Sundays) throughout summer, beginning at 8 P.M. outside City Hall. Each tour includes approximately eight stops and lasts a little more than a hour. While stories are historically documented, ghost sightings aren't guaranteed.

The city's annual New Year's Eve **First Night** is one of New Jersey's best, a great way for families to ring in the new year together with plenty of local food and entertainment, including music by the Ocean City Pops Orchestra and the opening of Wonderland's rides.

Sports and Recreation

Entertaining families for nearly 50 years, family-owned **Gillian's Wonderland Pier** (6th St. and Boardwalk, 609/399-7082, www.gillians .com) is Ocean City boardwalk's main attraction, an indoor-outdoor amusement park with everything from a glass house to a swinging galleon. Some of the rides, such as the Musik Express, City Jet Coaster, and fire engines, have been here for more than 30 years, while others like the bumper boats and log flume, only a decade or two. Wonderland is home to a giant 140-foot Ferris wheel—the tallest structure in Ocean City—as well as a 1926 carousel with a ring dispenser. Grab the gold ring and win a free ride. Rides cost a designated number of tickets (usually 2–6), and tickets run $1 each. Special half-price and discount days are scheduled throughout the season. Just down the boards is **Gillian's Island Waterpark** (6th St. and Boardwalk, 609/399-7082, www .gillians.com, daily 9:30 A.M.–6 P.M. mid-June–Labor Day, $22 adult, $18 child for 3 hours), offering thrilling waterslides and prime ocean views. Go for a quick soak on Shotgun Falls, hop a double tube along Skypond Journey, or take a ride down the lazy river.

Along with Wonderland, **Playland's**

Castaway Cove (1020 Boardwalk, 609/399-4751, www.boardwalkfun.com) has been around in one form or another seemingly forever. The cove is replete with outdoor rides geared mostly towards a younger crowd, although a series of not-for-the-faint-hearted thrill rides have been added recently. There's a Tilt-A-Whirl, bumper cars, and an upside-down roller coaster, and for those with an iron stomach, a Gravitron centrifugal spinning machine. The indoor arcade is home to a shooting gallery and an old-school photo booth, as well as the best skee ball in town. The lanes have recently been updated with 100-point holes, but 270 points still wins a free game. The Cove opens daily at 1 P.M. from late June to Labor Day; check the website for shoulder-season hours. Ride tickets never expire. Playland's other boardwalk properties include **Pier 9 Miniature Golf & Speedway Go-Karts,** and the two-course **Golden Galleon Pirate's Golf** at 12th Street ($5.50–6.50). Just look for the bearded Muffler Man with an eye patch.

Manicured miniature golf courses are everywhere these days, but if you're missing the giant fiberglass frogs, pink elephants, and spinning octopuses of yesteryear, you'll find them on Ocean City's boardwalk. Though my favorite fairy-tale course was demolished (*sigh*) in the 1980s, there are still enough old-school courses to make this ol' salt proud. One of them is **Tee Time Golf** (7th St. and Boardwalk, 609/398-6763), just south of Wonderland Pier. Be sure to check out the course's bit of wall humor while waiting for your friend to make that final putt. **Goofy Golf** (920 Boardwalk, 609/398-9662) may be home to the only fiberglass Teenage Mutant Ninja Turtle still existing. Don't forget to call last on the final hole—you'll want to savor the opportunity for a free game.

Built in 1928, the Spanish-style **Music Pier** (825 Boardwalk, 609/525-9245) is one of the boardwalk's most recognizable structures, adorning postcards and picture books throughout the city. It's also Ocean City's prime entertainment venue, hosting annual events like the Miss New Jersey pageant and concerts throughout summer, and serves as home base for the **Ocean City Pops Orchestra** (www .oceancitypops.org).

Originally opened as a bowling alley around 1901, Ocean City's historic **Moorlyn Theater** (820 Boardwalk, 609/399-0006) is now a partially rebuilt four-screen movie theater. Entrance to the theater is on the side, just off the boardwalk. Five-screen seasonal **Frank's Strand Theatre** (9th St. and Boardwalk, 609/398-6565) is the boardwalk's only other movie theater. Built in 1938, it was the flagship location of New Jersey's Shriver Theater chain.

Bikes and surreys are permitted on Ocean City's boardwalk daily before 11 A.M., and there are plenty of places to rent them throughout summer. The city's flat terrain makes bikes a good option on streets as well—just use caution at the intersections. **Surf Buggy Center** has rental locations at Eighth Street and the boardwalk and 12th Street and the boardwalk. A one-week single-speed adult rental costs $45. Others to try are **Ocean City Bike Center** (740 Atlantic Ave., 609/399-5550) and **Oves Bike Rental** (4th St. and Boardwalk, 609/398-3712).

For kayak rentals try **Bay Cats** (316 Bay Ave., 609/391-7960, www.baycats.com), which also offers two-hour guided tours of Ocean City's back bay. Trips—ideal for birders and nature lovers—leave daily each morning throughout summer. Private sailing lessons aboard Hobie catamarans are also available. **Wet-n-Wild Waverunner Rentals** (3rd St. and Bay Ave., 609/399-6527, www.wetand wildwaverunners.com) offers personal watercraft for use on the bay, daily 9 A.M.–sunset Memorial Day–Labor Day.

Fishers cast their lines from the toll bridge over **Corson's Inlet** (609/861-2404, www.state.nj .us/dep/parksandforests/parks/corsons.html), a 341-acre park along Ocean Drive between Ocean City and Strathmere. Quiet and inspiring, the inlet is a great place for walking, and its waters are ideal for sailing and kayaking.

Accommodations

HOTELS

Ocean City is well equipped to handle overnight stays, with dozens of independent motor lodges, hotels, guesthouses, and inns. Although lodging is scattered throughout the city, the area around the Ninth Street Bridge offers the most selection.

Impala Island Inn (1001 Ocean Ave., 609/399-7500, www.impalaislandinn.com, $151–196) offers standard rooms with cable TV and a fridge, and some have additional sleeper sofas. To really feel like you're on vacation, request a room overlooking the pool.

Watson's Regency Suites (Ocean and 9th St., 609/398-4300, www.watsonsregency.com, $219–229 s, $289–309 d) features spacious efficiencies each with a balcony and ample closet space, and decorated in the pastel greens and pinks you'd expect at the Jersey Shore. It's a good choice for extended stays.

Rising from the boardwalk like a pink saltwater taffy is the towering **Port-O-Call** (15th St. and Beach, 609/399-8812, www.portocall hotel.com, $295–430), an Ocean City stalwart. Many of the hotel's rooms offer wonderful ocean views, and all include air-conditioning, TV, and use of the in-ground pool. For guests not quite ready to leave the beach, shower rooms are available after checkout.

Centrally located along the boards is the historic **Flanders** (719 11th St., 609/399-1000, www.theflandershotel.com, $339–980), a grand 1923 Spanish-style hotel featuring one- and two-room bedroom suites, recently added promenade suites with hardwood floors and Americana decor, and penthouse suites. The Flanders is a popular place for weddings, and apparently ghosts: It's rumored to be haunted.

B&BS AND GUESTHOUSES

Ocean City will never rival Cape May when it comes to B&Bs, but there are several treasures if you know where to look. In general, the city's guesthouses range from comfortable to constricting. Those on the higher end are listed below.

Operated by a California surfer, the **Koo-Koo's Nest Bed & Breakfast** (615 Wesley Ave., 609/814-9032, www.kookoosnest.com, $105–135) features themed guest rooms—my favorites are Caribbean Rooms 6 and 7—and suites, most with private baths and fridges. Rooms are small, but they're also a steal. The family-owned **Osborne's Fairview Inn** (601 E. 15th St., 609/398-4319, www.osbornesinn.com, $100–140 summer) offers a handful of small well-kept guest rooms and a few weekly rental apartments, all with TVs, fans, air-conditioning, and private baths. It's a simple beachy sort of place, just down the block from the boards.

The three-story **Scarborough Inn** (720 Ocean Ave., 800/258-1558, www.scarboroughinn.com, $150–250) offers 24 individually styled guest rooms, along with a second-floor reading library and a sojourn room perfect for a game of Scrabble.

In the heart of downtown is **Atlantis Inn Luxury Bed & Breakfast** (601 Atlantic Ave., 609/399-9871, www.atlantisinn.com, $240–525), a suites-only Victorian originally built in 1905 and known for years as the Croft Hall Hotel, a vacationing home for Philadelphia's high society. The property was completely renovated in the early 2000s, transformed into 10 luxury suites and two apartments, each with a private bath, air-conditioning, a TV and DVD player, and access to an on-site spa offering hot-stone, deep-tissue, and Swedish massage. A spacious rooftop deck is ideal for winding out the day.

Most, if not all, of Ocean City's rental agencies cater to weekly or seasonal summer visitors. Some to try are **Grace Realty** (34th and Central, 800/296-4663), **Monihan Realty** (3201 Central Ave., 609/339-0998 or 800/255-0998, www.monihan.com), and **Berger Realty** (3160 Asbury Ave., 877/237-4371, www.bergerrealty.com).

Camping

Although it's a little more than a half-hour's drive to the beach, **Yogi Bear's Jellystone Park Camp-Resort** (1079 12th Ave., Mays Landing, 800/355-0264, www.atlanticcityjellystone.com) offers plenty to entertain kids—and their parents—without ever getting in the car. There's a playground, miniature golf course, and swimming pool, along with regular themed weekend celebrations mid-March–October—better pack your grass skirts and sneakers. No-hookup tent sites cost $37, and RV sites are $55. Barebones cabins ($100) and trailer rentals ($200) are also available.

Just three miles outside of Ocean City, **Whippoorwill Campground** (810 S. Shore Rd., Marmora, 609/390-3458 or 800/424-8275, www.campwhippoorwill.com, Apr.–Oct.) features sheltered wooded campsites along with an Olympic-size swimming pool, free hot showers, and themed events including Christmas in July and September's famed pig roast. Sites cost $50.50 per night based on two people.

Ten minutes from Ocean City is **Frontier Campground** (84 Tyler Rd., Ocean View, 609/390-3649, www.frontiercampground.com, mid-Apr.–mid-Oct.), a low-key place with shaded tent and RV sites. You'll find no bustling activities here—Frontier's all about relaxing. The campground also rents fully furnished "tree houses"—cabins on stilts—that each sleep five and include a kitchen ($100 for two people, $12 per night each additional adult). Basic campsites begin at $35 during the week.

Food

There's no room to argue: **Mack and Manco's** (609/399-2548, off-season hours typically 11:30–8:30 P.M. Mon.–Fri., until 10 or 10:30 P.M. Fri.–Sun., extended summer hours) serves the best slices of thin-crusted cheese pizza in existence. Ever. Take yours to go on a paper plate, grab a seat on a boardwalk bench, and devour it before the seagulls do. There are boardwalk locations at Eighth, Ninth (open year-round), and 12th Streets.

My dad never visits Ocean City without picking up a bucket of **Johnson's Popcorn** (1360 Boardwalk, 609/398-5404, www.johnsonspopcorn.com), New Jersey's most delicious caramel corn hands-down. A bucket is large enough to last a week, but expect it to be gone in a day.

For an authentic Ocean City experience, start your day at **Oves** (5th and Boardwalk, 609/398-3712, www.ovesrestaurant.com), serving some of the best breakfast on the boardwalk, including apple cider doughnuts ($0.75) baked on-site. Request a table on the upper deck, but watch your food—the seagulls aren't shy. When you're through noshing, rent one of their bikes ($5 per hour) and ride off the calories. Oves also serves a selection of lunch eats and dinner entrées, specializing in seafood ($17–24).

Originating in Hawaii, **Hula Grill** (940 Boardwalk, 609/399-2400, www.hulagrill oc.com) opened its now-expanded eatery on the Ocean City boards in 1999. In addition to casual eats, the restaurant serves a selection of intriguing entrées inspired by its home state, including a heaping pulled-pork plate ($8) doused in Hula Grill's own barbecue sauce, and grilled ahi tuna with pineapple salsa ($15.75). The Grill is open full-time seasonally; call ahead for hours April–May and September–October.

Around since 1937, **The Chatterbox** (500 9th St., 609/399-0013, Sun.–Thurs. 7 A.M.–10 P.M., Fri.–Sat. 7 A.M.–11 P.M., $9–18) is an institution—the city's best place to come for a burger and fries or a bit of local nostalgia. **Luigi's Restaurant** (300 9th St., 609/399-4937, $12–21) has been serving up traditional Italian dishes in a cozy corner locale for decades.

Owners of the original 4th Street Café have relocated to Asbury Avenue, where they've opened **Who's on First!** (100 Asbury Ave., 609/399-0764, daily 6 A.M.–9 P.M., $15–25), an incarnation of their popular coffeehouse-eatery. A loyal clientele smitten with the homemade scones has followed. Stop by **Dixie Picnic** (819 8th St., 609/399-1999, www.dixie picnic.com) for your fill of upcakes—delish upside-down cupcakes with icing on all three sides. Get a dozen ($16) to go or one of your favorites (mine's chocolate malted devil's food cake) inside a box lunch with a sandwich, potato salad, and a deviled egg ($8.25). Hours are Monday–Thursday 7 A.M.–9 P.M., Friday–Saturday 7 A.M.–10 P.M. in summer, with additional hours year-round.

Downtown's recently opened **TigerLilly Café & The Courtyard** (805 E. 8th St.,

609/391-7777, $17–28) has brought a new caliber of dining to Ocean City. Healthy helpings of Southern-inspired breakfast, lunch, and dinner dishes that change regularly have put this place on the foodie map. The restaurant is located within the Homestead Hotel; call for hours.

Information and Services

Ocean City's **Information Center** (800/232-2465) is located outside the island, along Route 52 on the Stainton Memorial Causeway, just over the Ninth Street Bridge. Public restrooms are located at First, Sixth, 12th, 34th, and 58th Streets and the beach, and also at the Music Pier along the boardwalk. Most streets close to the boardwalk have metered parking. If you drive around long enough it's possible to find free parking spaces, though they're usually a hike from the action. There are several manned parking lots close to the boards, including a lot at Ninth Street and the boardwalk and another at Fifth Street and the boardwalk.

It's been said that Ocean City has never served a drop of alcohol, but this doesn't mean you can't bring some in. Several liquor stores are situated just outside the city's boundaries, making import ridiculously easy. Two to try are **Circle Liquor** (Somers Point, 609/927-2921), on the west side of the Ninth Street Bridge, and **Boulevard Super Liquors** (501 Roosevelt Blvd., 609/390-1300), across the 34th Street Bridge.

For beachgoers with limited mobility, surf wheel chairs can be rented by calling 609/525-9304. Advance reservations are suggested.

Getting There

Ocean City is 20 minutes south of Atlantic City. It's located off Garden State Parkway's Exits 30 or 25 (southbound) or Exits 25 or 29 (northbound).

SEA ISLE CITY AND STRATHMERE

While Sea Isle has long been a haven for college students and weekend renters who see Miller Lite as the epitome of Shore life, things in this city are changing. The number of families setting up year-round residence has increased dramatically, and the summer bungalows once prevalent throughout the island are coming down and being replaced by million-dollar homes. This shift has been stirring since the new millennium when Fun City—Sea Isle's only amusement center—was torn down, and quiet zones were implemented citywide to keep noise to a minimum. Sea Isle's heading in a calmer direction, true, but its party scene is still going strong.

Just north of the city is Strathmere, a thin stretch of land usually mistaken for an extension of Sea Isle. Along with several eateries and bars, Strathmere is home to one of the Jersey coast's only free beaches. Landis Avenue is the main route between Sea Isle City and Strathmere, and is part of the larger Ocean Drive route connecting Atlantic City with Cape May. It's also a major crossing route for endangered diamondback terrapins making their way to higher ground to lay eggs. The majority of these crossings take place in June and July, so keep an eye out for them. Stone Harbor's Wetlands Institute suggests when you see one crossing the road, pick her up and help her along.

Promenade

Sea Isle's oceanfront paved Promenade (often referred to as a boardwalk) plays host to a couple of casino arcades, several sweatshirt and trinket shops, and casual eateries serving burgers, pizza, and ice cream. The bulk of businesses are situated along the bottom floor of the Spinnaker condo complex on the Promenade's north end. A few blocks south is a **Boardwalk Casino Arcade** (42nd and Boardwalk, 609/263-1377) and **Gunslingers Old Time Photos** (43rd and Boardwalk, 609/263-4771, www.seaislephotography.com/oldtime), where donning garters, flasks, chaps, and boas makes a great 8-by-10 souvenir.

Sand dunes and shrubbery separate the 1.5-mile-long Promenade from the beach. Bicycling, in-line skating, and skateboarding are allowed on the walkway

Monday–Friday 5 A.M.–3 P.M., summer weekends 5 A.M.–noon.

Beaches

Sea Isle's beach tags cost $5 daily, $10 weekly, and $20 for the season (quite a steal). Lifeguards are on duty daily 10 A.M.–5 P.M. throughout summer every few blocks—just walk until you find one. The city has several surfing beaches, including 26th Street, 42nd Street, 52nd Street, and 74th Street; rafting beaches at 24th Street, 45th Street, and 87th Street; and kayaking beaches at 30th Street, 56th Street, and 79th Street. Volleyball is allowed at 25th Street, 53rd Street, and 72nd Street, and surf fishing is allowed at the Townsend Inlet Bridge area south of 93rd Street and most city beaches north of 20th Street.

Entertainment and Nightlife

Cover bands and drink specials are the norm throughout Sea Isle. Most bars and clubs are open nightly in the summer months, but options diminish considerably during the off-season. The epitome of Sea Isle nightlife is the OD, or **Ocean Drive** (40th and Landis Ave., Sea Isle, 609-263-1000, http://theod.com, daily 10 A.M.–2 A.M. summer), centrally located just north of the island's causeway. The bar features a spacious dance floor, but that doesn't stop the place from packing wall-to-wall on weekends, especially when bands like **Love Seed Mama Jump** (http://loveseed.com) perform. Occasional events are hosted throughout the year.

The cavernous **Springfield Inn** (43rd and Pleasure Ave., Sea Isle, 609/263-4951, http://thespringfieldinn.com/main, Mon.–Fri. from 8 A.M., Sat.–Sun. from noon, summer) attracts a slightly older crowd with Wednesday trivia nights and half-price Heinekens. Its backyard open-air **Carousel Bar** (Mon.–Thurs. 11 A.M.–8 P.M., Fri.–Sat. 11 A.M.–10 P.M., Sun. noon–8 P.M.), adjacent to the Promenade, is the perfect place for sipping chill margaritas all afternoon. Just across the island causeway is **La Costa** (4000 Landis Ave., Sea Isle, 609/263-3611), a liquor store, lounge, and motel all rolled into one. The bar is known for its casual happy hour, but for something a bit more refined try the nearby **Dead Dog Saloon** (3809 Landis Ave., Sea Isle, 609/263-7600, http://seaislenightlife.com). This two-story tavern features a small menu of appetizers and sandwiches, along with live music, mixed drinks, and eight draft ales and stouts to choose from. Guys, if you want to enter after 6 P.M., make sure your shirt has a collar.

Plenty of people frequent **Braca Café** (Kennedy Blvd. and the beach, Sea Isle, 609/263-4271, www.bracacafe.com) for the food, but the property—which has belonged to the Braca family for more than a century—is best known to 20-somethings as the home of the 302, a mind-erasing mixture involving a Bacardi 151 double shot and a mean hangover.

Seasonal **Twisties Tavern** (232 S. Bayview Dr., Strathmere, 609/263-2200, www.twisties tavern.com, Wed.–Mon. noon–2 A.M. summer, closed Tues., $12–25) has never recovered from its speakeasy roots. A hidden bayside establishment revered among locals and virtually unknown to tourists, this wood-paneled bar and restaurant is as kitschy as it is kept. Nosh on scallops wrapped in bacon ($13) and fried calamari ($9.75) while admiring Twisties' mounted fish and chiseled coconut collections.

Sports and Recreation

Rent bikes and surreys, along with kayaks and surf chairs, at **Surf Buggy Center** (Kennedy Blvd. and Pleasure Blvd., Sea Isle, 609/628-0101 or 800/976-5679, www.surfbuggycenter .com). For more than 15 years **Sea Isle City Parasail** (86th St. and the bay, Sea Isle, 609/263-5555, www.seaisleparasail.com) has been lifting riders over ocean waters for spectacular views. On a clear day parasailers ($70 per person) can see all the way to Atlantic City. Boats depart from 86th Street and the bay every 1.5 hours throughout summer, beginning at 8 A.M.

Accommodations

Sea Isle's overnight options are limited. For more variety, head north into Ocean City or

set up outdoors at one the campground resorts west of the causeway bridge along Route 9.

The city's largest motel is **Sea Isle Inn** (6400 Landis Ave., Sea Isle, 609/263-4371, www.seaisleinn.com, $129–150), located at a busy intersection toward the island's south side. Rooms are standard, with TV, air-conditioning, a private balcony, and access to an outdoor swimming pool. The motel is next door to the lively **KIX McNutley's Bar** (www .kixmcnutleys.com), and both are better-suited for those preferring late nights to early mornings. Rates are less expensive with a stay of four or more nights.

Located one block from the beach, **The Colonnade Inn** (4600 Landis Ave., Sea Isle, 609/263-0460, www.thecolonnadeinn.com, $185–370) is a large Victorian guesthouse with 19 rentable rooms, ranging from studios to three-bedroom apartments, all with wireless Internet. Complimentary coffee and fresh baked goods are available each morning in the inn's great room.

Camping

Possibly home to New Jersey's largest number of campsites, **Ocean View Resort Campground** (2555 Rte. 9, 609/624-1675, www.ovresort .com, mid-Apr.–mid-Oct.) features 1,173 tent and RV sites on 180 wooded acres. Summer activities include clubhouse movies and a weekly Sunday flea market. The resort is located on the mainland just across Sea Isle's causeway bridge. Rates begin at $39 in early June, $59 late June–August. Lakeside sites cost extra.

On the mainland between Sea Isle and Ocean City, **Hidden Acres** (1142 Rte. 83, Cape May Court House, 609/624-9015 or 800/874-7576, www.hiddenacrescampground .com, mid-Apr.–mid-Oct., from $37) hosts 200 tent and RV sites and a freshwater lake for swimming. Two on-site rental cabins ($50–70) are also available.

Food

Several worthwhile seafood establishments are clustered around 43rd and the bay, but the finest of the bunch is **Mike's Seafood**

Market and Raw Bar (43rd and the bay, Sea Isle, 609/263-3458, www.mikesseafood.com, daily 9 A.M.–9 P.M. June–Aug., Sat.–Sun. 9 A.M.–9 P.M. off-season), voted best dock dining and best seafood raw bar by Sea Isle for nearly a dozen consecutive years. Start with a bucket of cheesy crab fries ($11), then settle in with a fresh steamed combo ($28) that includes large gulf shrimp, Nantucket sea scallops, and lobster tail. Directly behind the restaurant is **Mike's Crab Shack** (317 43rd St., Sea Isle, 609/263-1700), which along with grilled fish features salads and specialty wraps. Take note: Mike's is just as good to go.

Mildred's Strathmere Restaurant (Ocean Dr. and Prescott Rd., Strathmere, 609/263-8209, daily 4–10 P.M., $13–23) is one of the Shore's great old-school establishments, a cozy American restaurant that's been packing in crowds for more than 50 years.

For well over a century the upscale **Busch's Seafood** (8700 Anna Phillips Ln., Sea Isle, 609/263-8626, www.buschsseafood.com) has been feeding local denizens who flock here for the restaurant's signature crab dishes. Highlights include the crab imperial en casserole ($26.95) and Busch's famous she-crab soup ($7.50 per bowl), available Tuesdays and Sundays only. Dinner hours are Tuesday–Sunday from 4 P.M. late June–late September, closed Mondays. Call for additional hours.

Situated bayside at the foot of the inlet bridge is Strathmere's **Deauville Inn** (201 Willard St., Strathmere, 609/263-2080, www.deauvilleinn .com, $21–43), a local classic that's been drawing crowds with tasty American fare and summer weekly wings specials for years. Arrive by bike or by boat for bayside seating and brews along the beach. Monday–Saturday the Deauville opens at 11 A.M. year-round, Sunday at noon. Hungry for hotcakes? Hit up the '50s-themed **Shoobies Restaurant** (3915 Landis Ave., Sea Isle, 609/263-2000, call for hours, $7–17) in downtown Sea Isle. It's also a good spot for mint chocolate chip ice cream.

For late-night slices and pizza turnovers, try **Amici's** (38th and Landis Ave., Sea Isle, 609/263-2320, daily 11 A.M.–11 P.M., $7–24).

Their take-out window stays open until 3 A.M. summer weekends, and the restaurant's BYOB—so you can make a night of it. Bar crowds nurse their hangovers with hoagies from **McGowan's Food Market & Deli** (3900 Landis Ave., Sea Isle, 609/263-5500, daily 7 A.M.–8:30 P.M. summer, $6–9), home to the best sandwiches in Sea Isle.

Information and Services

Tourism information is available at www.seaisle tourism.org and at Sea Isle City Chamber of Commerce (121 42nd St., 609/263-9090, www.seaislechamber.com).

Acme at 63rd and Landis Avenue is the island's only large supermarket.

Public restrooms are located along the Promenade at 32nd Street, 40th Street, and 44th Street; along the beach at 85th Street; and at Townsends Inlet Park Beach at 94th Street.

Getting There

Sea Isle is located off Garden State Parkway Exit 17 (southbound) or 13 (northbound).

AVALON AND STONE HARBOR

Seven Mile Island, a barrier island approximately four blocks wide, is home to the wealthy seaside towns of Avalon and Stone Harbor. While Stone Harbor especially is known for its enormous beachfront homes, both towns are surprisingly accessible, with affordable restaurants, interesting shops, and some of the Cape's best nightlife. They're also environmentally friendly. Avalon hosts some of the state's tallest sand dunes, an important plant-life habitat, while Stone Harbor is known for its commitment to wildlife habitat conservation.

Avalon's downtown stretches along Dune Drive between the Avalon circle and 33rd Street; Stone Harbor's commercial district centers around 96th Street and Third Avenue.

Wetlands Institute

Across Stone Harbor's causeway bridge lies the 6,000-acre Wetlands Institute (1075 Stone Harbor Blvd., 609/368-1211, www

.wetlandsinstitute.org, $7 adult, $5 ages 2–11), a series of salt marshes, boardwalks, viewing platforms, and educational facilities and programs pertaining to the conservation and preservation of coastal ecosystems. The institute offers opportunities for self-guided wetlands tours and birding, along with an indoor saltwater aquarium featuring horseshoe crabs, seahorses, and moon snails. There's also a touch tank for kids. The on-site **Tidewater Museum Store** is a great spot for picking up field guides, Wings n' Waters posters, and binoculars, and for viewing a revolving display of carvings by local artists.

The Wetlands Institute works extensively with the local population of diamondback terrapins, rescuing the eggs of injured females and raising them on-site before rereleasing them. The turtles—often casualties of Jersey Shore drivers, especially along Ocean Drive—can live up to 40 years if they manage to avoid predators and cars.

Field science classes, daylong trips, and kayaking camps are offered during summer for kids and high school students. Call 609/368-1211 for further details.

The center is open Monday–Saturday 9:30 A.M.–4:30 P.M. and Sunday 10 A.M.–4 P.M. mid-May–mid-October, Tuesday–Saturday 9:30 A.M.–4:30 P.M. mid-October–mid-May, with extended midweek hours during July and August.

Stone Harbor Bird Sanctuary

Stone Harbor's 21-acre Bird Sanctuary (114th St. and 3rd Ave., 609/368-5102) is finally becoming human-friendly. For years the sectioned-off forest at Stone Harbor's southern end was strictly limited to birds: blue and green herons, yellow-crowned egrets, songbirds, and lately, two families of willets. But plans are in the works to add walking trails and a spring-fed freshwater pond. The trails are expected to be finished sometime in 2009; docent-led tours will begin soon after.

Beaches

Daily beach tags run $6 daily, $12 weekly for those age 12 and older, and can be used for both Avalon and Stone Harbor. Avalon's surfing beach is the 30th Street beach, and there are several raft beaches, including 12th Street, 24th Street, and 61st Street. Beach access is limited between 43rd Street and 58th Street, where the borough's multimillion-dollar mansions bump up to the sand. Most are blocked from street view by towering trees but can be gawked at from the beach. Just follow the marked trails allowing public beach access at varying intervals.

Avalon beaches are annual nesting spots for two endangered bird species: piping plovers and least terns. To learn more, pick up a brochure at the Community Hall (30th St. and the beach).

Entertainment and Nightlife

Avalon and Stone Harbor host a few of the Cape's most popular live-music venues. Bands let loose on the outdoor deck of **Fred's Tavern & Liquor Store** (314 96th St., Stone Harbor, 609/368-5591, Mon.–Sat. 10 A.M.–2 A.M., Sun. noon–2 A.M.), while regulars toss back beers in Fred's darkened innards until the early morning hours.

Seasonal party spot and local stalwart **Jack's Place** (3601 Ocean Dr., Avalon, 609/967-5001, www.jacksavalon.com, May–Labor Day) is the best place for catching bands like Liquid A and Mr. Greengenes. Another favorite drink spot is the newly expanded **Princeton Bar** (2008 Dune Dr., Avalon, 609/967-3457, www.princetonbar.com), now with a bar and grill, tavern, and rock room. On summer nights the Princeton runs a door-to-door shuttle throughout Avalon (5–10 P.M.) with service to and from the establishment. You can either call for pickup (609/741-1117) or flag it down along Ocean Drive on weekends.

For an alcohol-free evening, catch a film at **Frank Theatre-Stone Harbor 5** (271 96th St., Stone Harbor, 609/368-7731), Seven Mile Beach's only movie theater.

Sports and Recreation

Avalon and Stone Harbor boast several worthwhile seasonal attractions, including the 18-hole **Pirate Island Golf** (27th St. and Dune

Dr., Avalon, 609/368-8344, www.pirate islandgolf.com, additional locations in Sea Isle and Ocean City), an elaborate seafaring-themed miniature golf course worthy of the Caribbean.

Stone Harbor paddle shop **Harbor Outfitters** (354 96th St., Stone Harbor, 609/368-5501, www.harboroutfitters.com) runs two-hour guided ecotours ($40 adult, $30 child) through local wetlands, including Hereford and Townsend's inlets, with evening full-moon tours throughout summer. The shop also sells stand-up paddleboards, used kayaks, and wave skis (a surfboard-kayak combo), rents out single ($20 per hour) and double ($30 per hour) kayaks, stand-up paddleboards ($50 per day), and surfboards ($35 per day), and offers various learning workshops throughout summer.

Rent bikes at Stone Harbor's family-owned **Harbor Bike & Beach Shop** (9828 3rd Ave., Stone Harbor, 609/368-3691, http://harbor bike.com) between 98th and 99th Streets, or **Hollywood Bicycles** (2528 Dune Dr., Avalon, 609/967-5846, http://hollywoodbikeshop.com, closed Wed.) in Avalon.

Avalon is home to one of the East Coast's only high-dunes beaches. **The Wetlands Institute** (609/368-1211) hosts guided dune walks Wednesdays at 9 A.M. June–early September, leaving from the 48th Street dune path. Call for further details. The borough also hosts a half-mile beachfront walkway, which bicyclists are permitted to use daily 5–10 A.M.

Accommodations

The bulk of Seven Mile Island's overnight choices hover around 80th Street, where Avalon and Stone Harbor meet.

Now under new management, the 44-room **Avalon Inn Resort** (7929 Dune Dr., Avalon, 609/368-1543, www.avaloninn.org, $199–219) is a quiet motel with standard amenities and an outdoor pool.

Concord Suites (7800 Dune Dr., Avalon, 609/368-7800, www.concordsuites.com, May–Oct., $212) is Avalon's only all-suite hotel, a seasonal establishment about a one-block walk

to the beach. In addition to condo quarters, the hotel hosts an elevator, two swimming pools, and four sundecks.

Avalon's recently renovated **Windrift Hotel Resort** (80th St. and the beach, Avalon, 609/368-5175, www.windrifthotel.com, $230–310) provides overnight motel, efficiency, and condo accommodations, along with on-site amenities like an in-ground pool, a 50-foot oval bar, and a fun beach-garden patio perfect for evening cocktails. The hotel's restaurant offers an extensive American menu daily (breakfast–dinner).

In addition to superb ocean views and in-house Italian-inspired dining, Avalon's **Golden Inn Hotel & Resort** (Oceanfront at 78th St., 609/368-5155, www.goldeninn.com, $275–385) has a concierge who will book everything from sailing trips to parasailing equipment for you. If you can do without a view, the cost of a room is about $40 less.

Camping

On New Jersey's mainland just west of Avalon is **Avalon Campground** (1917 Rte. 9 N., Clermont, 609/624-0075 or 800/814-2267, www.avaloncampground.com, mid-Apr.–Sept.), offering wooded campsites for tents ($36) and RVs ($44–54). The campground also rents one- and two-bedroom log cabins ($80–90), and stationary trailers complete with air-conditioning and bathrooms ($1,025 weekly).

Food

Study the blackboard of daily offerings, then head right up to **Sea Grill's** (225 21st St., Avalon, 609/967-5511, www.seagrillrestaurant .com, daily from 5 P.M. year-round, $20–48) chef and place your steak or seafood order, along with a side or two. Despite the informalities, this ain't no fast-food place. One look at the wine list—and prices—will convince you otherwise.

Tiny BYO **Café Loren** (23rd St. and Dune Dr., Avalon, 609/967-8228, Tues.–Sun. 5:30–9 P.M., Memorial Day–Labor Day, $29–34) is a local fine-dining institution, serving first-rate meat and seafood dishes for more than 30 years.

Local breakfast haunt **Maggie's** (2619 Dune Dr., Avalon, 609/368-7422, daily from 6:30 A.M. summer, $7–12) serves French toast, omelets, and scrapple (yum!) along with lunch eats.

For fresh salads and banana-based smoothies, head to Stone Harbor's **Green Cuisine** (302 96th St., Stone Harbor, 609/368-1616, Mon.–Thurs. 10 A.M.–8 P.M., Fri.–Sun. 10 A.M.–8:30 P.M., $5–10), a nice alternative to the Shore's typical fried options.

Information and Services

Public restrooms are available at 10th St. and Dune Drive, Community Hall (30th St. and the beach, wheelchair accessible), the public safety building (31st St. and Dune Dr.), Borough Hall (32nd St. and Dune Dr.), and the tennis buildings (8th St. and 39th St.). There are public parking lots at 30th Street and Dune Drive, and 28th–20th Streets and the beach, among others.

Beach surf chairs for people with limited mobility can be rented through Avalon Beach Patrol (609/967-7587), or in Stone Harbor by phoning 609/368-5102.

Getting There

Avalon is located off Garden State Parkway Exit 13; for Stone Harbor, take Garden State Parkway Exit 10A (southbound) or 10B (northbound).

THE WILDWOODS

Collectively known as Wildwood-by-the-Sea or simply Wildwood, Five Mile Island consists of several towns, including North Wildwood, central Wildwood City, and southern Wildwood Crest. During the 1950s Wildwood earned the nickname "Little Vegas" due to its popularity as a vacation resort, party spot, and live-music venue. Bill Haley and His Comets publicly debuted "Rock Around the Clock" at the HofBrau Hotel at Atlantic and Oak Avenue; Chubby Checker performed his first twist at the Rainbow Club, just down the street; and

Bobby Rydell sang about his "Wildwood Days" on AM radio stations. Dick Clark even hosted *American Bandstand* from the Boardwalk's Starlight Ballroom during the summer months. At the same time hundreds of mom-and-pop motels sprung up around the island, most notably in Wildwood Crest, each trying to outdo the other with a more elaborate sign, higher-voltage lights, and plastic palm trees.

Sound tacky? That's what a lot of people thought, and the Wildwoods were pretty much left alone by investors and developers for years. Thankfully, this is what saved (or at least, postponed) Wildwood's affectionately dubbed doo-wop motels from destruction. Along with the boardwalk, it's these kitschy, campy structures that make Wildwood worth visiting in the first place. Now they're in danger, and so is Wildwood's allure.

Though the Wildwoods' "rediscovery" is evident in the upscale townhouses and condos popping up around the island and the demolition of doo-wop properties throughout, the place has managed to retain its working-class roots and remains the resort of choice for plenty South Jerseyans and Philadelphians.

Cheap eats, nightlife, and airbrushed fringed T-shirts are easy to come by, especially in Wildwood City, which feels more like a night at the fun house than a walk in the park. For now, the Wildwoods remain mostly seasonal, practically turning into a ghost town by late October and not kicking back in until May. Most restaurants and some hotels completely shut down for the winter, although come June you'll think the whole tristate region moved to town.

◖ Boardwalk

There is nothing quite like the Wildwood two-mile boardwalk, a smorgasbord of T-shirt shacks, gyro stands, arcades, amusements—one big buildup of color and kitsch. This extended carnival stand is one of New Jersey's best people-watching spots. In fact, there's little you won't find on these boards: Garlic fries, funnel cakes, giant stuffed Looney Tunes dolls, airbrushed T-shirts, and painted hermit crabs are all here, along with prophesizing iron-ons and temporary tattoos. Tramcars carrying weary vacationers up and down the walkway play pre-recorded warnings that'll stick with you all summer: "Watch the tram car, please. *Please,* watch the tram car." Though the Wildwoods are currently undergoing gentrification, this doesn't hold true for the boardwalk. Black, white, and Latino families, couples, and teens all fit in perfectly. I can't imagine it any other way.

One of the boardwalk's best attractions are its infamous **tram cars,** running the walkway's length in a continuous loop and picking up worn vacationers as they go. It seems these vehicles will stop for no one, so heed those warnings and "wa-wa-watch the tram car" or you may find you've become another boardwalk attraction. The transport stops wherever you like and costs $2 each way, although tokens will soon be required to pay.

Another great Wildwood staple is the multilevel **Boardwalk Mall** (3800 Boardwalk, 609/522-4260), the perfect shopping spot for flimsy gold rings, Hawaiian-print totes, and that Johnny Depp poster you've been pining for.

Ladies and gentleman, you ain't seen nothing like the boardwalk's **Seaport Aquarium** (3400 Boardwalk, 609/522-2700, $7–8 adult, $6–7 child), or so the employee standing outside with a live serpent draped over his neck would have you believe. This small attraction is home to several shark species, including lemon, sand tiger, and nurse sharks, along with alligators, crocs, pythons, and piranhas. It's just what you'd expect in Wildwood.

Amusement Piers

Wildwood's amusement piers are famous, at least around the Mid-Atlantic. These aren't all kiddie lands, mind you. This is serious stuff! The Morey family (www.moreyspiers.com), developers of the Wildwoods' first amusement pier, currently owns all three in operation as well as two beachfront water parks. Passes bought for one can be used at any, although some rides require an additional fee.

© LAURA KINIRY

Step right up and win a prize at Wildwood's famous boardwalk.

Situated at Spencer Avenue and the boardwalk, **Adventure Pier** hosts some of the boardwalk's most adrenaline-inducing rides, including one of the state's best roller coasters, the **Great White.** This wood and steel hybrid runs at 50 miles per hour and reaches heights of more than 100 feet. Additional rides include a human slingshot and the Inverter, carrying 24 people at a time up 50 feet and inverting them before returning to the ground. There's also a carousel, the kids-only Apache Helicopters, and the disorienting Chamber of Checkers, sort of like a glass house, but different.

For more excitement hit **Surfside Pier,** home to **AtmosFEAR,** a free-fall tower that keeps riders in the dark, literally. The pier recently updated its **Great Nor'easter Roller Coaster** with Freedom Flight seats—suspended seats placing riders on the outer loop. The coaster winds above Ocean Oasis Waterpark and does a double spin at up to 50 miles per hour. Surfside Pier is also home to a Formula 1 raceway, rideable for an additional fee, along with more than two dozen kid-friendly amusements and Dante's Dungeon, the boardwalk's obligatory dark ride.

Mariner's Landing Pier has gathered together some of the boardwalk's best rides, including the Pirates of the Wildwood's 3-D adventure and the **Giant Wheel,** an open-car 156-foot Ferris wheel that's one of the tallest in the state. At night the wheel lights up with over 200,000 LED bulbs. Mariner's Landing also features a climbing wall, paddleboats, bumper cars, and the Sea Serpent upside-down roller coaster.

Access to all Morey Piers is free, although rides are paid for through the purchase of wristbands or EZ tickets, which deduct individual ticket costs with each ride. A one-day wristband for all three piers costs $45 adult, $33 child. An EZ pass runs $50 for 70 tickets, $25 for 30.

Situated at the back of Surfside Pier is **Ocean Oasis Waterpark & Beach Club,** where you'll find a kid-friendly activity pool with walkable lily pads and a climbing cargo net, a lazy river, and high-speed waterslides like Riptide

Rapids and Sidewinders, two side-by-side slides that twist and turn while dropping 40 feet. Mariner's Landing **Raging Waters** features a rope swing, a Skypond Journey into four different elevated pools, and a Camp KidTastrophe equipped with water guns and water sprays. An all-day admission to both water parks is $33 adult, $25 child. Three hours at one water park costs $28 adult, $20 child.

A third Wildwood water park, this one visible from Wildwood streets, is the colorful **Splash Zone** (Schellenger Ave. and the boardwalk, 609/729-5600, www.splashzonewater park.com). The park has more than a dozen slides, rides, and attractions, including the Beast of the East, the Mid-Atlantic's only six-person raft ride; the torpedo-like Terminator; and a giant bucket that empties 1,000 gallons of water on park-goers every three minutes. A three-hour pass is $26 adult, $20 child, and an all-day pass goes for $28–30 adult, $21–24 child.

Other Sights

Just across the bridge from Stone Harbor is North Wildwood's **Hereford Inlet Lighthouse** (1st and Central Ave., 609/522-4520, www .herefordlighthouse.org, daily 9 A.M.–5 P.M. mid-May–mid-Oct., Wed.–Sun. 10 A.M.–4 P.M. mid-Oct.–mid-May, $4 adult, $1 child), a still-active Victorian lighthouse built in 1874. With five indoor fireplaces and English gardens that attract hundreds of butterflies annually, the property feels less like a lighthouse and more like that of a country home. Visitors are invited to tour the lighthouse and indoor museum, which includes the light's original whale-oil lamp. It's free to browse the gardens and gift shop. For those also planning a trip to nearby Cape May's lighthouse, combination tickets can be purchased at Hereford ($9 adult, $3 child under 11).

Beaches

Sure, the beaches are free. But at a half mile in width, it takes work to enjoy them. Really, it's not *so* bad. Benches are scattered along about midway from the ocean, offering nice respite for weary or scorched feet. Playgrounds, volleyball nets, and shuffleboard courts are also set up along the sand, notably alongside the boardwalk. North Wildwood's Moore's Inlet is the Wildwoods' only beach allowing dogs and barbecues. It's also a great spot for fishing and personal watercraft use.

There's a surfing beach between Eighth and 10th Avenues in North Wildwood, and another at Rambler Road in Wildwood Crest.

Festivals and Events

Since opening in 2002, the doo-wop-inspired **Wildwoods Convention Center** (4501 Boardwalk, 609/846-2631 or 800/992-9732) has brought the island new life by hosting close to 500 events each year, including October's annual **Fabulous '50s Weekend** (www.gwcoc.com), with musical performances by the likes of Ben E. King and the Del Vikings, and April's annual **Sensational '60s Weekend** (www.gwcoc.com), complete with a record hop deejayed by local radio icon Jerry "The Geator" Blavat.

Wildwood's long-running **National Marbles Tournament** (301/724-1297, www.nationalmarblestournament.org) occurs each June at a permanent beach location in front of the boardwalk. More than 1,000 games are played over the four-day tournament. You can also visit the city's **Marbles Hall of Fame** at the **George F. Boyer Historical Museum** (3907 Pacific Ave., 609/523-0277).

Held annually over Memorial Day weekend, the **Wildwood International Kite Fest** (Cresse Ave.–Burk Ave. on the beach and Wildwood Convention Hall, 609/729-4000, www.gwcoc.com) is the country's largest, featuring world-renowned kite builders, kite-making workshops and exhibits, and an illuminated Night Kite Fly. Kite Ballet, a takeoff on figure skating, is one of the weekend's more serious events—fliers come prepared for all weather conditions.

Recreation and Entertainment

Wildwood Crest's beachfront **Promenade** offers welcome relief from its northern boardwalk neighbor. Much more low-key, it's a

the Wildwoods Convention Center

good stretch for jogging or beach cruising. If you haven't brought your own ride, rent one at **Bradley's Bikes** (Rambler Rd. and Ocean St., 609/729-1444) across the street from the Admiral's Quarters restaurant. Bikes are allowed on the boards daily 5–11 A.M.

The borough's **New Jersey Surf Camps** (Ocean Outfitters, 6101 New Jersey Ave., 609/729-7400, www.newjerseysurfcamps .com) offers private ($45 per hour) and group surfing lessons for all ages year-round. A one-day surf "camp" runs $65 (weekdays 9:30 A.M.–noon or 2:30–5 P.M.), or spend the entire weekend catching waves (Sat.–Sun. 9–11 A.M., $130).

Atlantic Parasail Inc. (1025 Ocean Dr., 609/522-1869, www.atlanticparasail.com, $65 per person) offers tandem and single-harness rides above the ocean.

Billed as the world's fastest speedboat, the 70-foot-long, 147-passenger **Silver Bullet** (609/522-6060, www.silverbullettours.com) shoots across Wildwood waters at exhilarating speeds. Ninety-minute rides depart from the Wildwood Marina (Rio Grande and Susquehanna Aves.).

Accommodations

Many of Wildwoods' motels remain so old-school they're still advertising cable TV. This is a good thing, at least in theory. Motels and amusements are this Shore resort's top two attractions, but not many people want to stay in tiny rooms without hair dryers and central air when there's a fancy hotel up the street. That's why the best of Wildwood's bunch is upgrading and updating while keeping the funky neon signs, plastic palm trees, and 1950s flair that made them attractive in the first place. And if they're family-owned, even better. Book a room in a good Wildwood motel (and there are plenty of bad ones, believe me) and you're in for one of the most unique experiences along the Jersey Shore, let alone the country. Sure, such far-out places were all over the United States 50 years ago, but not anymore. Even in these parts doo-wop is endangered, so do your part to keep it around. Dig?

A good choice for families looking to spend time on the boardwalk, downtown Wildwood's **Le Voyageur Motel** (232 Andrews Ave., Wildwood, 609/522-6407, $99–175) offers standard motel rooms and efficiencies and hosts several outdoor decks, along with a heated pool. Known for its cleanliness, the two-part doo-wop-certified **Heart of Wildwood** (3915 Ocean Ave., Wildwood, 609/522-4090, www .heartofwildwood.com, $125–180) features both a 44-unit boardwalk location and a 30-room motel diagonally across the street on Ocean Avenue. All rooms are smoke-free, with air-conditioning, TVs, and DVD players. Both have heated pools *and* plastic palm trees.

With its plastic palms, angular roof, and kidney-shaped pool, the **Caribbean** (5600 Ocean Ave., Wildwood Crest, 609/522-8292, www.caribbeanmotel.com, $141–199) is a doo-wop classic—it's actually listed on the National Register of Historic Places. The motel has been completely renovated and revamped with an updated 1950s style: Its lounge combines

the neo-doo-wop Starlux Motel, Wildwood City

leopard-print furnishings with boomerang tables and complements them with a flat-screen TV; and guest rooms feature modern amenities enhanced by tropical-striped linens and lime rickey walls. And with shuffleboard and a panoramic sundeck, this place is hard to beat. Situated along the beach in Wildwood Crest, the seasonal **Fleur de Lis Resort Motel** (6105 Ocean Ave., Wildwood Crest, 609/552-0123, www.fleurdelismotel.com, May–mid-Oct., $130–366) features three stories of clean rooms, each with a kitchenette, air-conditioning, and wireless Internet. Highlights include a sundeck overlooking both the pool and the beach, and a game room with Ping-Pong.

It's impossible not to love North Wildwood's **Lollipop Motel** (23rd and Atlantic Aves., North Wildwood, 609/729-2800, www.lollipop motel.com, $189–217), if only for its roadside cherub-faced taffy sign and its candy-colored doors. Add to that Wi-Fi, a heated pool with a diving board, a patio with barbecue grills, and recently renovated rooms complete with kitchenettes, and you may find yourself gushing.

From its exterior, **The Pan American Hotel** (5901 Ocean Ave., Wildwood Crest, 609/522-6936, www.panamericanhotel .com, $186–240) looks *so* Miami Beach. There are palm trees (sh-h-h…plastic), private balconies, and a flashy ice-blue color scheme, along with a circular swimming pool that's as inviting as a Skyy martini. But head inside and this neo-doo-wop property is Wildwood all the way. There's nothing wrong with the Deja Blue rooms, but it's the renovated Summer Breeze rooms that'll make a doo-wop convert out of you, if you're not already.

Right on the beach, the family-friendly **Armada by-the-Sea** (6503 Ocean Ave., Wildwood Crest, 609/729-3000, www.armada motel.com, $182–335) is one of Wildwood's larger doo-wop properties, a three-story motel with pleasant rooms and an elevator, in the quiet part of town. Accommodations—ranging from single rooms to three-room suites—all have balconies with partial ocean views, along with microwaves and fridges. Armada's best

feature (besides its neon sign) is its Olympic-size heated pool, the perfect place for a swim while acclimating.

The first of Wildwood's neo-doo-wop properties, **C Starlux Motel** (305 E. Rio Grande Ave., 609/522-7412, www.thestarlux.com, $219–339) is the reincarnated former Wingate Motel, complete with an elevator, a whirlpool, and a hip modern take on the city's signature style. Designers salvaged throwaways from demolished doo-wop properties and recycled them into room furnishings and fabrics, complementing additional touches like lava lamps and Technicolor color schemes. Rooms are still small, but are much more of an experience. Besides, you can always spend your days at the heated pool or property's all-glass Astro Lounge. The motel also offers a couple of renovated Airstream trailers for overnight stays.

Camping

About 10 minutes west of Wildwood, **Acorn Campground** (Rte. 47, Green Creek, 609/886-7119, www.acorncampground.com, late May–early Sept., $40–45) features 330 wooded sites for tents and RVs. Perks include free hot showers, two swimming pools, and two license-free fishing ponds. At nearby **King Nummy Trail Campground** (205 Rte. 47 S., Cape May Court House, 609/465-4242, www.kingnummytrail .com, late Apr.–Oct.) families can throw horseshoes, compete at shuffleboard, or play badminton. Tent and RV sites run $32–36, and on-site cabins $50–90.

Food and Nightlife

While not a culinary hotspot, the Wildwoods hold their own when it comes to local favorites. Wildwood City's Schellenger Avenue hosts a couple of restaurants, including the kitschy **Schellenger's Restaurant** (3516 Atlantic Ave., Wildwood, 609/522-0533, daily from 3 P.M. summer, $15–29). Known as "Lobster City," this seasonal space serves seafood-heavy American eats in a nautically themed setting. You can't miss it: just look for the fiberglass lobster and a rooftop seaside-inspired menagerie. **Neil's Steak and Chowder House** (222

THE WILDWOODS' DESIGNS ON DOO-WOP

Wildwoods' motel boom happened in the 1950s, when autos ran rampant but air travel wasn't as ubiquitous as it is today. Americans were glimpsing faraway places on TV but didn't have the time or means to reach them. In stepped North Wildwood, Wildwood, and Wildwood Crest, beachside motels began evoking far-off places like Hawaii and Singapore, appealing to local families who wanted to feel like they were truly getting away. Most of these establishments were mom-and-pop-owned, ordinary cement buildings with smallish rooms and efficiencies. So in order to differentiate themselves from one another, they added oversize flashy neon signs, angular roofs, kidney-shaped pools, exotic themes (evident in larger-than-life names like Pink Champagne, Monaco, and Caribbean Breeze), "perks" like air-conditioning and television, and parking spots only a few feet away from the door. The kitschy decor ranged from pirate statues to futuristic motifs.

While it's true such places were popular throughout the United States, many are long since gone, either rebuilt as condos or replaced by homes. However, the Wildwoods were all but forgotten during much of the 1980s and 1990s, a lack of commercial attention that left these tacky jewels as diamonds in the rough just waiting to be uncovered.

In 1997 the late architect Steve Izenhour did just that. A proponent of Vegas-style kitsch (the Wildwoods were often referred to as "Little Vegas" during the 1950s), Izenhour was en-amored with the Wildwoods' wacky motels and first used the term "doo-wop" in talking about the Wildwoods' architectural offerings. (This style is also known as "populuxe," "California googie," and "Jetsonian" in other parts of the country.) Together with one of the Wildwoods' great founding sons, Jack Morey, Izenhour developed the **Doo Wop Preservation League**

© LAURA KINIRY

Cherubic faces welcome visitors to the Lollipop Motel, North Wildwood.

E. Schellenger Ave., Wildwood, 609/522-5226, daily 4:30–10 P.M. summer, Fri.–Sat. 4:30–9:30 P.M. shoulder seasons, $15–26) is a popular surf-and-turf where customers dine in dark wood booths under Tiffany-style lampshades. Free parking and an early-bird special are big draws.

Housed in a seemingly unlucky location along Atlantic Avenue, **Jersey Girl** (3601 Atlantic Ave., Wildwood, Wed.–Mon. 5 P.M.–midnight summer, closed Tues., 609/522-7747) is the newest incarnation in a long line of eateries, including Maureen's, Blue Olive, and Red Sky Cafe. The restaurant serves Shore classics like stuffed flounder ($20) and jumbo crab cakes ($20), along with pastas and specialty sandwiches. In keeping with one of the former establishments' themes, Jersey Girl offers a superb martini selection that alone is worth your visit.

Locals recommend Wildwood Crest's **Admiral's Quarters** (7200 Ocean Ave., Wildwood Crest, 609/729-1133, daily 7 A.M.–2 P.M. summer, $7–12) for omelets and

(www.doowopusa.org), a nonprofit aimed at highlighting and protecting the Wildwoods' unique architectural contribution.

Unfortunately, the league was formed just as the Wildwoods were being rediscovered as a beach resort, but not for their pop-culture attractions. As Preservation League members were attempting to inspire businesses to promote the doo-wop spirit, dozens of motels were meeting the wrecking ball, and what was once the largest collection of "midcentury commercial" architecture found in one place quickly began disappearing. Today the trend continues. Doo-wop is out of style, man, lacking many of the modern amenities that other Shore towns offer. Money is talking, and many motel owners are taking the more lucrative road when faced with the choice between selling or investing millions in a property that needs a complete overhaul.

In 2005, more than half of the Wildwoods' doo-wop properties had already been demolished; at the same time, local chain and independent businesses garnished themselves with doo-wop accessories, including the Harley Davidson shop and the Wawa convenience store along Rio Grande Avenue, as well as the Wildwood Convention Center, now featuring giant beach balls and a doo-wop-style sign out front. The entire doo-wop motel district was listed as one of **Preservation New Jersey's** (www.preservationnj.org) Ten Most Endangered Sites for 2005, and the area has been nominated for listing on the New Jersey State Register of Historic Places. The Caribbean became the first of the motels to gain an official historic listing in July 2005.

For those interested in doo-wop, there are a number of outlets. The Doo Wop Preservation League runs a doo-wop architectural bus tour through the Wildwoods' streets evenings June–August. Tickets ($10 adult, $5 child) may be purchased at the **Wildwood Convention Center** (4501 Boardwalk, 609/729-9000) ticket office, and buses leave across the street from in front of the new **Doo Wop Museum** (3201 Pacific Ave., 609 729-4000), home to a garden of neon signs preserved from former doo-wop properties, along with a café and a malt shop. Contact the Doo Wop Preservation League (609/729-4000, info@doowopusa. org) for further tour details and times. Doo-wop fans may also want to check out the 2003 documentary *Wildwood Days* by filmmaker Carolyn Travis, who spent her childhood summers vacationing in Wildwood. The movie is a nostalgic look into the Wildwoods' past and is heavy on the doo-wop shots. A book highlighting Wildwoods doo-wop with excellent color photos, Kirk Hasting's ***Doo Wop Motels: Architectural Treasures of the Wildwoods,*** is available at area bookstores. In addition, the **Wildwood Crest Historical Society** (116 E. Heather Rd., 609/729-4515, www.cresthistory.org) offers some information on the borough's doo-wop history, and visitors can pick up a map of current and former doo-wop properties at the Doo Wop Museum.

short stacks. The restaurant is tucked away on the bottom floor of the Admiral Resort Motel. Perhaps the Wildwoods' finest restaurant, upscale **Marie Nicole's** (9510 Pacific Ave., Wildwood, 609/522-5425, www.marienicoles .com, daily 5–10 P.M., closed Tues., $21–34) serves eclectic American cuisine in an intimate setting, with both a bar and a glass-enclosed dining room. Dishes include New Zealand rack of lamb ($34) and lemongrass encrusted ahi tuna ($29).

Looking for an authentic boardwalk snack?

Order a cup of fresh-cut **Curley's Fries** (822 Boardwalk, 609/398-4040, $5) with a side of cheese dip. C'mon, it's the Shore! For something a little more substantial, **Mack's Pizza** (4200 Boardwalk, 609/729-0244) serves the best slices in town. Just off the boardwalk is the bright pink **Laura's Fudge** (Wildwood and Ocean Aves., 609/729-1555, www.lauras fudgeshop.com), Wildwood's name in fudge since 1926.

For nightlife with your meal, stick to Wildwood and North Wildwood, where food is good and drinks are plenty. With a bit o' Irish luck you'll score a stool at **Tucker's Pub** (3301 Atlantic Ave., Wildwood, 609/846-1110, www.tuckers-pub.com) before the crowd packs in. Guinness, Harp, and Smithwicks are the resident beers, and the food recently got an upgrade with a new executive chef. Platters include shepherd's pie ($15) and bangers and mash ($13). At **Goodnight Irene's** (Poplar and Pacific Aves., Wildwood, 609/729-3861, www.goodnightirenes.com, daily 11 A.M.–3 A.M.) choose from dozens of draft beers and 60 in bottles, including Philadelphia Brewing Walt Wit, Landshark Lager, and Smuttynose Old Brown Dog Ale. Irene's also serves a menu of brick-oven pizzas with toppings like cheese steak and buffalo chicken. There are daily drink and dining specials throughout the week.

For a full-service waterfront meal or casual bayside dining, stop by the **Boathouse** (Rio Grande Ave., Wildwood, 609/729-5301, www.boathouseonline.net, $15–23) at the foot of the Rio Grande Bridge. In addition to a menu of meat and seafood entrées, along with deck dishes such as hot dogs ($3.25) and bacon cheeseburgers ($6.75), the Boathouse offers an interesting selection of frozen drinks, including the rum-spiked multifruit Tropicana and a mudslide made with Bailey's, ice cream, Kahlua, and vodka. Looks like you'll be spending the night. The Boathouse marina deck is open Tuesday–Thursday 11:30 A.M.–11 P.M., Friday–Saturday 11:30 A.M.–midnight. The dining room is open nightly 4–10 P.M. Call for off-season hours.

Information and Services

The **Great Wildwoods Tourism Improvement and Development Authority** is an umbrella organization for Wildwood City, Wildwood Crest, and North Wildwood, offering tourism info and hosting numerous events throughout the summer season. For more information, call 800/992-9732 or visit www.wildwoodsnj.com.

The **Greater Wildwood Hotel Motel Association** (800/786-4546 or 609/522-4546, info@wildwoods.org, www.wildwoods.org, Mon.–Fri. 9 A.M.–5 P.M., Sat.–Sun. 10 A.M.–2 P.M. summer, call for off-season hours) hosts an information center stocked with maps and brochures pertaining to the Wildwoods' motels, restaurants, and attractions. It's located on the south side of Route 47, just west of Wildwood.

Getting There and Around

Wildwood is accessible from Exit 4B southbound or Exit 4 northbound of the Garden State Parkway. You can also get here by taking Ocean Drive south from Stone Harbor or north from Cape May, and from the greater Philadelphia region by traveling Route 55 to Route 47 and continuing east into Wildwood City.

Cape May and Vicinity

What began as a prosperous 17th-century whaling town grew into the nation's "most famous seaside resort" by the 1850s, hosting such luminaries as Abraham Lincoln, Benjamin Harrison, and Franklin Pierce. Today, with its gaslit streets, horse-drawn carriages, and over 600 gingerbread Victorians, Cape May feels like a step back in time. But it wasn't always so: The city's architecture was considered outdated by the 1970s, and vacationers were bypassing Cape May for more modern towns like Ocean City and Beach Haven. Still, a group of concerned citizens and preservationists fought to use the city's Victorian excess to its advantage. There's no question as to whether it worked. Cape May's now home to more than 80 bed-and-breakfasts, along with dozens of tours, events, and festivals that center around the Victorian theme. And with the state's most moderate temperatures, Cape May's become a 10-month destination—a beachside resort as popular

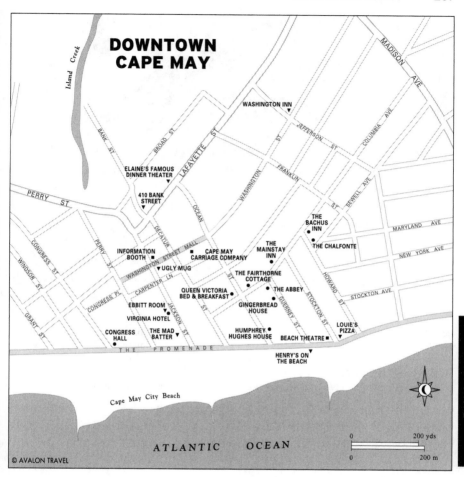

DOWNTOWN CAPE MAY

THE JERSEY SHORE

in December as in July. The city closes up shop come January, trickling to a start again in mid-February and slowly adding hours until summer's full schedule. Some of the best months for a Cape May visit are April–May and September–October, when there are fewer crowds and lower prices, and most of the shops and restaurants are still open. The winter holidays are also a great time to experience Cape May. It's cold as heck, but there are enough activities like candlelight house tours, heated trolley rides, and fireside cider drinks to make it all worthwhile.

SIGHTS
The Emlen Physick Estate

In 1970, on the verge of being demolished and replaced by modern homes, the Cape May Cottagers Association stepped in and saved the four-acre Physick Estate (1048 Washington St., 609/884-5404 or 800/275-4278, www .capemaymac.org) from the wrecking ball. Today, the estate is home to the very preservation group that spared it, though they now go by the name Mid-Atlantic Center for the Arts (MAC). Former home of Dr. Emlen Physick, a "father of American surgery" descendant, the

gingerbread architecture, Cape May

late-18th-century 18-room Victorian mansion and its surrounding property are Cape May's crowning jewels, a highlight on local trolley rides and Christmas tours and a centerpiece for festivals and events. The mansion's exterior is graced with exaggerated inverted chimneys and other unique adornments, while indoors are finely furnished Victorian rooms and changing exhibits on 18th-century life. The estate's Carriage House hosts a rotating gallery of art, along with the **Twinings Tea Room** (609/884-5404, ext. 138), serving a selection of finger foods, snacks, and sandwiches.

Tours of the estate ($10 adult, $5 child) take place daily 10:30 A.M.–3 P.M. May–October, daily 11 A.M.–3 P.M. November–December, and Friday–Saturday 11 A.M.–2 P.M. in January and March. Call for February hours. Two-hour combination trolley and estate tours ($18 adult, $9 child) are also available.

The Promenade

Lining Ocean Avenue's beachfront, Cape May's Promenade is home to a couple of arcades and some wonderful breakfast eateries. Look for **Morrow's Nut House** (609/884-4966), which sells warm roasted nuts and red fish candies perfect for snacking on a nearby bench, where the ocean view is unbeatable.

BEACHES

Cape May's beach tags cost $4 per day or $9 for three days. A season pass costs $25. Children 12 and under can use the beach for free. Beach chairs and umbrellas are available for rent right on the beach.

FESTIVALS AND EVENTS

As with the bulk of Cape May's tours, many of the city's events are sponsored by the Mid-Atlantic Center for the Arts.

Attending September's annual four-day **Cape May Food and Wine Festival** is a great way to sample the city's many culinary treats. Highlights include a gourmet marketplace with a people's choice chowder contest, a winery cellar tour, and a multiple-course beer-tasting dinner.

Since 2001 the **Cape May New Jersey**

State Film Festival (609/884-6700, www .njstatefilmfestival.com) has been drawing November crowds to the city for multiple-day showings of independent films, documentaries, shorts, and kids' cinema. Screenings take place throughout town at such venues as the Beach Theatre and Congress Hall.

For a true Victorian experience, nothing beats one of Cape May's **Sherlock Holmes Weekends** (609/884-5404 or 800/275-4278, www.capemaymac.org) held annually in March and November. Each sleuthing adventure features a cast of characters, including local turn-of-the-20th-century businessman John Wanamaker, as well as Holmes and his partner, Watson. Though period costumes aren't mandatory, there are prizes awarded for the best. Saturday's search for clues carries participants through some of the city's finest structures, and tickets for this event ($15) are sold separately for those who can only afford—both literally and figuratively—a couple of hours. If stepping back into a Victorian weekend is too short a time, visit Cape May during October's

Victorian Week (609/884-5404 or 800/275-4278, www.capemaymac.org), 10 days of antique shows, house tours, interactive murder mysteries, costume, dance, and a Victorian fashion show.

SHOPPING

Most Cape May shopping takes place along **Washington Street Mall** (609/884-2133, www.washingtonstreetmall.com), a pedestrian-only brick-paved stretch lined by specialty stores and restaurants. Antique items, lighthouse collectibles, Cape May logo hoodies, beach apparel, and footwear are in great supply here as well as within shops along the city's side streets. Stop by **Atlantic Books** (500 Washington St., 609/898-9694, www.atlanticbooks.us) for books on Cape May lore or trade paperbacks, then cross the mall to **Zoo Company** (421 Washington St., 609/884-8181, www.cape maypuppets.com) for inexpensive Schleich-made Smurfs and Hello Kitty mirrors. If you like to eat (and who doesn't?), why not show appreciation for the one who feeds you with a

THE JERSEY SHORE

© LAURA KINIHY

Washington Street Mall, Cape May

gift from **Love the Cook** (404 Washington St., 609/884-9292, www.lovethecook.com). **The Original Fudge Kitchen** (513 Washington St., 609/884-8814, www.fudgekitchens.com) almost always has an employee or two handing out free samples, but for a more substantial sweet **Dellas 5 & 10** (501-503 Washington St., 609/884-4568, www.Dellas5and10.com) features a back-of-the-store old-fashioned soda fountain serving sundaes, shakes, and floats, and **Uncle Charley's** (306 Washington St., 609/884-2197) scoops out 48 sherbet, sorbet, water ice, and ice cream flavors.

Just beyond the mall's east end is historic **Congress Hall** (251 Beach Ave.), where you'll find antique shops and history-themed souvenir stores. **Beach Avenue,** across the street from the ocean, hosts additional apparel and specialty stores.

RECREATION AND TOURS

Single cruisers and canopied surreys are available at **Shield's Bike Rentals** (11 Guerney St., 609/898-1818, daily 7 A.M.–7 P.M.), located across the street from the city's beachfront Promenade.

Newly relocated at the Nature Center of Cape May, **Aqua Trails** (1600 Delaware Ave., 609/884-5600, www.aquatrails.com) offers guided, sunset, and full-moon kayak nature tours ($46 individual, $80 double), and rents kayaks for use on the bay or the Atlantic. Rental rates are $20 for one hour with an individual kayak and $30 for a double, $75 and $85 for full-day or overnight use. A surf kayak, intended for ocean use, costs $75 for a full day.

Cape May Whale Watcher (609/884-5445 or 800/786-5445, www.capemaywhalewatcher .com) runs two- and three-hour whale and dolphin-watching tours on a 110-foot boat three times daily March–December. Trips leave from the Miss Chris Marina along the Cape May Canal, and cost $28–38 adult, $18–23 child 7–12, age 6 and under free. For wildlife tours along the Cape's backwaters, try **Salt Marsh Safari** (609/884-3100, www.skimmer.com, $27 adult, $15 child). Two-hour trips take place

aboard the Skimmer, a 41-passenger covered pontoon boat. Most depart from Cape May's Dolphin Cove Marina (just beyond the causeway toll bridge heading toward Wildwood Crest) daily at 10 A.M., 1:30 P.M., or 6 P.M. March–December, except Wednesday–Thursday mid-June–Labor Day, when trips depart from Stone Harbor's Wetlands Institute (Thursday's 6 P.M. trip departs from Dolphin Cove).

The Mid-Atlantic Center for the Arts (www .capemaymac.org) runs most Cape May tours. Information and tickets are available at the **Washington Street Mall Information Booth** (429 Washington St., 609/884-2368), staffed with volunteers happy to provide details on the day's offerings. MAC's website also lists updated schedules. Popular MAC tours include day and evening **Trolley Tours, Historic Walking Tours,** and the annual **Christmas Candlelight House Tours,** a regional favorite, so book ahead.

Across the street from the information booth is the boarding stop for the **Cape May Carriage Company** (641 Sunset Blvd., 609/884-4466, www.capemaycarriage.com), offering horse-drawn-carriage historic tours daily in summer (10 A.M.–3 P.M. and 6–10:30 P.M.), and on weekends in spring and fall. Private tours are available in December. Group tour rates are $10 adult, $5 child 2–11. Private carriage rides cost $40 for two passengers, $10 for each additional adult, $5 for an additional child 2–11.

The **Cape May Spa at Congress Hall** (609/898-2429, www.capemaydayspa.com) offers a variety of massages, facials, and bath and body treatments, along with manicures and pedicures. Specialty enhancements include a youthful lip treatment, and aromatherapy.

ENTERTAINMENT AND NIGHTLIFE

Not a nightlife hotspot per se, Cape May hosts several credible options for a good night out.

Locals like to hit up the Marquis De Lafayette's poolside **Fin Bar** (510 Beach Ave., 609/884-3500) late afternoons on their way home from the beach. Then it's on to the nearby **Rusty Nail** (Coachman's Motor Inn, 205 Beach

Ave., 609/884-0220, mid-May–mid-Oct.) for round 2. The Nail is also open daily for breakfast, lunch, and dinner throughout summer. It's quite casual, with live music on weekends. After a quick shower it's on to the evening's third stop, Congress Hall's **Brown Room** (251 Beach Ave., 609/884-8421, open nightly year-round). Not your typical beach establishment, this bar features chocolate-colored walls, a zebra-print rug, a massive stocked bookshelf, and some of the best drinks in town. Its open fireplace is the ideal spot to sit and sip martinis on a winter day. Tucked away in the hotel basement is the trendy **Boiler Room** (609/884-6507, mid-Apr.–Dec.) nightclub. Built into historic Congress Hall's original foundation, this bare-brick-walled and red-lit space is the place to come for dancing, jazz, reggae, and blues.

The **Ugly Mug** (426 Washington St., 609/884-3459, www.uglymugenterprises.com, Mon.–Fri. 10:30 A.M.–midnight, Sat.–Sun. 10:30 A.M.–1 A.M.) is Cape May's best place to chill with a draft any time of the year. Grab a stool at the center bar or slip into a booth, and be sure to bring plenty of change for the jukebox.

Cape May's historic **Beach Theatre** (711 Beach Ave., 800/838-3006) is in trouble. The first-run multiplex—and Cape May's only movie theater—is facing conversion into a mixed-use shopping space, although residents are trying to save it. For ways you can help, visit www.beachtheatre.org.

For a unique experience, try **Elaine's Famous Dinner Theater** (513 Lafayette St., 609/884-4358, www.elainesdinnertheater .com, $39.95 adult, $29.95 teen, $17.95 child), located within Elaine's Victorian Inn. Shows range from silly to scary depending on the season, and all take place throughout a three-course meal. Elaine's also hosts hour-long Victorian Ghost Tours (609/884-4358, $10 adult, $5 child) nightly throughout summer, leaving from the inn.

ACCOMMODATIONS
Hotels

While B&Bs are the crux of Cape May's overnight offerings, there are many hotels and a motel or two that offer the same level of luxury. A stay at one of the following establishments will make your trip just as memorable.

A standout even by Cape May standards is the boutique **Virginia Hotel** (25 Jackson St., 800/732-4236, virginiahotel.com, $290–520), a fully restored 1879 Victorian with 24 stylish guest rooms, each touting Belgian sheets, plasma TVs, terry robes, and minibars. The hotel offers both room service and valet parking, and houses one of the city's finest restaurants downstairs.

For more than 125 years, Cape May's historic 70-room **Chalfonte** (301 Howard St., 609/884-8409 or 888/411-1998, www .chalfonte.com, $217–278) has been welcoming visitors. Guests come to relax on the hotel's wraparound covered porches, dine in its Southern-style restaurant, read in the solarium, and forget about modern worries. You won't find heating, air-conditioning, or amenities like telephones or TVs here, and many of the rooms have shared baths (though they do have in-room sinks). Rates may seem a bit steep for your average getaway, but plenty will find the step back in time worth it. If you're intrigued by the thought but can't part with the cash, the Chalfonte offers spring and fall work weekends ($35 and 10 hours' labor), which include meals and a two-night stay.

Another Cape May beauty, the renovated and restored **Congress Hall** (251 W. Beach Ave., 609/884-8421 or 888/944-1816, www .congresshall.com, $345–565) once served as a summer White House for President Benjamin Harrison and hosted several other U.S. presidents over the years. In addition to numerous ground-floor shops and a restaurant, a lounge, a nightclub, and a day spa, Congress Hall features 107 modern yet subdued guest rooms that ideally accentuate their historic surrounds. All come with a TV and DVD player, Wi-Fi, and individual climate control, and are within steps to the ocean beach. If crossing the street feels too far, an in-ground pool and adjacent bar are just beyond the back door. Book well ahead for high season.

THE JERSEY SHORE

Bed-and-Breakfasts

Few places rival Cape May when it comes to B&Bs—the city offers one of the best selections on the planet. Many (if not most) of them offer modern guest room amenities such as TV, Wi-Fi, and air-conditioning, although some remain as Victorian as their architecture in terms of up-to-date offerings. Unfortunately, a city law bans the former practice of B&Bs providing complimentary beach tags to guests, although some places will allow visitors to "borrow" their personal stock. Many of the city's overnight establishments require a minimum stay during the high season, and parking is not always provided—it's best to check ahead.

Housed in a restored 1869 Gothic Victorian, **The Abbey** (34 Gurney St., 609/884-4506, www.abbeybedandbreakfast.com, $150–200) features seven period-decorated rooms, each named for an American city. There are plenty of interesting touches, including a displayed hat collection, an S-shaped conversation settee, and pull-chain toilets. Overnight stays come with full breakfast, private bath, and wireless Internet, along with free parking.

Recently expanded to include the former Brass Bed Inn, **The Bacchus Inn** (609/884-2129 or 866/844-2129, www.bacchusinn.com, $155–275) consists of two buildings: the Main House (710 Columbia Ave.), and the Cottage (710 Columbia Ave.). There are 13 rooms between the two, each with its own private bath and wireless Internet, and some with fireplaces and TVs. Named for the Roman god of wine, Bacchus Inn lives up to its moniker by offering complimentary afternoon wine and cheese, but the B&B's biggest perk is its Cottage billiards table.

The 19th-century carpenter Gothic–style **Gingerbread House** (28 Guerney St., 609/884-0211, www.gingerbreadinn.com, $148–298) features six antique-filled guest rooms, some with private baths and all with air-conditioning and flat-screen TVs. Owner and proprietor Fred Echevarria, a self-taught craftsman, has restored each of the inn's bathrooms, adding teakwood and glass shower doors. His handiwork exists throughout the house, along with wife Joan's bright color combos and antique collections.

Spread among two 1880s restored homes and an 1876 gambling parlor, the year-round ◖ **Queen Victoria Bed-and-Breakfast** (102 Ocean St., 609/884-8702, www.queenvictoria .com, $215–305) has everything you might want in a B&B: private baths, wireless Internet, and plentiful porches with rocking chairs and wicker swings. Each of the 32 rooms and suites comes equipped with a flat-screen TV and a fridge, and some have their own entrances. Modern amenities aside, the inn is filled with Victorian touches: period furnishings, handmade quilts, and wallpaper designed by arts and crafts figure William Morris for England's Queen Victoria. Afternoon tea and a breakfast buffet are offered daily.

Built in 1892 by a whaling captain, pretty **Fairthorne Cottage** (111 Ocean St., 609/884-8791 or 800/438-8742, www.fairthorne.com, $230–280) offers eight stylish guest rooms and one suite, all with a TV and VCR and a private bath. This colonial revival inn also features a wonderful wraparound porch lined with rocking chairs, and period decor that doesn't go overboard.

One of Cape May's largest freestanding B&Bs, the **Humphrey Hughes House** (29 Ocean St., 609/884-4428, www.humphrey hugheshouse.com, $299–350) features a sweeping veranda and 10 generously sized Victorian-inspired guest rooms. Amenities include comfy bathrobes and slippers, private baths, air-conditioning, and an on-site library. The elegant **Mainstay Inn** (635 Columbia Ave., 609/884-8690, www.mainstayinn.com, $295–360) consists of two buildings: a cottage and a 19th-century Italian villa once operated as a private gambling club. The two are joined together by a lovely outdoor garden. Guest rooms are filled with Victorian furnishings, some left over from clubhouse days, accented with updated offerings like wireless Internet and flat-screen TVs. In addition to complimentary breakfast, the Mainstay hosts daily afternoon tea, beginning at 4 P.M.

FOOD

Cape May is home to some of New Jersey's best restaurants. The selection is not ethnically diverse, but the quality is impressive. Restaurants run the gamut from beachside breakfast joints to grand Victorian dining rooms, with choices to fit every purse and tax bracket. So eat up; it's worth it.

Casual Eateries

Regardless of their recent franchise offerings, I'm a big fan of the ◖ **Ugly Mug** (426 Washington St., 609/884-3459, www.uglymug enterprises.com, Mon.–Fri. 10:30 A.M.–midnight, Sat.–Sun. 10:30A.M.–1 A.M. summer, $9–18), a local hangout serving up good American food, cold beer, and camaraderie. There's a well-stocked jukebox in back and a large bar in the center, perfect for whiling away a brisk winter day. Outdoor tables provide endless sightseeing throughout summer months, but if you're headed indoors, request a seat in the original dining room beneath the ceiling of hanging mugs (those of deceased Mug members face seaward)—the authentic atmosphere is worth it. Call ahead for off-season hours.

Cape May's best place for weekend brunch is **The Mad Batter** (19 Jackson St., 609/884-5970, www.madbatter.com, breakfast and lunch daily 8 A.M.–3 P.M., dinner daily from 5 P.M., $19.50–32), situated in the Carroll Villa B&B in downtown's historic district. Request a seat on the front porch for wonderful people-watching while you devour thick slices of orange and almond French toast ($7.50), washed down with fresh-squeezed apple juice ($3).

Tucked into Congress Hall's ground-floor corner is the **Blue Pig Tavern** (Congress Hall, 251 W. Beach Ave., 609/884-8421, breakfast Mon.–Fri. 7:30–11 A.M., Sat.–Sun. 7:30 A.M.–3 P.M., lunch Mon.–Fri. 11 A.M.–2 P.M., Sat.–Sun. 7:30 A.M.–3 P.M., dinner Sun.–Thurs. 5:30–9 P.M., Fri.–Sat. 5:30–10 P.M.), a stylish American eatery serving three meals daily. The restaurant features two distinct dining rooms—one reminiscent of a garden eatery, and the other a cozy tavern spilling onto the outdoor veranda during summer months. Fish and chips ($15) are a favorite.

Though something of a tourist trap, **The Lobster House** (Fisherman's Wharf, Schellenger Landing, 609/884-8296, call for hours, $18.50–39.95) remains a popular place for family outings, partially due to its dockside location and well-rounded meals. Entrées include shrimp scampi ($20), baked crab imperial ($20), and filet mignon ($25), and include vegetables, potatoes, and salad. There's also an on-site market. Hours vary throughout the year—call ahead.

Locals head to **Louie's Pizza** (711 Beach Ave., 609/884-0305, daily 10 A.M.–10 P.M., $3–17) for pizza pies and slices. Look for it at the start of a side street across from the Promenade.

My sister-in-law grew up in Cape May and swears by **McGlade's** (722 Beach Ave., 609/884-2614, $6–17) as the best breakfast in town. Known for their magnificent omelets, this beachfront property offers an unbeatable view of the Atlantic along with an endless ocean breeze. Open daily throughout the summer.

Fine Dining

Cape May offers some of the state's most rewarding restaurants. Most remain open the majority of the year, though hours tend to cut back gradually after Labor Day. They're really at their peak during July and August, when crowds can be heavy. Reserve your table early.

In business for more than 25 years, **Godmother's Restaurant** (413 S. Broadway, 609/884-4543, www.godmothersrestaurant .com, $16–28) prepares quality Italian dishes, including steak and seafood entrées, incorporating only the freshest Jersey produce. One of the kitchen's best offerings is its mix-and-match pastas and sauces. Godmother's is open daily 5–9 P.M. throughout summer, tapering off to weekends only as the year progresses, and is closed in January.

Serving as the main dining room for Cape May's boutique Virginia Hotel, the award-winning **Ebbitt Room** (25 Jackson St., 609/884-5700, www.virginiahotel.com, nightly

THE JERSEY SHORE

5–9 P.M., $24–34) has been completely renovated and restored to its original Victorian splendor. Highlights include an international wine list and New American dishes that include free range chicken with potato gnocchi ($26) and day-aged sirloin steak for two ($60).

Louisiana-style **410 Bank Street** (410 Bank St., 609/884-2127, daily 5–10 P.M. summer, call for off-season hours, $23–32) is a foodie mainstay and a haven among Manhattanites, serving up French-inspired Creole cuisine in a clapboard-cottage setting. Dining areas include a tropical garden and a vine-covered veranda, although overhead fans cool indoor patrons during summer months. Staff is knowledgeable and there is a small selection of New Jersey wines, otherwise BYO.

Reputed for its outstanding wine selection and a seasonally changing traditional American menu, the **Washington Inn** (801 Washington St., 609/884-5697, www.washingtoninn.com) is Cape May at its best. The restaurant occupies a former 19th-century plantation home in the heart of the city's historic district and features five dining rooms, including a summer patio. Dishes range from a herb crumb–crusted rack of lamb ($34) to pan-seared organic salmon ($27). Washington Inn opens at 5 P.M. daily during summer months, trickling off to weekends only by November; closing hours vary.

Removed from the bustling historic district is the romantic **Peter Shields Restaurant** (1304 W. Beach Ave., 609/884-9090, www.peter shieldsinn.com, nightly from 5 P.M., closed Mon. after Labor Day, $28–36), located on the first floor of the Georgian revival–style Peter Shields Inn. The restaurant features five dining areas, including an ocean-view veranda, and a rotating menu of New American dishes. Drinks are BYO, though a limited selection of Cape May Vineyard wines is available for purchase. A three-course fixed price menu ($38 per person) is offered Sunday–Thursday before 6 P.M.

GETTING THERE AND AROUND

Both Cape May and nearby Cape May Point are situated at the Garden State Parkway's southernmost point. To reach downtown Cape May from Wildwood Crest, take Route 621 (Ocean Drive) south over the causeway bridge and turn east onto Route 109 (Lafayette Street). Cape May Point is reachable from downtown Cape May by taking Sunset Boulevard west.

To reach either locale from South Jersey, take Route 47 (from Philly, take Route 42 to Route 55, which runs into Route 47) to Route 9 South and follow the signs to Cape May.

CAPE MAY POINT

Only 10 minutes west of Cape May City, the less-than-one-square-mile borough of Cape May Point has a decidedly different feel. With one general store and no bed-and-breakfasts, not to mention strict zoning laws keeping most homes for single-family use, the Point is quieter, less touristy, and more in tune with its natural surrounds. There are good opportunities for kayaking and sailing in local waters, and the Point offers one of the most varied and prolific birding opportunities in the entire country. Keep an eye out for hawks, falcons, eagles, ducks, geese, and herons, to name a few. In addition, Cape May Point is home to a state park, a lighthouse, one of New Jersey's most serene beaches, and tiny chunks of collectible quartz crystals found nowhere else on earth.

Cape May Point State Park

Windswept dunes, coastal woodlands, and freshwater marshes and ponds make up 235-acre Cape May Point State Park (Lighthouse Ave., Cape May Point, 609/884-2159, free), a key attraction on New Jersey's Coastal Heritage Trail. Constructed boardwalks and viewing platforms are great places for spotting waterfowl, songbirds, shorebirds, and raptors migrating through the area annually. The park is home to the romantic **Cape May Lighthouse,** a whitewashed tower standing 157 feet tall and that's more than 150 years old. One hundred ninety-nine cast-iron steps lead to a 360-degree lookout balcony, just below the active beacon. Both the lighthouse and the beach beneath are popular spots for couples to get engaged. The lighthouse is open for self-guided tours ($5 adult, $1 child) daily April–November, and usually on weekends the rest of the year. Just off the shore stands an old World War II defense bunker being battered by the sea.

In 2004–2005 the Army Corps of Engineers pumped the beach with millions of yards of sand to save migrating wildlife, concurrently rescuing it for public use from long Jersey Shore erosion.

Sunset Beach

The only beach in New Jersey where the sun both rises and sets over the Atlantic Ocean, Sunset Beach (800/757-6468, www.sunset beachnj.com) is also the only beach in the state (and the world) where you can find Cape May diamonds, bits of quartz crystals churned into creation by the sea. These tiny rocklike gems (you have to get 'em polished to make 'em sparkle) are sprinkled throughout the sand, plentiful and free. It is a gorgeous little beach, home to a cluster of shops and a flag-lowering ceremony held every evening at dusk. Fifty yards into the water are the still-visible remains of the *Atlantus,* a World War I concrete ship that the sea continues to slowly swallow.

Shop for candles, collectibles, and calendars, along with local literature and Shore-related tunes at **Sunset Beach Gift Shop** (502 Sunset Blvd., 609/884-7079). While Cape May jewelers will polish your diamond finds, you can purchase them here pre-polished for only a couple of dollars. The shop also sells necklaces, earrings, and rings adorned with Cape May diamonds. Additional Sunset Beach retailers include an apparel store and fossil shop, as well as a grill.

Higbee Beach

Just around the bend west of Sunset Beach is 1.5-mile Higbee Beach, a crescent-shaped sliver of white sand scattered with driftwood and lined by smooth blue ocean. In early summer dozens of horseshoe crab armors, their occupants victims of hungry shorebirds, often overtake the shore. Except for the ferry leaving for Delaware's Rehoboth Beach from the visible Cape May Canal, this beach feels truly remote,

perhaps the reason it operated as a nude beach (it no longer is) for so many years. Quiet and peaceful, it's an ideal getaway from the bustle happening along much of the Jersey Shore.

A coastal forest of holly, cedars, beach plums, and brush fields separates the parking area from the beach. In addition to straightaway access there are several nature trails within. Both the beach and the forest are part of the **Higbee Beach Wildlife Management Area** (609/628-2103, daily 5 A.M.–9 P.M.). Higbee Beach is dog-friendly.

Cape May–Lewes Ferry

One of the best routes into Cape May is aboard a ferry. The car and passenger Cape May–Lewes Ferry (Sandman Blvd. and Lincoln Dr., North Cape May, 800/643-3779, www.cape-maylewesferry.com) links the Cape May region to Delaware's Lewes, seven miles north of the Rehoboth Beach resort. Ferries run round-trip year-round (schedules vary seasonally) and take about 70 minutes each way. One-way fares are $7–9.50 adult, $3.50–4.75 child for vehicle and foot passengers, $28–34 for a car and driver, with discounts offered for round-trip fares. Shuttles to and from the ferry cost $3 for those age 6 and older.

Cape May Bird Observatory

Greater Cape May is a birder's paradise; the Audubon Center alone runs two local outposts, each part of the larger Cape May Bird Observatory. The first is **Northwood Center** (701 East Lake Dr., 609/884-2736, Thurs.–Mon. 9 A.M.–4:30 P.M.), located just up the road from the Cape May Lighthouse, and the second is Route 47's **Center for Research and Education** (609/861-0700, daily 1–4:30 P.M.), a model exhibit for creating your backyard wilderness, replete with hummingbirds. The observatory hosts public programs such as nature walks, butterfly and birding tours, and popular Back Bay Birding by Boat excursions at various times throughout the year. For details on where to meet and how to register, visit the Audubon Observatory website at www.njaudubon.org/Centers/CMBO, or call the Cape May Natural

History and Events Hotline at 609/861-0466. For updates on recent regional bird sightings dial 609/898-2473.

The **Nature Center of Cape May** (1600 Delaware Ave., 609/898-8848, www.nj audubon.org/Centers/NCCM, Tues.–Sat. 10 A.M.–3 P.M. Sept.–May, daily 9 A.M.–4 P.M. June–Aug.) is the Audubon Society's official local home, hosting several educational and volunteer programs year-round.

World Series of Birding

Never heard of the World Series of Birding (609/884-2736, www.njaudubon.org/WSB)? You're missing out. This annual Audubon event sees hundreds of teams competing to spot the most birds over a 24-hour period in May. Birding can be done one of two ways: either on a regulated platform, or by travel within a specified region. Everyone in the group has to see the bird for it to count, and teams must check in with their lists at Cape May Point State Park before the 24 hours are up. Think you can identify a Louisiana water thrush or a yellow-throated warbler? Then sign up: The competition's open to everyone.

Camping

Close to Cold Spring Village and minutes from downtown Cape May, 175-acre **Cape Island Resort** (709 Rte. 9, Cape May, 609/884-5777 or 800/437-7443, www.capeisland.com, May–Nov., from $30) hosts two large swimming pools, recreation facilities, and sites for both tents and RVs.

A bit north is **Seashore Campsites** (720 Seashore Rd., Cape May, 609/884-4010, www .seashorecampsites.com, mid-Apr.–Oct.), a 600-site resort tucked onto 90 wooded acres, complete with billiard tables, a heated pool, and a lake with its own bathing beach. Religious services are held on-site seasonally. Sites begin at $28 May–mid-June, $52 mid-June–August.

ROUTE 9: SOMERS POINT–CAPE MAY COURT HOUSE

More scenic than the Garden State Parkway and faster than Ocean Drive, Route 9 offers

© AVALON TRAVEL

its own array of attractions, including numerous seasonal ice cream stands and miniature golf courses. The stretch is also home to several hotels and camping resorts offering affordable alternatives to Shore towns. Though the roadway really comes alive during summer months (including often-heavy traffic), many of the antique stores leading to the lower route's "Antique Alley" remain open throughout winter. Beyond the Cape, Route 9 continues north into Atlantic County, passing Smithville and Brigantine Wildlife Refuge onto Forked River and Tuckerton, en route to Toms River.

Cold Spring Village

Cold Spring (720 Rte. 9, 609/898-2300, www

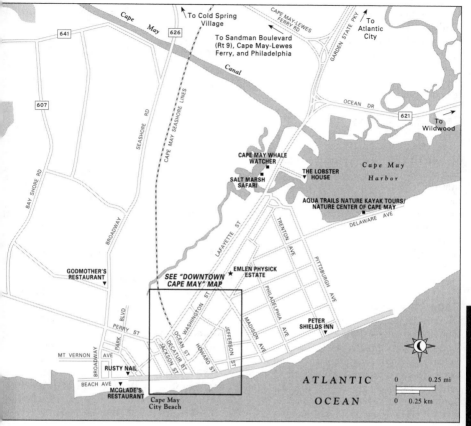

.hcsv.org, Sat.–Sun. 10:30 A.M.–4:30 P.M. Memorial Day–mid-June and Labor Day–mid-Sept., and Tues.–Sun. 10:30 A.M.–4:30 P.M. mid-June–Labor Day, $8 adult, $5 child) is the Cape's living history museum, a re-created 19th-century outdoor museum with 25 restored buildings and costumed interpreters demonstrating traditional crafts like bookbinding, weaving, and basket-making. The village houses both an ice cream parlor and an American restaurant (Wed.–Sun.), along with farm animals and a depot for the **Seashore Lines Train** (www.seashorelines.com, 609/884-2675, $5 adult, $4 child round-trip), which runs a loop between downtown Cape May and Cape May Zoo during high season.

Photographers may want to pit-stop at the striking **Cold Spring Cemetery** (780 Seashore Rd.), a Presbyterian cemetery open to all denominations located nearby.

Cape May National Wildlife Refuge

To see migratory flycatchers, orioles, tanagers, and endangered piping plovers in their natural habitat, visit Cape May National Wildlife Refuge (24 Kimbles Beach Rd., Cape May Court House, 609/463-0994, www.fws.gov/northeast/capemay). Opened in 1989, the refuge is home or temporary lodging for hundreds of bird species and dozens of reptiles, mammals, and amphibians, along with strictly sea creatures. During fall the refuge welcomes upwards of 15 raptor species. A handful of nature trails ideal for wildlife spotting and nature photography spread throughout the property. The headquarters are open Monday–Friday 8 A.M.–4:30 P.M., and the trails are open to the public daily.

Cape May County Zoo

Both kids and parents are fans of the free Cape May County Zoo (Rte. 9 and Pine Ln., 609/465-5271, www.capemaytimes.com/cape-may-county/zoo, daily 10 A.M.–4:45 P.M. summer, call for off-season hours), home to more than 100 animal species, including red pandas, giraffes, camels, bison, and tigers. Though small children may find the reptile house a bit scary, they'll flip over the new enclosed World of Birds. The zoo's part of a larger 200-acre wooded park filled with walking paths, fishing ponds, and playgrounds.

Cape May Court House

Don't let the name fool you. Cape May Court House is actually a town located along Route 9 north of Cape May Point. Downtown hosts a charming stretch of antique stores and small cafés. It's a good place for grabbing a cup of coffee. If you have time, stop by the **Cape May County Historical Museum** (504 Rte. 9 N., 609/465-3535, www.cmcmuseum.org) to learn about local maritime history and the Lenni-Lenape Indians.

Leaming's Run Gardens

With 25 themed gardens, an arboretum, a bamboo grove, bridges, ponds, and more, Leaming's Run (1845 Rte. 9 N., Swainton, 609/465-5871, www.leamingsrungardens.com, daily 9:30 A.M.–5 P.M. mid-May–mid-Oct., $8 adult, $4 child) comprises the country's largest annual gardens. Visitors can stroll among 30 acres and along a mile-long meandering walking path to view ever-changing flower displays, rediscover the 18th-century Colonial Farm, spot native frogs and turtles, and relax amid August's buzz of migrating ruby-throated hummingbirds. In late October Leaming's Run morphs into Screamings Run, hosting haunted candlelit tours (609/465-5871, $7) along the pathway.

Information and Services

A good site for gathering details on local happenings is **www.capemay.com.** Information is also available at **The Chamber of Commerce of Greater Cape May** (www.capemaychamber .com), which hosts the **Cape May Welcome & Information Center** (609 Lafayette St., 609/884-9562) in the city's downtown. **Cape May County Department of Tourism** (609/463-6415 or 800/227-2297) is accessible on the Web at www.thejerseycape.net.

CENTRAL JERSEY AND THE PINELANDS

With so much talk over where to draw the line between North and South Jersey, Central Jersey often gets the shaft. Travelers have long been passing through en route from Philly to New York on highway interstates and aboard Amtrak trains without a thought, and New Jersey residents are always overlooking gems like Bordentown and Freehold for the Skylands or the Shore. If Six Flags Great Adventure weren't smack-dab in the middle of the state, the region might be altogether forgotten. It's a shame, because in addition to pick-your-own orchards, quaint country towns, and a couple of distinguished universities, New Jersey's central stretch from Mercer to Monmouth County is steeped in history, and home to the pivotal turning point in the Revolutionary War.

While not a region of sharp geological contrast, Central Jersey is geographically diverse. Delaware River cities give way to rolling hills and horse farms; flower and produce centers stand between tiny hamlets and new developments, and heavily trafficked highways carve routes from one town to the next. Head east and the land fills with affluent suburbs and offbeat river towns.

Central Jersey's attractions are as diverse as its geography. You can spend a day touring Revolutionary War battlefields and New Jersey's Capitol, or driving through an African safari and visiting Bruce Springsteen's hometown instead. And foodies have a variety of eats to choose from, including Red Bank's swanky restaurants, Edison's Indian foods, Trenton's Italian dishes, and Middletown Township's Restaurant Nicholas, consistently topping New Jersey's "Best of" lists.

© LAURA KINIRY

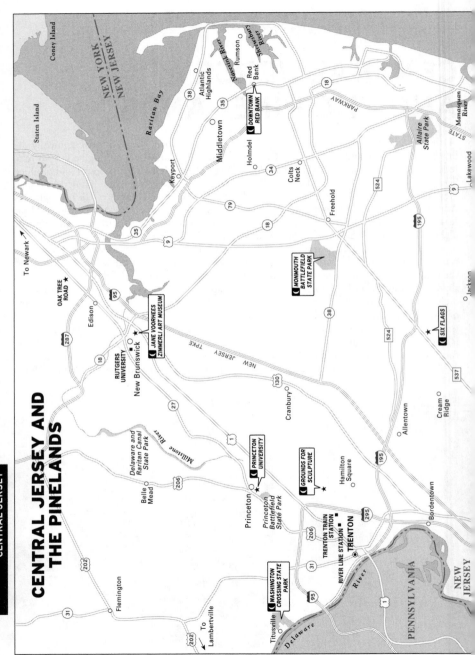

CENTRAL JERSEY

CENTRAL JERSEY AND THE PINELANDS

NEW YORK
NEW JERSEY

Coney Island

Staten Island

Raritan Bay

To Newark

Keyport

Atlantic Highlands

Middletown

Holmdel

Rumson

Red Bank

DOWNTOWN RED BANK

PARKWAY

Navesink River

Shrewsbury River

Manasquan River

Allaire State Park

STATE

Lakewood

Colts Neck

Freehold

MONMOUTH BATTLEFIELD STATE PARK

Jackson

SIX FLAGS

OAK TREE ROAD

Edison

RUTGERS UNIVERSITY

New Brunswick

JANE VOORHEES ZIMMERLI ART MUSEUM

NEW JERSEY TPKE

Cranbury

Allentown

Cream Ridge

Delaware and Raritan Canal State Park

Millstone River

Belle Mead

Princeton

PRINCETON UNIVERSITY

Princeton Battlefield State Park

GROUNDS FOR SCULPTURE

Hamilton Square

Flemington

Titusville

WASHINGTON CROSSING STATE PARK

TRENTON TRAIN STATION

RIVER LINE STATION

TRENTON

Bordentown

PENNSYLVANIA

NEW JERSEY

Delaware River

To Lambertville

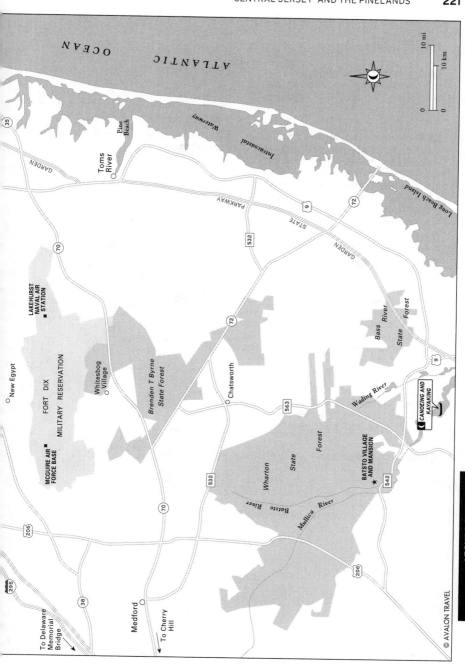

ATLANTIC OCEAN

Pine Beach

Toms River

Intracoastal Waterways

Long Beach Island

GARDEN

STATE PARKWAY

GARDEN STATE

35

70

9

72

532

New Egypt

LAKEHURST NAVAL AIR STATION ■

FORT DIX MILITARY RESERVATION

MCGUIRE AIR FORCE BASE ■

Whitesbog Village

Brenden T Byrne State Forest

Chatsworth

Bass River State Forest

Wading River

CANOEING AND KAYAKING

563

9

72

532

70

206

Wharton State Forest

Batsto River

Mullica River

BATSTO VILLAGE AND MANSION ★

542

Medford

To Cherry Hill

38

295

To Delaware Memorial Bridge

206

CENTRAL JERSEY

© AVALON TRAVEL

10 mi
10 km
0
0

HIGHLIGHTS

◖ **Grounds for Sculpture:** Jump into the Impressionist surrounds of this unique outdoor museum and delight in a world of mythical creatures, never-ending dinner parties, and sculpted parasols (page 228).

◖ **Following Washington's Footsteps:** General George was all over Central Jersey during the American Revolution, and there's no better place to be walking in his shoes. Follow him from **Washington Crossing State Park,** where he landed on his famous Delaware River crossing, into Trenton, Princeton, and onto **Monmouth Battlefield State Park,** commemorating the longest battle of the war (pages 231 and 258).

◖ **Princeton University:** One of the nation's oldest universities, this gorgeously Gothic campus features a world-class art museum, an administrative building once bombarded by cannons, and all the greenery you could ask for. Add to this a faculty that includes author Joyce Carol Oates and mathematician John Nash, as well as an alumni list for the history books, and you'll start thinking about returning to school (page 233).

◖ **Jane Voorhees Zimmerli Art Museum:** The largest collection of nonconformist ex-Soviet art in the West is in New Brunswick? You bet – and what a display (page 241).

◖ **Downtown Red Bank:** Those remembering "Dead Bank" are in for a change. Trendy restaurants, fun boutiques, and variety shops stocking everything from comic books to pink lawn flamingos have revamped this once down-and-out town into one of New Jersey's most happening places (page 247).

◖ **Six Flags:** Where else can you drive through an African safari, see Batman take on Catwoman, tackle more than a dozen roller coasters, and follow it up with a float down the river, all in one afternoon (page 261)?

◖ **Canoeing and Kayaking in the Pinelands:** The largest tract of forest from Maine to Virginia, and all the tea-colored water you can ask for. Grab a paddle and go (page 269)!

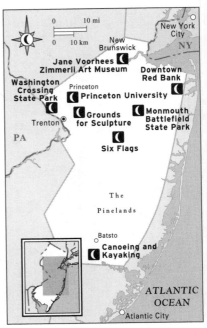

LOOK FOR ◖ TO FIND RECOMMENDED SIGHTS, ACTIVITIES, DINING, AND LODGING.

Central Jersey is home to both Ivy League Princeton University and Rutgers New Brunswick, considered New Jersey's state school. And the brains don't stop there. Physicist Albert Einstein and inventor Thomas Edison each spent large portions of their lives in Central Jersey, Einstein in Princeton (where he died at age 76) and Edison in Menlo Park, the birthplace of recorded sound.

For outdoor lovers, Central Jersey offers state park hiking trails, golf and horseback riding in the Central Plains, fossil hunting in Holmdel, and country roads ripe for cycling. Of course, some of the best outdoor opportunities are found in New Jersey's Pinelands, over a million acres of forests, rivers, and abandoned towns. Explore them but use caution, or you may find yourself face-to-face with the Jersey Devil himself. With a horselike face, cloven hoofs, and bat-like wings, this 13th child of Mrs. Leeds is unmistakable. And hungry.

PLANNING YOUR TIME

Like most of the state, Central Jersey's a great place for a weekend trip. If you're arriving from New York City, Red Bank is a good home base. Spend your evening downtown with dinner and drinks. The next day, take a drive along Rumson Road before heading north to explore the Bayshore, or west into Colts Neck, where you can pick up sandwiches for a picnic at one of Holmdel's parks.

If you're interested in history, Central Jersey offers several options. Base yourself in Trenton or Princeton to take full advantage of the region's Revolutionary War past. You can also brush up on the French and Indian War at Trenton's Old Barracks Museum, stroll down the city's State Street for a stop at the State Museum, or take a short drive north to Washington Crossing State Park, site of the general's famous Christmas morning river crossing. You'll find the best selection of restaurants in Trenton's Chambersburg section or Princeton Borough, where you can also visit the former home of Albert Einstein and Princeton University, one of the country's most architecturally stunning campuses. Before leaving, detour into nearby Cranbury for a walk around the historic village and a quick trip to Van Nest Park, home to the Orson Welles–inspired War of the Worlds monument.

Additional weekend possibilities include pairing Princeton shopping with a New Brunswick dinner and theater combo, followed with a day of fossil digging in Holmdel Park; a pop-culture tour of Freehold, Springsteen's hometown, followed by Red Bank, director Kevin Smith's alma mater, and later the Pinelands, home to the notorious Jersey Devil and site of the Hindenburg crash; or a New Jersey great minds tour featuring Albert Einstein's adopted home of Princeton, New Brunswick's Rutgers University, and Edison, former location of inventor Thomas Edison's most famous laboratory and current site of the small but interesting Edison museum and the Edison lightbulb tower.

INFORMATION

The **Molly Pitcher Travel Plaza and Information Center** (609/655-4330) is located along the New Jersey Turnpike at mile marker 71.9 South in Cranbury.

Trenton and the Capital Region

In 1721, wealthy Philadelphia merchant William Trent reestablished what was a small river settlement into the industrial township of "Trent's Town." Trent chose his location partially for its central proximity to Philadelphia and New York City. Today, New Jersey's state capital remains an essential Northeast Corridor crossroads, as well as a historic center for much of the state's Revolutionary War history. Although Trenton has seen better days, both aesthetically and financially, the city's downtown is surprisingly inviting and has a lot to offer visitors, including several fine museums and eateries, and a minor league baseball stadium.

Trenton's revitalized **Mill Hill** neighborhood is home to an excellent local theater company, and a bit further from downtown, the largely residential **Chambersburg District,** dubbed "Little Italy" and known locally (and to fans of mystery writer Janet Evanovich's Stephanie Plum series) as the Burg, is bursting with established and reputable Italian eateries.

Just outside Trenton, the capital region is one of the state's most trafficked hubs. Route 295 and I-195 are a crossroads of congestion leading drivers east and south across the state. Route 29 hugs the Delaware River north into the Skylands, while Route 1 diagonals northward, passing among university towns en route to the Hudson River. Historic villages, suburbs, and countryside share Trenton's surrounding space, offering numerous day-trip opportunities.

History

Trenton's famous motto "Trenton Makes, the World Takes," proclaimed in bold letters on the Delaware River Bridge, speaks of the city's continuing history as a major industrial center. In addition to rifles, ammunition, and Trenton Oyster Crackers, the city's known for its porcelain, pottery, rubber, and wire rope.

SIGHTS

As New Jersey's state capital, Trenton offers numerous sites of historic and political interest. It's a good spot to begin learning about New Jersey's past, as well as its future.

City Museums and Monuments

Trenton's downtown centers around **State Street.** The corner of State and New Warren Streets is a good starting point for a self-guided tour of nearby sites. While exploring, take note of the city's revitalization efforts.

Trenton's **Old Barracks** (Barrack St., 609/396-1776 or 609/777-3599 weekends, www.barracks.org, daily 10 A.M.–5 P.M., $8, $6 senior and student) were one of five U.S. barracks housing prisoners during the French and Indian War, and the only freestanding barracks to have survived. Used as a hospital during the American Revolution, the Barracks were once Trenton's largest building, divided into individual apartments after the war but later restored to its 1758 appearance. The Barracks are now an educational center for Colonial and American history, favored by grade school classes and historians. Inside is a display of period furniture and artifacts from the 18th century, including a working baker's oven. Baking demonstrations and various other events, including

school children in front of the New Jersey State House, Trenton

Revolutionary War reenactments, are scheduled throughout the year. A one-hour walking tour is available during museum hours.

Trenton City Museum (Parkside and Stuyvesant Aves., 609/989-3632, www.ellarslie.org, Tues.–Sat. 11 A.M.–3 P.M., Sun. 1–4 P.M., second Fri. of the month 11 A.M.–3 P.M. and 5–7 P.M., free) features permanent and changing art and craft exhibits, including a Trenton pottery display detailing the craft's local history. Since 1978 the museum has been housed in **Ellarslie Mansion,** a National Register of Historic Places 19th-century Italian villa located in **Cadwalader Park,** north of downtown's State Street.

Once home to the founder of Trent's Town, the 1719 period-restored **William Trent House** (15 Market St., 609/989-3027, www.williamtrenthouse.org, daily 12:30–4 P.M.) is Trenton's oldest remaining residence. Call ahead for tours.

At the intersection of North Broad and North Warren Streets stands the **Trenton Battle Monument** (609/737-0623, Sat. 10 A.M.–noon

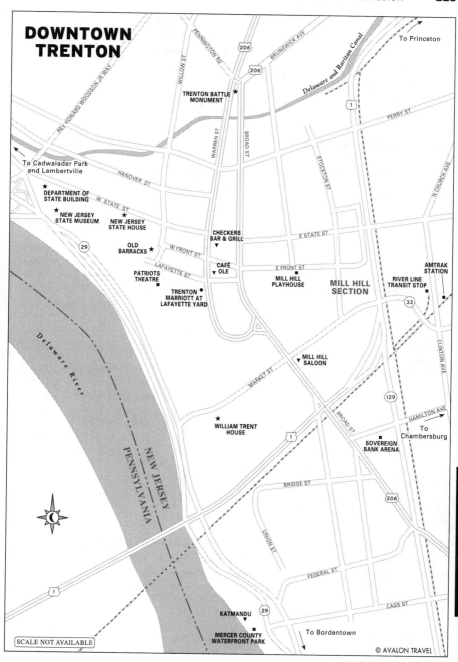

DOWNTOWN TRENTON

To Princeton

Delaware and Raritan Canal

PENNINGTON RD

206

206

BRUNSWICK AVE

PERRY ST

1

WILLOW ST

WARREN ST

BROAD ST

TRENTON BATTLE MONUMENT ★

REV HOWARD WOODSON JR WAY

HANOVER ST

To Cadwalader Park and Lambertville

STOCKTON ST

N CHURCH AVE

★ DEPARTMENT OF STATE BUILDING

W STATE ST

★ NEW JERSEY STATE MUSEUM

★ NEW JERSEY STATE HOUSE

E STATE ST

29

CHECKERS BAR & GRILL ▼

OLD BARRACKS ★

W FRONT ST

E FRONT ST

PATRIOTS THEATRE ■

LAFAYETTE ST

CAFÉ ▼ OLE

MILL HILL PLAYHOUSE ■

MILL HILL SECTION

RIVER LINE TRANSIT STOP ■

AMTRAK STATION ■

TRENTON MARRIOTT AT LAFAYETTE YARD ●

33

Delaware River

NEW JERSEY PENNSYLVANIA

MARKET ST

MILL HILL SALOON ▼

BROAD ST

129

HAMILTON AVE

CLINTON AVE

To Chambersburg

★ WILLIAM TRENT HOUSE

1

SOVEREIGN BANK ARENA ■

BRIDGE ST

206

UNION ST

FEDERAL ST

CASS ST

1

KATMANDU ▼

29

MERCER COUNTY WATERFRONT PARK ■

To Bordentown

To Chambersburg

SCALE NOT AVAILABLE

© AVALON TRAVEL

and 1–4 P.M., Sun. 1–4 P.M., free), a 148-foot granite beaux arts structure commemorating the December 26, 1776, American victory of the First Battle of Trenton. The monument was designed by John H. Duncan, architect of Grant's Tomb. An elevator carries visitors up to an outdoor pedestal, and a bird's-eye view of the city.

New Jersey State Museum
Following a multiyear renovation, the New Jersey State Museum's (225 W. State St., 609/292-6464, www.state.nj.us/state/museum/, Mon.–Sat. 9 A.M.–5 P.M., Sun. noon–5 P.M., donations accepted) main building reopened in spring 2008 with *Culture in Context,* an exhibit highlighting New Jersey's artistic and cultural life. The museum is a division of the Department of State and features everything from locally excavated fluorescent minerals to African American art to Native American tools, displayed among several floors. An on-site auditorium hosts lectures and films, including the 2008 Newark Black Film Festival. There's also a **planetarium,** but as of this writing it's still undergoing construction; call or visit the website for updates.

New Jersey State House
Originally built in 1792, the New Jersey State House (State St., 609/633-2709, www.njleg.state.nj.us, Mon.–Fri. 10 A.M.–3 P.M., Sat. noon–3 P.M.) is the country's second-oldest operating state house (the first is in Annapolis, Maryland). The structure, however, has been altered numerous times since its inception, and has suffered at least one major fire. Hour-long public tours, held during business hours, shed additional light on the State House's architectural history, along with details on the building's political and historical significance. Tours vary, but usually include the assembly and senate chamber, the State House annex, the rotunda, and the governor's office reception room.

An on-site cafeteria (609/392-2045) serves breakfast and lunch weekdays.

SPORTS AND ENTERTAINMENT
In downtown Trenton you'll find everything from neighborhood theaters to sports-size arenas hosting a wide range of plays, concerts, and athletic events.

The restored 1,807-seat **Patriots Theatre at War Memorial** (Memorial Dr., 609/984-8400, www.thewarmemorial.com) showcases music, dance, and comedy, such as the 1970s folk-rock group America. Located along Lafayette Street in downtown Stacy Park, right across from the visitors center, this 1932 Italian Renaissance structure has hosted the inauguration of every New Jersey governor since its opening. The Memorial also hosts seasonal outdoor concerts.

Sovereign Bank Arena (81 Hamilton Ave., 800/298-4200, www.sovereignbank-arena.com) is home to the **Trenton Devils** (609/656-3399, http://trentondevils.com), a minor league AA ice hockey team owned and operated by the New Jersey Devils. Opened in 1999, the venue hosts big name music acts like Bruce Springsteen and Elton John, ice shows, and the Ringling Bros. and Barnum & Bailey Circus. The 6,440-seat **Mercer County Waterfront Park** is home to Minor League Baseball's 2007 EL champions, **Trenton Thunder** (609/394-3300, www.trentonthunder.com), a Yankees AA farm club. Club seats run $10, terrace seats $6.

Passion Theatre Company (http://passagetheatre.org), Trenton's oldest professional theater group, performs at the cozy 120-seat **Mill Hill Playhouse** (Front and Montgomery Sts., 609/392-0766). This is the place to catch locally produced and directed drama, musicals, and comedy.

ACCOMMODATIONS
Oddly, there's only one hotel of interest in downtown Trenton. Many Capital City visitors opt to spend the night in nearby Princeton, easily reached by NJ Transit or by car in 20 minutes.

Don't worry about finding it—there are signs pointing the way to the [**Trenton Marriott at Lafayette Yard** (1 W. Lafayette

St., 609/421-4002, fax 609/421-4002, www .marriott.com, $109–179) throughout downtown. This seven-story hotel is ideal for both business travelers and tourists, featuring high-speed Internet (the lobby is wireless), in-house bar and restaurant, and incredibly comfy beds topped with a down comforter and pillows that you'll sink into. On-site parking is an additional $13 daily.

FOOD

Some of New Jersey's best Italian eateries are in Chambersburg, southeast of downtown's center. There are a few notable bistros around the Capital, along with a fun tropical-inspired restaurant near the river.

Downtown

For a light meal try **Café Olé** (126 S. Warren St., 609/396-2233, www.cafeolecoffee.com, Mon.–Fri. 7 A.M.–4 P.M., Sat. 8 A.M.–2 P.M., $4–7), a coffeehouse and eatery serving omelets and sandwiches, as casual as it is cute. Olé features a rotating display of artwork on its walls, and a daily soup special. Catering to government employees keeps it closed Sundays.

Trenton's historic Mill Hill neighborhood is home to **Mill Hill Saloon** (300 S. Broad St., 609/394-7222, Mon.–Fri. 11:30 A.M.–2 A.M., Sat. 5 P.M.–2 A.M., closed Sun., $9–20), although stalwarts still refer to it as "Joe's" in honor of the former owner. While more of a bar than a restaurant, the Saloon's a good place for lunch, serving standard American burgers and sandwiches along with a fine brew selection. City workers flock here during the day, but by night it morphs into one of Trenton's main music venues. There's also a brew basement for the late-night crowd.

Housed in a former Cooper & Hewitt machine shop next to Waterfront Park, the tropically-inspired **KatManDu** (Mercer Waterfront Park, 50 Riverview Dr., 609/393-7300, www .katmandutrenton.com, $9–20) offers a fun alternative to more standard eateries. The American-Caribbean fare is OK, but the frozen drinks are strong and sweet. A seasonal outdoor deck overlooking the Delaware River often features high-profile performers like Jimmy Buffet's Coral Reef Band. KatManDu opens Tuesday–Friday at 11:30 A.M., Saturday at 5 P.M., and Sunday at 10 A.M., closed Monday. Thursday–Saturday the bar stays open until 2 A.M.; closing hours vary the remainder of the week.

The Burg

Anyone who's read a book in Janet Evanovich's Stephanie Plum series is familiar with Chambersburg, or as locals call it, "The Burg." One of New Jersey's best-known Italian districts, the neighborhood is filled with row homes, front porches, and narrow streets, with restaurants tucked along residential blocks and into corner locales. Even with signs depicting knife, fork, and plate posted throughout the community, it's best to have an idea where you're heading before arriving. Street parking is limited, though several establishments offer valet services and small-ish lots.

Landmark **Marsilio's** (541 Roebling Ave., 609/695-1916, www.marsilios.com, Mon.–Fri. 11:30 A.M.–2 P.M. and 5–9 P.M., Sat. 5–10 P.M., closed Sun., $18–33) is a neighborhood and political-powerhouse favorite. Regulars come for the southern Italian fare, along with pinot and chardonnay served in personalized wine carafes. The restaurant is mentioned in several of Janet Evanovich's Stephanie Plum novels.

The local name in pizza is undeniably DeLorenzo's, but the question remains: which one? Trenton's two DeLorenzo's, both spurs of the same family line, are vastly different. Hudson Street's **DeLorenzo's Tomato Pies** (530 Hudson St., 609/695-9534, www .delorenzostomatopies.com, Thurs.–Sun. 4–9 P.M., closed Mon.–Wed.) serves a bevy of regulars crisp-crusted pies in a storefront setting, while **DeLorenzo's Pizza** (1007 Hamilton Ave., 609/393-2952, www.delorenzos pizza.com, Tues.–Thurs. 11 A.M.–1:30 P.M. and 4–8:45 P.M., Fri.–Sat. 11 A.M.–8:45 P.M., closed Sun.–Mon., $8–17) hosts spacious dining and a loyal clientele who pack the place for traditional pizza with extra cheese. Both

CENTRAL JERSEY

places are BYO, but only DeLorenzo's Pizza has a restroom.

For a casual bite try **Rossi's** (501 Morris Ave., 609/394-9089, www.rossiburger.com, Mon.–Sat. lunch 11:30 A.M.–2:30 P.M., dinner 5–10 P.M., closed Sun.), home of the infamous Rossiburger ($4.95)—Trenton's juiciest, fattest burger. The restaurant hosts a full bar with over 30 tap beers. **John Henry's** (2 Miffin St., 609/396-3083, www.johnhenrysseafood.com, lunch Mon.–Fri. 11:30 A.M.–2:30 P.M., dinner Tues.–Sat. 5–10 P.M., Sun. 3–9 P.M., $15–35) serves classic Italian cuisine and seafood dishes, including a fine fish and chips ($15). Although the decor's nothing spectacular, ingredients are fresh and portions are large.

Dishes at family-friendly **Amici Milano** (600 Chestnut Ave., 609/396-6300, www.amici milano.com, lunch Mon.–Fri. 11:30 A.M.–2:30 P.M., dinner Mon.–Thurs. 4–10 P.M., Fri.–Sat. 4–11 P.M., Sun. 1–10 P.M.) include broiled sea scallops ($16.95), pan-fried sausage with peppers, potatoes, onions, and mushrooms ($14.95), and vegetable ravioli ($12.95). There are three dining rooms and a piano player on weekends.

INFORMATION AND SERVICES

While in the area pick up a free copy of Trenton's *Downtowner* (available citywide) to get word on monthly happenings.

GETTING THERE AND AROUND

The **River LINE** (www.riverline.com), Amtrak's **Northeast Corridor Line** (800/872-7245, www.amtrak.com), and **New Jersey Transit's Northeast Corridor Line** run directly to Trenton, a central hub for much of New Jersey, as well as for travelers en-route from Philly to New York City. **Trenton Station** (72 S. Clinton Ave.), home to Amtrak and NJ Transit, and the River LINE stations are located across the street from each other.

The **Capital Connection** shuttle stops at all major points around the city, most notably the River LINE/Amtrak stations and the State House complex.

HAMILTON

Hamilton Township—nearly 40 square miles alongside Trenton—is one of New Jersey's fastest-growing suburbs, with a population slighter larger than its Capital City neighbor. Although Hamilton is without a downtown center, there are a few worthwhile attractions within its borders.

◖ Grounds for Sculpture

Created in 1992 by art collector, sculptor, and Johnson & Johnson heir J. Steward Johnson Jr., Grounds for Sculpture (18 Fairgrounds Rd., 609/586-0616, www.groundsforsculpture .org, Tues.–Sun. 10 A.M.–6 P.M., closed Mon., $10 adult, $8 student and senior, $6 child) is a sight to behold. One of the East Coast's most imaginative sculpture gardens, it features over 200 artworks both prominently displayed and intriguingly hidden across 35 flawlessly landscaped acres, making the possibility of stumbling upon something new with each visit a good one. Works range from a life-sized

a sculpture of a woman and man sitting in front of a lake at Grounds for Sculpture

impressionist-inspired garden party (including a sculpture of Johnson himself) to a rosy-cheeked shepherd tending a cartoonish flock of sheep, but they're all worth seeing.

While most works are displayed outdoors, there are also two spacious halls housing rotating exhibits, a museum gift shop, and a salad and sandwich café. An outdoor amphitheater and snack gazebo are both brought to life during summer months. On the other side of the grounds near Rat's Restaurant is **Toad Hall Shop and Gallery,** selling local and internationally designed artworks and featuring a changing exhibit of saleable art.

Sayen Gardens

Opened in 1912 by travel and gardening enthusiast Frederick Sayen, 30-acre Sayen Gardens (155 Hughes Dr., 609/587-7356, www.sayen gardens.org, daily dawn–dusk, free) features hundreds of azaleas and rhododendrons, many originating from strands Sayen picked up along his journeys. His self-constructed arts and crafts–style bungalow still stands, surrounded by nature trails, ponds, and pinewoods. The home is open to the public annually on Mother's Day.

Kuser Farm Mansion and Park

Built as a country home for the Kuser family, creators of Fox Film Industry (now 20th Century Fox) and founders of Prudential Life Insurance, the 17-room 1892 Victorian Kuser Mansion (2090 Greenwood Ave., 609/890-3630, Thurs.–Sun. 11 A.M.–3 P.M. May–Nov., Sat.–Sun. 11 A.M.–3 P.M. Feb.–Apr., free, donations accepted) offers public tours that include a look inside the family's private projection room. The mansion's surrounding 22-acre estate, known as "the Farm," is open during tour hours.

Food

For a special treat, stop by **Rat's** (16 Fairgrounds Rd., 609/584-7800, www.rats restaurant.org, Tues. 11:30 A.M.–8 P.M., Wed.–Fri. 11:30 A.M.–9 P.M., Sat. 11 A.M.–3 P.M. and 5:15–9 P.M., Sun. noon–7 P.M., $23–39), a

whimsical space that's right at home with the adjacent Grounds for Sculpture. Both the seasonal cuisine and aesthetics of this French restaurant are wonderfully creative. Enter through a red gypsy wagon in front—amid a rising-steam waterfall in back—into a decadent world of fine service, reserve wine, and delish dishes like organically raised salmon steamed in vermouth ($36). The decor is about the most imaginative you'll find in New Jersey.

Such luxury can be heavy on your wallet and hard on your clothes (proper attire is required), so for something more casual and affordable stop in for lunch as the restaurant's **(** **Kafe Kabul** (Tues. 11:30 A.M.–8 P.M., Wed.–Fri. 11:30 A.M.–9 P.M., Sat. 11 A.M.–3 P.M. and 5:15–9 P.M., Sun. noon–7 P.M.). The grilled organic burger is delicious ($13) as is the spring pea risotto with mint and piave ($17). The café's interior seems straight off the set of *Casablanca*.

Both Rat's and Kafe Kabul offer seasonal outdoor seating. Rat's hours are the same as Kafe Kabul, but only the café's dinner menu is available Tuesday and Sunday evenings. Both are closed Mondays. Free park entry comes with a Rat's meal.

BORDENTOWN

Known as a "hotbed of fervor" during the Revolutionary War, Bordentown's famous resident alumni include Francis Hopkinson, designer of NJ's State Seal and signer of the Declaration of Independence, and Thomas Paine, author of 1776's *Common Sense,* the first publication challenging Britain's authority over America. Today, riverfront Bordentown is a handsome community, home to a disproportionately large number of bookstores along with several fine art galleries and eateries.

Clara Barton School

In 1852, Clara Barton—who later founded the American Red Cross—established New Jersey's first free public school in downtown Bordentown. The schoolhouse, restored in 1921 with money raised by local schoolchildren, still stands and is owned by **Bordentown**

Historical Society (609/298-1740). Society walking tours include a stop at the small brick building (142 Crosswicks St.). Call for hours.

Art Galleries

Bordentown is popular place for artists to reside. Numerous galleries displaying their works exist along Farnsworth Avenue and its side streets.

The **Artful Deposit** (201 Farnsworth Ave., 609/298-6970, www.theartfuldeposit.com) displays the paintings of local and international artists. At **The Bordentown Gallery** (204 Farnsworth Ave., 609/298-5556) browse fine art and crafted wares, including etched glass and Raku pottery. Downtown's 1876 J. Reeves Building houses the **Pavs Gallery** (148 Farnsworth Ave., 609/298-7287), home to exquisite pieces of wearable textile art.

Down a short side path you'll find the **Firehouse Gallery** (8 Walnut St., 609/298-3742, www.firehousegallery.com), home to the exclusive works of local artist E. Gibbons. The gallery, also owned by Gibbons, is situated within an 1886 former firehouse and features his formal portraits, experimental Polaroid photography, and "automatic" or blind line drawings—a loose style of drawing associated with Matisse.

Entertainment and Events

In 2009 Bordentown's annual **Cranberry Festival** (www.downtownbordentown.com/cranberry.htm) celebrates 20 years. Held in early October, the weekend includes arts and crafts, live music, and a classic car show, along with the crowning of Miss Cranberry Fest.

Shopping

Bordentown features a couple of local bookstores specializing in used and antiquarian books, along with an independent record shop and a few collectible shops.

For mysteries, cookbooks, and military history try **Q.M. Dabney & Co. Booksellers** (300 Farnsworth Ave., 609/298-1003). The **Old Book Shop of Bordentown** (200 Farnsworth Ave., 609/324-9909) specializes in 19th- and

20th-century baseball and literary greats like Hemingway and Thomas Wolfe. For hard-to-find vinyls like Adam Ant's *Friend or Foe* along with CDs and rock-and-roll memorabilia, visit **The Record Collector** (358 Farnsworth Ave., 609/324-0880, www.the-record-collector.com).

Shoppe 202 (202 Farnsworth Ave., 609/298-1424, www.shoppe202.com) carries Yankee Candles, custom frames, and gargoyle statues, while **The Euphemia Gallery** (142 Farnsworth Ave., 609/324-1888) is the place for American-made crafts and limited-edition prints of fine art. Don't miss the selection of new and vintage motorcycles at **Cycle Icons** (102 Farnsworth Ave., 609/298-2633, www.cycleicons.com).

Food

A couple of good restaurants are situated along Farnsworth Avenue (an easy walk from the River LINE station), or head out to Route 130 for a great diner experience.

Casual **Jesters Cafe** (233 Farnsworth Ave., 609/298-9963, Mon.–Thurs. 11 A.M.–10:30 P.M., Fri.–Sat. 11 A.M.–11:30 P.M., $10.95–17.95) serves Italian and American cuisine, and features a full bar and live jazz throughout the week.

Housed in a three-story brick building, downtown's popular **Farnsworth House** (135 Farnsworth Ave., 609/291-9232, www.thefarnsworthhouse.com, lunch daily 11 A.M.–3 P.M., dinner Mon.–Sat. 3 P.M.–midnight, Sun. 3–10 P.M., $12–29) features fine Italian dishes and a varied red wine selection. Fifty-seat BYO **Oliver A Bistro** (218 Farnsworth Ave., 609/298-7177, www.oliverabistro.com, lunch Wed.–Sat. 11 A.M.–3 P.M., dinner Tues.–Sat. 5–10 P.M.) serves a fixed-price four-course meal of internationally-inspired dishes ($35) Tuesday–Thursday evenings along with an expanded menu ($16–26) throughout the week.

It may be a diner, but family-owned and operated **Mastoris** (Rtes. 130 and 206, 609/298-4650, www.mastoris.com, Mon.–Fri. 4 A.M.–2 A.M., Sat.–Sun. 4 A.M.–3 A.M. weekends, $4.50–17.95) is one of the best eats in

© LAURA KINIRY

Washington Crossing State Park

town. The menu is extensive, the portions are huge, and their complimentary cheese bread is legendary. You can get lost with so many dining rooms, but you'll never be lonely.

For morning brew try **Katie's Coffeehouse & Cafe** (1½ Crosswicks St., 609/324-7800), also showcasing live music Saturday evenings. Katie's features a full American menu with an all-day breakfast.

☾ WASHINGTON CROSSING STATE PARK

Hoping to surprise Hessian troops and gain some advancement in the American Revolution, General George Washington and 2,400 Continental soldiers traveled across the Delaware River from Pennsylvania to New Jersey in the early morning of December 25, 1776. After four hours on the icy water they landed at Johnson's Ferry, now known as Washington Crossing State Park (355 Washington Crossing–Pennington Rd., Titusville, 609/737-0623, www.state.nj.us/dep/parksandforests/parks/washcros.html), beginning what became a pivotal turning point in the Revolutionary War.

Over 700 artifacts interpreting the famous crossing and the 10 Crucial Days following are on display at the park's visitor center, situated on more than 3,000 acres of public lands that include red cedar and eastern white pine trees, long walking paths, and open fields. The park is a great place for birding and wildlife spotting. Hawks, owls, foxes, and deer are all common.

Adding to its historic value and beauty, Washington Crossing State Park offers numerous recreation opportunities, including 15 miles of multiuse trails used by walkers, hikers, mountain bikers, cross-county skiers, and horseback riders. Group camping is available during summer months (Apr.–Oct., $15–50), and picnicking is allowed year-round. The park is open daily dawn–dusk year-round and is free to enter the majority of time, although a $5 fee is charged weekends Memorial Day–Labor Day.

Washington Crossing Visitors Center Museum

The **Washington Crossing Visitors Center** (609/737-9303, daily 9 A.M.–4 P.M.) features two large galleries highlighting the

Revolutionary War's 10 Crucial Days turning point and New Jersey's larger role in the fight for independence. Ninety-nine percent of the exhibits is part of the **Swan Historical Foundation Collection,** including a historic gun display and a rare 18th-century soldier's uniform.

Johnson Ferry House

Once owned by 18th-century ferry operator Garret Johnson, the Johnson Ferry House (609/737-2515) is thought to have been used by General George Washington and his troops following their famous Delaware River crossing. Since restored as an 18th-century tavern and furnished with period pieces, the former farmhouse is open periodically during summer and fall (usually weekends), and often hosts living-history demonstrations; call for exact hours.

Events

A Christmas Day **Delaware River crossing reenactment** takes place annually at 1 P.M., depending on river conditions. Costumed actors steer authentically reconstructed vessels across the Delaware, beginning from Pennsylvania's Washington Crossing Historic Park. For more info, including event-day weather conditions (the event's been canceled more than once), contact Pennsylvania's Washington Crossing Historical Society (215/493-4076).

During summer months, the **Washington Crossing Open Air Theatre** (355 Washington Crossing–Pennington Rd., Rte. 546, 609/737-4323) hosts evening outdoor musicals like *Oklahoma, Carousel,* and *Grease.* Tickets are sold on-site and online (www.ticketbiscuit .com/WashingtonCrossing/) and run $12–14, and $8–10 for daytime children's theater performances.

Information and Services

The **Visitors Center** (609/737-9303) is open daily 9 A.M.–4 P.M. year-round. There's staff on hand to answer questions. Public restrooms are available.

HOWELL LIVING HISTORY FARM

One of New Jersey's several living-history farms, and one of its best, 130-acre Howell Living History Farm (70 Wooden's Ln., Titusville, 609/737-3299, www.howellfarm .org) authentically depicts 19th-century farm life, with period-dressed farmers working fields and tending resident chickens, horses, cows, and oxen. A few buildings are original to the site, including the large Philips Barn, and the farmhouse, both listed on the National Register of Historic Places. Various demos for kids and adults are held Saturdays year-round, including dairying, sheepshearing, and beekeeping. Each fall the farm hosts an enormous corn maze.

Parking and admission are free, though there's a fee for any additional activity (i.e. the corn maze). The farm is open Tuesday–Friday 10 A.M.–4 P.M. February–November, and Saturdays 10 A.M.–4 P.M. year-round, except on summer days when evening hayrides are held. Sunday hours are noon–4 P.M. April–November for self-guided tours only. Check the website for a complete list of updated activities.

Princeton and Vicinity

Princeton began as a stagecoach stop between the equidistant cities of Philadelphia and New York. The borough—and adjoining Princeton Township—later played a prominent role in the United States' fight for independence. Today, the two Princetons share a library and a health department, along with the campus of illustrious Princeton University. In addition to their historic sites and Ivy League school, boutique shops, fine restaurants, magnificent old homes, plentiful greenery, and fine dining, an interesting and diverse population makes stops in Princeton Borough and Princeton Township a must.

Nassau Street is the borough's main thoroughfare, housing everything from Indian take-out food to an Albert Einstein memorial tucked away in the back of a wool store. Princeton University is located directly across the street.

◖ PRINCETON UNIVERSITY

Princeton University was founded in Elizabeth in 1746 as The College of New Jersey, briefing making its way to Newark before ending at its present location in 1756. It wasn't until nearly a century and a half later that the school became known as Princeton University, and not until soon-to-be U.S. President Woodrow Wilson took over as university president in 1902 that Princeton became what it is today. Wilson implemented changes that carried the institution successfully into the 21st century, and along with faithful and generous alumni, he helped catapult Princeton into its position as one of the nation's leading academic institutions.

Princeton is also one of the country's oldest academic institutions, and for anyone who appreciates architecture, its exquisite Gothic buildings are aesthetically hard to beat. Take an opportunity to walk along the campus picking out arched windows, pointed steeples, stained glass windows, and gargoyles among its many ivy-covered structures.

Along with Yale, Dartmouth, and Brown,

Nassau Street, Princeton

© LAURA KINIRY

Princeton University is one of the country's eight Ivy League institutions and its alumni include such notables as James Madison, Aaron Burr Jr., Ralph Nader, Donald Rumsfeld, Brooke Shields, Jimmy Stewart, and F. Scott Fitzgerald (who didn't graduate). Professors include mathematician John Nash Jr. (portrayed in the film *A Beautiful Mind*), and authors John McPhee, Joyce Carol Oates, and Toni Morrison.

Nassau Hall

Arguably the University's best-known structure, Nassau Hall—set back from Nassau Street across from Princeton's borough's downtown shops—has been a campus mainstay since the school's local beginnings. Built in 1756, the hall acted as Princeton's entire campus—housing students, holding seminars—for almost 50 years. Today, it's an administrative building, though far more interesting were its years as a Revolutionary War

CENTRAL JERSEY

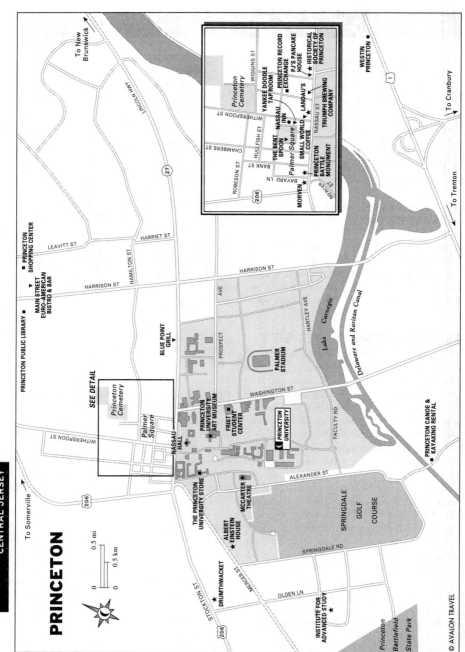

CENTRAL JERSEY

PRINCETON

© AVALON TRAVEL

IF I ONLY HAD A BRAIN . . .

Physicist Albert Einstein may not have been born in Princeton, but he certainly left his mark. Einstein, who was honored as a 2007 inaugural inductee into New Jersey's Hall of Fame along with Garden State greats like Yogi Berra and astronaut Buzz Aldrin, resided in the borough for more than 20 years. Here's an opportunity to follow in his footsteps:

Located at 112 Mercer Street, the **Albert Einstein House** was Einstein's home 1932-1955, the final years of his life. Today it's a private residence, but the sidewalk out front is a good place to begin an Einstein tour. During the time he worked in Princeton, Einstein worked nearby at the **Institute for Advanced Study** (Einstein Dr., 609/734-8000). Like the home, the center is off-limits to public viewing (a great mind is often a private mind), but visitors can explore the property's 588-acre **Institute Woods,** a community space adjacent to Princeton Battlefield State Park. While strolling the grounds, mull over the fact that Einstein's brain was immediately removed and preserved on his death at **Princeton Hospital,** but this fact wasn't revealed for another 20 years.

When you're through exercising your brain (and feet), head over to Nassau Street for a visit to family-run **Landau** (102 Nassau St., 609/924-3494, www.landauprinceton.com, Mon.-Sat. 9:30 A.M.-5:30 P.M., Sun. 11:30 A.M.-4 P.M.), a woolens shop offering deals on Princeton U. sweatshirts and mohair throws, and hosting a small Einstein museum in back. Strangely enough this memorial, filled with photos, news clippings, photocopied letters, and personal mementos loaned by Einstein's plumber and postmaster, happens to be Princeton's only museum dedicated to Einstein's life, although Princeton's Borough Hall did erect a 300-pound bronze Einstein bust in April 2005.

Further down the street, the **Historical Society of Princeton** (158 Nassau St., 609/921-6748, Tues.-Sun. noon-4 P.M.) displays Einstein's music stand in its Princeton History Room. In 2003 the society acquired 65 pieces of Einstein's furniture, including tables, chairs, cabinets, and a bed. As of 2008 they're still awaiting exhibit. To find out more, visit www.princetonhistory.org/einsteinfurniture.cfm.

barracks and hospital, and as the United States' capitol June–November 1783. According to *The Daily Princetonian,* one of numerous school legends describes students bowling cannonballs, left behind by Revolutionary War troops, down Nassau Halls' passageways.

Nassau Hall is a grand stone structure, a combination of architectural styles including colonial, Federal, and Italianate, resulting from a series of fires leading to its constant reconstruction. Although the hall boasts no large sign proclaiming its name, it's easily recognizable by two bronze tigers guarding the main entryway. Lions were the hall's original guardians, but when Princeton adopted orange and black school colors in the late 19th century the change made sense.

Ivy covers the entire front of the building, along with a back portion—gifts from the university's graduating classes.

Princeton University Art Museum

The celebrated collection of the 1882 Princeton University Art Museum (McCormick Hall, 609/258-3788, www.princetonartmuseum.org, Tues.–Sat. 10 A.M.–5 P.M., Sun. 1–5 P.M., free) spans a wide range of mediums, cultures, and time periods, including ancient art, pre-Columbian art, photographs, prints, and drawings. A museum highlight is its version of Monet's *Water Lilies and Japanese Bridge* (1899), one of 20 existing slightly different originals. Andy Warhol's 1962 *Blue Marilyn* silkscreen is also on display here, as are a number of Roman mosaics from Antioch.

McCarter Theatre

Built in 1929, beloved McCarter Theatre (91 University Pl., 609/258-2787 or 888/278-7932, www.mccarter.org) showcases both original works and wider-known stage, dance, and

CENTRAL JERSEY

musical acts. The theater began as a home for Princeton Triangle Club, the university's comedy and musical troupe whose famous alumni include Jimmy Stewart and Brooke Shields. Today, it is the residence of the American Repertory Ballet.

The recently renovated 1,100-seat Matthews Theatre serves as McCarter's main theater, with the intimate 360-seat Berlind Theatre added in 2003. The Berlind also includes a rehearsal hall doubling as a 75-seat performance space for new and experimental works and works in process. These performances are usually free.

An on-site theater-related store has hours coinciding with most shows.

Information and Services

One-hour **Orange Key Tours** of campus provide an overview of university life. Hosted by students, these tours are geared toward prospective undergrads and their families, although they do offer a bit on Princeton history and folklore. Tours leave weekdays from **Clio Hall,** weekends from **Frist Campus Center.** Reservations are not required. Call 609/258-3060 or visit www .princeton.edu for more details.

Shopping for University souvenirs? Stop by **Princeton University Store** (36 University Pl., 609/921-8500, ext. 238, www.pustore .com), home to alma mater sweatshirts, charms, and cuff links, stuffed tiger mascots, and personalized Princeton rocking chairs. The University also hosts a satellite store at 114-116 Nassau Street in the downtown borough. Hours are Monday–Saturday 9 A.M.–9 P.M., Sunday 11 A.M.–6 P.M. The campus shop is open 24/7 when classes are in session.

OTHER SIGHTS

Princeton has plenty of historic and culturally significant attractions worth seeing. I suggest spending a few hours, if not more, exploring them.

Historic Sites

For in-depth local history, stop by the borough's **Historical Society of Princeton** (158 Nassau St., 609/921-6748, www.princeton history.org, Tues.–Sun. noon–4 P.M., free), located in the 1766 **Bainbridge House** on the corner of Nassau Street and Greenview Avenue. The Society hosts a museum (look for Einstein's music stand in the Princeton History Room), library, local photo archive, and gift shop, along with various walking tours during warmer months. A historic house tour takes place in November.

Eighteenth-century **Princeton Cemetery** (29 Greenview Ave., 609/924-1369) serves as final resting place for many well-known Princeton residents, university alumni, and honorary Princetonians, including former U.S. president Grover Cleveland, third U.S. vice president Aaron Burr Jr., Paul Tulane (Tulane University), and African American jazz musician Donald Lambert. Be sure to stop by the Princeton University President's Plot, where all but four of the school's deceased presidents are buried. Cemetery maps are available at the entrance, although the groundskeepers will often assist in finding better-known sites.

gravesite of philanthropist Paul Tulane, Princeton Cemetery

© LAURA KINIRY

After serving as New Jersey's governor's mansion for 27 years (1953–1981), the 1759 Colonial-style **Morven** (55 Stockton St., 609/924-8144, www.historicmorven .org, Wed.–Fri. 11 A.M.–3 P.M., Sat.–Sun. noon–4 P.M., $5 adult, $4 senior and student) opened publicly in 2004 as a museum showcasing New Jersey's cultural heritage. Two exhibit floors feature artwork loaned from private collections and public institutions, like Trenton's State Museum and the New Jersey Historical Society in Newark. The mansion's own history is also on display. Visitors can tour the property gardens, which include 18th- and 19th-century annuals and a rotation of seasonal blooms.

Since its official inception as governor's mansion in 1982, **Drumthwacket** (354 Stockton St., 608/683-0057, www.drumthwacket.org) has only served as full-time residence for three New Jersey governors: Jim Florio (1990–1994), James McGreevey (2002–2004), and Acting Governor John O. Bennett (2002), in office for 3.5 days. Charles Smith Olden, who built the Greek Revival mansion in 1835, was the also the first state governor to live here. The mansion's long narrow layout seems more suitable for entertaining, perhaps the reason most New Jersey governors have chosen to reside, at least part-time, elsewhere.

Tours of Drumthwacket's first floor, including the library, governor's study, and solarium, are offered every Wednesday (tours for individuals begin at noon) and run approximately 45 minutes. Admission is free, although a $5 donation is suggested. Afterwards, visitors can wander the property's lovely outdoor gardens, or stop by the restored Olden House, the property's original farmhouse, currently housing a gift shop.

On the corner of Stockton Road (Rte. 206) and Bayard Street, next to Morven's eastern border, stands **Princeton Battle Monument,** a 1922 sculpture depicting what's often described as one of the Revolutionary War's fiercest battles. Despite a bloody theme, it makes a nice spot for a picnic lunch.

Princeton Battlefield State Park

On January 3, 1777, following the Second Battle of Trenton, General Washington and his troops headed toward Princeton, encountering Lord Cornwallis and his army in what is considered the Revolutionary War's fiercest battle of its size. Princeton Battlefield State Park (500 Mercer Rd., 609/921-0074, www.state.nj.us/dep/parksandforests/parks/ princeton.html) commemorates the battle, part of the 10 Crucial Days that were the Revolutionary War's turning point. Comprised of 100 mostly wide-open acres, the park offers a nice reprieve from downtown Princeton. Historic sights include the **Thomas Clark House** (609/921-0074, Sat. 10 A.M.–noon and 1–4 P.M., Sun. 1–4 P.M.), used as a postbattle hospital for both American and British troops, and the **Mercer Oak,** said to have sheltered General Hugh Mercer after he was impaled by a Brit's bayonet. The current Oak is actually a smallish acorn-grown offspring of the original, which crashed to the ground during a 2000 storm.

SPORTS AND RECREATION

Thirty-nine-acre **Charles H. Rogers Wildlife Refuge,** located alongside the Institute for Advanced Study's Institute Woods, is home to woodchucks, white-tailed deer, muskrats, frogs, and turtles, as well as a wide variety of plant life. The refuge hosts a few nature trails and an observation tower. For bicycle rentals try **Jay's Cycles** (249 Nassau St., 609/924-7233, www .jayscycles.com), part of the community since 1977. Bikes go for $8 per hour with a two-hour minimum, or $32 for a full day. **Princeton Canoe & Kayaking Rental** (483 Alexander St., Turning Basin Park, 609/452-2403, www .canoenj.com) provides vessels for use on the Delaware and Raritan Canal or nearby Lake Carnegie, training grounds for both Princeton University and the U.S. Olympic rowing teams—paying them heed comes with the territory. Canoes rent for $13 and kayaks for $10–16 (depending on the kayak) the first hour, $6 for each additional hour, and $20–40 for an all-day pass.

SHOPPING

As with most university towns, Princeton offers a wide range of shops catering to its

CENTRAL JERSEY

transient population, including clothing shops and boutiques, specialty stores, and a superb record exchange.

Downtown

It's easy to spend hours browsing Princeton's great selection of shops, mostly located around downtown's Palmer Square.

Still going strong since 1980, **Princeton Record Exchange** (20 S. Tulane St., 609/921-0881, www.prex.com) is the place to shop for vinyl, along with new and used CDs and DVDs. With more than 160,000 items in stock, this shop's reputation is as large as its selection.

Princeton borough's retail center is **Palmer Square** (800/644-3489, www.palmersquare .com), with more than 40 shops situated on four main streets—-Nassau Street, Palmer Square East and West, and Hulfish Street. Stores include national chains like J. Crew, Chico's, and Ann Taylor, along with local boutiques such as **Zoe** (11 Hulfish St., 609/497-0704), featuring the square's best Juicy Couture, Prada Sport, and Marc Jacobs selection, and **Jazams** (15 Hulfish St., 609/924-8697), home to Ugly Dolls, pinhole photography kits, and rockin' *Sesame Street* CDs.

Princeton Shopping Center

One-stop shoppers head to the township's **Princeton Shopping Center** (609/921-6234, www.shoppingprinceton.com) to stock up on home furnishings, greeting cards, and pet supplies, not to mention dermatology and dental visits. The center features over 50 businesses, including a sports store, Laundromat, and gourmet market. The only thing missing are clothing stores, which you'll find plenty of along Nassau Street.

ACCOMMODATIONS

Princeton offers some fine lodgings to choose from, but good luck booking a room during May graduation.

The pleasant **Hampton Inn Princeton** (4385 Rte. 1, 609/951-0066, www.hamptoninn.com, $109–169) offers 110 comfortable, clean guest rooms equipped with lap desks and high-speed Internet. Complimentary hot breakfast is available each morning, with a breakfast-to-go option on weekends.

At the heart of downtown Princeton borough is the 18th-century **Nassau Inn** (Palmer Sq., 609/921-7500, www.nassauinn.com, $200–300), one of the area's most illustrious accommodations. The inn features 203 rooms and suites, as well as 14 banquet rooms named after past locals like Paul Robeson and Albert Einstein. Rooms come equipped with high-speed Internet (wireless in common areas) and TV, and offer direct access to the famed Yankee Doodle Tap Room below. Special packages such as Escape to Romance, complete with chocolates and a four-course meal ($300–400) are available throughout the year.

About one mile from Princeton Borough is **Hyatt Regency Princeton** (102 Carnegie Center, 609/987-1234, http://princeton.hyatt .com, $209–294), tucked within an office complex just off Route 1. Rooms are newly renovated and include Wi-Fi and work areas; there's both a restaurant and a lounge on-site.

Westin Princeton (201 Village Blvd., 609/452-7900, www.westin.com/princeton, $249–315) offers 294 modern guest rooms, all with Wi-Fi and Heavenly bedding. The hotel is situated in the suburban Forrestal Village shopping center, a few short steps from shops, restaurants, and a spa. Additional perks include an indoor pool and local jogging maps designed by *Runner's World*.

FOOD

Princeton's eateries run the gamut from casual breakfast joints to fine-dining establishments. While it's not exactly a foodie hotspot, there are plenty of good options to choose from.

For carb overload try **Pj's Pancake House** (154 Nassau St., 609/924-1353, www.pancakes .com, Sun.–Thurs. 7 A.M.–10 P.M., Fri.–Sat. 7 A.M.–midnight, $7), a borough institution serving American eats and namesake dishes like banana pecan pancakes and pigs in a blanket—a buttermilk stack wrapped around link sausages. Breakfast is available all day, along with burgers and sandwiches after 11 A.M.

Small World Coffee (14 Witherspoon St., 609/924-4377, www.smallworldcoffee.com, Mon.–Thurs. 6:30 A.M.–10 P.M., Fri.–Sat. 6:30 A.M.–11 P.M., Sun. 7:30 A.M.–10 P.M., $3–7) serves pick-me-ups such as Morning Mocha and Tough Chai alongside breakfast goodies and a healthy selection of soups, salads, and sandwiches. The shop has two counters—one for food and the other for beverages—better to accommodate the hordes of locals, students, and lovable eccentrics stopping by.

A long hall off Nassau Street leads to the laid-back **Triumph Brewing Company** (138 Nassau St., 609/924-7855, www.triumphbrew .com, Mon.–Thurs. 11:30 A.M.–1 A.M., Fri.– Sat. 11:30 A.M.–2 A.M., Sun. noon–midnight), home to live music and daily drink specials. Meals at this microbrew are relatively inexpensive: try a ham and Brie panini ($10) for lunch; for dinner, the pumpkin ravioli ($15). Beneath Nassau Inn is the historic **Yankee Doodle Tap Room** (10 Palmer Sq., daily 7 A.M.–11 P.M., $16–36), a dark mahogany favorite sporting a massive stone fireplace and wood booths. The Tap Room received its name in 1937 after Norman Rockwell contributed a mural depicting Yankee Doodle that still hangs behind the bar. Peruse the framed photos of famed Princeton alums before settling in to dine on braised lamb shanks ($23) or a roasted half chicken ($19). The Tap Room's open for breakfast, lunch, and dinner.

Princeton borough's **Blue Point Grill** (258 Nassau St., 609/921-1211, www.bluepointgrill .com, Mon. 5–9:30 P.M., Tues.–Fri. 5–10 P.M., Sat.–Sun. 4:30–9:30 P.M., $19–24) serves an every-changing menu of fresh seafood, with daily chalkboard specials and alfresco seating in season. The restaurant's interior is bright and inviting; BYO and come with friends.

Located within Princeton Shopping Center, bustling **Main Street Euro-American Bistro and Bar** (301 N. Harrison St., 609/921-2779, www.mainstreetprinceton.com, Mon.–Thurs. 11:30 A.M.–9:30 P.M., Fri.–Sat. 11:30 A.M.– 10 P.M., Sun. 5–8:30 P.M., $9–21) features pasta, seafood, and lighter fare such as falafel pita ($9), along with fresh-baked goods.

Princeton has two superb ice cream shops, both located within Palmer Square. For organic ice cream and tasty sorbet try **The Bent Spoon** (35 Palmer Sq. W., 609/924-2368, www .thebentspoon.net). The long-running **Halo Pub** (9 Hulfish St., 609/921-1710) features more than 45 ice cream flavors, including chocolate-chocolate almond and peanut butter, and gets their dairy from nearby Halo Farm. Both stores are open year-round.

INFORMATION AND SERVICES

Princeton Public Library (65 Witherspoon St., 609/924-9529, www.princetonlibrary .org, Mon.–Thurs. 9 A.M.–9 P.M., Fri.–Sat. 9 A.M.–6 P.M., Sun. 1–6 P.M.) offers free Wi-Fi throughout—including the library's third floor, which has been turned into a space for teens and collegians to congregate. For additional wireless service, try chain eatery **Panera Bread** (136 Nassau St., 609/683-5222, www .paneranj.com) on Nassau Street.

Princeton's downtown parking garage, between Spring and Wiggins Streets, provides free parking for up to 30 minutes. For longer stays, pay on foot **Quick Pay Stations** are featured at all main garage entrances.

You can purchase **Smart Cards** at parking garages and Princeton Borough Hall. Use them on any of Princeton's parking meters and you'll be credited with whatever time you don't use. On-street parking is usually limited to two hours 8 A.M.–7 P.M. Borough parking is free on Sundays. For additional parking details and up-to-date changes, visit www.princetonparking.org.

GETTING THERE AND AROUND

Bicycles are the main transport route for many students, as traffic can be a nightmare. Cycling routes run along most roads, both in the borough and throughout the township.

Princeton's train station is located at University Place (one block north of Alexander Rd.), alongside campus and within walking distance to the borough's downtown shops. This station is unmanned but includes vending machines for ticket purchases, and bike racks. NJ Transit's **Northeast Corridor** train runs between Trenton and New York City, with stops in Princeton and Princeton Junction. Riders can also catch the Northeast Corridor into Trenton and connect with **SEPTA's** R7 rail (Southeastern Pennsylvania Transportation Authority) to downtown Philadelphia and 30th Street Station.

CRANBURY

Cranbury was founded in 1697 and served as one of George Washington's temporary headquarters during the American Revolution. Listed on both the National and State Registers of Historic Places, this historic village has retained much of its scenic history, evident in the whitewashed and faded pastel colonial clapboards lining its Main Street. Tucked inside them are several worthwhile shops and a couple of fine restaurants, including an 18th-century inn. Cranbury's **Brainerd Lake** is home to **Village Park,** where you'll find basketball and tennis courts, baseball diamonds, and a playground.

Along Cranbury Road west of the village is **Grover's Mill,** famous as the alien-invaded town cited in Orson Welles's famous—and fictitious—1938 *War of the Worlds* radio broadcast.

Cranbury Museum

Run by the **Cranbury Historical & Preservation Society** (609/860-1889), the circa-1834 **Cranbury Museum** (4 Park Pl. E., 609/655-2611, Sun. 1–4 P.M., $3 suggested donation) displays historic village artifacts like farming tools alongside items recovered from a downtown archaeological dig. A 12-panel quilt describing Cranbury's long history hangs in the museum's first floor.

Pick up Cranbury's self-guided walking tour brochure at the Society's History Center (6 South Main St.).

War of the Worlds

Those interested in popular culture should definitely check out the nearby town of **Grover's Mill.** There's not a lot to do here, but this was the fictitious site Orson Welles picked for his October 30, 1938, "Martians are landing" radio broadcast. Now known as the "Panic Broadcast," it was based on the 1889 science fiction novel *War of the Worlds* by H. G. Wells, and scared the shirts off locals and listeners nationwide.

Although the wooden water tower bearing bullet holes from that evening (the tower was supposedly mistaken for an approaching spaceship) has since been removed, you'll still find **Van Nest Park** (Cranbury Rd., 609/799-6141), a tiny community park that has a six-foot marker commemorating the event. The marker was erected in 1988 to honor the broadcast's 50th anniversary. If you can make it past the Canada geese often grazing in front of the statue, you'll see a plaque depicting Welles, a spaceship, and a very frightened family hovering together around their radio.

Food

Cranbury's dining is limited to the following favorable options.

Begun as a mid-18th-century tavern and stagecoach stop and later known as the United States Hotel, **The Cranbury Inn** (21 S. Main St., 609/655-5595, www.thecranburyinn .com, Mon.–Thurs. 11 A.M.–9 P.M., Fri.–Sat. 11 A.M.–10 P.M., Sun. 11 A.M.–9 P.M., $17–23) can't help but exude history. The traditional American eatery houses both a lounge and a liquor store, and a 220-seat high-ceilinged add-on. A champagne brunch takes place on Sundays 11 A.M.–2 P.M.

Opened at its present location in 2004, **Hannah & Mason's** (30 N. Main St., Cranbury, 609/655-3220, www.hannahandmasons.com, lunch Mon.–Sat. 11:30 A.M.–2:30 P.M., dinner Thurs.–Sat. 5–9:30 P.M., closed Sun., $14–22) serves contemporary American dishes like eggplant steak ($15) and Tuscan chicken ($16) inside a converted colonial home. This BYO recently received a subtle makeover on an episode of Chef Gordon Ramsey's *Kitchen Nightmares.*

New Brunswick and Vicinity

New Brunswick is home of Rutgers University, pharmaceutical and personal hygiene manufacturer Johnson & Johnson's world headquarters, and Robert Wood Johnson University Hospital, one of the country's leading academic medical centers. A well-known commuter hub and Middlesex's county seat, the city's also a vibrant cultural center, hosting a small but lively theater district and several excellent restaurants. Downtown consists of small-scale high-rises and narrow streets, with **George Street,** a difficult-to-navigate brick roadway, at the city center. Route 27 (French St.) cuts through New Brunswick, separating Rutgers's main campus from downtown and forming the city's Latino district.

New Brunswick's Raritan riverbank location makes it a popular spot for outdoor recreation, and the city is home to a couple neighborhood parks, including one hosting festivals throughout the year.

RUTGERS UNIVERSITY

Founded in 1766 as Queen's College, Rutgers (542 George St., 732/932-1766, www.rutgers.edu) is New Jersey's official state university. Though it hosts satellite campuses in Camden and Newark, and an agricultural school—Cook College—along the New Brunswick–Piscataway border, downtown's Old Queens–Voorhees Mall campus is the university's original, and much of its colonial architecture remains.

Free **Historic tours** of the downtown campus are offered by appointment Friday and Saturday at 11:30 A.M. during fall and spring semesters. Tours last about an hour and begin at **Riverstede** (542 George St., 732/932-9342), the campus information service center. Ghost tours, starting from the same point, are held in October. For further details on each, go to http://ruinfo.rutgers.edu/visitingRU/historictours/.

Rutgers Geology Museum

Inconspicuously located on the second floor of Old Queens campus's Geology Hall, Rutgers' Geology Museum (Geology Hall, 732/932-7243, http://geology.rutgers.edu/museum.shtml, Mon. 1–4 P.M., Tues.–Fri. 9 A.M.–noon, closed weekends summer, call for academic year weekend hours, free) is worth a detour. The century-old museum's exhibits include an Egyptian mummy, locally found dinosaur prints, and a nine-foot-tall mastodon skeleton discovered in Salem County in 1869. Most Rutgers students are oblivious that the museum exists. Good for you—you'll have this gem to yourself.

New Jersey Museum of Agriculture

Located on North Brunswick's Rutgers Cook Campus, just off Route 1, is the New Jersey Museum of Agriculture (103 College Farm Rd., North Brunswick, 732/249-2077, www.agriculturemuseum.org, Tues.–Sat. 10 A.M.–5 P.M., $4 adult, $2 child), dedicated to the state's farming history. Agricultural tools, butter churns, tractors, and a fully stocked general store are on display, along with several historic photo collections depicting agricultural research and rural life in New Jersey. Educational events, mostly geared toward kids, are held weekends year-round.

◖ Jane Voorhees Zimmerli Art Museum

The fourth-largest university art museum in the United States, Zimmerli Art Museum (71 Hamilton St., 732/932-7237, www.zimmerlimuseum.rutgers.edu, $3 adult, under 18 free) is home to the most impressive collection of nonconformist Soviet artwork outside Russia, much of it created underground during the Soviet regime. The museum's exhibit of Soviet Union theater posters is truly outstanding, as is its European printmaking collection, including a notable display of Belgian art nouveau posters. Additional museum highlights include an array of locally designed stained glass windows,

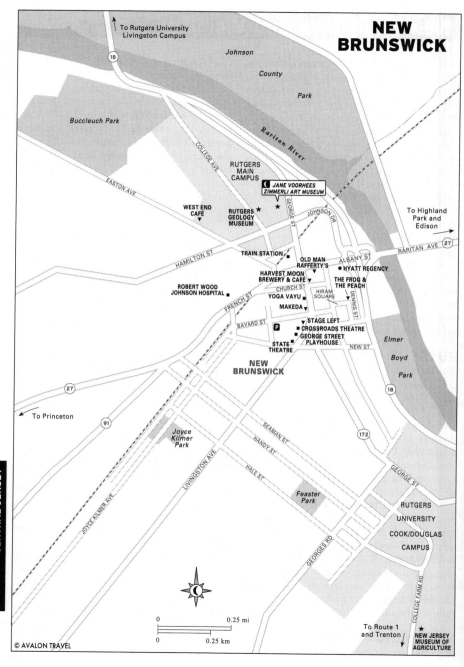

NEW BRUNSWICK

To Rutgers University Livingston Campus

18

Johnson

County

Park

Buccleuch Park

Raritan River

COLLEGE AVE

EASTON AVE

RUTGERS MAIN CAMPUS

JANE VOORHEES ZIMMERLI ART MUSEUM

WEST END CAFÉ

RUTGERS GEOLOGY MUSEUM

GEORGE ST

JOHNSON DR

To Highland Park and Edison

HAMILTON ST

RARITAN AVE 27

TRAIN STATION

ALBANY ST

OLD MAN RAFFERTY'S

HYATT REGENCY

HARVEST MOON BREWERY & CAFÉ

THE FROG & THE PEACH

ROBERT WOOD JOHNSON HOSPITAL

FRENCH ST

CHURCH ST

HIRAM SQUARE

YOGA VAYU

MAKEDA

DENNIS ST

BAYARD ST

P

STAGE LEFT

CROSSROADS THEATRE

GEORGE STREET PLAYHOUSE

STATE THEATRE

NEW ST

Elmer

Boyd

Park

18

NEW BRUNSWICK

27

To Princeton

91

SEAMAN ST

172

Joyce Kilmer Park

LIVINGSTON AVE

HANDY ST

HALE ST

JOYCE KILMER AVE

Feaster Park

GEORGE ST

RUTGERS

UNIVERSITY

COOK/DOUGLAS

CAMPUS

GEORGES RD

COLLEGE FARM RD

0   0.25 mi

0   0.25 km

To Route 1 and Trenton

NEW JERSEY MUSEUM OF AGRICULTURE

© AVALON TRAVEL

a collection of Japonisme—late 19th century Japanese and European paper art and ceramics—and a rare book library specializing in French art and society at the turn of the 19th century, open only by appointment.

A small gift shop and adjacent café are located on the museum's first floor. Both the museum and shop are open Tuesday–Friday 10 A.M.–4:30 P.M., Saturday–Sunday noon–5 P.M., closed Mondays year-round, closed Tuesdays in July, and closed August. Every first Sunday of the month is free.

ENTERTAINMENT AND EVENTS

New Brunswick boasts New Jersey's largest concentration of live-performance theaters and hosts a couple of popular festivals. Dinner and a show are great ways to enjoy the city's offerings.

Theaters

Just off of George Street is New Brunswick's theater row, occupying a block-long stretch of Livingston Avenue. There are nearby public parking lots on Banyard, Kirkpatrick, and Neilson Streets.

Founded in 1974 as New Brunswick's first professional theater, the **George Street Playhouse** (9 Livingston Ave., 732/246-7717, www.georgestplayhouse.org) has hosted dozens of independently produced plays and musicals since moving to its current location—a 375-seat theater—in 1984. Next door, the famed 1,800-seat **State Theatre** (15 Livingston Ave., 732/246-7469, www .statetheatrenj.org) has been completely renovated to recapture its 1921 vaudeville appearance. Recent performers include Lyle Lovett, late-night host Craig Ferguson, and Alvin Alley American Dance Theater.

Built in 1991, the 264-seat **Crossroads Theatre** (7 Livingston Ave., 732/545-8100, www.crossroadsnb.com) is home of the Crossroads Theatre Company, specializing in works examining the African American experience. The company was 1999's Tony recipient for Outstanding U.S. Regional Theatre.

They perform four plays on their main stage each season.

Festivals

Recently relocated to Piscataway's **Johnson Park** (River Rd.) from New Brunswick's Boyd Park, September's annual **Raritan River Festival** (www.raritanriverfest.com) has been a local tradition since 1980. The daylong event features food, live bands, kids' rides, and a cardboard-canoe race down the Raritan River.

For well over a decade the **New Jersey International Film Festival** (www.njfilm fest.com) has been offering residents a chance to view independent films, animation, shorts, documentaries, and experimental works from around the globe. The festival is held at various New Brunswick locations throughout June and July.

SPORTS AND RECREATION

New Brunswick is home to several parks, including 78-acre **Buccleuch Park.** Situated between the Raritan River and Easton Avenue, just above the main Rutgers campus, this neighborhood hangout hosts a 1.5-mile fitness trail, along with a couple of tennis courts and a baseball diamond. On the edge of the Raritan River, 20-acre **Boyd Park** features a nearly mile-long multiuse trail interspersed with signs providing details on local history, including information on the D&R Canal.

Yoga Vayu (354 George St. between Paterson and Banyard Sts., 732/249-8245, www.yogavayu.com) offers sessions in yoga, drumming, and dance—including belly dancing—and Reiki, a natural method of stress release. Massages are also available. Ask about student and senior discounts.

ACCOMMODATIONS

Located close to New Brunswick's theaters, Rutgers University, and the train station, the **Hyatt Regency** (2 Albany St., 732/873-1234, newbrunswick.hyatt.com, $149–289) is both stylish *and* convenient. Spacious rooms offer scenic balcony views along with wireless Internet and complimentary Neutrogena bath products. Meals are available via room service or downstairs in the hotel's Glass Woods Tavern & Lounge.

FOOD AND NIGHTLIFE

New Brunswick hosts a wonderful selection of eateries, ranging from lunch trucks to award-winning restaurants. You'll have no trouble finding a dining experience to suit your budget and needs. And as this is a university town, rest assured that both bars and drinks are plentiful.

Consistently ranked on New Jersey "Best of" lists, **Stage Left** (5 Livingston Ave. at George St., 732/828-4444, www.stageleft.com, lunch Fri. noon–2:30 P.M., dinner Mon. 5:30–9 P.M., Tues.–Thurs. 5:30–10 P.M., Fri.–Sat. 5:30–11 P.M., brunch Sun. 11:30 A.M.–2 P.M. summer, $22–39) serves outstanding New American dishes, both samplings and à la carte, along with an entire menu devoted to entrées prepared on their wood-burning grill. In addition to private dining rooms and its own wine shop, Stage Left has pioneered the state's green restaurant movement with the 2007 installation of rooftop solar panels.

For more than 25 years **The Frog and the Peach** (29 Dennis St. at Hiram Sq., 732/846-3216, www.frogandpeach.com, lunch Mon.–Fri. 11:30 A.M.–2:30 P.M., dinner Mon.–Thurs. 5:30–9:30 P.M., Fri.–Sat. 5:30–10 P.M., Sun. 4:30 P.M.–9 P.M., $19–38) has been pleasing crowds who flock to the industrial eatery for internationally inspired dishes like goat cheese tortellini ($24) and romance in the restaurant's glass-enclosed all-season garden.

The laid-back **Harvest Moon Brewery and Cafe** (392 George St., 732/249-6666, www.harvestmoonbrewery.com, Mon.–Wed. 11:30 A.M.–11 P.M., Thurs.–Sat. 11:30 A.M.–midnight, Sun. 11:30 A.M.–10 P.M., $14–25) serves up American eats alongside home-brewed beers like Harvest Hefeweizen and O'Leary's Irish Stout. An afterdinner menu is available for stragglers who stumble in for the live nightly music. Undergrads hit **Old Man Rafferty's** (106 Albany St., 732/846-6153, www.oldmanraffertys.com, Mon.–Thurs.

11:30 A.M.–11 P.M., Fri.–Sat. 11:30 A.M.–midnight, Sun. noon–midnight) flagship restaurant for sloppy joe sandwiches ($9.45) and chicken quesadillas ($7.95), while entrées like the New York strip steak ($24.95) are more appealing to the working crowd.

Named for the Queen of Sheba, stylish **Makeda** (338 George St., 732/545-5115, www.makedas.com, Mon.–Fri. 11:30 A.M.–10:30 P.M., Sat. noon–midnight, Sun. noon–3 P.M., $15.50–29) is New Jersey's first, perhaps only, Ethiopian restaurant. The menu features a nice selection of vegetarian dishes, and all meals come served with *injera*, a flatbread doubling as silverware. Live reggae and calypso music play on weekends.

With its comfy couches and late-night hours, **West End Café** (125 Easton Ave. Unit 1, 732/249-5282) is where Rutgers students go for their thrice-daily caffeine doses.

GETTING THERE AND AROUND

New Brunswick's train station (French and Albany Sts., Mon.–Fri. 5:30 A.M.–9 P.M., Sat.–Sun. 6:40 A.M.–8 P.M.), west of George Street, features bike racks and ticket vending machines. Both Amtrak and NJ Transit operate lines through the city (take NJ Transit for short distances). New Brunswick is 50 minutes by train from New York City. From South Jersey, hop the River LINE from Camden to Trenton, cross the street, and board NJ Transit.

If you're driving, several area businesses validate parking as long as you park in a lot run by **New Brunswick Parking Authority** (NBPA, 732/545-3118, www.njnbpa.org).

EDISON

In addition to being the birthplace of recorded sound, Edison Township is home to a large percentage of Indian and Chinese residents, reflected in the region's cultural and culinary offerings, and is one of the state's fastest growing areas. Formerly known as Raritan, Edison was renamed in 1954 to honor local inventor Thomas Alva Edison, who in the late 19th century built the world's first organized research facility in the township's Menlo Park section. Edison grew quickly as a manufacturing hub, developing like a doughnut around Metuchen borough but never forming its own town center. Still, the Edison Memorial Complex and Oak Tree Road, a six-block "Little India" located west of Route 27, offer more than enough reasons to visit.

Thomas Alva Edison Memorial Museum and Tower

Although Edison's famed research laboratory, where Edison invented the working phonograph is long gone, the Edison Menlo Park Museum, memorial tower, and information trail (37 Christie St., 732/549-3299, www.menloparkmuseum.com, Tues.–Sat. 10 A.M.–4 P.M., free) are fine reminders of what once stood in their place. Named for the section of Edison Township where the inventor worked, the Menlo Park Museum is a tiny two-room building bursting with Edison memorabilia, including numerous phonographs and photographs. The space is so tightly packed that funds are being raised for a new larger museum to be built in its place. To the museum's left stands the 131-foot Thomas A. Edison Memorial Tower, dedicated in 1938—seven years after Edison's death. Topped with a 13.5-foot working light bulb, the tower has become a popular roadside attraction.

Although small in overall size, the museum and surrounding grounds offer plenty to see, but it's the people working here who make this place. They're so well versed in Edison trivia and speak about his life with such enthusiasm that it's contagious. If you weren't already an Edison fan, you will be when you leave.

Oak Tree Road

Make an unassuming west turn onto Oak Tree Road from Route 27 and you'll find yourself in a land of sari shops, Bollywood video stores, and some of the best Indian cuisine in the tristate region. Though residents refer to it simply as Oak Tree, this six-block stretch running into nearby Iselin Township is one of New Jersey's two Little Indias (the other is in

Jersey City), a great place to dine, browse, and discover a new side to the state's offerings.

Food

Fast food and chain restaurants are in great supply around Edison, but one of the best reasons for visiting is the area's incredible ethnic cuisine. Most of these restaurants exist along Oak Tree Road, with a few located on Route 27.

Chowpatty (1349 Oak Tree Rd., 732/283-9020, www.chowpattyfoods.com, Tues.–Sun. 11:30 A.M.–10 P.M., $4–12) is both a restaurant and a sweets mart, serving an extensive menu of southern Indian vegetarian dishes along with a selection of *chaat,* savory snacks common at street stalls throughout India.

Reservations are recommended at **Ming** (ShopRite Plaza, 1655-185 Oak Tree Rd., 732/549-5051, www.mingrestaurants.com, Tues.–Thurs. and Sun. noon–2:45 P.M., 5:30–10 P.M., Fri.–Sat. noon–2:45 P.M., 5:30–10:30 P.M., $16–24), an upscale BYO serving spicy pan-Asian fare in Far East–inspired quarters. Next door is Ming's sister restaurant **Moghul** (ShopRite Plaza, 1655-195 Oak Tree Rd., 732/549-5050, www.moghul .com, lunch Tues.–Sun. noon–3 P.M., dinner Tues.–Thurs. and Sun. 5:30–10 P.M., Fri.–Sat. 5:30–10:30 P.M., closed Mon., $12–23), a BYO known for its Indian curries and lunch buffets ($10.95 weekdays, $12.95 weekends). Moghul also runs a fast-food eatery across the street called **Moghul Express** (1670A Oak Tree Rd., 732/549-6222, Tues.–Thurs. 11 A.M.–9:15 P.M., Fri.–Sun. 11 A.M.–9:30 P.M., $8), offering a variety of Indian, Chinese, and Thai dishes and a nice choice of vegetarian eats.

For traditional Cantonese cuisine try **Wonder Seafood Restaurant** (1984 Rte. 27, 732/287-6328, $15–25), a BYO that packs in on weekends (11 A.M.–3 P.M.) when exquisite dim sum selections are served.

Though the strip mall setting is pretty bare, it's the food that keeps customers returning to **Meemah** (Colonial Village Shopping Ctr., 9 Lincoln Hwy./Parsonage Rd., 732/906-2223,

Tues.–Thurs. 11:30 A.M.–10 P.M., Fri.–Sat. 11:30 A.M.–11 P.M., Sun. noon–9:30 P.M., $8–19), where Malaysian-Chinese dishes include Chinese eggplant with garlic sauce ($8.25) and golden-ginger chicken ($12.95).

Information and Services

Look for the free publication *Little India* (www.littleindia.com) in newspaper dispensers along Oak Tree Road. It offers ideas on where to shop in the area.

Red Bank and Vicinity

Red Bank seemed to be a lost cause in the 1980s. Its downtown was partially abandoned. Its population was dwindling. And people began referring to the borough as "Dead Bank." What could be worse? Today, Red Bank is one of New Jersey's most cosmopolitan communities. With boutique shops, trendy restaurants, coffeehouses, and an attractive main street, the riverfront borough has become a destination apart from the nearby Shore. That's not to say it has gone overboard flaunting its newfound confidence. You'll still find gritty pubs and budget dining, and you won't have to look far. Smaller than two square miles in size, Red Bank does have a few distinct neighborhoods, including an antiques district near the transit station and a Latino enclave along the borough's west side.

Red Bank's surrounding Bay and River region stretches north to Raritan and Sandy Hook Bays, west encompassing Middletown Township, and east, taking in Rumson borough before tapering off at the Shore's west border. A ferry connects bayside communities Keyport and Atlantic Highlands to Manhattan, a commuter benefit that likely accounts for the area's largely affluent inland community. Route 36 cuts horizontally across the region's northern portion, and Route 35 travels south, dividing Middletown Township and

Downtown Red Bank

© LAURA KINIRY

CENTRAL JERSEY

continuing on to Red Bank—a stop-and-go alternative to the parallel Garden State Parkway.

While you should save the bulk of your time for exploring Red Bank, the outlying area offers a few nice recreational opportunities and scenic drives.

DOWNTOWN RED BANK
Entertainment and Events

Named to honor the great jazz musician and Red Bank native, 1,575-seat **Count Basie Theatre** (99 Monmouth St., 732/842-9000, www.countbasietheatre.org) has been partially restored to its original 1926 appearance, including historically accurate theater seats and refreshed interior painting. There's also a new marquee. The restoration is an ongoing process, and recent fund-raisers included a benefit show by Bruce Springsteen, with raffle tickets going for $100 a piece. Primarily a venue for music, dance, and comedy, the theater has been reequipped to show films as well.

Catch stage performances like the sensual *Garden of Earthly Delights* and witty *Heartbreak House* at the 350-seat **Two River Theater** (21 Bridge Ave., 732/345-1455, www.trtc.org), home to Red Bank's eponymous theater company since 2005. The venue is an easy walk from the train station.

Just down the block from Broad Street is **Clearview Cinema** (36 White St., 732/777-3456, www.clearviewcinemas.com, $10.50 adult, $8.50 child), Red Bank's art film theater. Although constantly in a state of flux, downtown's mansard-roofed **Dublin House** (30 Monmouth St., 732/747-6699) features live local bands on weekends.

FESTIVALS AND EVENTS

Red Bank comes alive during the December holiday season with a series of events and attractions, beginning with a post-Thanksgiving **Window Walk.** Downtown's store windows are decorated with lights and festive displays and many feature live Barbizon models. While you're admiring, carolers, choirs, brass bands, and various other musicians provide free holiday entertainment along sidewalks, returning

to similar posts every Saturday afternoon before Christmas. **Horse & Carriage Rides** are also offered Saturday afternoons throughout December, leaving from Bridge Avenue.

Held annually during May or June, the **Red Bank Jazz & Blues Festival** (www.redbankfestival.com) features two days of crafts, food, and live jazz and blues performances on three outdoor stages.

The **Red Bank Farmers Market** (732/530-7300, Sun. 9 A.M.–2 P.M. May–Oct.) takes place at the Galleria on West Front Street and Bridge Avenue.

Shopping

Red Bank is home to several of New Jersey's more interesting independent shops, notably along Broad Street and Monmouth Street. It's fun to browse even if you're not a shopper. The borough is also known for its fine antique selection and art galleries.

ANTIQUE SHOPS AND ART GALLERIES

West Front Street, nicknamed Antique Alley, is home to several collectives hosting more than 150 antique dealers. Art galleries exist throughout the borough.

Located in the center of Red Bank's historic district, **Antique Center of Red Bank** (West Front St., 732/842-4336 or 732/842-3393, www.redbankantiques.com) encompasses three factory buildings filled with more than 100 antique dealer displays. Wares include Depression era glass, jewelry boxes, vintage furnishings, and artwork, but you'll also find venues offering furniture refinishing, phonograph repair, vintage clothing repair, and precious-metal purchase. Nearby **Monmouth Antique Shoppes** (217 W. Front St., 732/842-7377) provide room for over 50 antique dealers, including purveyors of classic coats and tableware.

The **Art Alliance of Monmouth County** (33 Monmouth St., 732/842-9403, www.artallianceofmonmouth.org) was originally located in the Count Basie Theatre when it opened in 1978, but moved to its present location in 1992. Its more than 300 members include sculptors, painters, photographers, fiber artists, digital artists, and art lovers whose works are displayed in rotating exhibits and within on-site galleries year-round.

The popular **Laurel Tracey Gallery** (10 White St., 732/224-0760, http://laureltracey gallery.com) features new paintings monthly. Past shows have included "'50s and '60s," "Shore Scenes," and "Small Works." **Art Forms** (16 Monmouth St., 732/530-4330, http://art formsgalleries.com) showcases contemporary American works by artists such as neo-Expressionist Paul Bennett Hirsch. For vintage 19th- and 20th-century movie, art deco, travel, and circus posters, don't miss **Inheritance Gallery** (27 Monmouth St., 732/530-5417, www .inheritancegallery.com), on the upper floor of the Downtown Antique Center.

SPECIALTY SHOPS AND BOUTIQUES

Red Bank has a fun selection of shops, mostly along Monmouth and Broad Streets.

Couldn't score *Soprano* Johnny Sachs's signature before he bit the dust? Get it at **Fameabilia** (42 Monmouth St., 732/450-8411, www.fameabilia.com), along with autographed photos and jerseys from practically every actor, politician, musician, and athlete you can think of. It's sort of like a museum—you can literally spend hours browsing the wares. The staff is helpful, but by no means overbearing.

For local boy Kevin Smith movie memorabilia, swing by **Jay and Silent Bob's Secret Stash** (35 Broad St., 732/758-0020, www .viewaskew.com), also home to a fine selection of comic books, *Year Without a Santa Claus* figures, and a mini Smith movie museum. A more boutiquish version of Urban Outfitters, **Funk and Standard Variety Store** (40 Broad St., 732/219-5885, www.funkandstandard.com) stocks pink lawn flamingos, crime scene Band-Aids, and Einstein action figures along with a modish selection of housewares and clothes.

Rumor has it that the Boss shops at **Jack's Music Shoppe** (30 Broad St., 732/842-0731, www.jacksmusicshop.com) for hard-to-find CDs. Jack's offers cash back for used CDs and DVDs, musical instruments, and surfboards. Watch for live events year-round.

Self-described "chic boutique" **Bees Knees** (24 Broad St., 732/758-1900, www.the beeskneesboutique.com) stocks Queen Beads bracelets and the pastel colored clothing of Lilly Pulitzer. There's a selection for guys and kids as well. The shop shares space with the **Jersey Shore Apparel Co.** (732/530-1048, www.jerseyshoreapparel.com), a subsidiary of the customized embroidery and screen-printing **Firehouse Specialty Shop,** located in the upstairs loft. Red Bank's one-stop shop for knitting supplies, crochet yarns, and stylish woolies is **Wooly Monmouth** (9 Monmouth St., 732/224-9276, www.woolymonmouth .com). In addition to hand-dyed natural fibers and custom written patterns, the shop hosts a range of knitting workshops for beginners up to advanced knitters year-round.

Fashionable **Marisa, The Art of Apparel** (67 Broad St., 732/933-9030, www.marisa boutique.com) carries designer Jovani gowns and Giavan necklaces. For men's and women's retro T-shirts and pencil-leg denim and ladies' jumpsuits, visit **Rok + Lola** (58 Broad St., 732/212-9696, www.rokandlola.com).

THE GALLERIA

With 80,000 square feet of retail and dining space adaptively reused from an old uniform factory, the Galleria (2 Bridge Ave., 732/842-9000, www.thegalleriaredbank.com) offers some worthwhile shopping ops, including the **Aristo-Tots Baby Boutique** (732/345-8500 or 800/651-6559, www.aristo-tots.com), **Buttercup Designs** (732/530-5627, www .buttercup-designs.com) children's furniture, and **Down to Basics** (732/741-6800 or 800/822-2135, www.downtobasics.com) bedding.

Accommodations

Along the Navesink River bank just off Route 35 is the 1928 **Molly Pitcher Inn** (88 Riverside Dr., 732/747-2500, www.mollypitcher-oyster point.com, $159–249), a boutique hotel with 106 rooms, a swimming pool, and a superb bar and restaurant—there's even a marina for guests arriving by sea. Next door is the inn's sister property, the smaller 58-room **Oyster**

Point Hotel (146 Bodman Pl., 732/530-8200, $179–219). Many of the hotel's guest rooms and suites offer the same river view, along with a basket of toiletries and complimentary home-baked cookies on your nightstand. What you don't get is coffee, although you can have a pot delivered for an additional fee. Both hotels are popular conference locales.

Both hotels are about a 10-minute walk from Broad Street, Red Bank's downtown center.

Food

Along with a great mix of shops, Red Bank is home to some of New Jersey's most cosmopolitan eateries. While the borough has most recently become known for its restaurant scene, it's also where you'll find familiar favorites that have been feeding the masses for years.

AMERICAN

No Joe Café (51 Broad St., 732/530-4040, www.nojoescafe.com, $5–14) is both No Ordinary Joe Coffee and Joe Mama's Soup-A-Rama: part coffeehouse, part eatery. It's a great place to kick back with a book weekday mornings, though once lunch hits, the menu (and crowd) expands: wraps, paninis, quesadillas, burgers, sandwiches, salads, and of course, soups, a selection of which changes daily. Joe's features a bevy of sidewalk seating during warmer months.

The country-style **River Edge Café** (35 Broad St., 732/741-7198, www.riversedge cafe.com, Mon.–Thurs. 8 A.M.–3 P.M., Fri.–Sat. 8 A.M.–10 P.M., Sun. 8 A.M.–4 P.M.) serves pancakes and omelets for breakfast and gourmet deli sandwiches for lunch, but returns to Chef Bob's Italian roots for dinner with dishes like linguini Bolognese ($16) and chicken Florentine ($19).

Visitors and locals alike insist the **Molly Pitcher Inn** (88 Riverside Dr., 732/747-2500, www.mollypitcher-oysterpoint.com, breakfast Mon.–Fri. 6:30–10:30 A.M., Sat.–Sun. 8–10:30 A.M., lunch daily 11:30 A.M.–3 P.M., dinner daily 5–9 P.M., $22–36) is the place to go for traditional American eats in Red Bank. The inn's former dining room (jackets

required after 5 P.M.) provides superb views of the Navesink River. Weekend brunch is an additional highlight.

For comfort food 24/7 stop by downtown's cozy **Broadway Diner** (45 Monmouth St., 732/224-1234, $7–21). The booths along the kitchen get the best service—the staff hardly has to move a muscle. Liven up your pancakes with pecans, followed with a tasty vanilla shake.

ECLECTIC

From nigiri sushi to lobster pancakes, Red Bank has eclectic cuisine covered.

Pan-Asian **Teak's** (64 Monmouth St., 732/747-5775, www.teakrestaurant.com, lunch Mon.–Fri. noon–3 P.M., dinner Mon.–Thurs. and Sun. 5–10 P.M., Fri.–Sat. 5–11 P.M., $21–29) sleek decor attracts local fashionistas who add to an already exclusive low-lit ambiance. While entrées are popular, it's the signature sushi rolls like the Jersey Girl, with salmon, mozzarella, and jalapeno ($13), and drinks such as pomegranate martinis and sangria that draw crowds.

The more causal **Bistro at Red Bank** (14 Broad St., 732/530-5553 or 732/530-5553, www.thebistroatredbank.com, lunch Mon.–Sat. 11:45 A.M.–3 P.M., dinner Mon.–Thurs. 5–9:30 P.M., Fri.–Sat. 5–11 P.M., Sun. 4–9 P.M.) serves a diverse menu ranging from pizza ($8–14) to lobster pancakes ($16) and sushi rolls ($6–15), all within a cool brick-walled space.

Another scene-stealer is Red Bank's swanky **Red** (3 Broad St., 732/741-3232, www.rednj.com, Mon.–Thurs. 5–10:30 P.M., Fri.–Sat. 5–11 P.M., Sun. 5–10 P.M., $18–31), serving New American dishes like seared sea scallops with orange coriander sauce ($21) and hanger steak with blue-cheese butter ($19). Dessert's Godiva chocolate cheesecake ($7) is a must. Afterward, head over to Red's lounge for a vanilla-bean martini and mingling. Lounge hours begin Wednesday at 6 P.M., Thursday–Saturday at 5 P.M., and Sunday at 8 P.M.

Cozy **Dish** (13 White St., 732/345-7070, lunch Mon.–Fri. 11:30 A.M.–2:30 P.M., dinner Tues.–Thurs. 5:30–9:30 P.M., Fri.–Sat.

CENTRAL JERSEY

5:30–10:30 P.M., Sun. 4:30–8:30 P.M.) uses fresh seasonal ingredients to prepare inspired American dishes like chicken penne vodka ($21) and grilled New York steak ($30). The decor is fairly low-key compared to the borough's other fine-dining choices.

Mediterranean favorite **Thyme Square** (45 Broad St., 732/450-1001, www.thymesquare restaurant.com, lunch Tues.–Fri. noon–2:30 P.M., dinner Tues.–Sat. from 5 P.M., Sun. from 4 P.M.) offers intriguing entrées like prosciutto-wrapped tuna ($28) along with delish sides including wild mushroom orzotto ($10) and chickpea polenta fries ($6).

Though a bit over-the-top, the kitschy and colorful **Carlos O'Connor's** (31 Monmouth St., 732/530-6663, Tues.–Thurs. 5–9 P.M., Fri. 5–9:30 P.M., Sat. 3–9:30 P.M., Sun. 3–9 P.M., closed Mon., $13–17) is undeniably fun. Dine on cheese-stuffed chili rellenos ($12.95) under a canopy of plush parrots, plastic peppers, and fruit baskets, and don't forget to leave a business card at this Irish-inspired Mexican BYO.

For authentic Mexican fare try **Juanito's** (159 Monmouth St., 732/747-9062, daily noon–10 P.M., $6–16), a popular eatery near the train station.

Information and Services
Red Bank's **Visitors Center** (732/741-9211, www.visit.redbank.com, Wed.–Fri. noon–5:30 P.M., Sat.–Sun. 10:30 A.M.–3:30 P.M.) is located at 17 East Front Street. The center hosts an additional information booth in the Red Bank Train Station (Monmouth St. and Bridge Ave., Mon.–Fri. 5:30–11 A.M.).

Getting There and Around
Red Bank is located along Route 35 on the tail end of the Navesink River. It's 48 miles south of New York City, eight miles east of the Jersey Shore, and 85 miles northeast of Philly. From the Garden State Parkway take Exit 109. If traveling by train from Philly, take NJ Transit's **North Jersey Coast Line** (800/772-2222, njtransit .com) to the Red Bank Train Station (Bridge Ave. between Monmouth and Oakland Sts.). Downtown is an easy walk from the station.

RUMSON
The only things that'll keep you from staring at the magnificent mansions along **Rumson Road** are the hedgerows blocking many of them from view. It doesn't help that one of them is rumored to belong to the Boss himself. Regardless of whether you're a Springsteen fanatic, Rumson's homes are something spectacular and make for a rewarding Sunday drive.

Fromagerie
One of the state's few dining venues where jackets are preferred is Rumson's excellent Fromagerie (26 Ridge Rd., 732/842-8088, www.fromagerierestaurant.com, lunch Fri. 11:30 A.M.–2:30 P.M., dinner Tues.–Thurs. 5–10 P.M., Fri.–Sat. 5–11 P.M., Sun. 10:30 A.M.–3 P.M. and 4–9 P.M.), a French restaurant occupying a former residential Victorian. Former employee and culinary demigod David Burke recently purchased Fromagerie from its original owners, updating both its decor and menu with dishes like roasted "soy honey" duck ($29), seaweed-soaked organic chicken ($26), and dry aged Florentine-style rib eye ($39).

KEYPORT–ATLANTIC HIGHLANDS
Situated along Raritan Bay, the small borough of Keyport was once an oyster-harvesting and shipbuilding capital. These days the "Pearl of the Bayshore" is determined to get its weathered downtown back up and running. Despite good efforts, Keyport offers little in the way of shops and restaurants. However, fishers and Bayshore enthusiasts will find worthwhile reasons to stop here.

Continue east along Route 36 to reach **Keansburg,** home to a boardwalk-style amusement park and water park, and the **Atlantic Highlands,** boasting the highest point on the entire Eastern Seaboard.

Steamboat Dock Museum
Keyport Historical Society runs the Steamboat Dock Museum (Broad St., Keyport, 732/739-6390), a seasonal institution dedicated

to the town's rich maritime history, including steamboat-building and the oyster industry. Well-researched exhibits and special events, such as a vintage swimsuit fashion show, are reasons for visiting. Hours are Sunday 1–4 P.M., Monday 10 A.M.–noon, or by appointment, mid-May–mid-September.

Keansburg Amusement Park

Situated on a few blocks of Bay-front property, carnival-style Keansburg Amusement Park (275 Beachway, Keansburg, 732/495-1400, www.keansburgamusementpark.com) has been entertaining crowds for more than a century, although both the park and its neighboring water park, **Runaway Rapids,** have updated with the times. Rides include a log flume, the Spook House, a balloon Ferris wheel, and the dizzying Chaos, while the water park features high-speed slides and a lazy river, along with a space specifically geared towards toddlers. The amusement park opens daily at 10 A.M. throughout summer and offers free admission; the cost of rides is based on the number of tickets each ride requires (a book of 100 tickets costs $42.95). Amusement park–water park combo tickets are your best deal: Three hours in Runaway Rapids plus unlimited amusement rides costs $33.95 ($31.95 for two hours). Runaway Rapids also opens daily at 10 A.M. throughout summer, weather permitting.

Mount Mitchell Scenic Overlook

At 266 feet above sea level, Mount Mitchell (Ocean Blvd., 732/842-4000, daily 8 A.M.–dusk) is—surprisingly—the Eastern Seaboard's highest point. The overlook provides a great view of Sandy Hook, the Raritan and Sandy Hook Bays, and—on a clear day—New York City's skyline. It also hosts a memorial to the many Monmouth County residents who died in the 9/11 terrorist attacks.

Sports and Recreation

Raritan Bay is home to a large striped bass population, and **fishing piers** are located in both Keyport and Keansburg. Area bait and tackle shops include **Crabby's Bait and Tackle**

(229 W. Front St., Keyport, http://fishbox.tv/crabbys, 732/335-9311), **Skipper's Shop** (35 1st Ave., Atlantic Highlands, 732/872-0367), and **Little Fish** (17 Ave. D, Atlantic Highlands, 732/872-2601).

The paved **Henry Hudson Bike Trail** is a 10-mile multiuse trail from Aberdeen, just east of the Garden State Parkway, continuing through the Raritan Bay towns along Route 36 until reaching the Atlantic Highlands. Plans are in the works to connect the trail south to Freehold; a portion of this stretch is already open.

Accommodations

Open in 2004, the boutique **Blue Bay Inn** (51 First Ave., 732/708-9600, www.bluebayinn.com, $216–329) offers a variety of rooms and room sizes, some with balcony and courtyard views, and all with Wi-Fi and complimentary daily breakfast. The inn is within walking distance of the ferry terminal, and includes both a restaurant and a lounge on-site.

Getting There

Seastreak (800/262-8743, www.seastreak.com, $45 round-trip peak, $37 round-trip off-peak, $26 one-way) runs a weekday commuter ferry from the Atlantic Highlands to New York City. The boat leaves from the Atlantic Highlands Municipal Marina at the bottom of First Avenue. The trip takes approximately 35 minutes.

MIDDLETOWN

Middletown Township's 41 square miles make up the Bay and River region's largest portion, stretching north toward Keyport, east along the Navesink River, and south past Red Bank. It's a mostly affluent suburb, home to both rocker Jon Bon Jovi and the Quick Stop Grocery immortalized in local director Kevin Smith's film *Clerks*. The township's Middletown Village, founded in 1613, is New Jersey's oldest settlement.

If you have the opportunity, drive or bicycle down the township's **Oak Hill Road** and past the grand estates lining **Navesink River Road**; they're impressive.

CENTRAL JERSEY

Quick Stop & RST Video

A must-stop for any Kevin Smith fan, Quick Stop & RST Video (58-60 Leonardo Ave., Leonardo) is the filming location for Jersey boy Smith's directorial debut, *Clerks*. Smith worked days at the Quick Stop and spent his late-night hours filming. RST Video has since closed and is currently used for storage. But it's the significance, right?

Monmouth Museum

Nestled into Brookdale Community College's campus, the Monmouth Museum (Newman Springs Rd., 732/747-2266, www.monmouth museum.org, Tues.–Sat. 10 A.M.–4:30 P.M., Sun. 1–5 P.M., $7) celebrates education, culture, and ideas with ever-changing exhibits like a New Jersey Emerging Artists series, and an outer space program with lectures by astronauts. Kid's have the Wonder Wing, a *Goonies*-type play area featuring a slide-through whale, a rope bridge, and a pirate ship. The museum is also home to one of North America's largest collections of 18th- and 19th-century sewing clamps. Also known as "bird clamps," these ornately designed pieces assisted sewers by keeping materials in place before sewing machines came about. Designs include snakes, dolphins, and cheeky-faced cherubs.

Recreation

Oak Hill Road is a popular stretch for cyclists. There's no set shoulder, but the road is wide enough to handle both automobiles and bicycles. Rather than continuing on Navesink Road, stick to the backstreets where traffic's lighter and the roads are generally safer for cycling. For a glimpse of the area's estates, cyclists may want to begin at nearby Red Bank and head east along **River Road** or **Rumson Road.**

Located along Oak Hill Road, 250-acre **Poricy Park** (345 Oak Hill Rd., 732/842-5966, www.poricypark.org) is a wild spread of open space housing fossil beds, wildlife, and the 18th-century **Murray Farmhouse** (last Sun. of the month 1–2:30 P.M.), which still contains its original beehive oven. For more than 35 years local nonprofit Poricy Park Conservancy has maintained the park, offering educational programs and activities like trail runs and ghost hunts, along with guided family and group fossil-bed visits to the park's Poricy Brook ($160, two hours). Self-guided fossil hunting is also an option (daily dawn–dusk Apr.–Oct.). The park is open daily dawn–10 P.M. year-round. An on-site nature center is open Monday–Friday 9 A.M.–4 P.M., with scheduled programs held most weekends.

Food

Middletown Township is a large place with no shortage of dining options. Those below offer a nice range of selections.

For a bit of Kevin Smith trivia to go with your burger and fries, stop by Belford's **Marina Diner** (Route 36 and Seeley Ave., 732/495-9749, $7–18), which makes a cameo in Smith's 1997 flick *Chasing Amy*. The diner is open Sunday–Thursday until midnight and Friday–Saturday 24 hours.

Recently undergoing major renovations, **Lincroft Inn** (700 Newman Springs Rd., Lincroft, 732/747-0890, www.lincroftinn.com, lunch daily 11:30 A.M.–4 P.M., dinner Mon.–Thurs. 4–10 P.M., Fri.–Sat. 4–11 P.M., Sun. 4–9 P.M., $16–32) serves continental dishes in a historic setting, a portion of which has been around since the late 17th century. The restaurant includes a popular separate sports bar with a tavern menu of burgers, pizza, salads, and sandwiches ($5–12).

Consistently topping the list of New Jersey's best restaurants, **Restaurant Nicholas** (160 Rte. 35 S., 732/345-9977, www.restaurant nicholas.com, Sun.–Thurs. 5:30–10 P.M., Fri.–Sat. 5:30–11 P.M., $59–79) is revered for its New American fixed-price menus and a superb wine list comprised of lesser known vintners and vintages. A 600-piece blown glass chandelier by local artist Bob Kuster hangs above the main dining room.

The Central Plains

Hills and horse farms occupy much of the plains stretching across Monmouth County's middle and lower portions. I-195 travels directly west from Allaire to Allentown, but regional back roads like Routes 524 and 537 are much more scenic, meandering past county parks, golf courses, orchards, and stables. The area's best restaurant selection is in Freehold, along with a pleasant B&B. For other accommodation options, try Jackson's camping resorts or New Egypt's excellent farm stay.

HOLMDEL

Once home to Mattel Toys, the rural suburb of Holmdel remains a major hub for Lucent Technologies' Bell Labs Innovations. It's also a great spot for fossil hunting. With several parks, a living-history farm, and the region's top outdoor amphitheater, Holmdel has a lot to offer anyone who likes a little fresh air. The town is also home to the country's first museum devoted entirely to the Vietnam War.

Sights

Located in Telegraph Hill Park at New Jersey Turnpike Exit 116, the **New Jersey Vietnam Veteran's Memorial and Vietnam Era Education Center** (732/335-0033 or 800/648-8387, www.njvvmf.org, Tues.–Sat. 10 A.M.–4 P.M., $4 adult, $2 senior and student, under age 10 free) was created to help educate the public about the Vietnam War. Exhibits include photographs and letters based on rotating war-related themes. There's also a resource gallery of books, videos, and other reference materials, and an outdoor memorial accessible 24/7 that pays tribute to the Americans, especially New Jerseyans, who died in Vietnam.

Holmdel Park's **Longstreet Farm** (732/946-3758, www.monmouthcountyparks.com, daily 9 A.M.–5 P.M. Memorial Day–Labor Day, daily

hogging it up at Longstreet Farm, Holmdel

© LAURA KINIRY

CENTRAL JERSEY

10 A.M.–4 P.M. Labor Day–Memorial Day, free, donations accepted) is a fun place to bring kids. This late-19th-century restored farming village is home to hogs, cows, horses, and sheep. Costumed interpreters demonstrate crafts such as lace-making and needlepoint on select weekends from several reconstructed and restored structures, including a 1770s 141-room farmhouse and Monmouth County's oldest Dutch barn.

PNC Bank Art Center
A popular summer music venue, 17,500-seat PNC Bank Art Center (732/203-2500, www .artscenter.com/main.html) showcases big-name performers like Eric Clapton and the Police along with more intimate acts, and stages a couple of festivals throughout the season. The outdoor amphitheater's strategic location at Garden State Parkway's Exit 116, adjacent to the Vietnam Education Center, draws crowds from up and down the Jersey Shore as well as New York City. Both reserved seats and general lawn admission are available.

Sports and Recreation
Holmdel Park (44 Longstreet Rd., 732/946-9562) features numerous nature trails that can be easily combined for longer hikes. These trails vary in length from the easy 0.4-mile Pond Walk Trail to the more moderately strenuous 3.1-mile Cross Country Trail. Bring along a picnic lunch and stop by the **Holmdel Arboretum** to dine in the shade of a crab apple tree. The park's hilly terrain is ideal for sledding during winter, and ice-skating is permitted on Lower Pond. Cross-country skiing is allowed on all nature trails.

For a healthy hike try the seven-mile **Ramanessin Greenway Trail** (www.holmdel enviro.org/ramtrail.htm), crossing Holmdel Township from **Phillips Park** to **Thompson Park** and running alongside the Ramanessin Brook. On the way you'll pass through woodlands and marshland, and beside steep slopes and deep ravines. The Greenway is an ongoing project of the Holmdel Environmental Commission (732/946-8997) and is not that

well marked in areas (specifically around Phillips Park), but guided walks—such as an Earth Day Walk and a Fall Foliage Tour—are scheduled throughout the year.

One of the sweetest things to do in Holmdel is to go fossil searching, and the best place to get started is at **Ramanessin Brook** (www .holmdelenviro.org, www.njfossils.net), where shark's teeth and arrowheads are plentiful. You have to supply your own equipment, such as rubber boots, shovel, and a sieve.

Food
Part of a local chain, BYO **It's Greek to Me** (2128 Hwy. 35, 732/275-0036, www.itsgreek tome.com, Mon.–Thurs. 11:30 A.M.–10 P.M., Fri.–Sat. 11:30 A.M.–11 P.M., Sun. 1–10 P.M., $7.75–20.95) is *the* place for dining on dolmades—stuffed grape leaves—and shrimp-filled pitas.

For delicious bento boxes—Japanese lunches packed with all sorts of interesting eats—and wonderfully fresh sushi try **K.O.B.E.** (The Commons at Holmdel, 2132 Rte. 35 S., 732/275-0025, www.kobecuisine.com, Tues.–Sat. 11 A.M.–10 P.M., Sun. 1–9 P.M., closed Mon., $30), a sleek modern BYO. Don't miss the gourmet tea selection, including hand-rolled full-bodied varieties.

COLTS NECK
You know you're in equestrian country when you reach Colts Neck. The township originally known as "Atlantic" changed to its current incarnation in 1962, and local streets bear names like "Hunt" and "Walling," referring to the chases and jumps associated with horses. On Sunday afternoons throughout summer, polo matches take place in a local park. Strict zoning laws and a limited water supply have helped Colts Neck stay exclusive, and what isn't used for housing is returned to the township for the creation of parks and golf courses. The intersection of Routes 537 and 34 acts as a makeshift town center, although there's little more than a general store, a steakhouse, a hotel, and a couple of garden and produce centers.

Polo Field

If you've never been to a Polo match (and even if you have), it's a worthwhile experience. Matches are held at Bucks Mill Park and Polo Field (105 Bucks Mill Rd., 732/946-4243, www.coltsneckpolo.com) Sunday afternoons throughout summer. Dress ranges from casual to formal (here's your chance to wear that pair of white hand gloves). Bring along lawn chairs and snacks ($5 per person), or reserve sideline parking ($30). Call or check the website for exact dates and times.

Produce and Garden Centers

Since 1911 **Delicious Orchards** (Rte. 34 S., 732/462-1989, www.deliciousorchardsnj.com, Tues.–Sun. 10 A.M.–6 P.M.) has been serving the Colts Neck community. A retail business was added in the 1950s, selling homemade pies, cakes, cookies, and apple cider doughnuts baked on the premises, as well as seasonal and organic produce and a selection of international cheeses.

Brock Farms (Rte. 34 S., 732/462-0900, www.brockfarms.com) provides for all your gardening needs and then some. In addition to a wide variety of plants, flowers, and produce, the center offers lawn and gardening workshops, and hosts a spectacular annual Christmas display.

Recreation

There are several area public golf courses, including the top-rated **Hominy Hill Golf Course** (92 Mercer Rd., Colts Neck, 732/462-9222), an 18-hole course designed by Robert Trent Jones, a highly regarded golf architect who designed about 500 courses worldwide in his lifetime. The Hal Purdy–designed 18-hole **Pebble Creek Golf Club** (40 Rte. 537 E., 732/303-9090, www.pebblecreekgolfclub.com) is known for its tall trees, sand traps, and a killer par-five eighth hole.

For horseback riding try **Jockey Hollow Farm** (64 Hominy Hill Rd., 732/761-0391).

Food

Opposite Delicious Orchards you'll find

Christopher's Café (41 Rte. 34, 732/308-3668, www.christopherscafe.com, Tues.–Fri. 11:30 A.M.–8:30 P.M., Sat. 8 A.M.–8:30 P.M., Sun. 8 A.M.–3:30 P.M.), a warm New American eatery known for its weekend breakfast sandwiches ($6.25–9.25) and fresh fruit crepes ($6.50). Dinner ranges from hand-pulled flatbread pizza ($8.95) to a French dip sandwich ($9.95).

ALLAIRE STATE PARK

Wall Township's 3,086-acre Allaire State Park (Route 524, 732/938-2371, www.state.nj.us/dep/parksandforests/parks/allaire.html, daily dawn–dusk) is a popular stop for naturalists and historians as well as families. In addition to opportunities for birding, bicycling, horseback riding, hiking, camping, and kayaking (not to mention nearby golf courses and skydiving), the park plays host to an antique steam train and a restored bog-iron village. A $5 park entrance fee is charged weekends only Memorial Day–Labor Day.

Historic Allaire Village

Originally known as Howell Works Company, James Peter Allaire created what is now Allaire Village (www.allairevillage.org) in 1822 to mine bog iron for his New York City steam-engine works. When cheaper, more efficient coal was later discovered in Pennsylvania's Allegheny Mountains, Allaire's pitch-pine charcoal furnaces were declared obsolete and the site became known as the "Deserted Village."

Today, Allaire Village is home to numerous historic structures, including a gristmill bakery, blacksmith and carpenter's shops, a blast furnace, and a working bakery with a beehive oven. Period-dressed interpreters provide demonstrations during summer months. There's a visitors center and museum located in one of the property's old row homes, and walking trails both within the working area and in the park surroundings.

Allaire Village is open Tuesday–Sunday 11 A.M.–5 P.M. in summer, and Saturday–Sunday 10 A.M.–4 P.M. in May and

NEW JERSEY SPEEDWAYS

Motor sports are a popular New Jersey pastime. While speedways are located statewide, you'll find the highest concentration in Central Jersey. Most are seasonal venues (Apr.–Nov.) that allow overnight camping without supervision or liability. The following speedways are currently open, along with the new **New Jersey Motorsports Park** (www.njmotorsportspark.com), which opened in Millville in 2008.

On the Pinelands' western outskirts is **Atco Raceway** (1000 Jackson Rd., Atco, 856/768-0900, www.atcorace.com), a quarter-mile drag racing strip and motocross park with bleacher stands and plenty of parking. The venue is home to **Jim Harrington's Drag Racing School** (732/690-3716, www.thedragraceschool.com). For information on weather and currently scheduled events, call the raceway's Weather and Information Hotline at 856/768-2167.

Resurrected in 1997, **New Egypt Speedway** (720 Rte. 539, New Egypt, 609/758-1900, www.newegyptspeedway.net) hosts a half-mile clay oval racing track. The speedway has plenty to offer in addition to racing, including kid-centric features like a monitored playground and weekly pit tours. Events take place Saturday evenings and occasionally during the week.

Old Bridge Township's long-running **Raceway Park** (230 Pension Rd., Englishtown, 732/446-7800, www.etownraceway.com) includes two drag racing strips — a quarter-mile National Hot Rod Association (NHRA) track and a one-eighth-mile junior track hosting the weekly NHRA Junior Drag Racing League Competition. There are also off-road facilities for motocross and paved go-kart courses. The park recently opened a 1.35-mile road course currently not used for sanctioned events and available for rental. Raceway Park is home to the annual spring and fall Sport Compact Nationals, and the Summer Sport Compact Slam.

The Skylands' **Island Dragway** (20 Island Rd., Great Meadows, 908/637-6060 during the week, 908/637-6536 during races, www.islanddragway.com) features a quarter-mile drag racing strip and weekly "street-legal racing," open to any and all automobiles for competition, every Friday and the first Wednesday of the month.

September–November. Admission is $5 adult, $2 child weekends May–October, free during all other times. The village visitors center is open daily 10 A.M.–5 P.M. Memorial Day–Labor Day, Wednesday–Sunday 10 A.M.–4 P.M. the rest of the year.

Pine Creek Railroad

The New Jersey Museum of Transportation runs an antique steam train along a 0.75-mile loop within the park on weekends March–December (every half hour noon–4:30 P.M., $4). Known as the Pine Creek Railroad, it has been operating for over 55 years. Volunteers stage themed productions, such as a great train robbery and a haunted express, aboard the locomotive throughout the year, but one of the most popular excursions is the afternoon Christmas Express ($7.50) held weekends during December.

Sports and Recreation

The park's four hiking trails range from 0.5 miles to a lengthy 16.5 miles. Each trail is marked with a different color code that rates its difficulty: red, yellow, and green are pedestrian-only; orange designates the longer multiuse trail.

Relatively smooth **Edgar Felix Bike Path** runs east from the park to Manasquan Inlet. Two wooden bridges carry cyclists above the Garden State Parkway.

Circle A Riding Academy (116 Herbertsville Rd., Howell, 732/938-2004, $35 per hour) gives guided horseback riding tours through Allaire State Park daily 9 A.M.–6 P.M. in summer and daily 9 A.M.–4 P.M. the rest of the year.

Skydive Jersey Shore (Monmouth Executive Airport, Rte. 34, 732/938-9002, www.skydivenjshore.com) offers tandem and solo jumps over Central Jersey—you may even catch a glimpse of the New York City skyline. Tandem jumps cost $215 weekends, $195 weekdays; solo jumps cost $190.

Consistently rated among the top 50 pubic golf courses in the United States, **Howell Park Golf Course** (Preventorium Rd., 732/938-4771, mid-March–Dec.) is a par-72 course with a well-maintained practice green. The course offers beginning and intermediate golf clinics during the season (732/842-4000). The year-round **Bel-Aire Golf Course** (3108 Allaire Rd., 732/449-6024) features 27 holes, including an 18-hole executive course. Tee times are first come, first served.

Camping

Allaire State Park features 45 tent and trailer campsites ($20), all within walking distance of showers and toilets. The trailer sanitary station is only open April 15–October 31, but campsites are accessible year-round. Allaire also hosts several group sites accommodating up to 250 people. Two smaller sites allow up to 25 people for $25 per night; four larger sites allow up to 50 people for $50 per night. Four circular yurts with skylights go for $30 per night, while six cabin-like shelters each cost $40 per night (closed January).

FREEHOLD

Freehold borough is best known as Bruce Springsteen's childhood home, although it was also dubbed the "Bicycling Capital of the World" in the late 19th century due to the large quantity of bicycles produced here. Today, the industrial borough hosts a revitalized downtown district as well as a sizeable Latino population. Most weekdays, Main Street fills with lawyers, clerks, and potential jurors from Freehold's downtown courthouse who file into neighborhood restaurants for a quick bite, or in summer, a seat at one of dozens of outdoor sidewalk tables.

Just outside Freehold borough is Freehold Township, home to several pick-your-own orchards and Monmouth Battlefield State Park, where one of the Revolutionary War's longest battles was fought.

Springsteen's lyrics contain details on Freehold's history, including the 1964 closing of the A&M Karagheusian Rug Mill. The textile mill, featured in "My Hometown," was once the region's largest employer.

Sights

When Springsteen sings about "My Hometown" on his 1984 *Born in the USA* album, it's Freehold he's talking about. Local authors Jean Mikle and Stan Goldstein give occasional Boss-centric tours of the borough, with a drive past the locations of Bruce's childhood homes (including the one on Institute Street), and a stop at the tree where he posed for the Born in the USA tour book. Mikle and Goldstein's joint publication, *Rock & Roll Tour of the Jersey Shore* (www.njrockmap.com), is available through their website. A self-guided **Monmouth County Music Heritage Map,** which includes some overlapping sites, is available in PDF format at www.freeholdcenter.com/pdf/musical_heritage_map.pdf.

Who says it's not about the bike? Anyone interested in bicycle history will love **Metz Bicycle Museum** (54 W. Main St., 732/462-7363, www.metzbicyclemuseum.com), home to a collection of antique high-wheels and wood-frame and tandem cycles dating back to the mid-19th century. Additional antiques such as toys, bike accessories, and a wonderful bottle opener collection are also displayed. The museum hosts the International Cycling History Conference in summer 2009. It's open by appointment only, so call ahead.

Freehold Raceway (Rtes. 9 and 33, www.freeholdraceway.com, free) is the nation's oldest daytime harness racetrack. Live harness racing around a half-mile track takes place August–May.

Pick-Your-Own Orchards

Despite recent residential and commercial development, pick-your-own farms remain prevalent in Freehold Township.

Located on the grounds of Monmouth Battlefield State Park is **Battleview Orchards**

(91 Wemrock Rd., 732/462-0756, www.battle vieworchards.com, daily 9 A.M.–6 P.M.), recently celebrating 100 years of farming. The orchards are open year-round and offer pick-your-own strawberries, sour cherries, nectarines, and pumpkins, depending on the season. There's an on-site store selling produce and baked goods, and hayrides during fall. A complete picking schedule is available at www.battlevieworchards.com/pickurown.htm. Best known for its freshly made fruit pies, **Wemrock Orchards** (300 Rte. 33 W., 732/431-2668, www.wemrockorchard.com, daily 9 A.M.–6 P.M.) allows guests to pick their own raspberries, blackberries, and strawberries. The farm hosts a haunted hayride and corn maze in autumn, when pick-your-own pumpkins are featured.

Shopping

New Jersey's second largest shopping center, **Freehold Raceway Mall** (3710 Rte. 9, 732/577-1144, www.freeholdracewaymall.com, Mon.–Sat. 10 A.M.–9:30 P.M., Sun. 11 A.M.–7 P.M.) home to dozens of stores, including Esprit, Apple, and Forever 21, along with a food court and a 96,000-square-foot open-air plaza simulating a downtown Main Street, opened in November 2007.

Don't miss nearby Englishtown's weekend **Englishtown Auction** (90 Wilson Ave., Englishtown, 732/446-9644, www.english townauction.com, Sat. 7 A.M.–4 P.M., Sun. 9 A.M.–4 P.M.). Established in 1929, this sprawling flea market has five indoor buildings and 40 acres of outdoor space. Rain or shine, the show goes on.

Food

Freehold is home to several established eateries and a number of newer haunts. Main Street springs to life during warmer months with ample sidewalk seating.

◖ **Tony's Freehold Grill** (59 E. Main St., 732/431-8607, Mon.–Fri. 6 A.M.–3 P.M., Sat. 6:30 A.M.–3 P.M., Sun. 6:30 A.M.–2 P.M., $8–17) has been a local staple for nearly three quarters of a century. It's a shoebox of a place, filled with booths, stools, and chrome steel, but the food is delicious—nothing fancy, just sandwiches and grilled eats. A framed Springsteen hangs on the wall, and tableside jukeboxes list his songs in handwritten script.

Main Street's casual **Olde Court Jester** (16 E. Main St., 732/462-1312, Mon.–Sat. 11:30 A.M.–2 A.M., Sun. noon–2 A.M., $12–20) serves burgers and well-seasoned fries. It can get crowded during the lunch hour when county workers compete for sidewalk tables. Another Freehold institution is **Federici's** (14 E. Main St., 732/462-1312, www.federicis.com, Mon.–Thurs. 11:30 A.M.–10:30 P.M., Fri.–Sat. 11:30 A.M.–11 P.M., Sun. noon–9:30 P.M., $5–20), home of the spicy pizza and a unanimous favorite among locals. Outdoor seating is the norm during warmer months.

Cozy **Sweet Lew's Hometown Café** (6 E. Main St., 732/308-1887, Tues.–Fri. 7:30 A.M.–2:30 P.M., Sat. 7 A.M.–2 P.M., Sun. 8 A.M.–1 P.M., closed Mon., $6–12) has been serving up blueberry pancakes, sandwiches, and homemade soups for years. Community hangout **Cornerstone Caffe and Restaurant** (2 E. Main St., 732/845-5300, Mon.–Thurs. 9 A.M.–9:30 P.M., Fri.–Sat. 9:30 A.M.–12:30 A.M., Sun. 10 A.M.–9:30 P.M., $9–22) serves espresso, pastries, and bona fide eats in an open space that plays host to an assortment of live musicians.

Accommodations

The area's best overnight option is Freehold borough's **Hepburn House** (15 Monument St., 732/462-7696, info@hepburnhouse.com, www.hepburnhouse.com, $115–175), a restored 1885 Victorian with five guest rooms and a covered porch, within walking distance of downtown and within sight of historic Monmouth Battlefield State Park. All rooms come with TV, wireless Internet access, and a private bath, and guests are treated to complimentary refreshments and a gourmet breakfast—with dishes like blueberry crumb French toast—during their stay.

◖ MONMOUTH BATTLEFIELD STATE PARK

Site of one of the longest battles of the Revolutionary War, 2,928-acre Monmouth

Battlefield State Park commemorates the conflict with an annual reenactment, a preserved farmhouse, and a variety of indoor displays. On June 28, 1778, General Washington and his troops took on British troops under the command of Sir Henry Clinton. The battle was a standoff, with Clinton calling off his troops due to strenuous heat and retreating after nightfall. The Battle of Monmouth produced legendary figure Molly Pitcher, who was said to have carried pitchers of water to fighting troops, later taking the place of her husband, who had been wounded in battle.

The expansive open park features numerous multiuse trails suitable for hiking, horseback riding, and cross-country skiing.

A park highlight is its **Historic Craig House,** an 18th-century farmhouse that belonged to farmer John Craig and his family during the time of the 1778 battle. The structure has since been restored and refurnished, and is occasionally open for tours. Check at the visitors center for updated details.

Visitors Center

In addition to providing park info, the Monmouth Battlefield Visitors Center (732/780-5782 or 732/462-9616, daily 9 A.M.–4 P.M.) hosts numerous displays and interpretive stations. There are rare coins and arrowheads found within the park, an archaeologist's cannonball analysis used to determine the length of the battle, and an interesting "Many Faces of George Washington" display showing more than 30 artist portrayals of the man "nobody could quite agree on." Depictions include the infamous "pig-eyed" portrait and a painting of a blue-eyed Washington, although his eyes were actually gray.

Battle of Monmouth Bike Route

The Battle of Monmouth Bike Route links Monmouth Battlefield with Holmdel park over a 28.5-mile loop. Most of the route is along roadways. To obtain a free route map from the New Jersey Department of Transportation, visit www.state.nj.us/transportation/commuter/bike/.

The Battle of Monmouth Reenactment

Hundreds of costumed actors and spectators take part in the reenactment of the Battle of Monmouth, held annually the last weekend of June.

ALLENTOWN AND CREAM RIDGE

Some time in the early 18th century, a man named Nathan Allen built three mills on land he'd acquired from proprietor Rob R. Burns and started "Allens Town." Today, the picturesque borough is filled with colonial, Federal, and Victorian homes and buildings, many that house specialty shops along Main Street. Allentown's downtown village hosts two small parks and an old mill, which stands as the borough's most prominent feature. Built on the site of one of Allen's original mills, it houses numerous shops and an excellent Bavarian restaurant.

Just east of Allentown is Cream Ridge, part of the largely rural Upper Freehold Township. The area's wide hillside stretches, bevy of horse

© LAURA KINIRY

Allentown's historic old mill

farms, and open sky make its proximity to a major highway hub seem almost impossible.

Sights

Centered around a restored and operating gristmill, 36-acre **Walnford** (609/259-6285, daily 8 A.M.–4 P.M., free) offers bits and pieces of its more than 250-year history as a farming and mill village, beginning in the 1730s. Most of the buildings have been reconstructed, and they include a former sawmill, carriage house, cow barn, and the 1773 Colonial **Waln House.** Walnford is located on the grounds of 1,046-acre **Crosswicks Creek Park** (Walnford Rd. off Rte. 539, 609/259-5794). Self-guided maps are available at the information center, located at the end of Walnford Road next to the parking lot.

The **Horse Park of New Jersey at Stone Tavern** (Rte. 524, Cream Ridge, 609/259-0170, www.horseparkofnewjersey.com) holds equine shows most weekends and some weekdays March–November.

Cream Ridge Winery (145 Rte. 539, Cream Ridge, 609/259-9797, www.creamridgewinery.com, Mon.–Sat. 11 A.M.–6 P.M., Sun. 11 A.M.–5 P.M.) offers tastings of more than a dozen wines, including specialty fruit wines crafted from locally grown cranberries and blueberries.

Specialty Shops

Allentown's walkable Main Street is where you'll find the area's best selection of specialty shops. Most stores and restaurants are closed Mondays, and some on Sundays.

The **Quilter's Cottage** (34 S. Main St., 609/259-2504) sells patterns, fabrics, and instructional books for beginning to advanced quilters, and hosts various quilting classes throughout the year. **Necessities for the Heart @ Wisteria** (28 S. Main St., 609/208-1349) carries a selection of handbags, totes, jewelry, and watches from such famed design names as Vera Bradley and Brighton. **Weaves** (35 S. Main St., 609/208-9990) stocks hand-embroidered items and rare linens for sale. **Allentown Feeding Co.** (42 S. Main St., 609/208-2050), known also as the Old Mill,

features several interesting shops, including **Pleasant Run Peddlers** (Bldg. 2, 609/259-0645), purveyor of Amish-made goods, and the **Old Mill Crafters Guild** (609/208-2050), carrying works of more than 20 local jewelers, potters, wood turners, and other artisans.

To *really* get a taste for Allentown, stop by **Chocolate N Dreams** (4-6 Church St., 609/259-4350, www.chocolatendreams.com), a local candy boutique specializing in handmade chocolates and gift baskets. The shop hosts a chocolate lounge next door, perfect for sipping chai or delighting in chocolate fondue. Candy-making classes are offered occasionally.

Accommodations

Located on the grounds of one of New Jersey's few organic farms is **Earth Friendly Bed & Breakfast** (17 Olde Noah Hunt Rd., Clarksburg, 609/259-9744, www.earthfriendlyorganicfarm.com, $95–115), a solar-powered inn with three guest rooms. The inn is actually a private home built in 1984, and the rooms, while bright and airy, feel as though you're bunking at a neighbor's. This changes once you get outside and start exploring the eight-acre farm. Blueberry bushes surround the property and are ripe for the picking late-June–September, along with blackberries and raspberries (Aug.–Sept.) and garden fresh veggies (mid-summer), and free-range chickens supply fresh eggs daily. Back inside, a greenhouse keeps things cozy with summer temps year-round.

Only minutes from downtown Main Street, elegant **Peace Fields Inn** (84 Walnford Rd., 609/259-3774, www.peacefieldsinn.com, $125–185) features five guest rooms, each with a private bath and TV. Proprietors Bill and Cathy, who moved to the 1850 Colonial in 2002, provide a full country breakfast each morning, along with use of their in-ground swimming pool mid-June–mid-September. They also offer boxed lunches for area exploring.

Food

There are several places to eat along Allentown's Main Street, but only a couple are standouts.

Located on the ground floor of the historic

Old Mill, **Black Forest Restaurant** (2 S. Main St., 609/259-3197, www.blackforestallentownnj .com, Tues.–Wed. 11:30 A.M.–3:30 P.M., Thurs.– Sat. 11:30 A.M.–9 P.M., Sun. noon–7 P.M., $13– 25) is easily one of the state's best Bavarian eateries. Hearty helping of potato dumplings and Wiener schnitzel do more than satisfy, but for a truly authentic German experience, BYO.

Allentown's cozy **Garden Tea Room** (4 S. Main St., 609/208-1880, www.inner harmonycenter.com/tearoom.html, Tues.– Sun. 11 A.M.–4 P.M.) provides the perfect shopping rejuvenation. Choose from a selection of sandwiches, quiche, and finger foods to accompany a steaming pot of herbal, green, or black tea.

Outer Ocean County

On the upper reaches of New Jersey's Pinelands sandy grounds start turning to suitable agricultural soil, and pick-your-own farms become plentiful. While blueberries and blackberries, both prominent further south, continue to grow here, fruits such as strawberries and nectarines flourish. Central Jersey's migrant workers find the bulk of their employment in this region.

Route 9 runs along the Pinelands' eastern border, separating them from land just west of the shore. The road carries vehicles south from Freehold through Lakewood and down into Toms River, a former seafaring town between barrens and beach. In these outer Pinelands, two-lane roads and sprawling shopping centers are the norm, and new development continues transforming the area's countrified suburbs.

◖ SIX FLAGS

Here's one thing that New Yorkers, Philadelphians, and New Jerseyans all have in common: New Jersey's extremely popular Six Flags theme park (1 Six Flags Blvd., 732/928-1821, www.sixflags.com), part of one of the world's largest amusement and theme park chains. Jackson's Six Flags opened in 1974 and today features three distinct parks that include more than a dozen roller coasters (one of them being the tallest and fastest in existence), a 350-acre drive-through safari, and one of the largest water parks in the United States. With at least a weekend's worth of attractions, Six Flags is a stand-alone destination.

Great Adventure

In 2001 Jackson's Six Flags Theme Park scored a Guinness World Record for the highest concentration of rides anywhere worldwide, an honor difficult to dispute. The park has become a favorite among roller coaster aficionados, who spend entire afternoons taking on Batman's inverted loops, braving Medusa's interlocking corkscrews, and bracing for El Toro's g-forces. But the park's most impressive coaster by far is Kingda Ka, the world's tallest and fastest as of 2008. Reaching a speed of 128 miles per hour in 3.5 seconds (ouch!) Kingda Ka takes about 50.6 seconds to complete, and at 456 feet tall is twice the size of the park's other hip highlight, the 230-foot Nitro, introduced in 2001. Great Adventure is constantly updating and adding, with recent additions including the indoor Dark Knight steel roller coaster, the Golden Kingdom subpark, and a glow-in-the-park night parade. Favorites such as Superman Ultimate Flight, the Big Wheel, Congo Rapids, and the Saw Mill log flume continue to attract crowds, as does the fairly new Bugs Bunny National Park for kids.

Great Adventure is known for its big-name concerts and varied theme shows, along with fireworks displays Saturday evenings throughout summer.

Wild Animal Safari

In business since the early 1970s, Six Flag's Wild Animal Safari is considered the largest drive-through safari outside Africa. Its 350 acres are home to over 1,200 animals, including elephants, giraffes, zebras, rhinos, kangaroos, and monkeys notorious for climbing over cars (the reason soft-top vehicles aren't allowed). Not that every animal is given completely free reign: lions, tigers, and bears are kept adequately away from through traffic, but close enough that they still feel up close and (perhaps a little too) personal. An air-conditioned safari tour bus with a guide is available for an additional fee, for those preferring not to risk their roadster's new paint job. Buses leave numerous times daily from the park entrance. For in-vehicle information tune into radio station 530 AM, which offers pertinent details on the park's wildlife. Plan on setting aside anywhere from 45 minutes to 1.5 hours to complete the safari tour.

Hurricane Harbor

Water parks are big business in New Jersey, and none more so than Six Flags' Hurricane Harbor (www.sixflags.com/parks/hurricaneharbornj, daily 10:30 A.M.–7 P.M. July–Aug., call for June hours), with dozens of slides, rides, and rivers ranging from lazy to crazy. While tobogganing through the eye of a makeshift storm is only *slightly* wild, the park's Cannonball, Wahini, and Jurahnimo Falls slides will have your heart thumping all the way to the bottom. Those in the market for slightly less thrill will want to stick with Reef Runner rapids or Taak It Eez Ee Creek, one of the longest, laziest rivers created, in the Island Village. The park also includes a giant wave pool and a water land especially for kids. Full-day tickets cost $29.99 adult, $24.99 child for Hurricane Harbor only, $39.99 adult, $34.99 child for the Harbor and Six Flags Safari.

Information and Services

Six Flags offers single and combo park passes for both adults and kids, as well as seasonal summer passes. A general admission Great Adventure one-day park pass runs $49.99 adult, $29.99 juniors under 54 inches tall. A Wild Safari upgrade with the purchase of a theme park ticket is $9.99, and a three-park admission is $89.99 adult, $49.99 child. One-day Wild Safari park admission is $19.99. Tickets are $10 cheaper if you purchase them online, or you can pick up a Six Flags coupon (many libraries carry them,

as does Burger King) for a $20 savings. Advance one-day parking tickets ($15) are available online (www.sixflags.com).

All three parks are open daily throughout summer and typically on weekends in May and September. Great Adventure hosts the ghoulish Fright Fest weekends in October, transforming the park into a bona fide monster mash.

Getting There

Six Flags is located off Exit 7A of the New Jersey Turnpike, I-195's Exit 16A, and Exit 98 of the Garden State Parkway.

JACKSON

At more than 100 square miles, Jackson is Ocean County's largest township—an expanse of horse fields and produce farms, cranberry bogs, recently constructed estate-style homes enveloping existing towns, and according to writer Susan Orlean, once "the highest concentration of tigers per square mile of anywhere in the world." Traversing upper Jackson, I-195 connects with major roadways transporting hundreds of thousands of visitors to the township each year. What's the big draw? Jackson's massive Six Flags theme park, the premier amusement park for one of the country's (and the world's) largest metropolitan centers. Unfortunately, regional accommodations are limited, and you may spend several sweltering hours in traffic only to find every room booked; call ahead.

Cassville

Clustered around the Routes 571 and 528 intersection is Jackson Township's Russian enclave, Cassville. There's not a lot to do here—downtown is nothing more than a couple of country stores and a tavern—but it's worth a look if you're in the area, especially for those interested in ethnic history. The village is home to two Russian Orthodox churches, including **St. Vladimir's Church** (Rova Farm Resort, 132 Perrineville Rd. off Rte. 571, 732/928-1337), an onion-domed structure with massive wooden doors, occupying a prominent piece of hilltop property. The church is especially interesting, even more so on Tuesday mornings when the

Rova Farms Flea Market (732/928-0928)—although not worthwhile in its own right—takes place on the grounds below.

Jackson Outlet Village

Jackson Outlet Village (537 Monmouth Rd., 732/833-0503, www.premiumoutlets.com/jackson/, Mon.–Sat. 10 A.M.–9 P.M., Sun. 10 A.M.–7 P.M.) is one of New Jersey's nicest outlet centers. It's clean and modern and hosts over 70 stores. Outlets include Banana Republic, Guess, and Nike.

Accommodations

One of the things preventing Jackson from becoming another Orlando, Florida, is its lack of accommodations. Other than camping facilities, the township offers nothing in the way of overnight options. Six Flags visitors will have to stay elsewhere if planning a multiday trip to the park. The Central Plains' New Egypt, Freehold, and Cream Ridge all offer recommendable lodging options, as do South Jersey's Mount Holly and Mount Laurel (40 miles away), conveniently located off Exit 4 of the New Jersey Turnpike.

Camping

There are several camping resorts within Jackson Township and most, if not all, offer Six Flags vacationer discounts. The campgrounds are all centrally located, providing easy access to both the theme park and the Shore.

Geared towards families, **Butterfly Camping Resort** (360 Butterfly Rd., 732/928-2107, www.butterflycamp.com, early Apr.–late Oct., from $46) features 135 tent and RV sites, along with a kiddie miniature golf course, lollipop hunts, and lawn chair movies throughout the season. The restrooms are in good shape, although "hot" showers tend to run more lukewarm. Butterfly Resort is located adjacent to Butterfly Bogs State Wildlife Refuge, which allows fishing and use of nonmotorized boats.

Tip Tam (301 Brewers Bridge Rd., 877/847-8261, www.tiptam.com, mid-Apr.–late Sept.) hosts 202 tent and RV sites. On-site activities include horseshoes and volleyball. There's also

a tiki bar, game room, rental pedal carts, and an in-ground swimming pool. Forgot your tent? No problem. Rental cabins are RVs are available. Rates start at $44 (online discounts are sometimes offered). Cabins begin at $70, RVs $100.

Toby's Hide-Away Campground (856 Green Valley Rd., 732/363-3662, early May–late Oct., from $25) has 50 full-service campsites over six acres. Many sites are wooded, and restrooms include hot showers.

Food

Finding good food in Jackson Township can be a chore. One place to try is **Java Moon Cafe** (1022 Anderson Rd. and Rte. 537, 732/928-3633, Mon.–Sat. 8 A.M.–10 P.M., Sun. 8 A.M.–8 P.M., $8–18), a local chain located just south of the outlets and a few miles' drive from Six Flags. The café's wide selection includes salads, meat, pasta, and chicken entrées, burgers, and signature specialties like the Harvest Moon Veggie Wrap. It makes a good place to go between shopping and tackling Six Flag's rides.

NEW EGYPT

Part of larger Plumstead Township, New Egypt lies at New Jersey's exact geographical center. Its small downtown offers little to do or see, although architecture buffs may enjoy the weathered saltbox structures lining Main Street. For others, New Egypt's appeal lies in the pick-your-own farms, an antique-filled barn, and a drag racing speedway on the town's outskirts.

Pick-Your-Own Farms

Pick-your-own farms are plentiful in Plumstead Township, a rural region largely committed to New Jersey's Farmland Preservation Program (www.state.nj.us/agriculture/sadc/about/), implemented to help preserve the state's agricultural landscape. **Hallocks U-Pick Farms and Greenhouse** (38 Fischer Rd., 609/758-8847, www.hallocksupick.com, Mon.–Fri. 7 A.M.–7:30 P.M., Sat.–Sun. and holidays 7 A.M.–5:30 P.M.) specializes in strawberry picking, along with tomatoes, beets, assorted greens, and other seasonal vegetables. A 30,000-square-foot greenhouse displays hundreds of flora species, including marigolds, geraniums, and candy corn plants. **De Wolf's U-Pick Farm** (10 W. Colliers Mills Rd., http://dewolfsupickfarm .com, 609/758-2424) grows pick-your-own strawberries, blackberries, and raspberries on more than 200 acres. De Wolf's is home to **Kim's Country Store** (609/758-6288), where you'll find home-baked pies, fresh-picked vegetables, and assortments of jams and jellies. Both the farm and store are open daily 9 A.M.–4 P.M. April and November, 7 A.M.–7 P.M. daily May–October; call ahead for holiday hours.

Emery's Berry Farm (346 Long Swamp Rd., 609/758-2424, daily 9 A.M.–5 P.M., www .netpie.com, late Mar.–late Dec.) is certified organic. They specialize in blueberries and raspberries, with an on-site market featuring freshly baked pies. Emery's runs blueberry- and pumpkin-picking hayrides throughout picking season, and is home several barnyard animals.

Accommodations

Located on a 250-acre working farm that features nature trails, seasonal wildflowers, and even a vineyard, **❰ Dancer Farm Bed & Breakfast** (19 Archertown Rd., 609/752-0303, www.dancerfarm.com, $190–310) makes a wonderful getaway. The farm once belonged to prominent area horse trainers and remains a Standard-bred boarding facility and training ground. A stunning 19th-century farmhouse provides 10 themed guest rooms for overnight lodging, each with a private bath, cable TV, and a phone. Some also feature a fireplace or fire stove and a balcony.

LAKEWOOD

Lakewood Township was once a wealthy retreat for high-profile New Yorkers like J. D. Rockefeller and boasted nearly 100 hotels. Today, it's a stretch of worn storefronts and shopping centers, although a few attractions do make a visit here worthwhile. Downtown centers along **Clifton Street,** mostly between Third and Fourth Streets—an ethnically diverse area home to several Latin groceries and a kosher deli. The town's most notable structure is a restored and operating vaudeville theater.

Sights

Georgian Court University (900 Lakewood Ave., 732/987-2263 or 800/458-8422, www.georgian .edu) was once the estate of railroad mogul George J. Gould. Now an institute of higher learning, its public grounds include a free arboretum with an Italian Garden, Formal Garden, and a Japanese Garden with blossoming cherry trees, a brook and waterfall, and a teahouse. Ninety-minute guided tours ($10) of Gould Mansion, the gardens, and additional campus highlights like **Raymond Hall,** home to the School of Education, are offered on selected Tuesday mornings throughout the academic year. The tours leave from Gould Mansion and require preregistration (732/987-2263).

Opened in 1922 at a vaudeville and silent movie theater, 1,100-seat **Historic Strand Theatre** (400 Clifton Ave., 732/367-7789, www .strandlakewood.com) was completely renovated and restored beginning in 2000, and now serves as stage for a variety of dance, music, comedy, and dramatic performances. The Strand is said to be one of the best acoustic theaters in the country. Off-hour tours can be arranged by calling ahead (ext. 207). These include backstage areas, dressing rooms, and a rumored secret tunnel.

Sports and Festivals

The Lakewood Blueclaws, a Philadelphia Phillies minor-league affiliate, take home field advantage at **FirstEnergy Park** (2 Stadium Way, 732/901-7000, www.lakewoodblueclaws .com, $6–9), where attendees will find a party deck, a playground, and plenty of general-admission Sod Squad seats.

September's annual **Renaissance Faire** (732/905-1065, www.lakewoodrenfaire.com) takes place along Country Club Lane in Pine Park, behind Lakewood Country Club. Don a medieval cloak and fasten up your corset for a weekend filled with jousting matches, jester antics, and roaming musicians. Browse among clothing and craft stalls, or grab yourself a turkey leg and settle in with a stein of beer.

TOMS RIVER

In 2006 Dover Township finally changed its name to Toms River (www.downtowntoms

river.com), reflecting the county seat village for which it has long been known. Toms River sits on the Pinelands' eastern border, lining a river that bears its name. The town's rich nautical history is preserved in museums along Washington and Main Streets, tucked among civic buildings and commercial stores, but it's wetland and river-based activities, a planetarium, and an ice cream festival that make the village and its surroundings noteworthy.

Sights

Ocean County College's **Robert J. Novins Planetarium** (College Dr., 732/255-0342, www.ocean.edu/campus/planetarium/) hosts programs ranging from local sky exploring to intergalactic star shows within a 188-seat 40-foot dome theater. All shows run about an hour and typically include a Q&A session with a student astronomer afterward. The planetarium's main office (732/255-0343) is open weekdays 9 A.M.–4 P.M., but most shows take place Friday and Saturday evenings and weekend afternoons. Robert J. Novins Planetarium is closed through 2008 for renovations; call for updates.

Cattus Island Park's **Cooper Environmental Center** (1170 Cattus Island Blvd., 732/270-6960 or 877/627-2757, daily 10 A.M.–4 P.M.) features several displays aimed at budding naturalists, along with snakes, reptiles, and an outdoor butterfly garden. Scheduled nature walks provide background on the area's bogs, swamps, and marshes, and Sunday's turtle feedings garner high marks from kids.

Entertainment and Events

The Mississippi-style **River Lady Cruise and Dinner Boat** (1 Robbins Pkwy., 732/349-8664, www.riverlady.com, $32–50 adult, $20–50 child) runs 2–3-hour cruises down Toms River daily throughout summer. Most trips include a communal meal.

Preorder a $5 tasting kit for July's annual **New Jersey Ice Cream Festival** (www.downtowntomsriver.com/icecream/festival.htm) and help choose Toms River's favorite brands and flavors. Past ice cream samplings have included Mrs. Walker's Blueberry Pie, Friendly's Hunka Chunks PB Fudge, and Applegate Farms' frozen hot chocolate.

Beginning boaters to old pros paddle it out along 8.5 miles of Toms River during October's **Ocean County's Canoe and Kayak Race.** For additional details contact the Ocean County Department of Parks and Recreation (877/627-2757, www.co.ocean.nj.us/parks/infopage.htm).

Sports and Recreation

Seaside Sailing Rides (Pier 1 Marina, 3430 Rte. 37 E., 732/830-9285, www.seasidesailing.com) hosts three-hour sailboat excursions on Toms River and Barnegat Bay for up to six people. Trips depart twice during the day and once in the evening throughout summer and cost $50 per person.

The Ocean County park system runs seasonal canoe trips along local estuaries and rivers, include Toms River and nearby Mullica River. For dates, times, and prices visit www.co.ocean.nj.us/Parks/default.htm or call 877/627-2757.

In addition to nature trails and birding opportunities, **Cattus Island Park** (1170 Cattus Island Blvd., 732/270-6960, www.co.ocean.nj.us/parks, $5–10) runs fishing and crabbing **Pontoon Boat Tours** (BYO traps, poles, and bait), Barnegat Bay nature tours, ornithology boat tours, and moonlight tours throughout summer.

Accommodations

With only five guest rooms, it's best to make advanced reservations at **Victoria on Main** (600 Main St., 732/818-7580, www.victoriaonmain.com, $130–190), a lovely B&B housed in a century-old Victorian. There are three public rooms available for mingling along with an on-site tearoom and an open-air wraparound porch. Business travelers will appreciate the inn's downtown location, as well as the writing desk and wireless Internet provided in each room.

The Pinelands

Starting in Central Jersey's Ocean Township and extending south along the Jersey Shore—encompassing portions of seven state counties and about 20 percent of New Jersey's total land area—the 1.4-million-acre **Pinelands National Reserve** (www.nps.gov/pine), also called the Pine Barrens (referring to the region's sandy, acidic, poor-growth soil) or Pinelands, is the East Coast's largest tract of uninterrupted forest from Boston to Richmond, Virginia. In 1983 the majority of the Pinelands was declared a United Nations International Biosphere Reserve, protecting it

from development. In addition to pitch pine, Atlantic white cedar, and scrub oak trees, this truly remarkable stretch is home to endangered tree frogs, forgotten towns, orchids, wetlands, cranberry bogs, blueberry bushels, carnivorous plants, wineries, army bases, and the legendary Jersey Devil, a horse-headed creature who's credited with wreaking havoc on the area for nearly three centuries.

Such a vast forest seems unusual in the country's most densely populated state, especially when you find out underneath it runs a pure and plentiful 17-trillion-gallon natural water

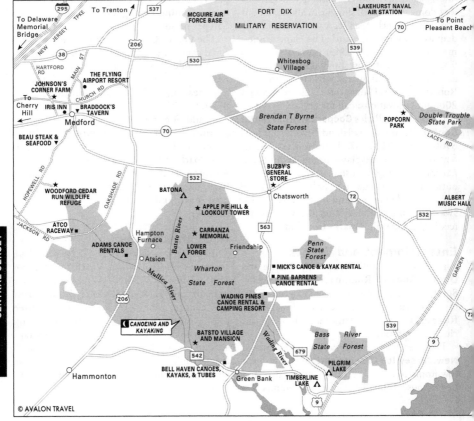

CENTRAL JERSEY

supply. Visitors can drive for miles without seeing another soul, although gun clubs tend to pop up every few miles. More than 700,000 people reside in the Pinelands, and many who call themselves "Pineys" live deep in the forests along back roads and rivers, and in the small towns scattered few and far between. The Pinelands were once a major supplier of bog iron, although most industry towns are now little more than furnace remains.

New Jersey's Pinelands are home to over 100 rare flora and fauna species, including floating heart, pennywort, hooded warbler, and northern kingfish, as well as ample recreational opportunities. Local rivers include the Batsto, Mullica, and Wading, and canoeing along

THE PINELANDS

their cedar-stained waters is a highlight of any Pinelands visit. The area also hosts numerous hiking trails and campsites, along with chances for swimming, fishing, hunting, and horseback riding. The Pineland's long flat stretches of empty roadway are ideal for cyclists.

TOURS

The Pinelands are uniquely New Jersey, and tours of the region are well worth the time and cost. Most guides are either Pineys or have studied Pinelands history extensively, so in addition to a bit of sightseeing you'll be learning too.

The nonprofit **Pinelands Preservation Alliance** (609/859-8860, www.pinelands alliance.org) hosts a wide range of events and excursions April–December, including canoe trips, ghost-town tours, daylong cougar hunts, and Pinelands navigation courses, but for a truly authentic Pine Barrens experience, catch one of naturalist Russ Juelg's **Jersey Devil Hunts** ($15) held one or two evenings each month. These hunts are really more of a guise for stirring interest in the region, and include an easy hike and some well-spent time around the campfire (bring your own marshmallows). Check the Alliance's website for an up-to-date listing.

Piney Power (609/698-2501, www.piney power.com) runs various Pinelands bus tours April–November, including four-hour discover tours ($38) with a stop in Chatsworth, Pinelands' self-proclaimed capital, and full-day and overnight tours. One of their most popular excursions is the Pine Barrens Winery Tour ($47), which includes cranberry wine tastings, Piney music, and a Piney trivia game. Call or visit the website for an updated schedule.

White Star Farms (888/272-6264, www .whitestarcs.com) hosts cranberry harvest tours of their working 150-year-old cranberry farm throughout October. Participants travel around the property in buses specially designed for off-road navigation, ensuring an up-close experience. Along the way tour guides offer valuable Piney insight into local culture and history.

For more than 30 years, outdoorsman Tom

CENTRAL JERSEY

walking along a nature path in the Pinelands' Batsto Natural Area

© LAURA KINIRY

Brown Jr. has been teaching people wilderness survival skills through training courses in New Jersey's Pinelands. Offerings at **Tom Brown Jr.'s Tracker School** (609/242-0350, www.trackerschool.com) cover a variety of disciplines, including teaching, healing, and visionary. Depending on the area of study, students may learn how to trap animals, build mud huts, collect water, or build a fire. Courses usually last a week, but intensives are offered some weekends. Call or visit the website for details.

The **Whitesbog Preservation Trust** (www.whitesbog.org) hosts events in and around Whitesbog Village throughout the year, including monthly volunteer workdays, moonlight walks, village tours, and an occasional lecture series. Visit the website for more details.

FORESTS

Much of New Jersey's Pinelands lie within protected state forests, namely Wharton, Brendan T. Byrne, and Bass River. These are also the best locations for Pinelands exploring. Each forest offers its own unique attractions and recreational opportunities.

Brendan T. Byrne State Forest

Old-timers may know it as Lebanon State Forest (named for a mid-19th-century glass factory that once operated here), but 37,000-acre Brendan T. Byrne State Forest (Rtes. 70 and 72, New Lisbon, 609/726-1191, www.state.nj.us/dep/parksandforests/parks/byrne.html, daily dawn–dusk, free) now bears the name of the New Jersey governor instrumental in turning the Pinelands into a national reserve. The Civilian Conservation Corps planted much of today's Pinelands forest in the early 20th century, replacing trees depleted through logging. A mix of oak trees, low-lying pitch pines, and Atlantic white cedar now thrive, most notably in the 735-acre **Cedar Swamp Natural Area,** just north of Route 72. Cedar Swamp is easily accessible from the Batona Trail, a portion of which makes up part of the forest's more than 25 miles of marked trails. These trails include easy nature walks, along with the wheelchair-accessible **Cranberry Trail,** as well as the **Mount Misery Trail,** accommodating both hikers and mountain bikers. Cross-country skiing, snowshoeing, and horseback riding are all popular forest activities.

Nineteenth-century Whitesbog Village, a semiactive agricultural town that's home of the cultivated blueberry, lies within Brendan T. Byrne Forest, along with remnants of several forgotten towns.

For additional park information, stop by the main office off Route 72, just east of the Four Mile Circle (the intersection of Routes 70 and 72).

Bass River State Forest

Acquired in 1905 as New Jersey's first state forest, Bass River State Forest (762 Stage Rd., New Gretna, 609/296-1114, www.state.nj.us/dep/parksandforests/parks/bass.html) has grown from 597 acres to more than 25,000. The forest, situated along the Pinelands' eastern edge, offers opportunities for fishing, boating, horseback riding, hunting, and easy hiking. Swimming is also allowed along 67-acre **Lake Absegami's** eastern shore during summer, with lifeguards on duty daily. The lake features a public boat launch, along with a seasonal concession stand renting rowboats.

Just east of the lake is 128-acre **Absegami Natural Area,** a former World War II U.S. military barracks. Absegami hosts a one-mile nature trail circling among pine, oak, red maple, Atlantic white cedar, and magnolia trees. A second natural area, 3,830-acre **West Pine Plains Natural Area,** is home to the freakishly short stunted-growth oaks and pines for which the Pinelands are known. Nicknamed the Pygmy Forest, the area is a must-see.

Bass River State Park is accessible from Exit 50 (North) or 52 (South) of the Garden State Parkway. There's a $5 weekday, $10 weekend parking fee Memorial Day–Labor Day, and walk-ins and cyclists are $2 each.

Wharton State Forest

Wharton (4110 Nesco Rd., Hammonton) is New Jersey's largest forest, 115,111 acres stretching from Burlington County south through Atlantic County and west into Camden County. One of the Pinelands' great highlights,

Wharton is home to both Atsion Recreation Area and Batsto Village, along with 9,949-acre **Batsto Natural Area** and 1,927-acre **Oswego River Natural Area,** prime endangered Pinelands tree frog habitat. Wharton offers opportunities for hiking, including a large portion of the 50-mile Batona Trail linking the forest to Bass River and Brendan T. Byrne State Forests, as well as miles of unpaved trails ideal for mountain biking and horseback riding. The Mullica, Batsto, Oswego, and Wading Rivers all wind through forest boundaries, reasons for taking advantage of the region's numerous canoeing and kayaking liveries. Swimming is allowed at **Atsion Lake** (744 Rte. 206, Shamong, Memorial Day–Labor Day, $5 weekdays, $10 weekends, $2 walk-in or bicycle), where lifeguards are on duty daily. The lake features a concession stand, bathhouse, and canoe and kayak rentals.

Wharton's abundant wildlife includes great horned owls, bluebirds, bald eagles, beavers, foxes, and river otters. The forest hosts several manmade attractions that take some sleuthing to find but are fun to uncover, including remains of former towns, an old lookout tower, and a memorial dedicated to the "Mexican Charles Lindbergh."

Park offices are located at Atsion Recreation Area (744 Rte. 206, 609/268-0444), and Batsto Village (Rte. 542, 609/561-0024).

◖ CANOEING AND KAYAKING

The Pinelands is probably New Jersey's best place for canoeing and kayaking. The Wading, Batsto, Mullica, and Oswego Rivers all wind through the reserve, and local canoe liveries (rental agencies) run excursions along at least one of them, providing transport both to and from the river. For those planning a canoe or kayaking trip, you'll benefit from starting early. Most trips (excluding overnighters) must be completed by 5 P.M. Each of the following liveries is dependable, so choosing one is a matter of convenience and personal preference. You'd be hard-pressed to find a better way of exploring the Pinelands. Most liveries offer shoulder-season discounts.

Wading Pines Canoe Rental (85 Godfrey Bridge Rd., Chatsworth, 888/726-1313, www.wadingpines.com) rents canoes and kayaks for use along the Wading River. Trips leave directly from the Wading Pines Camping Resort and vary in length and price from a one-hour excursion ($35 canoe, $25 kayak) to five hours ($50 canoe, $40 kayak). The two-hour trip ($40 canoe, $30 kayak) brings you directly back to the resort by way of the river, without any need for transport pickup.

Mick's Canoe and Kayak Rental (3107 Rte. 563, Chatsworth, 609/726-1380 or 800/281-1380, www.mickscanoerental.com) runs day trips down the Wading and Oswego Rivers ($48 canoe, $37 kayak), with drop-off and pickup transport. The livery opens Saturday–Sunday at 8:30 A.M., Monday–Friday at 9 A.M.

Pine Barrens Canoe Rental (3260 Rte. 563, Chatsworth, 609/726-1515 or 800/732-0793, www.pinebarrenscanoe.com) offers day-long canoeing and kayaking along the Wading and Oswego Rivers for $48 ($37 single kayak), as well as Batsto River advance-reservation trips (call ahead for rates). Overnight rentals are available for an additional fee.

Just east of Batsto, ◖ **Bell Haven Paddlesports** (1227 Rte. 542, Green Bank, 609/965-2205 or 800/445-0953, www.bellhavencanoe.com) runs several day-long canoe and kayak excursions along the Wading, Oswego, Batsto, and Mullica Rivers. Rates vary depending on the river ($48 and $56 canoe, $37 and $42 kayak). Overnight rentals are also available. If you're in the market for a ride of your own, Bell Haven features an indoor showroom (Tues.–Sun. 9 A.M.–5 P.M., Thurs. 9 A.M.–7 P.M., closed Mon.) of saleable canoes, kayaks, paddles, and accessories.

North of Hammonton and best reached by the Atlantic City Expressway, **Adams Canoe Rentals** (1005 Atsion Rd., Shamong, 609/268-0189, www.adamscanoerental.com) rents canoes ($75) and kayaks ($45) for 5–8 hour excursions along the Mullica and Batsto Rivers, with overnight rentals available ($55 Mullica

River, $90 Batsto). The livery also rents canoes for use on nearby Atsion Lake ($40).

OTHER RECREATION
Batona Trail
The Pinelands' best-known hiking trail, 50-mile Batona Trail commences at Brendan T. Byrne State Forest, winds south through Wharton State Forest, and ends in Bass River State Forest. It's a fairly easy, though lengthy, hike, but you can shorten it by starting from one of several intersecting access roads. The only real challenges are a few hills and wetlands. The trail is clearly marked and lined with huckleberries and orchids in spots. Keep an eye out for deer, waterfowl, and raptors. Several campgrounds are located along the way, and there are a few backcountry sites in the area.

Bike Route
The 42.6-mile **Pine Barrens River Ramble** is a bicycling loop along Pineland roads, routed by the New Jersey Department of Transportation. To obtain a free map, go to www.nj.gov/transportation/commuter/bike/tours.shtm.

FESTIVALS
Chatsworth's annual two-day **Cranberry Festival** (609/726-9237, www.cranfest.org/festival.html, $5 donation requested), taking place in October, features more than 100 artists and craftspeople as well as live music, antique dealers, and dozens of cranberry-filled pies, jams, jellies, and cakes. The annual June **Blueberry Festival,** held at Whitesbog Village, offers country crafts, Piney music, and blueberry picking, and for kids, the "Outrageously Messy" blueberry pie-eating contest.

SIGHTS
Naval Air Engineering Station at Lakehurst
On May 6, 1937, the German zeppelin *Hindenburg* burst into flames in Lakehurst, killing 36 of its 97 passengers. Reporters and cameramen had come to watch the 804-foot-long, 147-foot-tall, 135-foot-diameter aircraft

land at Lakehurst's naval air station (Rte. 547, 732/818-7520, www.lakehurst.navy.mil/nlweb/). Instead they witnessed one of the most famous aviation disasters in world history. The zeppelin cast a spark, setting its aluminum paint ablaze, and fire consumed the Hindenburg in a mere 34 seconds.

Navy Lakehurst Historical Society (732/818-7520, tours2@nlhs.com, www.nlhs.com) gives tours of the crash site, more impressive for its history than its current state, with two-week preregistration required. They include visits to historic Hangar 1, built to house the U.S. Navy's rigid airships, the control car mock-up created for Robert Wise's 1975 film *The Hindenburg,* starring George C. Scott and Anne Bancroft, and the exact spot the Hindenburg crashed, featuring a small monument and a 50th anniversary commemorative plaque. Tours take place the second Saturday of each month November–March and the second and fourth Saturday April–October. International travelers should call ahead for tour info.

Forgotten Towns

The Pinelands' sandy soil is notorious for "swallowing" villages abandoned after local bog-iron and glassmaking eras. The best way to recognize a lost town is to find nonnative ebony spleenwort, a smooth shiny red-brown stem plant that grows rampantly in places lime was used for building. Some forgotten towns, such as **Martha's Furnace** and **Hampton Furnace,** have left behind actual ruins, and in **Atsion,** a former bog-ore mining village, you'll still find several houses, the old iron-maker's mansion, and the company store, which now serves as a ranger station. Martha's Furnace, Hampton Furnace, and Atsion are all located in Wharton State Forest.

Albert Music Hall

Each Saturday night Piney music comes alive at Waretown's Albert Music Hall (125 Rte. 532, 609/971-1593, www.alberthall.org, $5 adult, $1 child under 12), just west of Route 9 along the Pinelands' eastern border. Local musicians perform bluegrass, country, and folk-inspired tunes, changing stage every half hour for an average seven-set total. Be sure to ask about the **Pickin Shed,** an on-site improv jam of fiddlers, washtub strummers, and dulcimer and banjo players—a true Piney experience. Albert Hall opens Saturday at 6:30 P.M., and the music begins at 7:30 P.M.

Carranza Memorial

On July 12, 1928, the 23-year-old Captain Emilio Carranza Rodriguez—known as the Mexican Charles Lindbergh—died in a plane crash over Wharton State Forest. Carranza was heading home from New York City on the final leg of a goodwill flight when his plane went down in an electrical storm. Today, a stone memorial erected two years after his death marks the spot, a sandy, otherwise nondescript roadside clearing. Each year since the tragedy, the Mount Holly American Legion and New York City's Mexican consulate have held a small on-site ceremony to honor Carranza's sacrifice (second Sunday in July at 1 P.M.). The memorial is located in Wharton State Forest along Carranza Road, a few miles south of Tabernacle, just past the turn-off for the juvenile correctional facility.

Apple Pie Hill and Lookout Tower

At 209 feet above sea level, Apple Pie Hill is the Pinelands'—and South Jersey's—highest point. Three miles from Chatsworth within Wharton State Forest, the hill is marked with a 60-foot lookout tower once used for spotting fires. Today, visitors can climb to the top for incredible views of the surrounding forests. Apple Pie Hill and Lookout Tower are reachable from the Carranza Memorial by way of the Batona Trail.

Batsto

No Pinelands trip is complete without a Batsto (Wharton State Forest, 4110 Nesco Rd., 609/561-0024, www.batstovillage.org, daily 9 A.M.–4 P.M.) visit. One of the region's premier attractions, this restored 19th-century village is a former bog-iron (and later glassmaking)

© LAURA KINIRY

Batsto village in the spring

center that mined bog ore from the area's rivers and streams. Located on the southern edge of Wharton State Forest, the village consists of 33 structures, including a general store, gristmill, sawmill, and a number of workers' quarters, along with a post office that's still in use. The property's main attraction is an Italianate-style 32-room mansion once home of ironmaster William Richards, who bought a controlling interest in Batsto in 1784 and subsequently, along with his son and grandson, built many of the buildings on the property today. The mansion was later purchased and remodeled to its current exterior by Joseph Wharton, a Philadelphia businessman who purchased numerous other Pineland properties as well. Wharton's legacy lives on in Wharton State Forest and in the mansion, which is closed for renovations as of this writing.

The village **nature center** (daily 9 A.M.–4 P.M. Memorial Day–Labor Day, Wed.–Sun. 9 A.M.–4 P.M. Labor Day–Memorial Day) offers guided canoe trips on Batsto's lake during summer months, and on the third Sunday in October the Batsto hosts

an annual **Country Living Fair,** complete with arts and crafts, pony rides, and chainsaw art. Sawmill demonstrations take place summer weekends at 1:30, 2, and 2:30 P.M. Additional activities include monthly hikes, star watches, and war reenactments.

Batsto's visitor center and gift shop are open daily 9 A.M.–4 P.M. It's a great place to stock up on New Jersey puzzles, Piney books, and maps of forgotten Pinelands towns. Restrooms are available.

Chatsworth

Once an iron-mining and glassmaking village, this self-proclaimed "Capital of the Pines" is today strictly agricultural, dominated by the region's two largest cranberry producers, A. R. DeMarco and Sons and **Ocean Spray.** Chatsworth has a big reputation for such a little place. When you finally do reach town (after miles passing woodlands and gun clubs), you'll hardly know you've arrived.

Centered on the crossroads of Routes 563 and 532, Chatsworth once served as a winter playground for New York high society, including the Astors, Vanderbilts, and Morgans. Although their country club has long since burned down, the 1860 **White Horse Inn,** which served as its annex, remains. The White Horse was originally built as a stagecoach stop but changed roles after Italian Prince Mario Ruspoli, introduced to the Pinelands by his in-laws, built the **Chatsworth Club.** Today, the two-story Colonial clapboard is somewhat di-lapidated, and is slowly undergoing renovations to reopen as a community center.

Down the road is the famous **Buzby's General Store** (First St. and Rte. 563), fea-tured in John McPhee's 1973 book *The Pine Barrens*. Although things have changed a lot in the 30-plus years since the book was writ-ten—the store no longer carries animal feed and kerosene—Buzby's continues to act as a makeshift information center for the area. For questions regarding Piney culture, this is the place to come. The store is also home to the **Cheshire Cat Gift Shop** (609/894-4415), stocked with books on Pinelands history, local cookbooks, works by regional artists, and goodies like homemade Cranberry mustard. Buzby's was added to the National Register of Historic Places in 2004.

Whitesbog Village

Joseph J. White founded Whitesbog Village (Mile Marker 13, Rte. 530) in 1870, and it quickly grew into a successful agricultural town. The streets were filled by workers' cot-tages, a packing and storing facility, and a com-pany store, while cranberry bogs and blueberry bushels occupied the surrounding land. It was here in 1916 that White's daughter Elizabeth cultivated the first blueberry ripe for sale, and the commercial blueberry was born.

Unlike most original Pineland towns, much of Whitesbog Village remains intact, and several of its homes continue to be inhab-ited. Whitesbog is owned by the state of New Jersey, who leases the village and surrounding land to the **Whitesbog Preservation Trust** (12103 Whitesbog Rd., Browns Mills, www .whitesbog.org), a nonprofit group that orga-nizes tours, events, and volunteer workdays to

help raise restoration money. Most events cost $5. Visit the Trust's website for an updated schedule.

CAMPING
Resorts

Along the Wading River just south of Chatsworth is the Pinelands' premier camp-ground, 50-acre **Wading Pines Camping Resort** (85 Godfrey Bridge Rd., 609/726-1313, www.wadingpines.com, Mar.–mid-Dec., $40–50 d), featuring 300 sites for tents and RVs, ranging from open field to pricier water-side sites. The resort also offers 26 log cabin rentals ($70), and canoe and kayak rentals from its on-site business.

Situated within Bass River State Forest, **Pilgrim Lake Campground** (Stage and Allan Rd., New Gretna, 609/296-4725 or 800/218-2267, early Apr.–late Oct., from $24) features 116 mostly wooded tent and RV sites, along with hot showers and a lake with a lifeguard for swimming.

Timberline Lake Camping Resort (365 Rte. 679, 609/296-7900, www.timberlinelake .com, early May–mid-Oct., from $35) offers 158 wooded and lakefront sites in addition to bingo nights and an August Hawaiian luau. On-site amenities include table tennis, boat rentals, and a lake for fishing and swimming.

Car Camping

There are road-accessible camping facilities in each of the Pinelands forests.

Brendan T. Byrne State Forest (609/726-1191) has year-round sites ($20) for more than 75 tents and trailers, all with restroom facilities located nearby. Three year-round group sites ($30) with fire rings, picnic tables, water, and flush toilets host up to 100 people. Visitors can also rent one of three cabins on Pakim Pond, each with a furnished living room and a fire-place, two bunk beds, full-facility kitchen, half baths, and electricity (Apr.–Oct., $45, $315 per week); or one of three wood-frame yurts (cir-cular tents with a skylight), each sleeping up to four ($30).

Bass River Forest (609/296-1114) offers

a variety of overnight facilities, including 176 family-style campsites (year-round, $20; trailer sanitation station open Mar.–Nov.) with flush toilets and six group campsites (year-round, $25) with pit toilets. There are also nine year-round lean-tos, each fully enclosed with hardwood floors, a wood-burning stove, and nearby restroom facilities ($30, up to six people), six lakeside shelters with nearby restrooms and two bunkrooms each (Apr.–Oct., $40, up to four people), and six Lake Absegami cabins, each with a screened porch, a living room, a bathroom, a fireplace, water, and electricity (Apr.–Oct., $65, $455 per week, up to six people).

Wharton State Forest (609/268-0444 or 609/561-0024) hosts 50 tent and trailer sites around Atsion Lake (Apr.–mid-Dec., $20), each with nearby restroom facilities, and 49 year-round primitive campsites ($20) at Godfrey Bridge, with water, picnic tables, and pit toilets. Several additional campsites are scattered throughout the forest, each equipped with a water hand pump and a pit toilet ($2 per person, 50–250 people). There are also nine furnished cabins along Atsion Lake, two accessible to those with disabilities. These cabins range in cost $45–85 or $315–595 per week, depending on the number of occupants (4–8).

To make reservations for any of the campsites above, visit www.state.nj.us/dep/parks andforests/parks/campreserv.html, or phone the specific park office.

Backcountry

Wharton State Forest hosts a couple of backcountry sites, accessible only on foot, by canoe or kayak, or on horseback. The **Lower Forge Wilderness Site** is situated just off Batona Trail along Batsto River, about 10 miles north of Batsto Village. It accommodates up to 50 people ($1 per person), but has no running water. The **Mullica River Wilderness Site**, located along the Mullica River, is 3.5 miles north of Batsto Village, 5.3 miles south of Atsion. It accommodates up to 100 people ($1 per person) and has running water. Pick up permits for either site at **Batsto Visitor Center** (Wharton State Forest, 4110 Nesco Rd., Hammonton, 609/561-0024) or the **Atsion Office** (Wharton State Forest, 744 Rte. 206, 609/268-0444).

FOOD

Your best bets for dining around the Pinelands are the outskirts: Medford and Mount Holly to the west, and Route 9 along the Pinelands' eastern border. Unfortunately, the inner Pinelands' most rewarding place for a meal, the campy Sweetwater Casino, burned down in 2008. It looks like casino cheese, murder mystery dinners, and Kelly Ripa autographs are a thing of Pinelands' past, for now.

MEDFORD

Medford skirts the Pinelands' western edge, spreading south to meet up with Camden County's retail hub. Now largely residential, the township was once home to several glass factories and mills. Only one mill remains, incorporated into Medford Village, the township's center. Main Street, lined by attractive Victorians housing specialty shops and eateries, feels like something out of a Rockwell painting, and it's a great place to walk around. The township hosts a few attractions worth a short drive, but for restaurants, shopping, and annual festivals, stick close to the village.

Historic Medford Village

Downtown Medford Village is filled with historic sites remaining from its days as a milling and glassworks town. **Cranberry Hall** (17 N. Main St., 609/654-2512), serving as the township's parks and recreation department, provides free self-guided walking tour brochures to the area's historic and architecturally significant structures. It's also a good place to pick up Pinelands' info. One of Medford Township's best-known attractions is **Kirby's Mill** (275 Church Rd., 609/654-7767), a 235-year-old working grist mill shut down in 1969. Today owned by the Medford Historical Society, plans are underway to construct an on-site period-style carriage house and restore some of the property's remaining historic structures. The mill hosts a small on-site museum.

Trimble Street, to Main Street's east, was once home to numerous Star Glassworks factory workers. Many of the original clapboard structures have since been restored.

Other Sights

A Medford staple since 1953, family-owned **Johnson's Corner Farm** (133 Church Rd., 609/654-8603, www.johnsonsfarm.com, daily 8 A.M.–7 P.M.) offers berry picking, hayrides, homemade pastries, and a seasonal ice cream window. There's also a Discovery Barnyard for young kids featuring climbing rocks, a pedal go-kart racetrack, and barnyard animals. Johnson's hosts events such as cotton-picking hayrides and Strawberry Jam Weekends throughout the year.

Woodford Cedar Run Wildlife Refuge (4 Sawmill Rd., 856/983-3329, www.cedarrun.org, Mon.–Sat. 10 A.M.–4 P.M., Sun. 1–4 P.M., $5 adult, $3 child) is a rescue and care center for injured wildlife. Founded in 1957 by James and Betty Woodford, the center—now run by their daughter, Jeanne—includes the interactive **Woodford Education Center,** home to amphibians, reptiles, and child-geared educational displays, wooded nature trails, and an outdoor compound for animals with insurmountable injuries.

Festivals and Events

A lot of towns hold holiday festivals, but not many can pull off Medford's December **Dickens Festival** (www.hmva.org), when the community completely transforms into a Victorian Christmas village. Area architecture and Medford's small-town feel provide an ideal setting for strolling period-dressed carolers, holiday music, a tree-lighting ceremony, and a visit from Santa himself. Additional yearly highlights include June's **Festival of Art and Music,** featuring jugglers, magicians, trolley rides, and multiple performance stages, and October's **Kirby's Mill Apple Festival,** with craft and blacksmith demos, an apple bake-off, and plenty of apple butter, apple cider doughnuts, and hot and cold drinks for purchase.

Shopping

For unique shopping options, stick to Medford Village. Although business along the village's traditional Main Street seems to be dwindling, the area is easy to navigate on foot and still hosts a nice array of specialty shops, interspersed with a few worthwhile eateries.

Creative Genius (32 N. Main St., 609/714-1131, www.creativegeniusonline.com) is a spacious store highlighting local artists' works, including photographs, handmade jewelry, and mosaics. The shop hosts art openings, trunk shows, and art workshops for both kids and adults year-round.

Voted 2007's Best South Jersey Knitting Store by the *Courier Post,* **The Knitting Room** (26 S. Main St., 609/654-9003, www.knittingroomnj.com) offers a wide selection of fine yarns and patterns, and hosts workshops on-site. **Catch the Wind** (23 S. Main St., 609/654-9393) sells, kites, wind chimes, and windsocks, along with Snow Babies and Disney collectibles. For antique and estate jewelry, including engagement rings, vintage compacts, and pocket watches from the 1920s, 1930s, and 1940s, check out **The Way We Were** (10 N. Main St., 609/654-0343, www.the-way-we-were.com).

Accommodations

The wonderfully kitsch **Flying W Airport Resort** (60 Fostertown Rd., 609/267-7673, www.flyingwairport.com, $89), built in the 1960s, includes an updated 38-room motel, restaurant, lounge, airplane landing strip, pilot gift shop, and an in-ground pool shaped like a Cessna. If this weren't enough, flying camps operate from the grounds during summer. The resort is quite popular with day guests who come for the restaurant's Sunday brunch, the summer doo-wop concerts, and then take off.

Conveniently located among Medford Village's shops and restaurants, the nine-bedroom **Iris Inn** (45 S. Main St., 609/654-7528, fax 609/714-0277, $95–175) serves a delicious complimentary and ever-changing breakfast prepared by Edie Wagner, innkeeper since 2006. The 1904 Victorian features modern amenities such as TV and a full bath in every room, and wireless Internet throughout.

Food

Medford offers a few good dining choices, both downtown and within the greater township.

Downtown Medford's **Mulberry Tea House** (60 S. Main St., 609/714-0640, www.mulberry teahouse.com, Tues.–Sun. 10 A.M.–4 P.M.) is an ideal place to spend a few afternoon hours. Bring some friends and snack on toast with Brie cheese ($7), or homemade crab and tomato quiche ($11), while sipping cups of gourmet tea.

In the heart of Medford Village, historic **Braddock's Tavern** (39 S. Main St., 609/654-1604, www.braddocks.com, lunch Tues.–Thurs. 11:30 A.M.–10 P.M., Fri.–Sat. 11:30 A.M.–11 P.M., Sun. noon–8 P.M., dinner Tues.–Thurs. 5–9 P.M., Fri.–Sat. 5–10 P.M., Sun. 4–8 P.M., $31–40) is an area institution that recently came under new ownership. While the colonial feel of this two-story eatery remains, traditional American entrées have been updated with a modern twist. The second-story veranda overlooking Main Street is a favorite dining locale.

Founded more than 30 years ago as the highly acclaimed French restaurant Beau Rivage, the newly reinvented **Beau Steak & Seafood** (Taunton Blvd., two miles east of 70/73 circle, 856/983-1999, www.beausteak .com, lunch Mon.–Fri. 11:30 A.M.–2:30 P.M., dinner Mon.–Sat. 4:30–9:30 P.M., Sun. 4–8 P.M., brunch Sun. 10:30 A.M.–2:30 P.M.) now offers a more global selection, including a raw bar and dishes like organic free-range chicken ($24) and Niman Ranch pork chops ($26). This lakeside establishment remains one of the region's most romantic, with a wine list of 400-plus bottles.

Getting There and Around

Medford Village is located along Route 541 north of Wharton State Forest. To reach the village and township from Chatsworth, take Route 532 west about 15.5 miles to Route 541 (where you'll find Medford Lakes), and head north for three miles. If traveling from Brendan T. Byrne State Forest, take Route 70 west for about 13 miles and turn south onto Route 541/Main Street.

SOUTH JERSEY

Far from New Jersey's exit-ramp and rest-stop reputation lies a quaint and countrified southern section that lives up to the Garden State motto. Often overlooked, South Jersey—as it's called locally—is a quiet reprieve filled with charming towns and back-road beauty, a treasure chest of environmental and cultural wealth only recently being discovered.

Stretching from the banks of the lower Delaware River eastward toward the Shore, and upward to include Camden and southwest Burlington Counties, South Jersey encompasses roughly one third of the state's landmass while housing only about one quarter of its residents. For many years the greater metropolitan region of South Jersey was little more than shopping centers and traffic jams, but revitalization has sparked new life in downtown centers from Mount Holly to Haddonfield. Still, there's great diversity among South Jersey's regions. The industrial cities of Gloucester and Pennsauken sit right down the road from the white-collar suburban stretch of Cherry Hill and Marlton, and the Delaware Bayshore—with vast wetlands that are a nature lover's paradise—is dotted with seafarers' settlements, strong with the scent of salty air. Seventeenth-century towns like Woodbury share county space with Washington Township, an area that has been developed for only 50 years, and in the counties of Gloucester, Salem, and Cumberland agriculture and farmlands are abundant. It's here the true Garden State can be found.

Visitors to New Jersey's southern half are surprised to find it so green and so well suited for outdoor recreation. Rivers and lakes are

© LAURA KINIRY

HIGHLIGHTS

◖ **Aunt Charlotte's Candies:** The downstairs candy store is a gorgeous sight, but it's what's happening upstairs that puts Aunt Charlotte's cocoa beans above the rest (page 288).

◖ **Camden Waterfront:** Roam the decks of a floating museum over three football fields in length, swim with sharks, and chill out to minor league ball with the Philadelphia skyline as your backdrop (page 294).

◖ **Haddonfield:** You'll find everything from snowboards to string lights to glass art while shopping in one of South Jersey's most picturesque, and historic, downtown centers (page 302).

◖ **Clementon Amusement Park and Splash World Water Park:** This century-old amusement park continues to pack 'em in with roller coaster thrill-rides, a new water park, and plenty of old-time favorites (page 307).

◖ **Mullica Hill:** South Jersey's filled with shopping ops, but no place embodies antiquing better than Mullica Hill Village. From the Yellow Garage to the Old Red Barn, it's a wonderful place to spend both money and an afternoon (page 315).

◖ **Cowtown Rodeo and Flea Market:** Cowboy up and mosey on down to the East Coast's longest continuously running rodeo, but don't let winter's inaction deter your spirits – there's always the flea market to wrangle you in (page 321).

◖ **Wheaton Arts & Cultural Center:** Glimpse into South Jersey's glass history with a guided Museum of American Glass tour and glassblowing demos. Or, sign up to create a paperweight of your own (page 332).

LOOK FOR ◖ TO FIND RECOMMENDED SIGHTS, ACTIVITIES, DINING, AND LODGING.

numerous in South Jersey's counties, and the scenic country roads of Gloucester and Cumberland Counties are perfect for two-wheeling. As the weather warms, stalls selling sweet Jersey corn, mouth-watering blueberries, and the plumpest and reddest of famous Jersey tomatoes appear by the roadside.

The southern half of New Jersey was originally settled by Lenape Indians and later Swedes, Finns, and Quakers, and it retains a history much different than the state's northern half. You won't drive far without coming

across signs for a Friends meeting house or passing a patch of land without a story to tell. In fact, there's such a distinction between South Jerseyans and their northern counterparts that you may think you've crossed into a different state. Down here the accents are softer, the pace a bit slower, and the tristate area includes Delaware and Pennsylvania rather than Connecticut and New York.

The state's industry planners believe that any new growth in New Jersey will take place in the south, although big-name businesses such

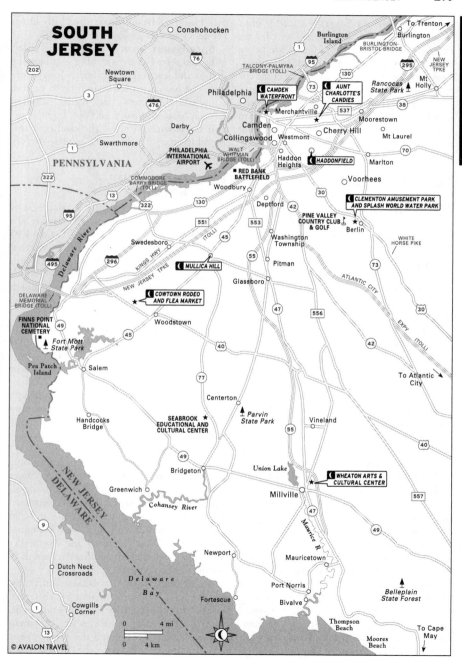

SOUTH JERSEY

To Trenton

Conshohocken

Burlington Island
Burlington
BURLINGTON-BRISTOL BRIDGE
NEW JERSEY TPKE

Newtown Square

TALCONY-PALMYRA BRIDGE (TOLL)

Philadelphia

(CAMDEN WATERFRONT

(AUNT CHARLOTTE'S CANDIES

Rancocas State Park
Mt Holly

Darby

Merchantville

Moorestown

Camden

Cherry Hill

Collingswood
Westmont

Mt Laurel

Swarthmore

PENNSYLVANIA

PHILADELPHIA INTERNATIONAL AIRPORT

WALT WHITMAN BRIDGE (TOLL)

Haddon Heights

(HADDONFIELD

Marlton

COMMODORE BARRY BRIDGE (TOLL)

■ RED BANK BATTLEFIELD

Woodbury

Voorhees

Deptford

(CLEMENTON AMUSEMENT PARK AND SPLASH WORLD WATER PARK

Delaware River

PINE VALLEY COUNTRY CLUB & GOLF

WHITE HORSE PIKE

Swedesboro

Washington Township

Berlin

KINGS HWY

(MULLICA HILL

Pitman

ATLANTIC CITY

Glassboro

DELAWARE MEMORIAL BRIDGE (TOLL)

NEW JERSEY TPKE

(COWTOWN RODEO AND FLEA MARKET

To Atlantic City

FINNS POINT NATIONAL CEMETERY

Woodstown

Fort Mott State Park

Pea Patch Island

Salem

Handcocks Bridge

Centerton

Parvin State Park

SEABROOK EDUCATIONAL AND CULTURAL CENTER

Vineland

NEW JERSEY
DELAWARE

Union Lake

(WHEATON ARTS & CULTURAL CENTER

Bridgeton

Greenwich

Millville

Cohansey River

Maurice R.

Dutch Neck Crossroads

Newport

Mauricetown

Delaware Bay

Belleplain State Forest

Port Norris

Cowgills Corner

Fortescue

Bivalve

Thompson Beach

To Cape May

Moores Beach

0   4 mi
0   4 km

© AVALON TRAVEL

as Subaru of America (Cherry Hill), NFL Films (Mount Laurel), and Sony Music (Sewell) have been based here for years. Houses are being built faster than they can be filled, and megastores are making their way onto some of the last remaining farmland—a potentially dangerous combination. Today, South Jersey is still part farmland, part suburbia, and it's often easy to feel you're in the middle of nowhere, or to put it another way, in a quiet refuge between a bustling urban center and weekend resorts.

PLANNING YOUR TIME

South Jersey offers several possibilities for day and weekend trips, although you should set aside at least four days to explore the region thoroughly. Consider giving a day to Burlington County, taking in the historic sites of Burlington City and Mount Holly. Chocolate lovers may want to detour into Camden County for a visit to Merchantville's Aunt Charlotte's Candies. Shoppers: head east into Marlton.

Pair Camden's waterfront attractions with an overnight stay at the Haddonfield Inn. The next day, stroll around Cooper River and tour Haddonfield's historic Indian King Tavern. Enjoy lunch along Haddon Avenue, and then take some time perusing Haddonfield's specialty shops and those in nearby Collingswood. Spend another evening in Haddonfield before heading home.

Gloucester, Salem, and Cumberland Counties host several worthwhile attractions, and they make a wonderful combined weekend trip. Begin Saturday morning bargain hunting at Cowtown Flea Market, and then head over to Fort Mott State Park along the Delaware River for a bit of historic exploring. Grab lunch at one of Salem's eateries or save your appetite for Mullica Hill, where you'll also want to set aside a few hours to browse the antique and collectible shops. When you're through, drive a short way east to Heritage Station and Winery for free wine tastings. A movie or performance at Pitman's excellent Broadway Theater will round out your night before booking into one of Deptford's hotels.

Still hungry? Hit up the nearby Philly Diner for delicious eats 24/7.

Spend your second day at Millville's Wheaton Arts Center watching glassblowing demos and learning about South Jersey folklore, but be sure to set aside time to explore Cumberland County's back roads, including stops at Mauricetown, East Point Lighthouse, and Greenwich—one of the country's few Revolutionary tea-burning towns—before heading home.

GETTING THERE AND AROUND

South Jersey is conveniently located east of Philadelphia and northeast of Delaware. To reach South Jersey from Delaware, take I-95 north to the Delaware Memorial Bridge. From Philadelphia International Airport, travel south along I-95 to Commodore Barry Bridge, which drops you onto Route 322, or travel north along I-95 towards Ben Franklin Bridge into Camden County.

Those traveling from North Jersey can use the New Jersey Turnpike, debarking at Exit 4 (Mount Laurel) or Exit 5 (Hwy. 541, midway between Burlington City and Mount Holly), or take I-295 or Route 130 south from Trenton. Outside of rush hour, when the highway's packed, I-295 is the quickest route. I wouldn't normally recommend Route 130 (it is a bumpy road lined by abandoned shopping centers), but for hungry travelers, it's the best route.

South Jersey's scenic drives include Route 47, from Deptford east to the Jersey Shore (although Route 55 is a quicker no-hassle alternative), and King's Highway's southern stretch, running north-south parallel to I-295 from Woodbury down to Delaware Memorial Bridge. East-West Route 49 and Route 45's southern portion, from Mullica Hill south to Salem, are also pleasant.

NJ Transit (www.njtransit.com) offers extensive bus service throughout South Jersey, connecting the majority of cities and towns, and also providing service to Philly. Towns along Haddon Avenue and the White-Horse Pike are linked to Philly by the **PATCO** (www

.ridepatco.org) high-speed line. PATCO connects with NJ Transit's **Atlantic City Line,** departing from Philadelphia's 30th Street Station, in Lindenwold, providing access to southern

Shore communities. NJ Transit's **River LINE** (www.riverline.com) connects Trenton with Burlington City and Camden, stopping along the way at various Delaware River towns.

Southwest Burlington County

Bordering the Delaware River northeast of Philadelphia, southern Burlington County is teeming with revitalized historic towns and modern commercial spreads. Route 130 runs north-south along the county's western border, linking Central Jersey's capital region with south Jersey's Salem County. While not as direct as Route 295, it offers a slower pace. For something more scenic, travel Route 537 west from Mount Holly, passing Victorian homes and through tiny downtown centers before intersecting with Route 73, which carries you south towards the lower Pinelands and the Shore. Along this route you'll find several restaurants, shopping centers, and hotels.

Getting There

From Philadelphia International Airport take I-95 north, crossing at either the Talcony-Palmyra Bridge (Route 73) or the Burlington-Bristol Bridge, which drops you just south of Burlington City's Historic District.

BURLINGTON

Burlington was the capital of West Jersey, and for a brief time was the county seat. Today, it's often overlooked by travelers en route from Trenton to Cherry Hill. But if you're a history buff or a fan of colonial architecture—the kind found in Williamsburg, Virginia, or Philadelphia's Society Hill—then Burlington

© LAURA KINIRY

High Street in downtown Burlington

is a must-see. The city boasts a one-square-mile historic district that has been carefully maintained and preserved and lists over 40 historic sights. Many of its buildings are red brick, trimmed in colonial shades of green, red, and blue, and date back over 200 years. Its convenient riverfront location made it a bustling port town in the early 1800s, but Burlington was soon bypassed for Philadelphia, further downriver but closer to shore. Still, many notable figures continued their association with Burlington, assuring the city a settled place in history.

New Jersey Firsts

Founded in 1677 by English Quakers, Burlington touts a large number of New Jersey firsts. Among them is the first recorded English settlement in New Jersey (1624) and the first recorded murder, both taking place on **Burlington Island,** a large landmass easily viewed from the city's one-mile riverfront walkway. At various times the island housed a school and an amusement park. Today, it sits vacant, but it is open to development. **The Revell House** (1685) at 213 Wood Street is the oldest building in Burlington, and is thought to be among the county's oldest residences. At 301 High Street is New Jersey's oldest continuously operating pharmacy, **The Burlington Pharmacy.** Now known as **Wheatley's,** it's believed to have been a stop on the Underground Railroad. And less than a block west on High Street is **Temple B'nai Israel,** one of South Jersey's oldest synagogues.

Neighborhoods

Burlington was one of the first planned towns in the United States. Richard Noble, an original colonist, mapped out the city in a well-laid grid stemming from High Street. Settlers were separated into neighborhoods according to their religious sects. To High Street's south went the **London** sect, and to the right the **Yorkshires.** These neighborhoods are still in use today, and Pearl Street, near the Delaware River, displays signs identifying them.

Historic Sites

Burlington's historic downtown centers around High Street, where a number of sites date back to the 18th century. Though some establishments no longer exist, their history is worth noting, and walking through this district is like taking a step back in time—an experience I recommend.

While strolling through the downtown district, take note of **206 High Street,** the former site of Isaac Collins Print Shop. At this spot, Benjamin Franklin printed New Jersey's first colonial currency. Though no longer a print shop, a historic plaque makes it easy to identify. On the southeast corner of High and Broad Streets is the former site of the **Blue Anchor Inn.** Established in 1750, it's now a seniors housing complex. History tells of an arm-wrestling match taking place here between then–presidential candidate Abraham Lincoln and one-day president Ulysses S. Grant. The **Ulysses S. Grant House** (1856), at 309 Wood Street, was home to General Grant and his family during the Civil War. It was here Grant learned President Lincoln had been shot at Ford's Theatre. On hearing the news, he rushed to the Blue Anchor Inn to catch a train to Washington, D.C. Two blocks north of Grant's house, at 114 East Union Street, is the **Oliver Cromwell House** (1798). This is the final residence of Cromwell, a black Revolutionary War soldier who crossed the Delaware with General George Washington on December 25, 1776.

The birth homes of two of Burlington's most famous historical sons stand side-by-side along High Street between Broad and Federal Streets. At 457 High Street is the **James Fenimore Cooper House** (1782). Cooper, author of *The Leatherstocking Tales,* was born on September 15, 1789. His family moved to what would become Cooperstown, New York, a year later. Next door at 459 High Street is the **Captain James Lawrence House** (1742). Captain Lawrence, a naval war hero whose dying words, "Tell the men to fire faster and not to give up the ship," were paraphrased "Don't Give Up the Ship" and adopted as the U.S. Navy's motto,

was born here October 1, 1781. Both houses, along with the **Bard-Howe House** (circa 1743) at 453 High Street, are part of the **Burlington County Historical Society** complex (451 High St., 609/386-4773, fax 609/386-4828, Tues.–Sat. 1–5 P.M., $3 adult, $1.50 age 12 and under). Forty-minute tours of the three homes ($3 adult, $1.50 child) are given every 50 minutes during the hours the Society is open.

Riverfront Park

Situated along Burlington City's downtown waterfront is mile-long Riverfront Park, a perfect picnic spot. The park hosts several events throughout the year, including a seasonal farmers market and an evening summer concert series. There's an amphitheater on-site, along with a permit-required seasonal boat launch towards its north end. Its southern end offers views of both historic Burlington Island and the Burlington-Bristol Bridge, connecting New Jersey with Pennsylvania. Riverfront Park serves as a central point for the **Delaware River Heritage Trail,** a 50-mile multiuse "work in progress" that, when finished, will form a loop between New Jersey and Pennsylvania.

Boat permits are available April–October at the park on weekends (8 A.M.–4 P.M.) or at **City Hall** (525 High St., Mon.–Fri. 9 A.M.–4 P.M.) during the week. Permits cost $15 per day for New Jersey residents, $25 per day for others.

Entertainment and Events

For a historic overview of the city given by guides in colonial garb, stop by the circa-1876 **Tour & Guide Office at the Carriage House** (12 Smith Ln., 609/386-3993, www.tourburlington.org). Tours are offered Fridays, Saturdays, and Sundays at 11:30 A.M. and 2 P.M. April–November ($5 adult, $3 senior, $3 child under 12), or by appointment throughout the year. Each tour lasts about 1.5 hours and includes moderate walking. If you'd rather explore the city's sights at your own pace, visit www.tourburlington.org/Us.html or call the Tour & Guide Office for a self-guided walking map.

The **Riverfront Summer Concert Series**

(Promenade Park, 609/386-0200 ext. 135) takes place Thursday nights in July and August. Admission is free, and music runs the gamut from jazz to big band to rock. For added comfort, bring along your own blanket and chairs. Call for performance schedules.

August's **Festival of Lights** (www.tourburlington.org/DoEvents.html) features arts and crafts, food, and live music throughout the day, culminating in an illuminated boat parade and fireworks display over the Delaware River.

Want the inside scoop on Burlington history? Take the annual December **Holiday House Tour** (609/386-7125) for a look into more than a dozen private residences and historical sites.

Shopping

Other than a handful of antique stores and Burlington Coat Factory's flagship store, Burlington's shopping options are mostly limited to commercial strips along Route 130.

ANTIQUE AND SPECIALTY STORES

Philip's Furniture and Antiques (307 High St., 609/386-7125, philsantiques.com) displays bedroom sets, sofas, armoires, cabinets, and dining-room tables on three floors. The shop is a community staple, located in Burlington for over 20 years. Farther east on High Street, **Burlington Antiques Emporium** (424 High St., 609/747-8333, www.antiquesnj.com, daily 10 A.M.–5 P.M.) offers wares from more than 80 antique dealers in over 14,000 square feet of space. The selection here is superb: grandfather clocks, antiquarian books, country decor, and Depression glass are among the thousands of salable items.

THE BURLINGTON COAT FACTORY OUTLET STORE

What began in 1972 as a single outlet grew into the nationwide Burlington Coat Factory (1250 Rte. 130 N., 609/386-3314, www.coat.com, Mon.–Fri. 10 A.M.–9 P.M., Sat. 10 A.M.–6 P.M., Sun. 11 A.M.–6 P.M.), with over 300 stores in 42 states. This is the original: a large, nondescript factory producing everything from baby products to home furnishings and, of course, coats. The Coat Factory is one of Burlington County's top 10 employers.

Food

Burlington hosts some lovely downtown restaurant and a couple of casual eateries along Route 130.

On the corner of High and Broad Streets in downtown's historic district is the **Birches** (345 High St., 609/239-5111, www.birches burlington.com, Tues.–Sat. 11:30 A.M.–10 P.M., closed Sun.–Mon., $19–39), formerly home to Thommy G's. Built as a bank, the building has retained many original touches, including the steel vault, available to private parties, and a wall of teller booths separating the bar from a more formal dining area, decorated with potted trees and white linens. Food offerings include a variety of meat, fish, and pasta dishes, along with a chef's tasting ($25) of three tapas-size selections like spicy tuna rolls or lobster potato skins.

Located on the corner of High and Pearl Streets in Burlington's downtown historic district, **Café Gallery** (219 High St. at Pearl St., 609/386-6150, www.cafegalleryburlington .com, lunch Mon.–Sat. 11:30 A.M.–4 P.M., dinner daily from 5 P.M., brunch Sun. 11:30 A.M.–3 P.M.) has been a community staple for 30 years. Serving French-American fare and offering sweeping Delaware River views from its second level, the café doubles as an art gallery, displaying works by local artists throughout its two stories. Request a seat outdoors near the fountain during warmer months, and don't miss Sunday brunch; it's spectacular.

There are plenty of diners along Route 130. Try the **Prince Inn Diner** (4520 Rte. 130, 609/386-5522) or further south, the **Harvest Diner-Restaurant** (2602 Rte. 130, 856/829-4499).

MOUNT HOLLY

Like nearby Burlington City, Mount Holly is built on history. A mix of storefront cottages, 18th-century structures, and darkened pubs all hovering at sidewalk's edge, its downtown

center is surprisingly pleasing. Consider taking a couple of hours to stroll High Street, perusing the shops, savoring the history, and stopping for a bite to eat before heading on to outlying attractions.

High Street

High Street, Mount Holly's main boulevard, is home to several notable 18th-century structures. These include **The Friend's Meeting House** (High and Garden Sts.), host to New Jersey's 1779 State Legislature assemblies during the township's temporary reign as state capital. A year earlier, the Meeting House was used as a commissary by British troops. Cleaver marks left by their butcher still adorn some of the benches.

Mount Holly is Burlington's county seat, and the township's original **Historic Burlington County Courthouse** stands at 120 High Street. Designed by Samuel Lewis, whose work includes Philadelphia's Congress Hall, the courthouse is a notable local landmark as well as a striking example of colonial architecture.

The Historic Burlington County Prison Museum

Designed by Washington Monument architect Robert Mills, Burlington County Prison (128 High St., 609/265-5476 or 609/518-7667, Thurs.–Sat. 10 A.M.–4 P.M., Sun. noon–4 P.M., $4 adult, $2 child) opened in 1811 and operated for 155 years before becoming a museum. When it closed it was the oldest running prison in the United States and was declared a National Historic Landmark in 1986. The structure features stone and brick walls and a vaulted ceiling of poured cement, and it's both fireproof and virtually maintenance-free. Not much about it has changed over the years—even its enormous front door and hinges are original. Docent-led tours providing historic insight, including details on prison life, are offered during open hours.

Smithville Mansion

Woodworking machinist and Bicycle Railroad

developer Hezekiah B. Smith and his wife Agnes owned Smithville Mansion (49 Rancocas Rd., 609/265-5068) during the late 1800s. Situated within Smithville Park on Mount Holly's northern outskirts, the Greek Revival mansion was once the center of a "model industrial town," created by Smith—considered a pioneer of sustainable employment—for his employees. The town included a factory complex, a dormitory, an opera house, a schoolhouse, and a public park for picnics. It was successful for decades after Smith's death in 1877, until the Great Depression. Many of its buildings remain.

Tours of the Smithville Mansion, listed on both the New Jersey and National Registers of Historic Places, take place Wednesday and Sunday 1–3 P.M. May–October ($5 adult, $4 senior, $3 student), and a popular evening candlelight tour is offered in December ($8 adult, $6 senior). The mansion grounds are open for unguided visits Monday–Friday 8 A.M.–5 P.M.

Smithville Park

As township parks go, this one's a pleaser. With 280 acres, Smithville Park (Smithville Rd., 609/265-5068, daily dawn–dusk) is home to Smithville Mansion and nearly five miles of nature trails, 170 acres of woodland, and a 22-acre lake popular with canoeists, kayakers, and fishers. Short hikes include the 0.5-mile **Ravine Nature Trail,** an interpretive trail incorporating a 600-foot floating path. Hikers can hike the trail down the park's main drive just past the mansion, or begin at the park entrance. Be on the lookout for deer, rabbits, red foxes, and wild turkeys—frequent park visitors—along with great blue herons and red-tailed hawks. Horses are allowed on the yellow-marked trail, accessible along West Rail Avenue or across the main road within Smithville Woods, which also hosts a birding vista. While there are no boat rental shops on or near park property, you can bring your own watercraft to launch on the lake or along Rancocas Creek. In winter the park allows snowshoeing and cross-country skiing.

Smithville Park is centerpiece to Burlington County's **Kinkora Trail,** a proposed 13-mile rails-to-trails project that when finished will link the Delaware River with the Pinelands.

Woolman House

The Woolman House (99 Branch St., www .woolmancentral.com) stands as a memorial and information center on the life of John Woolman, a Mount Holly resident, devout Quaker minister, and abolitionist well known for his journals condemning slavery. A small 18th-century brick structure located in one of Woolman's former apple orchards, the home is run by the John Woolman Memorial Association and is open for visits. Hours vary; call 609/267-3226 for more information.

Events

Still fairly new is Mount Holly's annual **Fire & Ice Festival** (www.mainstreetmountholly .com), where competing amateur ice carvers sculpt original artworks from 300-pound ice "vlocks." If it's warmth you're after, head indoors and test your inner strength in a chili-eating contest.

Shopping

Mount Holly's best shopping opportunities are housed within a small specialty village at the east end of High Street. The town is also home to a wonderful antique store. Since Mount Holly is considered an urban enterprise zone, state sales tax rates are cut in half.

Behind Robin's Nest restaurant stands the colorful **Mill Race Village** (www.millrace shops.com, www.millracevillage.com, Wed.– Fri. 11 A.M.–6 P.M., Sat. 10 A.M.–6 P.M., Sun. noon–4 P.M., closed Mon.–Tues.), nearly a dozen small specialty shops housed within a restored colonial mill village. Retailers include **Teddies of Mount Holly** (609/702-9386), stocked with artisanal teddy bears from around the globe. The two women running the shop also host bear-making workshops and tea parties. **Pinelands Folk Music & Basketry Center** (609/518-7600) carries mountain and hammered dulcimers, autoharps, flutes, mandolins, and various other folk instruments. Mary Carty, a descent of the region's original Piney Lenape inhabitants, makes all of the handcrafted baskets that are for sale. Basket-weaving workshops and private instrument lessons are available. **The Spirit of Christmas** (609/518-1700) features Byers' Choice figurines and Snowbabies, along with hundreds of other collectibles and ornaments, while **The Village Quilter** (609/265-0011) supplies quilting fabrics, tools, and instruction. Though specializing in kids' books and tween tales, the excellent **Bookery** (609/845-1396) also carries best-sellers and local reads.

On the downtown corner of Rancocas Road and King Street is the enormous **Center Stage Antiques** (609/261-0602, www.centerstage antiques.com). Center Stage specializes in antique furniture and collectibles. Come here for that Persian rug or Victorian love seat you've been pining for.

Accommodations

Conveniently located midway between Burlington and Mount Holly, the **Hampton Inn Mount Holly** (2024 Rte. 541, Westampton, 609/702-9888, fax 609/261-9370, www .hamptoninnmountholly.com, $139–159) provides clean quarters and free in-room movies. With an on-site setup that includes Internet, printing, copying, and fax machines, the inn also caters to business travelers. Complimentary 24-hour coffee, a hot breakfast bar, and seasonal heated pool access are included in the room rates.

Food and Nightlife

Mount Holly's restaurants mix dining and drinks, and there are several satisfying options.

Housed in a corner two-story cottage at the end of High Street, **The Robin's Nest** (2 Washington St., 609/261-6149, www.mount holly.com/robinsnest, lunch Mon.–Sat. 11 A.M.–2:30 P.M., dinner Tues.–Thurs. 4:30–9 P.M., Fri. 4:30–9:30 P.M., Sat. 5–9:30 P.M., Sun. 10 A.M.–6 P.M., $19–37) serves French-American cuisine in a cozy setting. If you're not drawn in by the ambiance, you will be by the display of daily fresh-baked desserts. Alfresco creek-side dining is available in warmer months, as is a waterfront happy hour and live music on Fridays.

Bridgetown Pub (44 High St., 609/261-6900, www.bridgetownpub.com, Mon.–Thurs. 11:30 A.M.–11 P.M., Fri. 11:30 A.M.–1 A.M., Sat. 3 P.M.–1 A.M., $7–15) serves some of the best French fries around, and that's saying a lot. Thick and crisp, cooked to perfection, it's obvious the kitchen cares. That's how the whole place feels, like someone took time to do things right. There's just enough new colonial decor in the low-lit space that it is not overdone, but if you want to see something special, head to the restrooms. It's easy to spend hours snacking on cheese fondue ($6) and fried clam strips ($5) and sipping on pints of Yuengling, so if you have somewhere to be, request one of the two brightly lit window-side tables. A bar next to the main dining area showcases live music on weekends.

Mount Holly's swanky two-story **High Street Grill** (68 High St., 609/265-9199, www.highstreetgrill.net, lunch Mon.–Sat. 11:30 A.M.–2:30 P.M., dinner Sun.–Thurs. 5:30–9 P.M., Fri.–Sat. 5:30–10 P.M.) features a downstairs tavern and an upstairs formal dining area. Dishes range from grilled Hawaiian butterfish ($21) to a veggie and polenta napoleon ($18), but the real highlight here is the piano player on weekends. Music begins at 7 P.M. in the main dining room, but drinkers needn't worry: The tavern also features a weekend late-night keyboardist.

RANCOCAS STATE PARK

One of New Jersey's less-visited state parks, 1,252-acre Rancocas State Park offers quiet woodlands ideal for birding and trail walking. Douglas firs and oak trees line the pathways, and Rancocas Creek meanders along the park's south portion, adding movement to a serene, oft-deserted landscape. Watch for white-tailed deer, beavers, and rabbits, especially within the park's 58-acre natural area. A nature center as well as an Indian reservation and museum are accessible from Rancocas Road, along the park's western border.

Rancocas Nature Center

Housed within an old whitewashed farmhouse, **Rancocas Nature Center** (794 Rancocas Rd., Mount Holly, 609/261-2495, www.njaudubon.org/Centers/Rancocas/, Tues.–Sat. 9 A.M.–5 P.M., Sun. noon–5 P.M. Mar. 16–Nov. 14, Tues.–Sat. 9 A.M.–4 P.M., Sun. noon–4 P.M. Nov. 15–Mar. 15, closed Mon.) is run by the local Audubon Chapter and its helpful volunteers. The center provides pamphlets and handouts on Rancocas State Park's hikes and wildlife, and it includes a small classroom, a nature store, and a museum with live native reptiles. Scheduled bird-watching excursions leave year-round from the trailheads outside. Check the website for updates.

Rankokus Indian Reservation

Just south of the nature center is Rankokus Indian Reservation (609/261-4747, www.powhatan.org), a 350-acre land parcel leased by the Powhatan Renape Nation, the area's original inhabitants. Along with a re-created traditional outdoor village and a quiet nature trail, the property is home to the **American Indian Heritage Museum,** where modern sculptures, wood carvings, and sketches done by American Indian artists and life-size dioramas depicting the lives of various Indian tribes are displayed. A gift shop selling woven rugs, feather head-dresses, and stationery is also on-site. Combined reservation and museum tours are offered the first and third Saturdays of the month 10 A.M.–3 P.M., and Tuesdays and Thursdays by appointment ($5 adult, $3 child).

Powhatan Renape Indian Arts Festival

The American Indian Arts Festival ($10 adult, $5 child, free under age 5) takes place on Rankokus Indian Reservation twice annually, spring and fall. Highlights include storytelling, more than 150 traditional and modern Indian arts and crafts, live music and dancing, and a variety of native foods. For more information,

including exact dates, visit the Powhatan Renape Nation website at www.powhatan.org.

MOORESTOWN

Any town voted the nation's "Best Place to Live" by *Money* magazine is worth a drive through. While there's not a lot to do in Moorestown (even the Moorestown Mall is a bit lackluster) there is some lovely architecture to see. Stately Victorians and Federal-style homes line either side of Route 537, set far back from the street on multiple-acre plots. Many former residences in old Moorestown (there's a more modern section to the east) have been converted into businesses. Downtown, Route 537 turns into Main Street, a row of brick buildings and Victorians housing mostly service centers and a few retail stores.

Philly Soft Pretzel Factory

Never pass up a doughy and dense Philly soft pretzel, ever. The Philly Soft Pretzel Factory (131 W. Main St., 856/642-1135, www.phillysoftpretzelfactory.com, Mon.–Fri. 6 A.M.–6 P.M., Sat. 6 A.M.–5 P.M., Sun. 8 A.M.–3 P.M.) is worth a pit stop. Besides, it'll save you a trip across the Delaware.

MERCHANTVILLE

Along Route 527 south of Moorestown lies Merchantville, another attractive borough of spacious Victorians, many with mansard roofs and intricate trimmings. At Centre Street and Maple Avenue, the borough's main intersection, is a small downtown strip with an Italian restaurant worth visiting, but you may consider saving your appetite for Merchantville's main attraction: a two-story candy store and chocolate factory west on Maple.

The Collins House

Housed in a historic brick building just north of downtown, the spacious **Collins House Restaurant** (2 S. Centre St., 856/661-8008, www.thecollinshouse.net, lunch and dinner Mon.–Fri. 11 A.M.–11 P.M., brunch Sat.–Sun. 10 A.M.–3 P.M., $11–29) serves internationally inspired Italian cuisine accompanied by an extensive wine list. This sister spot to Bordentown's Farnsworth House also cooks up a popular weekend brunch that includes frittatas, omelets, and spinach-stuffed phyllo triangles ($9).

◖ Aunt Charlotte's Candies

Can candy really be so special? Aunt Charlotte's Candies (5 W. Maple Ave., 856/662-0058, www.auntcharlottescandy.com) makes me believe so. With row upon row of boxed chocolates, a glass counter bursting with sweets, and clear giant bowls filled with twist-wrapped Ice Blue Mints and Cinnamon Buttons, I'm already in. But once I see the second-floor chocolate factory, I'm hooked. Don't expect an Oompa-Loompa to escort you up the stairs; you have to ask to visit the factory. They might say there's nothing up there to see, but insist. Drizzling syrupy chocolate and trays of nonpareils alone are worth a look.

Aunt Charlotte's got its start in 1920 when Charles Brooks Oakford Sr. began making candy at his home and selling it from the back of his truck before purchasing a small storefront. When Oakford died in 1945, his son, Charles Brooks Oakford Jr., took over the business and moved it to its current location, at the time a one-story grain shop. He and his wife, Bunny, added a second floor, which became the chocolate factory, in 1984. Today, a third generation of Oakfords runs the business.

While Willy Wonka–land it's not, you can't help but leave here happy.

MOUNT LAUREL

Situated along Route 73 where I-295 and Exit 4 of the New Jersey Turnpike meet, Mount Laurel is a popular stopping point for Eastern Seaboard travelers, and an affordable overnight alternative for business people doing work in Philly. The township is a mix of residential property and industrial parks, along with several hotels and fast-food chains. There is not a lot to see, but for convenience it's hard to beat.

PAWS Farm Nature Center

Most kids don't make it out the back door at **PAWS Farm Nature Center** (1105 Hainesport–Mount Laurel Rd., 856/778-8795, www.pawsfarm.com, Wed.–Sun. 10 A.M.–4 P.M., $6 adult, $4 child). They're too busy playing with the trains, games, and toys available inside. Too bad, because it's through the back room past Al the ferret and hedgehog Inessa that the real fun begins. PAWS is home to over 80 birds and animals, including Tipperary the miniature horse and a donkey named Cocomo, as well as a butterfly garden, hay jump, a dairy barn where kids can pretend grocery shop, and a farmhouse with a play veterinary clinic.

PAWS is intended for children eight and under and offers educational programs year-round.

Rancocas Woods

Near Mount Holly's Rancocas State Park is log-cabin shopping village Rancocas Woods (123 Creek Rd., 856/222-0346, www.rancocaswoods.net, daily 10 A.M.–5 P.M.), home to several specialty stores and art galleries. Businesses include used bookstore **Second Time Books** (856/234-9335), lace curtain and Byers Carolers purveyor **Craft Coleidescope** (856/778-0869), the **Toy Train Emporium** (856/273-0606), and the highly respected **William Spencer** (118 Creek Rd., 856/235-1830, www.williamspencerinc.com), a lighting and furniture center and Colonial Williamsburg shop.

Rancocas Woods hosts a monthly craft show (856/235-1830) on the second Saturday of each month 8 A.M.–4 P.M. The village also runs an annual candlelight shop tour in early December.

Accommodations

Easily accessible from New Jersey's major roadways, Mount Laurel is a smart place to stop for an overnight stay. Nearly a dozen lodging choices cluster around Exit 4 of the New Jersey Turnpike.

For an affordable overnight stay try the **Super 8 Mount Laurel** (554 Fellowship Rd., 856/802-2800, www.super8.com). Rooms are a bit small and open to the outdoors, but this may soon change: The motel closed in May 2008 for major renovations and is expected to reopen in early 2009. Pets are welcome for a small deposit. Call ahead for new rates.

The 10-story ◖ **Radisson Hotel Mount Laurel** (915 Rte. 73 N., 856/234-7194) features well-kept spacious rooms and a staff that's unbelievably helpful. As of 2008 the hotel is undergoing major renovations, including the addition of an indoor water park, so things can get a bit noisy. Hopefully that'll end soon, though with some of the most comfortable beds around you may hardly notice. There's a restaurant and sports bar on-site, and pets are welcome for a one-time $50 fee. Call for updated rates.

The **Courtyard by Marriott** (1000 Century Pkwy., 856/273-4400, $169–184) offers sizable rooms with work spaces and high-speed Internet. There's a heated indoor pool for relaxing, along with an on-site restaurant and 24-hour market. This smoke-free hotel has earned the EPA's Energy Star label for its energy efficiency.

MARLTON

Though Marlton is only a fraction of Evesham Township, their names are practically interchangeable. On the surface, Marlton—a word derived from the area's former marl pits—bears resemblance to nearby Cherry Hill, most notably in Route 70 shopping centers and traffic congestion. But unlike the latter, Marlton has retained an affinity with its natural surroundings, while also offering some of South Jersey's best shopping options.

Shopping

Shopping is what you do in Marlton, and thankfully, you can do it well. Route 73's **The Promenade at Sagemore** (Rte. 73, Sagemore Dr., 856/810-0085, www.thepromenadenj .com) is the township's best for one-stop shopping both in selection and appearance. The fashionable open-air market hosts such favorites as Lilly Pulitzer (Section E-02, 856/489-6751), J. Crew (Section A-12, 856/988-9046), Apple Computer (Section A-16, 856/810-3712), and Harry and David (Section E-03, 856/797-2030)

among its more than three dozen stores. Just north of the Promenade is the smaller, slightly older **Marlton Square** (300 Rte. 73), home to Pottery Barn (856/489-7110), Williams Sonoma (856/489-3941) and Chico's (856/988-1117). Across Route 73 is South Jersey's only **REI** outdoor store (501 Rte. 73 S., 856/810-1938).

Food

You won't go hungry in Marlton: There's food for every budget, ranging from fast-food chains to fine dining, but the following are some of your best options.

Sure, **Whole Foods Market** (Greentree Sq., Rte. 70 and Greentree Rd., 856/797-1115, www .wholefoodsmarket.com) is a chain, but it's one of the few large-scale specialty markets in South Jersey and a good place to shop for natural, organic, and ethnic foods. Situated alongside the Marlton Traffic Circle, **Olga's Diner** (Rtes. 70 and 73, 609/596-1700, closes daily 12:30 A.M., $17) makes a nice meeting point between South and Central Jersey. Food reviews are mixed, but desserts get high ratings. As of 2008 there are plans to eliminate the Marlton Circle, and Olga's owner is looking to sell; better squeeze into a booth while you can. Route 70's retro **Marlton Diner** (781 W. Rte. 70, 856/797-8858, daily 24 hours) gets plenty packed with locals who rave about the food and prices.

Tucked within the Marlton Crossing Shopping Center is the upscale **Food for Thought** (129 Rte. 70, 856/797-1126, Mon.– Sat. 11:30 A.M.–2:30 P.M. and 5:30–9:30 P.M., Sun. 4–8 P.M., $19–32), a New American BYO using fresh organic ingredients to create some of South Jersey's best dishes. Lavishly decorated dining rooms more than make up for the lackluster exterior.

Housed within a converted Victorian along Marlton's tiny Main Street, **Marlton Tavern** (65 E. Main St., 856/985-2424, daily 11 A.M.–2 A.M., $15–23) offers American eats in a relaxed setting. A downstairs pub and sun porch are ideal for those wanting to dine without missing the game. For something more intimate, request one of the two upstairs dining rooms.

Camden County

While often considered part of greater Philadelphia, Camden County maintains a personality all its own. South Jersey's most cosmopolitan region is known as much for its affluent communities as for Camden, one of the most crime-ridden cities in the United States. Haddon Avenue, one of the county's main thoroughfares, began as a Native American trail before becoming a toll road connecting Camden with Haddonfield. Today, Haddon Avenue is a shopping and dining destination, featuring award-winning restaurants, lax coffeehouses, and stretches ideal for window browsing and people-watching. The White Horse Pike, running parallel just south, offers an alternate route to Atlantic City for those wanting to avoid a portion of Atlantic City Expressway traffic. Traveling though former railway towns and past one of New Jersey's oldest operating amusement parks, it's also much more scenic. The two roads join together in Berlin, continuing through the vast Pinelands before overcrowding with restaurants, motels, and wineries as it nears the Shore.

CHERRY HILL

It's a given that you'll hit traffic in Cherry Hill, and when you do, you may find it hard to believe this was all once farmland—especially when you come upon the next stoplight, shopping center, or sign pointing the way to a housing development. But before it became a congested nightmare, Cherry Hill was known not only for its agriculture: It was considered an entertainment destination, second only to Atlantic City in South Jersey and the southern Shore.

Today, Cherry Hill is a residential and commercial suburb, home to numerous corporate centers and dozens of chain retailers sprawled along Route 70 with nearly nowhere left to build. Long without a cohesive town center, the township recently constructed its own version of one—an outdoor lifestyle center with 530,000 square feet (and counting) of retail space—where Garden State Racetrack once

stood, though locals continue to flock to their churches, synagogues, and the mall for a sense of community. Cherry Hill does offer a nice array of dining choices, along with some fine entertainment and lodging options. It also runs parallel to 345-acre **Cooper River Park,** the best outdoor stretch in Camden County.

Market Place Garden State Park

Cherry Hill's new downtown center (intersection of Routes 70, 38, and 295, www.gardenstatepark .net) stands at the heart of the community, where Garden State Race Track operated on and off for more than 50 years. Although it bears little resemblance to its former incarnation (save for a bronze horse statue commissioned during the track's 1985 reconstruction that now sits in an undeveloped field), this retail and residential mecca attracts just as many crowds. Dubbed a "power center" by its promoters, Market Place boasts dozens of big-name shops housed in eye-catching brick structures, all interspaced with outdoor paths and open space. Shops include Wegmans gourmet grocery, Barnes & Noble, Best Buy, and Dick's Sporting Goods dispersed among two distinct shopping centers. A trolley transports visitors between them.

Sights

Springdale Farms (1638 S. Springdale Rd., 856/424-8674, www.springdalefarms.com, daily 8 A.M.–6 P.M.), Cherry Hill's only remaining working farm, has been in operation for more than 50 years. Veggies, fruits, and herbs are all grown on-site. You can also pick up Jersey-made wine, cheese, gardening tools, or one of their wonderful homemade pies, over 60 varieties that change with the seasons. During fall the farm hosts hayrides and a corn maze, and events like a Strawberry Social and Fall Harvest Weekend take place annually.

The **Holocaust Education Center** (Jewish Community Center, 1301 Springdale Rd., 856/751-9500 ext. 224, www.holocaust educationcenter.com, Sun.–Thurs. 10 A.M.–

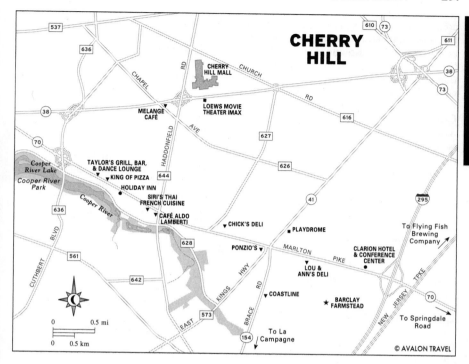

© AVALON TRAVEL

5 P.M., Fri. 10 A.M.–5 P.M., closed Sat. and Jewish holidays) hosts a permanent display of donated objects, letters, and photographs from World War II Holocaust survivors and their relatives. Although more of a community exhibit then a fully fleshed museum, the center offers valuable insight into the Holocaust on a local level. Those interested in individual research can visit the on-site lending library.

Built in 1816 by Quaker farmer Joseph Thorn, **Barclay Farmstead** (209 Barclay Ln., 856/795-6225, www.barclayfarmstead.org, Tues.–Fri. noon–4 P.M., $2 adult, $1 child) is listed on both the National and State Registers of Historic Places. In the township's care since 1974, the land boasts nature trails, a community garden, and a Federal-style brick farmhouse open for tours. Year-round events include a Living History Day, where visitors can churn butter and saw logs, and a summer music series under the stars. Don't be surprised if you see more than one "Barclay" sign en route to the farm—the surrounding development and a nearby shopping center share the name. In addition to its regular hours, the farmstead is open the first Sunday of each month 1–4 P.M.

Cooper River Park

I'm smitten with Cooper River Park (856/795-7275, www.ccparks.com). It's not just because my dad and I used to take walks here when he worked at nearby Unisys, or because I spent Philadelphia's 1985 Live Aid concert here listening to Madonna and Tina Turner across the Delaware River, or because my mother and I held Hands Across America on the park's western side. Cooper River is just a great park, that's all. At nearly 350 acres it hosts a four-mile multiuse loop trail, baseball diamonds, volleyball courts, even a miniature golf course (856/665-0505). The river itself is an excellent spot for sailing and plays host to major crew events, including the century-old **IRA National Collegiate Rowing Championships** (www.ecac.org), year-round. During summer free concerts are held at the park's **Commerce Bank River Stage** on North Park Drive, along with an evening Movies in the Park series.

Cherry Hill Mall

A description of Cherry Hill wouldn't be complete with mentioning Cherry Hill Mall (2000 Rte. 38, 856/662-7440, www.cherryhillmall .com), the East Coast's first indoor temperature-controlled mall. Since opening in 1961, the mall has served as sort of a community center. And as malls go it's pretty nice. Stores include Banana Republic, M.A.C., Coach, French Connection, and Abercrombie & Fitch, with Strawbridge's, Macy's, and J. C. Penney operating as anchors. There's also a food court and some miniature escalators perfect for a little pick-me-up.

Entertainment and Nightlife

Cherry Hill's favorite nightclub is **Taylors** (2031 Rte. 70 W., 856/486-1001, www.taylors cherryhill.com), a multistory space that has been around in one form or another forever. Past incarnations include Top Dog and the Iguana Beach Club. The layout is pretty much the same: Upstairs is a dance club; downstairs is a restaurant-bar often featuring cover bands and scantily clad women selling mixed-drink shots in test tubes and dancing on the bars. During summer Taylors opens an outdoor deck and dance floor. Expect long lines.

Favored both by recent college grads and senior citizens—though not usually at the same time—the **Coastline** (1240 Brace Rd., 856/795-1773, www.coastlinerestaurant bar.com, daily 11 A.M.–3 A.M.) offers something for everyone. Older crowds tend to dissipate after dinner, clearing the floor for nightly dance parties including Monday's best of the '60s, '70s, and '80s, and Friday's live radio broadcast. The Coastline fell into the national limelight in 2004 when it was sued for offering Ladies' Night drink specials. Though the court ruled in favor of the

prosecution, a new take on Ladies' Night has returned Friday evenings.

For the latest Will Smith blockbuster there's **Loews Movie Theater 24** (2121 Rte. 38, 856/486-1722), located across the road from the Cherry Hill Mall. The theater added an IMAX screen in August 2008. **Flying Fish Brewing Company** (1940 Olney Ave., 856/489-0061, info@flyingfish.com, www .flyingfish.com) is South Jersey's first microbrewery. In was originally founded in 1995 as a Web-only brewery, allowing site visitors a part in the brew-building process by naming beers and designing T-shirts. Today, Flying Fish is one of New Jersey's largest craft breweries, with free 40-minute tours and tastings held Saturday 1–4 P.M. If you're only in town on a weekday and would like a tour, email them; they may be able to fit you in.

Bowling is already fun, but even more so at Cherry Hill's **Playdrome** (1536 Kings Hwy., 856/429-0672). There's a pool hall and an on-site bar and grill, but the best thing about this place is Future Bowl. With black lights, fog machines, and a DJ spinning tunes from the 1970s, 1980s, and 1990s, you're in it for the long haul.

Accommodations

The **Holiday Inn-Cherry Hill** (Rte. 70 and Sayer Ave., 856/663-5300, www.holidaycherry hill.com, $118–155) features rooms both sizeable and reasonably priced, as well as a year-round indoor pool and a seasonal outdoor pool. With free wireless Internet, a car rental service located in the lobby, and the allowance of pets, it's a hotel worth considering. The popular barbecue restaurant chain **Red, Hot, and Blue** (856/665-7427) is adjacent to the hotel and often features live blues acts.

While the (**Clarion Hotel & Conference Center** (1450 Rte. 70 E., 856/428-2300, www .clarionofcherryhill.com, $120–389) has an abundance of spacious rooms with in-room safes and coffeemakers, the property's best feature is its eight "exotic" suites ($203–289). Named for and decorated to resemble faraway places like Greece, Venice, and the Artic, these suites also feature a whirlpool, wet bar, fireplace, and board games. My favorite is the Far East Suite, with its own Buddha statue and ceremonial arch. The hotel's additional amenities include an outdoor pool, tennis courts, a pool table, and a British-style restaurant-pub. Pets are welcome for an additional fee.

Food

A few of Cherry Hill's numerous dining options date back to the days this township was a must-stop for big name entertainers and musicians. To compete with the likes of Philadelphia and Atlantic City, Cherry Hill's food had to be *good,* and it still is. Don't bother traveling 'cross the river for a Philly cheesesteak; Cherry Hill's sandwiches are consistently voted some of the best in the tristate area. You'd better taste for yourself and decide.

CASUAL EATERIES

Stacked corned beef sandwiches are one reason to stop by the **Kibitz Room** (The Shops at Holly Ravine, 856/428-7878, www.thekibitz room.com, $8.50–13), but there are many, many more. *Philadelphia Magazine* voted this New York–style deli's pastrami and kugel as South Jersey's best. Family-run **Lou and Ann's Deli** (257 Rte. 70, 856/795-2307, Tues.–Sat. 8 A.M.–6 P.M.) is a Cherry Hill institution. Try the Italian hoagie, stuffed with meats and provolone cheese. Hidden down a nondescript side street is **Chick's Deli** (906 Township Ln., 856/429-2022, Mon.–Sat. 7 A.M.–5 P.M., closed Sun.), home to what has been called "the best Cheesesteak in South Jersey." It's a tiny place—only six tables—and hard to find, but worth it. To get here, take Route 70 heading east, past the three-way intersection with Brace Road and King's Highway, and turn right at Virginia Avenue before a quick left onto Township Lane.

Family-owned **Ponzio's** (7 Rte. 70 W., 856/428-4808, www.ponzios.com, daily 7 A.M.–1 A.M., $7–21) tops South Jersey's list of most revered diners, although it's less like a greasy spoon and more like a banquet space. Desserts made on-site are outstanding.

In Taylors' parking lot stands the famous **King of Pizza** (2300 Rte. 70, 856/665-4824, $6–14), a Cherry Hill landmark once owned and operated by singer Frankie Avalon. The King dates back the a time when Cherry Hill was legend, rivaling Atlantic City as South Jersey's premier hot spot and attracting names like Jackie Wilson and Tom Jones to its long-gone nightclubs. Sure, the King has since burned down and been rebuilt, but that hasn't changed its history or lessoned the quality of its pizza. Thin-crust slices rich with marinara remain especially good.

FINE DINING

Caffe Aldo Lamberti (2011 Rte. 70 W., 856/663-1747, www.lambertis.com, Mon.–Thurs. 11 A.M.–10 P.M., Fri. 11 A.M.–11 P.M., Sat. noon–11 P.M., Sun. 1–9 P.M., $15–36) is the original, and best, of the Lamberti family's tristate Italian eateries. The food is decadent, the atmosphere romantic, and perks include private-party wine cellar rooms and recently added alfresco seating.

Tucked into a shopping center just up the road is **Siri's Thai French Cuisine** (2117-19 Rte. 70 W., 856/663-6781 or 856/663-6128, www.siris-nj.com, lunch Mon.–Sat. 11:30 A.M.–3 P.M., dinner Sun.–Thurs. 3–10 P.M., Fri.–Sat. 3–11 P.M., $13–29), a BYO known for its eloquent dish execution and exquisite desserts. Prices range higher than a traditional Thai meal, but it's worth the added cost.

Perhaps the region's most romantic restaurant, **La Campagne** (312 Kresson Rd., 856/429-7647, www.lacampagne.com, Tues.–Thurs. 5–9 P.M., Fri.–Sat. 5–10 P.M., Sun. 5–8:30 P.M., brunch Sun. 11 A.M.–2 P.M., $26–36) occupies a rustic 150-year-old farmhouse with a working fireplace and hardwood floors. A seasonally changing French menu incorporates fresh local ingredients, and even the ice cream is homemade. The selection of artisanal and farmstead cheeses is an added bonus. Culinary classes take place upstairs.

For Southern-style cooking, including a seven-course tasting menu, make the trip to

Melange Café (1601 Chapel Ave., 856/663-7339 or 856/663-9493, www.melangecafe.com, Tues.–Thurs. 11 A.M.–10 P.M., Fri. 11 A.M.–11 P.M., Sat. 4–11 P.M., Sun. 2–10 P.M., $18–29). Award-winning chef Joe Brown creates dishes that are a blend of classic Italian and Bayou cuisine. The decor is nothing special, but the food is.

◖ CAMDEN WATERFRONT

Camden has a bad rep. I'm not saying it's undeserved, but regardless of the corruption, crime, and ultimately shabby living conditions, the city's waterfront is one of South Jersey's best entertainment venues. Although it offers little indication of what Camden is really like, this prime stretch of riverfront hosts quality attractions worth visiting. At its center is **Wiggins**

Park, a rounded marina that's a good starting point for exploring the area.

Signs leading to Camden's waterfront are clearly marked and easy to follow from the Route 676 North (from South Jersey) or Route 30 West (from North Jersey). By taking this route you'll avoid some of the city's less desirable neighborhoods, which is a good idea. Always use caution in Camden, especially when venturing away from the waterfront area. Nearby neighborhoods, such as the Rutgers University campus and the area surrounding the Walt Whitman house, are relatively safe—just know where you're going before you get there.

Both the Campbell Soup Company and the RCA-Victor Talking Machine Company originated in Camden, and the city was one of the

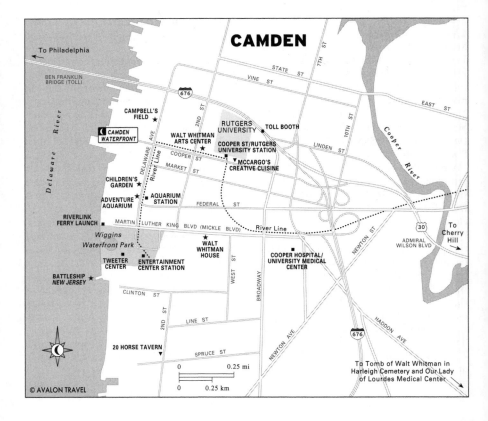

CAMPBELL'S CONDENSED HISTORY

Ever wonder who made cookin' up soup so easy? A few cans thrown into your backpack, to be opened and mixed with some water over the campfire, and voilà! You're enjoying that homemade taste as if Mom were sitting there next to you.

Condensed soup was invented by Dr. John T. Dorrance, a European-trained chemist whose uncle was the general manager of a small business called the Joseph A. Campbell Preserve Company, operated out of South Jersey's Camden. Joseph Campbell, a fresh-fruit sales-man, started the business in 1869 along with Abraham Anderson, a local ice-tray manufac-turer. Canned tomatoes and vegetables, pre-served fruits, condiments, and minced meats were its specialties — until Dorrance invented a way to take the water out of soup, lowering processing and shipping costs by one third. In-stantly, a new Campbell star was born. Camp-bell's condensed soup became so popular that "soup" was added to the business name, be-ginning what we know today as the Campbell Soup Company.

The Campbell Soup Kids welcome fans to Camden's Campbell Field, home of the minor-league Riversharks.

Quickly becoming a U.S. favorite, celebri-ties such as Jimmy Stewart, Donna Reed, and George Burns and Gracie Allen even took to touting the soup on radio and television. Two faces synonymous with Campbell Soup are the Campbell Soup Kids, whose advertising appeal and cherubic mugs paved the way for market-ing mascots like Snap, Crackle, and Pop; the Pillsbury Doughboy; and Punchy, the Hawaiian Punch boy. As famous from the Campbell Soup Company as chicken noodle and tomato soups, these kids were a welcome addition in 1904.

Another image associated with Campbell Soup is the red-and-white label on its cans. This color combo got its start when company executive Herbert Williams saw the new red-and-white uniforms Cornell University's foot-ball team wore. The uniforms so impressed Williams that he was able to persuade his em-ployer to adopt the colors as their own.

Campbell Soup soon became successful not only as a substantial meal but also as an individual ingredient in the baby-boom era's easy-to-prepare dishes. A staple of American culture, Campbell Soup found its way past con-sumers' tastes and into their hearts by spon-soring programs like *Lassie* and the *Campbell Playhouse Radio* series, previously known as *The Mercury Theater on the Air* and featuring well-known radio persona Orson Welles.

Of Camden's four world-class corporations enjoying great prestige (others were RCA, the New York Shipbuilding Corporation, and R. M. Hollingshead), Campbell Soup Company is the only remaining in the city. Although its main factory closed and was demolished in the early 1990s, its headquarters still operates along the waterfront, providing jobs to more than 1,200 employees.

The image of Campbell Soup cans became immortalized to the world in Andy Warhol's pop art, but for former factory employees, Campbell Soup holds deeper meaning. Many of them shared stories with local public broad-caster WHYY's Ed Cunningham, describing a time when "the streets in Camden literally ran red with tomato juice, and the air of all north Camden smelled sweet with soup."

Today, the Campbell Soup conglomerate includes Pepperidge Farms, V8 Vegetable Juices, and Godiva Chocolates.

first musical recording centers in the United States. After years of deterioration, Camden seems to be regaining some ground with its family-friendly waterfront, inviting arts centers, and eateries that aim to please.

Battleship *New Jersey*

When the **Battleship *New Jersey*** (62 Battleship Pl., 866/877-6262, www.battleship newjersey.org) made its final journey from the Philly Shipyard to Camden's waterfront, hundreds stood along the Delaware River banks in tribute. Battleship *New Jersey*, nicknamed "Big J," is the third largest battleship ever built, and the nation's most decorated. Nearly three football fields long (877 feet 7 inches) and eleven stories high, it's built of steel and teakwood and made to travel at a speed of 33-plus knots—approximately 38 miles an hour.

Along with the *Iowa, Wisconsin,* and *Missouri,* the USS *New Jersey* is one of only four Iowa-class battleships constructed during World War II. Though originally allotted 5–6 years to build, the U.S. involvement in

World War II called for quicker construction, and within a year and a half the battleship was ready for commissioning. Launched into action on December 7, 1942, the *New Jersey* went on to fight in World War II, the Korean and Vietnam Wars, Beirut, and the Middle East before being called out of service permanently in 1991.

Today, the battleship sits massive and majestic along the waterfront south of Wiggins Park. It has been completely restored by volunteers and now operates as a museum and host to an overnight "encampment" program for kids ($50.95 per person), who have the opportunity to sleep in its bunks, stow gear in its lockers, and eat in its mess hall. Ship tours are offered daily, take about two hours, and include the ship's upper and lower decks, combat engagement and communications centers, bridge, machine shop, and former admiral's and captain's cabins. A videotaped tour is available for those physically unable to walk the ship. Prices range from $17.50 adult, $13 senior and child for a general quarters tour to $18.50 adult, $13

Battleship *New Jersey,* Camden Waterfront

senior and child for a firepower tour, which also includes the BB 62's weapons systems, and $19.50 adult, $15 senior and child for the City at Sea tour, where you'll visit the medical and dental facilities, the post office, the TV studio, and a barbershop. Active service members receive free tour admission. The Battleship *New Jersey* is open daily 9:30 A.M.–3 P.M. March–April and September–December, and daily 9:30 A.M.–5 P.M. May–August. Call ahead for January and February hours and encampment program details.

Adventure Aquarium and Camden Children's Garden

Although it opened with much fanfare in 1992, New Jersey's official state aquarium immediately earned criticism. What was supposed to be at the forefront of Camden's revitalization was little more than a few local fish. But following extensive renovations, the newly named **Adventure Aquarium** (1 Riverside Dr., 856/365-3300, www.njaquarium.org, daily 9:30 A.M.–5 P.M., $18.95 adult, $14.95 child) reopened in May 2005 and has since secured its status as a bona fide destination. Innovative exhibits include the West African River Experience, where you can get up close and personal with 300-pound hippos Button and Genny in their glass-enclosed underwater surrounds, and a 40-foot walk-through shark tunnel with more than 20 *Jaws*-like creatures, including horn sharks, zebra sharks, and smooth dogfish. There's also a hands-on science lab, opportunities to feed sea turtles and seals, and a chance to swim (*dun-dun, dun-dun . . .*) with sharks ($165 per person age 12 and up).

After seeing Daddy swim with fishes, the kids may need a place to unwind. How about the four-acre **Camden Children's Garden** (3 Riverside Dr., 856/365-8733, www.camdenchildrensgarden.org, Tues.–Sun. 10 A.M.–5 P.M., $6 adult, $4 child), an interactive play and learning center adjacent to the aquarium. In addition to a treehouse, maze, dinosaur garden, and several fairy tale–themed gardens, there's an indoor educational center filled with more than 200 butterflies that soar, bask, and lay eggs in a climate-controlled environment. A train, carousel, and Spring Butterfly ride are also on-site (extra cost required).

Walt Whitman Sites

Walt Whitman, nicknamed the "Gray Poet," was one of Camden's most beloved residents. Whitman spent his final 18 years living in a two-story home on Mickle Boulevard, where he penned versions of his epic poem *Leaves of Grass* and received visitors such as Oscar Wilde and Bram Stoker. The home still stands, and now operates as a museum displaying many of Whitman's personal belongings, including books, papers, and the bed where he died. The **Walt Whitman House** (328 Mickle Blvd., 856/964-5383, www.state.nj.us/dep/parksandforests/historic/whitman/) is open Wednesday–Saturday 10 A.M.–noon and 1–4 P.M., Sunday 1–4 P.M.; reservations are required.

Whitman and his family are buried in a self-designed tomb at **Harleigh Cemetery,** just east of Our Lady of Lourdes Hospital and west of Route 130 along Haddon Avenue. The cemetery itself is lovely, filled with decorative headstones and dozens of family mausoleums, several built into hillsides. Signs to Whitman's tomb, located in the hospital's shadow, are well marked—just be sure to enter from the main entrance. The tomb's stone door has been opened and replaced with an iron gate so visitors can peek inside.

Sports and Entertainment

When 6,425-seat **Campbell Field** (856/963-2600, www.riversharks.com) opened along Camden's waterfront in 2001, the authentic baseball game was reborn. Not to say that the Phils across the river don't put on a great show, but they were still playing in the monstrosity that was Veteran's Stadium at the time. At Campbell Field, fans could once again get close to the game. The park includes a picnic pavilion, fun zone, and a fantastic view of central Philadelphia and the Ben Franklin Bridge. Besides, tickets are cheap: only $9–13. Don't miss the Campbell Soup Twins (www.campbell soup.com), the city's condensed legacy, at the field's main entrance.

Camden's **Tweeter Center** (1 Harbour Blvd., 856/365-1300, www.tweetercenter.com) opened in 1995, finally bringing live music to the South Jersey side. Seats are out in the open, meaning this place comes alive during warmer months when hordes of 20-somethings stream in to catch acts like Tom Petty and John Mayer under the stars. Like everywhere else along Camden's waterfront, your view of downtown Philly is unbeatable. The center converts from 25,000 seats to a climate-controlled theater seating 1,600–7,000 for local acts and regional events.

The Tweeter Center is home to **The South Jersey Performing Arts Center** (856/342-6633, www.sjpac.com), a theater coalition hosting area events year-round.

Food

Camden is not a place you'd visit just for the food, but if you're here and you're hungry, there are some surprisingly worthwhile options.

Close to both the courthouse and Rutgers University's campus is **McCargo's Creative Cuisine** (415 Cooper St., 856/964-7900, Mon.–Fri. 8 A.M.–3 P.M. summer, Mon.–Fri. 8 A.M.–5 P.M. the rest of the year), serving soul food–style American eats to a mixed clientele of locals, students, and city employees. The restaurant's founder and chef, Aaron McCargo Jr., left the job in June 2008 after winning the Food Network's reality show *The Next Food Network Star*. Here's hoping McCargo's continues dishing out delish foods in his fine tradition.

Housed within a former lumberyard stable is **20 Horse Tavern** (835 S. 2nd St., 856/365-9211, www.20horsetavern.com, $7–17), a refined eatery serving up a selection of burgers, wraps, and steak and seafood entrées. The restaurant's interior is impressive—exposed brick walls, white linens, and a display of historic photos and tools spread throughout the dining area—as is the beer selection, which includes brews by Flying Fish, Magic Hat, and Guinness. To get here, follow Clinton Street east from the riverfront (the Tweeter Center

is on your left) and turn right onto South Second Street. The tavern is on the northwest corner of Second and Spruce. Hours are Monday 11 A.M.–4 P.M., Tuesday–Thursday 11 A.M.–8 P.M., Friday 11 A.M.–9 P.M. fall and winter (the dining room closes daily at 3 P.M.), with extended spring and summer hours including Saturday 3–10 P.M.

Information and Services

Camden's **Parking Authority** (856/757-9300, www.camdenparking.net) operates a few garages in the city's more touristy areas, include one along the waterfront and another across from the Tweeter Center.

Getting There and Around

The **River LINE** (800/772-2222, www.river line.com, $1.35 one way) travels south from Trenton to Camden with numerous stops in between. Cars are clean and compact and run approximately every 30 minutes (every 15 minutes during peak weekday hours) Sunday–Friday and major holidays 6 A.M. to 10 P.M., Saturday 6 A.M.–midnight. Intercity stops include Cooper at Second Street (Rutgers University) and two waterfront stations. Most transit stations offer free parking.

The **Riverlink Ferry** (215/925-5465, www .riverlinkferry.org, $6 adult round-trip, $5 senior and child) runs between Pennsylvania's Penn's Landing and Camden's Waterfront, Monday–Thursday approximately every 40 minutes 9 A.M.–5 P.M., Friday–Sunday 9 A.M.–6:20 P.M. Parking is available on both sides of the river. An **Express Service** runs on Tweeter Center concert evenings, beginning at 6 P.M. and concluding about a half hour after the show.

COLLINGSWOOD

When it comes to downtown revitalization, Collingswood is queen. A decade ago the borough's main shopping district, Haddon Avenue, was pretty unremarkable, but keen-eyed developers saw potential. Attracted by Collingswood's walkable downtown, businesses began moving in. At the same time a gay community started establishing itself, drawn by affordable housing and the borough's proximity to Philadelphia (10 minutes from Center City by PATCO). Today, Collingswood is a role model for South Jersey towns struggling to revamp their downtown districts (although increasing rents have already caused some businesses to relocate). The neighborhood's cafés remain top-notch, and you'd be hard-pressed not to find an Italian restaurant that suits your needs. Specialty shops, boutiques, and antique stores offer an array of shopping opportunities, and most are within walking distance to the borough's PATCO transit station, connecting Collingswood to Westmont and Haddonfield to the east, and Camden and Philly to the west.

Entertainment

Like any good revitalized district, a café is essential to Collingswood's new streetscape. While it's currently the only coffeehouse in town (The Treehouse relocated to Audubon in 2008), trendy **Grooveground** (647 Haddon Ave., 856/869-9800, www.grooveground.com) would be worth a stop regardless. Although the tables are a little snug, you'll be too busy enjoying the music and Wi-Fi to notice. In addition to espresso drinks, virgin mixed drinks (BYO), gourmet sweets, and grilled eats, Grooveground does a bit of retail business, selling T-shirts, hipster button-downs, purses, and CDs.

Tucked back from the White Horse Pike's north side is the historic **Scottish Rite Auditorium** (315 White Horse Pike, 856/858-1000), a massive 1932 theater showcasing select music performances—many of them big-name acts—throughout the year. The theater seats up to 1,050 and keeps a working pipe organ in its main auditorium.

Specialty Shops

Collingswood has a good selection of shops worth browsing, although it's surprising how the selection has changed over the last few years. High rents have supposedly caused some stores to relocate to nearby towns like Audubon and Gloucester, but downtown remains vibrant, and several new shops have moved in.

Vintage Rose (720 Haddon Ave., 856/833-0900) stocks "a little bit of everything," including furniture, picture frames, and gifts for newborns.

Multistory **Jubili Beads & Yarns** (713 Haddon Ave., 856/858-7844, www.jubilibeadsandyarns.com) offers classes in crocheting, knitting, beading, flame-working, and weaving, and a first-floor shop brimming with bargain beads, craft books, hooks, knitting needles, and hundreds of other supplies.

Cheese Etc. & Gourmet Gifts (686 Haddon Ave., 856/858-1144, www.cheeseetc.com) meets epicurean needs with a varied selection that includes Gouda and aged cheddar cheeses along with dried pastas and fresh preserves. Nestled into a corner locale at the new Lumberyard Condos, **All Fired Up** (602 Haddon Ave., 856/833-1330, www.paintatallfiredup.com) hosts pottery-painting parties for all ages. The studio is stocked with hundreds of dinnerware items and designs to choose from, along with sponges, stencils, and stamps for the artistically disinclined. Modern **Fusion Gallery** (697 Haddon Ave., 609/410-8800, info@fusionnj.com, www.fusionnj.com) displays progressive works by emerging and renowned artists. The gallery's propAganda, a space within the space, carries functional, unique, and limited-run art glass, wearable art, and more.

The window display will lure you into **Ellis Antiques** (812 Haddon Ave., 856/854-6346, www.ellisantique.com), home to a fine collection of antique furniture, vintage tea sets, jewelry, toys, and home furnishings. For Parisian decor, vanity tables, and architecturally significant salvaged doors, stop by the lovely **Two Cherubs** (542 Haddon Ave., 856/287-5185, www.twocherubs.com). Styles from designers Kendra Scott, Melissa Masse, and Eileen Fisher are available at high-end women's boutique **Antionette Gabrielle** (802 Haddon Ave., 856/833-0606, www.antoinettegabrielle.com).

Food
CASUAL EATERIES
They just don't make 'em like **Weber's Drive-In** (Rte. 130 N., 856/456-4138,

Sun.–Thurs. 11 A.M.–10 P.M., Fri.–Sat. 11 A.M.–10:30 P.M., mid-Apr.–mid-Sept.) anymore. About a 10-minute drive from downtown Collingswood, this 1950s carhop eatery is strictly South Jersey, with three branches within 10 miles of each other. Cheeseburgers are cheap ($3) and simple, but tasty. Get one with a paper boat of stringy fries ($1.75) and a famous root beer float ($2.80) and you're set. After filling up on food, work it off on one of two miniature golf courses in back.

For unadulterated crab cakes without a pinch of filling, there's no better place than 🄲 **Bobby Chez** (33 W. Collings Ave., 856/869-8000, www.bobbychezcrabcakes .com, Tues.–Sat. 11 A.M.–7 P.M., $3.50–14), but one false move toward the counter before your number is called and hordes of salivating patrons will seriously stare you down. It's *that* good. One caveat: It's take-out only, and most items require heating. Make sure you've got an oven handy.

Patriarch of Collingswood's restaurant scene, family-friendly **Villa Barone** (753 Haddon Ave., 856/858-2999, Mon.–Thurs. 11:30 A.M.–10 P.M., Fri.–Sat. 11:30 A.M.–11 P.M., Sun. 11:30 A.M.–9 P.M., $12–19) serves southern Italian dishes in one of the coziest spots in town. A massive wood-burning oven keeps things toasty while you eat.

Collingswood hosts one of South Jersey's largest **Farmers Markets** (Irvin and Collings Ave., 856/854-6724, www.collingswoodmarket .com, Sat. 8 A.M.–noon May–Thanksgiving), with dozens of stalls selling organic produce, farm-made fruit and veggie pies, Italian-style baked goods, locally grown flowers, baked dog treats, and more. Chef's demonstrations take place throughout the season.

Although Collingswood had long been up-and-coming, things really improved once 🄲 **The Pop Shop** (729 Haddon Ave., 856/869-0111, www.thepopshopusa.com, Mon.–Thurs. 8 A.M.–9 P.M., Fri. 8 A.M.–10 P.M., Sat. 7:30 A.M.–10 P.M., Sun. 7:30 A.M.–8 P.M., $6–10) came to town. Since opening in 2006, this neighborhood soda fountain has served as a de facto community center. It's bright, open,

and loud with kids. The Pop Shop is famous for its extensive grilled-cheese selection—more than 30 varieties—one of which appeared on the Food Network's *Throwndown with Bobby Flay*. Kids' karaoke nights, pajama parties, and signature sundae contests all contribute to the allure.

FINE DINING

Over the past decade, and particularly the last few years, Haddon Avenue has morphed into a restaurant mecca. It's OK to be choosy—you have your pick.

For superb sushi, try **Sagami** (37 Crescent Blvd., 856/854-9773, lunch Tues.–Fri. noon–2 P.M., dinner Tues.–Thurs. 5:30–9:30 P.M., Fri. 5:30–10 P.M., Sat.–Sun. 5–10 P.M., $12–22), a South Jersey BYO favorite for over 30 years.

With an interior painted to look like an Italian piazza, **Nunzio's** (706 Haddon Ave., 856/858-9840, www.nunzioristoranterustico .com, lunch daily 11:30 A.M.–2:30 P.M., dinner Mon.–Thurs. 4:30–10 P.M., Fri.–Sat. 4:30–10:30 P.M., Sun. 3:30–9:30 P.M., $17.50–22) does its best to transport patrons to another time and place, complete with dishes like *pappardelle ai funghi,* bowtie pasta with mushrooms and cream sauce ($18.50), and a chef's table where talk centers around BYO vintages and desserts like panna cotta and crème brûlée.

Casual and airy **Brianna's** (712 Haddon Ave., 856/854-0660, Tues.–Thurs. 7:30 A.M.–9 P.M., Fri.–Sat. 7:30 A.M.–10 P.M., Sun. 8 A.M.–8 P.M., $12–18) serves some of the best sandwiches in town. Try the namesake sandwich, a combination of marinated mozzarella, roasted peppers, and olive oil on South Philly Sarcone bread. During warmer months take it alfresco in Brianna's backyard dining area.

If decadence is what you're after, **Word of Mouth** (729 Haddon Ave., 856/858-2228, lunch Tues.–Sat. 11:30 A.M.–2:30 P.M., dinner Tues.–Sat. 5–9:30 P.M., Sun. 4:30–8:30 P.M., closed Mon., $19–29) is your place. Occupying the former site of the Gordon Phillips Beauty School, this younger sibling to Marlton's Food for Thought serves up New American dishes like pan-seared striped bass and balsamic-glazed salmon using only fresh ingredients. Bring your own drinks, and don't skip the appetizers—they're the best part.

Locals line up to score seats at **The Tortilla Press** (703 Haddon Ave., 856/869-3345, www.thetortillapress.com, Mon.–Thurs. 11 A.M.–9 P.M., Fri.–Sat. 11 A.M.–10 P.M., Sun. 11 A.M.–8 P.M., $11–17), Collingswood's only gourmet Mexican eatery. Homemade chips and salsa accompany meals, which include a chicken and sweet potato burrito ($15) and grilled chicken *mole poblano* ($15), chicken topped with chocolate sauce. The decidedly upbeat atmosphere is accentuated by the availability of margaritas, although BYO tequila.

Water Lily (653 Haddon Ave., 856/833-0098, www.waterlilybistro.com, lunch Tues.–Fri. 11 A.M.–3 P.M., Sat. noon–3 P.M., dinner Tues.–Thurs. 5–9:30 P.M., Fri. and Sat. 5–10 P.M., Sun. 4–9 P.M., closed Mon., $17–26) serves innovate French Asian cuisine in a long dining space with both booths and tables. Start with the steamed veggie dumplings ($6), then move on to more succulent fare like the roasted crispy duckling ($21).

WESTMONT

Cross Cuthbert Boulevard heading south along Haddon Avenue and you're in Westmont, part of the larger Haddon Township. Sandwiched between bustling Collingswood and architecturally appealing Haddonfield, Westmont often gets the shaft. True, it's spread thin with no cohesive town center. But what it lacks in walkability and storefronts it makes up for in alcohol sales—Westmont's the only town on the block to allow sales or distribution of liquor.

Along Haddon Avenue, keep an eye out for the **Westmont Theater** (49 Haddon Ave.). Originally opened in 1927, it went through numerous incarnations before closing for good in 1986. For now the marquee still spells out Westmont in capital letters, and the township is currently mulling over potential adaptive reuse plans for the theater. It's said that director Steven Spielberg, who spent part of his childhood in Haddon Township, saw his first movie, *The Greatest Show on Earth,* at the Westmont, and actor Michael Landon once worked here as a doorman.

Food and Nightlife

I've never seen anything like **McMillan's** (15 Haddon Ave., 856/854-3094) cream donuts, so stuffed and puffed with filling it's hard to keep the tops on them. South Jersey's *Courier Post* says the bakery's donuts are so popular they're shipping them across the country. I believe it, because man, are they good!

Family-owned **Giumarello's** (329 Haddon Ave., 856/858-9400, www.giumarellos.com, lunch Tues.–Fri. 11:30 A.M.–2:30 P.M., dinner Tues.–Thurs. 5–9:30 P.M., Fri.–Sat. 5–10 P.M., closed Sun.–Mon., $18–27) serves Northern Italian cuisines in a crisp modern setting. Slip into a rounded booth and spend the evening sipping the famed martinis and slurping oysters, or settle onto the outdoor courtyard during summer months with a crab cocktail and an ice-cold draft. And don't forget to bring a date.

Somewhere between sports hangout and family restaurant is **P.J. Whelihan's Pub** (700 Haddon Ave., 856/427-7888, www .pjwhelihanspub.com, daily 11 A.M.–2 A.M.), with 16 televisions, two bars, and one of the best appetizer selections around, including pot stickers ($7), crab dip ($8), and mini burger sliders ($7 and $16). Fairly new **Dockhoppers** (703 Haddon Ave., 856/869-3345, Tues.–Sat. 11 A.M.–11 P.M., Sun. 1 P.M.–11 P.M., closed Mon., $7–17) sports chalkboard seafood specials along with a fantastic weekday happy hour (5–7 P.M.) and half-price appetizers earlier in the week.

Swanky **Cork** (90 Haddon Ave., 856/833-9800, www.corknj.com, Mon.–Fri. 11:30 A.M.–2 A.M., Sat.–Sun. 4 P.M.–2 A.M.) is Haddon Avenue's answer to Philadelphia dining and nightlife, without the traffic. Sip on Belgian brews and cucumber cosmos while snacking on calamari ($9), or head into the dining room for small plate samplings and entrées including salmon and rib eye steak.

Wednesdays are '80s nights, with Big Hair cocktails and Journey tunes; live jazz plays on weekends.

Additional nightlife options include local hangout **Pat's Pub** (239 Haddon Ave., 856/854-5545), and the fully stocked **Tom Fischer's Tavern** (18 W. Cuthbert Blvd., 856/854-6650, Mon.–Sat. 10 A.M.–2 A.M., Sun. 11 A.M.–2 A.M.), home to award-winning buffalo wings.

⬛ HADDONFIELD

Lovely Haddonfield is worth visiting for its architecture alone, though its downtown and a couple of interesting historic sites are just as impressive. The borough is easily recognizable by its colonial and Federal-style brick buildings, its tree-lined streets, and spacious Victorian estates. And if school's getting out, there'll be teenagers everywhere. Many families reside in Haddonfield, and it's a walkable kind of place.

Founded in 1701 by Elizabeth Haddon, whose courtship of a Quaker minister is described by Longfellow in his poem *Tales of a Wayside Inn,* Haddonfield has long been considered one of South Jersey's darlings. Downtown fell out of use for some years, but the borough never lost its appeal. Today, antique stores, art galleries, clothing boutiques, restaurants, and a large number of consignment shops fill the outlying intersection of Haddon Avenue and Kings Highway. It's where you'll also find the state's first designated historic site, and a dinosaur named Haddy.

Architecture

Between downtown's colonials and the outlying Victorian and Federal estates, Haddonfield's got some spectacular architecture. It's worth a drive around if you have time. The borough's grandest homes are along Kings Highway West and **Chews Landing Road,** reached from Haddon Avenue by making a right onto Kings Highway and veering left onto Chews Landing. During spring and summer the large buttonwood trees lining the sidewalks are in full bloom.

Indian King Tavern Museum

Situated along King's Highway East among several colonial structures is the 1750 Indian King Tavern Museum (223 Kings Hwy. E., 856/429-6792, www.levins.com/tavern.html, Wed.–Sat. 10 A.M.–noon and 1–4 P.M., Sun. 1–4 P.M., free), New Jersey's first designated historic site. The name "Indian King" honors the friendship between local Quakers and Lenape Indians, and this is where New Jersey's state seal was first adopted in 1777. Today's tavern has been completely restored to its Revolution-era appearance. While the furniture displayed is not original, the museum is still considered one of the country's best surviving examples of a traditional 18th-century tavern.

Hour-long guided tours of the tavern include its first two floors, but unfortunately not the underground cellars thought to have housed British prisoners during the Revolution. Regardless, the Indian King is a must-see.

Dinosaur Site

While vacationing in Haddonfield in 1858, fossil hobbyist William Parker Foulke happened upon the world's first nearly complete dinosaur skeleton, unearthing the bones from the bottom of a marl pit. The species was given the name *Hadrosaurus foulkii,* and the skeleton became the first set of dinosaur bones ever displayed in a museum. They remain on display at the **Philadelphia Academy of Natural Sciences,** right across the Delaware River. Although **Hadrosaurus Park,** where the skeleton was discovered, is easy to overlook, once you find it you'll come across two markers designating the historic find. The first is a stone-mounted marker placed here by a local Boy Scout in 1984, and the second is a mounted plaque erected in 1994 when the site became a National Historic Landmark.

To reach Hadrosaurus Park from Kings Highway East, turn west onto Grove Street, then right onto Maple Avenue.

Honoring Haddonfield's terrestrial history, a human-sized dinosaur sculpture (known as Haddy) has been placed on Lantern Lane just off Kings Highway West, in the borough's shopping district. Several local events center around Haddy, although he's nothing to go out of your way for.

Events and Festivals

A great time to visit Haddonfield is during the holiday season. A **Holiday House Tour** (856/216-7253) takes place annually. Lights adorn many of the homes and mansions, and extended **Candlelight Shopping** hours are offered throughout December. Costumed carolers, horse-drawn carriages, and an appearance by Santa are featured most weekends. Holiday festivities culminate at month's end with **First Night Haddonfield** (www.firstnighthaddonfield.org), a family-friendly block party ringing in the New Year.

July's annual **Craft and Fine Arts Festival** (856/216-7253) features over 200 knitters, painters, jewelry makers, fiber artists, and more displaying and selling their wares. Outdoor stalls are set up along Kings Highway, which is temporarily closed to traffic.

Entertainment

While most of Haddonfield's shops close early, a wonderful coffeehouse and a nonprofit theater are both reasons to come to town in the evening.

Ain't nothing fancy about **Three Beans Coffee Co.** (140 N. Haddon Ave., 856/354-2220, Mon.–Thurs. 6:30 A.M.–10 P.M., Fri. 6:30 A.M.–11 P.M., Sat. 7:30 A.M.–11 P.M., Sun. 8 A.M.–8 P.M.), which is why it's so great. Floppy couches, mismatched tables, and books lie around—there's even a pool table. Service can be slow, but there's more to a coffee shop then an uninspired barista.

Since 1935, **Haddonfield Play and Players** (957 S. Atlantic Ave., 856/429-8139, www.haddonfieldplayers.com, $18) has been putting on top-notch comedy, musical, mystery, and children's performances for the local community. Recent productions include *Dial M for Murder* and *Bat Boy: The Musical.*

Shopping

Haddonfield is a great place for shopping,

with dozens of boutiques, specialty shops, and a couple of upscale chains. There are also several consignment shops in the area, and stores catering to kids and teens.

At **Woolplay** (22 N. Haddon Ave., 856/428-0110, www.woolplay.com, closed Sun.–Mon.) choose from more than 100 yarn varieties, including Artyarns, Dancing Fibers, and Blue Sky Alpacas. The shop hosts occasional knitting classes.

Regional chain **Benjamin Lovell Shoes** (212 E. Kings Hwy., 856/429-7801, www.benjaminlovellshoes.com) carries the latest in Merrell, Cole Haan, and Camper comfort.

Velvet Paws (107 E. Kings Hwy., 856/428-8889, www.velvetpaws.com) has all you need to pamper your pet, including freshly baked treats, raingear, sweaters, and sunglasses.

Women rule at **Her Sport** (114 E. Kings Hwy., 856/795-7514, www.hersport.com), where a wide selection of designer styles, sneakers, accessories, and equipment is available for athletes from field hockey players to cheerleaders. For one-of-a-kind women's wear, try vintage consignment shop **Secrets** (10 Mechanic St., 856/354-9111), one of Haddonfield's many, which also include **Evergreen Furniture** (36 Ellis St., 856/857-1880), **Nifty Thrifties** (413 N. Haddon Ave., 856/795-9085), and **Raks Thrift Avenue** (43 Kings Hwy. E. Unit A3, 856/429-6777). The oh-so-urban **Six** (6 Mechanic St., 856/216-0666) carries progressive styles for women from designers like James Jeans and Rock & Republic. Snow bunnies and surf Betties love **The Powder Room** (112 E. Kings Hwy., 856/216-1670), stocking women's boards, designer threads, and accessories for all seasons. Brands include Roxy, Billabong, and Obey.

For baseball cards and sports memorabilia, stop by **Post Game Memories** (138 E. Kings Hwy., 856/216-9881). Corner-spot **Happy Hippo** (201 E. Kings Hwy., 856/429-2308) carries toys for both kids and adults, including LEGO, board games, Madame Alexander dolls, and Radio Flyer wagons.

ANTIQUES AND ART GALLERIES

You'll find vintage maps, glass vases, rare coins,

and books at **Haddonfield Antique Center** (9 E. Kings Hwy., 856/429-1929). **N.K. Thaine Gallery** (150 E. Kings Hwy., 856/428-6961, www.nkthaine.com) is an interesting fine arts and crafts gallery stocking everything from canine-themed papier-mâché wall clocks to footstools with actual feet. **Accent Studio** (207 E. Kings Hwy., 856/795-8800, www.accent-studio.com) displays contemporary glass art that's both functional and fun, along with fine art paintings. The studio also offers custom framing and art restoration.

Accommodations

Housed in a Queen Anne Victorian within walking distance to the borough's shops and transit line, the ◖ **Haddonfield Inn** (44 West End Ave., 856/428-2195 or 800/269-0014, fax 856/354-1273, www.haddonfieldinn.com, $249–349) is really something special. Not only does it offer an ideal stay for area visitors, it's also the perfect escape for local residents who just want to get away. The inn features eight guest rooms and one suite, all individually themed to call to mind nearby Shore towns and exotic faraway places. My favorites are the woodsy Mallard Room, the Cape May Room (just right for a bluesy winter day), and the Dublin Room, with a canopy bed and a mural. Each room has a private bath, wireless Internet, a TV, and a telephone, along with access to a wraparound porch and DVD library. Dogs are permitted in some rooms for a $35 fee, and an elevator provides access for disabled people.

Food

Haddonfield is known more for retail options and architecture than for restaurants, although it's not difficult find somewhere to eat if you're hungry. For something sit-down, there are a couple of in-town choices. For a larger selection, drive west along Haddon Avenue (or hop on the PATCO heading west) into Westmont or on to Collingwood.

In 2005 **The Little Tuna** (141 Kings Hwy. E., 856/795-0888, www.thelittletuna.com, Tues.–Thurs. 11 A.M.–9 P.M., Fri.–Sat. 11 A.M.–10 P.M., Sun. 5–9 P.M., $21–28) relocated to its present larger space among downtown's shops, and things have been on the way up since. The restaurant specializes in fish but also offers various steak and pasta dishes, along with a lunch menu that includes burgers, wraps, and sandwiches. Seasonal sidewalk seating at this trendy BYO provides great people-watching opportunities.

With a name that means "energy," **Animo Juice** (113 Kings Hwy. E., 856/427-9070, www.animojuicecafe.com) delivers the goods. In addition to fresh-pressed juices like carrot and orange-pineapple, this strictly organic café serves up hot soups, signature vitolicious drink blends, and shots of wheatgrass that'll boost your vitality. Detour (on foot) from the main shopping drag to reach **Gracie's Water Ice & Ice Cream** (9 Kings Ct., 856/427-9239, Sun.–Thurs. 12:30–10 P.M., Fri.–Sat. 12:30–10:30 P.M.), an old-fashioned parlor serving chocolate-covered pretzels and delicious banana splits. Take yours to go, or savor it in the court's outdoor gazebo.

Better arrive at **Franco's** (67 Ellis St., 856/857-9889, Mon.–Thurs. 9 A.M.–9 P.M., Fri. 9 A.M.–10 P.M., Sat. 11 A.M.–9 P.M., and Sun. noon–7 P.M., $10–24) with an appetite: Their plain or stuffed deep-fried *panzarottis,* or pizza turnovers, are a lot of meal, but they're oh-so-amazing. Be prepared to wait—Franco's has a dining room, although many prefer these masterpieces to go.

Tristate locals rave about **Fuji** (116 Kings Hwy. E., 856/354-8200, www.fujirestaurant.com, $17–30), a BYO Japanese and sushi restaurant recently relocated from Cinnaminson. Fuji's is open for lunch 11:30 A.M.–2 P.M. Tuesday–Saturday and dinner 5–9:30 P.M. Tuesday–Thursday, 5–10:30 P.M. Friday and Saturday, and 4–9 P.M. Sunday. Closed Monday.

Information and Services

Haddonfield Visitors Center (2 Kings Ct., 856/216-7253, www.haddonfieldnj.org, daily noon–4 P.M.), in the center of the downtown business district, provides free maps and pamphlets, as well as restrooms.

All levels are welcome to the hour-long

classes at **Yoga Center of Haddonfield** (20 Haddon Ave., 856/428-9955, www.haddon fieldyogacenter.com, $15, $3 more for extra half hour, meditation $10). Check their website for a complete schedule.

Getting There

Downtown Haddonfield is located at the intersection of Haddon Avenue (Rte. 561) and Kings Highway (Hwy. 551), just east of Westmont (about a five-minute drive) along Haddon Avenue.

It takes approximately 20 minutes to reach Haddonfield from Philadelphia's Center City on PATCO, which drops you off downtown at Washington Avenue and Kings Highway.

VOORHEES

Voorhees Township (about 10 minutes' drive east from Haddonfield along Haddon Ave./Haddonfield-Berlin Rd.) is home to a significantly large Asian population, reflected in the fine selection of ethnic restaurants scattered throughout the area.

Showcase at the Ritz Center

The Ritz (900 Haddonfield-Berlin Rd., Voorhees, 856/770-9065) ain't what it used to be, but it remains South Jersey's only place for catching first-run art-house movies. Most of the 16 theaters show mainstream hits, with stadium seating and digital surround sound in each. The popular "no kids" and "no unaccompanied teens" rules have been abolished, so choose your seats wisely at showtime.

Food

Voorhees offers a nice mix of restaurants, along with a great pre- or postdinner hangout.

Coffee Works Roastery & Café (910 Berlin Rd., 856/784-5282, www.coffee-works.com) serves a mean cup o' joe, roasted on-site using 100 percent Arabica green coffee beans. Teas, sandwiches, and salads are also in supply, along with an impressive selection of muffins, cookies, and pastries. Tuesdays are open-mic night, but for music a bit more refined stop by weekend evenings. The café offers free Wi-Fi.

For authentic Thai, there's no better place than **Bangkok City** (700 Berlin Rd., 856/309-0459, lunch Mon.–Sat. 11 A.M.–3 P.M., dinner Sun.–Thurs. 4:30–10 P.M., Fri.–Sat. 4:30–11 P.M., $10–20), a BYO located in the Eagle Plaza Shopping Center.

Despite its shopping-plaza locale, **A Little Café** (Plaza Shoppes, 118 White Horse Rd. E., 856/784-3344, http://alittlecafenj.com, dinner Tues.–Thurs. 5–9 P.M., Fri.–Sat. 5–10 P.M., $25–31) is a great spot for romance. With its intimate tables and creative Asian-influenced cuisine—including out-of-this-world appetizers like crepe-wrapped crab "cigarettes" ($14.95)—you'll want to savor the experience. BYO two bottles this time.

Fieni's Ristorante (800 S. Burnt Mill Rd., 856/428-2700, www.fieni.com, Mon.–Thurs. 11 A.M.–10:30 P.M., Fri. 11 A.M.–11 P.M., Sat. 3 P.M.–11 P.M., Sun. 3–9:30 P.M., $17–23), located across the street from the Voorhees Town Center, is a casual BYO serving homestyle Italian dishes. Most everything here is made from scratch, including breads, sauces, and desserts, and the award-winning scarpel soup—a light chicken broth filled with spiraled crepes—will convert you for life.

Featured on the Food Network's *Best of* show, BYO **Ritz Seafood** (910 Rte. 561, 856/566-6650, www.ritzseafood.com, lunch Tues.–Sat. 11:30 A.M.–2:30 P.M., dinner Tues.–Sun. 4:30–10 P.M., closed Mon., $18–39) serves internationally inspired seafood dishes that are simply outstanding, accompanied by an extensive tea selection. A special four-course menu is available daily. For dessert, don't miss the wok-fried Oreos.

WHITE HORSE PIKE

Originally known as Lonaconing ("where waters meet") Trail, the White Horse Pike (Rte. 30) was once an Indian travel route stretching from the Delaware River to the Atlantic Ocean. It later developed into a paved thoroughfare—a major Shore roadway before the Atlantic City Expressway opened. Today, Shore travelers use it as a slower, though more visually interesting, alternative. With its local and chain retailers, chrome diners, and neighborhood pubs, it's far more intriguing than a toll road, and there are several stop-worthy towns and worthwhile detours en route.

The White Horse Pike is accessible from Route 130. From there, it continues east through South Jersey and across the lower Pinelands, eventually reaching Absecon before ending at Atlantic City. It's about 60 miles from beginning to end, and takes a little over one hour to complete when driving straight through. Stopping for a midday meal or a visit to the Peter Mott Museum adds a couple more hours.

Oaklyn

From Route 130, White Horse Pike extends east through Southern Collingswood, past the massive Heights of Collingswood apartments and into Oaklyn borough. On your left will be the **Ritz Theatre** (915 White Horse Pike, 856/858-5230, www.ritztheatreco.org), with its eye-catching red and white marquee. This restored 1927 Greek Revival theater, now listed on the National Register of Historic Places,

puts on classic and children's musicals year-round, hosts comedy nights, and showcases monthly art exhibits. It has been home to the Ritz Theatre Company performance group for nearly 30 years.

For a nearby bite to eat, try **Aunt Berta's Kitchen** (639 White Horse Pike, 856/858-7009, www.auntbertaskitchen.com, Wed.–Thurs. 11 A.M.–9 P.M., Fri.–Sat. 7 A.M.–10 P.M., Sun. 7 A.M.–7:30 P.M.). It's a tiny place with counter seats, a few front tables, and a small dining area. Aunt Berta's specializes in down-home-style soul food, including baked mac and cheese ($4), the rib sandwich ($9) and sweet potato pie ($2). Weekends include an all-you-can-eat brunch with fresh biscuits and grits.

Haddon Heights

There's plenty to like about Haddon Heights, a former railway town about 1.5 miles east of Oaklyn. The main street is pleasant, and so are the people; there's a nice park for picnicking on the edge of town. There's even a refurbished train station honoring the community's

Haddon Heights train station

history as a railway town. The main stretch of Station Avenue, just south of Haddon Avenue, is lined with shops, eateries, and cafés, many worth visiting. They all lead toward 74-acre **Haddon Lake Park,** a neighborhood park with bicycle paths, picnic tables, playgrounds, and an outdoor amphitheater. While in town, stop by **John's Friendly Market** (856/547-6132), the town's unofficial meeting place, and pick up some snacks. For something a bit more substantial, there's **Station House Restaurant** (600 Station Ave., 856/547-5517, Mon.–Sat. 7 A.M.–3 P.M., Sun. 7 A.M.–2 P.M., $6–18), a cozy restaurant serving country-style meals, including breakfast.

Elements Café (517 Station Ave., 856/546-8840, www.elementscafe.com, lunch Tues.–Sat. 11:30 A.M.–3 P.M., dinner Tues.–Fri. 4:30–9 P.M., Sat. 5–10 P.M., closed Sun.–Mon.) is a great place to stop with friends. This BYO serves sampling-sized New American tapas like smoked sea scallops ($12) and chorizo beignets ($8). Eat as much or as little as you like.

Lawnside

Originally known as Snow Hill, Lawnside is the only historically African American incorporated municipality in the United States. Once a haven of jazz clubs and music, the borough was also a significant player in the Underground Railroad. Today, visitor's can tour the **Peter Mott House** (26 Kings Ct., 856/546-8850, www.petermotthouse.org, Sat. noon–3 P.M., Mon.–Fri. by appointment only, $5 adult, $2 student), former home of Peter Mott, a free black 19th-century farmer and minister, and an Underground Railroad stop operated by the Lawnside Historical Society. It's also Lawnside's oldest home and houses a collection of local memorabilia.

Stratford

While not exactly a destination, Stratford does have a couple of noteworthy spots, including the popular **Stratford Diner** (19 S. White Horse Pike, 856/435-4300), where both the staff—and the turkey burger ($7)—receive high ratings. Stratford's **PATCO Park and**

Ride is South Jersey's access station for NJ Transit into Atlantic City. If you're going down the Shore and don't want to drive, begin your journey here. A bit past the PATCO turn-off, look for **La Martinique Bowling Alley** (501 S. White Horse Pike, 856/783-0558, www .lamartiniquelanes.com). Featuring 80 lanes, La Martinique was voted by South Jersey's *Courier Post* as one of the top bowling alleys in the region.

Clementon Amusement Park and Splash World Water Park

Opened in 1907, Clementon Amusement Park (144 Berlin Rd., 856/783-0263, www.clementon park.com, $25–34) is one of the few New Jersey amusement parks that have survived the times, likely due to loyal patrons and Clementon's ability to adapt. Recent years have seen the addition of a water park and 2004's Jackrabbit Two—now known as Hell Cat—a hybrid wood and steel roller coaster with one

PINE VALLEY

Just beyond Clementon Lake is a small community hidden from view by a dense stand of trees and protected from the street by a large iron gate and a stoic security guard. Don't even think about trespassing; this borough, population 20, has its own police force. Welcome to Pine Valley, the country's most consistently rated number-one private golf course and one of the top 10 courses in the world. Why so special? Amateur architect George Crump developed the course in such a way that no one hole sits parallel to the next. Add to this the sandy soil of New Jersey's coastal plains, ample woodland, and a hole known as "Hell's Half Acre," and you've got yourself a course that has hosted presidents, celebrities, and the best golfers in the world. Rarely does this ultraexclusive establishment see an ordinary joe. Mondays are reserved for staff members and their guests, and women are limited to Sunday afternoons.

of the steepest vertical drops of any wooden roller coaster in North America. (The park's original Jack Rabbit was the world's longest continuously operating ride in the same location before it shut down in 2002.) As the state's second oldest amusement park, it has really done well, growing from a tiny fun park into a full-blown theme park, complete with the brand-new Laguna Kahuna, a 13,000 square foot Polynesian-inspired water attraction with eight slides, 10 play platforms, and a 50-foot-tall tiki-like water bucket dumping 422 gallons of water at a time on unsuspecting visitors. The older rides, including the giant Ferris wheel, classic carousel, and a log flume built entirely over Clementon Lake, are still my favorites, but newer rides like the Inverter, an upside-down circular ride not for the faint-hearted, are just as popular. The park opens for long weekends in June and daily in July and August, but call ahead—occasionally groups rent out the park for company picnics. Weekend evenings in October are a good time to visit, as the park transforms into a Halloween fun house complete with a haunted trail, railway, and mansion. Discount entry coupons for the season are often available online or in local newspapers.

For a nearby dine-in meal, try **Cotardo's Ristorante Italiano** (1468 Blackwood-Clementon Rd., Clementon, 609/627-2755, www.cotardosrestaurant.com, Mon.–Thurs. 11 A.M.–9:30 P.M., Fri.–Sat. 11 A.M.–10:30 P.M., Sun. noon–9 P.M., $16–32), a popular southern Italian eatery with a steady clientele. Regulars can't get enough of the seafood pescatore ($32 and $60), a mound of pasta served on a double-sized plate, covered in red or white sauce with mussels, clams, scallops, shrimp, lobster tail, and crab legs. The restaurant's shopping-strip location doesn't prevent couples from lining up out the door with their bottles of wine, so get here early.

Berlin Market

From Clementon Park, travel the Berlin-Clementon Road south a few miles for the Berlin Farmers Market (41 Clementon Rd., Berlin, 856/767-1284, www.berlinfarmersmarket.com). This is one of those places you'll either love or hate, but either way it's an experience. Established in 1940, the market consists of a large indoor mart and a weekends-only outdoor flea market with over 700 stalls (if you're claustrophobic, this isn't the place for you). A lot of it is junk, but it's worth a go-through. Come here for that off-the-wall item you can't find elsewhere.

Nothing like a mall, the indoor mart consists of two long aisles tightly packed with stores, each having numerous entryways. One store worth a visit is **Sam's Fabric Center** (store 120, 856/767-2552, www.samsfabrics.com), offering an expansive selection of fabric, drapery, vinyl, even foam rubber. Sam's is consistently regarded as South Jersey's favorite fabric center.

Berlin's indoor mart is open Thursday–Saturday 10 A.M.–9 P.M., Sunday 10 A.M.–6 P.M. The outdoor flea market runs Saturday–Sunday 8 A.M.–4 P.M., weather permitting.

Gloucester County

A conglomeration of small towns, suburbs, farmland, and ample greenery, Gloucester County is both touched with history and rampant with new development. Shopping centers, big-box stores, and locally owned institutions share space with produce stands and county parks, not to mention 19th-century homes and 18th-century inns. Major local throughways include Route 45, traveling south from Camden County's Route 130 past strip malls and through picturesque towns en route to Salem County, and Route 47, running through Deptford's retail center into tiny Pitman Borough and the university town of Glassboro before continuing on to Cumberland County. Route 322 stretches west-east from Pennsylvania's **Commodore Barry Bridge** through the antique village of Mullica Hill, heading on to the Shore. Straightforward routes sparse with scenery but heavy with local exits include Route 295 and Route 55.

DEPTFORD

Deptford Township is known for two things: a balloon landing and the Deptford Mall. While the landing of Jean Pierre Blanchard's hot-air balloon, which took off from Philadelphia and traveled 15 miles to become the first manned aerial flight in the United States, is the one that's featured on the township's seal, it is the mall that has most defined this community. The 1975 opening of the **Deptford Mall** (1750 Deptford Center Rd., 856/848-6400) began the township's transition from pig farms to shopping centers, chain restaurants, and multiplexes. There's not a lot to see, but it makes a convenient overnight stop (workers doing business in Philly stay here) or a shopping stop.

Deptford's most famous resident is perhaps Jonas Cattell (although rock singer Patti Smith spent her preteen and teen years in Deptford and graduated from Deptford High). Cattell was a well-known hunter and woodsmen and spotter for the Gloucester County Fox Hunting Club, a popular 18th-century area club. On October 22, 1777, Cattell ran from Haddonfield to Fort Mercer in present-day National Park (see Woodbury) to inform the American Army about approaching Hessian soldiers. Today, Cattell Road runs through one of Deptford's few remaining wooded areas. Its namesake and his family are buried at a small private cemetery in Deptford's Gardenville neighborhood.

Accommodations

Deptford's hotels were built in the late 1990s to accommodate the growing number of workers and other visitors to the Philadelphia Metropolitan Area. They offer the best overnight options for exploring Gloucester County, and are both only steps away from numerous restaurants, shops, and movie theaters.

Right behind Deptford Mall near the Route 42 off-ramp is the basic **Fairfield Inn** (1160 Hurffville Rd., 856/686-9050, marriott.com/ fairfieldinn, $129–149), a smoke-free hotel with wireless Internet and complimentary continental breakfast.

Adjacent to the Fairfield, **Residence Inn by Marriott** (1154 Hurffville Rd., 856/686-9188, www.marriott.com, $159–229), caters to business travelers with a full kitchen, a work desk, and wireless Internet in every room. This smoke-free inn also features a heated indoor pool and an exercise room. Pets are welcome for an additional $75 fee.

Food and Entertainment

Deptford has a ton of fast-food and chain restaurants in the area, but for something unique try **Filomena Lakeview** (1738 Cooper St., 856/228-4235, www.filomenalakeview .com, lunch Mon.–Fri. 11:30 A.M.–3 P.M., Sat. 11:30 A.M.–2 P.M., Sun. 11 A.M.–3 P.M. in the bar, dinner Mon.–Thurs. 4–10 P.M., Fri.–Sat. 4–11 P.M., Sun. 3–9 P.M., $16–36), a renovated historic inn with restored ceiling beams, hardwood floors, and fireplaces, not to mention fine Italian dishes. The two-story eatery offers evening piano accompaniment for meals throughout the week.

For late-night dining there's no place better than Runnemede's 24-hour ◖ **Phily Diner** (31 S. Black Horse Pike, Runnemede, 856/939-4322, daily 24 hours, $7–18), just a short drive from Deptford Mall. More like a neodiner, its classic chrome and neon shine brighter than any old-school haunt, and its burgers are bigger and juicier than most. My dad's not a diner fan, but he likes it here. To reach Phily Diner take Clements Bridge Road west and turn right on the Black Horse Pike (Rte. 42); the sign is on your right.

WASHINGTON TOWNSHIP

For 45 years South Philadelphians longing for manicured lawns, good schools, and designated parking spots have settled on the once-farmlands of South Jersey's Washington Township, one of several such-named townships in the state. The 23-square-mile "South Philly South" or "Township," as its often called, is made up mostly of residential and retail development interspersed with the occasional country road, but a few worthwhile attractions exist. To get a feel for local life before the SUVs and soccer moms, visit one of the remaining area farms, which still manage to do good business. Township's oldest standing structure, **The Old Stone House** (856/227-9681), and its small surrounding village are open for tours on weekends.

Duffield's Farm

One of only a handful of farms still operating in Washington Township, family-run Duffield's Farm (280 Chapel Heights Rd., Sewell, 856/589-7090, www.duffieldsfarm .com, Mon.–Sat. 9 A.M.–7 P.M. during summer, 9 A.M.–6 P.M. the remainder of the year) sells fresh produce, meats and cheeses, and a variety of pies and breads baked fresh on the premises. Delicious apple-cider doughnuts are a farm specialty, and definitely worth any added calories.

Duffield's hosts activities for kids year-round, including Halloween hayrides and Easter-egg hunts, as well as pick-your-own strawberries, peas, and pumpkins in season for adults. The farm also hosts a craft fair featuring more than 100 artisans annually in the fall. And don't worry about Duffield's disappearing; they're enrolled in New Jersey's Farmland Preservation program, so regardless of encroaching development, they'll continue to remain a farm.

Commerce Bank Arts Centre

Originally designed as an auditorium for Washington Township High School's student overflow, 2,500-seat Commerce Bank Arts Centre (529 Hurffville-Crosskeys Rd., 856/218-8902, www.sjlivearts.com) also serves as a public venue, hosting the likes of Bill Cosby, Tony Bennett, and the Beach Boys, along with plays and musicals. The center is a convenient entertainment alternative to driving into Philly.

Skydive Cross Keys

I never thought of South Jersey as a skydiving locale, but with so many open fields and so much farmland, it only makes sense. Skydive Cross Keys (300 Dahlia Ave., 856/629-7553, skydive@freefalladventures.com, www.cross keysskydiving.com) is apparently ahead of the curve. Planes take off from Williamstown's Cross Keys Airport, reaching 14,000 feet before releasing you to the skies. Tandem dives cost $165 in person, $149 online, with an additional $30 gear-rental fee. For an added thrill, book an extreme tandem skydive ($299), performed from a turbine helicopter hovering steady. You accelerate from zero to 120 miles per hour in a heartbeat. Skydive Cross Keys opens Monday–Friday at 10 A.M., Saturday–Sunday at 9 A.M. (occasionally 8 A.M.).

Hospitality Creek Campground and Swim Club

Hospitality Creek Campground (117 Coles Mill Rd., 856/629-5140, www.hospitality creek.com, mid-Apr.–Sept., from $49) hosts more than 200 tent and RV sites, along with a 30-acre lake for swimming, fishing, and boating (boat rentals are available). In 2006 the campground opened an activity pool, complete with hoppable lily pads, water-dumping buckets, and a log slide, designed for families with younger kids. A swim-club membership is open to area residents without additional overnight fees.

Food

You'll find plenty of chain restaurants in Washington Township, mostly along the Black Horse Pike. Family-owned Italian eateries are also in great supply. Lately, Township has been working to establish its niche in fine dining, and while results are slow going, they're definitely beginning to pay off.

Why should Hoboken get all the Frank? At the Rat Pack–inspired **Blue Eyes** (130 Egg Harbor Rd., 856/227-5656, www.blueeyes restaurant.com, Mon.–Wed. 11:30 A.M.– 10 P.M., Thurs. 11:30 A.M.–11 P.M., Fri. 11:30 A.M.–midnight, Sat. 4 P.M.–1 A.M., Sun. 3–9 P.M., $18–42) even South Jerseyans can live the highball life. Order a martini, snag a high-backed booth, and sway to a Friday-night song sung by a wannabe Sinatra crooner. This is a steak-and-potatoes kind of place where Sunday best is required, although rumor has it that the dress code isn't as strict as some swingers would like. An outdoor patio has been added for sultry summer nights.

Sal's Pizza (404 Egg Harbor Rd., 856/468-2226, Mon.–Sat. 11 A.M.–11 P.M. and Sun. noon–10 P.M.) has been serving up superb pepperoni pies for more than two decades. For an easy bite, this is your place.

PITMAN

Pitman is a small unpretentious borough situated in the heart of Gloucester County. Named for the famous Methodist preacher Reverend Charles Pitman, the town began in the late 1800s as a Methodist summer camp. Homes were seasonal at first, but many families eventually decided to live in them year-round. Although the borough is no longer a Methodist retreat, the religious influence is still apparent, most notably in laws restricting liquor sales.

Pitman is filled with narrow streets and front-porch cottages, and its main thoroughfare, Broadway, is a pleasant mix of commercial and mom-and-pop shops with the feel of a mid-century small town. In 2005 the borough celebrated its 100th anniversary as an incorporated community.

Pitman is home to the regionally famous **Original Hobo Band** (www.originalhoboband .org), a 40-piece marching band whose members dress in ragtag costumes and hole-punched hats, part of the neighborhood since 1946.

Broadway

Pitman's downtown centers around Broadway, where you'll find the borough's small selection of shops and eateries. This main street is also home to Pitman's Broadway Theatre, a venue that's more than worth your time.

The best place to begin exploring is on the downtown corner of Pitman Avenue and Broadway, at **Bob's Hobbies and Crafts** (67 S. Broadway, 856/589-1777). Bob's shelves are stocked with everything from coin-collecting booklets to wooden race-car parts. If you're thinking of acquiring a hobby, this is the place to come.

North of Bob's is the wonderful **Broadway Theatre** (43 S. Broadway, 856/384-8381, www.thebroadwaytheatre.org), a restored 1920s vaudeville house and single screen that after several owners closed its doors in 2005, only to reopen in fall 2006 with movies, musicals, concerts, and children's theater. Most films shown are second-run, although not too far out of initial release. One Wednesday each month the theater runs a classic matinee series, featuring films like *Bonnie and Clyde* and Hitchcock's *Rear Window,* along with pipe-organ performances by the South Jersey Theatre Organ Society. You're not going to wax poetic about the seats, but considering the theater's history and the overall experience, a little discomfort is worth it.

Looking for dressage coats, shipping boots, and saddle bags? Stop by **Pegasus Closet** (17 S. Broadway, 856/218-7770, http://pegasus closet.com), a unique equestrian boutique. The shop also does a brisk online business.

Occupying a former Victorian residence, **My Fair Lady Consignment Shoppe** (20 S. Broadway, 856/256-0111) displays women's fashions according to rooms. Eveningwear is shown off in an upstairs bedroom, while lingerie hangs in the bathroom above a claw-foot tub. The shop also sells a wide selection of global and locally made jewelry.

Pitman Grove

Pitman Grove was the borough's original Methodist summer camp, a series of twelve cottage-lined walkways, said to represent the 12 apostles, radiating from a central pavilion. Many of those first homes are still in use and are in decent shape. Visitors are free to walk along the pathways, and it's something I recommend doing. All of the homes face inward, and without traffic distracting you, it's easy to imagine these same structures as they were a century before. The grove is listed on both New Jersey's and the National Register of

Historic Places. You can enter at the intersection of Broadway and Pitman Avenue.

Food

Pitman's few eateries are mostly local establishments serving breakfast and lunch. This isn't the place for gourmet foodies, but it makes for a pleasant break.

Downtown's gingham-dressed **Broadway Café** (13 S. Broadway, 856/589-2669, Mon.–Fri. 8 A.M.–2 P.M., Sat. 8 A.M.–noon, Sun. 8:30 A.M.–12:30 P.M.) is both cozy and cute, serving up simple breakfast and lunch dishes for less than $10.

For something sweet, including sticky buns and ice cream, stop by **Pitman Bakery** (130 S. Broadway, 856/589-4276), a local institution. **Jim & Mike's Pizzeria & Restaurant** (7 S. Broadway, 856/582-8044) serves up pies, cheesesteaks, and pizza turnovers to a regular clientele. The in-town place for hoagies is **Pal Joey's Deli** (58 S. Broadway, 856/256-1333).

GLASSBORO

South of Pitman, where Broadway turns into Main, is Glassboro, a university town with a long history in glassworks. Glassboro, or "Glass Town" as it was originally called, was founded as a glass factory by German immigrant Solomon Stanger, a former employee of Salem County's Wistar Glassworks. For several decades Glassboro was South Jersey's leading glass producer. Today, the town's primary focus is Rowan University and getting its downtown—a noncohesive group of eateries and service stores hovering around Main and 11th Streets—back on track with the help of the Main Street New Jersey revitalization program, aimed at improving downtown districts. In the meantime, there are some places worth a stop on your way through town.

Rowan University

Founded in 1923 as a training school for teachers and expanded into Glassboro State College in the 1950s, it wasn't until the 1990s that Rowan College, later Rowan University, came into being. Rowan is Glassboro's centerpiece, occupying much of the land once owned by the town's founder, Solomon Stanger, along with what later became Whitney Glassworks. The Whitney family's 1840s Italian–style villa,

Bunce Hall, Rowan University, Glassboro

© DREW KINIRY

Hollybush Mansion, has since been used as a dormitory, an administrative building, a museum, and is currently a reception space. In July 1967 the mansion was the site of a last-minute Cold War summit between President Lyndon B. Johnson and Soviet Premier Aleksey Kosygin.

Sights

Glassboro's recently renovated **Heritage Glass Museum** (High and Center Sts., 856/881-7468, Sat. 11 A.M.–2 P.M., last Sun. of every month 1–4 P.M.) is worth a stop if you're in the area. The small museum offers a peek into South Jersey's extensive glass heritage, and its collection includes amber bottles and jars blown at Whitney Glassworks, on whose original property the museum now sits. Free docent-led tours on Glassboro's glass history are held some Saturdays during summer months; call ahead.

Heritage Station and Winery (480 Rte. 322, Richwood, 856/589-4474, www.heritage stationfruit.com) is one of the few New Jersey wineries in the Philadelphia region. The property hosts a mix of fruit trees and grapevines, and in turn some of their specialty wines include peach, blueberry, and sugarplum. The main store (open through winter) sells stuffed gift baskets and fresh-baked goods, and offers free wine tasting. Apple picking, pumpkin picking, hayrides, and a corn maze are some of the events hosted throughout the year.

Recreation

Can't stand the humidity? Head down Route 553 to **Lake Garrison** (Monroeville, 856/881-2972, daily Fathers Day–Labor Day, $9 Mon.–Fri., $10 weekends and holidays), a favorite local watering hole. Grab a picnic table in the shade or take a boat (rowboat, canoe, or paddleboat $6 per half hour) out on the water; just be sure to lather on that sunscreen. Swimming is limited to a small section along the shore.

Scotland Run Park (980 Academy St., Rte. 610, Franklinville, 856/881-0845), located in nearby Franklinville, is 940 acres of meadows and marshes with numerous nature trails and an 80-acre lake ideal for fishing and boating.

Food and Entertainment

Glassboro's eateries cater mostly to university students and a local crowd.

Since 1946 **Angelo's Glassboro Diner** (26 N. Main St., 856/881-9854, Mon.–Sat. 5 A.M.–9 P.M., Sun. 5 A.M.–8 P.M., $4–15) has been hashing out an authentic South Jersey experience. Small and worn with only one row of booths and counter seating, it's home to a bevy of regulars who like their eggs how they like 'em. Angelo's is closed the week between Christmas and New Year's.

Situated on the longest continuously running tavern spot in Glassboro (dating back to 1781), **Landmark Tap and Grill** (1 East/West St., 856/863-6600, www.landmarkamericana .com, Mon.–Sat. 11 A.M.–2 A.M., Sun. noon–midnight, $12–20) is a restaurant, bar, dance club, and liquor store combined. While students tends to congregate around the massive central bar, families, couples, and seniors relax with burgers and sandwiches in the quieter outskirts of the main dining area. Landmark is best known for its three-feet-high beer towers, which have numerous taps and are served with several pitchers. Cold rods run through the tower's middle to keep the beer—a ridiculous amount of it, really—cold.

Adjoining Landmark is **Spot Dance Club,** featuring DJ music and drink specials weekly. The club mostly caters to a university crowd, as evidenced by its MySpace page.

WOODBURY

Like Philadelphia across the river, Woodbury exudes history. It's much smaller than the City of Brotherly Love, granted, but its past is just as apparent. Colonial brick and century-old structures line Broad Street (Route 45), the city's main thoroughfare, and grand homes on spacious lots lie west along Delaware Avenue toward the river. It's easy to envision Hessian Soldiers marching through town as they did more than 200 years ago en route to fight Revolutionary soldiers at Fort Mercer in nearby National Park. But Woodbury's position as Gloucester County's political seat takes precedence over history, and power lunches are the norm at area restaurants and cafés. Over the last decade the city has experienced new life with help from New Jersey's Main Street improvement program, although things seem to be at a standstill. Many of Broad Street's structures are still awaiting makeovers, others stand tenantless, and crime is a problem on the east side of town. Still, the city has several sights of historic interest, both downtown and nearby, as well as a café and a few shops making it worth the trip.

Driving east along Cooper Street or west onto Delaware from Broad Street will give you a good feel for the city's history. Many of the homes you'll see are colonials with Victorian additions, and each is unique.

Sights

Woodbury is brimming with history. Drive around the city or walk along downtown Broad and Delaware Streets to take in some of the historic sights.

On the east side of Broad Street is the 1715 **Friends Meeting House** (120 N. Broad St.), a gathering place for Quakers. Although the structure's eastern side was added in 1785, its western portion is considered one of South Jersey's oldest meetinghouses. The structure was used as a makeshift hospital for Hessian soldiers during the nearby Battle of Red Bank, and was once used as a barracks for British soldiers. A bit south is the **Hunter-Lawrence-Jessup House** (58 N. Broad St., 856/848-8531, $2 adult, free age 12 and under), an attractive brick colonial built in 1765 and since updated numerous times, including with the addition of a mansard roof. Revolutionary Army chaplain Reverend Andrew Hunter once owned the house, which was also the boyhood home of Captain James "Don't Give Up the Ship!" Lawrence, a Burlington City native. In the 1800s judge and civic leader John S. Jessup owned it. Today, the **Gloucester County Historical Society** operates the house as an 18-room museum, open to the public Monday, Wednesday, and Friday 1–4 P.M., and the last Saturday and Sunday of the month 2–5 P.M. The Historical Society's library (856/845-

4771) is located in a smaller building at 17 Hunter Street, and is open Monday–Friday 1–4 P.M., Tuesday and Friday 6–9:30 P.M., with additional hours the first Saturday of the month 10 A.M.–4 P.M., and the last Sunday of the month 2–5 P.M.

Woodbury's historic district stretches from Woodbury Creek south to Kings Highway and includes the **Gloucester County Courthouse** (1 N. Broad St.), an 1885 Romanesque-style brownstone standing at the corner of Broad and Delaware Streets. The structure's clock tower is one of the city's most recognizable sights, and often displays Santa during December. Next door on Delaware is the limestone and granite **Courthouse Annex,** built in 1925, and across the street is the colonial revival–style **City Hall.** Its lower eastern portion was once Woodbury's Society of Friends' first permanent school.

Originally founded in 1799, **Woodbury Fire Co.** (29 Delaware St.) resides in a 1920s building located next door. Behind the fire hall is a small museum filled with firefighter memorabilia, including photos, helmets, and badges. To arrange a tour of the museum and firehouse call 856/845-0066; the museum is open to the public Monday–Friday.

The former opera house **G.G. Green Building** stands unoccupied on the western corner or Broad and Centre Streets. Green, a pharmaceutical manufacturer and prominent local figure, was responsible for much of Woodbury's growth between 1880 and 1900. His patent medicines stopped production after World War II, but many of his workers-quarters homes remain.

Red Bank Battlefield

In addition to its playgrounds, open fields, and a narrow riverfront beach, National Park's Red Bank Park (100 Hessian Ave., National Park, 856/853-5120) was the site of a historic October 22, 1777, battle between more than 1,000 Hessian soldiers and 600 Revolutionary troops. Marching from Haddonfield, the British-service Hessians hoped to surprise American soldiers stationed at Red Bank's Fort Mercer, a fort protecting nearby Philadelphia. The fore-warned Americans claimed victory instead, resulting in nearly 500 Hessian casualties. Red Bank's **Ann Whitall House** (856/853-5120, Wed.–Sun. 1–4 P.M. Apr.–Sept., Wed.–Fri. 9 A.M.–noon and 1–4 P.M. Oct.–Mar.), a 1748 colonial farmhouse that survived the battle, now operates as a museum. It is said that Mrs. Whitall waited out the battle inside her home, tending to wounded soldiers afterward. Tours of the home are free.

Red Bank Park is a great place to watch the sun set over the Delaware or airplanes descend into Philadelphia International Airport (PHL), just across the river. Some planes are flying so low you can practically see the passengers. The park hosts numerous events year-round, including a costumed battle reenactment the third Saturday in October and the Jonas Cattell Run, a 10K race recreating Cattell's famous jaunt (see *Deptford* in this chapter) from Haddonfield to Fort Mercer, warning Revolutionary soldiers of the approaching Hessians.

Food and Entertainment

Diners are the norm around these parts. Fast food is rampant in Woodbury's outlying areas, but the selection is such that you shouldn't need to go down that road.

Although not much to look at from the outside, 24-hour **Colonial Diner Restaurant** (924 N. Broad St., 609/848-6732, $4–15) serves one of the best breakfasts in town (ooh, the hotcakes!), complete with an endless pot of coffee. The front room, with its booths and counter seating, is best.

On the corner of Broad Street and Delaware is **CHC Coffee Shop** (1 S. Broad St., 856/845-0607, Mon.–Fri. 7 A.M.–5 P.M., Sat. 9 A.M.–5 P.M., closed Sun.), a local coffeehouse filled with cozy couches, gourmet coffee dispensers, and a mix of city employees and students from the nearby public high school. It's a great place to come for your caffeine fix, along with toasted bagels and Wi-Fi.

Woodbury's local **Farmers Market** (Cooper St. and Railroad Ave., 856/845-1300 ext. 123, mid-June–Oct.) is held Thursdays 2–6 P.M. in the train station parking lot. Shop for oyster mushrooms, brown eggs, heirloom tomatoes, homemade jams, organic produce, and more—including Italian ices.

South along Route 45 is the **Hollywood Cafe Diner** (940 Rte. 45, 856/251-0011, www.hollywoodcafeandsportsbar.com, call for hours, $7–18), a bright neon beacon that only *looks* like a diner, although it does have a similar menu and layout. The place makes a mean BLT, and the bathrooms are spotless. There's also an attached sports bar.

◖ MULLICA HILL

Mullica Hill is an adorable village filled with historic colonial and Victorian structures, each occupied by antique shops, specialty stores, and a couple of fine cafés and eateries. The town straddles Route 45 midway between Woodbury and Salem. A Finn named Eric Molica founded Mullica Hill with his brothers in the late 1700s. They originally purchased the land and its surrounding acres for farming, and the area remains largely rural today.

While street parking is hard to come by, many of the shops provide lots or spaces in back. Mullica Hill is not exactly walkable. Traffic on Main Street (Rte. 45) can be heavy, and shops are spread out along a fairly steep hill. I suggest parking in one of the lots and exploring the shops in that area.

Antiques and Specialty Shops

Since many Mullica Hill stores are closed Monday–Tuesday, it makes sense to save your visit for later in the week. But be warned: during summer months the traffic along Route 322, which snakes through the village center, can be nightmarish with Pennsylvania folks heading to and from the shore. To save yourself trouble, arrive early.

Housed in a former bus terminal, the magnificent 6,500-square-foot **Yellow Garage Antiques** (66 S. Main St., 856/478-0300, www.yellowgarageantiques.com, Wed.–Sun. 11 A.M.–5 P.M.) features the wares of 35 antique dealers. The shop provides props and furniture for many M. Night Shyamalan films.

HISTORIC INNS OF SOUTH JERSEY

Throughout New Jersey, inns were traditionally built at major crossroads to act as rest stops, meetinghouses, dining halls, and taverns for travelers making arduous multiday journeys from one destination to the next, such as from Philadelphia to the Jersey Shore. Although many of those established statewide during the 18th and 19th centuries still stand today, South Jersey's numbers are particularly prolific. These inns serve as restaurants and bars oozing history from every wall, window, cellar, and ceiling tile. Most serve traditional American fare, and while a few have been updated with modern amenities and decor, their past remains easily recognizable. For a romantic glimpse into South Jersey history and a walk in America's footsteps, stop by one of the following haunts.

Once known as the Spread Eagle, the 1720 **Barnsboro Inn** (699 Main St., Sewell, 856/468-3557, www.barnsboroinn.com, lunch Tues.-Sat. 11 A.M.-2:30 P.M., dinner Tues.-Thurs. 4:30-9:30 P.M., Fri.-Sat. 4:30-10 P.M., Sun. 3-8 P.M., $22-27) originated as a hotel but obtained its first tavern license in 1776. Situated at a five-way intersection west of Gloucester County's Pitman, the inn's original portion acts as a bar – dark and narrow with a low beam ceiling, plenty of stools, a dartboard, and a CD jukebox. The adjoining restaurant is more formal – a favorite among couples who come to dine on clams casino ($8) and prime rib ($27). A garden patio was added in 2005. The bar remains open until 1 A.M. Monday-Thursday, until 2 A.M. Friday and Saturday, and until midnight Sunday.

Occupying a prime piece of property along Swedesboro's Main Street, **Swedes Cafe Bar and Restaurant** (301 Kings Hwy., Swedesboro, 856/467-2032, www.swedesinn.com, Mon.-Thurs. 4 P.M.-midnight, Fri. 11:30 A.M.-2 A.M., Sat. 4 P.M.-2 A.M., Sun. 3-10 P.M., $19-34) was built and licensed as a tavern in 1771. The inn is housed in a pine-green colonial that has been touched with Victorian fixtures, including a front porch and mansard roof. Indoors, however, it is decidedly modern, especially the café, with large windows originally installed for a 1950s car showroom, muraled walls, and an art deco bar. There's even a setup for live music on weekends. The inn stood vacant for 35 years until owner Mark Beltz purchased it in 1979 – sufficient time for Edith, the resident ghost of a 12-year-old girl, to get comfortable living on her own.

At first glance, the **Franklinville Inn** (Delsea Dr./Rte. 47 and County Rd. 538, Franklinville, 856/694-1577, www.franklinvilleinn.com, Tues.-Thurs. 4-9 P.M., Fri.-Sat. 4-10 P.M., $19-32) seems like just another building, perhaps due to its large size and resemblance to many South Jersey suburban homes. But inside it's an entirely different story. Wood-paneled walls, historic paintings, mounted rifles, and low ceilings reveal the past of this traditional inn, once acting as a stagecoach stop between Cape May and Philadelphia. Originally known as Cake's Tavern, the inn dates back to the beginning of the 19th century, operating as a hotel and restaurant until the mid-20th century.

At the intersection of Routes 553 and 540, just northwest of Parvin State Park, stands **Ye Olde Centerton Inn** (1136 Almond Rd., Pittsgrove, 856/358-3201, www.centertoninn.com, Mon. 4-9 P.M., Tues.-Thurs. 4:30-9:30 P.M., Fri.-Sat. 4:30-10 P.M., Sun. 9:30 A.M.-2:30 P.M., $15-30), a former stagecoach stop and freight shop between Cumberland County's Greenwich and Philadelphia. This is South Jersey's oldest surviving inn, dating back to 1706. Its exterior looks a little worse for wear – with peeling paint and chipping clapboard – but its interior is authentically colonial and surprisingly spacious, with eight dining rooms on two floors and an extensive wine cellar. Beneath the inn are the graves of three Revolutionary War soldiers, who share haunting privileges with a female ghost named Margaret.

Kings Row Antique Center (46 N. Main St., 856/478-4361, www.kingsrowantique center.com) is home to numerous proprietors of Victorian furnishings, vintage textiles, books, postcards, and kitchenware.

De Ja Vu Antiques Gift Gallery (38 S. Main St., 856/478-9994) carries Christopher Radko and Old World Christmas ornaments, Camille Beckman toiletries, and Ty collectibles. Search for the perfect display cabinet or 20th-century oil painting at **Front Porch Antiques** (21 S. Main St., 856/478-6556, www.thefrontporchantiques.com).

Just north of the turnoff for Route 322 East is **The Old Mill Antique Mall** (1 S. Main St., 856/478-9810, daily 11 A.M.–5 P.M.), a large barn that's home to more than 50 antiques and collectibles dealers selling everything from Barbie dolls to mid-century dinette sets to locally produced glass bottles.

Purchase paper dolls, doll clothing and accessories, and collectibles designed by Madame Alexander and Effanbee at **Debra's Dolls** (20 N. Main St., 856/478-9778, www.debrasdolls .com, Thurs.–Sat. noon–4 P.M., other days by appointment), housed in one of Mullica Hill's oldest structures. The shop also offers doll restoration.

One of my favorite Mullica Hill shops is **Murphy's Loft** (53 N. Main St., 856/478-4928), a wonderful store packed with vintage magazines, maps, postcards, and period sheet music, along with tens of thousands of used books. You can literally spend hours here. The loft occupies an old barn set back from Main Street, and parking is available on-site.

Mood's Farm Market

From Mullica Hill, take Route 77 east a few miles, passing apple and peach-tree groves to reach Mood's Farm Market (901 Rte. 77, 856/478-2500, www.moodsfarmmarket.com, Mon.–Sat. from 8 A.M., closed Sun., June–Thanksgiving). Mood's offers hayrides and a large selection of pick-your-own fruit, including blackberries, sweet plums, raspberries, and pears. They also sell delicious farm-made apple cider and roasted peanuts on-site.

Food

Opened in December 2005 by Philadelphia native and professionally trained chef James Malaby, ☾ **Blue Plate** (47 S. Main St., 856/478-2112, breakfast Mon.–Fri. 6 A.M.–11:30 A.M., Sat. 6 A.M.–4 P.M., Sun. 7 A.M.–4 P.M., lunch Mon.–Fri. 11:30 A.M.–3 P.M., Sat.–Sun. 11:30 A.M.–4 P.M., dinner Tues.–Sun. 5–9 P.M.) serves casual dishes by morning and day, and by night transforms into a cozy BYO dishing out upscale French-inspired American fare. The decor hasn't changed much from the space's former incarnation as the country-style Hilltop Restaurant, but the evening's dishes are more refined and well worth it. Try a fried onion cheesesteak with waffle fries ($7.25) for lunch, or for dinner begin with a pear and oak-leaf salad (6.75) and continue with handmade potato gnocchi and andouille sausage (19.50).

At the northern junction of Routes 322 and 45 sits the **Harrison House** (Rtes. 45 and 322, 856/478-6077, www.harrisonhousediner.com, daily 6 A.M.–11 P.M., $5–16.95), a popular stop en route for Jersey Shore travelers. With its redbrick exterior and spacious dining area, it's hard to believe the restaurant originated as a moveable diner, relocated to its present (and permanent) location in 1985. Breakfast is available throughout the day, along with a large selection of sandwiches, pasta, and meat dishes. A coffee counter serving mochas, espresso, flavored coffees, and smoothies is a recent addition.

My mom and I make a point to visit **Amelia's Teas & Holly** (26 S. Main St., 856/223-0404, www.ameliasteasandholly.com, Wed.–Sat. 11 A.M.–4 P.M., Sun. noon–4 P.M., closed Mon.–Tues.) together whenever I'm in town. Housed in a circa-1840 two-story home with a gift shop up front, the tearoom is lavished with Victorian touches: high-backed chairs, painted portraits, decorative end tables and cabinets—the ideal setting for sipping gunpowder tea and nibbling on scones. And the crustless egg-salad sandwiches? Don't even get me started.

Just a brief detour from downtown's main stretch is **Crescent Moon Coffee & Tea** (Mullica Hill Plaza, 141 Rte. 77, Store D,

856/223-1237, www.cmcoffee.com, Mon.–Fri. 6:30 A.M.–6 P.M., Sat. 7:30 A.M.–6 P.M., Sun. 8:30 A.M.–2 P.M.), a comfortable place serving artisanal and organic coffees, loose-leaf teas, and panini sandwiches. With a cozy couch and free Wi-Fi, you can make an afternoon of it.

Getting There

Take Route 322 West to reach Mullica Hill from Glassboro, or east from Swedesboro and the Commodore Barry Bridge to Pennsylvania. From Salem and Woodstown take Route 45 North, or Route 45 South from Woodbury.

KINGS HIGHWAY SOUTH

A scenic alternative to both the New Jersey Turnpike and I-295 heading into Salem County, Kings Highway (Hwy. 551) passes through farmland and alongside small storefronts and country homes, with a few historic sites of interest (and seasonal farm stands) along the way. You can pick up the highway along Broad Street in Woodbury or further south along Route 45 in Mantua. Just turn right (west) on Ogden Road to connect.

Roadside Sights

While driving along Kings Highway, keep your eyes peeled for these roadside attractions:

Approximately 2.5 miles from downtown Woodbury on the highway's western side is the Colonial stone **Death of the Fox Inn** (217 Kings Hwy.). Now a private residence, the inn was built in the early 1700s and named for the Gloucester County Fox Hunting Club—one of the country's first fox hunting clubs—whose members would gather there after fox chases. Notable club members included Deptford's Jonas Cattell and Dr. Bodo Otto Jr., whose former residence is just a couple of miles south. While approaching Dr. Otto's home (which will be on your left), look for signs pointing the way to **Haines Pork Shop** (521 Kings Hwy., 856/423-1192), a butcher shop

and smokehouse hidden behind a Victorian home. Locals rave about this place, which sells only the freshest cuts of ribs and tenderloin. People travel from throughout the tristate region to purchase their pork here. Across the street is the **Bodo Otto House.** Dr. Otto was a well-known surgeon who accompanied General George Washington during the Battle of Valley Forge. This house is also privately occupied, and rumored to be haunted. A blue marker in front of the property offers additional background info.

Swedesboro

About five miles south of the Bodo Otto House is Swedesboro, a tiny borough at the heart of Woolwich Township. Swedesboro was settled by Swedes in 1638, and the **"Old Swedes" Trinity Episcopal Church** (208 Kings Hwy., 856/467-1227, Mon.–Sat. by appointment) remains one of downtown's most prominent features. Though the current structure wasn't built until 1784, replacing a damaged log cabin church that stood in its place, it stands on South Jersey's oldest deeded church property. A walk around back reveals a graveyard where many of South Jersey's original Swede settlers are laid to rest, along with Dr. Bodo Otto Jr. and Eric Molica, founder of nearby Mullica Hill. Swedesboro has a small main stretch of commercial storefronts dominated by the distinctive Swedes Café Bar and Restaurant, a historic inn serving New American cuisine and drinks in a modernized setting.

For a nice side trip, take Swedesboro Road east from downtown Swedesboro about eight miles to the **C.A. Nothnagle Log House** (406 Swedesboro Rd., Gibbstown, 856/423-0916, by appointment, free). Built in 1638 by Swedish and Finnish settlers, it's the country's oldest surviving log cabin. While it doesn't look like much from the outside, it's the history that's important. This is a truly unique piece of early settlement history in the United States.

Salem County

Salem County is New Jersey's least populated county, a rural stretch of fruit orchards and farmland and an area with deep historic roots. The county (its name derives from the Hebrew word for peace, *shalom*) was once part of the New Sweden settlement established by Finns and Swedes in the early 17th century, but later became a primary Quaker colony and port of arrival. Located in the state's southwesternmost corner, Salem was originally connected with Burlington City by way of Kings Highway. Today, it retains its relative isolation as farther areas become increasingly burdened with new development.

Filled with silos, farmhouses, and a large number of patterned brick homes built during the 18th century, the county has more of a connection with its neighbors across the river in Delaware and Pennsylvania's Brandywine Valley than with those in New Jersey. Salem retains an agricultural charm unlike anywhere else in the state, although that's not to say industry hasn't touched here. Glassmaking and ice cream production were once big businesses, and **DuPont,** a chemical developing company located along the Delaware River in **Carneys Point,** is one of the county's major manufacturers. Salem is also home to the nation's second-largest nuclear complex, the **Salem/Hope Creek Nuclear Power Plant,** an interesting juxtaposition to its large number of wildlife preserves.

SIGHTS

Salem County's architectural and historic significance is evident, especially in and around the city sharing its name. It's one of the state's most agricultural regions, and it is home to the longest continuously running rodeo on the East Coast.

Salem

Salem is one of South Jersey's oldest cities, founded by English Quaker John Fenwick in 1675. Today, it stands somewhere between

manufacturing community and agricultural town, with red-brick warehouses clustered around its downtown center, and spaciously set colonial farmhouses lining the streets beyond. Salem's history is one of its most enduring features. In fact, the downtown streets Market and Broadway are those Fenwick originally laid out, and they are now listed on the National Register of Historic Places. Salem's starting to emerge as an antiques shopping center, but the city's main draw remains its own history, both traditional and cultural.

Founded in 1884, the **Salem County Historical Society** (79-83 Market St., 856/935-5004, schs@verizon.net, www.salemcountyhistoricalsociety.com, Tues.–Sat. noon–4 P.M.) contains a superb collection of local archival materials, including photographs, diaries, and oral histories, as well as a museum featuring a wonderful display on Wistarburgh Glass. The Society is made up of four historic structures: the **Alexander Grant House** (1721), the **John Jones Law Office** (1721), the **Stone Barn Museum,** and the **Log Cabin Educational Center.** It hosts an annual Salem County historic home and garden tour the first Saturday in May.

Just west of downtown's Market and Broadway intersection is **Friend's Burial Ground,** home to the **Salem Oak.** It was under this hauntingly beautiful white oak tree that John Fenwick acquired soon-to-be Salem from local Lenape Indians. The tree remains one of the city's most revered features.

Salem is considered the birthplace of the "edible tomato." It's said that in 1820 Colonel Robert Gibbon Johnson, a College of New Jersey (now Princeton University) graduate, declared he would eat an entire bushel of tomatoes on the steps of the **Salem County Courthouse** (92 Market St.). Since tomatoes were widely thought to be poisonous, a large crowd gathered to watch Johnson die. He didn't, and tomatoes became part of the American diet. Although the story is likely a legend, it hasn't kept the edible tomato from becoming a bona fide part of Jersey history.

Salem was also home to **Wistarburgh,** the country's first successful glass factory. Although the factory's long gone, the city has retained its glass industry connection. **Salem Community College** (460 Hollywood Ave., 856/299-2100, www.salemcc.org), in nearby Carney's Point, offers the only associate degree in scientific glassblowing in the country. Facilities include the **Paul J. Stankard Gallery,** a showcase of glass art and scientific glass pieces named for internationally acclaimed alum and local resident Paul Stankard, best known for his intricate botanical paperweights.

Just east of Salem is the **Hancock House** (Hancock's Bridge Rd. off Rte. 27, 856/935-4373, www.fohh.20fr.com, donations welcome), a historic site and former residence also known for its architectural significance. In 1778 the home was site of a brutal massacre by British troops led by local loyalists who entered and bayoneted to death nearly 30 colonial militia sleeping in the upstairs attic. Among those killed with the home's owner, Judge William Hancock, himself a British faithful.

Built in 1734 by Judge Hancock's parents, William and Sarah, the home is an excellent example of British Quaker patterned brickwork associated with the local region. William and Sarah's initials, along with the year of the home's construction, adorn the structure's western exterior through a series of interspersed glazed bricks; a glazed-brick herringbone design decorates its exterior side walls. Regular hours are Wednesday–Saturday 10 A.M.–noon and 1–4 P.M., Sunday 1–4 P.M.; these can sometimes vary—call ahead.

Fort Mott State Park

Settled on the banks of the lower Delaware River, Fort Mott State Park (856/935-3218, daily dawn–dusk, free) was once a self-contained military community, built in the late 1800s as part of a three-fort coastal defense system. Today, the 104-acre state park is home to picnic areas, nature trails, and original fort remnants, as well as a visitors center serving as a **Regional Welcome Center** for the **New Jersey Coastal Heritage Trail Route** (NJCHTR). The park hosts year-round interpretive programs, including an all-access tour, and maps for self-guided tours are available at the visitors center.

Drive down Cemetery Road—a striking tree-lined street no wider than a walking path—or stroll along **Finns Point Interpretive Trail** through the **Killcohook Wildlife Refuge** to reach **Finns Point National Cemetery.** This small cemetery, secluded by tall reeds and marshes, is the resting place for nearly 2,500 Confederate soldiers, many of whom died as Pea Patch Island prisoners during the Civil War and are buried together in a mass grave on the cemetery's western side. Union soldiers are also buried here, as are veterans from other wars.

The **Three Forts Ferry** connects Fort Mott to Pea Patch Island's Fort Delaware (the second of three Delaware River defensive forts) during summer months. Ferries depart Saturday–Sunday every two hours 10:30 A.M.–4:30 P.M. until mid-June, and Wednesday–Sunday July–August.

Finns Point Rear Range Lighthouse

At the nearby intersection of Fort Mott and Lighthouse Roads is Finns Point Rear Range Lighthouse (Pennsville, 856/935-1487), part of the greater Supawna Meadows Wildlife Refuge. This 115-foot-tall externally supported structure was built as part of a two-light system, operating in conjunction with a front range light. Ship captains would line up the two lights to guarantee safe travel. Dredging of the Delaware River in the 1950s rendered both lights useless; they were decommissioned and the front one taken down. From the outside, Finns Point Rear Range is hardly anything to look at—it reminds me of a lifeless Jack from *Nightmare Before Christmas*—but you can't deny its history. Call ahead for tours.

New Jersey Coastal Heritage Trail Route

New Jersey's Coastal Heritage Trail is a U.S.-

designated auto and bicycle route highlighting coastal cultural and natural sights from Fort Mott east to Cape May, and north to Central Jersey's Perth Amboy. Stops along the way include lighthouses, estuaries and Pineland forests, patterned brick architecture, and roadside attractions. It's a work in progress with only a couple of regional offices currently open, including Fort Mott's **Delsea Region Welcome Center** (856/935-3218, hours vary). Stop in for brochures, maps, and an information video highlighting the trail. If the Delsea center is closed, you might also try **Cape May Region Welcome Center** (609/624-0918, www.visitnj .org, daily 9 A.M.–4 P.M.), located at the Ocean View Service Area (Milepost 18.3) along the Garden State Parkway.

Woodstown

About 10 miles north of Salem en route to Mullica Hill is the small settlement of Woodstown, a country borough dotted with colonial homes and simple Victorians, surrounded by farms and open countryside. Each December the **Pilesgrove-Woodstown Historical Society** (856/769-4588, www .historicwoodstown.org/hist-soc.html) hosts a candlelight tour highlighting several of its historic homes and downtown structures. The Society's museum (42 N. Main St.) is open Saturday 10 A.M.–1 P.M. year-round.

To get a better feel for the area, head west of town along Route 40 and stop in to **Cowtown Cowboy Outfitters** (Rte. 40 W., 856/769-1761, www.cowtowncowboy.com). Peruse the stock of cowboy boots, Wrangler jeans, silver belt buckles, and felt hats, then mosey across the street to New Jersey's most famous rodeo and flea market.

◖ Cowtown Rodeo and Flea Market

For more than half a century Cowtown Rodeo (780 Rte. 40, Pilesgrove, 856/769-3200, www .cowtownrodeo.com) has been wrangling in crowds who pile into its 4,000-seat stadium for the East Coast's longest continuously running rodeo show. Although it's South Jersey, this ain't no joke: Cowtown rivals anything you'd see in Texas or Wyoming. These here are real cowboys—both on their horses and in the stands—and they're serious. Every Saturday night from Memorial Day to mid-September expect bull riding, team roping, steer wrestling, and women's barrel racing. Cowtown is not hard to find—just look for the giant fiberglass cowboy smiling down over Route 40.

A Cowtown highlight is its year-round Tuesday and Saturday flea market (8 A.M.–4 P.M.). More than 500 vendors set up along dirt paths, touting everything from fringed shirts to supersized beach towels. You may have to dig to find what you're looking for, but the price will be right. Graze on fish and chips or snack on funnel cake while browsing the wares—this indoor-outdoor market is by no means fancy, just good fun.

Cowtown also hosts a livestock auction every Tuesday at noon.

RECREATION

Its proximity to both Delaware Bay and the Delaware River make Salem County a natural for marshes and wetlands, a few that make good fishing and birding locales.

Natural Areas

Supawna Meadows (609/463-0994, http:// northeast.fws.gov/nj/spm.htm, daily dawn–dusk) is a few thousand acres of protected wetland intended for the feeding, nesting, and resting of migratory birds, including waterfowl, ospreys, and bald eagles. The refuge is part of the Cape May National Wildlife Refuge Complex and offers nature trails, as well as opportunities for fishing, crabbing, hunting, and wildlife observation. Eighty percent of the Meadows are marshland, accessible only by boat (you provide your own).

Additional local wetlands include **Stow Creek Viewing Area** (between Hancock House and Greenwich, off Rte. 623, 609/628-2103, daily dawn–dusk), a bald eagle nesting place and educational facility featuring both a boardwalk and interpretive exhibits, and the **Alloway Creek Watershed** (888/627-7437, daily dawn–dusk), which offers observation platforms and a nature trail.

Parvin State Park

At the border with Cumberland County is Parvin State Park (791 Almond Rd., Pittsgrove, 856/358-8616, www.state.nj.us/dep/parksand forests/parks/parvin.html, daily year-round, $2 bicycle or walk-in Memorial Day–Labor Day), nearly 2,000 acres filled with pine and swamp hardwood forests and home to more than 200 flowering plant species. Parvin has 15 miles of hiking trails, many of them suitable for mountain bikes and horses, 16 rental cabins for overnight stays, and opportunities for fishing, canoeing, and swimming in **Parvin Lake,** the larger of the park's two lakes, which hosts an open snack bar and accessible boat ramp during summer months. One of the best ways to spend an afternoon at Parvin is to rent a canoe (or bring your own) and paddle along the park's **Muddy Run,** a tributary of Parvin Lake, to the nearby town of **Canterton.**

Fifty-six campsites (year-round, $20) for tents and trailers are located on Parvin Lake's south side, along with four group sites ($1 per person) that each accommodate up to 25. There are 18 cabins (Apr.–Oct.) with living rooms and fireplaces ($45) or stoves ($65) on the north shore of Thundergust Lake, the smaller of the park's two lakes.

The park has an interesting history, including its 1940s use as a day camp for the children of displaced Japanese Americans, and during the same decade as a camp for German prisoners of war relocated from Fort Dix to work on area farms and in factories. The remains of several Indian encampments have been found within park boundaries over the years.

ENTERTAINMENT AND EVENTS
Appel Farm

Founded in 1960 as a private summer arts camp for kids, the nonprofit Appel Farm Arts and Music Center (457 Shirley Rd., Elmer, 856/358-6513 or 800/394-1211, www.appel farm.org) has expanded to hosting visual and performing arts workshops for all ages, along with a series of musical performers, including folk singers, country stars, and classic violinists, year-round. The center is located on 176 out-of-the-way wooded and open acres—a great place for catching one of their summer outdoor shows. Each June, Appel Farm puts on a daylong **Arts and Music Festival** ($40) with a craft fair and a dozen musical acts. 2008's show featured Suzanne Vega, They Might Be Giants, and the Smithereens.

Appel Farm is located just off Route 77 on Route 611 (Shirley Rd.).

Festivals

Route 40's **Salem County Fairgrounds** hosts Labor Day weekend's annual **Delaware Valley Bluegrass Festival** (www.brandywinefriends .org), three days of bluegrass performances, improv jams, and on-site camping. Tickets run $67.50 adult, $35 student age 12–16 in advance, $80 adult, $40 student at the gate.

ACCOMMODATIONS

Located just beyond the Delaware Memorial Bridge, Pennsville's **Hampton Inn** (429 N. Broadway, 856/351-1700, fax 856/351-9554, www.hamptoninnpennsville.com, $129–179) shares its parking lot with the popular chain restaurant Cracker Barrel. The hotel provides free wireless Internet and seasonal access to an outdoor pool. An on-site bar hosts a weekday happy hour geared towards business travelers. Romeos will want to request the romance package, complete with Belgian chocolates, comfy robes and slippers, and champagne. The fairly new **Comfort Inn & Suites** (634 Sodder's Rd., Carneys Point, 856/299-8282, $90–150) shares its quiet street with a horse farm. Rooms are pet-friendly ($15 extra) and come complete with high-speed Internet, microwaves and fridges, and a deluxe pancake breakfast. Rooms at the **Holiday Inn Express Hotel and Suites** (506 Pennsville-Auburn Rd., Carneys Point, 856/351-9222, $125) are nothing special, but its location just east of I-295 is convenient and its bathrooms are large.

Camping

Yogi Bear's Jellystone Park at Tall Pines (49 Beal Rd., Elmer, 856/451-7479 or 800/252-2890, www.tallpines.com, Apr.–Oct., from $42) is the perfect family campground. Kids stay free, pets are welcome, and events like September's *Survivor* Weekend cater to all ages. Rental cabins are also available.

FOOD

There aren't a lot of restaurants to choose from in Salem County, but those listed below offer good food and pleasant surroundings. For a wider variety, head north into Gloucester and Camden Counties.

To reach the heart of Salem County, head straight to the **Salem Oak Diner** (113 W. Broadway, Salem, 856/935-1305, Mon.–Fri. 5 A.M.–9 P.M., Sat.–Sun. 6 A.M.–9 P.M., $4–14). A local hangout since 1955, the Silk City establishment has changed ownership several times recently, even closing down for a short spell in

2006. Thankfully the diner's quality food and community feel remain.

For fine dining, try **JG Cook's Riverview Inn** (60 Main St., Pennsville, 856/678-3700, www .riverviewinn.net, Wed.–Thurs. 11:30 A.M.–10 P.M., Fri.–Sat. 11:30 A.M.–11 P.M., Sun. 2–9 P.M., $19–27), situated along the Delaware River next to Riverview Park. The lobby displays classic photos of the long-gone Riverview Amusement Park, which once occupied the neighboring space before closing in the 1960s. American entrées include filet mignon ($27) and roasted deep-sea scallops ($19), or you can sit back with a Texas chicken wrap ($7.25) on the outdoor deck overlooking the Delaware.

Best known for its ice cream, **Richman's Restaurant** (849 Rte. 40, 856/769-0356, daily 6 A.M.–9 P.M., $7–10) is a wonderful stop for a step back in time. With well-worn booths, counter service, and a seasonal ice cream window, not to mention a menu filled with budget selections like grilled cheese and burgers, it feels like the 1940s.

Cumberland County

Cumberland County, or "the Bayshore Region," is filled with wetlands, fishing villages, and charming river towns. It's also home to numerous historic districts, a budding arts scene, and New Jersey's largest city in terms of land mass, Vineland. Once one of the world's leading oyster harvesters, Cumberland County has held tight to its maritime heritage and remains a prime locale for boating, crabbing, and fishing. The region's scenic river, estuaries, salt marshes, and coastal meadows offer excellent opportunities for spotting egrets, red-tailed hawks, blue jays, and American bald eagles, and along the open fields visitors may glimpse eastern coyotes and white-tailed deer. During summer months the region hosts produce stands on seemingly every corner, and fresh seafood markets are found in most community towns. Like much of South Jersey, Cumberland's glass industry roots run deep, the tradition's output evident in local shops and galleries.

Often bypassed by South Jersey visitors, this surprisingly diverse region should definitely be explored for its culture and beauty, as well as its people.

Information and Services

The **Bridgeton-Cumberland Tourist Association** (50 E. Broad St., Bridgeton, 856/451-4802) is a self-service center located in downtown Bridgeton at the intersection of Routes 77 and 49. If you'd rather speak with a live person, the staff at the nearby **Cumberland County Library** (800 E. Commerce St., 856/453-2210, www.clueslibs .org) is extremely helpful.

The **New Jersey Department of Agriculture**'s website (www.state.nj.us/jersey fresh/) offers updated information on roadside markets, community farmers markets, and pick-your-own farms within the county and throughout New Jersey. For a full list of

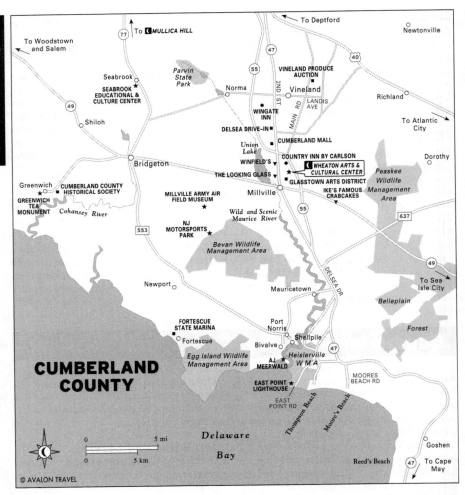

CUMBERLAND COUNTY

Cumberland County marinas, charter boat companies, and favorite fishing spots, visit www.co.cumberland.nj.us.

Getting There and Around

Route 55 runs south from Philadelphia (I-295), Camden County, and Gloucester County directly into Cumberland County, with Millville and Vineland exits. The road eventually leads to Route 47, which has turnoffs for Mauricetown, the Bayshore beaches, and East Point Lighthouse.

For an alternate route take Route 47, commonly called **Delsea Drive,** south straight through from Deptford. This commercial stretch received its name from a newspaper reporter who quipped the road ran from the "Del"-aware River to the Atlantic "Sea."

BRIDGETON AND VICINITY

Cumberland's County seat, Bridgeton boasts New Jersey's largest continuous historic district: over 2,000 colonial, Federal, and Victorian structures. Unfortunately many of them look like crash pads, and the city feels somewhat forgotten, although massive road work may lead to a few uplifting changes. Bridgeton lays claim to a number of New Jersey firsts: The state's first zoo is still in operation, and New Jersey's first newspaper, *The Plain Dealer* (1775–1776), was written at the city's **Potter's Tavern** (W. Broad St., 856/451-4802, Sat. noon–4 P.M. Apr.–Oct., $1), today a restored museum.

Like so many South Jersey communities, Bridgeton is trying to revitalize its downtown, but progress is slow. Many storefronts remain empty, and foot traffic is minimal. **The Bridgeton Renaissance League** (856/455-3230, www.bridgetonrenaissanceleague.org), formed in 2003 to promote the "arts, history, and beautification of Bridgeton," is hoping to jump-start things by implementing numerous beautification and aspirational projects, including constructing a downtown Victorian sitting-park, along with an annual Christmas Historic House Tour. Still, Bridgeton is not a place you'd want to spend the night, but its numerous attractions are worth an afternoon visit.

The Cohansey River runs through the city center, and during warmer months **Bridgeton Riverfront** pops to life hosting various events, most notably a Friday **farmers market** (10 A.M.–2 P.M.). Apple and peach orchards, spacious farms, seafaring towns, and a unique shopping village are all part of Bridgeton's surroundings, offering plenty of scenic drives. Just be sure to take it slow—most area roads are curvy and narrow.

Bridgeton City Park

West of Bridgeton's downtown center is 1,100-acre Bridgeton City Park (Mayor Aitken Dr., 856/455-3230), home to several of the city's museums, a free zoo, and an outdoor amphitheater where summer concerts are held. The park's river-fed **Sunset Lake** is open for swimming during summer months, with seasonal canoe rentals available at **Bridgeton Canoe House** (Washington and Mayor Aitken Dr., 856/451-8687). There are also a handful of walking trails.

Bridgeton's an odd place to find a white tiger, but it's here, along with a puma, lemurs, monkeys, and nearly 100 birds, reptiles, amphibians, and other animals. Located within Bridgeton City Park, **Cohanzick Zoo** (856/455-3230, daily 9 A.M.–5 P.M. spring–summer, daily 9 A.M.–4 P.M. fall–winter, free) opened in 1934 as New Jersey's first municipal zoo. It's a small place but definitely worth a walk through. Just keep an eye on those pesky peacocks.

Museums

Bridgeton City Park is home to several attractions, including the **Nail Mill Museum** (1 Mayor Aitken Dr., 856/455-4100, Tues.–Sat. 10:30 A.M.–3:30 P.M., free), an unassuming building once home to Cumberland Nail and Iron Works. The museum displays items relating to local history, including examples of Bridgeton glass and South Jersey's oldest public clock. Nearby stands the **New Sweden Farmstead Museum** (Bridgeton City Park, Mayor Aitken Dr., 856/455-9785, Sat.

Bridgeton's free zoo

© LAURA KINIRY

11 A.M.–5 P.M., Sun. noon–5 P.M. mid-May–Labor Day, open to reserved tours year-round), an outdoor replica of a 17th-century Swedish farmstead. The circular log village includes a stable, a blacksmith shop, a bathhouse, a smokehouse, and the main residence. Sweden's king and queen officially opened the farmstead in 1988 to honor the 350th anniversary of Swedish settlement in the United States.

Just past the baseball diamonds off Babe Ruth Drive, skirting the park's outer border, is a small white building resembling an American Legion post. This is the **Bridgeton Hall of Fame All Sports Museum** (Bridgeton Recreation Center, Burt St., 856/451-7300, daily 10 A.M.–noon and 1–2 P.M. spring–summer, daily 10 A.M.–noon and 1–3 P.M. fall–winter, free), exhibiting memorabilia from both regional and national amateur and professional sports teams. For such an out-of-the-way place, the museum's collection is surprisingly well rounded. Displays include a Cincinnati Reds bat collection, Willie Mays's 1960 Golden Glove, and items relating to the 1980 World Series Champs, the Philadelphia Phillies.

Located on the lower level of downtown's **Bridgeton Public Library** (150 E. Commerce St.), the **George Woodruff Indian Museum** (856/451-2620, Mon., Fri. 10 A.M.–5 P.M., Tues.–Thurs. 10 A.M.–8 P.M., Sat. 10 A.M.–2 P.M. summer, Mon., Fri. 10 A.M.–5 P.M., Tues.–Thurs. 10 A.M.–8 P.M., Sat. 10 A.M.–2 P.M. other seasons, closed Sun.) collection includes more than 25,000 Indian arrowheads discovered in South Jersey, along with additional artifacts relating to the area's original Lenni-Lenape inhabitants. For additional books on the Lenape, visit the Cumberland County Library.

Dutch Neck Village

South of Bridgeton is Dutch Neck Village (97 Trench Rd., Bridgeton, 856/451-2188, www.dutchneckvillage.com), a country-themed open-air shopping village selling crafts, knick-knacks, and Red Hat Society wares. The village centers around a walking path that connects stores with a restaurant serving comfort cuisine and baked breads, and a small **Country Living Museum** displaying old sewing machines, typewriters, clothing, and books depicting 20th-century regional lifestyles. It's an easy walk among the shops, and there's an arboretum on-site for relaxing and picnicking during warmer months. The village was established in 1976 and plays host to a few long-running annual festivals: June's **Strawberry Festival,** August's **Peach Festival,** and December's three-week **Walk of Lights.**

Dutch Neck's shops are open Monday–Saturday 10 A.M.–5 P.M., and the café and restaurant are open daily. To get here from Bridgeton, take Route 49 to Fayette Street and turn left, driving approximately one mile to a fork in the road and bearing right onto Cubby Holly Road. Make a right at the first crossroad, Trench Road.

Seabrook Educational and Cultural Center

When Charles F. Seabrook turned his father's 57-acre farm into a vegetable growing, processing, and freezing facility in the 1940s, he needed employees. Instead of putting an ad in the paper, Seabrook recruited interned Japanese Americans, offering room, board, and children's education to anyone agreeing to a six-month commitment. Over the ensuing years Seabrook employed Caribbean migrant workers, African Americans, Italians, and Eastern Europeans, all brought together in a unique farming village. Today's Seabrook Education and Cultural Center (Upper Deerfield Township Municipal Building, 1325 State Hwy. 77, Seabrook, 856/451-8393, www.seabrookeducation.org, Mon.–Thurs. 9 A.M.–3 P.M.) is a nonprofit museum honoring Seabrook Farms. The museum, founded by Japanese Americans—who remained Seabrook's largest ethnic community—features photographs and memorabilia, along with a model display of Seabrook Farms as it looked in the 1950s and educational materials relating to the Seabrook community. The center offers an interesting and often overlooked glimpse into South Jersey's past.

Greenwich

Southwest of Bridgeton is scenic Greenwich (pronounced GREEN-which), a former boat-building town that's home to some of the region's finest colonial architecture—definitely worth a side trip. Along with Boston, Greenwich was one of the country's few 18th-century tea-burning towns. On December 22, 1774, local revolutionaries stole tea from a nearby cellar and burned it outdoors, protesting British-imposed taxes. The **Greenwich Tea Monument** on Ye Greate Street commemorates this site.

Greenwich is also home to the **Cumberland County Historical Society** (981 Ye Greate St., 856/455-4055, www.cchistsoc.org). Established in 1908, it consists of a historical research library (Wed. 10 A.M.–4 P.M., Fri.–Sun. 1–4 P.M.) and several museums, including the 1730 **Gibbon House Museum** (Tues.–Sat. 1–4 P.M. Apr.–Dec.) of 18th- and 19th-century furnishings, and the **John DuBois Maritime Museum** (by appointment only), showcasing maritime artifacts from the 19th and 20th centuries.

© LAURA KINIRY

Greenwich Tea Monument

Events

Bridgeton comes alive during the summer months, especially at Sunset Lake's **Donald Rainear Amphitheater** (800/319-3379), which hosts outdoor movies and family-oriented theater shows throughout summer. Outdoor concerts take place Sundays in summer along the riverfront.

Food

Family-owned and operated since 1888, **Weber's Candy** (16 S. Laurel St., 856/451-7811) is a Bridgeton treasure. The peanut clusters are famous, but the peanut brittle is just as delicious. For a bit of old-school try **Angie's Bridgeton Grille** (1½ E. Broad St., 856/451-0220, early morning–2 P.M. Mon.–Thurs., 7 P.M. Fri., 10 P.M. Saturday, and noon Sun.), a local institution since 1940. This Silk City diner and converted caboose is looking better than ever, and locals continue to flock here for the best breakfast in town.

DELAWARE BAYSHORE

One of the state's most underrated regions, the Delaware Bayshore in teeming with tiny fishing villages, miles of wetlands, and practically deserted bayside beaches. The area has been described as one of the Northeast Corridor's least disturbed ecosystems, and it is one of the best places in the state for spotting migrating raptors and shorebirds. The **Wild and Scenic Maurice River** flows south from Millville through to the Delaware Bay, cutting through the region and providing an ideal path for boaters and fishers. On the river's west side is Commercial Township, once one of the world's leading oyster harvesters. While disease has wiped out much of the local oyster population, the township has turned to other seafaring endeavors to fuel its economy, namely crabbing, fishing, and maritime tourism. This livelihood is evident in tiny fishing communities and small port towns scattered throughout the Bayshore.

With Mauricetown as the exception, the area has little to offer architecturally, but it does provide some great wildlife viewing opportunities, as well as excellent cycling routes, stunning natural scenery, and maritime history galore.

Sights

South off Route 47 is Commercial Township's crown jewel, **Mauricetown,** a charming waterfront village filled with brightly painted saltbox structures, many with gingerbread add-ons, once belonging to 19th century oystermen and sea captains. The names of these original occupants—along with each home's year of construction—are carved into plaques adorning their exteriors: 1862—CAPTAIN DAVID P. HALEY; 1860—CAPTAIN SETH BOWEN. At the village center stands **Mauricetown M.E. Church** (9574 Noble St.), a large 19th-century United Methodist church with a tall white steeple visible from Mauricetown's entry bridge, and lovely stained glass windows. At water's edge sits the tiny **Maurice Waterfront Park,** one of the best spots for viewing the Maurice River.

When you arrive at **Bivalve, Port Norris,** and **Shellpile** villages, you won't think you've arrived to much. Former oyster station shacks stand haggard upon the waterfront docks, fishing vessels sit lifelessly in port, and quiet homes are tucked away like nesting birds among the region's tall wetland reeds. But this gritty place is home territory for New Jersey's official tall ship, a 1928 oyster schooner named the **A.J. Meerwald** (2800 High St., Bivalve, 856/785-2060 or 800/485-3072, www.ajmeerwald .org). This boat is impressive: 155 feet long with room for up to 45 passengers, it's used as a sailing classroom by the **Bayshore Discovery Project,** a local nonprofit that also operates a small maritime museum just a few hundred yards away. Both adults and children can set sail on the *Meerwald,* learning about local maritime culture while acquiring skills needed to operate an oyster vessel. The schooner can also be chartered for private events. In addition to 2.5-hour public summer sails ($30 adult, $15 ages 2–12 morning and afternoon sails, $35 all tickets evenings) the *Meerwald* hosts special sails, including birding sails, a lighthouse

Delaware Bayshore's East Point Lighthouse

cruise, and a Halloween pirate sail. Check the website for a complete schedule.

Plan ahead before arriving in Bivalve. The *A.J. Meerwald* is often out of port for overnight stays (secondary ports include Burlington, Camden, and Cape May), and although the Discovery Project maintains a small dockside maritime museum (Sat.–Sun. 1–4 P.M. Apr.–Oct.), there's not a whole lot to do in the area aside from bicycling, birding, and nature walks.

Situated within **Heislerville Wildlife Management Area** by the foot of the Maurice River, **East Point Lighthouse** (East Point Rd. off Rte. 47, Heislerville, 856/327-3714) is typically regarded as a favorite among lighthouse enthusiasts for its unique and photogenic Cape Cod appearance. Built in 1849, it's New Jersey's second-oldest lighthouse, standing vacant for nearly 40 years until 1980, when the U.S. Coast Guard restored it for use at public request. East Point is the state's last operating lighthouse on Delaware Bay. Its unrestored interior is open to visitors the third Sunday of each month, and during New Jersey's annual October Lighthouse Challenge.

Sports and Recreation

The Bayshore is a great place for **bicycling.** Roads are flat, traffic is light, and BIKE ROUTE and SHARE THE ROAD signs are everywhere. Since the region is filled with marshes and wetlands, bugs can be a problem during warmer months. Bring along insect repellent, as well as a map: Route signage isn't so hot around here, and getting lost is easy. Muskrats cross the roads occasionally; keep an eye out that they don't get in front of your wheels. Although often heavy with Shore traffic, Route 47's wide shoulder, green scenery, and access to both Gloucester County and the Jersey Shore make it a popular cycling route, but you should use caution. Bivalve hosts a bike route–nature trail across from the *A.J. Meerwald* dock.

Dubbed the "Weakfish Capital of the World," **Fortescue** bayside village is the site of a state-owned marina and several bait and tackle shops, including the friendly **Al's Bait**

downtown Fortescue

& Tackle (63 Creek Ave., 856/447-3566). It's a great little spot for surf fishing, night fishing, and birding, and several charter boats are available for half-day and full-day rentals. While there's not a lot to see, Fortescue appears to be up-and-coming, and it's beaches, although small, have got to be some of the state's most isolated—and peaceful.

One of the area's most intriguing events occurs annually in late May–early June, when thousands of horseshoe crabs crawl onto Delaware Bay beaches to lay eggs and hungry shorebirds enjoy quite a feast. The best places to see this magnificent phenomenon are **Heislerville Wildlife Management Area** east of the Maurice River, **Thompsons Beach** and **Reed's Beach,** both easily reachable by way of Route 47 east of Mauricetown, and **Fortescue.** Spectators only, please.

Filled with tidal marsh, tall reeds, and mud flats, **Heislerville Wildlife Management Area** is a great place for spotting snowy and great egrets, great blue and green herons, and the occasional bald eagle. Thompson Road en route to **Thompson's Beach** is billed as a wildlife viewing driving tour. Along the way you'll see a pull-off platform for birding. Look for ospreys nesting in the trees.

The Bayshore's **Reed's Beach** is a single-lane road lined with beachfront bungalows, shacks, and trailers—many built directly above the water—and surrounded by marshland. At the end of the road is a small fee parking area for shorebird viewing. It's a short walk to the viewing platform.

Keep an eye out for turtles and monarch butterflies in late summer and early fall, especially within the **Egg Island Wildlife Management Area** and around East Point Lighthouse. Songbirds migrate through in spring and autumn, and raptors frequent the area in autumn and winter.

Thompson's Beach and East Point are good places to spot migrating shorebirds in May. Bald eagles fly over the **Wild and Scenic Maurice River** (http://mauriceriver.igc.org) in winter. The river is a migratory path for shorebirds, raptors, waterfowl, and fish.

Events

Mauricetown is home base for the region's annual **Winter Eagle Festival** (Mauricetown Firehall, 856/453-2177), a daylong birding festival taking place in February.

Delaware Bay Days (856/785-2060, www.ajmeerwald.org) is the area's largest free festival, a two-day June celebration of the Bay region's rich maritime history. Activities and events, which include boat parades, river tours, wetland walks, live bands, fresh seafood, and dozens of arts and crafts, are spread throughout Port Norris, Bivalve, Shellpile, and Maurice Township's East Point Lighthouse, and are sponsored by the Bayshore Discovery Project.

Getting There and Around

While the following directions will come in handy, a New Jersey State or Cumberland County map is essential for navigating the area.

It's about a five-mile drive from Mauricetown to Port Norris. To reach Greenwich, take County Road 607 south from Bridgeton approximately seven miles, or follow the Coastal Heritage Trail east from Salem along County Road 658 to 623, about 10 miles.

To reach Fortescue from Bridgeton, take Route 49 east and turn right onto Route 553 south, continuing until you arrive at Route 732. Turn right and you'll reach Newport. Drive approximately 10 more minutes south along County Road 637 to get to Fortescue.

Located at the mouth of the Maurice River, the East Point Lighthouse is even more remote. From Mauricetown, take the Mauricetown Bypass East to Route 47 (Delsea Drive), turn right, and continue south onto County Road 616. About 15 minutes down the road you'll come to the town of Heislerville. Turn right onto East Point Road, traveling through Heislerville Wildlife Management Area en route to East Point Lighthouse.

MILLVILLE

Over the last decade the industrial city of Millville (nicknamed the "Holly City" for its extensive cultivation of holly trees) has established itself as a major South Jersey arts community. Centered around downtown's High Street, the city's revitalized district is filled with multistory brick structures housing art galleries, collectible shops, a used bookstore with a café, and a wide variety of restaurants. Among them stands an old vaudeville theater (www.levoy.org) waiting to be restored.

Despite its downtown renaissance, Millville's surrounding neighborhoods aren't so tourist-friendly; best to stick to the Glasstown Arts District and nearby attractions.

Glasstown Arts District

Attempting to revamp a dilapidated downtown district and boost a floundering economy, locals created the **Glasstown Arts District** in 2001 as a way of attracting artists and new area businesses. Their efforts paid off. Today, High Street's once half-empty storefronts, from Main to Broad Street, are now filled with galleries, gift shops, artists' studios, and educational facilities, including **Clay College** (106 N. High St., 856/765-0988, www.cccnj.net/clay college/), Cumberland County College's satellite ceramic art studio offering both credited courses and scheduled afternoon workshops, and the **Riverfront Renaissance Center for the Arts** (22 N. High St., 856/327-4500, www.riverfrontcenter.org), a regional hub hosting exhibits, lectures, and classes, and providing studio time for artists.

The idea of turning Millville into an arts community wasn't far-fetched. The glass industry has been rooted in the city for over two centuries, and **The Barn Studio of Art** (814 Whitaker Ave., 856/825-5025, www.barn studio.org), an "anything goes" fine arts center founded by much-loved "Wetlands Painter" Pat Witt, has been part of Millville for over 45 years.

There's plenty of parking available in the arts district, both in lots and on nearby streets.

Air Force History

The **Millville Army Air Field Museum** (Bldg. 1, Millville Municipal Airport, 856/327-2347, www.p47millville.org, Tues.–Sun. 10 A.M.–4 P.M.) is dedicated to the history of local and national aviation. Located at the Millville Airport, known as "America's first defense airport" and operated as an army airfield for three years during World War II, the museum showcases a large collection of aviation memorabilia, including uniforms and photographs, and offers tours focusing on Millville's role in aviation history, often led by World War II veterans. Each May the airport hosts the **Millville Wings and Wheels Show,** a two-day festival with performance planes, fighter demonstrations, and a classic car display.

To reach the airport, take Route 49 west from Millville's downtown center and turn left onto Dividing Creek Road (County Road 555). The airport's access road is approximately three miles from the turn.

On the side of Millville's City Hall at the corner of High and Main Streets is the **Wall of Remembrance,** a mural dedicated to Millville's 14 fallen World War II pilots.

NJ Motorsports Park

During its summer 2008 inaugural season, NJ Motorsports Park (8000 Dividing Creek Rd., 866/550-6567, www.njmotor sportspark.com) opened the first phase of its 700 acre park with two world-class road race courses and a karting track allowing visitors to feel the thrill of racing firsthand. Purchase a day license ($10) and test your speed during open lapping sessions ($55 per half-hour), which include complete racing attire, a corner worker, and fuel. If spectator is more your speed, catch events at the 14-turn Thunderbolt raceway or the smaller 1.9 mile Lighting raceway. Restaurants, hotels, a research facility, and a racing school are all in the works for the future.

Recreation

Just west of the Glasstown Arts District at the intersection of High and Broad Streets is the **Millville Riverwalk,** a walkway along the Maurice River leading toward a public boat ramp and the Millville Marina. To the north is **Union Lake,** South Jersey's largest freshwater lake and a good spot for boating and swimming.

Events

One of Millville's most popular events is **Third Fridays** (800/887-4957, www.3rdfriday.org), when the arts district's galleries, shops, and restaurants extend regular hours and resident artists open their doors to the public. A variety of live music entertains crowds strolling High Street, sampling free wine and hors d'oeuvres. The event takes place in the evening the third Friday of each month. Most businesses stay open until 9 P.M.

Food and Entertainment

Millville offers Cumberland County's best restaurant selection.

Locals rave about the sushi at **Peking Tokyo** (101 E. Main St., 856/765-1818, Mon.–Thurs. 11 A.M.–10 P.M., Fri.–Sat. 11 A.M.–11 P.M., Sun. noon–10 P.M., $7–14), a restaurant serving both Chinese and Japanese cuisine. Next door is **Jim's Lunch** (105 E. Main St., 856/327-1299, http://new .enterit.com/JimLunch1299/, Mon.–Thurs., Sat. 6 A.M.–6 P.M., Sun. 6 A.M.–7 P.M. fall–spring), a Millville institution family-owned and operated for 75 years. Jim's cheeseburgers ($2.25), doused in a special brown sauce, are incredible, but you can also choose from an inexpensive variety of steaks, seafood, and daily specials. The decor is luncheon simple, with counter seating and some orange booths. Closed in summer, it's packed the remainder of the year.

High Street's trendy **Looking Glass** is the perfect spot for savoring a cup of coffee or settling in for a tasty Chianti Salad—greens topped with prosciutto and provolone and garnished with beets and blue cheese ($8). This café-coffeehouse is open Monday–Tuesday and Saturday 7:45 A.M.–3 P.M., Wednesday–Friday 7:45 A.M.–8 P.M. and is closed Sunday.

Situated in High Street's former F. W. Woolworth's building, **Winfield's Restaurant** (106 N. High St., 856/327-0909, www.winfields restaurant.com, Tues.–Sat. 4:30–10 P.M., Sun. 4–9 P.M., $17–29) is Millville's fine dining establishment, serving meat, seafood, and pasta dishes accompanied by a full bar selection.

Settle into a booth for casual beers and burgers at the **Old Oar House Brewery** (123 N. High St., 856/293-1200, www.oldoarhouse brewery.com, Mon.–Sat. 11 A.M.–2 A.M., Sun. 5 P.M.–2 A.M., $7–12), a Philadelphia-inspired Irish-style pub serving delish appetizers and sandwiches along with a full diner menu. The cigar-friendly brewery hosts a seasonal outdoor garden and live music on weekends. For fine dining, head **Next Oar** (127 N. High St., 856/293-1360, Thurs.–Sat. 5–10 P.M.) for ever-changing entrées like spinach ravioli ($17) and rosemary chicken ($18).

◖ WHEATON ARTS & CULTURAL CENTER

Formerly called Wheaton Village, Wheaton Arts & Cultural Center is a remarkable glass and crafts village two miles northeast of Millville's Glasstown Arts District. Since 1968 Wheaton has been educating and entertaining visitors with demonstrations in glass arts and exhibits detailing South Jersey's craft history. This walkable village is home to an excellent glass art museum as well as numerous shops selling art-glass jewelry, glass paperweights, and blown glass ornaments, a museum highlighting the crafts and culture of New Jersey's southernmost counties, and a playground and general store. Each of the shops, museums, and artist facilities lie along an oval pathway, lending the place a small-town feel. It's worth an afternoon to explore.

Sights

As a working re-creation of Millville's 1888 T. C. Wheaton Glass Factory, Wheaton Arts' **Glass Studio** has been entertaining front-and-center audiences with glassblowing demonstrations for decades. Resident artists assist one another in creating exquisite sculptures, goblets, and vases by gathering molten glass from the massive furnace, using a blowpipe to expand the glass, working it, reheating it in a glory hole, shaping it, and eventually placing the finished glass form in an annealing oven to cool. Want to be part of the action? Visitors have the opportunity to make their own paperweight with an instructor's aid (advance booking is required: 856/825-6800 ext. 2744).

At the village center is the sizable **Museum of American Glass,** providing insight into American and local glass history from the 18th century through Tiffany, Carnival, and the Studio Glass Art Movement. Be sure to catch one of the docent-led tours offered throughout the day.

Established in 1994, the **Down-Jersey Folklife Center** celebrates South Jersey's somewhat covert cultural diversity with changing exhibits highlighting the arts, crafts, and lifestyles of the state's eight southernmost counties. The center hosts occasional dance and music demonstrations and has a large audio and visual archive focusing on South Jersey traditions.

A Wheaton Center highlight is its old-time **General Store,** featuring loads of small souvenirs, including machine-made marbles, as well as an awesome penny-candy counter and working nickelodeon. After satisfying your sweet tooth, continue around the grounds to catch wheel-throwing and flame-working demos, browse salable books, jewelry, and the works of resident artists, and take a ride on a miniature train (extra cost).

Glass Weekend

One of the best times to visit Wheaton Arts is during its biennial **Glass Weekend,** held in July in odd-numbered years. World-renowned glass artists are on hand demonstrating their craft, and some of the finest glass art in existence is on display. Things can get pretty crowded, but for glass lovers, students, and anyone who appreciates art, it's worth it.

Accommodations

Adjacent to Wheaton Arts is the pleasant **Country Inn by Carlson** (1125 Village Dr., Millville, 856/825-3100, $95–110). This quiet two-story hotel (no elevator) has a front porch, lending library, and swimming pool. A family-style restaurant and lounge are located next door.

Information

Wheaton Arts & Cultural Center is open Friday–Sunday 10 A.M.–5 P.M. January–March ($9 adult, $6 child), and Tuesday–Sunday 10 A.M.–5 P.M. April–December ($10 adult, $7 child). It's also open Memorial Day, July 4th, and Labor Day. It's free to walk around the grounds and visit shops.

VINELAND

Originally settled as a planned agricultural community in 1861, Vineland has since morphed into a mix of urban-suburban sprawl. Landis Avenue is the city's main thoroughfare, a wide road lined by nondescript storefronts that give way to large Southern-style homes. Most retail shopping takes place at nearby **Cumberland Mall** (3849 S. Delsea Dr., 856/825-9507).

Vineland has gone through numerous incarnations over the years. Named for the area vines that led to the creation of Welch's grape juice, the city later became known as a poultry producer and earned the nickname "the egg basket of America." More recently Vineland's been dubbed the country's "Dandelion Capital," even hosting an annual spring dinner (856/691-7400) incorporating the plant as its main culinary ingredient. Through it all, the city has continued as an agricultural center. The Vineland Produce Auction (1088 N. Main Rd., 856/691-0721, www.vineland produce.com), a local co-op with hundreds of members, supplies fresh fruits and vegetables to farm stands throughout the area, including **Arbittier Farms** (344 N. Main Rd., 856/697-3200).

Vineland's cultural diversity is reflected in local shops, markets, and restaurants. The city is home to large Italian and Latino populations. Cultural heritage celebrations are hosted for these and other ethnic communities throughout the year.

Delsea Drive-In Theatre

New Jersey invented drive-in theaters. Funny, because the Delsea Drive-In (2203 S. Delsea Dr., 856/696-0011, www.delseadrive-in.com)

is now the state's one and only, reopening in 2004 after being closed for 13 years. Sporting a 120-by-85-foot screen, the theater presents first-run double features evenings throughout summer ($8). There's a concession stand on-site selling burgers, sodas, snacks, and novelty items like yo-yo lights and glow bracelets, although bringing your own food requires a $7 permit fee.

Accommodations

Vineland is home to several hotels and motels, but only one worthy of an overnight stay. For an additional choice visit Millville.

Vineland's best hotel is the newer **Wingate Inn** (2196 W. Landis Ave., 856/690-9900, $119–194), conveniently located between Exits 32A and 32B off Route 55. Guest-room amenities include work areas and Neutrogena bath products, and there's a heated pool and Bennigan's restaurant on-site. Complimentary continental breakfast is served daily.

BELLEPLAIN STATE FOREST

Along the Pinelands' southern outskirts stands Belleplain State Forest (Rte. 550, Woodbine, 609/861-2404), more than 20,000 acres filled with oak, pitch pine, and Atlantic white cedar trees, two lakes—including a cranberry bog turned swimming lake—and ample recreational opportunities. The forest stretches across Cumberland's county line into Cape May County and lies about 30 miles north of Cape May City. Tall trees line its entryway, leading to a visitors center, trailheads, and vehicle pathways that extend toward campsites and a wildlife viewing area. In addition to over 40

miles of marked and unmarked trails, the forest is a popular spot for fishing, hunting, mountain biking, horseback riding, camping, and winter sports like snowmobiling, cross-country skiing, and ice fishing. Belleplain is free to enter during the off-season and $5 weekdays, $10 weekends Memorial Day–Labor Day.

Recreation

Belleplain has numerous hiking paths and multiuse trails, but the **East Creek Trail** is a local favorite. Surrounding East Creek Pond, the forest's largest body of water, this easy seven-mile trail takes only a few hours to complete, passing among pine and cedar trees and alongside greenbrier and laurel. Ticks can be a problem, so dress accordingly. The trail begins on Champion Road next to Lake Nummy.

Lake Nummy, a former cranberry bog, is one of Belleplain's highlights. During summer months it's a popular canoeing and swimming area with a lifeguard, complete with a floating dock. There's a concession stand, canoe rentals, and shower facilities nearby. The lake is surrounding by campsites and hiking trails.

A boat access ramp is situated on the western shore of East Creek Pond.

Camping

Belleplain has nearly 200 campsites (Mar.–Nov., $60), including 14 lean-tos (year-round, $25) and five yurts ($30)—domed, lockable structures each with two sets of bunks and a skylight—for rent. All are equipped with a picnic table, outside fire pit, and grill. Restrooms and showers are located nearby. A group cabin accommodating up to 30 people ($155) is also available.

BACKGROUND

The Land

About midway along the United States' Eastern Seaboard below New York State, east of Pennsylvania, and north of Delaware sits New Jersey, a peninsula-like landmass with a larger-than-life reputation and a geographic makeup that varies both physically and culturally. In the north you'll find mountainous terrain, hard rock, and valleys, all formed by glaciers thousands of years before, while in the south you'll see flat land never rising more than a few hundred feet above sea level—a fertile landscape radiating south and east to become sandy and barren soil. New Jersey is heavily urban but also exceedingly natural, with unique flora and fauna, abundant sea life and

birds, and a larger black bear population than you might expect.

GEOGRAPHY

With 7,417 square miles of land, New Jersey is the United States' fourth-smallest state. Although best known for its intricate highway system and a heavily industrialized northeastern section, only one third of New Jersey is developed land. The rest is filled with salt marshes, protected estuaries, swamps, forests, mountain and river valleys, white sand beaches, and fruitful agricultural land. New Jersey is separated into four main land regions: the Appalachian Ridge and Valley Region, the

© LAURA KINIRY

Highlands, the Piedmont, and the Atlantic Coastal Plain.

Ridge and Valley

Nestled in the state's northwestern corner, the Ridge and Valley is part of the East Coast's larger Appalachian range and covers only about 8 percent of New Jersey's landmass. Mountains—most notably the Kittatinny Mountain Ridge—slope down into low-lying valleys, the largest of which is the Kittatinny Valley. New Jersey's highest point, aptly named High Point (1,803 feet), lies in this region. Along the Ridge and Valley's western edge, the Delaware River carves a route between New Jersey and Pennsylvania.

Highlands

The Highlands are part of the Blue Ridge Mountain range stretching from New England to Pennsylvania, and are home to most of New Jersey's glacier-formed lakes, along with flat-top rock ridges, crystal formations, and the remnants of old mining towns. Although the area was once heavily deforested to provide fuel for the prospering mining industry, much of the woodlands have since grown back.

This new geologic landmass isolates the Ridge and Valley into New Jersey's northwest corner, extending south from the mountainous New York border into the central lake region, east from the Ramapo Mountains into Vernon Valley, and west, encompassing Warren County. The Highlands' average elevation is about 1,000 feet above sea level, and the area provides water for about 15 percent of the Northeast Corridor.

Piedmont

The Piedmont ("foothill") makes up the lowlands of the state's Appalachian region, which are 40 percent of New Jersey's landmass and its entire northern portion. It stretches southwest from New York's state line and through the urban northeast toward Trenton, with a system of faults lining its western edge. The Raritan, Passaic, and Hackensack Rivers run through the area, emptying along the state's eastern coast. The Piedmont also goes by the name Newark Basin.

Atlantic Coastal Plain

New Jersey's final land region—known collectively as the Atlantic Coastal Plain—encompasses a whopping 60 percent of the state's landmass, expanding south from Central Jersey to include all of South Jersey, the Pinelands, and the Jersey Shore. Land here is flat with low-lying hills, and more than half of the region is less than 100 feet above sea level. Barrier islands line much of the eastern coastline, separated from the mainland by wetlands, back bays, and canals.

The Atlantic Coastal Plain can be divided into two sections: the Outer and Inner Coastal Plains. In the Outer Coastal Plains, barren sands give way to reeds and marshlands. This section is highly developed with a couple of pristine wildlife habitats and relatively untouched lands, including Sandy Hook, Island Beach State Park, and both E. B. Forsythe Wildlife Refuges. The Inner Coastal Plains offer some of New Jersey's most fertile farming soil.

Geology

Three glaciers have shaped North Jersey over the past two million years. Their limestone remains exist in Sussex, Passaic, Hudson, Essex, Somerset, Hunterdon, and Mercer Counties. Ancient glacial deposits mark Jenny Jump State Forest's terrain, and natural lakes fill the landscape.

New Jersey is abundant with metal ores, with the Highlands containing minerals found nowhere else in the world along with iron, zinc, and marble. Copper is easily readable in land north of Trenton. Silica sand ideal for glassmaking exists throughout South and Central Jersey, and Cape May Diamonds—a unique type of quartz pebble—are isolated to Sunset Beach along New Jersey's southern coast.

Bodies of Water

Water plays a leading role in New Jersey's geographic and cultural make-up, from the surrounding ocean and bays to the inland rivers, lakes, and wetlands. The Raritan (1,105 square miles), Passaic (949 square miles), and Maurice (570 square miles) Rivers are the state's three largest; others include the Delaware, Hudson, Mullica, Maurice, and Musconetcong. Lake Hopatcong is New Jersey's largest natural lake; notable artificial lakes include South Jersey's Union Lake in Millville, and Sparta's Lake Mohawk in the Skylands.

New Jersey has bountiful wetlands that play an essential role in the state's ecosystem. They prevent soil erosion and floods, improve water quality, and provide important habitat for migratory birds, fish, and other wildlife. Atlantic, Ocean, and Cape May Counties host the state's largest concentration of wetlands. The best wetlands to visit include the E. B. Forsythe National Wildlife Refuge Brigantine Division, the Meadowlands, and the Great Swamp of Morris County.

Stretching along the Atlantic coastline from Boston south to Key West, Florida, the Intracoastal Waterway is a series of bays and inlets providing a protective passageway for fishing and leisure boats. New Jersey's portion flows between its barrier islands and the mainland, extending from Manasquan Inlet south along the Barnegat Peninsula and on to Cape May and the Delaware Bay.

CLIMATE

New Jersey enjoys a temperate climate and is a relatively easy place to negotiate during all seasons. The state has four distinct seasons, with temperatures ranging from the high 90s in summer to below freezing in winter. January is the coldest month, and August the warmest. Fall and spring offer moderate weather. The northwestern Highlands tend to see the coldest temperatures and heaviest precipitation, while the Jersey Shore gets the least amount of snowfall and offers the state's most judicious climate. Rain is common statewide throughout the year, turning to snow during colder months and often accompanied by thunder and lightning in summer, when humidity levels are high. The state's average rainfall is 45 inches per year.

Hurricanes are possible in New Jersey, although most weaken considerably before arriving over land. Areas along the shore have been evacuated numerous times over the last 20 years, and a heavy storm can do thousands of dollars in damage to the coastline. Hurricanes occur June–November, and nor'easters (counterclockwise storms that can result in blizzard-like conditions) arrive September–April. In years past, severe weather conditions have caused serious flooding, most recently in Medford, the Gateway Region, and the Delaware River towns.

ENVIRONMENTAL ISSUES

As a main throughway and essential contributor to the Great Northeast Corridor, not to mention being a major pharmaceutical manufacturer and having an over-the-top population density, New Jersey—not surprisingly—has issues with pollution. For years its Meadowlands region—a marshy landmass that once seemed uninhabitable—served as a dumping ground for trash, toxic waste, and the occasional body, earning its nickname "The Armpit of America." Today, New Jersey hosts over 100 Superfund sites, more than anywhere else in the country (for a complete list, go to www.epa.gov/super fund/sites). While efforts to restore some sites have met with great success—such as Pitman's Lipari Landfill—others continue to have problems, most notably a section of Ringwood that despite earlier cleanup efforts remains contaminated with paint sludge left behind by Ford Motor Company.

Mercury in the rivers and streams of New Jersey's northeast corner has also been a major concern over the last couple of decades. This toxic chemical is the offshoot of industrial smokestacks located in the area, and it threatens the region's fish supply and those who eat them. Contamination also occurs throughout the state from the leachate runoff of landfills, farms, and waste sites that seep into water supplies.

New Jersey's Atlantic coastline has its fair share of environmental concerns. In 1988 a number of the state's beaches were indefinitely closed when hypodermic needles dumped in the sea began washing up along their shores. Measures have since been taken to prevent such incidents in future. Beach erosion is another serious issue. Storms cause many of the state's beaches to reduce in size, their sands relocating out to sea or to towns farther south. The Army Corps of Engineers is constantly pumping the shore with sand, and creating dunes to act as barriers between ocean waters and beachfront homes.

Sprawl is prevalent throughout New Jersey. Shopping centers are abandoned and homes and megastores built faster than they're occupied, even during the recent economic slowdown. South Jersey is currently receiving the brunt of new development, and new construction is swallowing many of the region's remaining farmlands.

The Pinelands and the Highlands

John McPhee's 1973 book *The Pine Barrens* changed the way many people looked at New Jersey, including then-governor Brendan T. Byrne (in office 1974–1982), who enacted legislation designating over one million central and south Jersey acres as "America's first National Reserve." Today, the New Jersey Pinelands Commission oversees the region, also called the Pinelands, which remains relatively unchanged, although interior preservation efforts have negatively affected some outlying areas. Pinelands' legislation states development in the reserve's central region be highly regulated, but to a lesser extent in the outlying Protection Area (the perimeter), meaning any new Pinelands' construction—and taxes—are relocated to surrounding boroughs, cities, and towns.

The Highlands, a section of New Jersey's Skylands supplying water to a large percentage of the Northeast Corridor, are experiencing a similar situation. In efforts to preserve this area's delicate ecosystem, the government introduced the Highlands Water Protection and Planning Act in 2004, a law shielding much of the Highlands region from future development. Unfortunately, this preservation effort interferes with local building rights and zoning laws, and those living on the Highlands' outskirts fear they'll be faced with an onslaught of construction and an increase in taxes. Numerous legal challenges to the act have since been filed.

Flora and Fauna

New Jersey boasts more than 2,600 native and introduced plants species. Forests cover approximately 40 percent of the state, and flowers include 50 orchid species, 30 violet species, and the endangered swamp pink perennial wildflower native to the Pinelands. The state tree is the red oak, and the state flower is the purple violet.

New Jersey is also an ideal habitat for a varied array of fauna, including 325 bird species, 90 mammal species, 79 reptile and amphibian species, and more than 400 fish species. The state hosts a number of rare and endangered species as well, such as the blue-spotted salamander, the piping plover, and the Pine Barrens tree frog.

TREES AND SHRUBS

Overall, the state's forests are dominated by oak trees, but in the Skylands, where the soil is wetter and more nutrient-rich, sugar maple, white ash, and black birch are also prominent. The ridges and the Pinelands feature pitch pine and scrub oak. You may see pygmy pines—dwarf pine trees topping off at 4–6 feet tall—in other regions, but they're a major Pinelands attraction.

Wetland forests vary throughout the state, but they often include red maple and Atlantic white cedar. Lowland blueberry, black huckleberry, and mountain laurel grow alongside tree growth statewide. Sandy Hook, at the Jersey Shore's northern tip, has the largest American holly forest on the East Coast.

flora of the Delaware Bayshore

FERNS AND GRASSES

New Jersey has over 70 grass varieties, including beach grass, used to ward off storm damage, and the considerably invasive phragmites—tall reed grass once used by Native Americans for thatching, its seeds used for flour—prominent in the Meadowlands and along the coast in areas like Cape May and Sea Isle. The state uses restoration ecology to ward off phragmites' aggressive growth while replenishing land, stopping erosion, restoring groundwater, and providing wildlife habitat.

Pinelands grasses include switchgrass, Indian grass, wild rice, sweet vernal grass (a scented grass), and Pine Barrens reed-grass. One way to recognize Pinelands sites where former communities stood is to identify ebony spleenwort, a green semigloss fern with a dark-brown stem that is invasive to Pineland soil. It is plentiful throughout the region, but only exists where lime had been used to build structures.

SALT MARSHES AND LIMESTONE SINKS

New Jersey has 245,000 acres of salt marshes, and salt hay is harvested as cattle feed, packing material, and insulation. In the Skylands' Kittatinny Mountain region there are limestone sinks, formed when acidic groundwater eats away at the earth and creates cavities into which the topsoil collapses. These sinkholes often contain ponds with fluctuating water levels, creating a hotbed for unique vegetation.

MAMMALS

New Jersey is home to a surprising mix of wildlife, including many animals that you wouldn't expect in a place with such an urban reputation. The reason for this array of species is twofold: The state lies at both the southern and northern borders of wildlife terrain, and its varied landscape and large swaths of connected land give these mammals plenty of room to roam. Many of the state's wildlife populations are increasing, such as those of beavers, eastern coyotes, and black bears (the latter leading to New Jersey's bear hunt to be reinstated, the first in 33 years, amid massive protest, in 2003).

New Jersey's coastal waters host a large array of seals, dolphins, and whales, and notable species such as the harbor seal, beluga whale, Atlantic killer whale, and endangered blue and humpback whales. Smaller mammals prolific throughout the state include hairy-tailed moles; gray, red, and flying squirrels; striped skunks; and the southern bog lemming.

While not native to New Jersey, eastern coyotes were introduced to the state in the early 1900s and today number about 3,000. They're found in every one of New Jersey's 21 counties; their howls have even been known to keep Cape May Point campers up at night; and their scraggly figures "haunt" Gloucester County graveyards.

New Jersey is home to over 1,000 black bears, and their numbers are currently increasing. Once prominent throughout the state, Europeans reduced the population until it was limited to the state's upper northwest, although in recent years bears have made their way east into the urban outskirts, and as far south as Cumberland and Cape May Counties. Black bears are known to inhabit forested regions but often venture into suburbs, foraging inside improperly sealed garbage cans and disturbing camping resorts where food has not been suitably contained.

Bobcats are rare in New Jersey but have been spotted, increasingly so over the past few years.

New Jersey has about 200,000 white-tailed deer, often seen in backyards, natural areas such as state and county parks, and scampering along roadsides, especially around dusk. Their numbers are decreasing, partially due to the large number of traffic accidents they are involved in. Use extreme caution while driving, especially in the Skylands region, where you're sure to spot a recent casualty every few miles.

New Jersey is home to nine bat species, including six that are year-round residents. They reside in attics, barns, under bridges, and in deep dark caves in the Skylands.

MARINE LIFE

Lined on three sides by water and filled with lakes, rivers, and streams, it's no wonder New Jersey has some interesting sea life. The state fish is the brook trout, and trout—both stocked and natural—are plentiful in the state's inland waters. Oysters and shellfish were once prominent in the Delaware Bayshore (as well as the Raritan Bay), but disease and overharvesting have wiped out much of the population. Shad—river herrings long-disappeared from a polluted Delaware River—are returning to swim upstream every April. Along the coast you'll often spot dolphins, whales, and the occasional shark. Seals, porpoises, sea turtles, and seaweed are all prominent in coastal waters as well. Jellyfish appear along the shore in July and August, sometimes resulting in beach closures.

Blue crabs are delicacies prominent in Atlantic waters, and they are found in both the ocean and the bays. They molt in order to grow, and are considered highly prized softshell crabs in the day or two it takes to do so. Sometimes called the "king crab," horseshoe crabs are hard-shelled invertebrates featuring long tail spines and oversized black back-shells resembling suits of armor. One of the world's largest horseshoe crab populations exists along the Delaware Bayshore, and during May and June thousands of horseshoe crabs ascend onto the beaches to lay their eggs.

New Jersey waters host three clam species. Hard-shell clams, including littleneck, chowder, cherrystone, and top-neck, live in the bays and are harvested in small amounts with hand utensils. Surf clams and ocean quahogs are native to the Atlantic and are dredged from the ocean floor for cuisine.

BIRDS

A major stop along the Atlantic Flyway, New Jersey offers some of the best bird-watching in the country. The number of species that nest, breed, or migrate through the state is in the hundreds, and along with sea life, accounts for the bulk of the state's fauna. The state bird is the eastern goldfinch, a tiny songbird that transforms from a dull-brown color into a yellow-coated black-winged beauty during summer. Songbirds, shorebirds, and raptors all make their home here or migrate through. Members of New Jersey's native population include sparrows, cardinals, mourning doves, seagulls, warblers, and turkey vultures.

Canada geese, once only a migratory species within the state, are now year-round residents. They're identifiable by their long black necks and distinctive squawk, and they tend to wreak havoc in county parks, soiling grass and chasing away anyone who comes within a short distance.

Raptors

A raptor is a predatory bird with keen eyesight, sharp talons, and a hooked beak. Species seen within New Jersey include red-tailed hawks (the state's most commonly sighted year-round raptor), ospreys, peregrine falcons, American kestrels (falcons), bald and golden eagles, merlins, and broad-winged and sharp-shinned hawks. The state's annual fall hawk migration occurs from northwest New Jersey downward to Cape May and the Delaware Bayshore.

Peregrine falcons are listed on the state's endangered species list. They nest on tall cliffs as well as artificially constructed platforms like buildings and bridges. These attractive birds may be gray, slate blue, or white with yellow features, and they dine on small birds.

Shorebirds

New Jersey is home to three gull species—herring, laughing, and black-backed—found along the shore, around inland bodies of water, and often dining on heaps of trash. Along the state's shoreline, gulls have earned an aggressive rep, swarming innocent strollers and helping themselves to people's meals. Before 1900, laughing gulls were the state's only prevalent gull species.

Shorebirds are common along the Atlantic coast, and at least 20 species migrate through New Jersey regularly during spring and fall. Five species breed along the coasts, including the piping plover. One of the shorebirds' primary stops north on the way to arctic breeding grounds is Cape May and the Delaware Bayshore region. They usually arrive for three weeks each May to feast on horseshoe crab eggs. Spotted sandpipers nest near ponds, and killdeers—ring-necked plovers—nest in short-grass fields, as well as in front lawns and

© LAURA KINIRY

one of New Jersey's many web-footed friends

driveways. The piping plover, pale brown with a white underbelly and black features, is a federally listed endangered species that nests along the shore and within the Pinelands.

Herons and Egrets

The best places for spotting herons and egrets are along the coastal marshlands and estuaries, and the Delaware Bayshore. These birds fly south for the winter and return around April, nesting in colonies that are often large and noisy. The great blue heron is the most eye-catching, and it exists inland as well as along the coast. Additional state species include the snowy egret, great egret, and glossy ibis. Herons and egrets eat fish as well as small delicacies like frogs, mice, and eggs.

REPTILES

New Jersey's native reptiles consist almost entirely of turtles and snakes along with a few lizard species, including the northern fence lizard and the ground skink. Most of the snakes are nonpoisonous, although the Skylands' northern copperheads and timber rattle-snakes—found in South Jersey, the Pinelands, and the Skylands—are New Jersey's two venomous species. Loss of habitat and illegal killing has endangered the state's population of timber rattlesnakes, and their numbers are dwindling.

New Jersey has 15 native turtle species, including the common snapping turtle, the stinkpot, the eastern mud turtle, and the bog turtle. Endangered species include the Atlantic loggerhead and the Atlantic leatherback. The endangered northern diamondback terrapin is the only marine turtle species to favor both saltwater and freshwater environments. Unfortunately, female diamondbacks crawling ashore to bury their eggs (late May–July) are often killed crossing the busy coastal roads.

INSECTS

With all of the state's marshlands, woodlands, and orchards, it's easy to see why New Jersey's insect population thrives. Once referred to as "The Mosquito State," its namesake insect infested everything from coastal inlets and estuaries to the Meadowlands and Morris County's Great Swamp. Thankfully, air-conditioned automobiles, bug spray, and other technological advances have helped ease the pain, although New Jersey's mosquitoes remain alive and well. The green-headed fly, a nasty little biting creature with a bulbous transparent head, breeds in wetlands as well and prospers during July and August. Deer ticks, those infamous little spreaders of Lyme disease, are also prominent statewide.

New Jersey's insects aren't all so bloodthirsty. More than 100 butterfly species are common to the state, especially within the Pinelands and Cape May County during warmer months. Monarch butterflies en route to Mexico pass through New Jersey in fall, and they are easy to spot in the Cape May region.

The honeybee is New Jersey's state insect, although it's not a local native. And one of the state's most highly regarded insects, the firefly, only appears in summer. Also known as "lightening bugs," they're beetles equipped with a flashing yellow light that brightens the evening sky.

AMPHIBIANS

New Jersey hosts 32 amphibian species, 16 of which are salamanders—including the endangered blue-spotted salamander. The mountain dusky and the northern red salamander exist only in the state's northern counties. Frogs and toads are prominent statewide but most notably within the Pinelands, home to the endangered Pine Barrens tree frog, a tiny plum-and-green species with bright yellow on its underside and suction cups on its toes. It's found around the Pinelands' acidic water, preferring fish-free waters and bogs, and it has a very distinct call consisting of a series of rapid nasal honks. You'll most likely hear it in summer.

History

EARLY HISTORY

New Jersey's land was originally home to Lenni Lenape Indians, also called Delaware Indians. European settlers later turned the Lenni Lenape's paths for hunting, foraging, and coastal access into roads.

The Dutch were the first Europeans to arrive in present-day New Jersey, establishing a trading post in 1618 in what is now Bergen County as part of the larger New Netherland settlement, encompassing the nearby island of Manhattan. In 1638 Swedes and Finns founded the state's first settlement along the banks of the Delaware Bay. Together with Delaware's and Pennsylvania's waterfront portions it was known as New Sweden, a port for the tobacco and fur trades. In 1654 the Dutch, under the rule of Peter Stuyvesant, easily overtook New Jersey's southern half and incorporated it into New Netherland. This held together for 10 years before the British claimed the entire region as their own.

By 1676 the Brits had separated New Jersey's land into two colonies: East and West Jersey, named for the British Isle of Jersey. The two provinces were joined under a royal governor in 1703. For the next 35 years, the colony of New Jersey shared its governor with New York.

REVOLUTIONARY YEARS

With no large cities brimming with revolutionary fervor like Boston and Philadelphia, New Jersey was not a key player in the fight for independence (although South Jersey's Greenwich did host one of the 13 colonies' infamous tea-burning parties), and a large percentage of the population remained loyal to the British crown. As a war became imminent, the colony's Royal Governor William Franklin (the illegitimate son of Benjamin Franklin and a steadfast loyalist) became increasingly remote. He was arrested in June 1776, marking New Jersey's tentative acceptance of the Revolution.

While New Jersey did not play a large part in prerevolutionary events, it made up for the lack once the war began. A central location between New York and Philadelphia guaranteed its place as a major crossroads for both British and American soldiers during the early years of battle, and General George Washington spent more time in New Jersey than in any other colony during the war. Still, much of the population shied away from involvement. Many Quakers, prevalent on New Jersey's western side, opposed the war and remained pacifist, while the New Jersey militia proved less than adequate.

On November 20, 1776, the British attacked New Jersey. As General Howe and his troops captured Fort Lee along the Hudson River, General Cornwallis and a British army of 6,000 scaled the Palisades cliffs and headed west, sending Washington and his men on a retreat across the colony and into Pennsylvania, where they spent a long and discouraging month at Valley Forge. The morale of the Continental Army had reached an all-time low, and in New Jersey, fearful rebels signed oaths to the crown

under British soldiers' watchful eyes. The fight for the cause was looking defeated.

Ten Crucial Days

The Revolution's turning point began December 26, 1776, on New Jersey land. In the early morning hours, General Washington and an army of 2,400 crossed the Delaware River north of Trenton and arrived at present-day Washington Crossing State Park, in Titusville, before turning south toward Trenton. They separated into two groups and attacked a Hessian brigade in Trenton at 8 A.M. The Americans won this battle with no casualties and only a few injuries.

Washington and his men retreated back to Pennsylvania, but finding Trenton deserted, they returned to New Jersey later that week. In the interim, General Cornwallis and his army were drawn from nearby Princeton, and on January 2, 1777, the Second Battle of Trenton ensued. Later that evening Washington and his men escaped over back roads and continued on to Princeton, where under General Hugh Mercer's leadership they fought British troops at a local orchard. Mercer was killed, but Washington rallied the troops to continue on and defeat the British. Collectively known as the 10 Crucial Days, this became the turning point of the war. Bruised and battered, the British retreated through the state, leaving New Jersey almost entirely by year's end.

Other Revolutionary Events

The British later tried returning to New Jersey through Philadelphia, leading to the Battle of Fort Mercer in present-day Gloucester County (Red Bank Battlefield park now occupies the site). Although their attempt was unsuccessful, British troops eventually returned to the colony via a southern route. General Washington and his army followed closely behind and engaged them at the Battle of Monmouth, the longest battle of the American Revolution. The outcome was not decisive, but significantly it was the northern colonies' last major battle. One last assault on New Jersey took place in June 1780 where

Elizabeth (south of Newark) stands today. Americans resisted British and Hessian takeover, but nearby towns were torched.

New Jersey wasn't just a place for major revolutionary battles. South Jersey was home to several skirmishes, and Salem County's Hancock House was site of an assumed rebel massacre by British soldiers. Bergen County, in New Jersey's upper northeast corner, saw fighting between Tories and loyalists result in bloodshed. General Washington spent nights in present-day Lambertville and Somerville, among numerous other towns, as well as two long winters in Morristown—one of them at the Ford Mansion.

The war ended in 1783, and New Jersey entered into statehood on December 18, 1787, as the nation's third state. On November 20, 1789, New Jersey became the first state to ratify the Bill of Rights.

NEW JERSEY'S INDUSTRIAL REVOLUTION

With its strategic position along the Northeast Corridor and a large number of immigrants looking for employment, New Jersey was primed to become a significant contributor to the nation's Industrial Revolution. During the 18th century, southern areas like Gloucester and Cumberland Counties grew prosperous with glass factories profiting from the region's sandy silica terrain and heavily wooded areas that provided furnace fuel. During the same period, iron was being mined throughout the state. In fact, it was Newark inventor Seth Boyden who changed the world's iron industry by developing a way to produce malleable cast iron in 1826.

But it was when Alexander Hamilton established Paterson in 1791 that New Jersey's industrial revolution truly began. Wanting to build a planned industrial town, Hamilton decided Paterson's Great Falls were just the resource needed to do it. (Paterson later earned the nickname "Silk City" from the textile industry that grew up there.) Thereafter, New Jersey blossomed with manufacturing, invention, and industry. Today, it remains one of the most industrialized states in the nation.

© LAURA KINIRY

Now a museum, Burlington County Prison opened in 1811.

Newark in particular prospered as a manufacturing center. Breweries were a big city industry throughout the 1800s and into the 20th century, becoming the city's fourth-largest industry by the time of Prohibition. Leather was another of Newark's major manufactured items. Tanneries were plentiful, and patent leather was a local specialty. Outside the manufacturing sector, the city was also home to insurance providers such as Prudential.

With its prime location along the Delaware River, Trenton also flourished. The city contributed significantly to the country's rubber industry, and it was also center to the state's ceramics industry, fueled by northeastern New Jersey's clay resources. Trenton was the nation's headquarters for Sanitary Ware in the late 1800s and early 1900s, manufacturing porcelain toilets, sinks, bathtubs, and kitchen appliances.

Canals

During the early half of the 19th century, canals were a main mode of industrial transport across New Jersey. Completed in 1834, the Delaware & Raritan Canal carried goods, mainly coal from Pennsylvania, from Bordentown along the Delaware River up to Trenton, turning east to New Brunswick, where it connected with the Raritan River. A feeder canal entering at Trenton flowed down from the river town of Stockton. The D&R mainly served as a cargo carrier. It flourished for decades, although by the turn of the 20th century it began facing increasing competition from railroad carriers. The D&R finally closed for transport in 1932, but its length now acts as a popular state park.

Completed one year earlier, the Morris Canal carried goods from Phillipsburg to Newark across the state's northern portion. It was later expanded to reach Jersey City and the nearby Hudson River. The canal featured a 760-foot incline from the west and a 914-foot decline to the east, reaching a total elevation change of 1,674 feet—more than any other canal in the world. Like the D&R, the canal's main cargo was coal from Pennsylvania, and also like its neighbor to the south, it

thrived during the 1860s and 1870s, eventually succumbing to the railroads' success by 1924. Today, portions of the canal are found throughout the Skylands and Gateway regions. (In Newark the subway travels through a stretch of the former canal.)

CIVIL WAR YEARS

New Jersey's Civil War efforts receive mixed reviews. Some claim the state sympathized with the South. In fact, New Jersey was slow granting rights to blacks and slaves. By 1860, nearly 20 slaves still existed in New Jersey, making it the last northern state to abolish slavery. And by the time of the Civil War, New Jersey's population was evenly divided down the middle. Still, when the Union Army needed fighters, the state responded.

The Civil War ensued from 1861 to 1865. After it ended, 1870's 15th Amendment granted black males the right to vote. Perth Amboy's Thomas Mundy Peterson became the country's first African American to cast a ballot under the new law.

The Underground Railroad

Whatever its legislature's stance on slavery, New Jersey played an important role on the eastern line of the Underground Railroad, which traveled up the Atlantic coast from as far south as Florida. Along this route slaves entered New Jersey from the south through Delaware, or east from Pennsylvania, and continued north to New York. Stops have been traced to several New Jersey towns and cities, including South Jersey's Lawnside and Burlington City.

New Jersey holds ties to two famous Underground Railroad figures, Harriet Ross Tubman and William Sill. Tubman worked as a cook in numerous Cape May hotels during the period 1849–1852, and she used money earned to operate as a Railroad conductor, assisting slaves en route. Her nickname, "Black Moses," comes from her part in helping more than 300 slaves to freedom. William Sill grew up in New Jersey, later moving to Philadelphia, where he became head of the General Vigilance Committee, an organization that aided runaway slaves.

THE GROWTH OF THE SHORE

While steamboats were responsible for the first development along New Jersey's shore, in cities like Cape May and Long Branch, it's the railroad that created the coast we know today. New Jersey's first train line, the Camden and Amboy Railroad, opened in the early 1830s, but it wasn't until after the Civil War that the state's railroads really began taking off and shore towns began to grow.

Before the railroad, most people deemed Jersey's coast inaccessible. To even reach the shore, visitors had to endure a long open carriage ride in sweltering hear through mosquito and greenfly swarms. But with the advent of the train, people could go down the shore for an afternoon and arrive home later that evening, in time for work the following day. Atlantic City's first train arrived in 1851, sparking the birth of "America's Playground." Train lines were soon built across South and Central Jersey and down the coast from New York City, turning empty stretches of barren sand into New Jersey's most prolific tourist industry. New towns were popping up all along the coastline, continuing until the turn of the 20th century. Trains prospered until after World War II, when competition from automobiles and buses led to line consolidation, and train travel petered out.

THE EARLY 20TH CENTURY

The major movements and events of the early 20th century affected New Jersey in countless ways.

Woodrow Wilson

The Progressive Era (1890–1920), begun as a reaction to the country's swift industrial growth, saw New Jersey singled out for its political corruption, corporate bullying, and violence resulting from labor movements seeking fair wages and working conditions. But things changed when Woodrow Wilson became governor. The former President of Princeton University (where he completely revised the curriculum to its current form) won the governorship with the support of Democratic bosses, whom he quickly abandoned after being elected. He soon put forth a series of progressive ideals—establishing a corrupt practices act, Public Utilities Commission, workers compensation, and laws assisting schools and labor. Although Wilson went into the governorship top-strong and failed to produce toward the end of his term, he left the position with a substantial Progressive following that eventually scored him the U.S. presidency.

World War I

When World War I led to the banning of all imported German products, including the textiles the United States heavily relied on, New Jersey's industries were called on to produce. Salem County's DuPont became the country's number 1 dye maker, and pharmaceutical companies began expanding their research. Women found employment with ships and railways, and local soldiers traveled overseas to fight after receiving training. All the while New Jersey's cities were experiencing huge demographic changes as growing numbers of blacks migrated from the South to take advantage of the state's increasing number of factory jobs, and German persecution remained ongoing. Many businesses and towns even dropped their German names.

Prohibition and Women's Suffrage

Prohibition didn't do much to deter New Jerseyans. In fact, New Jersey was one of three states that refused to ratify the 18th Amendment. Both sides of the Hudson River earned a reputation for rum smuggling and speakeasies, and the mob took control of the region's liquor trade. (Prohibition was repealed in 1933 with the passage of the 21st Amendment.)

The state accorded voting rights to women—unintentionally—before the 20th Amendment was passed in 1920. New Jersey's constitution, hastily written at the onset of the American Revolution, gave "adult residents worth 50 pounds" the right to vote, and women were known to cast ballots until the loophole was sealed in 1807. The battle for women's suffrage, however, continued on with Alice Paul, a Mount Laurel native, leading the National Woman's Party in the fight for female suffrage at the federal level.

The Great Depression

The great stock market crash of October 29, 1929, sent the nation reeling in a downward spiral, and New Jersey was no exception. The state suffered severely, especially African Americans who moved to New Jersey from the South during World War I in search of employment. New Jersey would not bounce back until World War II.

WORLD WAR II

Like the First World War, the Second World War created heavy industrial demands on New Jersey. The New York Shipbuilding Yard provided more than 100 ships for the war effort. Blacks poured into the state's cities in even greater numbers to take advantage of job opportunities, and they propelled New Jersey legislation in terms of antidiscrimination laws.

German U-boats were positioned off the Jersey Coast during each of the wars, posing a threat to merchant ships, especially during 1942. Many American vessels sank, torn by torpedoes or accidentally crashing into other ships while running a zigzag (and often miscalculated) course to avoid enemy fire. U-boats were able to identify American vessels by the backlights that shone from the coast and illuminated them in the night sky, but towns refused to extinguish their lights for fear of losing tourists until they were absolutely required to do so. The U.S. Navy eventually employed information obtained by the British, who'd captured a U-boat in 1940, preventing future surprise attacks.

After World War II, the GI Bill brought an influx of soldiers to study at Rutgers, leading to the school's designation as New Jersey's state university, and home-loan provisions further altered the state's physical and cultural geographic makeup. Although suburbanization had been occurring since the arrival of the railway, there became a substantial shift from urban getaways like Lakewood to year-round homes located far from train routes.

CONTEMPORARY TIMES
The Automobile

Although trolley cars were responsible for the state's first suburbs, nothing changed the face of New Jersey like the automobile. With the popularity of cars, suburbia took on a whole new form, especially in this state already considered a main transport route. The onslaught of the auto saw the end of expansive railway transport. With cars, people began moving farther from city centers and abandoned older suburbs (contributing to "white flight"), a distance requiring a new dependency on New Jersey roads.

Bridges, tunnels, and interstate highways were constructed to link New York with Philadelphia, and New Jersey's barrier islands to the mainland. Much of the state's bridge building took place during the early–mid 20th century.

State Governor Alfred E. Driscoll proposed the New Jersey Turnpike, today one of the busiest highways in the world, in 1947. Its first 118 of 148 miles opened by 1952. This infamous toll road, New Jersey's first, now stretches like nylon across the state, connecting Delaware Memorial Bridge to New York with over two dozen exits, rest stops named "Vince Lombardi," "Clara Barton," and "Molly Pitcher" (all famous New Jerseyans at some point in their lives), and four to 12 lanes across.

The state's system of highways and interstates grew into one of the country's most intense, with notorious bumper-to-bumper traffic and throughways constantly needing expanding to meet impending demands.

Civil Rights

For a state slow to abolish slavery, New Jersey was quite progressive, although this didn't prevent Newark's 1967 riots or Camden's riots in later years. Incidents of racial discrimination continued to occur throughout the state, including the controversial arrest of Rubin

"Hurricane" Carter, immortalized by Bob Dylan and later by Denzel Washington.

The Late 20th Century

New Jersey's economy saw a few major changes during the 20th century's final few decades, including 1976's opening of the Meadowlands Sports Arena, 1978's legalization of gambling in Atlantic City, and the rise of pharmaceutical manufacturing companies. The state's century-old organized crime organizations prospered in metropolitan regions like Newark, Camden, and Atlantic City, with the tristate area's arguably most-famous mobster, Little Nicky Scarfo, banished to New Jersey before receiving a life sentence.

GOVERNMENT

Like the federal government, New Jersey has executive, legislative, and judicial branches. Its governor is one of the few in the nation to be elected in odd-numbered years. New Jersey's best-known governors include Woodrow Wilson (1911–1913), who went on to become U.S. President; Alfred E. Driscoll (1947–1954), responsible for the New Jersey Turnpike; Brendan T. Byrne (1974–1982), "Savior of the Pinelands"; Christine Todd Whitman (1994–2001), New Jersey's first female governor; and James E. McGreevey, who announced himself a "gay American" before resigning from office (because of "out-of-tune" governmental appointments) in fall 2004.

New Jersey is sometimes considered a swing state, but it leans Democrat. The more urban areas around New York City, Philly, and Trenton have the largest Democratic demographics, and rural counties such as Warren, Sussex, and Ocean (along the coast) are considerably Republican.

Townships and Boroughs

New Jersey towns are often described as townships or boroughs. A township is a geographic area incorporating several smaller towns and neighborhoods. They usually range 6–54 square miles, and they're often used to designate school districts and public works. Sometimes part of a larger township, boroughs are small (less than four square miles) self-governing areas with their own mayor and council.

New Jersey State Capitol, Trenton

© LAURA KINIRY

Economy

In 2004 New Jersey's per capita personal income was $41,332, third highest in the country behind Connecticut and Massachusetts, with 8.5 percent of New Jerseyans living below the poverty level, the fifth-lowest percentage in the country. The reason for these impressive statistics is the state's prime location between Philadelphia and New York City. As a double-edged sword, New Jersey also has some of the highest property taxes in the country. The state's economy has shifted over the years from focusing on agriculture to manufacturing to service, although pharmaceuticals are currently the state's number 1 industry.

AGRICULTURE

About 17 percent of New Jersey's land is currently used for agriculture, which makes up 0.2 percent of the state's economy. The bulk of the production comes from South Jersey's Cumberland, Salem, and Gloucester Counties, the bogs and bushels of Atlantic and Burlington Counties, and Central Jersey's Monmouth County.

The state's central region raises large numbers of standardbred horses for racing and recreation, so it's unsurprising that the horse is New Jersey's official animal. New Jersey is said to have more horses per square mile than anywhere else in the country.

During the 1800s, Vineland native John Mason invented the mason jar as a way of preserving perishables. Soon canned fruits and vegetables became a large part of New Jersey's economy, especially with the founding of the Campbell Soup Company in Camden. The state's focus on produce paved the way for Welch's grape juice, begun in Vineland, and Ocean Spray, which started as a Pinelands' cranberry co-op.

Produce

New Jersey is home to the cultivated blueberry, "invented" by Elizabeth White of Whitesbog in 1916, and today ranks second in the nation in blueberry production. The blueberry was declared New Jersey's official state fruit in 2003. The peach has replaced the apple as New Jersey's number 1 fruit (although you'll see both kinds of orchards throughout South Jersey).

New Jersey ranks second in the nation in potato production and third behind Massachusetts and Wisconsin in the production of cranberries, harvested throughout Burlington, Ocean, and Atlantic Counties.

It is botanically a fruit, but the tomato was designated a vegetable in the 1800s for reasons of taxation, and for all intents and purposes remains a veggie throughout the Garden State, a place that even raised legislation to make it the state vegetable. Today, most every roadside stand advertises Jersey tomatoes that are locally, if not nationally, famous.

Corn is another item with a large in-state following, and most locals have a favorite produce stand where they head for sweet white Jersey corn. Most heavily produced in South Jersey, the Skylands, and Monmouth County, corn is increasing in cultivation with the popularity of maize mazes in summer and fall.

MANUFACTURING AND INDUSTRY

New Jersey was at the forefront of the country's industrial revolution, and early manufacturing included iron, glass, textiles, and paper. Today, the state's number 1 manufacturing industry is pharmaceuticals—their research, development, and production. Most of the industry is centered in New Jersey's urban northeast. Johnson & Johnson, one of the country's leading suppliers of health care products, was founded and remains in New Brunswick.

Oil refineries make up one of the state's most visible industries, and there are currently six in the state—three in the Gateway and three in South Jersey (two in Paulsboro and one in Westville on the way to Gloucester).

Notable businesses that help define New

Jersey's economy include Subaru of America, headquartered in Cherry Hill and begun as the Japanese carmaker's U.S. distributor, and NFL Films, which films every game for the National Football League and has been a major Mount Laurel employer since 1979. Atlantic City's casinos are also leading state contributors, creating jobs and supporting businesses.

TOURISM

The state's second-largest industry, New Jersey tourism dates back to the late 1800s when New York and Philadelphia steamboats would carry visitors along the coast to Long Branch and Cape May. With the coming of railways, the Shore was developed and inland resorts like Lake Hopatcong and Lake Mohawk prospered. Air travel carried some of the industry out of state, but coastal towns have bounced back, especially with the recent trend of travelers staying closer to home. Although most tourism capital comes from Shore resorts—Atlantic City is the state's number 1 destination—the Skylands places second in attracting crowds.

The People

In 2004 New Jersey had an estimated population of 8.5 million, ranking 10th among the 50 states. At 1,172 people per square mile it's the United States' most densely populated state and exceeds the density of both China (360 people per square mile) and India (927 people per square mile). Still, on a drive through New Jersey it doesn't seem densely populated, with about two people per square mile in some parts of the Pinelands.

Immigration plays a large role in the state's population. Even before Ellis Island welcomed inhabitants to the New World, New Jersey, with its prime locale along the Eastern Seaboard and Northeast Corridor, was an ideal stop for the country's new arrivals and for those searching for employment.

After New Jersey's initial settlement of Dutch, Swedes, and the British, the state's first wave of immigration was mostly Irish and German. Germans arrived in the late 19th century and earlier, working as craftsmen such as glassmakers and ironworkers in South Jersey and the upper Highlands. The Irish came to New Jersey in massive numbers during their country's Great Potato Famine (1845–1851), continuing through the 19th century and well into the 20th century, although they have been arriving in the state since its beginning.

Irish immigrants gained positions as political powerhouses throughout New Jersey, setting up neighborhoods in Newark's Ironbound, in Jersey City, Trenton, and Morristown's and Paterson's "Dublin sections."

Italians, today New Jersey's largest ancestry group, didn't really begin arriving until the late 19th century, mostly from southern Italy. Most originally worked on South Jersey farms, eventually seeking work in the state's northeast. Italian populations settled in Newark's First Ward, Trenton's Chambersburg, Camden, Morristown, and Paterson. Large numbers of Western, Eastern, and Northern Europeans also came to New Jersey around this time.

The state's African American population increased dramatically during the two World Wars, as blacks from Southern states were drawn by industrial opportunities. Many settled into impoverished sections of Camden and Trenton, and in Newark's Third Ward, then home to a large Jewish population.

New Jersey's Cuban population soared after Castro came to power. Today, the state hosts the country's second-largest Cuban population, after Florida. New Jersey is also home to Indian, Bangladeshi, Colombian, Dominican, Asian, Latin American, and Middle Eastern populations, all arriving in the latter half of the 20th century.

Arts and Culture

Local culture depends on where you are in the state: Set foot in South Jersey's Deptford, say, and you're in Philadelphia territory—where Philly sports teams get prime air time; cheesesteaks, soft pretzels, and hoagies are common food staples; water-ice is sold at seasonal stands; ice cream comes topped with jimmies; and if you refer to the tristate region, you're talking about New Jersey, Pennsylvania, and Delaware. But take a ride up to Bergen County in the state's northern half and suddenly you love the Yankees, you eat Italian ice and dine on subs, you top your ice cream with sprinkles, and the tristate region now includes New York and Connecticut.

New Jersey may seem divided across the middle, but its similarities transcend its differences. If you're a girl from New Jersey, you're a "Jersey Girl" across the state; going "down the Shore" is what all New Jerseyans do; and Jersey jokes are general enough to encompass everyone, no matter whether you're from Hoboken or Cherry Hill. It's okay to call it "Jersey"; in fact, many locals do. New Jersey's rep precedes it, and its residents are proud.

ARTS, CRAFTS, AND FOLK TRADITIONS

New Jersey is home to several living-history farms demonstrating mostly forgotten ways of life, such as butter churning and beekeeping. These include Central Jersey's Howell Living History Farm, Longstreet Farm, and Historic Allaire Village; Cape May County's Cold Spring Village; and Morristown's Fosterfield's Living History Farm. For a better understanding of folk traditions spanning New Jersey's eight southernmost counties, stop by Wheaton Arts & Cultural Center's Down Jersey Folklife Center. Tuckerton Seaport offers good insight into the Jersey Shore's maritime history, and the Delaware Bayshore Project runs educational outings on the state's official tall ship—the *A.J. Meerwald*—while teaching visitors about local culture and history.

South Jersey's prosperous glassmaking history lives on at Wheaton Arts & Cultural Center, where resident artisans work and later display their creations. For a complete overview of New Jersey arts, check out **Discover Jersey Arts** (800/843-2787, www.jerseyarts.com), a guide to theater, dance, galleries, and entertainment venues statewide, along with details on local craft fairs and festivals.

LITERATURE

New Jersey has hosted a large number of writers and acted as muse for numerous authors. Poets William Carlos Williams and Allen Ginsberg drew inspiration from Paterson, where one lived and the other was born, while poet Amiri Baraka writes about Newark. Former Poet Laureate Robert Pinsky is a Long Branch native, and New Yorker Walt Whitman spent his last years in Camden, where he is buried. Stephen Crane (*The Red Badge of Courage*), another writer heavily associated with New York, was born and raised in Asbury Park in the late 19th century and began his career writing commentary for a local paper.

Modern-day authors inspired by New Jersey include Philip Roth, who grew up in Newark's Third Ward when it was primarily a Jewish neighborhood. Roth's Newark experiences play pivotal role in his works like *Goodbye, Columbus,* and the Pulitzer Prize–winning *American Pastoral.* Joyce Carol Oates's writings hold lots of Garden State ties, most notably *The Barrens,* a mystery written under her pseudonym Rosamond Smith.

Although Janet Evanovich lives in New Hampshire, her best-known bail-bond enforcer, Stephanie Plum, is a Jersey Girl through and through. Evanovich's highly successful series follows Plum through numerous love interests, car explosions, and family dinners at her parents' home in Trenton's Chambersburg district. Author Joshua Braff is one of the latest New Jersey writers inspired by his home state. His fictional *The Unthinkable Thoughts of Jacob Green* is set in the Gateway Region.

the tomb of the "Good Gray Poet," Walt Whitman, Camden

© LAURA KINIRY

Other literary greats who've left their mark on the Garden State include F. Scott Fitzgerald, whose *This Side of Paradise*'s main character is a Princeton University undergrad; Toni Morrison, who wrote *Beloved* while living in New Jersey; and Dorothy Parker, who employed a table at Hunterdon County's Stockton Inn as a "country" Algonquin Round Table.

MUSIC

New Jersey's music history is prolific. Frank Sinatra, Frankie Valli, Sandra Dee, Connie Francis, Pete Yorn, Whitney Houston, Sarah Vaughan, Count Basie, Queen Latifah, Redman, Kool and the Gang, and Lauryn Hill are all from here. The state has inspired huge hip-hop and jazz movements, as well as an entire genre known as Jersey Shore Music, which produced Jon Bon Jovi, Little Steven Van Zandt, Southside Johnny, Patty Scialfa, Gary U.S. Bonds, and the mighty master, Bruce Springsteen. Rocker Patti Smith, though not a New Jersey native, spent her formative years in Deptford, an experience she continues to recall today. Like those of Nashville and New Orleans, New Jersey musicians take pride in their environment and are heavily influenced by it, creating a sound that's like no other.

Asbury Park and Wildwood stand as New Jersey's musical testaments. The former remains the best place in New Jersey to see up-and-coming local bands; the latter changed music history during the 1950s. Wildwood saw the live debut of Bill Haley and His Comets' rock-and-roll classic "Rock Around the Clock" and hosted the first-ever "Twist" by Chubby Checker. The city also served as summertime host to Dick Clark's *American Bandstand*.

New Jersey's cities, people, and culture have inspired countless songs, including Springsteen's "Atlantic City"; "Jersey Girl," written by Tom Waits; Bobby Rydell's "Wildwood Days"; and the shore standard "On the Way to Cape May," best performed by Philadelphia TV personality Al Alberts. The entire soundtrack of *Eddie and the Cruisers* can be considered a Jersey Shore anthem.

Not to be overlooked, the Pinelands produces

a unique sound called Piney music, a blend of country and bluegrass that includes stringed instruments and washtubs. Waretown's Albert Music Hall is the place to hear these lively sounds every Saturday night.

TV AND FILM

A New Jersey overview wouldn't be complete without mentioning the state's role in motion pictures and television. New Jersey was home to the world's first film studio. Known as "The Black Maria," it was built by Thomas Edison on the grounds of his West Orange Laboratory. For a brief time in the early 20th century, New Jersey was the center of the silent picture industry, and the term *cliffhanger* was coined in reference to a series of films shot on location at the Palisades cliffs. Studios eventually moved to California for year-round production ability and more control, but not before New Jersey, and specifically Fort Lee, earned its place in history. Less than two decades later, the world's first drive-in movie opened along South Jersey's Admiral Wilson Boulevard between Camden and Pennsauken. It was 1933, and the film was *Wife Beware.*

New Jersey has produced numerous big- and small-screen actors, among them Paul Robeson (Princeton), Jack Nicholson (Neptune), Danny DeVito (Asbury Park), Meryl Streep (Summit), Bud Abbott (Asbury Park) and Lou Costello (Paterson), Bette Midler (Paterson), Bruce Willis (Penns Grove), James Gandolfini (Westwood), and Kelly Ripa (Stratford). In addition, the Shore was a summer haunt of Grace Kelly (Ocean City), Kevin Bacon (Ocean City), and Will Smith (Wildwood). Michael Landon attended Collingswood High, Jimmy Stewart and Brooke Shields attended Princeton, and Steven Spielberg is said to have seen his first movie in Haddon Township.

Films in which New Jersey or its cities have played a starring role include *On the Waterfront* (Hoboken), *The King of Marvin Gardens* (Atlantic City), *Atlantic City* (Atlantic City), *Eddie and the Cruisers* (South Jersey), *Friday the 13th* (Blairstown), *The Station Agent* (Skylands), and most recently *Garden State* (Gateway region). Director Kevin Smith's New Jersey trilogy—comprising *Clerks, Mallrats,* and *Chasing Amy*—casts New Jersey as a leading character, but the state's most award-worthy performance goes to its role in the HBO television series *The Sopranos.*

ESSENTIALS

Getting There

Its relatively small size and location between two of the Eastern Seaboard's most prosperous cities make New Jersey one of the most convenient places to travel in the United States.

BY AIR

Both **Newark Liberty International Airport** (888/397-4636, www.panynj.com) and New York's JFK, or **John F. Kennedy International Airport** (718/244-4080 or 800/247-7433, www.kennedyairport.com), serve the state's northern half, while those exploring South Jersey or the southern shore can either fly into **Philadelphia International Airport** (215/580-7800 or 215/937-6800, www.philadelphia-phl.com) or the smaller **Atlantic City International Airport** (609/645-7895, www.acairport.com), served by **Spirit Airlines** (www.spiritair.com). I won't go so far as to say it's fun trying to configure the cheapest flight from your starting point to New Jersey, but with so many points to choose from it's almost always easy to find an inexpensive flight. **Southwest** (www.southwest.com) flies to Philly, while **Jet Blue** (www.jetblue.com) offers flights into JFK and Newark. If you're traveling from many places in Europe, a direct flight into JFK will most likely be the cheapest and most direct route, although flights to Philly from London's Heathrow can run fairly low during off-season. Cross-country

flights into the three major airports often offer rock-bottom deals, running about $250 (with taxes) round-trip. Pennsylvania's **Lehigh Valley International Airport** (3311 Airport Rd., Allentown, PA, www.lvia.org) is the closest airport to the Skylands, only a 40-minute drive to Clinton and an hour to Flemington. **Continental** (www.continental.com) and **Northwest** (www.nwa.com) both fly here. New Jersey has dozens of smaller airports, including ones in Princeton, Medford, and Sussex, and a handful of airports throughout the Skylands that are equipped for hot air balloons.

BY CAR

If arriving by motor vehicle, I-95 is a direct toll-route along the East Coast from Maine south to Florida, turning into New Jersey's famed Turnpike on its leg through the state. In an east-west direction, I-80 can be taken from the Gateway region's Fort Lee across the country to Oakland, California, if you're up for the drive. Cars are allowed on the **Cape May-Lewes Ferry** (609/889-7200, www.cape may-lewesferry.com), connecting Delaware and Cape May.

BY TRAIN

Amtrak (800/872-7245, www.amtrak.com) offers service to both Philadelphia and New York City, with transfer stops in numerous places statewide, including Trenton, Princeton, New Brunswick, Cherry Hill, Atlantic City, and Newark. If you have the time, I recommend train travel, which offers discounts for students, seniors, veterans, children, and international travelers. Check Amtrak's website for more info. Philadelphia's **30th Street Station**

is reachable from the city's airport by **SEPTA** (215/580-7800, www.septa.org). Amtrak has a station at Newark Liberty International Airport, and offers bus connections from JFK.

NJ Transit (800/772-2222 North Jersey, 800/582-5946 South Jersey, 973/762-5100 out of state, www.njtransit.state.nj.us) runs trains out of New York City and into the Garden State with stops in the eastern Skylands, throughout the Gateway Region, and along the Jersey Shore's northern coast.

BY BUS

America's ultimate hippie bus, the **Green Tortoise** (www.greentortoise.com), offers 10-day and two-week cross-country trips arriving in New York City, just a hop, skip, and jump from New Jersey's Gateway Region. **Greyhound** (800/231-2222, www.greyhound .com) is an inexpensive albeit boring (and often scary) bus alternative for in-state arrivals, and has stations in Atlantic City, Mount Laurel, Newark, and Trenton, among others.

From New York City, **Transbridge Lines** (www.transbridgebus.com) operates daily bus service to Newark Airport, as well as the Skylands' Clinton, Flemington, Phillipsburg, and Frenchtown.

BY BOAT

For those looking to arrive by sea, **Cunard Cruises** (www.cunard.com) offers transatlantic cruises that end in New York City, an excellent starting point for exploring New Jersey. If you have your own water vessel, the state is part of the Intracoastal Waterway running along the Atlantic seaboard down to the Gulf of Mexico that offers protected passage for sea travelers.

Getting Around

BY CAR

To really delve into New Jersey, it's essential to have a car. Rental agencies are located at each of the airports, though its often cheaper to rent in-state, away from the urban areas. Some to try are **Alamo** (800/327-9633, www .alamo.com), **Hertz** (800/654-3131, www .hertz.com), **Avis** (800/831-2847, www.avis .com), and **Budget** (800/527-0700, www .drivebudget.com). Anyone renting a car in New Jersey, and any additional drivers added to the rental agreement, must be 25 or older.

Taxis are available in most of the state's larger cities. Atlantic City has its own 24-hour **jitneys** (609/344-8642, www.jitneys .net)—transport buses that run approximately every 15 minutes and stop at all the major locations—and many of the Shore towns operate trolleys during summer months.

Roadways

New Jersey's major roadways have the well-deserved reputation of being traffic-heavy nightmares. It's best to avoid these interstates and highways—which include Interstates 295, 195, 282, 80, Route 1, and the infamous New Jersey Turnpike—if at all possible during rush hours. The Atlantic City Expressway (Rte. 446, though unsigned) and the Garden State Parkway (Rte. 444, unsigned) should be added to the list, with the further suggestion to steer clear of them in the direction of the Shore at all costs on Friday evenings and Saturday mornings during summer. The introduction of E-Z Passes, allowing drivers to slowly drive through, instead of stopping at, tolls, and electronically deducting the fare from a prepaid account, has sped things up somewhat, but not by much.

Shore traffic occurs elsewhere as well, including Route 72 en route to Long Beach Island (and the island's only existing entry), Route 322 from the Delaware River's Commodore Barry Bridge across the state to Atlantic City, and Route 55, a highway connecting Route 47

to the southern Shore towns. If you're planning a weekend down the Shore, heading out early on a Friday afternoon or at the crack of dawn on Saturday should help alleviate some of the bumper-to-bumper pain. From South Jersey, an alternative to the Garden State Parkway for reaching Northern Shore towns is to take Route 70 through the Pinelands from Marlton. It's a

BARRIERS AND CIRCLES

New Jersey roads are responsible for one well-known invention and known for one frightening feature: the Jersey barrier and the traffic circle. The Jersey barrier is that short movable wall standing between lanes of oncoming traffic along major roadways – a few feet tall and tapering as it rises to prevent vehicles from rolling over. It was developed as a way to prevent trucks from jumping lanes, which had resulted in head-on collisions.

While not developed here, the traffic circle is synonymous with New Jersey roadways. The state's first circle was Pennsauken's Airport Circle, built in the early 1900s. Similar to the British roundabout, drivers enter the circle from a feeder road and either skirt the outer lane, where they're poured onto another joining roadway, or they merge into the inner circle (which is daunting) to avoid additional entering traffic (and out-of-state drivers) until they're again ready to rejoin the straight-lane world. Although many circles have been replaced with traffic lights and corner edges (sometimes just as dangerous), you'll still find quite a number of them throughout New Jersey; there are three in the Flemington area alone. As if circles weren't enough, the state also features a large number of LEFT TURNS FROM RIGHT LANE ONLY intersections, called jughandles.

long, straight—though somewhat mundane—two-lane road that will eventually lead you to Point Pleasant Beach and the surrounding Shore towns. Still, as toll roads go, the 173-mile Garden State Parkway, extending from New York State's border south to Cape May, is actually quite nice (sans traffic), with snaking curves, green islands and borders, and enough natural bumps to provide your ride with a rhythmic *Dukes of Hazzard* feel. Also disregarding traffic, Route 55 is one of the nicest roads for reaching the shores of Cape May County. It connects with Route 47 and travels along the Delaware Bayshore region through heavy woods and past farms and wetlands, eventually carrying traffic right to Wildwood and Cape May. Drivers can disembark early from Route 55 onto Route 49 east to reach Ocean City, but like other back routes to the shore, this two-lane road gets pretty dark at night.

Some of the state's older roads, like Route 17 (the Gateway Region), Route 130 (from Camden County to Bordentown), and Route 1 (Trenton to South Brunswick) all experience heavy traffic and are laden with stop lights and abandoned shopping centers. Fortunately, famed Jersey diners seem to exist alongside them every few miles, making the driving experience a bit more worthwhile.

Roads both pleasant and easy to navigate include Route 29 north of Lambertville, Route 537 from Merchantville northeast to Freehold (a good back route for reaching Jackson Township's Six Flags), I-22, and Route 206, from South Jersey's Hammonton north through the Pinelands and on to the state's northwest corner. Route 9 north from Cape May is a nice alternative to the Garden State Parkway, and is lined with campgrounds, shopping centers, miniature golf courses, and individual antique shops, and the road starts to get a bit congested as it enters Ocean County. I-287 is a modern, easy route traveling south from New York State through the center of North Jersey (bypassing the Gateway congestion) and connecting with the Turnpike and the Garden State Parkway near Perth Amboy, along Raritan Bay. It's an easy way to get to many Skylands and Gateway locations and a good access route to the rest of New Jersey.

Tolls are collected along the **Garden State Parkway** (732/442-8600), the **New Jersey Turnpike** (732/247-0900, www.state.nj.us/turnpike), the **Atlantic City Expressway** (609/965-6060, www.acexpressway.com), and many of the bridges connecting the coastal barrier islands in the southern half of the state. New Jersey is connected to Delaware, Philadelphia, and New York City by bridges, most of which require a one-way toll paid when leaving the state. Many of the bridges connecting the Skylands to Pennsylvania's Lehigh Valley are free.

One thing New Jersey lacks are sufficient roadside rest stops. Other than toll roads, your best bets for a bathroom break are gas stations and fast-food eateries.

Helpful Hints

The **New Jersey Department of Transportation** website offers real-time traffic updates statewide at www.state.nj.us/transportation/commuter/trafficinfo, and significant road construction updates in the New York metropolitan region at www.state.nj.us/transportation/commuter/roads/. For information on road closures and traffic throughout the Philadelphia metropolitan area, including much of South Jersey, try AM radio news station **KYW 1060**. On the FM dial, New Jersey 101.5 broadcasts traffic throughout Central Jersey and the outlying regions. In the Gateway Region, tune to AM **1010 WINS** (www.1010wins.com).

New Jersey allows the use of the E-Z Pass on all major toll roads and participating bridges, which include all those in the New York City and Philly regions, and along the upper Delaware River traveling west to Pennsylvania's Lehigh Valley. E-Z Passes can also be used in New York, Massachusetts, Pennsylvania, Delaware, Maryland, and West Virginia.

Don't even think about pumping your own gas in New Jersey—it has been illegal since 1949. New Jersey and Oregon are the only two U.S. states requiring full service. Just pull up, specify the amount and type of gas you want, and let yourself be pampered. You'll need the extra energy for navigating the nearly 100 traffic circles New Jersey roads are known for.

PUBLIC TRANSPORTATION

NJ Transit (800/772-2222 North Jersey, 800/582-5946 South Jersey, 973/762-5100 out of state, www.njtransit.state.nj.us) operates buses throughout the state, serving even the hard-to-reach Skylands region, as well as rail service in the New York City metropolitan region, and a transit line between Philadelphia and Atlantic City (connecting with PATCO). Additional NJ Transit services include the Gateway's Gold Coast **Hudson-Bergen Light Rail,** the Newark Subway, and the **River LINE** (800/626-7433, www.riverline.com), operating along the Delaware River between Camden and Trenton.

PATCO (856/772-6900, www.drpa.org/patco), a division of the Delaware River Port Authority, is an easy way to get from Philly to numerous Camden County locations, including Camden, Collingswood, and Haddonfield,

or if you'd rather travel by boat the **Riverlink Ferry** (215/925-5465, www.riverlink.org) connects Philly's Penn's Landing to the Camden Waterfront (Mar.–Dec.), where you can easily board the River LINE to Trenton's Amtrak Station. In North Jersey, the Port Authority Trans-Hudson, or **PATH** (800/234-7284, www.panynj.gov/path/) operates between New York City and Hoboken, Jersey City, and Newark. The **New York Waterway** (800/533-3779, www.nywaterway.com) runs ferries from New York to points all along New Jersey's Gold Coast, including Weehawkin, Hoboken, Jersey City, and Belford, along Raritan Bay, and **Seastreak** serves the Atlantic Highlands.

TOURS

Tours encompassing the entire state are not yet offered, but specialized tours—best-known are those to Atlantic City—are available. Trips to the casinos are often senior-centric excursions aboard charter buses run by schools, churches, and other organizations, though quite a few are regularly scheduled trips geared toward a more

the River LINE heading southbound from Trenton to Camden

© LAURA KINIRY

eclectic crowd leaving from Philly or New York City. Bus trips to AC often include vouchers for food and drink, or cash back in the form of casino coins and chips. One to try is **Academy** (www.academybus.com), offering daily bus service from Philly, New York City, and numerous places throughout Central and North Jersey, with packages that include cash-back bonuses.

Other popular New Jersey tours include *The Sopranos* filming locales and Pinelands bus trips, as well as walking tours of Princeton and Rutgers Universities.

Transbridge Lines (908/859-1125, www .transbridgebus.com) runs scheduled one-day tours throughout Central and South Jersey and along the Jersey Shore, including trips to Atlantic City, Wildwood, Camden's Adventure Aquarium, Cape May (a multiday tour), and Ocean City. All trips leave from Phillipsburg in the state's Skylands region.

Bicycle Touring

Bike touring is a wonderful way to experience New Jersey's back routes and small towns, and it is becoming increasingly popular, as is cycling itself. Relatively low elevation, wide shoulders, and winding roads that are light on traffic make for some great rides statewide. For those planning to explore New Jersey by bicycle, a wonderful resource is the **Adventure Cycling Association** (www.adventure cycling.com). Bicycles are allowed on most NJ Transit lines during off-peak hours, and on the company's buses that are "bike friendly"— about half, including all those that run within South Jersey. Bikes are also permitted on all PATCO lines running from Philly through South Jersey, connecting with NJ Transit en route to Atlantic City. A limited number of bicycles are allowed on PATH trains during off-peak hours.

Sports and Recreation

With 39 state parks, 11 forests, and three recreation areas, not to mention miles and miles of coastline, New Jersey is a haven for outdoor enthusiasts. State parks sometimes require a fee, most notably between Memorial Day and Labor Day. Prices are usually a bit more on weekends throughout the season, although plenty of county parks throughout New Jersey don't cost a penny. All cyclists, in-line skaters, and skateboarders age 12 and under are required by law to wear helmets.

GENERAL RESOURCES

A good place to get an overview of New Jersey's recreational offerings is the **Department of Environmental Protection**'s website at www .state.nj.us/dep/. The Department of Parks and Forestry link provides information on many of the state's natural resources, which you can search by location or activity. The website also offers insight into local environmental concerns and supplies up-to-date details on fishing and hunting licenses and seasons.

The **National Park Service** (www.nps.gov, then search for a park) provides an overview of the state's national recreation areas, historic sites, parks, routes, and scenic trails, including links to the **Delaware Water Gap National Recreation Area** and the **New Jersey Pinelands National Reserve**.

The **New Jersey Sierra Club** (139 W. Hanover St., Trenton, 609/656-7612, www .newjersey.sierraclub.org), a local chapter of the San Francisco–based organization, sets out to "explore, enjoy, and protect the planet." Local events and activities include coastal cleanups, hikes, canoe trips, and river tubing, all open to both club members and nonmembers. More localized Sierra groups exist throughout the state, each representing a number of counties, and they often host their own meetings and events. Many excursions are free, although sometimes a nominal fee, such as a park entrance fee, is charged.

The **Outdoor Club of South Jersey** (856/427-7777, www.ocsj.org) is an excellent organization running trips in everything from

boating on the Delaware River

cycling, mountain biking, and hiking to overnight wilderness and survival outings. A one-year membership ($20) allows participation in all events offered throughout the year. It's open to anyone, regardless of your place of residence. Most of the activities take place in the South Jersey region, though a number of North Jersey and out-of-state trips are also organized.

The **Appalachian Mountain Club New York/North Jersey Chapter** (www.amc-ny .org) hosts hiking events, as well as other excursions, in the New York tristate area, while the **Appalachian Mountain Club Delaware Valley Chapter** (www.amcdv.org) is better suited for those in the Philadelphia and Trenton metropolitan areas. Membership is not required in either group to participate in many of the activities.

For outdoor leadership skills, one of the top schools in the country is **Tom Brown Jr.'s Tracker School** (www.trackerschool.com) in the Pinelands.

AGRITOURISM AND ECOTOURISM
The **New Jersey Department of Agriculture** (www.state.nj.us/jerseyfresh/) provides information on in-season produce, locations of pick-your-own farms and roadside stands, horseback riding facilities, wineries, and gardens within the state. Another website with a list of pick-your-own farms is www.pickyourown.org/ NJ.htm. The nonprofit **Surfrider Foundation** (www.surfrider.org), dedicated to protecting the country's coastal waters and beaches, has two New Jersey chapters—the Jersey Shore chapter in Belmar (www.surfrider.org/jersey shore/) and the South Jersey chapter (www .surfrider.org/southjersey/), which centers around the Cape. Both websites list numerous area activities open to the public. Two of the last remaining relatively untouched stretches along the Eastern Seaboard are New Jersey's Sandy Hook (732/872-5970, www.nps.gov/ gate) and Island Beach State Park (732/793-0506, www.state.nj.us/dep/forestry/parks).

FISHING
New Jersey offers numerous opportunities for fishing, including rivers and streams, state park waters, wildlife management areas, coastal shores, back bays, and deep-sea charter boats. The state sponsors two free fishing days (908/637-4125, www.nj.gov/dep/fgw/ffd .htm) each June, although anglers remain accountable for catch size and limits regularly

© LAURA KINIRY

implemented within the state. During the rest of the year anyone between the ages of 16 and 69 must have a valid freshwater fishing license, including for the use of privately owned bodies of water, and trout fishing requires an additional stamp. Both licenses and stamps can be obtained online, by post, or at area municipal offices and some sporting goods stores.

Resident fishing licenses are $22.50 ($34 nonresident) and additional trout stamps are $10.50 ($20 nonresident). Nonresidents can also purchase a seven-day ($19.50) or two-day ($9) fishing license. All fishers must abide by the size and catch requirements set forth by the New Jersey Department of Fish and Wildlife. There are no license requirements for saltwater fishing, although they are needed for crabbing ($3), clamming ($11 resident, $21 nonresident), and the collection of oysters ($11).

The Department of Environmental Protection stocks freshwater fish annually, and some places ideal for trout fishing include the trophy lakes of the Round Valley Recreation Area and Lake Aeroflex in Kittatinny State Park, and the streams of Big Flatbrook, Toms River, Manasquan River, Pequest River, and the lower Musconetcong. New Jersey waters are popular among fly-fishers, and Big Flatbrook has four miles of "fly-fishing only" waters beginning just above Stokes State Forest's park office along Route 206. Wild trout streams include Van Campens Brook, which runs within the Delaware Water Gap National Recreation Area.

Saltwater fishing can be enjoyed from piers, docks, jetties, private and commercial boats, beaches, and in the bays, ocean, and other coastal waterways. Fishing for blue crabs is most popular in the bay regions, namely Barnegat, Delaware, and Little Egg Harbor, and can be done from a boat, dock, or on land. Towns to visit for commercial fleets include Keyport, Point Pleasant Beach, Cape May, and Fortescue. Fishing piers exist at coastal towns such as Margate, Ocean City, Beach Haven, Keyport, Keansburg, and Seaside Heights.

New Jersey operates four public marinas: the Leonardo State Marina along the Raritan Bay, Forked River State Marina near Point Pleasant, Senator Frank S. Farley State Marina outside of Atlantic City, and the Fortescue State Marina along the Delaware Bayshore. The Belmar Marina is one of the state's largest, and one of the East Coast's best.

HUNTING

Hunting opportunities in New Jersey include deer, wild turkeys, waterfowl and migratory birds, and small game. Resident licenses require six months' residency or proof of current serving status in the armed forces. Under standard requirements, one-day licenses may be purchased at licensed commercial shooting preserves. License costs are as follows: A firearm hunting license is $27.50 resident, $135.50 nonresident; bow and arrow hunting is $31.50 resident, $135.50 nonresident; trapping is $32.50 resident, $200.50 nonresident. Additional stamps are required for waterfowl, pheasant, quail, and turkeys, as are permits for rifles, bows, shotguns, and muzzleloaders. Those between the ages of 10 and 16 must register for a free youth license, and seniors over 65 can apply for discounted licenses.

HIKING

Hiking in New Jersey runs the gamut from easy, flat-terrain loop trails to rugged, high-elevation throughways designed for only the most experienced. **Rails to Trails** (www .railtrails.org) converts the state's old railway beds (there are plenty) into multiuse tracks that connect towns and sometimes counties, ranging in length 1–87 miles. The **New York/ New Jersey Trail Conference** (www.nynjtc .org) maintains the regular hiking trails in the North Jersey vicinity, including the **Highland Trail,** a work in progress that on completion is set to extend 150 miles from New York's Storm King Mountain along the Hudson River southwest to Phillipsburg, along the Delaware River. The trail connects with some already in existence, including a portion of the Appalachian Trail, and there are some newly established stretches. Other New Jersey trails cared for by the conference, which is a conglomeration of numerous hiking clubs, environmental groups, and individuals, include those in Palisades Interstate Park, High Point State Park, and the Delaware Water Gap National Recreation Area.

Seventy-four miles of the **Appalachian Trail,** one of the country's best-known through-hikes running from Georgia north to Maine, lie within New Jersey, cutting northeast from Pennsylvania through the Kittatinny Mountain Range and along the state's northern border before heading into New York.

CAMPING

Camping is available in many of New Jersey's state parks, as well as in private, often seasonal resorts clustered along Route 9 in Cape May County and within the state's upper northwest corner. A few backcountry camping facilities are available in the Pinelands as well as the Skylands' Round Valley Recreation Area. State park camping facilities are relatively inexpensive and are often equipped with restrooms and showers. The resorts offer more of a home-away-from-home feel, usually with

laundry, electricity, and (somewhat) hot showers. Most of the state's private and public campgrounds are listed in the annual **New Jersey Campground & RV Guide** (www.newjersey campgrounds.com), which includes a list of amenities and current prices.

There are plenty of resorts that accommodate RV campers, and even a few RV-only parks, including one in the Gateway Region. Some of these resorts require seasonal stays, so check ahead.

CYCLING

The **New Jersey Department of Transportation** provides excellent free maps for road cycling routes. To obtain them, visit www.state.nj.us/transportation/commuter/ bike and click on "Free Information." If you're interested in cycle touring, a nationwide organization to try is **Adventure Cycling** (www.adventurecycling.org). **Morris County Trails Conservancy** (http://morris trails.org) lists a handful of mountain biking trails in the area.

© LAURA KINIRY

cyclists gathering to ride alongside the Delaware River

SPECTATOR SPORTS

When it comes to professional sports, most New Jerseyans are fans of either New York teams—like pro football's Giants or Jets and baseball's Yankees—or teams from Philadelphia, like the Flyers (hockey), Eagles (football), Sixers (basketball), and Phillies (baseball). Although for now both the Giants and the Jets play their home games in New Jersey's Meadowlands, the state has only a handful of pro teams it can truly call its own: hockey's **New Jersey Devils** (www.newjerseydevils.com), basketball's **New Jersey Nets** (www.nba.com/nets/), and lacrosse's **New Jersey Pride** (http://new jerseypride.com), who play at Kean University Alumni Stadium in the Gateway's Union.

New Jersey has seven minor league baseball teams and stadiums, including those in Atlantic City, Newark, Montclair, and Camden.

FESTIVALS AND EVENTS

At any time during the year, you'll find festivals and events occurring somewhere in New Jersey. The state celebrates its four seasons with a variety of happenings, ranging from afternoon outings to weeklong activities, and new festivals come into play annually. Each city and town seems to hosts some sort of local event, whether it's a neighborhood street fair, an arts and crafts festival, or a holiday house tour, but the following is a list of New Jersey's largest and most notable happenings. For more detailed information on local events, check out the regional chapters of this book.

Spring

New Jersey hosts numerous events highlighting the spring season, beginning with Newark's annual **Cherry Blossom Festival** (973/268-3500, www.branchbrookpark.org), held in the city's Branch Brook Park in April. This three-week event features thousands of cherry trees and demonstrations of traditional Japanese crafts. Also in April is Lambertville's annual two-day **Shad Festival** (609/397-0055, www .lambertville.org), a celebration of the Delaware River's restoration. Food, crafts, and live music are included in the festivities. The **New Jersey Marathon** (732/578-1771, www.njmarathon .org) takes place starting from Long Branch, along the Jersey Shore, in April.

In May the New Jersey Audubon Society sponsors Cape May County's **World Series of Birding** (609/884-2736, www.njaudubon .org/wsb). Participating groups have 24 hours to spot and record as many birds as possible while competing for title of World Series champs. Each Memorial Day weekend Skylands' Somerville hosts the four-day **Tour of Somerville** (www.tourofsomerville.org), the United States' oldest bike race.

Summer

New Jersey truly comes alive Memorial Day–Labor Day, as evidenced by the number of festivals and events taking place statewide. Held in South Jersey's Cumberland County during early June, **Delaware Bay Days** (856/785-2060, www.ajmeerwald.org) is a free two-day festival celebrating the Delaware Bay region's maritime history with parades, walks, and river tours.

June is a popular time for festivities, beginning with the **Red Bank Jazz & Blues Festival** (www.redbankfestival.com), an annual two-day event highlighting the region's musical heritage. The state's largest seafood festival is also held this weekend: Belmar's **New Jersey Seafood Festival** (800/523-2587, www.belmar.com), featuring local catch and cuisine. **Michael Arnone's Crawfish Festival** is a three-day annual June event held at the Skylands' Sussex County Fairgrounds. Music, camping, and Big Easy eats are just a few of the helpings you'll find here.

As the birthplace of motion pictures, New Jersey celebrates with a number of film-related events, including the Rutgers Film Co-op/New Jersey Media Arts Center **New Jersey Film Festival** (www.njfilmfest.com), held throughout June and July. The Pinelands' Whitesbog Village holds its annual **Blueberry Festival** (www.whitesbog.org), which celebrates the home of the cultivated blueberry, for one day in late June.

July is just as eventful with one of the state's most popular arts and crafts fairs,

Haddonfield's **Craft and Fine Arts Festival** (856/216-7253, www.haddonfieldnj.org/eventscrafts.php), occurring the second weekend in July. The shore's Ocean City celebrates a **Weekend in Venice** in late July, beginning with a Friday night seafood block party followed on day 2 by a spectacular lighted boat parade along the barrier island's back-bay waters. At the end of the month the Skylands puts on the three-day **Quick Chek Festival of Ballooning** (800/468-2479, http://quickchk.balloonfestival.com) honoring hot air balloons, frequent visitors to area skies. The event takes place at Solberg Airport in Readington, between Clinton and Somerville.

One of the state's most unique events is held in August off Atlantic City waters: The **Around the Island Marathon Swim** (www.acswim.org) is a 22.5-mile race around Absecon Island. Known for many years as the Sussex County Horse and Farm Show, the annual August **New Jersey State Fair** (Sussex County Fairgrounds, 973/948-5500, www.newjerseystatefair.org) is a week's worth of rides, crafts, cuisine, and agricultural competitions.

Fall

Although summer is winding down, New Jersey sees no shortage of festivals in the fall. In addition to hay rides, pumpkin picking, corn mazes, and Halloween fright nights, the state hosts a number of weekend and weeklong events, beginning with South Jersey's annual **Delaware Valley Bluegrass Festival** (www.brandywinefriends.org), a music and camping extravaganza held at the Salem County Fairgrounds over Labor Day weekend. The following weekend in North Jersey is the **Hoboken Italian Festival** (www.hobokenitalianfestival.com), a celebration of dining, desserts, tradition, and music, capped off with evening fireworks. The shore's Cape May extends its summer season with a number of events and festivals, including the four-day **Cape May Food & Wine Festival** (www.capemaymac.org), highlighting the city's reputation as a foodie destination. In October Cape May hosts a 10-day **Victorian Week** (www.capemaymac.org), featuring everything from haunted house tours to a vintage ball, where proper Victorian dress is encouraged.

The **New Jersey Lighthouse Challenge** (856/546-0514, www.njlhs.org) takes place in mid-October. Partakers have two days to visit and climb the state's 11 participating lighthouses, after which they receive a commemorative souvenir. Around this time Chatsworth—the self-proclaimed "capital of the Pinelands"—hosts the region's annual two-day **Cranberry Festival** (609/726-9237, www.cranfest.org/festival.html), with arts, crafts, and cranberry treats. South Jersey's Rankokus Indian Reservation, located within Rancocas State Park, is host to October's three-day **Indian Arts Festival** (www.powhatan.org), highlighting traditional and modern Native American culture, including storytelling, music, and dance. A second annual festival takes place in the spring.

Winter

Most of the state's winter festivities are held in South and Central Jersey and along the Jersey Shore, where temperatures are more moderate than in northern sections. During the month of December, Cape May transforms into a full-fledged holiday town, with carriage rides, candlelight house tours, and a spectacular light display. For additional holiday lights, check out the Atlantic City region's **Storybook Land** (www.storybookland.com). This fairy-tale village also hosts Santa and his reindeer throughout December. The Pineland's Medford Village holds its annual **Dickens Festival** (www.hmva.org) the first Friday in December, complete with costumed carolers, late-night shopping, and a tree-lighting ceremony.

On December 31 South Jersey's Haddonfield starts the New Year off with **First Night Haddonfield** (www.firstnighthaddonfield.org), a block party intended for the entire family. Mount Holly holds a **Fire & Ice Festival** (www.mainstreetmountholly.com), with ice carving and chili eating in late January. By February the state's winter temperatures have taken their toll, inciting hundreds of disillusioned types to strip down and dunk themselves in freezing ocean waters for Point Pleasant Beach's annual **Polar Bear Plunge** (732/213-5387, www.njpolarplunge.org), in the name of charity, of course. Cumberland County's Delaware Bayshore hosts the **Winter Eagle Festival** (856/453-2180), a daylong birding event, in early February.

March's big event is Belmar's **St. Patrick's Day Parade** (732/280-2648, www.belmar parade.com), beginning a daylong celebration complete with a beauty pageant, bagpipes, and all the corned beef you can stomach.

Accommodations

New Jersey has hundreds of overnight lodging options ranging from wonderfully elegant to downright seedy. In general, many of the older motels existing along once-frequented roadways that are now home to roadside attractions and prevalent with potholes are not the kind of place you want to check into. I found that it's best to stick to chain hotels, small-town establishments, and B&Bs, and to steer clear of independently owned motels *unless* you're at the Shore—that's a whole other ball game.

RATES

Rates listed in this book are for double occupancy, weekday high-season rooms (and are subject to change). New Jersey visitors, most notably those heading down the Shore, can save a ton of money by booking ahead, planning their vacation during the shoulder season, or even staying over a couple of weekday nights rather than weekends. Some Shore accommodations slash prices in half—sometimes by two thirds—after the summer rush, although not all remain open throughout the year. In-season you can save a good deal of cash simply by booking a room on the mainland and driving to the beach, instead of staying at the center of town. If you're looking to break your bank account, book a last-minute room on a weekend evening (a two-night minimum is

© LAURA KINIRY

Cape May's luxurious and historic Congress Hall

often required) during July or August in any of the Shore towns. You won't be able to afford food for a month.

ALTERNATIVE ACCOMMODATION OPTIONS

Home exchanges are one economical way to find accommodations. **Home Exchange** (www.homeexchange.com), a membership-based organization that acts as a middleman, introduces potential home swappers to one another early on with the intention of establishing mutual trust. All swappers must be members, and a one-year membership costs $99.95. If you're presently without a home to trade (but will soon have one to offer) and you don't mind living in someone else's while they're there too, two websites that can help are www.globalfreeloaders.com and www.couchsurfing.com. Both online communities highlight people willing to offer a night of couch surfing on their IKEA sleeper for one on yours—or someone like you—in the future. Global Freeloaders requires anyone crashing in someone else's crib to have one of their own to offer within six months time (it's all about karma), but Couch Surfing can be just that.

Renting a home at the Shore is another alternative to hotels and motels. Most Shore rental units are actually bought as second properties for the purpose of renting them out during the summer season, and come decorated in distinct Jersey Shore decor: pastel pinks and greens, seashell paintings and ocean scenes, lighthouses, ship wheels, and a thickly matted light-colored rug that works especially well at hiding sand. Menus of local seafood delivery and pizza places are fanned out on the dining table upon your arrival, and behind the house there's usually an enclosed outdoor shower and a low-lying faucet for guests to wash off their gritty feet. Renting a house for a week at the Shore is considerably pricey, but many people get around this by going in on seasonal rentals with a dozen or more people, some of whom will only be down on weekends and others who schedule one week for themselves and their families when no one else is around—a situation similar to a time-share.

Food and Drink

New Jersey is not traditionally known for its cuisine, although that's changing. It has also become a place where you can find almost anything if you look hard enough. The state's unique foods include diner fare and boardwalk eats. Depending on where you are in New Jersey, you can get yourself a hearty sub or a stuffed hoagie, and if you're anywhere near Philly, say Cherry Hill, you can delve into one of the best cheesesteaks around. Philadelphia soft pretzels are a common staple in the South Jersey diet, and Tastykakes—cakes, cupcakes, and pies—are now purchasable statewide.

BOARDWALK EATS

New Jersey's boardwalks offer a makeshift menu of all the so-bad-it's-good food you can think of. Pizza slices, funnel cake, gyros, grilled sandwiches, soft-serve ice cream, cotton candy, saltwater taffy, and fudge are traditional board favorites. Deep-fried Oreo cookies are one of the latest boardwalk additions.

DINERS

For a true New Jersey experience, eating at a diner is a must. The state is said to have more than 600 of them, the highest concentration in the country, and they range from shiny chrome and neon railcars to stationary stone-walled structures. Diners include cheap eats, an extensive menu, and often 24-hour service. They usually feature long counters lined with stools, and many of the older ones host comfy worn booths with tabletop jukeboxes that don't usually work. Rotating glass dessert displays often stand ready to greet you upon entry, and cashier counters host bowls of powdered mints. Diners serve as after-church excursions, power-lunch spots, writers' havens, conversational hangouts, and late-night joints. It's not uncommon to walk into a diner at 2:20 in the morning and find the place packed, since it's about the time most New Jersey bars let out. This is when coffee hotpots, crocks of French onion soup, Greek salads, and the lemon meringue pie all have their glory runs. Diner specialties include cheese fries with gravy, Taylor pork roll sandwiches, and all-day breakfast meals with pancakes, eggs, and scrapple.

ETHNIC FOOD

With Italians claiming the state's largest ethnic heritage, it's no wonder that Italian cuisine is intertwined with New Jersey culture. Many who move out of state claim a good Italian meal is hard to come by elsewhere, as is a good slice of thin-crust pizza. Trenton's Chambersburg district is perhaps the state's best-known neighborhood for Italian eats, but family-owned restaurants are found statewide.

The state's diverse population hosts a large number of ethnic enclaves that specialize in particular cuisines. Cherry Hill and Lakewood are good places to find kosher food, and authentic Mexican eats are prevalent in Lakewood and Red Bank. For Indian cuisine you can't go wrong along Edison's Oak Tree Road or Jersey City's western portion of Newark Avenue. Fort Lee is known for its Korean cuisine, while the state's finest Spanish, Brazilian, and Portuguese cuisine, along with soul food, is found in Newark. Cuban eats are prevalent throughout Union City, and Middle Eastern markets are common in Paterson. In much of the state, especially South Jersey and the Skylands, you'll find historic taverns serving traditional American fare. Seafood, notably crab cakes, flounder, and shellfish, is the choice cuisine along the shore.

FOR FOODIES

New Jersey's foodie towns include Hoboken, Red Bank, Cape May, Morristown, Collingswood, and lately Atlantic City. Two excellent online message boards for food lovers are the **eGullet Society for Culinary Arts & Letters,** or eG Forums (http://forums.egullet .com), and Chow's **Chowhound** Mid-Atlantic message board (http://chowhound.chow.com). Vegetarians may want to check out the online **New Jersey Vegetarian Travel Guide** (www.vegetarianusa.com/city/NewJersey .html), a list of vegetarian-friendly restaurants, farmers markets, farms, and co-ops. A few of the links are outdated, but it's a good overall source. For written resources look for *Ed Hitzel's Restaurant Magazine* (www.edhitzel .com), a free publication focusing on Central and South Jersey and the Shore and found at area restaurants, and *New Jersey Tables* (www .njtables.com), a biannual publication featuring select North and Central Jersey restaurant menus, available for purchase in bookstores or free at area restaurants.

CONVENIENCE STORES

New Jerseyans love their convenience stores, which they frequent for their sandwiches, snacks, and coffee. In the state's southern half **Wawa** (www.wawa.com) is on every few blocks. These omnipresent stores were a gift from Pennsylvania and have recently begun converting into megasized convenience centers complete with gas stations. Wawa is the place to go for a quick cup of coffee, an inexpensive hoagie, or a Philly soft pretzel, which many stores have delivered fresh each morning. Also in South Jersey, more localized to the Philadelphia metropolitan area, are **Heritage's Dairy Stores** (www.heritages.com), another great place to grab a sandwich to go. The Skylands convenience equivalent is **Quick Chek** (www.qchek.com), easily recognized by its forest-green sign.

For convenient ice cream, there's nothing better than the seasonal **Mister Softee** (www .mistersoftee.com), a must if he happens to be driving through your area. Although these soft-serve ice cream trucks exist in other states, their home base is in South Jersey. When you hear his song (don't worry, you'll recognize it) go running toward the tune.

DRINK

New Jersey has dozens of brewpubs, microbrews, and wineries, as well as numerous BYOs scattered throughout the state. Age 21 is the legal drinking age. New Jersey law allows for unfinished bottles of wine to be recorked, bagged, and carried out from restaurants, and for packaged goods to be sold by licensed retailers daily 9 A.M.–10 P.M. The sale of liquor varies statewide, with some towns prohibiting alcohol sales before 1 P.M. on Sunday, and designated liquor stores replacing supermarket sales in the southern half of the state. If you want a six-pack after 10 P.M., you often have to purchase it directly from a bar.

Coffee shops are finally catching on in New Jersey, although they haven't made a clean sweep of the state (the convenience stores still occupy that business). To find one in the region you're planning to visit, try **The Delocator** (www.delocator.net), an online site allowing users to punch in a zip code and view a list of all the independent cafés in the area, alongside a separate list of nearby Starbucks. The point is to support local business while seeing the power of corporations to take over a neighborhood, but someone has to enter the cafés into the database, and so far states like New Jersey, especially in the more rural areas, are misrepresented. Still—it's a handy tool to use.

Shopping

In general, New Jersey employs a 6 percent sales tax, although its 31 Urban Enterprise Zones, usually located in areas seeking revitalization, offer 3 percent sales tax. Clothes and shoes as well as newspapers and magazines are not taxed in New Jersey.

As many New Jerseyans can attest, shopping is a popular local pastime. Malls hold a prominent place in the state—in fact, New Jersey's reputation is as intricately tied to the shopping mall as it is with thick accents and big hair, and it has been since the Cherry Hill Mall—the East Coast's first indoor climate-controlled shopping center—opened in 1961. Some of the state's best malls include the Mall at Short Hills, the aforementioned Cherry Hill Mall, Freehold Mall, the three-story Bridgewater Commons, and the more modern "lifestyle centers" featuring upscale shops, each with a drive-up entrance, an example of which is Marlton's Promenade.

You'll find plenty of outlets, antique stores, flea markets, and independent boutiques throughout New Jersey as well. Mullica Hill, Chester, Long Beach Island, Asbury Park, Red Bank, Lambertville, and along Route 9 in Cape May County are wonderful places to go exploring for antiques, and twice a year the Atlantic City Convention Center hosts **Atlantique City** (www.atlantiquecity.com). Flea markets are just as popular in New Jersey. You can find the state's finest in Central Jersey (the Englishtown Auction), Lambertville (the Golden Nugget Antique & Collectible Flea Market), Berlin (the Berlin Market), and Woodstown (Cowtown).

Outlets exist statewide and include multiple locations in Flemington and Secaucus, centers in Elizabeth and Jackson, and Atlantic City's fairly new Walk. The state's best street shopping, including independent boutiques and specialty shops, is in Haddonfield, Red Bank, Lambertville, Hoboken, Spring Lake, and Atlantic City.

Yard sales are posted in the paper come spring, and many New Jerseyans make a sport out of prowling the neighborhoods scouting out unbeatable deals. For the best selection, arrive early. During summer months the state is filled with roadside fruit and veggie stands—you'll find them all along back roads throughout South, Central, and northwest Jersey. There's no better place to pick up a bushel of tomatoes and a few ears of sweet Jersey corn.

Tips for Travelers

The American Automobile Association, better known as **AAA** (www.aaa.com), offers members substantial benefits, including 24-hour emergency service, free and discounted maps, discounts on theater and sports tickets, and cheaper rates on hotels, to name a few.

A photo ID is required to get into many nightlife establishments, and you must be 21 years of age to purchase alcohol.

OPPORTUNITIES FOR EMPLOYMENT

Getting a seasonal job down the Jersey Shore is a rite of passage and a great way to spend the summer. International recruits, including Russians, French, Irish, Italians, and Canadians, have arrived in large numbers over the past decade, running the prize booths, staffing casino arcades, and working as servers and bar backs, but Shore employment is open to everyone. There is, however, one minor caveat: Seasonal housing is pricey, and it's not uncommon to find yourself in a rental situation with too many occupants and too few beds.

An organization that sets up jobs between international recruits and Jersey Shore companies is the Council on International Educational Exchange (www.ciee.org).

ACCESS FOR TRAVELERS WITH DISABILITIES

These days it's required that any establishment making upgrades be accessible to visitors with disabilities, and since New Jersey is constantly changing its appearance, it's becoming less frequent to find a place not adhering to required standards. Generally speaking, the state has made great progress, especially down the Shore, where some bicycle rental businesses have begun carrying electric wheelchairs, and towns such as Wildwood provide plastic chairs with large tires ideal for navigating through sand. Manasquan is the Shore town most accessible for travelers with disabilities, with a walkway that runs the length of the beach to its inlet waters. **Seniors on the**

Go (35 S. Main St., Pleasantville, 609/569-0443, www.sog-inc.com) rents electric wheelchairs to visitors to the southern Shore towns and does a large business in Atlantic City.

Although 99 percent of NJ Transit buses are wheelchair accessible, only 61 of the state's 161 commuter platforms offer a convenient method of boarding, like a ramp or elevator. To find out more go to www.njtransit.com/as.shtml. NJ Transit does offer reduced fares for travelers with disabilities.

TRAVELING WITH CHILDREN

New Jersey is a family-friendly state that has a ton to offer those traveling with children, most notably on the Jersey Shore. One thing you should understand: Get a kid hooked on the Shore and they'll be hooked for life. In addition to the Shore's attractions, the state has numerous amusement parks, some specifically geared toward children such as Hope's Land of Make Believe and Atlantic County's Storybook Land, while others like Six Flags' Great Adventure have loads of family-friendly entertainment—in this case a drive-through safari where giraffes and monkeys have full run of the roads. There are a handful of zoos, a couple of aquariums, and plenty of educational facilities, including the Liberty Science Center in Jersey City's Liberty State Park, the Old Barracks in Trenton, and Morristown National Historic Park. And of course, kids score discounts at most places.

A few thing to note: Kids under one year of age are required to ride in a rear-facing car seat in the backseat of an auto, and they are required by state law to continue using a car seat until they weigh 40 pounds, at which time they switch to a booster until they're eight years old. Those under age 12 must wear a helmet while bicycling, in-line skating, or skateboarding.

SENIOR TRAVELERS

Senior discounts are available at many of the state's parks, museums, and attractions, but there are also benefits to being a member of the American Association of Retired Persons, or **AARP** (888/687-2277, www.aarp.org), which provides additional hotel, auto, and travel discounts to those over 50 for a $12.50 annual fee. Seniors can also take advantage of national and local transit discount rates. Those 62 and older are eligible for free admission and parking at all of New Jersey's state parks, historic sites, and recreational facilities, as well as a $2 deduction on overnight fees at state camping facilities. However, you must first apply with the New Jersey Division of Parks and Forestry by calling 800/843-6420 or downloading a PDF application, available to print at www.state.nj.us/dep/parksandforests/parks/#discounts.

WOMEN TRAVELING ALONE

Women should use the same precautions they use elsewhere when traveling alone, including being aware of one's surroundings, steering clear of poorly lit areas, back stairs, and parking garages, and always using caution. Some women may feel uncomfortable traveling to certain cities alone, but while some areas of Camden, Jersey City, Newark, Trenton, Union City, Paterson, and even Asbury Park and Atlantic City are best avoided altogether, you'll have little trouble during the day as long as you stick to your destination. Know where you're going ahead of time—places like the Pinelands seem innocent enough, but many of its roads go on forever and lead nowhere. Having a map and a cell phone handy and traveling during daylight hours are ways to ease discomfort. New Jersey is just like anywhere else—exercise good judgment and you'll be fine.

GAY AND LESBIAN TRAVELERS

You might be surprised to find that New Jersey is at the country's forefront when it comes to gay rights. In 2004 the state signed a gay partnership law, and is one of several states in the country that currently recognizes a form of same-sex unions, along with Maine, Vermont, Massachusetts, California, and Connecticut. For a short while in February 2004, Asbury Park was one of the few cities nationwide allowing same-sex marriages to take place. Over the last decade the state has seen an influx of gay residents drawn by New Jersey's proximity to Philadelphia and New York City, affordable housing, and open space, and towns and cities with a noticeable gay population include Collingswood, Haddonfield, Moorestown, Trenton, Maplewood, Asbury Park, South Orange, and Jersey City. Local resources for gay and lesbian visitors include **New Jersey Gay Life** (www.njgaylife.com), which hosts a directory of gay- and lesbian-friendly and gay- and lesbian-owned businesses throughout the state, and **Gay Asbury Park** (www.gay asburypark.com).

INTERNATIONAL TRAVELERS

International travelers to New Jersey must adhere to U.S. visa requirements. Canadians and citizens from 27 Visa Waiver Program countries do not need visas. Citizens from other countries are required to have a nonimmigrant visa, which costs about $100 to process. Nearby New York City is where both visitor and student visas are issued, and where the embassies and consulates of most countries are located.

For those visiting the United States, I suggest carrying both travel insurance and an **International Student ID Card** (www.isic .org). The former is essential when visiting the United States, where the cost of health care is sky-high—shop around for a policy that best suits you. The latter holds the key to substantial savings for full-time students, teachers, and professors, and those age 26 and younger, and it can be used the world over after your trek through the Garden State. Obtain it at travel offices around the globe.

Health and Safety

Crime in New Jersey is similar to other parts of the country, with the state's larger cities seeming to host the highest crime rates. Always be aware of your surroundings, especially in such areas as Camden, Paterson, Newark, Trenton, Jersey City, and Atlantic City. Many Shore towns can give you the feeling of being in la-la land, and for the most part you are, but just be aware. *Sopranos*-like organized crime is nothing for the average traveler to worry about, but there's no reason to be hanging around downtown Camden at night unless you're looking for trouble. If you have a cell phone, keep it on you—it's easy to get lost (though not *really* lost) in the state, especially with all the recent roadwork that requires drivers to detour. Remember—Jersey's not that big, and head east, west, or south and you'll eventually hit water. Head north and once you reach New York State you'll know you've gone too far.

ROAD SAFETY
HAZARDS AND WILDLIFE

New Jersey roads have a reputation for aggressive drivers. I'm not saying they're all state residents (many of the highways are overtaken by throughway traffic), but especially in the Gateway Region, proceed with caution—roads can be downright hellish. While driving at night, particularly in the Skylands, be on the lookout for deer. I can't tell you the number of roadside carcasses I've seen while driving in the area, but it's more than I'd ever cared to see. If that's what happened to the deer, I hate to think what happened to the cars and drivers.

Take note of wildlife acting erratically. Species such as bats, skunks, raccoons, even dogs are known to carry rabies, a fatal virus that without treatment results in death. If a wild animal bites you, call 911 immediately. Black bears primarily inhabit the state's northwest region but have been making their way south through the Pinelands and even into Cape May County. Although many have grown accustomed to humans, they'll generally steer clear

if they hear people approaching. It's a good idea to make noise while hiking, especially if you're hiking alone (not recommended). According to the New Jersey Department of Fish and Wildlife brochure, if you do encounter a bear, yell and use whatever you have handy to make noise. Never turn your back on a bear—if one's being aggressive, slowly back away and report the incident immediately. You can further prevent bear encounters by keeping food, makeup, and anything that produces a scent in a tightly sealed storage container. *Never* camp with food or drink in your tent, or cook in your tent, and always wash utensils immediately after use.

New Jersey is home to two species of poisonous snakes: northern copperheads and timber rattlesnakes. Northern copperheads live in the state's Skylands region and are mostly found in Sussex, Warren, Hunterdon, and Passaic Counties. They are active May–October, have a distinct reddish-brown color with hourglass bands, and according to the New Jersey state website, favor "rotting woodpiles in rocky wooded areas that are usually mountainous." New Jersey's timber rattlesnakes are either yellow-colored with dark V-shaped crossbands or entirely black or darkened. They're also active May–October and reside in both the Pinelands and in the state's upper northwest corner.

INSECTS AND PLANTS

Mosquitoes are common in New Jersey, especially on summer evenings and near still bodies of water. Although malaria in the state has long been controlled, mosquitoes—besides being pesky and annoying—are now known to carry West Nile virus, an infection that increases the risk of illness mostly in the elderly and those with weakened immune systems. To avoid contracting the virus, use bug spray and keep away from wetlands and marshes during summer months. Lyme disease, transmitted by deer ticks, is a problem in the Eastern United States, and New Jersey has one of the highest numbers of reported cases in the country. If you notice a bull's-eye–like rash anywhere on your skin, see a doctor immediately. Lyme disease is treatable if cared for right away, but left on its own the symptoms are nasty, incurable, and will continue to worsen. May and June are the worst months for ticks, but if you are heading outside, there are preventative measures you can take: dress in light-colored clothes in order to notice ticks more clearly, along with a hat or a bandanna to protect your head, and if you're out for a hike, wear long pants and tuck them into your socks (I know, *I know*). Always stay on trails, keep away from tall grass, and avoid marshlands and wetlands during summer months—they're full-on breeding grounds for ticks and mosquitoes. It's also a good idea to use insect repellent and to check yourself (or have someone check you) for ticks after being outside. Ticks are tiny eight-legged arachnids that try to bury themselves in your skin—feel around for any unusual bumps and look for dark spots.

Another reason to avoid still water is greenflies. These vile creatures have large, almost transparent green heads and a stinging bite, and they reside all along the East Coast and across to Texas. Greenflies are most associated with the humid sticky months of July and August. They breed in the salt marshes that line much of the western side of the Jersey Shore, and they are not shy about attacking as you lay quietly on the beach. Use insect repellent to keep these buggers at bay; it's when the wind blows east from the bay that you'll encounter the worst of them. One website cites Brigantine, just north of Atlantic City, as having the most greenflies "on the planet."

Poison ivy is common throughout New Jersey. As the old adage states, "Leaves of three, let it be."

SUN, TEMPERATURE, AND NEW JERSEY WATERS

Don't let the jokes about New Jersey smog fool you—the state gets plenty of sun. Cloudy days are oftentimes the worst because sunbathers along the Shore don't realize the sun's rays are coming through all that overcast. The sun is strongest 10 A.M.–2 P.M.—avoid laying out during this time and always use sunscreen, preferably SPF 30 or higher, reapplying it every few hours, especially after a dip in the ocean or a pool.

Summer months can be brutally hot and humid in New Jersey—always drink plenty of water, and when the sun is at its peak, find some shade (or at least wear a hat or a visor). Dehydration occurs more often than you may think, and it's not worth the nausea. Winter temperatures often drop below freezing, and it's important to be adequately prepared. If you're going out for a hike, always carry extra layers, bottled water, and some snacks, and tell someone where you'll going and when you plan to return. Freak snowstorms have been known to occur.

Swimming in the ocean is a favorite New Jersey pastime, and one where you should encounter few problems as long as you take a couple of precautions. Beaches employ lifeguards up and down the coast Memorial Day–Labor Day—swim in the designated areas only, as the ocean can have a mean undertow and instantly suck you out to sea without anyone knowing you were even in the water. Shark sightings are a rare though not unheard-of occurrence off Jersey's coast, and in 2005 a surfer was bitten on the foot off the coast from Long Beach Island's Surf City. If the lifeguard yells "shark," get out of the water, but otherwise don't think too much about it—it's a big ocean out there. You may encounter the occasional crab along the ocean floor, but the biggest problem is the jellyfish hovering along the coastline during July and August. A beach will occasionally close because of them. New Jersey's jellyfish aren't poisonous—but they do sting. Ouch!

SMOKING

New Jersey has banned smoking in bars and restaurants since April 2006. A ban for smoking on casino floors is set to go into effect in October 2008. It's also against the law to smoke in the state's public buildings, and many boardwalks have declared designated smoking sections, although it's unclear how well enforced these are.

HOSPITALS AND PHARMACIES

Hospitals exist in all of New Jersey's counties, although the greatest concentrations lie in the Philadelphia and NY metropolitan regions. Cape May County has only one hospital. The **New Jersey Hospital Association** provides a list of the state's hospital systems alphabetically, by county, or on a downloadable PDF map on its website, www.njha.com. For overseas visitors and those traveling without a provider, I highly recommend travel insurance—health care in the United States is overwhelmingly expensive, especially if you don't have good coverage. Your local travel agency can help you out with this—a good place to try is **STA Travel** (www.statravel.com), with locations worldwide.

With its reputation as a pharmaceutical giant, you'll have little trouble finding a pharmacy anywhere in the state. **Rite Aid** (www.riteaid.com), **Walgreens** (www.walgreens.com), and **CVS** (www.cvs.com) all offer 24-hour prescription-filling locations in New Jersey.

Information and Services

MONEY

ATMs (automatic teller machines) are readily available throughout New Jersey and accept most cards. Those located in Wawa convenience stores (which seem to multiply like bunnies throughout the southern half of the state) or Quick Chek in the Skylands region don't charge a processing fee. Overseas travelers will have no trouble exchanging their currency at JFK, Philadelphia, or Newark Liberty International Airports, but for those already on the road, **American Express** (http://home.americanexpress.com) has travel offices throughout the state, including currency exchange centers in Newark (at the airport), Fort Lee, and Summit.

One bank with a large New Jersey presence is **Commerce Bank** (www.commerceonline.com), a Cherry Hill–based business whose perks include seven-day banking and longer hours for nine-to-fivers. Other banks in the state include **PNC Bank** (www.pncbank.com) and **Bank of America** (www.bankofamerica.com).

Credit Cards

Many establishments, especially along the Shore, don't take credit cards. It's always smart to have a bit of cash on hand.

Tipping

Tipping is a common practice in the state's service industries, and many employees depend on the money they earn from tips to survive. At New Jersey restaurants, it is common to tip waitstaff 15–20 percent on top of your total bill, depending on the quality of service, and taxi drivers and hairdressers usually receive 15–20 percent as well. A couple of dollars is common to leave in your hotel room for the cleaning staff, and it is also a common tip for valet parkers and airport porters. At cafés and coffeehouses, spare change is customary for an espresso drink (just how much depends on the drink's complexity), or a couple of dollars for a round of drinks or a prepared meal. Bartenders usually receive a dollar for a mixed drink, or a few dollars for a round of drinks (although a round of beers would require less of a tip then a round of cosmopolitans). New Jersey's gas station attendants are paid per hour and are not usually tipped.

MAPS AND TOURIST INFORMATION
Tourist Information Offices

New Jersey has numerous information and welcome centers. State Welcome Centers are located in Jersey City (Liberty State Park, Central Railroad Terminal, NJ Turnpike Exit 14B, 201/915-3400), Newark (Newark Liberty International Airport Terminal B, International Arrivals, 973/623-5052), Flemington (Liberty

Village Premium Outlets, 1 Church St., 908/782-8550), and Jackson (Jackson Outlet Village Information Center, 537 Monmouth Rd., 732/833-0503 ext. 7). The greater tourism councils for regions divided by the New Jersey Office of Travel and Tourism (800/847-4865, www.visitnj.org) are the Greater Atlantic City Tourism Council (866/719-8687, www.ac tourism.org), Delaware River Regional Tourism Council (856/757-9400, www.visitsouth jersey.com), Gateway Regional Tourism Council (877/428-3930), Shore Regional Tourism Council (800/722-0201 ext. 200), Skylands Regional Tourism Council (800/475-5263, www.skylandstourism.org), and Southern Shore Regional Tourism Council (800/277-2297, www.njsouthernshore.com). On New Jersey's official state website (www.state.nj.us) you'll find information regarding government, economy, and local flora and fauna.

COMMUNICATIONS AND MEDIA
Internet
Many—if not all—of New Jersey's public libraries offer Internet access of some form, whether hookup or wireless, and most provide computers for public use. To search for libraries in South Jersey that offer Wi-Fi connections, log onto www.sjrlc.org/wireless. Many Burger Kings and McDonald's statewide offer wireless connections, but I'd recommend supporting the local cafés and coffeehouses that also offer Internet—they're something that the state could use more of. Many hotels have wireless access in both guest rooms and public areas, and some will allow you to connect for a short bit even if you're not staying there (if you ask nicely). Other hotels features in-room data ports, and lobby computers requiring a fee—these can add up quickly. The website www.wififreespot.com/nj.html provides up-to-date listings of wireless access throughout New Jersey.

Phones and Area Codes
New Jersey has six area codes currently in use: 201, covering much of the Gateway Region; 732, used for the Northern Shore and much of eastern Central Jersey; 973, covering the mid-portion of North Jersey where the Gateway and Skylands meet; 908, used for the greater western Skylands; 609, covering the Pinelands, the Cape, the Greater Atlantic City Region, Central Jersey's western portion, and a small part of the Skylands; and 856, covering the Philadelphia metropolitan region.

Cell Phones
Like elsewhere in the country, cell phones have seemingly overtaken New Jersey. It's illegal in the state to drive while talking on a handheld phone, and the law is enforced. Be grateful: The state's drivers have a bad enough rep as it is (although *we all know* it's really those Pennsylvania and New York drivers mucking up the roads), and the phone-to-hand-to-head doesn't help.

A number of New Jersey's restaurants have decided to ban cell phone usage in dining areas.

Radio and TV
Many of New Jersey's television stations are broadcast from either New York or Pennsylvania, and in-state offerings are slim. The state does have its own public television station, **NJN** (www.njn.net), which features shows pertaining to New Jersey history and culture, as well as Jersey-centric news coverage; it is accessible statewide.

Magazines and Newspapers
New Jersey is home to dozens of publications, both newspapers and magazines, that cater to the state and its specific regions. Both Pennsylvania's *Philadelphia Inquirer* (www.philly.com) and Manhattan's *New York Times* (www.nytimes.com) are distributed in New Jersey and feature local news sections pertaining to the state's greater metropolitan suburbs as well as occasional stories about the Jersey Shore.

Some of New Jersey's best-known newspapers include the Gateway's *Star-Ledger* (www.nj.com/starledger); the *Trenton Times* (www.njtimes.com), keeping readers up-to-date on New Jersey's capital city; and the *Press of Atlantic City* (www.pressofatlanticcity.com).

For complete New Jersey news coverage, log on to **www.nj.com.**

Booksellers find it difficult to keep issues of *Weird N.J.* (www.weirdnj.com) in stock. This wonderful publication focuses on all that's odd and offbeat in the Garden State (there's plenty) and has developed quite a cult following. The magazine's readers supply the majority of its stories, and features range from thought-provoking pieces on albino villages to coverage of haunted asylums.

New Jersey Monthly (www.njmonthly.com) is perhaps the state's most established publication, a well-written monthly filled with up-to-date restaurant info, local profiles, and in-depth articles pertaining to New Jersey culture, life, and politics. The magazine features an annual "Best of the Shore" issue each June.

Upstage magazine (www.upstagemagazine .com) is a free publication listing local nightclubs, nightlife happenings, music venues—really anything to do with entertainment. Reviews and interviews are a substantial part of the magazine, which is distributed throughout Central Jersey and the northern Jersey Shore.

Although you have a better chance finding it in New Jersey bookstores than elsewhere in the country, *Backstreets* (www.backstreets .com) is more of a subscription-type magazine. It is the ultimate Springsteen resource, a fan-based publication centered on the Boss that has been distributed since 1980. *Backstreets* updates its website daily with current set lists, news, and the latest in possible Springsteen-centric purchases.

RESOURCES

Suggested Reading

GENERAL INFORMATION

Genovese, Peter. *Jersey Diners.* Rivergate Books, 2006. While not the diner's birthplace, New Jersey hosts approximately 600 of these pre-fab eateries within the state's borders, making it the diner's de facto home. Now in paperback, Peter Genovese's homage to the establishment most strongly associated with the state (besides malls) is a must for any roadside food fan.

Gillespie, Angus K., and Michael A. Rockland. *Looking for America on the New Jersey Turnpike.* Rutgers University Press, 1993. A fascinating historical ride along one of New Jersey's most infamous landmarks. Who knew it was illegal to snap a photo on the Turnpike?

Lurie, Maxine N., and Marc Mappen. *Encyclopedia of New Jersey.* Rutgers University Press, 2004. Everything and anything you'd like to know about New Jersey. Want to find out where Leo, the MGM lion, died? Curious about Garden State sweet corn? Or maybe you'd like to learn the legends regarding saltwater taffy? It's all here, and it's interesting.

Sceurman, Mark, and Mark Morean. *Weird N.J.: Your Travel Guide to New Jersey's Local Legends and Best-kept Secrets.* Barnes & Noble, 2003. The *Weird N.J.* boys picked the state's best self-taught superheroes, abandoned missile sites, lizard creatures, and little villages

and brought them together in one hardcover book. Need more? Pick up *Weird N.J., Volume II,* Sterling, 2006. Both are bibles for the offbeat planner.

LITERATURE, FICTION, AND CULTURAL STUDIES

Capuzzo, Michael. *Close to Shore.* Broadway, 2002. Capuzzo uses dozens of resources, including historic newspapers, magazines, journals, and interviews, to piece together the events of July 1916, when one of history's worst shark attacks occurred in New Jersey waters. A page-turner.

Evanovich, Janet. *Stephanie Plum* series. St. Martin's Press, 1995–present. Cake lover, fast-food eater, man magnet: Stephanie Plum is the ultimate Jersey Girl, a big-haired, ill-fashioned bounty hunter who's misshaped her way through more then a dozen easy reads. There's not a lot of substance, but the entertainment factor is high.

Kalita, S. Mitra. *Suburban Sahibs* Rutgers University Press, 2005. A modern-day cultural study of three Indian families living in the Central Jersey suburb of Edison.

McPhee, John. *The Pine Barrens.* Farrar, Straus, & Giroux, 1968. McPhee's groundbreaking work on the New Jersey Pinelands thrust the fragile ecosystem into the limelight and led to the establishment of the country's first National Reserve.

Roth, Phillip. *American Pastoral.* Vintage, 1998. Roth's Pulitzer Prize–winning novel explores a fictional yet familiar America from the eyes of a Newark-based Swede.

Roth, Phillip. *Goodbye Columbus, and Five Short Stories.* New York City: Vintage, 1994. A collection of Roth's earlier short stories, set in Newark and the surrounding Gateway Region at a time when Essex County's suburbs were developing their own identity.

Smith, Rosamond. *The Barrens.* Carroll & Graf, 2002. Under the Smith pseudonym, New Jersey–based author Joyce Carol Oates writes one of the state's most chilling fictional tales—read it *after* you visit the Pinelands.

Sullivan, Robert. *The Meadowlands: Wilderness Adventures on the Edge of a City.* Anchor, 1999. One man's passionate journey through the backwaters of New Jersey's Meadowlands, the oft-described "Armpit of America," is both a humorous and educational account of New Jersey's famed swampland.

Talese, Gay. *Unto the Sons.* Random House Trade Paperbacks, 2006. An epic and potent novel intertwining the story of Talese's Ocean City childhood with that of his Italian ancestors.

PHOTOGRAPHY, MUSIC, AND HISTORY

Buchholz, Margaret Thomas. *New Jersey Shipwrecks: 350 Years in the Graveyard of the Atlantic.* Down the Shore Publishing, 2004. A coffee-table book telling the stories of New Jersey's hundreds of shipwrecks with surprisingly strong text and captivating black-and-white photos.

Cunningham, John T. *Four Seasons at the Shore: Photographs of the Jersey Shore.* Down the Shore Publishing, 2004. An inspiring look at the Jersey Shore as it travels through time; packed with gorgeous images.

Goldstein, Stan, and Jean Mickle. *Rock & Roll Tour of the Jersey Shore.* June 2008. The expanded third edition of this hard-to-find book is packed with historic rock-and-roll sites throughout Monmouth, Ocean, and Middlesex Counties. Look for it in area stores or order online at www.njrockmap.com. It's a great resource for followers of Jersey Shore music.

Kirst, Bob. *Down the Shore: A Photo Tour of the Jersey Coast.* Photo Tour Books, 2005. One of the most inspiring photo anthologies of the New Jersey Shore, this book captures the state's coastal spirit in a lovely still journey worth the price.

Pike, Helen-Chantal. *Asbury Park's Glory Days: The Story of an American Resort.* Rutgers University Press, 2007. Relive Asbury Park's history from its founding as a temperate seaside town, through its days as Queen of the Shore, to its role as the birthplace of Jersey Shore music. Vintage photos are spread throughout.

Springsteen, Bruce. *Songs.* Harper Paperbacks, 2003. Well over 100 sheets of song lyrics interspersed with the Boss's own commentary on what was truly going on behind the music. With some great Springsteen shots.

Van Meter, Jonathan. *The Last Good Time.* Three Rivers Press, 2004. The life and times of Paul "Skinny" D'Amato, an Atlantic City entrepreneur who owned and operated the city's famed 500 Club. Friends with Sinatra, DiMaggio, and mob boss Sam Giancana, D'Amato and his past are page-turners. I couldn't put this book down.

Waltzer, Jim, and Tom Wilk. *Tales of South Jersey: Profiles and Personalities.* Rutgers University Press, 2001. Want to learn about Atlantic City's Club Harlem, the history of skeeball, and Pitman's Broadway Theatre in a way that feels like you're reading a collection of short stories? The interesting and informative *Tales of South Jersey* is the way to do it.

Wien, Gary. *Beyond the Palace*. Trafford Publishing, 2006. A well-researched book highlighting Asbury Park's music scene, written by the publisher of *Upstage* magazine.

OUTDOORS

Boyle Jr., William J. *A Guide to Bird Finding in New Jersey*. Rutgers University Press, 2002. An excellent birding guide, easy to navigate and providing in-depth coverage statewide.

Javins, Marie. *The Best in Tent Camping: New Jersey*. Menasha Ridge Press, May 2005. Javins points readers to the state's quiet spots to set up for the night. A must for anyone who enjoys privacy with their scenery.

Parnes, Robert. *Paddling the New Jersey Pine Barrens*. Falcon, 2002. A good accompaniment for navigating the state's Pinelands rivers.

Santelli, Robert. *Short Bike Rides in New Jersey*, fourth edition. Globe Pequot, 1998. A pocket-size and easy-to-read book encompassing New Jersey's most scenic bike rides, heavy on the Skylands and interspersed with factual tidbits.

Scherer, Glenn. *Nature Walks in New Jersey: AMC Guides to the Best Trails from the Highlands to Cape May*, second edition. Appalachian Mountain Club Books 2003. New Jersey is a true hiker's paradise if you know where to look; this book assists by exploring 40 of the state's best trails.

Internet Resources

GENERAL INFORMATION

New Jersey Motion Picture & Television Commission
www.njfilm.org
Providing information on all New Jersey filming locations past and present, as well as a comprehensive list of movies and TV shows shot in the state.

New Jersey State Website
www.state.nj.us
New Jersey's official state website, with information on local transit, Jersey fresh produce, state government, and tourism. The site offers free maps and travel guides as well as interactive New Jersey–based games and trivia for kids.

NJ.com
www.nj.com
The ultimate New Jersey resource, with local and statewide news, sports, and weather, restaurant listings and reviews, and online access to numerous state newspapers.

HISTORIC PRESERVATION

Doo Wop Preservation League
www.doowopusa.org
A site devoted to the preservation and utilization of the Wildwoods wacky—and wonderful—architectural contribution. For learning about doo-wop and getting involved, there's no better site around.

Cinema Treasures
http://cinematreasures.org
A wonderful site dedicated to old movie houses and theaters across the United States, providing brief histories and current status for all single screens (even those since demolished) and converted multiplexes. Each listing includes a message board and most often photos. *Definitely* worth visiting, though watch the time—it's easy to spend hours here.

New Jersey Lighthouse Society
www.njlhs.org/
A nonprofit dedicated to preserving New Jersey's more than one dozen lighthouses.

The organization sponsors the state's annual October Lighthouse Challenge.

Palace Museum Online
www.palaceamusements.com

Asbury Park's now-demolished Palace Amusements lives on in this well-crafted online museum, put together by **Save Tillie** (www.savetillie.com), a nonprofit devoted to saving all of the city's landmarks.

Preservation New Jersey
www.preservationnj.org

A private organization focused on saving New Jersey's endangered historical, cultural, and architectural sights. Some of the state's most endangered in 2008 include Cape May's Beach Theatre and Morristown's Speedwell Avenue.

OUTDOORS

New Jersey Audubon Society
www.njaudubon.org

New Jersey's top birding website provides information on Audubon centers throughout the state, local birding activities and events, and Cape May's annual World Series of Birding.

Tracker School
www.trackerschool.com

Wilderness survival guide Tom Brown Jr. is no stranger to the Pinelands—he's been hosting courses here for years. This website provides a listing of all current classes and prices. If you're looking to get lost in the Pines, Tracker School is the way to go.

Pinelands Preservation Alliance
www.pinelandsalliance.org

A nonprofit committed to preserving the Pinelands for future generations, the site features up-to-date newsletters and a schedule of upcoming Alliance events, including Jersey Devil hunts, Pineland ghost town tours, and wilderness survival training courses.

OFFBEAT SITES

New Jersey Diners
www.njdiners.com

Looking for a diner in New Jersey? Start here. I'm not sure how often it's updated, but the site does provide a pretty comprehensive list of diners in each of the state's five regions. Check in every once in a while and you'll never be without roadside assistance.

Roadside America
www.roadsideamerica.com

The website for all that's truly tacky and kitsch—it's no secret that Jersey's a hotbed for this kind of stuff. Muffler Men; storybook castles; giant stuffed grizzlies—if it's odd, you'll find it here.

Soprano Sue Sightings
www.sopranosuesightings.com

The best place to uncover the goings-on of New Jersey's favorite mob family, even after the vague finale. The site includes updated news, information on cast and characters, *Sopranos* trivia, and a listing of local sites that have appeared in the show.

Index

List of Maps

Acknowledgments

Thanks again to my parents: Mom, for keeping an eye on local news and a pair of scissors handy; and Dad, for being the most eager, accepting, and wide-eyed travel companion a person could ask for. You're a true rock star. Drew--a belated thank you for believing in me from the beginning--and to both you and Tanya, thanks for the Curly Fries poses (next time, chum!). Mike and Patti Simmons, Chris and Mary Borzell, Alicia Kiniry, Jim Greenhalgh, and Rebecca Marsh, thank you many times over for your knowledge, input, and assistance; and to the entire Avalon Travel staff, including Elizabeth Hansen, Kathryn Ettinger, Kevin Anglin, Grace Fujimoto, Jane Musser, the publicity department, and the wonderful Stefano Boni. The work you've all put into shaping this book is endlessly appreciated.

My nephews, David, Tommy, and Patrick, I love you guys so much. You are *my* New Jersey highlight. Matthew, I don't know how you do it. For a boy from San Jose, you've learned more about NJ than you probably ever dreamed. Thank you! You're my best friend, always.

This book is dedicated to Tracy Exler, a true Jersey girl and a wonderful person; Grandmom—I'll never visit Atlantic City without thinking of you; Uncle Hank, my number one fan, with love from your only niece; Ken Whelan, you continue smiling down on me; and Uncle Jerry, the true New Jersey wanderer. I love you, too.

www.moon.com

DESTINATIONS | ACTIVITIES | BLOGS | MAPS | BOOKS

MOON.COM is all new, and ready to help plan your next trip! Filled with fresh trip ideas and strategies, author interviews, informative blogs, a detailed map library, and descriptions of all the Moon guidebooks, Moon.com is all you need to get out and explore the world—or even places in your own backyard. As always, when you travel with Moon, expect an experience that

MAP SYMBOLS

▦▦▦	Expressway	◖	Highlight	✗	Airfield	⚲	Golf Course
▦▦▦	Primary Road	○	City/Town	✈	Airport	Ⓟ	Parking Area
▦▦▦	Secondary Road	◉	State Capital	▲	Mountain	▰	Archaeological Site
- - - -	Unpaved Road	⊛	National Capital	✛	Unique Natural Feature	⚑	Church
- - - - -	Trail	★	Point of Interest			⬛	Gas Station
··········	Ferry	•	Accommodation	≋	Waterfall	◡	Glacier
▬▬▬	Railroad	▼	Restaurant/Bar	⬥	Park	~	Mangrove
▦▦▦	Pedestrian Walkway	■	Other Location	◗	Trailhead	▨	Reef
⬚⬚⬚	Stairs	⋀	Campground	⏃	Skiing Area	◢	Swamp

CONVERSION TABLES

°C = (°F - 32) / 1.8
°F = (°C x 1.8) + 32
1 inch = 2.54 centimeters (cm)
1 foot = 0.304 meters (m)
1 yard = 0.914 meters
1 mile = 1.6093 kilometers (km)
1 km = 0.6214 miles
1 fathom = 1.8288 m
1 chain = 20.1168 m
1 furlong = 201.168 m
1 acre = 0.4047 hectares
1 sq km = 100 hectares
1 sq mile = 2.59 square km
1 ounce = 28.35 grams
1 pound = 0.4536 kilograms
1 short ton = 0.90718 metric ton
1 short ton = 2,000 pounds
1 long ton = 1.016 metric tons
1 long ton = 2,240 pounds
1 metric ton = 1,000 kilograms
1 quart = 0.94635 liters
1 US gallon = 3.7854 liters
1 Imperial gallon = 4.5459 liters
1 nautical mile = 1.852 km

MOON NEW JERSEY

Avalon Travel
a member of the Perseus Books Group
1700 Fourth Street
Berkeley, CA 94710, USA
www.moon.com

Editor: Elizabeth Hollis Hansen
Series Manager: Kathryn Ettinger
Copy Editor: Christopher Church
Graphics Coordinators: Kathryn Osgood,
    Stefano Boni
Production Coordinator: Darren Alessi
Cover Designer: Kathryn Osgood
Map Editor: Kevin Anglin
Cartographers: Kat Bennett, Chris Markiewicz
Cartography Director: Mike Morgenfeld
Indexer: Rachel Kuhn

ISBN-13: 978-1-59880-156-9
ISSN: 1930-2630

Printing History
1st Edition – 2006
2nd Edition – April 2009
5 4 3 2 1

Some photos and illustrations are used by permission and are the property of the original copyright owners.

Front cover photo: © Steve Gottlieb, drr.net
Title page photo: carousel horse, Ocean City
    © Laura Kiniry
Interior color photos: All photos © Laura Kiniry, except pg. 7 © Save Lucy Commitee, Inc. 2005 All rights reserved. Any duplication without authorization is prohibited. Photo courtesy Larry Sieg, Atlantic City Convention & Visitors Authority.

Printed in the United States by RR Donnelley

KEEPING CURRENT

If you have a favorite gem you'd like to see included in the next edition, or see anything that needs updating, clarification, or correction, please drop us a line. Send your comments via email to feedback@moon.com, or use the address above.